The L

GEORGE
WHITEFIELD

The Life and Times of

GEORGE
WHITEFIELD

Robert Philip

THE BANNER OF TRUTH TRUST

THE BANNER OF TRUTH TRUST
3 Murrayfield Road, Edinburgh EH12 6EL, UK
P.O. Box 621, Carlisle, PA 17013, USA

*

First published 1837
First Banner of Truth edition 2007
Reprinted 2009

ISBN: 978 0 85151 960 9

*

Printed in the U.S.A. by
Versa Press, Inc.,
East Peoria, IL

INTRODUCTION

There can be few Christians who changed the life of nations only to be as little remembered as George Whitefield (1714–70). In part this was because he founded no denomination. Except for the short biography by the Scotsman, John Gillies (published two years after his death), Whitefield's memory was left largely in the hands of those who wished to attribute his influence to 'theatrical talent' and fanaticism. The English evangelical, Thomas Wilson, who died in 1794, called for a fuller biography, but nothing came until Robert Philip's volume in 1837. After Philip's work there was a turning of the tide, and by 1852 J. C. Ryle was among those popularizing the belief that 'Whitefield was one of the most powerful and extraordinary preachers the world has ever seen.' Later and more definitive biographies were to confirm this opinion, notably the two volumes of Luke Tyerman, 1876–77, and of Arnold Dallimore in 1970 and 1980.

Philip's work, however, has not been displaced. It remains the best account to be found in a single volume. As a biographer he has his own distinctive merits. Although Whitefield was dead more than twenty years before he was born, Philip knew and spoke with those who had a personal knowledge of his subject. From them, and from his own extensive study of Whitefield's Journals, letters and sermons, he grasped the great lesson of his life, namely, that it is the Holy Spirit who makes preachers. In a brief personal allusion, Philip tells us (pp. 553–5) how he first saw this as a youth in Huntly, Scotland, where his minister, George Cowie, preached 'bathed in tears of love' – the result of 'tender and intense love to souls'. Not without cause was Cowie called 'the Whitefield of the north', yet, as a child, Philip was present in September 1799 when the Synod of the Anti-burgher Presbyterians excommunicated him. His fault lay in no weakening of Calvinistic orthodoxy; it was for his recognition of evangelists outside his denomination whose preaching was owned of God. Cowie led Philip into the secret of Whitefield's life: effective preaching is more than the demonstration of truth; it must be 'in demonstration of the Holy Spirit and power'. 'God makes ministers a blessing to others, by blessing themselves first. He works in them, in order to work by them.'

Philip is not an uncritical writer, and he is ready to note weaknesses and failures that admirers of Whitefield have sometimes passed over. But the great feature of his work is the way in which he leaves his subject to speak for himself. He seems to have absorbed all that Whitefield ever said and wrote, and his selection brings us into direct contact with the man. Thus Philip can truthfully write: 'This work is chiefly from Whitefield's own pen. So far as it is mine, it is in his own spirit.'

For those who want a work of quiet scholarship, Philip is not their man. But where the desire is for the evangelical flame – for words that burn, and reach heart and soul – this is a volume that shows why the gospel can turn the world upside down.

Philip's *Life and Times of Whitefield* was one of the first biographies I read as a young Christian and I never return to it without being stirred afresh by its enduring message.

IAIN H. MURRAY
June 2007

ROBERT PHILIP (1791–1858)[1]

Robert Philip, Maberly Chapel, Kingsland, was born in the year 1791, at the village of Huntly, Aberdeenshire. His father was an elder in the church of the Rev. G. Cowie, who was the founder and first promoter of Independency in the north of Scotland. The principles of this form of church government were, as a natural consequence, early instilled into the mind of the subject of this memoir, and to these he firmly adhered throughout the whole of his life. He was, by the grace of God, led to an early decision for Christ; so that, although he was deprived of his father's care at the age of eleven years, the truths that had been impressed on his youthful heart continued to exert the strongest influence over him. Very shortly after the death of his father, the gifts and powers which characterised his later life began rapidly to develop themselves. In the course of a few years he left his native place for Aberdeen, where he had obtained a situation as clerk in the Grandholm works [a flax mill]. While there, he was admitted into the church of the Rev. Dr Philip, under whose guidance and counsel he was induced to devote himself to the work of the ministry of the gospel, and at the age of nineteen he was admitted a student of Hoxton Academy, in the year 1811. After four years' laborious and successful study in that institution, he commenced his ministerial life at Liverpool, where he was for eleven years pastor of the church over which the youthful but fervent Spencer had previously presided.

During his pastorate here, much of his time and energies were devoted, and with much success, to the spiritual improvement of the sailors frequenting the port of that town. A small volume of sermons to seamen,

[1] From the *Congregational Year Book*, 1859: *Notices of Ministers Deceased.*

which he published at this time, under the title of the '*Bethel Flag*', evinces, to a striking degree, the remarkable power which he possessed of adapting his style, language and illustration to the capacities, occupations and habits of his audience.

On the 1st January 1826, he came to London to take the pastorate of a church which had been formed under his superintendence at Maberly Chapel, Kingsland, and here the remainder of his life was spent. During thirty-one years he carried on his labours here with unremitting vigour and constancy. He was seldom away from his own pulpit, rarely leaving it for any other purpose than to advocate the claims of the London Missionary Society. To this Society he was always strongly attached, and energetically endeavoured to extend its operations, especially in China. The fearful results of the East Indian trade in opium with that country were a source of deep and bitter lamentation to him. He made himself master of all the arguments that could be brought to bear against this pernicious traffic, and published a pamphlet on the subject.

Although while at Maberly he was indefatigable in the discharge of his pastoral duties, his pen was never idle. Among the numerous works which he then produced, a series of small volumes, separately issued under the name of *Guides*, obtained a very large circulation; another series, similar in plan, but addressed to a different class of readers, and published under the collective title of the *Young Man's Closet Library*, was received with equal favour both in this country and in America, where both series were ably edited and prefaced with essays by the Rev. Albert Barnes of Philadelphia. His statements of truth were clear, terse, and vigorous; the arguments and appeals by which they were enforced were conclusive, convincing, and solemn; a spirit of deep earnestness and high-toned piety pervades them all. Many traces may be found in his writings of those peculiar features of his character which all who knew him were well acquainted with; viewed, however, apart from these occasional peculiarities, none can better stand the test of the severest criticism. His biographical works were *The Life of Bunyan, The Life and Times of Whitefield,* and *The Life of Dr Milne of China.* He published also a series of lectures, forming a sequel to the *Guides*, in one volume, under the title of *The Eternal; or, the Attributes of Jehovah.*

For nearly thirty years he continued sole pastor of Maberly church; but after this period his health, which had for some time been slowly giving way, begin rapidly to decline. The relief afforded by a co-pastorate was insufficient to rally him. His strength and natural spirits yielded before the encroachments of premature old age, induced by the severe studies of his life, and the acute sufferings of its last years. About the middle of April, 1858, it became apparent to his beloved family and friends that the termination of his sufferings was near at hand. He was, however, able to get up, and, with some assistance, to reach his study, in which he most delighted to sit, till within fourteen days of his decease. After taking to his bed, his sufferings became so acute, and the difficulty of breathing under which he laboured so great, that it was almost impossible for him to communicate his thoughts and feelings to those who were around him. Oftentimes his all but inarticulate utterances were intelligible only to her who had been the faithful, devoted, and loving partner of his life for nearly forty years. As his end approached, he gradually sank into a state of unconsciousness; but ere the messenger of death – to him the messenger of life – summoned his spirit to the presence of his Lord and Master, there were given him a few moments of rest from pain, and of perfect consciousness; so that he departed hence in undisturbed peace both of body and of mind, no sigh nor struggle marking the moment when his spirit took its flight to the mansions of his Father's house. He died early in the morning of the first of May [1858], in the 67th year of his age.

George Whitefield.

Late of Pembroke College, Oxford, & Chaplain
to the Countess of Huntingdon.

London, Geo. Virtue, 26, Ivy Lane.

TO

JOSHUA WILSON, ESQ.

THIS WORK,

SUGGESTED BY HIS VENERABLE FATHER,

THE FOUNDER AND TREASURER

OF

HIGHBURY COLLEGE,

AND

ENRICHED FROM HIS OWN VALUABLE LIBRARY,

IS INSCRIBED,

BY HIS OLD FRIEND,

THE AUTHOR.

NEWINGTON GREEN,
MAY 10, 1837.

PREFACE.

THIS Work is chiefly from Whitefield's own pen. So far as it is mine, it is in his own spirit. It will, therefore, help all that is good, and expose not a little of what is wrong, in all churches; and thus, like his actual life, *tell* upon both. At least, if it fail to do this, my object will be defeated. Should its *honest* catholicity commend it, it may be followed by similar " Annals and Illustrations of Evangelical Preaching," from the dawn of the Reformation to the close of the last century.

In regard to the *style* of this Work I have nothing to say; except that it is my *own* way of telling the facts of personal history. The time is not yet come, for the *philosophy* of Whitefield's Life. It is, however, fast approaching: and, therefore, my mass of facts will soon be turned to good account by myself, or by some one. In the mean time, Whitefield will be *known* to the public; which he was not until now.

R. P.

CONTENTS.

CONTENTS.

CONTENTS.

WHITEFIELD'S LIFE AND TIMES.

CHAPTER I.

WHITEFIELD'S EARLY LIFE, EDUCATION, AND ORDINATION.

"I WAS born in Gloucestershire, in the month of December, 1714. My father and mother kept the *Bell Inn*." In this unassuming manner Whitefield commences a brief memoir of himself. It will not, however, be uninteresting to add some particulars respecting his family. His great-grandfather, the Rev. Samuel Whitefield, born at Wantage, in Berkshire, was rector of North Ledyard, in Wiltshire, and afterwards of Rockhampton. In the latter charge he was succeeded by his son, Samuel, who died without issue. Two of his daughters were married to clergymen. Andrew, Whitefield's grandfather, was a private gentleman, and lived retired upon his estate. He had fourteen children; Thomas, the eldest, was the father of the Rev. George Whitefield. Mr. Thomas Whitefield was bred to the business of a wine merchant, in Bristol, but afterwards kept an inn in the city of Gloucester. . While in Bristol he married Miss Elizabeth Edwards, a lady related to the families of Blackwell and Dinmour, of that city. He had six sons, of whom George was the youngest, and one daughter.

Concerning his father and mother, Whitefield writes : " The former died when I was two years old ; the latter is now alive,

B

(she died in December, 1751, in the 71st year of her age,) and has often told me how she endured fourteen weeks' sickness, after she brought me into the world; but was used to say, even when I was an infant, that she expected more comfort from me than from any other of her children. This, with the circumstance of my being born in an inn, has been often of service to me, in exciting my endeavours to make good my mother's expectations, and so follow the example of my dear Saviour, who was born in a manger belonging to an inn."

This amiable solicitude to realize his mother's "expectations," is the more worthy of notice, because, whatever she was as a mother, she was not distinguished as a christian. This seems *more* than implied in the following lamentation, extracted from one of his letters : " Why is my honoured mother so solicitous about a few paltry things, that will quickly perish? Why will she not come and see her youngest son, who will endeavour to be a Joseph to her, before she dies?" Such was his suspense in regard to the spiritual state of his parent; and yet he gratefully owns the salutary influence of her maternal hopes upon his mind, and, while afar off on the Atlantic, commemorates her tenderness. " My mother was very careful of my education, and always kept me, in my tender years, (for which I never can sufficiently thank her,) from intermeddling in the least with the tavern business." (This paragraph was written on board the *Elizabeth*, during the voyage to Philadelphia.) Now these acknowledgments were penned during the heat of his zeal and the height of his popularity; at a period when recent converts are prone to speak with harshness of their unconverted relatives, and to sink the child in the champion towards them. This is so common, and, to say nothing of its cruelty, so unwise, that I could not record this pleasing exception, without holding it up to general imitation. " The servant of the Lord must not strive ; but be gentle towards all,—apt to teach,—patient ; in meekness instructing those that oppose themselves; if God, peradventure, will give them repentance to the acknowledging of the truth."

Whitefield's humiliating recollections of his own early and inveterate opposition to " the truth," contributed, no doubt, to moderate his natural impatience towards others. The following is his own narrative of that period.

" My infant years must necessarily not be mentioned; yet I can remember such early stirrings of corruption in my heart, as abundantly convince me that I was conceived and born in sin; that in me dwelleth no good thing by nature; and that, if God had not freely prevented me by his grace, I must have been for ever banished from his presence. I was so brutish as to hate instruction; and used, purposely, to shun all opportunities of receiving it. I soon gave pregnant proofs of an impudent temper. Lying, filthy talking, and foolish jesting, I was much addicted to, even when very young. Sometimes I used to curse, if not swear. Stealing from my mother I thought no theft at all, and used to make no scruple of taking money out of her pockets before she was up. I have frequently betrayed my trust, and have more than once spent money I took in the house, in buying fruit, tarts, &c. to satisfy my sensual appetite. Numbers of sabbaths have I broken, and generally used to behave myself very irreverently in God's sanctuary. Much money have I spent in plays, and in the common amusements of the age. Cards, and reading romances, were my heart's delight. Often have I joined with others in playing roguish tricks; but was generally, if not always, *happily detected:* for *this* I have often since, and do now, bless and praise God."

This enumeration of youthful vices and follies, is certainly minute, and, in one sense, gratuitous; but, when the spirit and design of the confessions are duly weighed, no man will venture to laugh at them, except those who regard sin as a " *light matter.*" Every candid mind must be conscious of seeing *itself* in young Whitefield, " as in a glass;" and every *spiritual* mind will not fail to deplore these early exhibitions of depravity, nor to mark this modern exemplification of an ancient truth, " Thou makest me to possess the iniquities of my youth." (Job xiii. 26.) Were these acknowledgments written in the spirit, or for the same purpose, as Rousseau's unblushing " Confessions," I should despise myself, as well as insult the public, were I inclined to transcribe them. Were they even calculated to suggest the bare idea of uncommon sins, I should not have hesitated to

merge the particulars in some general charge of corruption:
but, besides carrying their antidote along with them, in their
penitential tone and spirit, they are but too common, however
melancholy. Bishop Lavington, indeed, affects great horror
and disgust at them, and compares them with the confessions
of " the wild and fanatical *Theresa*," in his treatise " On the Enthusiasm of Methodists and Papists ;"—a book, to which his own
description of Whitefield's confessions is far more applicable ;
" so ludicrous, filthy, and shameless, as quite defiles paper, and
is shocking to decency and modesty." Such a " perfect Jakes "
of ribaldry never issued from the episcopal bench; and yet it
found an editor in the vicar of Manaccan, in 1820!

I shall have occasion, more than once, to refer to both the
bishop and the vicar. In the mean time, I cannot but allow
Whitefield to speak for himself, on the subject of his early life.
" It would be endless to recount the sins and offences of my
younger days. ' *They are more in number than the hairs of my
head.*' My heart would fail me at the remembrance of them,
was I not assured that my Redeemer liveth to make intercession for me! However the young man in the gospel might
boast, that he had kept the commandments from his ' youth
up,' with shame and confusion of face I confess that I have
broken them all from *my* youth. Whatever foreseen fitness for
salvation others may talk of and glory in, I disclaim any such
thing : if I trace myself from my cradle to my manhood, I can
see nothing in me but a fitness to be damned. ' *I speak the
truth in Christ : I lie not !*' If the Almighty had not prevented
me by his grace, and wrought most powerfully on my soul—
quickening me by his free Spirit, when dead in trespasses and
sins, I had now either been sitting in darkness and in the
shadow of death,—or condemned, as the due reward of my
crimes, to be for ever lifting up my eyes in torments. But such
was the free grace of God to me, that though corruption worked
so strongly in my soul, and produced such early and bitter
fruits,—yet I can recollect, very early, movings of the blessed
Spirit upon my heart. I had, early, some convictions of sin.
Once, I remember, when some persons (as they frequently did)
made it their business to tease me, I immediately retired to

my room, and kneeling down, with many tears, prayed over the 118th Psalm."

It appears from the narrative, that, on this occasion, the mind of young Whitefield fastened chiefly upon the words, " *In the name of the Lord will I destroy them.*" This, of course, he applied to his *teasing* enemies, who had " compassed him about like bees :" a coincidence likely to be noticed by an irritated boy, of quick perceptions. Even *men* are but too prone, when injured, to appropriate the Messiah's weapons to their own warfare ;—as if revenge could be sanctified by the use of sacred language. But what is pitiable in the boy, is contemptible in the man. This happened when Whitefield was only ten years old ; but the following hint will account for the facility with which he turned to a psalm suited to his purpose. " I was always fond of being a clergyman, and used frequently to imitate the minister's reading prayers, &c." Such being his favourite habit at the time, he was sure to be familiar with the *imprecatory psalms*, of which so many occur in the book of Common Prayer.

We have seen that he was addicted to petty thefts. The manner in which he seems to have reconciled his conscience to them, is not peculiar to boys. "Part of the money I used to steal from my mother I gave to the *poor*, and some books I privately took from others (for which I have since restored fourfold) I remember were books of *devotion.*"

" When I was about twelve, I was placed at a school, called St. Mary De Crypt, in Gloucester : the last grammar school I ever went to. Having a good elocution and memory, I was remarked for making speeches before the corporation, at their annual visitation. During the time of my being at school, I was very fond of reading plays, and have kept from school for days together, to prepare myself for acting them. My master, seeing how mine and my schoolfellows' vein ran, composed something of this kind for us himself, and caused me to dress myself in girls' clothes, (which I had often done,) to act a part before the corporation." Thus he contracted that taste for theatrical amusements, which gave rise to the well-known insinuation, that he learned his peculiar style of oratory upon the

stage. This, however, is not the fact : his acting was confined
to the boards of St. Mary De Crypt, and to his own chamber.
But his fondness for this species of amusement was not left at
school. When seventeen years of age, he was not weaned from
this folly. Even while at college he says, "I was not fully
satisfied of the sin of reading plays, until God, upon a fast day,
was pleased to convince me. Taking a play, to read a passage
out of it to a friend, God struck my heart with such power, that
I was obliged to lay it down again."

How deeply he deplored the cause and consequences of this
habit, appears from the following remarks. "I cannot but
observe here, with much concern of mind, how this way of
training up youth has a natural tendency to debauch the mind,
to raise ill passions, and to stuff the memory with things as
contrary to the gospel of Christ, as darkness to light—hell to
heaven." This fatal "tendency" was but too fully exemplified when at school. "I got acquainted with such a set of debauched, abandoned, atheistical youths, that if God, by his free,
unmerited, and special grace, had not delivered me out of their
hands, I should have sat in the scorners' chair, and made a
mock at sin. By keeping company with them, my thoughts of
religion grew more and more like theirs. I went to public
service only to make sport, and walk about. I took pleasure in their lewd conversation. I began to reason as they did,
and to ask, why God had given me passions, and not permitted
me to gratify them? In short, I soon made great proficiency
in the school of the devil. I affected to look rakish, and was in
a fair way of being as infamous as the worst of them." This,
not oratory, was what young Whitefield learned from plays and
acting. He fell into sins, of which he says,—"*their dismal effects I have felt and groaned under ever since.*"

Of course, this progress in vice was gradual. During his
first two years at school, he bought, and read with much attention, *Ken's Manual for Winchester Scholars :* a book commended to him by the use made of it by his mother in her
afflictions. He was also a diligent scholar, and for some time
made considerable progress in the Latin classics. But the
amusements which alienated his heart from virtue, gradually

impaired his taste for education. "Before I was fifteen, having, as I thought, made sufficient progress in the classics, and, at the bottom, longing to be set at liberty from the confinement of a school, I one day told my mother,—that since her circumstances would not permit her to give me a University education, more learning, I thought, would spoil me for a tradesman, and therefore I judged it best not to learn Latin any longer. She at first refused to consent, but my corruptions soon got the better of her good nature. Hereupon for some time I went to learn to write only. But my mother's circumstances being much on the decline; and, being tractable that way, I began to assist her occasionally in the public-house, till at length I put on my blue apron and my snuffers—washed mops—cleaned rooms, and in one word, became professed and common *drawer* for nigh a year and a half."

Thus he exchanged the confinement of a school for the imprisonment of an inn; and, as might be expected in such a place, he was twice or thrice intoxicated. It does not appear, however, that he was addicted to drinking.—"He who was with David when he was '*following the ewes big with young,*' was with me here. For, notwithstanding I was thus employed in a common inn, and had sometimes the care of the whole house upon my hands, yet *I composed two or three sermons,* and dedicated one of them, in particular, to my elder brother. One time, I remember, I was much pressed to self-examination, but found myself very unwilling to look into my heart. Frequently I read the Bible, while sitting up at night. Seeing the boys go by to school, has often cut me to the heart. And a dear youth would often come, entreating me, whilst serving at the bar, to go to Oxford. My general answer was,—I wish I could."

" After I had continued about a year in servile employment, my mother was obliged to leave the inn. My brother, who had been bred up for the business, married; whereupon all was made over to him ; and I being accustomed to the house, it was agreed that I should continue there as an assistant. But God's thoughts were not as our thoughts. By his good providence it happened, that my sister-in-law and I could by no means agree ; and, at length, the resentment grew to such a height, that my proud heart would scarce suffer me to speak to her for three weeks together. But, notwithstanding I was much to blame, yet I used to retire and weep before the Lord, as Hagar when flying from Sarah : little thinking that God, by this means, was forcing me out of the public business, and calling me from drawing *wine* for drunkards, to draw water from the wells of salvation for the refreshment of his spiritual Israel. After continuing for a long time under this burden of mind, I at length resolved (thinking my absence would make all things easy) to go away. Accordingly, by the advice of my brother and consent of my mother, I went to see my elder brother, then settled in Bristol."

During a residence of two months in Bristol, Whitefield experienced some awakenings of conscience. Once, in St. John's church, he was so affected by the sermon, that he resolved to prepare himself for the sacrament, and decided against returning to the inn. This latter resolution he communicated by letter to his mother ; and the former was so strong, that, during his stay in Bristol, reading *Thomas a Kempis* was his chief delight. " And I was always impatient till the bell rung to call me to tread the courts of the Lord's house. But in the midst of these illuminations, something surely whispered,—*this would not last*. And, indeed, it so happened. For (oh that I could write it in tears of blood !) when I left Bristol and returned to Gloucester, I changed my devotion with my place. Alas, all my fervour went off. I had no inclination to go to church, or draw nigh to God. In short, my heart was far from him. However, I had so much religion left, as to persist in my resolution not to live in the inn; and, therefore, my mother gave me leave, though she had but a little income, to have a bed on the ground, and live at her house, till Providence should point out a place for me.

" Having now, as I thought, nothing to do, it was a proper season for Satan to tempt me. Much of my time I spent in reading plays, and in sauntering from place to place. I was careful to adorn my body, but took little pains to deck and beautify my soul. Evil communications with my old schoolfellows, soon corrupted my good manners. By seeing their evil practices, the sense of the divine presence, I had vouchsafed unto me, insensibly wore off my mind. But God would let nothing pluck me out of his hands, though I was continually doing despite to the Spirit of grace. He even gave me some foresight of his providing for me. One morning as I was reading a play to my sister, said I, ' Sister, God intends something for me, which we know not of. As I have been diligent in business, I believe many would gladly have me for an apprentice, but every way seems to be barred up ; so that I think God will provide for me some way or other, that we cannot apprehend.'

" Having thus lived with my mother for some considerable time, a young student, who was once my schoolfellow, and then a servitor of Pembroke College, Oxford, came to pay my mother a visit. Amongst other conversation, he told her, how he had discharged all college expenses that quarter, and saved a penny. Upon that my mother immediately cried out, ' *This will do for my son !*' Then turning to me, she said, ' *Will you go to Oxford, George?*' I replied, ' *With all my heart.*' Whereupon, having the same friends that this young student had, my mother, without delay, waited on them. They promised their interest, to get me a servitor's place in the same college. She then applied to my old master, who much approved of my coming to school again. In about a week, I went and re-entered myself ; and being grown much in stature, my master addressed me thus : ' *I see, George, you are advanced in stature, but your better part must needs have gone backward.*' This made me blush. He set me something to translate into Latin, and though I had made no application to my classics for so long a time, yet I had but one inconsiderable fault in my exercises. This, I believe, somewhat surprised my master.

" Being re-settled at school, I spared no pains to go forward in my book. I learned much faster than I did before." But, whilst thus assiduously preparing himself for college, it does not appear that he *began* to study, with an express view to the ministry : if, however, this was his object at the time, and if he never, altogether, relinquished the design, which the composition of sermons betrayed, then the following events furnish a melancholy insight, not only into the presumption of his own heart, but into the prevailing maxims of that age—upon the subject of

the christian ministry. These must have been low and lax in
the extreme, if they allowed *such* a young man to anticipate
office in the church. He was, indeed, diligent in studying the
classics, but he was, at the same time, living in the indulgence
of secret and open profligacy. " I got acquainted with a set of
debauched, abandoned, and atheistical youths—I took pleasure
in their lewd conversation—I affected to look rakish, and was
in a fair way of being as infamous as the worst of them." It is
hardly possible to conceive that, while in this state, he should
have contemplated the ministry as his object ; and yet there is
reason to fear that the tone of public feeling, at the time, was
such as to impose little check upon the morals of ministerial
candidates.   Even *now* holy character is not indispensable,
either in college halls, or at national altars ; and *then*, as we
shall see, it was still less so.   Certain it is, that Whitefield's
reformation was neither suggested nor enforced, in the first instance, by any thing moral or religious which *the general practice* of the church insisted upon.   Whatever the *letter* of her
requirements calls for in candidates, the *spirit* of them was, in
a great measure, evaporated in that age.

    I have, already, said that Whitefield is silent upon the subject
of his express design in preparing himself for the University ;
but, there being no evidence that he ever contemplated any
other profession than the ministerial, and it being the only one
for which he had evinced the shadow of a partiality, or was
likely to succeed in, under his circumstances,—we must conclude, that he had it in view from the beginning.   Such, in all
probability, being the fact, it might be expected, that the bare
idea of becoming a minister would, of itself, have imposed a
restraint upon his passions ;—but neither its own solemnity,
nor the tone of ecclesiastical feeling at the time, had any moral
influence upon him.   " I went," he says, " to public service only
to make sport and walk about."   At this time he was nearly
seventeen years of age : a period of life when he must have been
capable of understanding what is expected from a clergyman.
And yet, nothing which he saw or heard on this subject seems
to have suggested the necessity of reformation.   " God stopped
me when running on in a full career of vice.   For, just as I

was upon the brink of ruin, He gave me such a distaste of their (his companions') principles and practices, that I discovered them to my master, who soon put a stop to their proceedings."

I have been the more minute in recording this event, because without clear and correct ideas of the prevailing tone of public and ecclesiastical feeling, at the time, no fair estimate can be formed of the spirit in which methodism originated at Oxford.

The breaking up of that vicious combination which existed in the school of St. Mary de Crypt produced an important change in the morals of Whitefield. "Being thus delivered out of the snare of the devil, I began to be more and more serious, and felt God at different times working powerfully and convincingly upon my soul." This improvement of character was so evident, that his friends did not fail to welcome it. It was, however, but external at first. "One day as I was coming down-stairs, and overheard my friends speaking well of me, God deeply convicted me of hypocrisy." This timely discovery fixed his attention upon the state of his heart, and gave to his reformation a more religious character.

"Being now near the seventeenth year of my age, I was resolved to prepare myself for the holy sacrament; which I received on Christmas day. I began now to be more watchful over my thoughts, words, and actions. I kept the following Lent, fasting Wednesday and Friday, thirty-six hours together. My evenings, when I had done waiting upon my mother, were generally spent in acts of devotion, reading Drelincourt ' upon Death,' and other practical books, and I constantly went to public worship twice a day. Being now upper boy, I made some reformation amongst my schoolfellows. I was very diligent in reading and learning the classics, and in studying my Greek Testament; but I was not yet convinced of the absolute unlawfulness of playing at cards, and of reading and seeing plays; though I began to have some scruples about it. Near this time, I dreamed that I was to see God on mount Sinai; but was afraid to meet him. This made a great impression upon me, and a gentlewoman to whom I told it, said, " *George, this is a call from God.*"

Whatever may be thought of the dream, or of the interpretation, such *hints* have more frequently determined the character and

pursuits of young men, than more rational means. There is, to
a susceptible mind, a peculiar fascination in these mysterious
oracles; and, after all that has been said of their folly and fallacy, they continue to govern the choice of many, and are still
followed as leading stars,—whilst sober advice is regarded as a
dull finger-post on the road of life. In the present instance
the imaginary omens were not useless. " I grew more serious
after my dream; but yet hypocrisy crept into every action.
As once I affected to look more rakish, I now strove to look
more grave, than I really was. However, an uncommon concern and alteration was visible in my behaviour, and I often
used to find fault with the lightness of others. · One night as I
was going on an errand for my mother, an unaccountable but
very strong impression was made upon my heart, that I should
preach quickly. When I came home, I innocently told my
mother what had befallen me; but she (like Joseph's parents,
when he told them his dream) turned short upon me, crying out,
' *What does the boy mean ? Prithee, hold thy tongue !*'
" For a twelvemonth I went on in a round of duties, receiving the sacrament monthly, fasting frequently, attending constantly on public worship, and praying, often more than twice
a day, in private. One of my brothers used to tell me, he feared this would not hold long, and that I should forget all when
I went to Oxford. This caution did me much service; for it
set me on praying for perseverance. Being now near eighteen
years old, it was judged proper for me to go to the University. God
had sweetly prepared my way. The friends before applied to,
recommended me to the master of Pembroke College. Another friend took up ten pounds upon bond (which I have since
repaid) to defray the first expense of entering; and the master,
contrary to all expectation, admitted me servitor immediately."
When Whitefield entered the University of Oxford, that seat
of learning had not shaken off the moral lethargy which followed
the ejectment of the 2000 nonconformists. The *Bartholomew
Bushel,* under which those burning and shining lights were
placed, proved an extinguisher to the zeal of the luminaries that
struck into the orbit of uniformity. Those of them who retained their light lost their heat. During the seventy years, which

had elapsed since the expulsion of the nonconformists, the Isis had been changing into a Dead sea, upon the banks of which the tree of life shrivelled into a tree of mere human knowledge ; and, in the adjacent halls, the doctrines of the Reformation were superseded, in a great measure, by high church principles. Even irreligion and infidelity were so prevalent at both Universities, that when the statue of the age was chiselled by that moral Phidias, BUTLER, they seem to have furnished the model. " It is come, I know not how, to be taken for granted by many persons, that christianity is not so much as a subject of inquiry, but that it is now at length discovered to be fictitious ; and, accordingly, they treat it as if, in the present age, this were an agreed point among all people of discernment ; and nothing remained but to set it up as a principal subject of mirth and ridicule, as it were by way of reprisals for its having so long interrupted the pleasures of the world." *Bishop Butler's Analogy.*

So much was this the character of the after-dinner conversations at Oxford, that the recent change from gross ribaldry to decorum, used to be appealed to with triumph, by Coleridge, and other modern advocates : a fact, which betrays the former state of things. Even the defences of christianity, which issued from the University press during that age, betray the fatal secret, that they were as much wanted for the gownsmen, as for the public. Bishop Butler says of this state of things, " It is come, I know not how ;" but he might have known soon, if he had studied the " *analogy*" between it and the discipline of the colleges. What else could be expected from a nation or a university, after seeing the brightest ornaments of the church sacrificed to rites and ceremonies ; after seeing talents, learning, and piety reckoned " as the small dust in the balance," when weighed against robes and forms ? After witnessing diocesan and state patronage withdrawn, and exchanged for penalties *on such grounds*, it was not likely that christianity would be better treated by the nation, than its faithful ministers were by the government. From that time, down to the year 1734, when Whitefield entered at Pembroke College, the motto of the University might have been, " We care less for character than for conformity."

" A dissolution of all bonds ensued ;
The curbs invented for the mulish mouth
Of headstrong youth were broken ; bolts and bars
Grew rusty by disuse ; and massy gates
Forgot their office, opening with a touch ;
Till gowns at length are found mere masquerade ;
The tasselled cap, and the spruce band, a jest,
A mockery of the world ! "   *Cowper.*

Such Whitefield found the general character of the Oxford
students to be. " I was quickly solicited to join in their excess
of riot, by several who lay in the same room. Once in particular, it being cold, my limbs were so benumbed by sitting alone
in my study, because I would not go out amongst them, that I
could scarce sleep all night. I had no sooner received the sacrament publicly on a week day, at St. Mary's, but I was set up
as a mark for all the polite students, that knew me, to shoot at ;
for though there is a sacrament at the beginning of every term,
at which all, especially the seniors, are by statute obliged to be
present ; yet, so dreadfully has that once faithful city played
the harlot, that very few masters, no graduates, (but the methodists,) attended upon it."

I quote the latter part of this extract, not to deplore the falling off in attendance, as Whitefield does : the sacrament was

" More honoured in the breach, than the observance "

of the statute, by such men ; but the breach illustrates both the
state of discipline and of religion at the time. There were,
however, some lilies among the rank thorns of Oxford. Of
these solitary exceptions, the Wesleys and their associates were
the most exemplary. This little band had then existed during
five years, and were called, in derision, methodists. Their regular habits and rigid virtue, were proverbial throughout the
University and the city. They were the friends of the poor,
and the patrons of the serious. But, with all these excellences
of character, the Wesleys united much enthusiasm, and an
almost incredible degree of ignorance in regard to the gospel.
Their avowed object, in all their voluntary privations and zealous efforts, was, *to save their souls, and to live wholly to the glory*

of God : a noble enterprise, certainly; but undertaken by them from erroneous motives, and upon wrong principles. For any relief which their consciences seem to have obtained from the death of the Son of God, and the free salvation proclaimed in virtue of it, the gospel might have been altogether untrue or unknown; so grossly ignorant were the whole band at one time. And yet, at this period, Mr. John Wesley was a fellow of Lincoln College, and teaching others. Nine years before, he had been ordained by Dr. Potter, who was afterwards archbishop of Canterbury.

This fact reveals one of two things : either, that the young men were very inattentive to the *theological* lectures delivered from the divinity chair, or that the lectures themselves were very unscriptural. Perhaps the fault lay partly on both sides; for it is highly probable, that such young men would underrate the cold, systematic lectures of a professor. I am led to form this opinion, because the celebrated mystic, *William Law,* was, at the time, their oracle. They imitated his ascetic habits, and imbibed his spirit of *quietism.* He had said to John Wesley, who was likely to circulate the notion, " You would have a philosophical religion, but there can be no such thing. Religion is the most simple thing : it is only, We love Him because he first loved us." Such indefinite maxims assimilated, but too readily, with the mystic temper of the persons they were addressed to ; and silent contemplation, in solitude, being the very spirit of LAW's system, Wesley and his associates were not likely to relish argumentative theology, however excellent.

The following account of their devotional habits, will illustrate the true character of their religious sentiments, at the time of Whitefield's arrival from Gloucester. " They interrogate themselves whether they have been *simple* and recollected; whether they have prayed with fervour, Monday, Wednesday, Friday, and on Saturday noon; if they have used a collect at nine, twelve, and three o'clock; duly meditated on Sunday, from three to four, on Thomas a Kempis ; or mused on Wednesday and Friday, from twelve to one, on the Passion." Thus were they *monks* in almost every thing except the name.

It was necessary to delineate thus minutely the original cha-

racter of methodism, that its natural influence upon the susceptible mind of Whitefield may be anticipated. Suffering and
smarting, as he did, from vicious indulgence, and now seriously
bent upon the ministry, he was not likely to associate with the
profligate or the profane in the University. He did not. " God
gave me grace to withstand, when they solicited me to join in
their excess of riot. When they perceived they could not prevail, they let me alone, as a singular, odd fellow." He did not,
however, join himself to the methodists at once. " The young
men, so called, were then much talked of at Oxford. I heard
of and loved them before I came to the University; and so
strenuously defended them, when I heard them reviled by
the students, that they began to think that I also, in time,
should be one of them. For above a twelvemonth, my soul
longed to be acquainted with some of them, and I was strongly
pressed to follow their good example, when I saw them go
through a ridiculing crowd, to receive the holy eucharist at St.
Mary's."

How much he was prepared to enter into their peculiar spirit
when he did join them, will appear also from the following hint.
" Before I went to the University, I met with *Mr. Law's* ' Serious Call to Devout Life,' but had not money to purchase it.
Soon after my coming up to the University, seeing a small
edition of it in a friend's hand, I soon procured it. God worked
powerfully upon my soul by that excellent treatise." Thus, like
two drops of water, they were quite prepared to unite whenever
they came in contact. And this soon occurred. " It happened
that a poor woman, in one of the workhouses, had attempted to
cut her throat, but was happily prevented. Upon hearing of
this, and knowing that the two Mr. Wesleys were ready to every
good work, I sent a poor aged apple-woman of our college, to
inform Mr. Charles Wesley of it; charging her not to discover
who sent her. She went; but, contrary to my orders, told my
name. He having heard of my coming to the castle, and to a
parish church sacrament, and having met me frequently walking
by myself, followed the woman when she was gone away, and
sent an invitation to me by her, to come to breakfast with him
the next morning. I thankfully embraced the opportunity. My

soul, at that time, was athirst for some spiritual friends to lift up my hands when hung down, and to strengthen my feeble knees. He soon discovered it, and, like a wise winner of souls, made all his discourses tend that way. And when he put into my hands Professor Frank's ' Treatise against the Fear of Man,' and ' The Country Parson's Advice to his Parishioners,' I took my leave.

" In a short time he let me have another book, entitled, ' The Life of God in the Soul of Man ;' and though I had fasted, watched, and prayed, and received the sacrament so long, yet I never knew what *true religion* was, till God sent me that excellent treatise, by the hands of my never-to-be-forgotten friend. At my first reading it, I wondered what the author meant by saying, ' That some falsely placed religion in going to church, doing hurt to no one, being constant in the duties of the closet, and now and then reaching out their hands to give alms to their poor neighbours.' Alas ! thought I, if this be not religion, what is ? God soon showed me ; for in reading a few lines further, ' *that true religion was a union of the soul with God, and Christ formed within us,*' a ray of divine light was instantaneously darted in upon my soul, and from that moment, but not till then, did I know that I must be a new creature."

This was an important era in Whitefield's experience ; and, if he had been left to the guidance of the book that suggested the necessity of regeneration, his feet might soon have stood upon the Rock of ages. He was now in the right track to Calvary ; and, with his anxiety to " be born again," would have held on, until he had discovered that, " to as many as received Him, Christ gave power to become the sons of God ; even to them that believe on his name." But, unhappily, Whitefield was not left to follow out his own convictions : Charles Wesley —" *ignorant of God's righteousness, and going about to establish his own righteousness* "—interfered with the young convert, and inoculated him with the *virus* of legality and quietism. Before Whitefield had time to acquire from the gospel the relief which his heavy-laden conscience longed for, he was introduced to the methodists ; from kind motives on the part of his zealous friend, no doubt ; but unhappily for himself.

The intimacy well nigh proved fatal to his life, and to his reason.

" From time to time, Mr. Wesley permitted me to come unto him, and instructed me as I was able to bear it. By degrees he introduced me to the rest of his christian brethren. I now began, like them, to live by rule, and to pick up every fragment of my time, that not a moment of it might be lost. Like them, having no weekly sacrament (although the Rubrick required it) at our own college, I received every Sunday at Christ-Church. I joined with them in keeping the stations, by fasting Wednesdays and Fridays, and left no means unused which I thought would lead me nearer to Jesus Christ. By degrees I began to leave off eating fruits and such like, and gave the money I usually spent in that way to the poor. Afterward I always chose the worst sort of food, though my place furnished me with variety. My apparel was mean. I thought it unbecoming a penitent to have his hair powdered. I wore woollen gloves, a patched gown, and dirty shoes ; and though I was then convinced that the kingdom of God did not consist in meats and drinks, yet I resolutely persisted in these voluntary acts of self-denial, because I found them great promoters of the spiritual life. It was now suggested to me, that Jesus Christ was amongst the *wild beasts* when he was tempted, and that I ought to follow his example ; and being willing, as I thought, to imitate Jesus Christ, after supper I went into Christ-Church walk, near our college, and continued in silent prayer nearly two hours ; sometimes lying flat on my face, sometimes kneeling upon my knees. The night being stormy, it gave me awful thoughts of the day of judgment. The next night I repeated the same exercise at the same place. Soon after this, the holy season of Lent came on, which our friends kept very strictly ; eating no flesh during the six weeks, except on Saturdays and Sundays. I abstained frequently on Saturdays also, and ate nothing on the other days (except Sunday) but *sage-tea* without sugar, and coarse bread. I constantly walked out in the cold mornings, till part of one of my hands was quite *black*. This, with my continued abstinence, and inward conflicts, at length so emaciated my body, that, at Passion-week, finding I could scarce creep up-stairs, I was obliged to inform my kind tutor of my condition, who immediately sent for a physician to me."

While it is impossible to read this catalogue of extravagances, without pitying the wretched sufferer and his superstitious friends, it is equally impossible to refrain from smiling and frowning, alternately, at the gross absurdities of *quietism*, and the foolish requirements of the Rubrick. Many of both are equal outrages upon common sense; to say nothing of their being unscriptural. But these were not the only baneful effects of Whitefield's intimacy with the methodists. " The course of my studies I soon entirely changed: whereas, before, I was busied in studying the dry sciences, and books that went no farther than the surface, I now resolved to read only such as entered into the heart of religion. Meeting with Castanza's ' Spiritual Combat,' in which he says, that ' he that is employed in mortifying his will, was as well employed as though he was converting the Indians,' Satan so imposed upon my understanding, that he persuaded me to shut myself up in my study, till I could do good with a single eye; lest in endeavouring to save others, I should, at last, by pride and self-complacence, lose myself. When Castanza advised to talk but little, Satan said, I must not talk at all; so that I, who used to be the most forward in exhorting my companions, have sat whole nights without speaking at all. Again, when Castanza advised to endeavour after a silent recollection, and waiting upon God, Satan told me, I must leave all forms, and not use my voice in prayer at all." These habits soon affected his college exercises also. " Whenever I endeavoured to compose my theme, I had no power to write a word, nor so much as to tell my christian friends of my inability to do it. All power of meditating, or even thinking, was taken from me. My memory quite failed me. And I could fancy myself to be like nothing so much as a man locked up in iron armour."

Having twice neglected to produce the weekly theme, his tutor called him into the common room, after fining him, and kindly inquired whether any calamity had befallen him, or what was the reason of his neglect? " I burst into tears, and assured him, that it was not out of contempt of authority, but that I could not act otherwise. Then, at length, he said, he believed I could not; and, when he left me, told a friend (as he very well might) that he took me to be *really mad*. This friend, hearing what had happened from my tutor, came to me, urging the command in Scripture, ' to be subject to the higher powers.' I answered, *Yes; but I had a new revelation*. Lord. what is man!"

During the progress of this direful malady, the Wesleys were not wanting, either in attention or tenderness, to their unhappy friend; and if, like Job's friends, they were miserable comforters, still, their motives claim the highest respect. They would have brought him " water from the well of Bethlehem" at any expense; but, like Hagar weeping over her fainting child in the wilderness, their own eyes were not then opened to see that well. It is only bare justice to make this acknowledgment. I have exposed and censured, freely, the ignorance, mysticism, and superstition of the Wesleys; I have deplored, in strong terms, the intimacy which Whitefield formed with the Oxford methodists; and traced to their maxims and habits, as the direct cause, a great part of his extravagances; but, in all this, I have been actuated by no prejudice against his friends, nor do my remarks upon methodism embrace the system as it now exists : they are, hitherto, entirely confined to its character at Oxford. *Then,* its influence, according to Mr. John Wesley's own acknowledgment, was that " of leading him into the desert to be tempted and humbled, and shown what was in his heart." Even Dr. Coke says of him, it is certain that he was then very little acquainted with true experimental religion. This is very obvious from the advice which he gave to Whitefield, when his case was so pitiable, that Charles Wesley was afraid to prescribe. " He advised me to resume *all my externals,* though not to *depend* on them in the least." Now, however wise the latter clause of this rule may be, the former part is pitiable : " all" Whitefield's " externals" included many of the very habits which had unhinged his mind, and ruined his health. He did, however, " resume" them, and the result was, " a fit of sickness which continued during seven weeks." His tutor seems to have been the only person about him who acted wisely. Charles Wesley referred him to chapters in *A Kempis:* John, to the maxims of quietism. "My tutor lent me books, gave me money, visited me, and furnished me with a physician : in short, he behaved in all respects like a father."

The reader must not suppose, however, that Whitefield himself arraigns the imprudence of his young friends ; or that he contrasts, as I have ventured to do, their measures with those of his tutor : no, indeed ; he records both with equal gratitude, and uniformly pronounces benedictions upon the authors. Even when he became the opponent of John Wesley, on the subject of "free grace," and *might* have pointed his arguments by an appeal to the early errors of his rival, he does not so much as hint at them, but prefaces his letter by declaring, " *Was nature to speak, I had rather die than write against you.*" I, however, have no such scruples on this head : but, while I shall avoid doing injustice to the Wesleys, I shall canvass as freely their influence upon Whitefield, as that of any other persons with whom he came in contact. The formation of *his character* must be shown, without regard to the light in which it may exhibit the forces that determined it.

The seven weeks of sickness, already mentioned, Whitefield calls, "a glorious visitation." "The blessed Spirit was all this time purifying my soul. All my former gross, notorious, and even my heart sins also, were now set home upon me ; of which I wrote down some remembrances immediately, and confessed them before God morning and evening." This exercise, although more humiliating and mortifying than even his fasts and austerities, was infinitely more useful. While they led him only to *Castanza* and *A Kempis*—this led him direct to the gospel, and to the throne of grace. Unable to sustain such views of the evil of sin, and having failed, in all his former efforts, to remove a sense of guilt by a series of observances, he was now *shut up to the faith.* "Though weak, I often spent two hours in my evening retirements, and prayed over my *Greek Testament,* and Bishop Hall's most excellent ' Contemplations.' " While thus engaged in searching the Scriptures, he discovered the true grounds of a sinner's hope and justification. The testimony of God concerning his Son became "*power unto salvation.*" "I

found and felt in myself, that I was delivered from the burden
that had so heavily oppressed me.   The spirit of mourning was
taken from me, and I knew what it was truly to rejoice in God
my Saviour.   For some time I could not avoid singing psalms
wherever I was; but my joy became gradually more settled.
Thus were the days of my mourning ended : after a long night
of desertion and temptation, the star, which I had seen at a distance before, began to appear again : the day-star arose in my
heart."

Such is the history of Whitefield's conversion : in this manner
was he rescued from the malignant snares of the devil, and from
the blind guidance of friends who were unconsciously strengthening these snares, and unintentionally enabling the arch-de-
ceiver to keep this brand in the burning.   This, I am aware, is
strong language ; and, by many, will be considered unwarrantable : but, as Whitefield will ever be a grand object of attention
in the church of Christ ; and as myriads, yet unborn, will study
his character or hear of his conversion ; it shall not be my fault,
if that conversion is misunderstood by posterity, or any thing
gathered from it in behalf of *such* methodism as he was
led into then.

I duly appreciate the benevolence, the zeal, and the sincerity
of the Wesleys ; but, in this instance, and at that time, those
virtues rank no higher in them, than the same virtues in Ma-
homedans or Hindoos ;—amount to no more at *Oxford* than
they would at *Mecca* or *Benares*.   Now if, instead of the Wesleys, the same number of *Wahabees* had been about Whitefield,
inculcating their simplified Islamism; who would have ascribed
to them, or to it, any *usefulness ?*   Both would have been
arraigned, as diverting him from the gospel of Christ ; nor would
the sincerity of the Wahabees, or the self-denying character of
their habits, have shielded either from severe reprehension.   The
only apology that any one would have thought of offering for
them, would have been, " *I wot that through ignorance ye did
it.*"   In like manner I am quite ready to say of the Wesleys,
" I bear them record, that they had a zeal of God ; *but not according to knowledge :*" a fact, which neutralizes their Oxford
piety into well-meant superstition.   Such explanations are

wanted, now that devotion apart from faith, and penitential feeling apart from the knowledge of " the truth," are often hailed as conversion to God. This is a sore evil under the sun ; and one not easily touched, without seeming to slight symptoms of piety. I must, however, attempt to unmask this plausible " form of godliness," whatever suspicions my freedom may awaken.

Whitefield, in the simplicity of his heart, calls the events of this period " the dealings of God" with him, and records them as the gradual steps by which he was led to believe in Christ for righteousness. And, so far as they were made instrumental in discovering to him his own weakness, and in weaning him from sin and vanity, they were " the dealings of God ;" but, so far as his maxims and habits were superstitious and unscriptural, God must not be identified with them, nor even implicated in the least. All the hand He had in this part of the transaction was, that he made these austerities and superstitions their own punishment, and prevented them from ruining an ignorant young man. So far as their own natural influence went, it increased the spirit of bondage, and diverted the sinner from God's appointed remedy. We have seen from Whitefield's own acknowledgments, and Wesley's too, that the further such measures were pursued, the further the methodists were from solid relief. Now, it cannot be supposed for a moment, that God's dealings with the soul divert it from the Saviour ; nor that any thing is the work of His Spirit on the heart, which leads to absurdities and extravagance. And if this be granted, then a great part of those things in the experience of Whitefield, which strike the mind so forcibly, lose all their importance, except as *facts*. As feelings, motives, or maxims in religion, they have no weight ; but were, while they continued, the actual rivals of faith and evangelical repentance. For any thing, therefore, which appears to the contrary, his *conversion* would not have been less genuine, if he had never gone through the exercise of mind produced by *these* causes. The horror, the depression, the despair, which preceded his being born again, were neither elementary nor necessary parts of regeneration. Humanly speaking, a clear exhibition of the plan of salvation, if presented to him when he entered Oxford, would have relieved his mind at once, and introduced him into the liberty of the sons of God. He was not, indeed, so fully prepared to prize the gospel then, as when he did believe it with the heart; but, although less humble, less in earnest, at the time of his arrival, even then he was awakened to a sense of his guilt and danger. Now, the question is, would not the gospel itself, if it had been preached to him at this time, have effected a change of heart? Would not the glad tidings of a finished salvation, addressed to him, as he was, have melted, humbled, and converted him, without the preliminary process he went through? The only thing valuable in that process is, the humbling effect of it; but if the same kind and degree of humility would result from believing the gospel, then, *faith* in Christ ought to be the *first* step pressed upon an awakened sinner.

I have been induced to throw out these hints, because so many persons imagine that they have no warrant for believing in Christ, until they experience such convictions, and possess such feelings, as converts like Whitefield did. The consequence is, that they live on, looking for what *they* call "a day of power," which shall qualify them for the exercise of faith. This false and fatal maxim must not be allowed to shelter itself in the example of Whitefield; and that it may not intrench itself there, I have felt it my duty to expose the true character of his preliminary experience. It was useful; but how? Not by its own direct influence; that was injurious in every sense; but its usefulness in humbling, and in emptying him of self-dependence, arose from its being overruled for good by the Spirit of God. This being the fact, let no one quote Whitefield's experience in proof of the necessity of going through such a process of awakening as he underwent. The gospel itself is "power unto salvation to every one that believeth;" and nothing is *religion*, which precedes the belief of it, except such exercises as naturally lead to faith.

Although I have grouped, into one view, the mental aberrations and bodily sufferings of Whitefield whilst at Oxford, there were, during the period it embraces, calm and lucid intervals, in which he combined with his studies, efforts to do good in the city. Like his friends, he was the friend of the poor ; but not without giving offence to his superiors.

" I incurred the displeasure of the master of the college, who frequently chid, and once threatened to expel me, if I ever visited the poor again. Being surprised by this treatment, and overawed by his authority, I spake unadvisedly with my lips, and said, if it displeased him, I would not. My conscience soon smote me for this sinful compliance. I immediately repented, and visited the poor the first opportunity, and told my companions, if ever I was called to a *stake* for Christ's sake, I would serve my tongue as Archbishop Cranmer served his hand,—*make that burn first.*" Nor were his efforts confined to private houses : he constantly visited the town gaol to read and pray with the prisoners. One instance of this is too remarkable to be passed over.

" As I was walking along, I met with a poor woman whose husband was then in *bocardo,* Oxford town gaol. Seeing her much discomposed, I inquired the cause. She told me, that not being able to bear the crying of her children, and having nothing to relieve them, she had been to drown herself; but was mercifully prevented ; and said, she was coming to my room to inform me of it. I gave her some immediate relief, and desired her to meet me at the prison with her husband in the afternoon. She came ; and there God visited them both by his free grace. She was powerfully quickened; and when I had done reading, he came to me like the trembling jailer, and grasping my hand, cried out, ' *I am upon the brink of hell !* ' From this time forward both of them grew in grace. God, by his providence, soon delivered him from his confinement. Though notorious offenders against God and one another before, yet now they became helps meet for each other in the great work of their salvation."

In the same spirit he also exerted himself on behalf of his relations and friends at Gloucester. His discovery of the necessity of regeneration, like Melancthon's discovery of the truth, led him to imagine, that no one could resist the evidence which convinced his own mind. " Upon this, like the woman of Samaria when Christ revealed himself to her at the well, I had no rest in my soul, till I wrote letters to my relations, telling them there was such a thing as the *new birth*. I imagined they would have gladly received it; but alas! my words seemed to them as idle tales. They thought I was going beside myself."

I have not been able to obtain any of the letters on this subject, which he addressed to his own family; but the following extract from one to a friend, will be a sufficient specimen of their character.

" Lest you should imagine that true religion consists in any thing besides an entire renewal of our nature into the image of God, I have sent you a book entitled, " The Life of God in the Soul of Man," written by a young, but an eminent christian;— which will inform you what true religion is, and how you may attain it; as, likewise, how wretchedly most people err in their sentiments about it, who suppose it to be nothing else (as he tells us, page 3) but a mere model of outward performances; without ever considering, that all our corrupt passions must be subdued, and a complex habit of virtues—such as meekness, lowliness, faith, hope, and the love of God and of man—be implanted in their room, before we can have the least title to enter into the kingdom of God. Our divine Master having expressly told us, that unless we "renounce ourselves, and take up our cross daily, we cannot be his disciples." And again, " unless we have the spirit of Christ, we are none of his."

This advice met, we are informed, " with a cold reception," and was an ungrateful subject to his friend at first; and yet, even while it was so, such were his own confused notions of religion, that he urges his friend to receive " the holy communion" frequently; assuring him that " nothing so much bedwarfs us in religion, as staying away from the heavenly banquet." As if a man who had no relish for the doctrine of regeneration, could have any religion!

Having thus noticed the line of conduct which, notwithstanding all his crude notions, he pursued at Oxford,—I proceed now to record the means by which he was supported during his stay at the University. It will be recollected that his chief dependence was upon the emoluments of servitorship.

" Soon after my acceptance I went and resided, and found my having been used to a public-house was now of service to me. For, many of the servitors being sick, at my first coming up, by my diligent and steady attendance, I ingratiated myself into the gentlemen's favour so far, that many who had it in their power chose me to be their servitor. This much lessened my expense ; and, indeed, God was so gracious, that with the profits of my place, and some little presents made me by my kind tutor, for almost the first three years I did not put all my relations together to above £24 expense." When he joined himself to the methodists, the profits of his place were, as might be expected, diminished: a number " took away their pay from me ;" but other sources of supply were soon opened for him. Some of the methodists having left Oxford about this time, and being solicitous to keep up the society, wrote to Sir John Philips of London, commending Whitefield to his patronage, " as a proper person" to stay and encourage their friends in fighting the good fight of faith. " Accordingly he immediately offered me an annuity of twenty pounds. To show his disinterestedness, he has promised me *that,* whether I continue here or not ; and if I resolve to stay at *Oxon,* he'll give me thirty pounds a year. If that will not do, I may have more." In this manner was he provided for, when his original resources failed.

The state of his health, however, compelled him to quit, for a time, his " sweet retirement" at Oxford. So long as he could, he resisted all the persuasions of his tutor and physician, and all the invitations of his mother to visit Gloucester. Their urgency at length prevailed, and he returned home. " My friends were surprised to see me look and behave so cheerfully, after the many reports they had heard concerning me."

" However, I soon found myself to be as a sheep sent forth amongst wolves in sheep's clothing ; for they immediately endeavoured to dissuade me from a constant use of the means of grace ; especially from weekly abstinence, and receiving the blessed sacrament. But God enabled me to resist them, stedfast in the faith ; and, by keeping close to him in his holy ordinances, I was made to triumph over all."

" Being unaccustomed for some time to live without spiritual companions, and finding none that would heartily join me—no, not one—I watched unto prayer all the day long; beseeching God to raise me some religious associates in his own way and time. ' *I will endeavour either to find or make a friend*' had been my resolution now for some time, and therefore after importunate prayer one day, I resolved to go to the house of one Mrs. W——, to whom I had formerly read plays, Spectators, Pope's Homer, and such-like trifling books; hoping the alteration she now would find in my sentiments, might, under God, influence her soul. God was pleased to bless the visit with the desired effect: she received the word gladly: she wanted to be taught the way of God more perfectly, and soon became ' a fool for Christ's sake.' Not long after, God made me instrumental to awaken several young persons, who soon formed themselves into a little society, and had quickly the honour of being despised at Gloucester, as we had been before them at Oxford. Thus, *all* that will live godly in Christ Jesus, must suffer persecution."

As his efforts and usefulness, during the period of this visit to Gloucester, may be viewed as the *dawn* of his future zeal and success, it will be proper, before enumerating more instances, to record, distinctly, the manner in which he prepared himself for doing good to others.

" My mind being now more open and enlarged, I began to read the holy Scriptures upon my knees; laying aside all other books, and praying over, if possible, every line and word. This proved meat indeed, and drink indeed, to my soul. I daily received fresh life, light, and power from above. I got more true knowledge from reading the book of God, in one month, than I could *ever* have acquired from all the writings of men. In one word, I found it profitable for reproof, for correction, for instruction; every way sufficient to make the man of God perfect, throughly furnished for every good work and word. About this time God was pleased to enlighten my soul, and bring me into the knowledge of his free grace—and the necessity of being *justified in His sight by faith only.* This was more extraordinary, because my friends at Oxford had rather inclined to the *mystic divinity.* Burkitt's and Henry's

Expositions were of admirable use, to lead me into *this* and all other gospel truths. *It is* the good old doctrine of the church of England; it is what the holy martyrs, in Queen Mary's time, sealed with their blood." To these habits of reading, Whitefield added much secret prayer. " Oh, what sweet communion had I daily vouchsafed with God in prayer after my coming to Gloucester! How often have I been carried out beyond myself, when meditating in the fields! How assuredly I felt that Christ dwelt in me and I in Him, and how daily did I walk in the comforts of the Holy Ghost, and was edified and refreshed in the multitude of peace!"

Such were Whitefield's private habits while attempting to be useful in public. His zeal and success will now be understood.

" I always observed that as my inward strength increased, so my outward sphere of action increased proportionably. In a short time, therefore, I began to read to some poor people twice or thrice a week. I likewise visited two other little societies besides my own. Occasionally as business and opportunity permitted, I generally visited one or two sick persons every day; and though silver and gold I had little of my own, yet in imitation of my Lord's disciples, who entreated in behalf of the fainting multitude, I used to pray unto Him; and he, from time to time, inclined several that were rich in this world, to give me money; so that I generally had a little stock for the poor always in my hand. One of the poor, whom I visited in this manner, was called effectually by God at the eleventh hour: she was a woman above threescore years old; and I really believe, died in the true faith of Jesus Christ."

" At my first coming to Gloucester, being used to visit the prisoners at Oxford, I prayed most earnestly that God would open a door for me to visit the prisoners here also. Quickly after, I dreamed that one of the prisoners came to be instructed by me: it was much impressed upon my heart. In the morning I went to the door of the county gaol;—I knocked, but nobody came to open it. I waited still upon God in prayer; and in some months after, came a letter from a friend at Oxford, desiring me to go to one *Pebworth*, who had broken out of Oxford gaol, and was retaken at Gloucester. As soon as I read this letter, it appeared to me that my prayer was now answered. Immediately I went to the prison : I met with the person, and finding him and some others willing to hear the word of God, (having gained leave of the keeper and two ordinaries,) I constantly read to and prayed with them, every day I was in town. I also begged money for them, whereby I was enabled to release some of them, and cause provision to be distributed weekly among them ; as also to put such books into their hands as I judged most proper. I cannot say that any one of the prisoners was effectually wrought upon ; however, much evil was prevented, many were convinced, and my own soul was much edified and strengthened in the love of God and man."

" During my stay here, God enabled me to give a public testimony of my repentance,—as to seeing and acting plays ; for, hearing the strollers had come to town, and knowing what an egregious offender I had been, I was stirred up to extract Mr. Law's excellent treatise, entitled ' The Absolute Unlawfulness of the Stage Entertainment.' The printer at my request put a little of it in the news, for six weeks successively ; and God was pleased to give it his blessing." In this manner Whitefield employed himself during nine months ; and one effect of pursuing such plans was, that " the partition-wall of bigotry and sect religion was soon broken down" in his heart. " I loved all, of whatever denomination, that loved the Lord Jesus in sincerity." This acknowledgment stands, in his diary, connected with an account of the benefit he derived from studying the works of the nonconformists. Baxter's " Call" and Allein's " Alarm," accorded so with his own ideas of fidelity and *unction*, that wherever he recognised *their spirit* he acknowledged " a brother beloved."

Upon this portion of his history, the mind dwells with almost unmixed delight : the only drawback is, the undue importance attached by him to dreams ; and even those, considered as an *index* to his waking thoughts, are interesting ; revealing, as they do, his deep solicitude on behalf of souls. His zeal was now according to knowledge ;—his object, at once, definite and scriptural ;—his measures direct and rational,—and his motives truly evangelical. Drawing his own hope and consolation immediately from the oracles of God, he led others direct to the same source; shutting up to the faith those he associated with. In this respect Whitefield presents a striking contrast to Wesley, at the commencement of his public exertions. The latter, although equally conscientious, was so crazed with the crude notions of the mystics, that when he left Oxford to visit Georgia, Law's "Christian Perfection" was almost his text-book, while instructing his fellow-passengers. Accordingly the *success* of the two, at the time, was as different as the means which they severally adopted. While Whitefield won souls by reading the Scriptures, Wesley, by inculcating the austerities of the ascetics, laboured in vain: he was long "esteemed an Ishmael; for his hand was against every man, and every man's hand was against him."

During the latter part of Whitefield's residence in Gloucester, although " despised" by many, his friends multiplied in spite of all the odium which his opinions and practice called forth. They became urgent for his immediate ordination, and solicitous to see him in a sphere worthy of his talents and zeal. But such were, *now*, his views of the ministry, that he put a decided negative upon all their applications; intrenching his refusal in a resolution of the diocesans, " not to ordain any under twenty-three years of age." He was not yet twenty-one. This apparently insurmountable objection was, however, soon removed. He obtained, about this time, an introduction to Lady Selwyn, who had marked her approbation of him by a handsome present of money, and by an immediate application to the bishop on his behalf. The character she seems to have given of him had its due weight with Dr. Benson. " As I was coming from the cathedral prayers, thinking of no such thing, one of the vergers called after me, and said, the bishop desired to speak with me. I immediately turned back, considering within myself, what I had done to deserve his Lordship's displeasure. When I came to the top of the palace stairs, the bishop took me by the hand, told me he was glad to see me, and bid me wait a little, till he had put off his habit, and he would return to me again. This gave me an opportunity of praying to God for his assistance, and adoring him for his providence over me. At his coming again into the room, the bishop told me that he had heard of my character, liked my behaviour at church; and, inquiring my age, said, ' *notwithstanding I have declared I would not ordain any one under three and twenty, yet I shall think it my duty to ordain you, whenever you come for holy orders.*' He then made me a present of five guineas to buy me a book." Thus was the chief external hinderance removed at once; and with it, his hesitation vanished. " From the time I first entered the University, especially from the time I knew what was true and undefiled christianity, I entertained high thoughts of the importance of the ministerial office, and was not solicitous what place should be prepared for me, but how I should be prepared for a place. That saying of the apostle, ' *Not a novice, lest being puffed up with pride, he fall into the condemnation of the devil;*' and that first question of our excellent ordination office, ' Do you trust that you are inwardly moved by the Holy Ghost to take upon you this office and administration?' used even to make me tremble, whenever I thought of entering into the ministry. The shyness of Moses and some other prophets, when God sent them out in a public capacity, I thought was sufficient to teach me, not to run until I was called. He who knoweth the hearts of men, is witness that I never prayed more earnestly against any thing, than I did against entering into this service of the church, *so soon.* Oftentimes I have been in an agony in prayer, when under convictions of my insufficiency for so great a work;—with strong cries and tears, I have frequently said, ' *Lord, I am a youth of uncircumcised lips: Lord, send me not into thy vineyard yet!*' And sometimes I had reason to think God was angry with me for resisting his will. However, I was resolved to pray *thus* as long as I could. If God did not grant my request in keeping me *out of it,* I knew his grace would be sufficient to support and strengthen me whenever he sent me into the ministry."

" To my prayers I added my endeavours, and wrote letters to my friends at Oxford, beseeching them to pray to God to disappoint my country friends, who were for my taking orders as soon as possible. Their answer was, ' Pray we the Lord of

the harvest to send thee and many more labourers into his harvest.' Another old and worthy minister of Christ, when I
wrote to him about the meaning of the word *novice,* answered,
it meant a novice in grace, and not in years ; and he was pleased
to add—if St. Paul were then at Gloucester, he believed St.
Paul would ordain me. All this did not satisfy me : I still continued instant in prayer against going into holy orders, and was
not thoroughly convinced it was the divine will, till God by his
providence brought me acquainted with the bishop of Gloucester." " Before I came home, the news had reached my
friends, who being fond of my having such a great man's favour,
were very solicitous to know the event of my visit. Many
things I hid from them ; but when they pressed me hard, I was
obliged to tell them how the bishop, of his own accord, had
offered to give me holy orders whenever I would. On which
they, knowing how I had depended on the declaration his Lordship had made some time ago, said, and I then began to think
myself, that, if I held out any longer, I should fight against
God. At length I came to a resolution, by God's leave, to
offer myself for holy orders the next Ember-days."

Having thus surmounted his difficulties, he proceeded at
once to prepare himself for ordination. He had, before, satisfied himself of the truth of the Thirty-nine Articles, by comparing them with the Scriptures ; but it does not appear that
the Prayer Book, as a whole, was submitted to the same test :
he seems to have taken its truth for granted. This is the more
remarkable, because in every thing else he was conscientious.

" I strictly examined myself by the qualifications required
for a minister, in St. Paul's Epistle to Timothy, and also by
every question that I knew would be put to me at the time of
my ordination. *This* latter, I drew out in writing at large, and
sealed my approbation of it every Sunday at the blessed sacrament. At length, Trinity Sunday being near at hand, and
having my testimonials from the college, I went, a fortnight
beforehand, to Gloucester, intending to compose some sermons,
and to give myself more particularly to prayer. When I came
to Gloucester, notwithstanding I strove and prayed for several
days, and had matter enough in my heart, yet I was so restrain-

ed, that I could not compose any thing at all. I mentioned my
case to a clergyman : he said, I was an *enthusiast*. I wrote to
another, who was experienced in the divine life : he gave me
some reasons, why God might deal with me in that manner ;
and, withal, promised me his prayers. The remainder of the
fortnight I spent in reading the several missions of the prophets and apostles, and wrestled with God to give me grace to
follow their good examples.

" About three days before the time appointed for ordination,
the bishop came to town. The next evening I sent his Lordship an abstract of my private examination upon these two
questions : ' *Do you trust that you are inwardly moved by the
Holy Ghost, to take upon you this office and administration?* '
And, ' *Are you called according to the will of our Lord Jesus
Christ and the laws of this realm ?* ' The next morning I waited
upon the bishop. He received me with much love; telling me,
he was glad I was come, and that he was satisfied with the
preparation I had made. Upon this I took my leave ; abashed
with God's goodness to such a wretch, but, withal, exceedingly
rejoiced, that, in every circumstance, he made my way into the
ministry so very plain before my face ! This, I think, was on
Friday. The day following I continued in abstinence and
prayer. In the evening, I retired to a hill near the town, and
prayed fervently, for about two hours, on behalf of myself and
those that were to be ordained with me. On Sunday morning
I rose early, and prayed over St. Paul's Epistle to Timothy, and
more particularly over *that* precept, ' *Let no one despise thy
youth.*' When I went up to the altar, I could think of nothing
but *Samuel's* standing a little child before the Lord, with a
linen ephod. When the bishop laid his hands upon my head,
my heart was melted down, and I offered up my whole spirit,
soul, and body, to the service of God's sanctuary. I read the
gospel, at the bishop's command, with power, and afterward
sealed the good confession I had made before many witnesses,
by partaking of the holy sacrament."

His feelings and views upon this solemn occasion, are recorded, still more forcibly, in two letters to a friend. The first is
so excellent, that no apology is required for inserting it here entire.

"Gloucester, June 20th, 1736.
"My dear friend,

This is a day much to be remembered, O, my soul! for, about noon, I was solemnly admitted by good Bishop Benson, before many witnesses, into holy orders; and was, blessed be God! kept composed both before and after imposition of hands. I endeavoured to behave with unaffected devotion; but not suitable enough to the greatness of the office I was to undertake. At the same time, I trust, I answered to every question from the bottom of my heart, and heartily prayed that God might say, Amen. I hope the good of souls will be my only principle of action. Let come what will—life or death, depth or height— I shall henceforward live like one who this day, in the presence of men and angels, took the holy sacrament, upon the profession of being inwardly moved by the Holy Ghost to take upon me that ministration in the church. This I began with reading prayers to the prisoners in the county gaol. Whether I myself shall ever have the honour of styling myself—' a prisoner of the Lord,' I know not; but indeed, my dear friend, I can call heaven and earth to witness, that when the bishop laid his hand upon me, I gave myself up to be a martyr for Him who hung upon the cross for me. Known unto Him are all future events and contingencies. I have thrown myself blindfold, and, I trust, without reserve, into his almighty hands; only I would have you observe—*that till you hear of my dying for or in my work, you will not be apprized of all the preferment that is expected by*

G. W."

TO THE SAME.

"June 23.
"Dear friend,

Never a poor creature set up with so small a stock. * *
* * My intention was, to make at least a hundred sermons, with which to begin the ministry; but this is so far from being the case, that I have not a single one by me, except that which I made for a small christian society, and which I sent to a neighbouring clergyman, to convince him how unfit I was to take upon me the important work of preaching. He kept it for

a fortnight, and then sent it back, with a guinea for the loan of it; telling me, he had divided it into two, and had preached it morning and evening to his congregation. With this sermon I intend to begin, God willing, next Sunday. * * * * Help, help me, my dear friend, with your warmest addresses to the throne of grace, that I may not only find mercy, but grace to help in time of need. * * * * O, cease not; for I must again repeat it, cease not to pray for

. G. W."

The intense energy of these appeals to God and man, forms a striking contrast to his first views of the ministry, and leads the mind to expect a corresponding energy in his preaching.

" Being restrained from writing, I could not preach in the afternoon, though much solicited thereto. But I read prayers to the poor prisoners; being willing to let the *first* act of my ministerial office be an act of charity. The next morning, waiting upon God in prayer, to know what he would have me to do, these words, ' *Speak out, Paul,*' came with great power to my soul. Immediately my heart was enlarged; and I preached on the Sunday following to a very crowded audience, with as much freedom as though I had been a preacher for some years."

The following letter illustrates the truth of this statement, and excites curiosity about the sermon itself.

" My dear friend,

Glory! glory! glory! be ascribed to an Almighty Triune God. Last Sunday, in the afternoon, I preached my first sermon in the church of St. Mary De Crypt, where I was baptized, and also first received the sacrament of the Lord's supper. Curiosity, as you may easily guess, drew a large congregation together on the occasion. The sight, at first, a little awed me; but I was comforted by a heartfelt sense of the divine presence, and soon found the unspeakable advantage of having been accustomed to public speaking when a boy at school; and of exhorting and teaching the prisoners, and poor people at their private houses, whilst at the University. By these means I was kept from being daunted overmuch. As I proceeded, I perceived the

fire kindled, till at last, though so young, and amidst a crowd
of those who knew me in my infant, childish days, I trust I was
enabled to speak with some degree of gospel authority. Some
few mocked, but most, for the present, seemed struck; and I
have since heard, that a complaint had been made to the bishop,
that I drove fifteen mad by the first sermon. The worthy prelate, as I am informed, wished that the madness might not be
forgotten before next Sunday. Before then, I hope my sermon
upon 'He that is in Christ is a new creature,' will be completed.
Blessed be God, I now find freedom in writing. Glorious
Jesus!

> ' Unloose my stammering tongue to tell
> Thy love immense, unsearchable!'

Being thus engaged, I must hasten to subscribe myself

G. W."

The sermon was on " The Necessity and Benefits of Religious
Society," from Eccles. iv. 9—12, " Two are better than one,"
&c. That Whitefield should have chosen to commence his
public ministry with such a subject, can only be accounted for
by a reference to his peculiar circumstances. The social religion of the Oxford methodists, and of the society he had
formed in Gloucester, was a *new thing*, the principles of which
required to be explained and defended. He had to leave, that
week, the little flock collected during his visit. They were to
be as sheep without a shepherd; and that they might not disperse on his departure, he wisely vindicated the object of such
meetings, and removed some of the odium attached to them.
In this point of view, the subject was well chosen, and quite
consistent with his determination to know nothing among men,
save Jesus Christ, and him crucified. The sermon will be
found in the fifth volume of his works; but as it is not printed
from his own manuscript, it would be unfair to quote from it
any specimens of his style. And yet, even in its present form,
it breathes, in no ordinary degree, that freshness and warmth
which characterize all his writings. It is not rolled from that
" *secret place of thunder*," which the foregoing letters disclose

in his bosom, and which afterward pealed like the cloud on
Sinai; but it contains earnests of his future energy.

It is not generally known, and this is not the place to explain
it, but it is the fact, that whilst Whitefield never lost sight of
his ordination vows, his views of the form of episcopal ordination underwent such a change, that he declared to Ralph Erskine, of his own accord, " I knew of no other way then; but I
would not have it in that way again, for a thousand worlds."
The letter containing this acknowledgment, will be found in
the Scotch part of his history.

Perhaps no mind, since the apostolic age, has been more
deeply affected, or suitably exercised, by " the laying on of
hands," than Whitefield's was. A supernatural unction from the
Holy One, could hardly have produced greater *moral* effects.
That high sense of responsibility, that singleness of heart, that
entire and intense devotedness of soul, body, and spirit, which
characterized the first ambassadors of Christ, seems revived in
him. Accordingly, after reading the narrative of his ordination,
we naturally expect from Whitefield a sort of apostolic career.
This would be anticipated, were we utterly ignorant of the result. After witnessing at the altar, a spirit wound up to the
highest pitch of ardour, throbbing and thrilling with strong
emotions, and, like a renovated eagle, impatient to burst off, we
naturally look for a corresponding swiftness of flight and width
of sweep; and feel that we shall not be surprised by any thing
which follows. His unbosomings of himself disclose in his
heart a " secret place of thunder," and " a fountain of tears,"
from which we expect alternate bursts of terror and tenderness
—bolts of Sinai, and dew of Hermon; and we shall not be disappointed. Agreeably to his engagement with Sir John Philips,
Whitefield returned to Oxford, and took out his bachelor's degree. During his residence, he resumed the care of the methodist society, and of the poor. His stay at Oxford was, however, but short. He received and accepted an invitation to
officiate for a time in the chapel of the Tower of London.
His first sermon in the metropolis was, however, preached in
Bishopsgate church. On entering the pulpit, his juvenile aspect
excited a general sneer of contempt; but he had not spoken

long, when the sneer gave place to universal symptoms of wonder and pleasure. The sermon stamped his character at once; and from that time his popularity in London continued to increase. During his stay, which only extended to two months, he maintained his usual habits of visiting the prisoners and the poor.

About this time, letters were received from the Wesleys and Ingham, then in Georgia. Their descriptions of the moral condition of the British colonies in America, affected his heart powerfully, and awakened in him a strong desire to preach the gospel abroad. It was an undertaking suited to his energetic and enterprising character; and therefore sunk deeply amongst his thoughts. He could not, however, come to a final determination then, and therefore he returned to Oxford again. There, Whitefield devoted the chief part of his time to the study of Henry's Commentary; which seems to have been a favourite book amongst his associates in the University. "God," says he, "works by him (Henry) greatly here." How highly he prized his own copy, may be judged from his gratitude when he was able to pay for it. To the friend who furnished it, he writes, "Herewith I send you seven pounds to pay for Mr. Henry's Commentary. Dear Esqr. Thorold made me a present of ten guineas, so that now (for ever blessed be divine goodness!) I can send you more than I thought for." In a former letter he had said, "I hope to send you, in a short time, two guineas towards paying for Henry's Exposition."

The study of this invaluable work was soon interrupted, by an invitation to officiate for a short time at Dummer in Hampshire. This was a very different sphere to any he had been accustomed. The people were equally poor and illiterate; but he was soon reconciled to them, and acknowledged that during his stay he had " reaped much spiritual benefit." While he continued at Dummer, he adhered rigidly to his system of economizing time; dividing the day into *three* equal parts; eight hours for sleep and meals; eight for public prayers, catechising, and visiting; and eight for study and devotional retirement.

While thus occupied in obscurity, he was not forgotten in London: a profitable curacy in the metropolis was offered to

him ; but the chord touched by the spiritual wants of Georgia,
had not ceased to vibrate in his inmost soul. From the moment
it was struck, Oxford had no magnet, Hampshire no charms,
the metropolis no fascination, for the young evangelist. He
promptly and decidedly declined the lucrative and attractive
curacy, being intent on going abroad. And an opportunity of
gratifying his truly missionary spirit soon presented itself.
" He received letters," says Dr. Gillies, " containing what *he*
thought to be an invitation to go to Georgia, from Mr. John
Wesley, whose brother came over about this time to procure
more labourers." The doctor might have said " letters containing
what *was* an invitation :" for although, at a future period, it
was insinuated that Whitefield had intruded himself upon the
sphere of the Wesleys in America, the imputation is unwarranted. Charles Wesley both urged and encouraged him to leave
England. The following extracts are from a poem addressed
to Whitefield by Charles Wesley, at the time.

1.

" Servant of God, the summons hear ;
Thy Master calls—arise, obey !
The tokens of his will appear,
His providence points out the way.

*   *   *   *   *   *

8.

" Champion of God, thy Lord proclaim ;
Jesus alone resolve to know ;
Tread down thy foes in Jesus' name ;
Go! conquering and to conquer, go.

9.

" Through racks and fires pursue thy way ;
Be mindful of a dying God ;
Finish thy course, and win the day ;
Look up—and seal the truth with blood ! "

This impassioned adjuration to proceed to America, proves
that Whitefield did not intrude himself on the mission, nor run
unsent. Had Dr. Southey observed those lines, he would not
have said, that " Charles did not invite him to the undertaking." The truth is, both brothers appealed to him in the form
most likely to win his consent ; making the call appear to be

from God. "Only Mr. Delamotte is with me," says John, "until God shall stir up the hearts of some of his servants to come over and help us. What if thou art the man, Mr. Whitefield? Do you ask me what you shall have? Food to eat, and raiment to put on; a house to lay your head in, such as your Lord had not; and a crown of glory that fadeth not away." This is a *real* invitation, or mockery; and precisely in that spirit which Whitefield could not resist. Accordingly, on reading it, "his heart," he says, "leaped within him, and, as it were, echoed to the call." A concurrence of favourable circumstances at the time, enabled him, thus promptly, to embrace the proposal, and embark in the undertaking. Mr. Kinchin, the minister of Dummer, had been chosen dean of Corpus Christi College, and was willing to take upon him the charge of the prisoners at Oxford; Harvey undertook to supply his place in the curacy; and in Georgia, the novel sphere of usefulness, and the warm friendship of Wesley, were equally attractive, as inducements to leave England. The resolution thus formed, he solemnly confirmed by prayer; and, that it might not be shaken by his relations at Gloucester, he wrote to assure them, that unless they would promise not to dissuade him, he would embark without seeing them. This promise they gave; but they forgot it when he arrived. His aged mother, as might be expected, wept sorely; and others, as Dr. Southey observes, who had no such cause to justify their interference, represented to him what " pretty preferment" he might have if he would stay at home. But, none of these things moved him: their influence was defeated by his own prayers, and by the weight of the bishop's opinion; who, as usual, received him like a father, approved of his determination, and expressed his confidence that God would enable him to do much good abroad. From Gloucester he went to take leave of his friends at Bristol. During this visit, the mayor appointed him to preach before the corporation: even the quakers thronged to hear him. But the effect of his farewell sermons will be best told in his own words. " What shall I say? Methinks it would be almost sinful to leave Bristol at this critical juncture. The whole city seems to be alarmed. Churches are as full on week-days, as they use to be on Sundays, and on Sundays so full, that many, very many are obliged to go away because they cannot come in. Oh that God would keep me always humble, and fully convinced that I am nothing without him; and that all the good done upon earth, God himself doth it."—" The word was sharper than a two-edged sword; the doctrine of the new birth made its way like lightning into the hearers' consciences. Sanctify it, Holy Father! to thine own glory and thy people's good."

Similar impressions were made in Bath and Gloucester, and unprecedented collections obtained for charitable objects. His stay was, however, short : he was called up to London to appear before General Oglethorpe, and the trustees of Georgia. Having been accepted by them, he was presented to the bishop and primate, who both highly approved of his mission. But his departure from England was delayed for some months, owing to the vessel in which he was to sail not being ready at the time expected. He therefore undertook to serve, for a while, the church of one of his friends at Stonehouse. In this retirement his communion with God was, at once, intimate and habitual. Could the trees of the wood speak, he says, they would tell what sweet communion he and his christian brethren had, under their shade, enjoyed with their God. " Sometimes as I have been walking," he continues, " my soul would make such sallies, that I thought it would go out of the body. At other times I would be so overpowered with a sense of God's infinite majesty, that I would be constrained to throw myself prostrate on the ground, and offer my soul as a blank in his hands, to write on it what he pleased. One night was a time never to be forgotten. It happened to lighten exceedingly. I had been expounding to many people, and some being afraid to go home, I thought it my duty to accompany them, and improve the occasion, to stir them up to prepare for the coming of the Son of man. In my return to the parsonage, whilst others were rising from their beds, and frightened almost to death to see the lightning run upon the ground, I and another, a poor but pious countryman, were in the field, praising, praying to, and exulting in our God, and longing for that time when Jesus shall be revealed from heaven ' in flaming fire.' Oh that my soul may

be in a like frame when he shall actually come to call me!"
He refers to this scene in one of his letters. "Honest *James*
and I were out in the midst of the lightning, and never were
more delighted in our lives. May we be as well pleased, when
the Son of God cometh to judgment."

He came glowing from this mount of communion to Bristol
again, prepared to preach the gospel with new energy; and the
people were prepared to hear it with new interest; for such was
the impatience for his return, that multitudes on foot, and some
in coaches, were waiting to meet him, a mile from the city; and
a still greater number welcomed him, as he passed along the
streets. And if the city was alarmed during his former visit, it
was now electrified: persons of all ranks and denominations
crowded to hear him; and such was the pressure in every church,
that he could hardly make his way to the reading desk. "Some
hung upon the rails of the organ loft, others climbed upon the
leads of the church, and altogether made the church so hot
with their breath, that the steam would fall from the pillars
like drops of rain." When he preached his farewell sermon,
and said to the people that perhaps they might "see his face no
more," high and low, young and old, burst into tears. Multitudes followed him home with tears, and many with entreaties
that he would remain in England; but he was firm to his purpose, and merely consented to spend the next day in speaking
with those who had been awakened under his ministry. This
he did from seven in the morning until midnight, when he stole
away secretly to avoid the parade of a public escort.

After some brief intermediate visits, he arrived again in London. Here invitations to preach and administer the sacrament
poured in upon him from so many churches, and were so promptly
accepted by him, that his friends were afraid for his health;
the crowds at each church being so overwhelming. But his
answer was, "I find by experience that the more I do, the more
I may do, for God." This was said when he was in the habit
of preaching four times on the sabbath, and had often to walk
ten or twelve miles in going from one church to another, and
to preach five times in the week besides. Such unprecedented
labours might well be, as they were, called "mighty deeds" by

the newspapers ; but, this kind of notice hurt his feelings.   In a letter to a friend he expresses himself on the subject thus : " I suppose you have heard of my *mighty deeds,* falsely so called by the newspapers ; for I find some *back-friend* has published abroad my preaching four times in a day ; but I beseech Mr. Raikes, the printer, never to put me in his news again upon any such account, for it is quite contrary to my inclinations and positive orders."   To his friends, however, he was not reserved in communicating either the extent of his labours, or the symptoms of their success.   In another letter to the same person he writes, " Last week, save one, I preached ten times in different churches ; and the last week, seven ; and yesterday four times, and read prayers twice, though I slept not an hour the night before, which was spent in religious conversation, &c.   God still works more and more by my unworthy ministry.   Many youths here sincerely love our Lord Jesus Christ ; and thousands, I hope, are quickened, strengthened, and confirmed by the word preached.   Last Sunday (in St. Dunstan's) at six in the morning, when I gave my farewell, the whole church was drowned in tears : they wept and cried aloud, as a mother weepeth for her first-born.   Since that, there is no end of persons coming and weeping, telling me what God has done for their souls : others again beg little books, and desire me to write their names in them.   The time would fail me, were I to relate how many have been awakened, and how many pray for me. The great day will discover all ! "   This will be more minutely detailed in the next chapter.

Having thus traced the amazing effects of Whitefield's *first* sermons, it will now be interesting to examine their general character, and to ascertain what were the truths which thus arrested and aroused the public mind.   Three of these successful sermons can, happily, be identified with these " times of refreshing ;" and they may be depended on, as specimens of both the letter and the spirit of his preaching, because they were printed from his own manuscripts : that " *On Early Piety ;*" that " *On Regeneration ;*" and that " *On Intercession.*"   Whoever will read these appeals, realizing the circumstances under which they were made, will hardly wonder at the effect produced by them ;

the topics of the second and third, and the tone of all the three, are so different from the matter and manner of sermonizing, to which the public had been long accustomed. They do not surprise us at all; because, happily, neither the topics nor the tone of them are " strange things to our ears." Both were, however, novelties, even in the metropolis, at that time. When—where had an appeal like the following been made in London? " I beseech you, in love and compassion, to come to Jesus. Indeed, all I say is in love to your souls. And if I could be but an instrument of bringing you to Jesus, I should not envy but rejoice in your happiness, however much you were exalted. If I was to make up the *last* of the train of the companions of the blessed Jesus, it would rejoice me to see you above me in glory. I would willingly go to prison or to death for you, so I could but bring one soul from the devil's strong holds, into the salvation which is by Christ Jesus. Come then to Christ, every one that hears me this night. Come, come, my guilty brethren : I beseech you for your immortal souls' sake, for Christ's sake, come to Christ ! Methinks I could speak till midnight unto you ; I am full of love towards you. Would you have me go and tell my Master, that you will not come, and that I have spent my strength in vain ? I cannot bear to carry such a message to him ! I would not, indeed I would not, be a swift witness against you at the great day of account : but if you will refuse these gracious invitations, I must do it."

In this spirit (not very prevalent even now) Whitefield began his ministry. And there is a fascination as well as fervour in some of his early sermons. How bold and beautiful is the peroration of that on Intercession ! Referring to the holy impatience of " the souls under the altar," for the coming of the kingdom of God, he exclaims, " And shall not we who are on earth, be often exercised in this divine employ with the glorious company of the spirits of just men made perfect ? Since our happiness is so much to consist in the communion of saints, in the church triumphant above, shall we not frequently intercede for the church militant below ; and earnestly beg, that we may be all one ? To provoke you to this work and labour of love, remember, that it is the never-ceasing employment of

the holy and highly exalted Jesus himself: so that he who is
constantly interceding for others, is doing that on earth, which
the eternal Son of God is always doing in heaven.   Imagine,
therefore, when you are lifting up holy hands for one another,
that you see the heavens opened, and the Son of God in all his
glory, as the great High Priest of your salvation, pleading for
you the all-sufficient merit of his sacrifice before the throne.
Join your intercessions with His!   The imagination will
strengthen your faith, and excite a holy earnestness in your
prayers."

CHAPTER II.

WHITEFIELD's ministry in London began at the Tower—an un-likely quarter for attraction or effect. The curate of the Tower, who had been his friend at college, having occasion to officiate in Hampshire for a season, invited him to supply during his absence. Sir John Philips also sanctioned the re-quest, and joined in it. Little did either of these good men, and still less did Whitefield himself, foresee the remote, or even the immediate, consequences of this invitation. And it is well they did not! For had they foreseen Whitefield's splen-did irregularities in Moorfields and Blackheath, or his spacious tabernacles in London, or even his moderate Calvinism, they would not have countenanced him. He himself, notwithstand-ing all his constitutional bravery and conscientious simplicity, would not have hazarded the experiment, had he suspected the result.

How little he did so, will be best told in his own words. " On Wednesday, August 4th, 1737, with fear and trembling I obeyed the summons, and went in the stage coach to London ; and the Sunday following, in the afternoon, preached at Bi-shopsgate church. As I went up the pulpit stairs, almost all seemed to sneer at me, on account of my youth. But they soon grew serious in the time of my preaching ; and after I came down, showed me great tokens of respect, blessed me as I passed, and made great inquiry who I was. The question no one could answer ; for I was quite a stranger : and, by passing speedily through the crowd, returned to the Tower without having my name discovered."

" Here (at the Tower) I continued for the space of two
months, reading prayers twice a week, catechising and preaching once, besides visiting the soldiers in the infirmary and barracks daily. I also read prayers every evening in Wapping
chapel." (It was, no doubt, in going between the Tower and
Wapping chapel, that his well known expression, " *Wapping
sinners*," was first forced upon him.) " I preached at Ludgate
prison every Tuesday." (This also, together with his visits to
the castle at Oxford, will account for the frequency of the forms
of judicial trial and condemnation, in his sermons to the ungodly.) " God was pleased to give me favour in the eyes of
the inhabitants of the Tower. The chapel was crowded on
Lord's days. Religious friends from various parts of the town
attended the word, and several young men on Lord's-day morning, under serious impressions, came to converse with me on the
new birth."

So far all is pleasing; but there was nothing surprising
marked Whitefield's first visit to London. That it made no
great impression on himself, is evident from the perfect simplicity with which he records its close : " Having staid in London
until Mr. B. came out of the country, I returned to my little
charge at Oxford, and waited on my deaconship according to
the measure of grace imparted to me." Even when he was
invited to " a very profitable curacy" in London, and urged to
accept it, he says, " I had no inclination to accept it. At
Dummer I soon began to be as much delighted with the artless
conversation of the poor illiterate people, as I had been formerly
with the company of my Oxford friends; and frequently learnt
as much by an afternoon's visit, as by a week's study."

It was therefore for the sake of Georgia, solely, that he came
back to London. The metropolis was to Whitefield, then,
merely the way to America. Accordingly, he did not seek for
engagements, nor volunteer his services, on his arrival from
Oxford. Indeed, he does not seem to have contemplated
preaching. " I followed my usual practice of reading and
praying over the word of God on my knees. Sweet was this
retirement to my soul—but it was not of long continuance. Invitations were given me to preach at several places." Not,

however, that he was unwilling to preach. All I want to show is, that he had no *designs* upon London, and no idea of creating a sensation in it. He could not, however, be hid long. His former visit was not forgotten, and his fame in Bristol had reached the metropolis. " The stewards and members of the religious societies" found him out, and forced him out, on behalf of their charity schools : a work which their successors carry on, with great fidelity and perseverance, to this hour ! I mean no reflection upon stewards. They thus call out ministers, who would otherwise shrink from publicity ; and extend over London the influence of talents and piety, which must otherwise have been confined to a corner. It is not their fault, if another Whitefield has not been found out. Had there been another in the empire since, the nets of religious societies would have caught him : and, whenever there is another, they are sure to bring him into full notice and employment ! Whitefield says, with great simplicity, " The stewards of religious societies were very fond of hearing me." No wonder: he collected upwards of a thousand pounds for the schools alone ; " in those days," says Dr. Southey, " a prodigious sum; larger collections being made than had ever *before* been known on like occasions."

Whitefield himself has drawn a distinction between the feelings with which he accepted invitations from societies, and the feelings with which he assisted clergymen on the sabbath. " I *embraced* the invitations to preach and assist in administering the sacrament." " With great *reluctance* I was prevailed on to preach a charity sermon at Wapping chapel." On both occasions he was, however, equally successful. " So many came" to the sacrament at Cripplegate, St. Anne's, and Foster Lane, " that sometimes we were obliged to consecrate fresh elements twice or thrice, and the stewards found it somewhat difficult to carry the offerings to the communion table." In like manner, " more was collected at Wapping chapel, for the charity, than had been for many years." At St. Swithin's also, instead of ten shillings, as formerly, " eight pounds were collected."

This was too great a novelty then to be concealed. " Next morning as I was at breakfast with a friend at the Tower, I read in one of the newspapers, that there was a young gentleman going

E

volunteer to Georgia, had preached at St. Swithin's, and collected eight pounds, instead of ten shillings; three pounds of
which were in halfpence; and that he would preach next Wednesday before the societies, at their general quarterly meeting.
This advertisement chagrined me very much. I immediately
sent to the printer, desiring he would put me in his paper no
more. His answer was, that he was paid for doing it, and
would not lose two shillings for any body. By this means people's curiosity was stirred up more and more. On Wednesday
evening Bow church, in Cheapside, was crowded exceedingly.
I preached my sermon on Early Piety; and at the request of
the societies printed it. Henceforward, for nearly three months
successively, there was no end of people's flocking to hear the
word of God. Sometimes constables were obliged to be
placed at the doors, without and within. One might, as it were,
walk upon the people's heads. Thousands went away from the
largest churches for want of room. I now preached generally
nine times a-week. The people were all attention, as hearing
for eternity! The early sacraments were exceedingly awful!
Oh how often at Cripplegate, St. Anne's, and Foster-lane,
have we seen Jesus Christ crucified and evidently set forth before us! On Sunday mornings, long before day, you might see
streets filled with people going to church, with their lanthorns
in their hands; and hear them conversing about the things of
God."

By thus specifying the spot where Whitefield preached his
first published sermon, Bow church will be *reconsecrated*, in the
estimation of many, and Bow bells sound more sweetly. Such
is the force of association. Its laws, like those of nature, can
neither be set aside nor weakened. Only hallowed men can
make hallowed ground; and no minister becomes hallowed to
posterity, but "he that winneth souls." Accordingly, Bow
bells remind us of no one but Whitefield. His one sermon in-
vests that church with more sacredness than its consecration,
and with more interest than the whole series of its corporation
sermons.

There is neither venom nor vapouring in this remark. Visitors
from the country, and from America, pause even in Cheapside

to gaze at the spire under which George Whitefield preached. They remember no one else. Why? Because no one else has "so preached" there, "that many believed." Thus it is only the salvation of immortal souls that stamps religious immortality upon "solemn temples." Accordingly, not all the talent and piety which graced the pulpit at Whitehall during the Protectorate, nor all the rank which has been in it and around it since, can awaken one *spiritual* emotion or recollection. Even Baxter, Owen, and Howe, can hardly be realized there, as ministers of the glorious gospel. A *barn*, where either of them had preached Christ to the poor and the perishing, would make our hearts burn within us; but in the chapel-royal, they are remembered only as great men. Had Simeon of Cambridge, that "Paul the aged," preached there but once, before singing his *Nunc dimittis,* he would have been more remembered by posterity, than all his late predecessors put together. It is utterly in vain to sneer or reason against this law of association. Nothing gains or retains a hallowed hold upon the sympathies of the pious, but usefulness. Mere talent and heartless orthodoxy can no more endear or dignify a church now, than *relics* from Rome or Jerusalem.

But, to return. Whitefield had soon to pay the usual price of popularity. "As my popularity and usefulness increased, opposition increased proportionably. At first, many of the clergy were my hearers and admirers; but some soon grew angry, and complaints were made that there was no room for the parishioners, and that the pews were spoiled. Some called me a spiritual pickpocket; and others thought I made use of a charm to get the people's money. A report was spread abroad that the bishop of London, upon the complaint of the clergy, intended to silence me. I immediately waited upon his Lordship, and inquired whether any complaint of this nature had been lodged against me. He answered, No. I asked his Lordship whether any objection could be made against my doctrine? He said, 'No: for he knew a clergyman who heard me preach a plain scriptural sermon.' I asked his Lordship whether he would grant me a license? He said, 'I needed none, as I was going to Georgia.' I replied—'Then your Lord-

ship would not forbid me.' He gave me a satisfactory answer
—and I took my leave."

Why has Dr. Southey stripped the bishop's courtesy of all
its grace? He says of the bishop, " Evidently he thought this
(Georgia) a happy destination for one whose fervent spirit was
likely to lead him into extravagances of doctrine as well as of
life." This is no compliment to his Lordship's wisdom, whatever it be to his policy. Even his policy was bad, if this be
true; for what could be worse in principle or policy, than letting loose upon an infant colony an extravagant chaplain?
Thus Dr. Southey has imputed to the bishop, unwittingly, a
heartless, if not reckless, indifference to the religious interests
of Georgia; for if Whitefield was dangerous even in London,
where he could easily be counteracted, if not controlled, how
much more dangerous he must have been in a distant colony!
This inference is inevitable, if there was any real danger to be
apprehended from Whitefield's doctrine or example. It is easy
to say, that "the whole force of his enthusiasm might *safely*
expend itself" in Georgia; but Dr. Southey should not have
said this; for he had just said before, of the disorders raised in
the colony, that Charles Wesley had, " in truth, been the occasion of them, by his injudicious zeal." But, enough of this.
Southey is no doubt right in saying, that the bishop was glad,
and that some of the clergy rejoiced "in Whitefield's departure," as a happy riddance. He guessed well, although he
reasons ill, in this instance. Accordingly, the bishop's " satisfactory answer" to Whitefield did not prevent some of the
London clergy from shutting their pulpits against him. " Soon
after this, two clergymen sent for me, and told me they would
not let me preach in their pulpits any more, unless I renounced
that part of the preface of my sermon on Regeneration,
wherein I wished, that my brethren would entertain their auditories oftener with discourses on the new birth. This I had
not freedom to do—and so they continued my opposers."

" What, I believe, irritated some of my enemies the more,
was my free conversation with many of the serious dissenters,
who invited me to their houses; and told me repeatedly, ' that
if the doctrine of the new birth and justification by faith was

preached powerfully in the church, there would be but few dissenters in England.' Who the dissenters were that said this,
cannot now be ascertained : but, certainly, they were not *serious
dissenters*, nor sound reasoners, however serious they may have
been as christians ; for wherever these doctrines are powerfully
preached in the church, there are many dissenters. The progress of . both dissent and methodism keeps pace with the
progress of evangelical sentiment in the church, and ever must
do whilst they continue evangelical. Whitefield was, however,
simple enough to believe what he wished, and honest enough to
act accordingly, in this instance. " My practice in visiting and
associating with (these dissenters) I thought was quite agreeable to the word of God. Their conversation was savoury ; and
I judged, (' rightly,' says Dr. Southey,) that the best way to
bring them over, was not by bigotry and railing, but by moderation and love, and undissembled holiness of life."

"But these reasons were of no avail. One minister called
me a *pragmatical rascal*, and vehemently inveighed against me
and the whole body of dissenters together." Dr. Southey explains the "serious offence" thus taken by the clergy, by saying,—"for the evils which puritanism had brought on this
kingdom were at that time neither forgotten nor forgiven."
No thanks to the Doctor, if ever they should be so ! He has
done all he could to perpetuate their memory. It will not,
however, live long. The accidental evils of puritanism, like
those of the Reformation, will soon be forgiven, and forgotten
too, in the enjoyment of the truth and liberty which the puritans bought and sealed with their blood. Wycliffe and Baxter,
Latimer and Owen, Cranmer and Howe, will be associated and
enshrined names in the temple of christianity, when all who
have hindered their identification will be nameless, or named
only to be pitied and wondered at for ever.

Whitefield found pulpits in London, until he embarked for
America. Not many, indeed, seem to have been shut against
him. "I have been wearied almost to death," he says, "in
preaching." "The nearer the time of my embarkation approached, the more affectionate and eager people grew. All
ranks gave vent to their passion. Thousands and thousands of

prayers were put up for me. The people would run and stop me in the alleys of the churches, hug me in their arms, and follow me with wishful looks. Such a sacrament I never saw before, as at St. Dunstan's. The tears of the communicants mingled with the cup: and had not Jesus given us some of his ' new wine,' our parting would have been insupportable.

"At length having preached in a good part of the London churches, collected about a thousand pounds for the charity schools, and got upwards of three hundred pounds for the poor in Georgia, I left London on Dec. 28th, 1737, in the twenty-third year of my age, and went in the strength of God, as a poor pilgrim, on board the Whitaker."

CHAPTER III.

THE settlement of Georgia was begun in 1733, by a number of English people, who were brought over by General Oglethorpe. On the first of February of that year, General Oglethorpe and his colony entered the Savannah river, and the same night the tents were first pitched where the city of Savannah now stands. For several days the people were employed in erecting a fortification, and in felling the woods, while the general marked out the town. The first house was begun on the ninth; and the town, after the Indian name of the river which ran by it, was called Savannah. The fort being completed, the guns mounted, and the colony put into a state of safety, the next object of Oglethorpe's attention was, to treat with the Indians for a share of their possessions.

In his intercourse with the Indians, he was greatly assisted by an Indian woman, whom he found in Savannah, of the name of Mary Musgrove. She had resided among the English, in another part of the country, and was well acquainted with their language. She was of great use, therefore, to General Oglethorpe, in interpreting what he said to the Indians, and what they said to him. For this service he gave her a hundred pounds a year.

" Among those who came over with General Oglethorpe was a man named Thomas Bosomworth, who was the chaplain, or minister, of the colony. Soon after his arrival he married the above-mentioned Indian woman, Mary Musgrove. Unhappily, Bosomworth was, at heart, a bad man, although by profession he was a minister of the gospel. He was distinguished for his pride, and love of riches and influence. At the same time, he was very artful. Yet, on account of his profession, he was, for a time, much respected by the Indians.

" At one of the great councils of the Indians, this artful man induced some of the chiefs to crown Malatche, one of the greatest among them, and to declare him prince and emperor of all the Creeks. After this, he made his wife call herself the eldest sister of Malatche; and she told the Indians that one of her grandfathers had been made king, by the Great Spirit, over all the Creeks. The Indians believed what Mary told them; for, since General Oglethorpe had been so kind to her, they had become very proud of her. They called a great meeting of the chiefs together, and Mary made them a long talk. She told them that they had been injured by the whites—that they were getting away the lands of the Indians, and would soon drive them from all their possessions. She said, ' We must assert our rights—we must arm ourselves against them—we must drive them from our territories. Let us call forth our warriors —I will head them. Stand by me, and the houses which they have erected shall smoke in ruins.'

" The spirit of Queen Mary was contagious. Every chief present declared himself ready to defend her to the last drop of his blood.

" After due preparation, the warriors were called forth. They had painted themselves afresh, and sharpened anew their toma-hawks for the battle. The march was now commenced. Queen Mary, attended by her infamous and wicked husband, the real author of all their discontent, headed the savage throng.

" Before they reached Savannah, their approach was an-nounced. The people were justly alarmed—they were few in number, and though they had a fortification and cannon, they had no good reason to hope that they should be able to ward off the deadly blow which was aimed against them.

" By this time the savages were in sight of Savannah. At this critical moment an Englishman, by the name of Noble Jones, a bold and daring man, rode forth, with a few spirited men on horseback, to meet them. As he approached them, he exclaimed in a voice like thunder : ' Ground your arms !

ground your arms! not an armed Indian shall set his foot in this town.'

" Awe-struck by his lofty tone, and perceiving him and his companions ready to dash in among them, they paused, and soon after laid down their arms. Bosomworth and his queen were now summoned to march into the city, and it was permitted the chiefs and other Indians to follow, but without their arms.

" On reaching the parade ground, the thunder of fifteen cannon fired at the same moment, told them what they might expect should they persist in their hostile designs. The Indians were now marched to the house of the president of the council, in Savannah. Bosomworth was required to leave the Indians while the president had a friendly talk with them.

" In his address to them he assured them of the kindness of the English, and demanded what they meant by coming in this warlike manner.

" In reply, they told the president ' that they heard that Mary was to be sent over the great waters, and they had come to learn why they were to lose their queen.'

" Finding that the Indians had been deceived, and that Bosomworth was the author of all the trouble—that he had even intended to get possession of the magazine, and to destroy the whites, the council directed him to be seized, and to be thrown into prison.

" This step Mary resented with great spirit. Rushing forth among the Indians, she openly cursed General Oglethorpe, although he had raised her from poverty and distress, and declared that the whole world should know that the ground she trod upon was her own.

" The warlike spirit of the Indians being thus likely to be renewed, it was thought advisable to imprison Mary also. This was accordingly carried into effect. At the same time, to appease the Indians, a sumptuous feast was made for the chiefs by the president, who during the better state of feeling, which seemed to prevail, took occasion to explain to them the wickedness of Bosomworth, and how by falsehood and cunning he had led them to believe that Mary was really their queen—a descendant of one of their great chiefs. 'Brothers,' said he, 'it is no such thing. Queen Mary is no other than Mary Musgrove, whom I found poor, and who has been made the dupe of the artful Bosomworth; and you, brothers, the dupes of both.'

" The aspect of things was now pleasant. The Indians were beginning to be satisfied of the villany of Bosomworth, and of the real character of Mary. But at this moment the door was thrown open, and, to the surprise of all, Mary burst into the room. She had made her escape from prison; and, learning what was going on, she rushed forward with the fury of a tigress, exclaiming as she entered, 'Seize your arms! seize your arms! Remember your promise, and defend your queen.'

" The sight of their queen seemed, in a moment, to bring back all the original ardour of the enterprise. In an instant, every chief had seized his tomahawk, and sprung from the ground to rally at the call of their queen.

" At this moment Captain Jones, who was present, perceiving the danger of the president, and the other whites, drew his sword and demanded peace. The majesty of his countenance, the fire of his eye, and the glittering of his sword, told Queen Mary what she might expect, should she attempt to raise any higher the feverish spirit of her subjects.

" The Indians cast an eye towards Mary, as if to inquire what they should do. Her countenance fell. Perceiving his advantage, Captain Jones stepped forward, and in the presence of the Indians, standing round, again conducted Mary back to prison.

" A short imprisonment so far humbled both Bosomworth and Mary, that each wrote a letter, in which they confessed the wrong they had done, and promised, if released, that they would conduct themselves with more propriety in future. The people kindly forgave both, and they left the city.

" But they did not perform their promise. Again Bosomworth tried to make Mary queen, and to get possession of three large islands, called Ossalaw, Sapelo, and St. Catharine's. He pretended that they had been given to him by the Indians. Being, however, unable to make himself master of them, he went over

to England with Mary, where he instituted a law-suit for their
recovery. At length, having obtained St. Catharine's island
by a judgment of the court, he returned with his wife, and
took up his residence upon that island. There Mary died.
Some time after, Bosomworth married one of his own servants,
who did not survive him. At length, he finished his own inglo-
rious life, and was buried between his two wives, upon the island
which had given him so much trouble."

Such (it is said in America) was the first specimen of a
chaplain, which the Indians and colonists at Savannah had before their eyes. No wonder Oglethorpe and the trustees of
Georgia turned their eyes upon another kind of men! The
Oxford methodists were, accordingly, fixed upon, " as men who
appeared to possess the habits and qualities requisite" for
preaching the gospel to settlers and the Indians. Dr. Butler,
of Corpus Christi College, sounded the Wesleys on the subject,
and introduced them to Oglethorpe. This was going to the
opposite extreme. Accordingly, on their arrival in the colony,
they soon proved their unfitness for the religious management
of an infant settlement. They certainly meant well, and were
shamefully treated: but it is equally true, that they were both
very imprudent. Dr. Southey, however, implicates Charles
Wesley too deeply in the mutinies of the period: for he ought
to have known, that Oglethorpe acquitted him of this charge,
and offered to build him a house, and to allow him a deputy, if
he would return to the colony. This is just as true, and was
as easily ascertained, as that Oglethorpe, who had been "brutal
enough to give away from under" Charles, the old bedstead on
which he lay in a fever, afterwards " embraced and kissed him
with cordial affection." The Doctor even says, " that the explanation then given so satisfied the general, that his feelings
were entirely changed: all his old love and confidence returned:" and yet, he says that Charles " had in truth been the occasion of the disorders by his injudicious zeal." On the other
hand, however, Watson has admitted into his answer to
Southey, a vindication of Charles Wesley, from the pen of his
daughter, somewhat inconsistent with the acknowledgment, that
the Wesleys " held the reins of ecclesiastical discipline with a

tightness unsuitable to infant colonists especially, and which tended to provoke resistance."

But the character of neither brother should be judged of from their career in Georgia. I quite agree with Watson, that "their integrity of heart, and the purity of their intentions, came forth without a stain:" for although I have heard reports, and been told of letters, which implicate John in more than imprudence, I have found no one to authenticate the reports, or to produce the letters. Besides, Whitefield returned from Georgia unchanged in his love or esteem for Wesley: a conclusive proof that he found nothing to justify the *fama clamosa.* Nothing in his journals, letters, or diary, indicates a suspicion. (I have learnt, since I wrote this paragraph, that Wesley's private journals of the *Causton* affair have been discovered by the Conference ; and that they justify my argument.)

It was to this new colony, then in danger from the Spaniards, and irritated by the Wesleys, that Whitefield went forth so cheerfully, although solemnly. He does not, indeed, say that he knew the distracted state of the people : but it is quite evident from the way in which he prepared for his work, and from the spirit in which he began his labours, that Oglethorpe, or some of the trustees, had apprized him of the rocks on which his predecessors had split. Both his hopes and his fears prove that he was not ignorant of what he had to do, nor of what he had to undo. All his conduct, and especially his utter disregard of Wesley's oracular " *Let him return to London,*" shows clearly that his heart was set upon healing the breaches in the colony ; that thus the benevolent and pure designs of its founders might be carried into effect.

In this spirit, and for this purpose, Whitefield embarked for Georgia, in the latter end of December, 1737. It was, however, the end of January, 1738, before the vessel was fairly on her way ; owing to contrary winds. His reception on board was, as might be expected from a motley group of soldiers and sailors, of a mixed kind. The captains of both, with the surgeon and cadet, treated him, for a time, as an impostor ; and, to mark their contempt for him, turned the vessel into a gambling-house, during the whole first sabbath. The fact is, he had begun, the day before, to read prayers on deck : but he added to this a short sermon on the text, " I am determined to know nothing among you, save Jesus Christ, and him crucified." This gave offence. The officers and soldiers " attended with decency and reverence" to the prayers : but when he told them in the sermon what his " future conduct would be," they were indignant; and, to prove it, began the sabbath with the hautboy, and spent it in card-playing and blasphemy.

He seems to have foreseen this burst of opposition; and he wisely escaped from it. " Sunday, Jan. 1. Rose early in the morning, and retired to an adjacent hill with my friends to prayer." That day, however, he also preached three times (once extempore ; for he had only taken *two* sermons with him) in the church at Gravesend. This was not cowardice. He himself was unwilling to leave his " own flock in the ship," and he did not leave them without reading prayers again on the Saturday evening. He yielded, however, to the urgency of his friends ; and very properly.

This does not appear from his journals, because he would not leave a reflection upon a crew which afterwards treated him respectfully : but it appears from his private diary. Dr. Gillies says truly, " It is worth while to observe, with what prudence he was helped to behave, and how God was pleased to bless his patient and persevering endeavours to do good." This retreat from a premeditated storm, was one of his prudent steps.

In the same spirit, he began his usual work on board, on Monday, without upbraiding. Wherever there was sickness in the ship, he visited, counselled, and prayed. When he could not assemble the crew to prayers on deck, he read prayers and expounded any where between decks. When the soldiers could not or would not attend, he devoted himself to the religious education of their children. When he could *say* nothing to the swearing officers, he turned a *look* upon them which they understood. Thus he was never idle, nor unamiable.

Whilst thus employed, a heavy gale sprung up at the Nore, which created some alarm and more sickness. Even the officers felt thankful that the vessel was at the Nore, and not in

the Downs, (for she had "dragged her anchor two miles,")
which they had been trying to reach. Accordingly, they requested Whitefield to read prayers to them in the grand cabin
on Sunday, in addition to the service on deck. What a different aspect the ship wore on the preceding sabbath! But he
had endeared himself during the week by courtesy and kindness, and had spent the whole morning of this sabbath in going
from hammock to hammock amongst the sea-sick, administering *sage-tea* to them, as well as good advice.

He availed himself of this favourable turn of feeling, to obtain for himself more accommodation in the ship; for, hitherto,
he had no place of retirement for prayer or study. He seems,
however, to have been somewhat afraid of a refusal; for he
offered the captain money for the occasional use of his cabin.
This was not in good taste, but the captain overlooked that, and
politely granted his request.

The military captain also (whom Whitefield dreaded most)
sent him an invitation to take coffee in his cabin. He went;
and took the opportunity of saying to him, "that he thought it
a little *odd* to pray and preach to the servants, and not to the
master!" This good-humoured hint he followed up by pro-
posing to read "a collect now and then to him and the other
gentlemen, in the great cabin." At first the captain shook his
head; but, after a pause, he said, "I think we may, when we
have nothing *else* to do."

When the ship reached Margate, another storm arose at
midnight, accompanied by vivid lightning, which seemed to set
the sea on fire. The long-boat was lost, and many of the soldiers taken very ill. Whitefield became, literally, the *nurse* of
his "red-coated parishioners," as he called the soldiers. He
superintended the making of sage-tea and broth, and distributed them amongst the sick with his own hands.

Whilst thus employed he gained the esteem of the surgeon;
and so ingratiated himself with the wives of the soldiers, that
fifteen of them agreed to meet, to hear him explain the Catechism. Even the captains again requested him to read prayers
in the state cabin, and expressed "their approbation" of his
conduct.

Whilst the vessel was lying in the Downs, he ventured one day to remove " The Independent Whig" from the captain's pillow, and replace it with a book called " The *Self-Deceiver.*" Next morning the captain came to him smiling, and asked who had made the exchange? Whitefield confessed the charge, and begged his acceptance of the book. It produced a visible change. The military captain also, without being again asked, requested that " they might have public service and expounding twice a day in the great cabin."

In this manner, with occasional preaching on shore, he spent the month, during which the ship was waiting for a fair wind; and in that time, not a few of both the soldiers and sailors became very serious, and the ship's company at large orderly. At length the wind changed, and sailing orders were given. In the hurry of this movement, Whitefield fell down the stairs of the steerage ; but received " little or no hurt." In a few days after, the vessel had a very narrow escape. " The men upon deck not keeping a good look-out, an East Indiaman ran so very near, that had not Captain Whiting been upon deck, and beseeched them to tack about, the ships must inevitably have split one against another."

Altogether it was a perilous voyage to Gibraltar : but although the scene was new, and the labour trying, Whitefield's patience never failed. The following sketch is very characteristic. " Feb. 14th. May I never forget this day's mercies, since the Lord has dealt so lovingly with me ! About twelve at night a fresh gale arose, which increased so very much by four in the morning, that the waves raged horribly indeed, and broke in like a great river on many of the poor soldiers, who lay near the main hatchway. Friend Habersham and I knew nothing of it ; but perceived ourselves very restless, and could not sleep at all. I arose, and called on God for myself and all that sailed with me, absent friends, and all mankind. After this I went on deck—but surely a more noble and awful sight my eyes never beheld ; for the waves rose more than mountain high, and sometimes came on the quarter-deck. I endeavoured all the while to magnify God for making his 'power to be known!' And then, creeping on my *knees*—for I knew not how else to go—I went between decks, and sung psalms, and comforted the poor *wet* people. After this I read prayers in the great cabin. Then, I laid myself across a chair reading. But God was so good, that though things were tumbling, the ship rocking, persons falling down around me, I was never more cheerful in my life. I also finished a sermon before I went to bed, though in the midst of company."

On his arrival at Gibraltar, he was courteously received and hospitably entertained by the governor first, and then by Major Sabine and General Columbine. Gillies reverses the *order* of this reception. Sabine did not seek out Whitefield, until some days after he had visited the governor. But whilst all these attentions gratified him, he was most interested by a little group of pious soldiers, who, for twelve years, had been the *methodists* of Gibraltar. At first, they had assembled secretly in dens and caves of the rock, for prayer and conversation. The character and spirit of the venerable governor, soon led them, however, to apply for permission to build a house of prayer for themselves. But instead of granting this, he gave them the free use of the church; and there they statedly met for worship three times a day. They seem to have been nonconformists; and thus were called "*new lights:*" whilst another society of the Scotch church were called "dark *lanthorns.*"

Besides visiting the popish chapel, and preaching frequently in the protestant church, he attended the Jewish synagogue, and was agreeably surprised when one of the rulers showed him into the chief seat. The rabbi had heard him preach the day before against swearing, and now thanked him for his sermon. Whitefield remained in the synagogue during the whole service, engaged, he says, "in secret prayer, that the veil might be taken from the heart of the Jews, and they graffed again into their own olive tree."

His success at Gibraltar was remarkable. He says quaintly, "Samson's riddle was fulfilled there: out of the strong came forth sweetness. Who more unlikely to be wrought upon than soldiers! And yet, amongst any set of people I have not been where God has made his power more known. Many that were quite stark blind have received their sight; many that had

fallen back, have repented and turned to the Lord again; many
that were ashamed to own Christ openly, have waxen bold;
and many saints had their hearts filled with joy unspeakable
and full of glory."

When the journal of this revival was first published in England, it called forth an answer from some T. G. even more
foolish than any thing Tristram Land, M. A. had written.
Taking the words, " many that were quite stark blind have received their sight," literally, he says with all gravity,—" This
being a thing so seldom heard of, it seems likely to be a *falsity;*
and, that he inserted it here, to have the world think that God
worked this miracle on his account!" Straws show how the
wind blows; and, therefore, I will add a few specimens of this
first commentary on Whitefield's first journal. Because he
had lamented the want of the divine presence, on one occasion;
and had rejoiced on its return; T. G. says, " What he means
will puzzle any one; for by God's being with him at one time,
and not at another, seems to infer as if he denied the omni-
presence of the Deity!" When Whitefield says, that he " was
enlarged in intercession," T. G. remarks, " An odd expression
this, and inexplicable; but it frequently occurs!" Whitefield
says of a dying christian, " His soul seems full of God;" T. G.
observes, " An odd expression this, and needs explanation."
T. G. concludes by recommending, in the words of Sylvester,
" That we should go to our BAPTISM for the *date* of our regeneration." What must have been the state of popular sentiment and feeling, when such nonsense could obtain readers?
And yet, the authorship of this anonymous pamphlet was
ascribed to an ex-fellow of a college; who, although he disclaimed it, did not object to its principles or spirit. " *Land's
Letter to the Religious Societies,*" 1739.

Early in March the vessels left Gibraltar, and proceeded on
their voyage: and being soon in the trade-winds, they often
joined at the hours of public worship. On one occasion, Captain Mackay, after Whitefield had preached against drunkenness, urged the men to attend to the things that had been
spoken; telling them, that he had been a notorious swearer
until he had done so; and beseeching them, for Christ's sake,

F

to give up their sins. On another occasion, whilst marrying a couple on deck, Whitefield suddenly shut the prayer book in the midst of the ceremony, because the bridegroom had behaved with levity : and not until the laughter was turned into weeping, would he proceed. At the close, he gave the bride a Bible.

The ships were now almost as orderly as churches, when the weather allowed of worship. The drum summoned them to morning and evening prayers. The captains vied in kindness and attention to the chaplain. Cards and profane books were thrown overboard, in exchange for religious books. The women, in the Whitaker, exclaimed, " What a change in our captain ! " An oath became a strange thing. The soldiers began to learn to read and write, and the children to repeat their prayers regularly. This general impression was deepened by the prevalence of a fever on board ; during which, Captain Whiting accompanied Whitefield in crawling between decks, to administer medicine and cordials to the sailors.

One of the sufferers, a negro boy, had never been baptized. Whiting pledged Whitefield to instruct and baptize him, in the event of his recovery. The poor lad, however, died, and was buried without the service being read over him. The chaplain was afraid to venture upon such a canonical irregularity, although he was no believer in baptismal regeneration. The *drum*, however, was beaten on the occasion, and an address given to the whole ship's crew, calling on them to prepare for the time when the sea shall give up its dead.

Many little traits of Whitefield's character may be traced in his journals of this voyage. I only mention another ;—his tact in turning every incident into a lesson for himself or others. When a shark was caught, with five pilot-fish clinging to its fins, he says, " Go to the pilot-fish, thou that forsakest a friend in adversity ; consider his ways, and be abashed." When a dolphin was caught, the change of its hues from lovely to livid, reminds him, that " just so is man ; he flourishes for a little, but when death cometh, how quickly his beauty is gone ! A christian may learn instruction from every thing he meets with." When darkness came on whilst he was preaching, on Good

Friday, he says, " It put me in mind of that darkness which overwhelmed the world, when the God of nature suffered."

The fever, which only three or four in the ship escaped, at length laid hold upon Whitefield, and confined him to his bed for a week. The attack, though short, must have been severe; for besides blisters and vomit, he was bled three times. During his illness the captain gave up his own bed to him; Habersham watched him day and night; and (which delighted him most) the sick between decks, whom he had perilled his life to console, prayed fervently for him. He soon recovered, and repaid the kindness of all.

At length, on May 5th, they came in sight of Savannah river, and sent off for a pilot; and such was the joy of all when they came to anchor at Tyby island, that he could not help exclaiming, " How infinitely more joyful will the children of God be, when, having passed through the waves of this troublesome world, they arrive at the haven of everlasting rest ! " Though still weak, he preached a farewell sermon to his " red-coated and blue-jacketed parishioners," as he called his military and naval congregation. It was heard with floods of tears.

" Upon this voyage," says Gillies, " he made the following reflections many years after."—" Even at this distance of time, the remembrance of the happy hours I enjoyed in religious exercises on deck, is refreshing to my soul; and although nature sometimes relented at being taken from my friends, and I was little accustomed to the inconvenience of a sea life, yet, a consciousness that I had the glory of God and the good of souls in view, afforded me, from time to time, unspeakable satisfaction."

Whitefield was cordially welcomed at Savannah by Delamotte and other friends of Wesley. The magistrates also offered to wait upon him, to pay their respects. This he declined, and waited on them; when they agreed to build him a tabernacle and house at Frederica, and to accept his services at Savannah as long as he pleased. He was soon laid aside again, however, by a return of his fever, which terminated in ague. This attack brought him so low for a few days, and made such an alteration in his person, that he says, " Had my friends seen me at that hour, they might have learnt not to have any man's person in admiration, and not to think more highly of me than they ought to think."

The first thing he did after his recovery was to visit *Tomo-Chichi*, the Indian king, then on his death-bed. This was the micoe, or king, whom Oglethorpe brought to England in 1734, and introduced to George II. He was accompanied by his wife and son, and seven other Indians of the Creek nation. His eloquent speech to the king and queen is well known; and was so well received at court, that he was loaded with presents, and even sent in one of the royal carriages to Gravesend when he had to embark again.

He now lay, says Whitefield, " on a blanket, thin and meagre ; little else but skin and bones. Senanki, his wife, sat by, fanning him with Indian feathers. There was no one could talk English, so I could only shake hands with him and leave him." A few days after Whitefield went again to visit Tomo-Chichi, and found that his nephew, Tooanoowee, could speak English. " I desired him to ask his uncle, whether he thought he should die; who answered, I cannot tell. I then asked, where he thought he should go after death? He replied, to heaven. But, alas, how can a drunkard enter there ! I then exhorted Tooanoowee (who is a tall, proper youth) not to get drunk; telling him, that he understood English, and therefore would be punished the more, if he did not live better. I then asked him, whether he believed a heaven? He said, Yes. I then asked, whether he believed a hell? and described it by pointing to the fire. He replied, No. From whence we may easily gather, how natural it is to all mankind to believe there is a place of happiness, because they wish it to be so; and on the contrary, how averse they are to believe a place of torment, because they wish it may not be so. But God is just and true ; and as surely as the righteous shall go away into everlasting happiness, so the impenitently wicked shall go into everlasting punishment."

Dr. Southey has quoted part of this paragraph in a note, and prefaced it thus : " Whitefield was not so likely (as Wesley) to have led these Indians into the right way, if we may judge from his conference with poor Tomo-Chichi, when that chief was at the point of death." If the Doctor mean, that Whitefield should have shown a dying drunkard how pardon might be obtained, instead of exclaiming, "Alas, how shall a drunkard enter heaven!" I quite agree with him. He mistakes, however, if he supposes that this exclamation was addressed to the chief. It is Whitefield's own private reflection on the case, when he wrote an account of it; and distinguished, like all his private reflections of a solemn kind, by *italics*. Besides, it is highly improbable that Whitefield, the man who had just been teaching soldiers and sailors the way to heaven, would have thus abruptly shut the door on a dying Indian! He who warned the young nephew, would not forget to woo the old uncle; although the *result* only, and not the process, appears in his journal.

When Whitefield was sufficiently recovered to survey the colony, the state of the *children* affected him deeply. The idea of an orphan-house in Georgia had been suggested to him by Charles Wesley, "before he himself had any thought of going abroad;" and now that he saw the condition of the colonists, he said, "nothing but an orphan-house can effect" the education of the children. From this moment he set his heart upon founding one, as soon as he could raise funds. In the mean time, he did what he could : he opened a school for the villages of Highgate and Hampstead; and one for girls at Savannah. He then visited the Saltzburghers' orphan school at Ebenezer ; and if any thing was wanting to perfect his own design, or to inflame his zeal, he found it there. The Saltzburghers themselves were exiles for conscience' sake, and eminent for piety and industry. Their ministers, Grenaw and Boltzius, were truly evangelical. Their asylum, which they had been enabled to found by English benevolence, for widows and orphans, was flourishing. Whitefield was so delighted with the order and harmony of Ebenezer, that he gave a share of his own " poor's-store" to Boltzius, for his orphans. Then came the scene— which completed Whitefield's purpose. Boltzius "called all the children before him : catechised and exhorted them to give God thanks for his good providence towards them : then prayed with them, and made them pray after him : then sung a psalm. Afterwards, the *little lambs came and shook me by the*

hand one by one; and so we parted! " From this moment
Whitefield made his purpose his fate.

After spending a few weeks at Savannah, labouring as hard
as his health would permit, he went to Frederica, where he was
gladly received; the people having " had a famine of the word
for a long season." They had no sanctuary : and therefore he
had to preach under a tree, or in Habersham's house. This
visit, although short, endeared him to all the people ; and he
had the satisfaction before he left, to see them " sawing timber
for a commodious place of worship, until a church could be
built."

His return to Savannah was hastened by a circumstance
which Gillies overlooked. One of his friends (he does not say
which) had lost himself in the woods, and was missing from
Tuesday to Friday. The great guns had been fired in vain to
direct the wanderer. Some of the people had searched day
and night for him, without success. This report was sent to
Whitefield, and it hurried him away from Frederica. He had
the pleasure, however, on his arrival at Savannah, to find his
" lost sheep."

Here an instance of refusing to read the burial service occurred, which is more creditable to him than its omission in
the case of the poor negro boy. It will be best told in his own
words. " I was obliged to-day to express my resentment
against infidelity, by refusing to read the Burial Office over the
most professed unbeliever I ever yet met with. God was
pleased to visit him with lingering illness ; during which I went
to see him frequently. About five weeks ago, I asked him,
what religion he was of ? He answered, ' Religion was of so
many sects, he knew not which to choose.' Another time, I
offered to pray with him ; but he would not accept it. Upon
which I resolved to go to see him no more. But being told,
two days before he died, that he had an inclination to see me, I
went again, and after a little conversation, put the following
questions to him : ' Do you believe Jesus Christ to be God,
and the one Mediator between God and man ? ' He said, ' I
believe Jesus Christ was a good man.' ' Do you believe the
holy Scriptures ? ' ' I believe something of the Old Testa-

ment: the New, I do not believe at all.' 'Do you believe, sir, a judgment to come?' He turned himself about, and replied, 'I know not what to say to that.' 'Alas, sir,' said I— 'if all these things should be true, what—?' which words, I believe, gave him great concern; for he seemed after to be very uneasy, grew delirious, and in a day or two departed. Unhappy man—how quickly he was convinced! The day after his decease he was carried to the ground, and I refused to read the office over him;—but I went to the grave, and told the people what had passed between him and me : and, warning all against infidelity, I asked them, whether I could safely say,— 'As our hope is, this our brother doth?' Upon which, I believe, they were thoroughly satisfied that I had done right." This was equally creditable to the preacher and the people!

A few days after this event, Whitefield preached his farewell sermon at Savannah; it being necessary for him to return to England. How much he loved and was beloved, although only "as a wayfaring man turning aside to tarry for a night," may be judged from his own account. "I preached my farewell sermon, to the great grief of my dear parishioners, whose hearts were full as well as mine, which we all showed by many tears. But a sensible alteration appeared in their countenances, when I promised them solemnly, before God, to return as soon as possible."

Next day he went to Charleston, in South Carolina, to embark for England. Gillies says, that Commissary Garden entreated him to preach in the church. This is true : but Garden was the *ecclesiastical*, not the civil, commissary. I mention this, because his kindness to Whitefield was great at first. It is thus recorded in the revised journals : " The bishop of London's commissary, the Rev. Mr. G. received me very courteously, and offered me a lodging. How does God raise up friends wherever I go!" Gillies's account will now be better appreciated : " Mr. G. thanked him most cordially, (he had preached twice in the church,) and assured him that he would defend him with his life and property, should the same arbitrary proceedings commence against him, which Mr. Wesley met with in Georgia. He also said something about the colony

of Georgia, which much encouraged Whitefield ; as if he
thought its flourishing not far off;" and instanced Charleston
" as now fifteen times bigger than when he came there." This
" life and fortune" friend put on a new face afterwards !

Gillies sums up Whitefield's labours in Georgia thus : " It
had been his practice to read prayers and expound (besides
visiting the sick) twice a day. On Sunday, he expounded at
five in the morning ; at ten, read prayers and preached ; and at
three in the afternoon; and at seven in the evening, he expounded
the Church Catechism. How much easier it is for the clergy
in England, Scotland, and Ireland, to find fault with such a
faithful brother in the ministry, than to follow his example ! "

The following note from Whitefield's diary will explain, in
some measure, how he bore the hardships of his perilous voyage
home. " During my stay (in Georgia) the weather was most
intensely hot, burning me almost through my shoes. Seeing
others do it, who were as unable, I determined to inure myself
to hardships, by lying constantly on the ground ; which, by use,
I found to be so far from being a hardship, that afterwards it
became so to lie on a *bed*." It was well it did : for all the way
home, he had no bed, until he reached Ireland. Nor was this
his only privation on the voyage. At the outset they were
tossed from " bar to bar," for nearly a fortnight, by contrary
winds. Their provision began to fail before they had accomplished a third of the passage : and when they reached Ireland,
they were so worn out by famine and fatigue, that Whitefield
says, " they were weak and hollow-eyed," even in the great cabin.
On landing, however, he soon rallied, and preached with great
power at Limerick and Dublin for some days. The account of
his reception and success will be found in the chapter, " Whitefield in Ireland."

CHAPTER IV.

THESE had so much influence upon his subsequent character and career, that I shall not interrupt their narrative, by his occasional excursions into the country, until his position in the metropolis is fully understood. That was, indeed, influenced by his proceedings in Bristol and Wales : but he would have become a field preacher, even if he had not begun at Bristol.

He arrived in London again at the close of 1738, after a perilous voyage. This sudden return was forced upon him ; not sought by him. " I was really happy in my little foreign cure, and could have cheerfully remained among them, had I not been obliged to return to England, to receive priest's orders, and make a beginning towards laying the foundation of the orphan-house. And thus—the place where I intended to hide myself in, became, through my being obliged to return for these purposes, a mean of increasing that popularity which was already begun ;—but which by me was absolutely unforeseen, and absolutely undesigned."

His diary at sea, written amidst hurricanes and famine, illustrates the truth of this explanation. " Had I my own will, I could wish myself a speedy passage, that I might return the sooner to those few sheep I have left in Savannah." It was thus with a single eye and a simple purpose, that Whitefield returned to London.

The first thing he did on his arrival, was, to wait on the archbishop of Canterbury, and the bishop of London. Dr. Gillies says, " he was coldly received by them :" Whitefield himself says, " I met with a favourable reception from both ; but was not so civilly treated by some of the clergy ; for five churches have been already (in two days) denied me.   However, I had an opportunity of preaching at St. Helen's and at Islington, to large congregations indeed; and in the evening (of that first sabbath) I went to a society in Fetter Lane, where we had, what might not be improperly called, a love feast ; eating a little bread and water, and spending two hours in singing and prayers."

It was now Christmas, and he spent almost every evening in expounding to, and praying with, societies of this kind.   On Christmas eve, he continued the exercise until *four* in the morning.   " At six," he says, with his characteristic simplicity, " I went to another in Crutched Friars, and expounded as well as I could ;—but (no wonder !) perceived myself a little oppressed with *drowsiness*."   He had been from four till six o'clock that morning in a large meeting in Red Cross Street ; which is memorable from the fact, that there, for the first time in his life, he ventured to pray *extempore*, " before many witnesses."   He mentions this fact in a note of his diary.   " Dec. 25. The first time I ever prayed extempore, before such a number."   Extempore preaching soon followed this prayer !

On new-year's day he writes thus: " Received the holy sacrament, preached twice, and expounded twice ; and found this the happiest new-year's day that I ever saw.   Afterwards spent the whole night in close prayer, psalms, and thanksgivings, with the Fetter Lane society."   Well might Dr. Gillies say, of Whitefield and his friends, " religious exercises seemed to be their meat and drink."

As might be expected, work of this kind offended many.   It was shared, however, for a time, by some of the clergy.   " Jan. 5th. Held a conference at Islington, concerning many things of importance, with seven ministers of Jesus Christ, despised methodists, whom God in his providence brought together.   We continued in fasting and prayer till three o'clock ; and then parted with a full conviction that God was about to do great things amongst us.   Oh that we may be in any way instrumental to his glory !   Oh that he would make the vessels pure and holy ; meet for such a dear Master's use !"

Such were Whitefield's habits, and such the state of his mind, when he went to Oxford to be ordained a priest. "He was ordained," says Gillies, "by his good friend Bishop Benson." Benson deserved this epithet from Whitefield's biographer. It is well known, however, that he afterwards repented, for a time, of having "ever laid his hands upon George Whitefield:" but he repented of this repentance; and sent, from his dying bed to Whitefield, a present, with a kind request to be remembered in his prayers.

The ordinary explanation of all this seems to be warranted by fact. Benson had been tutor to Lord Huntingdon, and was thus naturally sent for to reason with the countess, when she became a methodist. Her Ladyship, however, reasoned with the bishop; and so plied him with articles and homilies in favour of her creed, and with the solemn responsibilities of his own office, that she offended him. "He rose up in haste (says my authority) to depart, bitterly lamenting that he had ever laid hands on George Whitefield; to whom he imputed, though without cause, the change wrought on her Ladyship. She called him back: 'My Lord,' said she, 'mark my words: when you come to your dying bed, that will be one of the few ordinations you will reflect upon with complacency.'"

As before, Whitefield was deeply affected by his ordination. He went from the altar to the pulpit that very day, "to begin to make proof" of his ministry; and preached twice in Oxford, and expounded at Carfax in the evening, and attended a prayer-meeting at night.

On his return to London, he was alternately in the pulpit, and at these private meetings: and it is difficult to say which of the two spheres of labour had most influence upon his mind and movements at this time. It was certainly the crowding at church, that first suggested to him the idea of preaching in the open air. "When I was informed that nearly a thousand people stood out in the churchyard, and that hundreds returned home, this put me first upon thinking of preaching without-doors. I mentioned it to some friends, who looked upon it as a *mad* motion. However, we kneeled down and prayed, that nothing might be done rashly. Hear and answer, O Lord, for thy name's sake." It is evident from this prayer, that Whitefield himself did not think his design " a mad motion." But still, although a crowded church suggested it, crowded prayer-meetings produced the spirit of the enterprise. It was by expounding and praying extempore, that he discovered his own power over himself and others; and found out that the divine presence might be calculated upon, whenever the divine glory was consulted. These Pentecostal seasons in private made him feel through all his soul, that he ought to do every thing to win souls, and that he *could* do any thing he might attempt.

The influence of these meetings upon Whitefield has never been fully appreciated. They were to him, however, what the wilderness was to John the Baptist; the school of his spirit There he caught the holy and heroic impulse, which prepared him to challenge the scribes and Pharisees any where, and determined him to warn them, in common with publicans and sinners, every where, to " flee from the wrath to come." I might go further, and without extravagance say, that prayer-meetings were to Whitefield what the " third heavens " were to Paul; the *finishing* school of his ministerial education. He was as much indebted to them for his unction and enterprise, as to Pembroke Hall for his learning; or as to the Oxford methodists for his piety; or as to Benson for his ordination to the priesthood; (for what other bishop would have laid his hands on him then ?) WESLEY also caught the primitive flame of evangelization, in one of these private societies at Bristol: for until he saw how " the Spirit moved on the face " of these meetings, he was so tenacious of every thing relating to clerical order and decorum, that he would have counted it " almost a sin to save souls out of a church." Watson, without seeming at all struck by the coincidence, says, " Mr. Wesley first expounded to a little society in Nicholas Street,—and *next day* he overcame his scruples, and preached abroad, on an eminence near Bristol, to more than two thousand persons ! " In all this, indeed, he was only following the example of Whitefield, who had just preceded him, as well as proved both the safety and the success of the experiment: but still if these things encouraged Wesley, it was the social meeting that convinced and determined him. " I have *since*," he says, " seen abundant reason to adore the wise providence of God herein, in thus making a way for myriads of people, who never troubled any church, or were likely to do so, to hear that word which they soon found the power of God unto salvation." These facts are as instructive as they are interesting. Private devotional meetings were thus the cradle of field preaching, as surely as field preaching was the morning star of England's *second* reformation! How often, in grace as in nature, God hangs the greatest weights on the smallest wires! I mean, on wires *accounted* the smallest by the wisdom of this world, and by the folly of the church : for social prayer-meetings are the strongest wires in all the machinery of the moral universe. God hung upon them all the weighty gifts, and all the weightier grace and glory, of PENTECOST! God hung upon them all that is great and good in the American revivals, and all that is amazing in the success of foreign missions. It was when the British churches were as the heart of one man in prayer, that African slavery was abolished throughout the British dominions. The *spiritual* destiny of America now hangs on her prayer-meetings!

It is not a *misnomer* to call the religious societies, which Whitefield and Wesley found in London and Bristol, prayer-meetings. Whitefield often mentions the prayers he united in before he ventured to pray extempore. Bishop Hopkins and Dr. Horneck were the authors of them. The members met, however, for other purposes. They were bound by their rules to meet weekly, " for good discourse ; for the promotion of schools and catechising ; for the relief of the poor ; and to discourse only on subjects tending to practical holiness, and to avoid all controversy."

These societies originated in 1667, in consequence of the success of Dr. Horneck's ministry, and the morning lectures in Cornhill ; which brought many young men to a very affecting sense of their sins, and to a very serious way of treating religion. The meetings were so well conducted, and their influence on public morals so beneficial, that on the accession of William and Mary, they were patronized by the queen and a few of the bishops. They gradually, however, fell into decay. Instead of

forty in London, which was their number at the beginning of
the eighteenth century, I can only trace about ten in Whitefield's journals, in vigorous or healthy action. In these, however, there was evidently much vital godliness, when Whitefield
began to expound and pray in them. Even his devotional spirit
was improved by them, as well as appreciated in them. They
not only sympathized in all the fervency of his first love, but
also fanned it into the blaze of apostolic zeal. Could there be
better proof of their spiritual health or discernment? How
vividly and fondly he remembered the " times of refreshing from
the presence of the Lord," vouchsafed in these little sanctuaries,
may be judged from the following note in his diary : " Often
have we been filled as with new wine. Often have I seen them
overwhelmed with the divine presence ; and crying out, Will
God indeed dwell with men upon earth ? How dreadful is this
place ! This is no other than the house of God, and the gate of
heaven." He also published a letter to them. Whilst thus
engaged and affected in London, persecution began to assail
him. One clergyman attacked him by a scurrilous pamphlet,
(of which Whitefield merely says, " Thou shalt answer for me,
my Lord and my God,") and others from the pulpit. Gillies
says, " Pulpits rung with invectives against him, and the parish
priests threatened some of their parishioners with prosecutions,
for letting him expound and pray in their houses." Whitefield
himself, however, records only one instance of threatened prosecution, in his corrected journals. " Jan. 30th. Expounded
twice on Dowgate Hill, where the people pressed mightily to
come in. The minister of the parish threatens the master of
the house with a prosecution. But, blessed be God, we breathe
in a *free* air ! "

I quote this memorandum for the sake of the closing exclamation. He had seen enough of bigotry and intolerance in the
course of *one* month in London, to turn his attention to the
shields of liberty. Besides, during that month, Whitefield had
visited " some dissenting christian brethren ;" and only a week
before writing his thanksgiving for the " free air" of religious
liberty, he had enjoyed an interview with Dr. Watts, at Stoke
Newington. " Jan. 24. Went to Newington to see Dr. Watts,

who received me most cordially." This record does not, indeed, imply that any thing passed between him and the dissenters, on the subject of freedom ; but still the coincidence is remarkable, because none of his former visits with dissenters drew forth any apostrophe to liberty. Then, however, he was only personally assailed ; but now that his converts were threatened with prosecutions, nothing was more likely to lead his thoughts to the subject, than a visit to Dr. Watts, even if nothing was said on the subject. For Whitefield could not but see that he must soon need for himself and his adherents, the whole panoply of toleration, if he preached in the open air : and that, he had made up his mind to do, two days *before* he penned his apostrophe. " Jan. 28th, Sunday. Received the sacrament at Crooked Lane church : afterwards went and preached at Ironmonger's Alms-houses—not doubting, but there would be hundreds more than the chapel would hold. I took *two* written sermons with me—one for *within*—and the other for *without*. But to my surprise (he might have said disappointment, for he wished to get out!) found no more than could conveniently hear me from the pulpit." In the course of a few days, he also exhorted the society at Dowgate Hill, particularly, " not to forsake the assembling of themselves together, *notwithstanding* the people of the house had been threatened with a prosecution." Thus, wherever Whitefield caught the love of religious liberty, he soon both cherished and spread the sacred flame, when intolerance menaced his friends.

In the space of a fortnight from this time, Whitefield was preaching to the Bristol colliers, on Hannam Mount, at Rose Green ; and on the twenty-seventh of April, he preached in Islington churchyard. The churchwarden of Islington had demanded him to produce his licence, although he went there by the vicar's appointment, to officiate. " For peace' sake, I declined preaching in the church ; and after the communion, preached in the churchyard ; being assured my Master *now* called me out here, as well as at Bristol." Next day he writes thus : " Preached again in Islington churchyard, to a congregation nearly as large again as yesterday. The second lesson was very applicable ; being Acts xxv. I can say with St. Paul,

' Neither against the temple, nor against Cæsar, have I done any thing ;' and yet I am cast out and reviled as an evil-doer : but the Scriptures must be fulfilled—' If they have persecuted Me, they will also persecute you.' " The people must have been struck by this coincidence : for they had given Whitefield a collection for his orphan-house, amounting to £22, only a few weeks before ; and nothing had happened in the interval to disqualify him for the pulpit, but field preaching ; and that had not startled the vicar. The fact is, *Stonehouse,* the vicar, was friendly to the methodists, and disliked by the heads of the parish. I have seen some of his sermons, the fidelity of which is almost ferocious.

At this time, too, all London was ringing with the announcement, that Whitefield would preach next day (Sunday) in MOORFIELDS. " The thing being new and singular," says Gillies, " he found, on coming out of the coach, an incredible number of people assembled. Many had told him that he should never come out of that place alive. He went in, however, between two friends, who by the pressure of the crowd were soon parted from him entirely, and obliged to leave him to the mercy of the rabble. But these, instead of hurting him, formed a lane for him, and carried him along to the middle of the fields, where a table had been placed, (which was broken in pieces by the crowd,) and afterwards back again to the wall that then parted the upper and lower Moorfields ; from which he preached without molestation, to an exceeding great multitude, in the lower fields."

This is not too oratorically told for the greatness of the occasion. That was worthy of a more graphic and glowing pen, than has yet tried to depict the scene. Whitefield himself, however, summed up the whole matter, in his corrected journals, thus : " Sunday, April 29. Begun to be yet more vile this day ; for I preached at Moorfields to an exceeding great multitude : and, at five in the evening, went and preached at Kennington Common, where upwards of twenty thousand people were supposed to be present. The wind being for me, it carried my voice to the extremest part of the audience. All stood attentive, and joined in the psalm and the Lord's prayer so regularly, that I scarce ever preached with more quietness in a church. Many were much affected.

> For this—let men revile my name,
> I'd shun no cross, I'd fear no shame,
> All hail, reproach, and welcome, pain !
> Only thy terrors, Lord, restrain."

Such was his own bulletin of this " great field day," when he wrote for posterity :—for this is part of his autobiography. When he wrote for his public journals, he merely said, " Preached in the morning at Moorfields to an exceeding great multitude." Then, as if he had done no great thing, he adds, " Went to Christ-Church, and heard Dr. Trapp preach most virulently against me and my friends, from these words, ' Be not righteous over-much.' God gave me great serenity of mind ; but, alas, the preacher was not so calm as I wished him."

It is remarkable that none of his letters, at this time, refer to the enterprise. Two days before it, he wrote to a friend, " To-day my Master, by his providence and Spirit, compelled me to preach in the churchyard of Islington. To-morrow I am to repeat that mad trick, and on Sunday to go out into Moorfields. I preach until I sweat through and through." Even his diary contains nothing on the subject, but the following simple note : " Words cannot well express the glorious displays of divine grace, which we saw, and heard of, and felt," this day. He had, however, a decided opinion upon both the measure and its success. " All agreed," he says, " that it was never seen on this ways before. I hope a good inroad has been made into the devil's kingdom this day. Lord, not unto me, but unto thy name be all the glory." *Journals.*

Even all this, with all the prospects which it must have opened of London as a sphere for vast usefulness, did not divert nor divide Whitefield's heart from his " poor orphans or his little flock " in the colony ; for on the very day after, he refused to preach at all, that he might devote himself to their interests. " April 30. Received letters from Georgia this evening, telling me of the affairs of the colony. They have a melancholy aspect at present ; but our extremity is God's opportunity. *Lord, thou callest me : lo, I come !* "

" For several months after this," says Gillies, " Moorfields, Kennington Common, and Blackheath, were the chief scenes of action. At a moderate computation, the auditories often consisted of above twenty thousand. It is said their singing could be heard two miles off, and his voice nearly a mile. Sometimes there were upwards of a hundred coaches, besides waggons, scaffolds, and other contrivances, which persons let out for the convenience of the audience." The rising ground on Blackheath, from which Whitefield preached, is still known as " Whitefield's Mount." After his death, one of his *noble* friends (I believe) planted it with fir-trees. Many spots in the country, also, are thus hallowed by his name ; and of these, none is more hallowed than a field at Gornal in Staffordshire. When I visited that " hill of Zion," Whitefield's park was the first object pointed out to me, although the hill of Gornal is crowned with the most complete establishment for religious instruction I have ever seen in a rural district. The reason was obvious : Whitefield had laid the foundation of that establishment. And Gornal is just the spot that was sure to arrest him ! He could not have looked down from that mount, into the vast *cup* of the surrounding valley, without weeping over the population. He must have wished his mighty voice mightier, that he might *cry* down to them all ! He did what he could ;—set a lamp upon the hill.

But to return to the metropolis. He was much disappointed and grieved to find that, notwithstanding all the money he had formerly obtained for the London charities, he was not allowed to collect for Georgia, except in a few churches. He had, therefore, to carry his " begging case " into the fields with him. Gillies says, " Having no other method to take, he was obliged to collect for the orphan-house in the fields, or not at all, which was humbling to himself, and to the friends who assisted him in that work ; but the readiness with which the people gave, and the prayers they put up while throwing in their mites, were very encouraging." They were so : for he thus obtained upwards of a thousand pounds for his orphan-house. He himself says, "The readiness with which the people gave is inexpressible: for I think they could not have expressed more earnestness, or taken more pains, had they all been to have received an alms. One sign this, I hope, that the word of God has taken hold of their hearts."

On one occasion he collected in Moorfields, £52 19s. 6d., "of which, above twenty pounds was in halfpence." On another, at Kennington, sixteen, of £47, was in copper. He says, "I was one of the collectors; and methinks it would have delighted almost any one to have seen with what eagerness the people came up both sides of the eminence on which I stood, and afterwards to the coach doors, to throw in their mites!" He saw, however, how all this would seem to the Pharisees, and anticipated them thus, in his public journal: "Preached to nearly sixty thousand people in Moorfields, and collected £29 17s. 8d. and came home deeply humbled with a sense of what God had done for my soul. I doubt not but many self-righteous bigots, when they see me spreading out my hands to offer Jesus Christ freely to all, are ready to cry out,— 'How glorious did the Reverend Mr. Whitefield look to-day, when, neglecting the dignity of a clergyman, he stood venting his enthusiastic ravings in a gown and cassock, and collecting mites from the poor people!' But if this be vile, Lord, grant that I may be more vile! Ye scoffers, mock on: I rejoice, yea, and will rejoice." (He calls them "Pharisees," in his public journal; but in his Life, he calls them bigots and scoffers.)

On this memorable day, he received the first letter from Ralph Erskine, "a field preacher of the Scots church, and a noble soldier of the Lord Jesus Christ," as he calls him then. He had added to this record, in his public journal, "Oh that all that are truly zealous knew one another! It must greatly strengthen each other's hands." Whitefield, however, did not find all he expected from this mutual knowledge; and therefore excluded the whole record from his revised journals, in 1756. By that time, he knew more about the Erskines; and though he still venerated their christian character highly, he was too honest to compliment their spirit.

Amongst other coincidences in this memorable week, none

G 2

gratified him more than the grant of five hundred acres of land to himself and his successors for ever, for the use of the orphan-house, by the honourable trustees for Georgia. " They received me with the utmost civility, and agreed to every thing I asked." This, be it remembered, was done at the very time when all the city was moved by his " mad trick" in the fields; and he returned the compliment to the Honourable Board, by leaving them, to preach that evening to twenty thousand people at Kennington, where (judging from the collection after the sermon) he seems to have mentioned the grant made to him in the morning. " At night," he says, " my heart was so full, that I could not well speak. I could only pour it out in *awful silence*. Oh the happiness of communion with God! "

It was also at the height and heat of this crisis, that he engaged a passage for himself and eleven others, on board the Elizabeth, to Pennsylvania; that he might preach the gospel and provide for the orphan-house, on his way to Georgia :—so little was Whitefield's original purpose affected by his popularity. In fact, he never lost sight of it for a moment; for the delay in sailing arose from an embargo.

A singular incident occurred at this time, which Whitefield has recorded at considerable length in his journals. A young man, Joseph Periam, who had read his sermon on Regeneration, and been impressed by it, prayed so loud, and fasted so long, and sold " all he had" so literally, that his family sent him to Bethlehem mad-house. There he was treated as methodistically mad, and as " one of Whitefield's gang." The keepers threw him down, and thrust a key into his mouth, that they might drench him with medicine. He was then placed in a cold room, without windows, and with a damp cellar under it.

Periam, however, found some way of conveying a letter to Whitefield, requesting both advice and a visit. Both were promptly given. Whitefield soon discovered that Periam was not mad; and, taking Mr. Seward and some other friends with him, he went before the committee of the hospital to explain the case. Seward seems to have been the chief speaker; and he so astounded the committee by quoting Scripture, that they pronounced him as mad as the young man! It must have been a ludicrous scene. The doctors told the whole deputation frankly, that, in their opinion, Whitefield and his followers were "really beside themselves." It was, however, agreed that if Whitefield would take Periam out to Georgia, a release would be granted. Thus the conference ended; and the young man went out as a schoolmaster at the orphan-house. There he was useful and exemplary to the last; and when he died, two of his sons were received into the school.

Whilst the embargo continued, Whitefield made some running excursions into the country, with great success. Before leaving London, however, he went to St. Paul's, with the Fetter Lane society, and received the sacrament as " a testimony," he says, "that we adhered to the church of England." He was perfectly sincere in this; but many churchmen thought it a *strange* adherence, when he went from St. Paul's to Moorfields and Kennington Common, and preached to 30,000 people! This was adherence to Christ and Paul only.

After spending a week about Northamptonshire, where Doddridge received him "most courteously," he returned to London, and added *Hackney* Fields to the list of his preaching stations. There he made that tremendous attack upon " the impiety of the *letter-learned* teachers, who count the doctrine of the new birth enthusiasm," which drew upon him the wrath of the clergy. " I could not help," he says, " exposing the impiety of these vile teachers, who say we are not now to receive the Holy Ghost. Out of your own mouths I will condemn you, ye blind guides! Did you not, at the time of ordination, tell the bishop that you—were inwardly moved by the Holy Ghost, to take upon you the administration of the church? Surely at that time you acted the part of Ananias and Sapphira over again. Surely, says Bishop Burnet, you lied not only unto man but unto God."

This is the revised form of the charge. As he first published it, he did not quote Burnet, nor use the word " vile." That word he substituted for the epithet " letter-learned," because Warburton and others represented him as a despiser of learning.

The *first* answer given to his sermon on Regeneration, was by Tristram Land, A. M. curate of St. James's, *Garlickhithe.*

Whitefield deemed it unworthy of notice. I do not. It is a fair specimen of the general tone of sentiment and feeling at the time. It was written in 1737, although not published ("for private reasons") until 1739; by which time, Whitefield and Wesley had compelled theologians, at least, to *mask* their battery somewhat, in assailing the doctrine of the new birth. TRISTRAM, however, has nothing to conceal. With inimitable inanity and frankness, he says to Whitefield, "I hope you'll please to alter your practice, and no longer preach up the necessity of the new birth, until you better understand the nature and commencement of it: for to tell christians they must be born again, who in the *soundest* sense were born again in their infancy, is, at least, a great impropriety. And besides, your time would be much better spent, after having given so much just occasion of offence to your brethren, if, instead of regeneration, you insist more upon repentance and amendment."

"You tell your readers, 'It is plain beyond all contradiction, that comparatively but few of those that are born of water are born of the Spirit likewise; or, to use another Scriptural way of speaking, many of those that are baptized with water, are not effectually, at least, baptized with the Holy Ghost.' But prithee, Sir, attend now to these few following places which I set before you, to confront your ill-grounded assertion." Tristram then quotes the Office of Baptism, and the Rubrick at the end of it, and adds triumphantly, "All this, Sir, I take to be direct evidence against you, not to be evaded by the word 'effectually,' with which you thought proper to guard your assertion. All the members of our church were baptized in infancy. She declares them regenerate; and gives hearty thanks to God, that it has pleased him to regenerate such infants with his Holy Spirit. The church supposes they have already been born again, and so does not command them to be baptized or born again a second time: for to be born more than once in a spiritual sense, is just as impossible as to be born twice in a natural.

"Perhaps, Sir, at another opportunity, I may make it my business to point out some more mistakes in your writings and conduct; but if I should not, I dare say you'll excuse your humble servant, Tristram Land."

When Whitefield read this letter, he wrote in his diary, " Thou shalt answer for me, O Lord." He saw that it was unanswerable, if the Office of Baptism, and the Catechism, be true ; and he was not prepared then to impeach them by name.

The clergy seem to have been ashamed of the bald defence published by this honest—" Fellow of Clare Hall, Cambridge :" for Whitefield's next opponent, on this subject, was no less a person than Dr. Stebbing, his Majesty's chaplain in ordinary, and preacher to the honourable society of Gray's Inn. (At both Gray's and Lincoln's Inn, sermons against Whitefield and Wesley seem to have been popular amongst the lawyers, and means of obtaining preferment at court. See Warburton's.) Dr. Stebbing's sermon, entitled " A Caution against Religious Delusion," went through two or three editions in 1739. It is the production of a scholar and a gentleman ; and so far of a divine too, that it is silent on the subject of baptismal regeneration. Indeed, it is a dexterous attempt to prove, that the new birth is only another expression for " the new man," which is, the Doctor says, the figurative name of " practical righteousness." This sermon the bishop of Gloucester sent to Whitefield, with a kind letter of caution and advice. The letter itself he answered with equal firmness and courtesy ; but the Doctor, without ceremony. " Dr. Stebbing's sermon (for which I thank your Lordship) confirms me more and more in my opinion, that I ought to be instant in season and out of season. For to me, he seems to know no more of the true nature of regeneration, than Nicodemus did, when he came to Jesus by night. Your Lordship may observe, that he does not speak a word of original sin, or the dreadful consequences of our fall in Adam, upon which the doctrine of the new birth is entirely founded. No ; like other polite preachers, he seems to think that St. Paul's description of the wickedness of the heathen, is only to be referred to past ages : whereas, I affirm, we are all included under the guilt and consequences of sin, as much as they were ;—and if any man preach any other doctrine, he shall bear his punishment, whosoever he be.

" Again, my Lord, the Doctor entirely mistakes us, when we talk of the sensible manifestations of the Holy Ghost. Indeed, I know not that we use the word *sensible :* but, if we do, we do not mean that God's Spirit does manifest itself to our *senses,* but that it may be perceived by the soul, as really as any sensible impression made upon the body. But to disprove this, the Doctor brings our Lord's allusion to the *wind ;* which is one of the best texts to prove it ; for if the analogy of our Lord's discourse be carried on, it amounts to this much,—that although the operations of the Spirit can no more be accounted for, than how the wind cometh, and whither it goeth, yet may they as easily be felt by the soul, as the wind by the body. But he understands us as the carnal Jews understood Christ, when He talked of giving them that bread which came down from heaven. But the Doctor, and the rest of my reverend brethren, are welcome to judge of me as they please. Yet a little while, and we shall all appear before the great Shepherd of our souls ! "

We can scarcely appreciate now the value of this solemn and decided stand for the truth as it is in Jesus. Had Whitefield conceded an iota to Stebbing, he would have stultified his grand object. Regeneration by the Holy Spirit had to be maintained by its champion then, as Luther fought for justification by faith ;—giving no quarter to the vulgar or the refined opponents of it. Stebbing's sermon could do no injury now. It is even calculated to do real good, wherever more stress is laid upon strong emotions, than upon personal holiness ; but then, it was as much a moral *" go-by"* to the question, as baptism was a ceremonial one. Whitefield had, therefore, no alternative but to abandon the necessity of spiritual conversion, or to refute Stebbing.

His next opponent, at this time, was the bishop of London, who made him, he says, "the chief subject matter" of a pastoral letter. That letter charges him with "professing to plant and propagate a new gospel, unknown to the *generality* of ministers and people, in a christian country." Whitefield, very properly, admits the charge. "Mine is a new gospel—and will be always unknown to the generality, if your Lordship's clergy follow your Lordship's directions. Your Lordship exhorts your clergy to preach justification by faith alone—and quotes the 11th Ar-

ticle of our church, which tells us, we are justified by faith only,
and not for our works or deservings :' at the same time,—your
Lordship bids them 'explain it in such a manner, as to leave
no doubt upon their minds, whether good works are a necessary
condition of their being justified in the sight of God.' Your
Lordship, in my opinion, could not well be guilty of a greater
inconsistency. This, my Lord, is truly a *new* gospel! It is
as contrary to the doctrine of the church of England, as light is
contrary to darkness."

This reply, happily, committed Whitefield as fully upon the
question of justification, as his letter to the bishop of Gloucester had upon the question of regeneration : for, until Gibson's
Letter appeared, Whitefield himself had but confused notions of
the subject. But the bishop's errors made him aware of his
own mistakes. In his early sermons, he had used such expressions as, " washing away the guilt of sin, by the tears of a sincere repentance, joined with faith in the blood of Christ ;"
" depending on the righteousness of Christ imputed to and
inherent in" us ; " things necessary to *qualify* us for being
savingly in Christ." The fact is, he had not " read a single
book on the doctrine of free justification," when he began to
preach. " No wonder, then," he says, " that I was not so clear
in some points, at my first setting out. I think it no dishonour
to retract some expressions that dropped from my pen, before
God gave me a more clear knowledge of the doctrines of grace.
St. Austin, I think, did so before me." *A Letter to some Church
Members of the Presbyterian Persuasion. New York,* 1740. Both
American and Scotch presbyterians helped to teach him " the
way of God more perfectly," at this time. Dr. Watts also had
some influence upon him, about this time ; although less than
he wished. The Doctor did not, indeed, take any public part in
the controversy ; but he *privately* sustained Bishop Gibson, and
thus placed himself in a false position, which for ever after prevented him from being more than the *private* friend of Whitefield. The bishop had sent him a copy of his Pastoral Letter
against Whitefield : and, in answer to it, he says, " Your Lordship's distinction of the ordinary and extraordinary influences
of the Holy Spirit is so very necessary, that I think the New

Testament cannot be understood without it : and I wish Mr.
Whitefield would not have risen above any pretence to the ordinary influence, unless he could have given better evidences of it.
He has acknowledged to me in conversation, that it is such an
impression upon his own mind, that he knows to be divine,
though he cannot give me any convincing proof of it.

" I said many things to warn him of the danger of delusion,
and to guard him against the irregularities and imprudences
which youth and zeal might lead him into; and told him plainly,
that though I believed him very sincere, and desiring to do good
to souls, yet I was not convinced of any extraordinary call he
had to some parts of his conduct :—and he seemed to take this
free discourse in a very candid manner." *Milner's Life of Watts*,
p. 638. In an evil hour this was written ; for however true, it
was ill timed. No matter that the letter contains some faithful remonstrances to the bishop, about his clergy : it contains
none against Gibson's " new gospel," as Whitefield well calls
it ; and it abets him (unintentionally, indeed) in confounding
regeneration with the extraordinary influences of the Spirit.
For that was the real point at issue between Gibson and Whitefield. Accordingly, Gibson took the letter in good part. He
wrote thus : " Good Sir, it had been well for Mr. Whitefield, if
he had taken the wise advice and cautions you gave him : but
from the time that men imagine themselves singled out by God
for extraordinary purposes, and in consequence of that, to be
guided by extraordinary impulses and operations, all human
advice is lost upon them.—I am, with great affection and esteem,
your very faithful servant, EDM. LOND."

Watts did not see the bearing of all this ; but it so committed
him upon the bishop's side of the question, that he could not
espouse Whitefield's side of it publicly, even when that was no
longer encumbered with crude notions of impulses and impressions.

This incident deserves far more consideration than it has ever
received. It is often asked, with wonder, why the orthodox
dissenters of that time did not rally around Whitefield, and
open their pulpits to him, when he was excluded from the
churches? The author of the " Life and Times of Watts " says,

" The co-operation of such men as Watts and Doddridge was forfeited by the want of a conciliating spirit, and the good will they tendered was lost by causeless and imprudent reflections" (on the part of the methodists). " When their churches were denounced as companies of banded formalists,—when their ministers were proclaimed as feeding the flock with husks, instead of salutary food,—it is not surprising if the majority stood aloof, or retired disgusted by the exhibition of such censoriousness."

But what has all this tirade against the methodists to do with Whitefield ? He never spoke in this manner or spirit against Watts or Doddridge. He revered and loved both from the first. Milner surely does not mean, when he says that " Whitefield in middle age saw his error," that *this* was the " youthful intemperance he acknowledged." He did acknowledge, with great candour and self-condemnation, that he had spoken both hastily and harshly of many ministers. For this he publicly asked pardon of God and man. But it was never of such men as Watts and Doddridge, and especially not of these men, he had ever been an accuser. Indeed, both of them had said of him what was not exactly kind or wise, however well meant. Doddridge called him " a very weak man," though " very honest ;" and, " a little intoxicated with popularity." He might also have found " a more excellent way " of appeasing the brethren who were " angry" with him for the respect he showed to Whitefield, than by saying to Coward's trustees, " I am not so zealously attached to him, as to be disposed to celebrate him as one of the greatest men of the age, or to think that he is the pillar that bears up the whole interest of religion among us." *Letters to Dr. Wood and Nath. Neal, Esq.* vol. iv. This was playing too far into the hands of Whitefield's dissenting opponents, just as Watts conceded too much to Gibson. Watts went so far in his courtesy to the bishop, as to tell him, not only how to " make all the *Whitefields* less regarded, and less dangerous to the church," but also how " to lessen separation" from the church: " Induce the ministers under your care, to preach and converse among their people with that evangelical spirit, that zeal for the honour of God and the success of the gospel, and with that compassion for the souls of men, that your Lordship so much

approves and advises in your pious and excellent charge."
Milner, p. 639.

All this may surprise some: but the fact is, that the dissenters
of these times were, in their own way, almost as great sticklers
for " order " as the bishops.   Field preaching was as alarming to
the *board* as to the bench.   The primate would have as soon
quitted his throne, as a leading nonconformist his desk, to
preach from a horse-block or a table, in the open air.   Indeed,
aggression was no part of the character of dissent, in these days.
No wonder !   Dissenters had been so long persecuted even in
their secluded and obscure chapels, that they were glad to *sit
still* under their vine and their fig-tree ; thankful for their own
safety, and neither daring nor dreaming to go into the highways or hedges.   It was methodism made dissent aggressive
upon the strong holds of Satan.   Indeed, until the chief of them
were carried by storm, by Whitefield and Wesley, dissenters
must have dreaded all co-operation with methodism, as perilous
to their own peace and safety.   They did.   Accordingly, all the
remonstrances addressed to Doddridge, by Coward's trustees
and the London ministers, harp chiefly upon the string, that the
church will not think so well of the dissenting interest, if she see
it countenancing Whitefield.   Doddridge nobly despised this
fear ; but still, it was long and deeply felt by many of the nonconformists.   This was not, however, their only reason.   They
did fear for their own standing with the church ; but they feared
more for the ark of God ; which, they thought, was in danger of
being " swallowed up in a sea of deism," if the enthusiasm of
methodism obtained countenance " from prudent christians."
See Neal's Letters to Doddridge, vol. iv.

Do I then regret that Whitefield was not adopted by the
dissenters, when the church cast him out? No, in nowise ! They
would have spoiled him by their *orderliness ;* and he might have
confused them by his splendid irregularities.   Ralph Erskine
well said to Whitefield, " I see a beauty in the providence of
your being in communion with the English church : otherwise,
such great confluences from among them had not attended your
ministry ; nor, consequently, reaped the advantage which so
many have done."   *Fraser's Life of R. Erskine.*

The Scotch dissenters, the Seceders, would, indeed, have gladly adopted Whitefield, if they could have had a monopoly of his labour: but they, too, were better without him. His *reaction* upon the secession in Scotland, as upon the dissenters of England, multiplied and strengthened both eventually, far more than his exclusive services could have done.

This digression, though long, and somewhat out of place, will be found useful in its bearings upon his future positions. At this time, however, whilst doctors differed, he carried the great questions at issue into the midst of *"multitudes, multitudes in the valley of* DECISION!" He also preached frequently in the church at Bexley, and administered the sacrament. The vicar of Bexley, Mr. Peers, was much attached to him; but was compelled at last, by the diocesan, to deny him the use of the pulpit. But the good man went no further than the *letter* of the injunction: he employed Whitefield in the desk, and at the altar, when he could no longer admit him into the pulpit. " Read prayers and assisted in administering the sacrament at Bexley church. Many came from far, and expected to hear me." The pulpit being denied, " I preached in the afternoon, in Justice D.'s yard, to about three hundred people; and in the evening, at Blackheath, to upwards of twenty thousand, on these words, ' *And they cast him out.*' I recommended to the people the example of the blind beggar, and reminded them to prepare for a gathering *storm!*"

A few days before this expulsion from the pulpit at Bexley, he had introduced Mr. Wesley to Blackheath. This afforded him great pleasure. He regarded it " as another fresh inroad made into Satan's kingdom," that his " honoured and reverend friend, Mr. John Wesley," was "following him in field preaching in London, as well as in Bristol." " The Lord give him ten thousand times more success than he has given me."

Next week, when he himself went to preach at Blackheath in the evening, instead of twenty or thirty thousand people as usual, there were not one thousand. This arose from a report that Whitefield was dead. He does not explain the report in any of his journals; but merely says of it, " Wherever I came, I found people much surprised and rejoiced to see me alive."

Next night, however, the heath was again swarming with thousands.

On the following day he went on a tour into Gloucestershire, for nearly a month. During his absence, the work was carried on by his " honoured friend and fellow-labourer, Charles Wesley." On his return, he says, " The poor souls were ready to leap for joy," at Kennington Common. At Moorfields, " A greater power than ever was amongst us. I collected £24 17s. for the school-house at Kingswood."

Whitefield little knew, whilst thus occupied, how narrowly his life had escaped at Basingstoke, two days before. He had, indeed, been told by one, as he went out to preach in a field, that he " should not go alive out of Basingstoke ;" but he heeded not the threat, as he had claimed protection from the mayor. He would not, perhaps, have thought of it again, had not a quaker, at whose house he slept, sent the following letter : " I am truly glad that thou wert preserved out of the hands of cruel and unreasonable men. Thou heardst of the threatenings of many; but the malice and blind zeal of some went further. For hadst thou went to my friend H—— to bed, or elsewhere towards that part of the town, (which I believe was expected,) there were ten or twelve men lying in wait to do thee a private mischief : which I know by the testimony of one of those very men ; who boasted to me—' *We would have given him a secret blow, and prevented him making disturbances.*' This confession came out to me in the warmth of his zeal ; as thinking, perhaps, that I could hate, at least, if not destroy, (like him,) all that were not of my own party." *Revised Journals.*

Gillies has not mentioned this escape. He merely refers to the " groundless fictions," then afloat, about Whitefield's murder or wounds ; for *report* killed or wounded him, whenever he left London for a few days. Gillies has, however, marked a coincidence which, although I durst not have noticed in the way he has done, I dare not altogether suppress. He says, " The bishop of London laid hold of *this* occasion for publishing a charge to his clergy, to avoid the extremes of enthusiasm and lukewarmness." And that the charge was ill-timed, and calculated to endanger Whitefield, cannot be doubted ; for he was made, as he himself says, " the chief subject matter " of it, and thus held up to public odium; but it certainly was not intended to injure him, except in his reputation and influence. Bishops, however, should take care how they bark, when *curs* are inclined to bite. Well might Whitefield say at this crisis, " People wonder at me, that I should talk of persecution, now the world is become christian : but, alas, were Jesus Christ to come down from heaven at this time, he would be treated as formerly. And whoever goes forth to preach the gospel in his Spirit, must expect the same treatment as his first apostles met with. Lord, prepare us for all events."

But if he saw danger, he did not shrink from it. In one instance, at this time, he almost courted insult, as well as exposed himself to it. Having heard that there was to be a horse-race at Hackney Marsh, he says, " I appointed, *purposely*, to preach there, because the race was to be in the same field." He did preach to ten thousand people; and " very few left the sermon :" some who did, " returned back quickly," and them he addressed personally. This was certainly imprudent. The whole affair, however, passed off quietly.

Marybone Fields and Stoke Newington Common then became the chief scene of his labours, until his embarkation : and they were scenes of triumph. Many scoffers were arrested and overpowered by the gospel, and more formalists roused to flee from the wrath to come. He himself has not hazarded any computation of the precise number of avowed converts, won by field preaching, in and around London; but, judging from the time he spent in speaking with the awakened, during the intervals of preaching, and from the letters and notes he acknowledges, the numbers must have been great. He says in his revised journal, at the close of this grand campaign to win souls, " Great things God has already done: for it is *unknown* how many have come to me under strong convictions of their fallen state; desiring to be (more) awakened to a sense of sin, and giving thanks for the benefits God has imparted to them by the ministry of his word." His last sermon, before leaving London to embark, brought so many of these amongst the crowd at Kennington Common, and they were so " exceedingly affected," that he was " almost prevented from making any *application* " of the subject.   But whatever was the number of his converts then, TOPLADY, who was not inclined to give an exaggerated answer to the question, " Are there many that be saved ? " gave Whitefield credit for having been, in the course of his entire ministry, useful to " *tens* of thousands besides " himself.

CHAPTER V.

WHATEVER disadvantages may attend the mode in which I trace the first labours and influence of Whitefield, the divisions I have adopted will enable the reader to follow him without effort or confusion, and to judge fairly of each of his successive spheres; many of which were very dissimilar, however much alike were the effects of his preaching in them. Besides, it is much easier to realize the changes which passed upon his spirit as he moved from country to country, and from spot to spot, in the glory or gloom of circumstances, than to realize places, however vividly characterized; for they seldom gave a character to his preaching. I mean, that he did not exactly adapt himself to localities; but came into a new field in the spirit he had left the old one. He preached "the common salvation" every where, although with varied power. According to "the brook in the way," he "lifted up the head." He came to London under the Bristol impulse; and he embarked for America under the London impulse. This is evident from his journals. He had no plans, but for winning souls; and these, although they could never be set aside by circumstances, could be inflamed by them. Accordingly, whilst the vessel was detained in the river or on the coast, he was never idle. Wherever he could land, he preached; and when on board, he read prayers and expounded daily; just as might be expected from a man fresh from the impulses of London.

His work in England, as distinguished from London and its immediate vicinity, began on his return from Georgia; and then, he was full of his orphan school: an institution which, if

H

it did little for the colony, led him to do much for the mother country! Humanly speaking, but for that school, and the college he intended to graft upon it, Whitefield would never have traversed England as he did, nor visited Scotland so often. It compelled him to travel, and inspired him to preach. It was his *hobby*, certainly; but by riding it well, he made it like " the white horse" of the Apocalypse, the means of going "forth conquering and to conquer."

Having been ordained a priest at Oxford, and received a " liberal benefaction" from the bishop of Gloucester for Georgia, his first visit was to Windsor. There he could find only a school-room to expound in; but such was the impression made by his address, that he exclaimed on leaving, " Not unto me, O Lord, not unto me; but unto thy name be all the glory."

Next morning he went to Basingstoke, and expounded to about a hundred very attentive hearers, in the dining-room of the inn; but on the evening of the next day, the crowd outside was noisy, and threw stones at the windows. This roused Whitefield's zeal and the curiosity of the town. On the following day, he had three large rooms nearly filled; and although some interrupted him, many were so struck and overawed, that they said they would " never oppose again."*

At this time he visited and revisited Dummer, where he had once been so useful and happy amongst the poor. " I found," says he, that " they had not forgotten their former love. We took exceeding sweet counsel, prayed, and sang psalms, and eat our bread with gladness and singleness of heart. How did Jesus comfort us by the way! *Monstrare nequeo sentio tantum!* Lord, melt down my frozen heart, with a sense of thy unmerited love."

From Dummer he went to Salisbury, and there visited " an old disciple, Mr. Wesley's mother;" but found no opportunity for preaching. He then went to Bath, with the hope of preaching in the abbey church for the orphan-house, the trustees having obtained leave of the bishop; but Dr. C. would not permit him. "He was pleased" (so Whitefield expresses it) " to

---

* See Letter 51. Works, vol. i.

give me an absolute refusal to preach either on that or any
other occasion, without a positive *order* from the king or the
bishop. I asked him his reasons. He said he was not obliged
to give me any. I therefore withdrew, and reached Bristol."
There a welcome awaited him ; and he felt the difference.
" Who can express the *joy* with which I was received ? " It
was not long, however, unmixed joy. He was refused the use
of Redcliffe church, although he had the promise of it. The
clergyman pretended that " he could not lend his church without a special order from the chancellor." Whitefield, with his
usual promptitude, put this excuse to the test at once. " I immediately waited on the chancellor, who told me frankly, that
he would neither give positive leave, nor would he *prohibit* any
one that should lend me a church ; but he would advise me to
withdraw to some other place, till he heard from the bishop,
and not to preach on any other occasion. I asked him his reasons. He answered,—' Why will you press so hard upon me ?
The thing has given general dislike.' I replied, ' Not the orphan-
house ; even those that disagree with me in other particulars,
approve of that. And as for the gospel—when was it preached
without dislike ? '

" Soon after this I waited upon the reverend the dean, who
received me with great civility. When I had shown him my
Georgia accounts, and answered him a question or two about
the colony, I asked him, whether there could be any just objection against my preaching in churches for the orphan-house?
After a pause for a considerable time, he said, he could not
tell. Somebody knocking at the door, he replied, ' Mr. Whitefield, I will give you an answer some other time : now I expect
company.' ' Will you be pleased to fix any time, Sir,' said I.
' I will send to you,' says the dean. O christian simplicity,
whither art thou fled ? "

Whitefield himself *fled*, that afternoon, to the Newgate of
Bristol, and obtained the jailer's permission to preach there to
the prisoners. " I preached a sermon on the Penitent Thief,
and collected fifteen shillings for them." On the following
sabbath he preached at St. Werburgh's church to a large audience. Even St. Mary Redcliffe was open to him soon, though

not for a collection. " Blessed be God,—I thought yesterday
I should not have the use of any pulpit; but God has the hearts
of all men in his hands." The old effects accompanied this
new visit to Bristol. " Great numbers were melted down.
Thousands could not find room." He thus verified a prediction
which had been sent from London to Bristol, by some raving
blasphemer ;—" Whitefield has set the town on fire, and now he
is gone to kindle a flame in the country. I think the devil in
hell is in you all."

The flame was kindled in Bristol; and the devil had certainly something to do with those who tried to extinguish it.
" The chancellor told me plainly, that he intended to stop my
proceedings. ' I have sent for the registrar here, Sir, to take
down your answers.' He asked me, by what authority I
preached in the diocess of Bristol without a licence? I answered, ' I thought that custom was grown obsolete. Why, pray,
Sir, did not you ask the clergyman, who preached for you last
Thursday, this question?' He said, that was nothing to me?"
Dr. Southey says, that Whitefield's reply to the chancellor was
given " without the slightest sense of its impropriety or its irrelevance." But where is its irrelevance? It is certainly quite
ad rem, whatever it may be as etiquette, when curates argue
with chancellors; and in all respects, it is more gentlemanly
than the chancellor's "*what is that to you.*" That is real
vulgarity.

The Doctor narrates the remainder of this high-church
scene, with more discrimination. " The chancellor then read
to him those canons which forbade any minister from preaching
in a private house. Whitefield answered, he apprehended they
did not apply to professed ministers of the church of England.
When he was informed of his mistake, he said, ' There is also
a canon forbidding all clergymen to frequent taverns and play
at cards : why is not that put in execution?' And he added,
that notwithstanding these canons, he could not but speak the
things he knew, and that he was resolved to proceed as usual."
Now, if the Doctor pleases, Whitefield is as *unpolite*, as the
apostles were to the chancellor of the Jewish sanhedrim! " His
answer was written down, and the chancellor then said, ' I am

resolved, Sir, if you preach or expound any where in this diocess till you have a licence, I will first suspend, and then excommunicate you.' With this declaration of war they parted: but the advantage was wholly on the side of Whitefield; for the day of ecclesiastical discipline was gone by." *Southey's Wesley.*

Whitefield says, they parted politely. "He waited upon me very civilly to the door, and told me, 'What he did was in the name of the clergy and laity *(laity* indeed!) of the city of Bristol;' and so we parted. Immediately I went and expounded at Newgate as usual!"

The *unusual,* as might be expected, soon followed this Bartholomew day in Bristol. Ejected from the churches, Whitefield betook himself to the fields at once. "All the churches being now shut—and if open, not able to contain half that came to hear—I went to Kingswood, amongst the colliers." There he took his station upon Hannam Mount, on Rose Green, and preached, not, as Dr. Gillies says, from the sermon on the mount, but from John iii. 3, on regeneration, his favourite subject. The other text was on a subsequent occasion. "I thought" (says he) "it would be doing the service of my Creator, who had a mountain for his pulpit, and the heavens for his sounding-board; and who, when his gospel was refused by the Jews, sent his servants into the highways and hedges."

In thus renewing a practice which, as Dr. Southey says, "had not been seen in England since the dissolution of the monastic orders," and by commencing it at Kingswood, Whitefield dared not a little danger. The colliers were numerous and utterly uncultivated. They had no place of worship. Few ventured to walk even in their neighbourhood; and when provoked, they were the terror of Bristol. But "none of these things moved" Whitefield, although he was told them all by his timid friends. The fact is, the chancellor had told him something he dreaded more than insult,—that he must be *silent;* and that, he could not endure. Instead of insult or opposition at Kingswood, however, "the barbarous people," although they had never been in a church, "showed him no small kindness." His first audience amounted to nearly two thousand, who heard him with great attention and decorum for nearly an hour. His third audience increased to five thousand; and thus they went on increasing to ten, fourteen, and twenty thousand. On one of these occasions he says, " The day was fine—the sun shone very bright—and the people standing in such an awful manner around the mount, in the profoundest silence, filled me with holy admiration. Blessed be God for such a plentiful harvest. Lord, do thou send forth more labourers into thy harvest."

Although Whitefield had thus drawn the sword against the obsolete canons of the church, he had not " thrown away the scabbard;" for, on the morning of the very next day, he waited again on the chancellor, and showed him a letter he had received from the bishop of London. " After usual salutations, I asked why he did not write to the bishop, according to his promise ? I think he answered,—he was to blame. I then insisted on his proving I had preached false doctrine, and reminded him of his threatening to excommunicate me in the name of the clergy and laity of the city of Bristol. But he would have me think—that he had said no such thing; and confessed, that to this day he had neither heard me preach, nor read any of my writings." Thus, it seems, Whitefield was charged with heresy, and threatened with excommunication— and that by a chancellor on mere hearsay evidence ! This reply to Whitefield was surely not given " without the slightest sense of its impropriety or its irrelevance ! " *Southey's Wesley.*

He wrote an account of this shameful affair to the bishop of Bristol. " To-day I showed your Lordship's letter to the chancellor, who (notwithstanding he promised not to prohibit my preaching for the orphan-house, if your Lordship was only *neuter* in the affair) has influenced most of the clergy to deny me their pulpits, either on that or any other occasion. Last week, he charged me with false doctrine. To day, he is pleased to forget that he said so. He also threatened to excommunicate me for preaching in your Lordship's diocess. I offered to take a licence, but was denied. If your Lordship ask, what evil I have done, I answer,—none; save that I visit the religious societies, preach to the prisoners in Newgate, and to the poor colliers at Kingswood, who, they tell me, are little better than heathens. I am charged with being a dissenter ! although many are brought to church by my preaching, and not one taken from it.

" I am sorry to give your Lordship this trouble, but I thought proper to mention these particulars, that I might know of your Lordship wherein my conduct is exceptionable." A copy of this letter he sent to the chancellor, with the following note ; " The enclosed I sent to the bishop of Bristol : be pleased to peruse it, and see if any thing contrary to truth is there related."

How the matter ended, I know not ; except that there was an end to Whitefield's preaching in the churches of Bristol. That led, however, to what he calls, his " *beginning to begin* " to be a preacher. " I hasted to Kingswood. At a moderate computation, there were above ten thousand people. The trees and hedges were full. All was hush when I began. The sun shone bright, and God enabled me to preach with great power, and so loud, that all (I was told) could hear me. Blessed be God, Mr. —— spoke right—the fire is kindled in the country. May the gates of hell never be able to prevail against it ! To behold such crowds standing together in such awful silence, and to hear the echo of their singing run from one end of them to the other, was very solemn and striking. How infinitely more solemn and striking will the general assembly of the spirits of just men made perfect be, when they join in singing the song of Moses and the Lamb in heaven !—As the scene was new, and I had just began to be an extempore preacher, it often occasioned many inward conflicts. Sometimes when twenty thousand people were before me, I had not, in my own apprehension, a word to say either to God or them ! But I was never totally deserted ; and frequently (for to deny it would be to sin against God) so assisted, that I knew by happy experience what our Lord meant by saying, ' Out of his belly shall flow rivers of living waters.' The gladness and eagerness with which these poor despised outcasts, who had never been in a church in their lives, received the truth, is beyond description ! Having no righteousness of their own to renounce, they were glad to hear of a Jesus, who was the friend of publicans, and came not to call the righteous, but sinners to repentance. The first discovery of their being affected, was to see the *white gutters* made by their tears, which plentifully fell down their black faces ; black as they came out of the coal-pits. Hundreds and hundreds of them were soon brought under deep conviction, which, as the event proved, ended in a sound and thorough conversion. The change was visible to all ; though numbers chose to impute it to any thing rather than the finger of God."

Neither the bishop, nor the chancellor, threw any hinderance in the way of this mighty work. Would they had helped it on ! What an effect would have been produced, had the bishop preached to the colliers in the cathedral ! They were in his diocess, though without both a fold and a shepherd ; and he was more responsible to God for them, than for the dignity of the episcopal throne, where " the traditions of men " had seated him. Prelacy, if above " the work of an evangelist," is beneath the acceptance of good men.

Though somewhat embarrassed at first by his novel situation, Whitefield soon found himself in his native element. In churches, however large, there was not room for his mighty voice ; and thus not full scope for his mightier feelings. Both were cramped, although he knew it not, until the horizon was their circle, and the firmament their roof. Immensity above and around him, expanded his spirit to all its width, in all its warmth ; whilst the scenery touched all his sensibilities. Then he knew both his power and his weakness. " The open firmament above me," says he,—" the prospect of the adjacent fields, with the sight of thousands and thousands, some in coaches, some on horseback, and some in the trees,—and at times, all affected and drenched in tears together ;—to which sometimes was added the solemnity of the approaching evening,—was almost too much for me, and quite overcame me."

In recording this impressive scene, Dr. Southey, notwithstanding all his recollections of Bristol scenery, has not ascribed to it any part of the impression made by Whitefield upon the people. He does not say of him, as of Wesley, that " he himself perceived that *natural* influences operated upon the multitude, like the pomp and circumstances of Romish worship :" and yet, Whitefield, although less refined than Wesley, was equally alive to the influence of scenery and seasons ; and often chose situations as bold as the amphitheatre of Gwenap, or as beautiful as the groves of Heptenstal. Watson never wrote with greater severity, nor with more truth, than when he exposed the fallacy of ascribing the effect of Wesley's preaching to picturesque scenery. " It is not upon uncultivated minds," he justly says, " that such scenes operate strongly." Besides, " we are not informed how similar effects were produced, when no rocks reared their frowning heads, and when the sea was too far off to mix its murmurs with the preacher's voice; when no ruined castle nodded over the scene, and when the birds were so provokingly timid as to hasten away to an undisturbed solitude."

Whitefield could turn both scenery and circumstances, whatever they were, to good account. On one occasion, whilst preaching at the Bristol glass-houses, he says, " I heard many people behind me hallooing, and making a noise; and supposed they were set on to disturb me by somebody. I bless God, I was not in the least moved, but rather increased more in strength. When I was done, I inquired the cause of the noise : I found a gentleman (?) being drunk, had taken the liberty to call me a *dog*, and say, ' that I ought to be whipped at cart's tail;' and offered money to any that would pelt me. Instead of that, the boys and people near began to cast stones and dirt at him." This retaliation Whitefield reprobated in strong terms, before he left the ground; slyly reminding the people, however, of " the sorry wages the devil gives his servants." Some days after he visited this ungentlemanly disturber, to condole with him upon his punishment. The visit was well received, and they parted " very friendly." *Journals.*

After some hasty trips into Wales, from Bristol, he went to his native city, where the congregations were so large, that the clergyman refused him the church on week days. He, therefore, preached in his " brother's field" to the crowd. He felt deeply for Gloucester, and threw all his soul into his sermons, that he might " save some " where he was born. " To-day," he says, " I felt such an intense love, that I could have almost wished myself accursed (anathema) for my brethren according to the flesh." Such was his zeal to win souls in this city, that he preached alternately in the Boothall and the fields, almost

every day, during his visit. This encroachment upon the time
of the people, drew upon him the charge of encouraging idle-
ness;—which, with his usual readiness, though not with his
usual prudence, he retorted by saying, " Ye are idle, ye are idle,
say the Pharaohs of this generation; therefore ye say, *Let us
go and worship the Lord*." He was, however, permitted by the
bishop to baptize an old quaker in the church of St. Mary De
Crypt, where he himself had been baptized: and there, he did not
confine himself to the book; but, giving way to the emotions
awakened by the font where he himself had been presented before the Lord in infancy, he poured out his heart in a free and
fervent exhortation to the spectators; " proving the necessity
of the new birth from the Office."

From Gloucester he went to Cheltenham, where his acquaintance with the *Seward* family began, although they had to follow him to the bowling-green and the market-cross, the churches
being all shut against him. And Oxford, to which he went
next, completed and sealed this expulsion. " The vice-chancellor came in person to the house" where Whitefield was exhorting, and accosted him thus: " ' Have you, Sir, a name in
any book here ?' ' Yes, Sir,' said I ; ' but I intend to take it out
soon.' He replied, ' Yes, and you had best take yourself out too,
or otherwise I will lay you by the *heels*. What do you mean by
going about, and alienating the people's affections from their
proper pastors ? Your works are full of vanity and nonsense.
You pretend to inspiration. If ever you come again in this
manner among these people, I will lay you first by the heels,
and these shall follow.' " It does not appear that Whitefield
returned any answer to this paltry threat. A few days after it,
he preached in Moorfields: and from that moment, he cared
nothing about chancellors or vice-chancellors, when they stood
in the way of the gospel.

In the course of his short excursions into the country, whilst
the embargo prevented him from sailing, he visited Olney, where
he was " not a little comforted," by meeting, as a field preacher,
Mr. R—— of Bedford, who had been both expelled and imprisoned for preaching the Scriptural doctrines of justification and
regeneration. " I believe," says Whitefield, " we are the first

professed ministers of the church of England, that were so soon, and without cause, excluded every pulpit. Whether our brethren can justify such conduct, the last day will determine." An *earlier* day determined the question! The people of Bedford had made up their minds upon it at the time: for thousands assembled regularly around the windmill to hear their expelled minister preach from the stairs ;—" Mr. R——'s pulpit," as Whitefield calls it. *Journals.*

During this journey he visited Northampton; but, although " courteously received by Dr. Doddridge," he had to preach upon the common, " from the starting post." Indeed, he was not *welcome* to the Doctor's pulpit, even when he did preach there afterwards. Doddridge was so far from " seeking his preaching," that he took " all the steps he could prudently venture on to prevent it." *The Doddridge Diary and Correspondence.*

The clergy having thus shut their pulpits against him, and the dissenters not opened theirs to him, the country magistrates followed in the train of his opponents, and even the inn-keepers were afraid to admit him. At Tewkesbury he found four constables waiting to apprehend him, and the whole town in alarm. Happily, a lawyer in the crowd demanded a sight of the warrant ; and the constables having none, Whitefield determined to preach at all hazards, though beyond the liberties of the town. He did preach in the evening, in the field of a neighbouring gentleman, and two or three thousand people attended. Next morning he waited on one of the town-bailiffs, and meekly remonstrated against the attempted outrage. The bailiff told him, that the whole council were against him ; and that a judge had declared him a vagrant, whom he would apprehend.

It was now a crisis ; and Whitefield determined to bring the question to an issue. He claimed the protection of the laws. The bailiff's answer was equivocal : " If you preach here to-morrow, you shall have the constables to *attend* you." Whether this was a threat or a promise, he knew not, and cared not. He did preach next day, in another field, to six thousand people ; " but saw no constables to molest or attend " him.

The reports of this affair spread in all forms ; alarming his friends for his safety, and preparing his enemies for his approach. At Basingstoke, the mayor (a butcher) sent him a warning by the hands of a constable. This led to an amusing correspondence, as well as to interviews, between the parties; in which the mayor boasted of what he would do, " although he was a butcher ;" and Whitefield told him what he ought to do as a magistrate.

It was the time of the revel at Basingstoke, and many of the people were riotous. Whitefield, however, preached in a field, although he was unprotected, and even told that he would not come out alive. Indeed, it was confessed, some days after, by one of the ringleaders, that a party were pledged to " give him a *secret blow*, and prevent his disturbances." He was, however, only grossly insulted.

The fact is, the magistrates and the booth-keepers were afraid that he would spoil the revel: and he evidently intended to preach at the fair, although he did not exactly say so ; for he repeatedly urged the mayor to prevent the scenes of cudgelling and wrestling, which were going forward. Failing in this, he set out to go to London; but when he saw the stage for the cudgellers and wrestlers, he could not proceed.

The following account of his " mad prank," is too characteristic of him to be suppressed, although he himself erased it from his journals. " As I passed by on horseback, I saw a stage ; and as I rode further, I met divers coming to the revel ; which affected me so much, that I had no rest in my spirit. And therefore having asked counsel of God, and perceiving an unusual warmth and power enter my soul,—though I was gone above a mile,—I could not bear to see so many dear souls, for whom Christ had died, ready to perish, and no minister or magistrate interpose. Upon this I told my dear fellow-travellers, that I was resolved to follow the example of Howel Harris in Wales, (he had just come from a tour with him in Wales,) and to bear my testimony against such lying vanities,—let the consequences, as to my own private person, be what they would. They immediately consenting, I rode back to town, got upon the stage erected for the wrestlers, and began to show them the error of their ways. Many seemed ready to hear what I had to say ; but one more zealous than the rest for his master, and fearing conviction every time I attempted to speak, set the boys on repeating their *huzzahs*.

" My soul, I perceived, was in a sweet frame, willing to be offered up, so that I might save some of those to whom I was about to speak : but all in vain! While I was on the stage, one struck me with his cudgel, which I received with the *utmost love*. At last, finding the devil would not permit them to give me audience, I got off, and after much pushing and thronging me I got on my horse,—with unspeakable satisfaction within myself, that I had now begun to attack the devil in his strongest holds, and had borne my testimony against the detestable diversions of this generation." *Original Journals.*

The reason why Whitefield excluded this event from his revised journals, was, perhaps, the tremendous severity of the following reflections. " Ye masters in Israel, what are ye doing ? Ye magistrates, that are gods in Scripture, why sleep ye ? Why do ye bear the sword in vain ? Why count ye me a troubler in Israel, and why say ye, I teach people to be idle, when ye connive at, if not subscribe to, such hellish meetings as these, which not only draw people from their bodily work, but directly tend to destroy their precious and immortal souls ? Surely I shall appear against you at the judgment-seat of Christ ; for these diversions keep people from true christianity, as much as paganism itself. And I doubt not, but it will require as much courage and power to divert people from these things, as the apostles had to exert in converting the heathen from dumb idols. However, in the strength of my Master, I will now enter the lists, and begin an offensive war with Satan and all his host. If I perish, I perish ! I shall have the testimony of a good conscience : I shall be free from the blood of all men." It is easier to find fault with the severity of this invective, than to prove that any lower tone of feeling could have sustained any man, in grappling with such national enormities. Whitefield struck the first blow at them, and thus led the way to their abandonment ; an issue which may well excuse even the wildfire of his zeal.

Such was his position in London and the country, when he sailed for America the second time. He then left enough for the nation to think about until his return.

CHAPTER VI.

THE following singular account of the commencement of methodism and dissent in Wales, is translated from the "Trysorva," by
Johnes. " In the reign of James I. a clergyman of the name of
Wroth was vicar of Llanvaches, in Monmouthshire. Being of a
joyous temper, and like most of his countrymen, passionately fond
of music, he was sometimes carried beyond the bounds of propriety by this enthusiasm. On one occasion, a gentleman with
whom he was on terms of intimacy, having presented him with
a new harp, fixed a day on which, in company with some friends,
he would visit him, and hear him perform upon it. The day appointed came, and Wroth was anxiously expecting his visitor, when
a messenger appeared to inform him that his friend was no more!
This incident affected him so deeply, that, repenting the levity
of his youth, from a gay clerical troubadour he became all at
once a sad but zealous divine. With these impressions, he determined to commence preaching to his congregation, a practice
then almost unknown in the churches of the principality. As
a preacher, he soon distinguished himself so much, that the
Welch peasantry flocked from all the neighbouring counties to
hear him. His audience, being frequently too numerous for
his church to contain—on such occasions, he was in the habit
of addressing them in the churchyard. It is said that Sir Lewis
Mansel, of Margam, a man illustrious for his exalted religious
and patriotic zeal, was often one of his congregation.

" The irregularity alluded to at last exposed him to the
censure of his diocesan, who, on one occasion, asked him, in
anger, how he could vindicate his infringement of the rules of

the church? To this reprimand Wroth replied, by appealing, with tears in his eyes, to the religious ignorance which prevailed throughout the country, and to the necessity of employing every means to dissipate it : by which answer, the bishop is said to have been deeply affected. Eventually, however, by refusing to read the ' Book of Sports,' and by the general tenor of his con- duct, he rendered himself so obnoxious to the dignitaries of the church, that he was deprived of his benefice. After his expul- sion, he continued to preach in secret to his old followers, and at last he formed, from amongst them, a regular dissenting con- gregation, on the independent model. From Llanvaches, the opinions of its pastor soon spread themselves into the remotest corners of Wales : during his life, this village was regarded as the rallying point of the Welch nonconformists. Wroth, never- theless, seems to have cherished to the last some feeling of affec- tion towards the church, of which he had once been a minister ; for, on his death, which occurred in 1640, he was buried, at his own request, under the threshold of the church of Llanvaches. During the civil wars, which broke out soon afterwards, the independents were not only tolerated, but predominant. In Cromwell's time, an attempt was made to get rid of every thing like an establishment, and to substitute a few itinerant minis- ters in its place. The modicum of preachers proposed to be given by this plan of economical piety was six to a county ; it was lost in the House of Commons, by a majority of two voices. It was felt, however, that the bright thought was too precious to be discarded without an experiment ; and, accordingly, it was partly carried into effect in Wales, under Hugh Peters and Vavasor Powel, and a confiscation of church property in that country ensued, to an enormous amount ; for, unhappily, under all the various forms of civil and ecclesiastical polity which have prevailed in England, the Welch church has been treated as a fair field for experiments, no less injurious to the general cause of religion than to Wales.

" In the times of the Stuarts, dissent from the episcopal church became once more an object of persecution ; but the ministers of the Welch nonconformists still continued to traverse the wild hills of the principality, braving all dangers for the sake of their few and scattered followers. Their congregations still occasionally met, but it was in fear and trembling, generally at midnight, or in woods and caverns, amid the gloomy recesses of the mountains.

" At the revolution, these dissenters exhausted their strength by controversies amongst themselves on the rite of baptism; on which subject a difference of opinion had long existed amongst them, though persecution had prevented them from making it a ground of disunion. Till the breaking out of methodism, their cause continued to decline.

" In the year 1736, there were only six dissenting chapels in all North Wales. In this year an incident occurred which forms an interesting link between the history of the early Welch dissenters (the followers of Wroth) and that of the methodists, connecting together the darkening prospects of the former and the first symptoms of that more powerful impulse which was communicated by the latter. One Sunday, Mr. Lewis Rees, a dissenting minister from South Wales, and father of the celebrated author of the Cyclopædia, visited Pwllheli, a town in the promontory of Llëyn, in Caernarvonshire, and one of the few places in which the independents still possessed a chapel. After the service, the congregation, collecting around him, complained bitterly, that their numbers were rapidly diminishing, that the few who yet remained were for the most part poor, and that every thing looked gloomy to their cause. To which the minister replied, ' The dawn of true religion is again breaking in South Wales,—a great man, named Howel Harris, has recently risen up, who goes about instructing the people in the truths of the gospel.' Nor was he mistaken, either in his anticipation that dissent was on the eve of bursting forth with tenfold vigour in Wales, nor in the man from whom he expected this result: the first elements of methodism were already at work ; Howel Harris was its founder, and one of its most distinguished champions. Properly speaking, the history of methodism is the history of dissent in Wales : before entering, however, upon this interesting subject, it will be necessary to give a cursory view of the state of the church in Wales at the time of its origin, as hardly a doubt can be entertained that the predisposing causes to methodism were to be found in the inefficiency of the establishment.

"The following is a translation of an 'Account of the State of Religion in Wales about the middle of the Eighteenth Century.' It was taken from the mouth of a very old Welch methodist, and published in 1799, in the 'Trysorva,' a Welch periodical, edited by the Rev. Thomas Charles, of Bala; and I have high authority for asserting that the descriptions it affords are in no respect exaggerated." *Johnes.*

"'In those days,' says the narrator, 'the land was dark indeed! Hardly any of the lower ranks could read at all. The morals of the country were very corrupt; and in this respect there was no difference between gentle and simple, layman and clergyman. Gluttony, drunkenness, and licentiousness, prevailed through the whole country. Nor were the operations of the church at all calculated to repress these evils. From the pulpit the name of the Redeemer was hardly ever heard; nor was much mention made of the natural sinfulness of man, nor of the influence of the Spirit. On Sunday mornings, the poor were more constant in their attendance at church than the gentry; but the Sunday evenings were spent by all in idle amusements. Every sabbath there was what was called 'Achwaren-gamp,' a sort of sport in which all the young men of the neighbourhood had a trial of strength, and the people assembled from the surrounding country to see their feats. On Saturday night, particularly in the summer, the young men and maids held what they called 'Singing eves' (nosweithian cann); that is, they met together and diverted themselves by singing in turns to the harp, till the dawn of the sabbath. In this town they used to employ the Sundays in dancing and singing to the harp, and in playing tennis against the town-hall. In every corner of the town some sport or other went on, till the light of the sabbath day had faded away. In the summer, 'interludes' (a kind of rustic drama) were performed, gentlemen and peasants sharing the diversion together. A set of vagabonds, called the 'bobl gerdded,' (walking people,) used to traverse the country, begging with impunity, to the disgrace of the law of the land.'

"Such, then, was the state of Welch society, and the Welch

church in the middle of the last century; and it is a singular instance of the impression left by the vice and levity of this period, that the sounds of our national instrument are still associated, in the minds of many, with the extravagances of which it was formerly an accompaniment, though, apart from adventitious associations, its simple and pensive tones are certainly far more congenial with devotional feeling, than with levity or with joy. I have frequently heard, that the late Mr. Charles, of Bala, was so much under the sway of these recollections, that it was quite painful to him to remain in a room in which any one was playing upon the harp.

" At first sight, nothing would appear more improbable than that methodism should find proselytes among a people so gay and thoughtless, as the Welch of that period; or that the joyous group which assembled at Bala on a Sunday evening, should become, as was shortly afterwards the case, a leading congregation of modern puritans. But the religion of the Welch, and their fondness for national music, arose from the same cause, an earnest and imaginative frame of mind. A disposition to melancholy, disguised by external gaiety of manner, is characteristic of all Celtic nations.

' As a beam o'er the face of the waters may glow,
Though the stream runs in darkness and coldness below.'

" With all their social sprightliness, the Welch were then a superstitious and, consequently, a gloomy race. The influence of the church had confessedly done little to civilize the people; they still retained many habits apparently derived from paganism, and not a few of the practices of popery. Their funerals, like those of the Irish, were scenes of riot and wassail. When the methodists first came into North Wales, the peasantry expressed their horror of them and their opinions, by the truly popish gesture of crossing their foreheads; they also paid great veneration to a tale called ' Brenddwyd Mair,' (Mary's dream,) obviously a popish legend. Children were taught, even within my recollection, to repeat a rhyme like the following, as soon as they had been put into bed at night :

' There are four corners to my bed,
And four angels there are spread;
Matthew, Mark, Luke, and John;
God bless the bed that I lie on.'

" Some of their customs and notions were extremely fanciful. On the Sunday after a funeral, each relation of the deceased knelt on his grave, exclaiming, ' Nevoedd iddo,' (literally, Heaven to him,) that is, ' May he soon reach heaven.' This is plainly a relic of the popish custom of praying the soul out of purgatory. If children died before their parents, the parents regarded them as so many candles to light them to paradise. When Wesley came into Wales, he found the ignorance of the people so great, that he pronounced them ' as little versed in the principles of christianity, as a Creek or Cherokee Indian.' To this declaration he adds the striking expression, that, notwithstanding their superstition and ignorance, the people ' were ripe for the gospel,' and most enthusiastically anxious to avail themselves of every opportunity of instruction;—an interesting proof, that the necessary tendency of the corruptions of the Welch church to produce the consequences which have since ensued, was sufficiently obvious, even to the cursory view of a stranger.

" It was quite clear, then, to those who lived while methodism was yet in its infancy in Wales, that the country was about to become the scene of a great religious change. There was evidently a movement in the minds of the people—a longing for the extension of their spiritual advantages, which would ultimately lead them out from the establishment, unless provided with food from within. In such a state of popular feeling towards existing institutions, whether civil or ecclesiastical, it often happens that the most trivial deviation from ordinary routine becomes the basis of a series of innovations, and serves to impart an impetus and a direction to the dormant elements of disunion. It is only by keeping these considerations steadily in view, that we can clearly comprehend the early history of methodism in Wales, and avoid the confused ideas that are sometimes entertained as to the conduct of those with whom it commenced, and the exact date of its commencement. The

I 2

real truth is, that the separation of the Welch methodists from the church took place by insensible degrees. The first symptom was an unusual and somewhat irregular zeal in a certain body of clergy in the church itself; and these first faint traces of irregularity (which probably at the time excited little notice) gradually, and in the course of generations, widened into a broad line of demarcation. It was in this manner that the breaking out of methodism was undoubtedly hastened by the exertions of two eminent divines, whose only intention was to infuse new vigour into the established church,—I mean the Rev. Rhees Pritchard, and the Rev. Griffith Jones.

" The former, who is familiarly known to his countrymen under the name of ' Vicar Pritchard,' was vicar of the parish of Llanddyvri, in Caermarthenshire, in the time of James the First and Charles the First.

" Of the particulars of his life, little is known, except that whilst he stood high in the estimation of his countrymen, as a preacher, he was at the same time an object of peculiar favour with the ruling powers of the day,—honours which his countrymen in recent times have rarely seen enjoyed by the same individual. Though, like Wroth, he is said to have attracted numerous congregations, and to have occasionally preached in his churchyard, still he had the good fortune to be made chaplain to the Earl of Essex, received from James the First the living of Llanedi, and eventually became chancellor of the diocess of St. David's. As a proof of his charitable disposition, and of his anxiety to enlighten his countrymen, we are informed that he gave a donation of twenty pounds a year, charged upon land, to establish a school in his parish of Llanddyvri, and also a house for the schoolmaster. This endowment (no insignificant one in those days) went on prosperously for some time, but on the death of the founder's son, Thomas Manwaring, son of Dr. Manwaring, bishop of St. David's, who had married ' the vicar's ' granddaughter, took possession of the land belonging to the school, undertaking to pay the schoolmaster himself, which he did for a year or two, and then withheld from it all support. His biographer adds, that in 1682, the land was still in the possession of the Manwaring family,—

and that the school-house had been swept away by an inundation of the river Tyrvi!

"But the veneration still felt in Wales for the memory of 'Vicar Pritchard,' is mainly attributable to a small volume of poems, which are not a little remarkable, as a summary of christian doctrine and duty, at once simple, poetical, and concise. No book, except the Bible, has been there so much and so enthusiastically studied: its author may justly be styled the Watts of his native country; and, notwithstanding the unhappy divisions that have since his day distracted her, the undiminished popularity of his little book proves that there is even yet no schism in the principality as far as the 'Divine Poems' of 'Vicar Pritchard' are concerned.

"After the poet's death, his works were collected and published by Stephen Hughes, a worthy nonconformist, who zealously disseminated them through Caermarthenshire, and the adjacent parts of South Wales. In almost every cottage where the Scriptures were to be found, 'the vicar's' little volume occupied a place beside them: it became a class-book in every school, and its most striking passages passed into proverbs among the peasantry. Hence, at the beginning of the last century, a spirit had sprung up in certain districts of South Wales, that formed a strong contrast to the general ignorance which at that time pervaded the principality. The effect of poetry on minds left unoccupied by other reading has in all ages been remarked: thus, we are told that the great Bishop Bull, when bishop of St. David's, was so much struck with the impression made on the minds of the people by the writings of 'Vicar Pritchard,' that he expressed a wish to be buried in the same grave with him!

"Griffith Jones was born at Kilrhedin, also in the county of Caermarthen.* Even in his boyhood, he evinced a strong sense of religion, which has sometimes, though erroneously, been thought incompatible with the unformed views and elastic spirits of our earlier years. Like Bishop Heber, he might justly be termed a 'religious child:' whilst yet a boy at Caer-

* Trysorva, vol. ii. p. 1.

marthen school, he was in the habit of retiring from the pas-
times of his play-fellows for the purpose of secret prayer.   In
the year 1709, he was ordained by Bishop Bull ; on which occasion he experienced marks of peculiar kindness and approbation from that illustrious prelate, the recollection of which continued ever after a source of gratitude and delight to him.   In
1711, he was presented to the living of Llandeilo Abercowyn,
and in 1716, Llanddowror was added to it by the patron, Sir
John Phillips, of Picton Castle, in Pembrokeshire, with whom
he was connected by marriage.

" His constitution was naturally delicate, and he describes
himself as having been in early youth so much afflicted with
asthma, that he could not walk across a room without pain and
difficulty ; but his was a mind which seemed capable of impart-
ing a portion of its own energy, even to his debilitated frame ;
as he advanced in life, this infirmity, in a great measure, forsook him ; and of this we have ample proof in the various labours he accomplished.

" The fame of Griffith Jones chiefly rests on an institution
he devised for the diffusion of education in Wales, still known
under the name of the ' Welch Circulating Schools.'   The main
feature of this plan is the instruction of the people by means of
itinerant schoolmasters.   It was first suggested to him by the
following train of circumstances :—On the Saturday previous to
sacrament Sunday, it was his practice to assemble his flock together, and read to them the service of the church.

" At the conclusion of the second lesson, he would ask in a
mild and familiar tone, if any one present wished an explanation of any part of the chapter they had just heard; and on a
difficult verse being mentioned, he would expound it in plain
and simple language, adapted to the capacities of his hearers.
On the day following, before admitting communicants to the
sacrament, he used to examine them on their ideas of christian
doctrines, and as to their general moral conduct.   On these
occasions, his church was generally crowded : numbers came
from the neighbouring districts, and it frequently happened that
twenty or thirty persons were publicly examined by him before
receiving the communion.   But he found that those who were

likely to derive most benefit from this plan of instruction—men who had grown up in ignorance—were deterred from attending by a consciousness of their inability to answer the questions that might be put to them. To remedy this, he made a practice of fixing the Saturday before the sacrament Sunday, for the distribution among the poor of the bread purchased by the money collected at the previous sacrament. Having by this means brought them together, he arranged them in a class, and proceeded to ask them a few easy questions, with an affability and kindness of manner that immediately removed all embarrassment and reserve; and pursuant to an arrangement he had previously made, these questions were answered by some of the more advanced scholars. In a little time the humbler classes became willing and constant attendants at the altar. And for the purpose of still further grounding his flock in religious knowledge, he was in the habit of requesting them to commit to memory every month a certain portion of the Bible. Thus it became a regular custom among his poor parishioners, to repeat each a verse of Scripture on receiving the bread purchased with the sacrament money.

" This system of examination had the effect of affording him a very clear insight into the notions and attainments of the peasantry, the result of which was an opinion that preaching was calculated to convey only vague and imperfect views to the minds of the poorer classes, unless combined with catechising and other methods of instruction. Following up these impressions, he was led to consider the incalculable benefit that would result, were a well-organized system of schools extended over the whole surface of his native country. These were the steps by which he arrived at the first conception of that noble machinery which he soon afterwards set in motion. At first, it would seem that he looked upon his plan rather in the light of a favourite day-dream, than as a project which had the slightest chance of success. Nevertheless, he had too much ' moral chivalry ' to despair,—too much of that imaginative love of enterprise, without which no great impression has ever been made on the people with whom he had to deal. Accordingly, a beginning was made. In the year 1730, the first school was founded, with the sacrament money of the parish of Lland-dowror; and it answered so well, that a second was established shortly afterwards; and this again was attended with such admirable effects, that several benevolent individuals, both in Wales and England, were induced to support the scheme with a liberality that enabled their founder to realize his fondest anticipations. The Society for promoting Christian Knowledge voted him a very generous donation of Bibles and other books. Thus supported, the schools continued rapidly to increase: from an account published in August, 1741, that is, about ten years after their commencement, it appears, that the number of schools in existence during the past year had amounted to 128, and the number of persons instructed in them to 7595. The plan on which Griffith Jones proceeded was simply this: he first engaged a body of schoolmasters, and then distributed them in different directions over the country. The duty of these men was to teach the people to read the Scriptures in the Welch language, to catechise them, to instruct them in psalmody, and to promote their religious advancement by every means in their power. They were sent, in the first instance, to the nearest town or village where their assistance had been requested; and then, having taught all who were desirous of instruction, they were to pass on to the next district where a similar feeling had been manifested. In the course of time, they were to revisit the localities whence they had at first started, and resume the work of education anew on the youth who had sprung up in their absence; and thus making a continual circuit of the whole country, to present to every generation as it arose the means of knowledge, and the incentives to virtuous principle.

" Griffith Jones seems to have been in his day the most popular and indefatigable preacher in the principality. He was, in consequence, often solicited by his clerical brethren with applications to preach in their pulpits, with which he was in the habit of complying, by making a kind of tour through the neighbouring districts of South Wales, and preaching in the churches as he passed. Like Wroth and ' Vicar Pritchard,' he would sometimes forsake the pulpit for the tombstone or the green sward, when he found the church too small for his audience.

" He generally managed to make these excursions during the Easter and Whitsun-week, as he had a greater chance, at these seasons, of falling in with some of those scenes of pugnacious uproar, and drunken frolic, which were at that time so much in vogue in his native country, and which it was always his object to discourage. When he met with one of these rustic carnivals, he would attempt to disperse it with all the arguments he could employ ; and we are told by an individual who frequently accompanied him on these occasions, that though the beginning of his address was generally received with looks of anger and churlish disdain, its conclusion was always marked by symptoms of strong emotion, and by an expression of reverence and awe, from the whole assembled multitude. The great number of persons whose conversion (and I use the word in the sense of a change, not of opinion, but of conduct—a fundamental, moral revolution of the motives of the heart) is traceable to him, furnishes a strong additional proof, that there was something peculiarly impressive in the eloquence of Griffith Jones. His biographer has very forcibly described the distinctive excellence of his pulpit oratory, by saying, it was ' gavaelgar ar y gydwybod,' that is, it possessed a ' *grasp on the conscience ;*' and, he adds, that the commencement of his discourses were generally familiar and unadorned ; but that, as he went on, his spirit seemed to kindle and burn, ' gwresogi a thaniaw,' with his subject. Indeed, his merits, as a preacher, seem to have been held in high estimation beyond the limits of his native country ; for it is an interesting incident in his history, that at one period of his life, he received an invitation from the Society for the Propagation of the Gospel in Foreign Parts, to become one of their missionaries. Ultimately, as we have seen, he decided that his path of duty lay in the humble land of his birth.

" After accomplishing a variety of labours, which might have seemed quite incompatible with his delicate health,—and establishing his favourite schools in almost every parish of Wales,— this excellent man breathed his last in the month of April, 1761, leaving behind him, in the religious regeneration and the religious gratitude of a nation of mountaineers, a memorial, which will be envied most by those who are at once the greatest and the humblest of mankind, and which will endure when the ostentatious monuments of worldly power shall melt away ' like the baseless fabric of a vision.'

" It may now be asked," says Johnes, " with what degree of propriety the rise of dissent in Wales can be connected with the name of Griffith Jones—a man whose whole life was spent in exertions to render the establishment impregnable against dissent on the one hand, and the more fearful encroachments of sin, ignorance, and superstition, on the other? One answer only can be given: it is a melancholy truth—a truth, nevertheless, but too well sanctioned by experience, that a few pious ministers are the weakness, and not the strength, of an establishment, when the majority of its ministers are sunk in indifference to their sacred duties! The zeal of the few only serves to cast into darker shade the apathy of the many; and, by raising the moral sentiment of the people, to make them more sensitively intolerant of the abuses that surround them. It is upon this principle only, that we can explain whence it was, that methodism broke out first, and most extensively, in that division of Wales where the poems of Rhees Pritchard and the schools of Griffith Jones had exerted the most powerful influence. And hence it was, that so many of those clergymen, who had been connected with the latter, became eventually the missionaries of methodism; and it may also be remarked, that the irregularities of the methodist clergy, which led in the end to systematic itinerancy, appear to have begun by the practice of preaching from church to church, which they seem to have adopted in imitation of Griffith Jones's ' Easter and Whitsun ' circuits."

Whitefield's connexion with Howel Harris of Trevecca led to results which deserve to be traced step by step. It began by a letter from Whitefield; which has, happily, been preserved at Trevecca. " London, Dec. 1738. My dear brother, Though I am unknown to you in person, yet I have long been united to you in spirit; and have been rejoiced to hear how the good pleasure of the Lord prospered in your hands."—" Go on, go on; He that sent you will assist, comfort, and protect you, and make you more than conqueror through his great love. I am a living monument of this truth."—" I love you, and wish you may be the spiritual father of thousands, and shine as the sun in the kingdom of your heavenly Father. Oh how I shall joy to meet you—at the judgment seat! How you would honour me, if you would send a line to your affectionate though unworthy brother, G. W."

Harris's answer was prompt and cordial. I am happy to be able to furnish extracts from it. "Glamorgan, Jan. 8th, 1739. Dear brother, I was most agreeably surprised last night by a letter from you. The character you bear, the spirit I see and feel in your work, and the close union of my soul and spirit to yours, will not allow me to use any apology in my return to you. Though this is the first time of our correspondence, yet I can assure you I am no stranger to you. When I first heard of you, and your labours and success, my soul was united to you, and engaged to send addresses to heaven on your behalf. When I read your diary, I had some uncommon influence of the divine presence shining upon my poor soul, almost continually. And my soul was, in an uncommon manner, drawn out on your account:—but I little thought our good Lord and Master intended I should ever see your hand-writing." (In his journal Harris wrote, " About this time, I heard from a friend that came from London, of a young clergyman, namely, Mr. Whitefield, that preached four times a day, and was much blessed. In hearing this, my heart was united to him in such a manner, that I never felt the like connexion with any one before: but yet I had not the least prospect of ever seeing him; being informed that he had gone beyond sea to America. I was agreeably surprised, in the beginning of January, by a letter from him: he having providentially heard of me, wrote to me to encourage me to go on. I was at this time greatly distressed in respect to my itinerary way of preaching :—yet I prosecuted my work with the utmost activity.") " Sure, no person is under such obligations to advance the glory of free goodness and grace, as this poor prodigal,"—himself. " Oh how ravishing it is to hear of the divine love and favour to London! And to make your joy greater still, I have some more good news to send you from Wales. There is a great revival in Cardiganshire, through one Mr. D. Rowlands, a church clergyman, who has been much

owned and blessed in Caermarthenshire also. We have also a
sweet prospect in Breconshire, and part of Monmouthshire."
—" I hint this in general, as I could not testify my love any
way more agreeably to your soul, than to let you know how the
interest of our good, gracious, and dear Saviour prospers here-
abouts."—" Were you to come to Wales, it would not be labour
in vain. I hope the faithful account I have given you, will excite you to send again a line to him, that would be sincerely
yours, in Jesus Christ, whilst H. H."

In this way Whitefield and Howel Harris attracted each
other. How much they influenced each other also, will be best
told in their own words. In the mean time, however, I must
give some account of Howel; for he is too little known. Dr.
Gillies knew him merely " as one Howel Harris, a layman;"
and the Doctor's editors and annotators have not amplified this
account of him.

Howel Harris was born at Trevecca, Brecknockshire, in 1714.
He was intended for the church, by his family ; and had flattering prospects of patronage. Up to the twenty-first year of
his age, he had, however, no serious views of his character, or
of his destined profession. His first thoughtfulness was awakened in Talgarth church, by a sermon on the neglect of the
sacrament. He had been a very irregular attendant, and thus
was conscience-struck when the clergyman exclaimed, " If you
are unfit to visit the table of the Lord, you are unfit to visit the
church, you are unfit to live, you are unfit to die."

From this time, his vague convictions deepened and settled
into vital principles. On the very day, whilst going home after
the sermon, he met with a person whom he had offended, and
both confessed the offence and begged forgiveness. For a time,
however, he was the victim of great mental anguish. Remorse
darkened and depressed his spirit, although he had abandoned
all his old sins, and solemnly resolved to make the service of
God " the key-stone of his conduct." Happily for himself, he
did not forget the souls of others, whilst brooding over his own
fears : but as soon as he caught a glimpse of his way to the
cross, he began to instruct and invite his neighbours to flee from
the wrath to come. In this work, he found so much comfort

for himself, and saw so much good done by it, that it became " the sole occupation of his life."

In November, 1735, he went to Oxford, to finish his studies, with an express view to ordination : but he was so much disgusted with the immorality of the University, that he staid only one term. He returned home, and renewed his visits and exhortations in the cottages of the poor, and commenced field preaching. And such was the effect, that in the course of a year, " so many had become embued with serious impressions," that he began to form them into religious societies. " In the formation of these associations," he says, " I followed the rules of Dr. Woodward, in a work written by him on that subject. Previously to this, no societies of the kind had been founded either in Wales or England. The English methodists had not become famous as yet, although, as I afterwards learnt, several of them in Oxford were at that time under strong religious in- fluences." Harris had organized thirty of these societies, before Whitefield or Wesley visited Wales: not, however, as dissenting or methodist congregations ; nor, indeed, with any view of their ever separating from the church. The revival of religion in the church was his avowed object from the first, and his professed object through life.

Whitefield and Howel Harris met for the first time at Cardiff, in 1739 ; just whilst the former was glowing with the recollections of what he had seen and felt amongst the colliers at Bristol ; and whilst the latter was girding himself for a new campaign in Wales. On his way from Bristol to Cardiff, Whitefield was delayed, by contrary winds, at the New Passage. " At the inn," he says, " there was an unhappy clergyman, who would not go over in the passage boat, because I was in it. Alas, thought I, this very temper would make heaven itself unpleasant to that man, if he saw me there. I was told, that he charged me with being a dissenter. I saw him, soon after, shaking his elbows over a gaming-table. I heartily wish those who charge me causelessly with schism, and being righteous over-much, would consider that the canon of our church forbids the clergy to frequent taverns, to play at cards or dice, or any other unlawful games. Their indulging themselves in these things is a stumblingblock to thousands.

At Cardiff, Whitefield preached in the town-hall, from the judges' seat. Harris was there. " After I came from the seat," he says, " I was much refreshed with the sight of Mr. Howel Harris; whom, though I knew not in person, I have long loved, and have often felt my soul drawn out in prayer in his behalf.

" A burning and shining light has he been in those parts; a barrier against profaneness and immorality, and an indefatigable promoter of the gospel of Jesus Christ. About three or four years, God has inclined him to go about doing good. He is now about twenty-five years of age. Twice he has applied (being in every way qualified) for holy orders; but was refused. About a month ago he offered himself again, but was put off. Upon this, he was and is resolved to go on in his work; and indefatigable zeal has he shown in his Master's service! For these three years (as he told me with his own mouth) he has discoursed almost twice every day, for three or four hours together. He has been, I think, in seven counties, and has made it his business to go to wakes, &c. to turn people from lying vanities. Many alehouse people, fiddlers, and harpers, Demetrius-like, sadly cry out against him for spoiling their business. He has been made the subject of many sermons, has been threatened with public prosecutions, and had constables sent to apprehend him. But God has blessed him with inflexible courage; and he still goes on from conquering to conquer. Many call and own him as their spiritual father. He discourses generally in a field; but, at other times, in a house; from a wall, a table, or any thing else. He has established nearly thirty societies in South Wales, and still his sphere of action is enlarged daily. He is full of faith and the Holy Ghost. He is of a most catholic spirit; loves all who love the Lord Jesus Christ; and therefore he is styled, by bigots, a dissenter. He is contemned by all that are lovers of pleasure more than lovers of God; but God has greatly blessed his pious endeavours.

" When I first saw him, my heart was knit closely to him. I wanted to catch some of his fire, and gave him the right hand of fellowship with my whole heart. After I had saluted him, and given an exhortation to a great number of people, who followed me to the inn, we spent the remainder of the evening in taking sweet counsel together, and telling one another what God

had done for our souls.   A divine and strong sympathy seemed
to be between us, and I was resolved to promote his interest
with all my might.   Accordingly, we took an account of the
several societies, and agreed on such measures as seemed most
conducive to promote the common interest of our Lord.   Blessed
be God ! there seems a noble spirit gone out into Wales ; and
I believe that, ere long, there will be more visible fruits of it.
What inclines me strongly to think so is, that the partition
wall of bigotry and party spirit is broken down, and ministers
and teachers of different communions join with one heart and
one mind, to carry on the kingdom of Jesus Christ.   The Lord
make all the christian world thus minded; for until this is done,
we must, I fear, despair of any great reformation in the church
of God."

Any thing that would lessen the impression of these concluding remarks, would be ill-timed, and in bad taste ; but still, it
would be improper, even if it were possible, to forget that this
fall of " the partition wall of bigotry and party spirit " has, like
the fall of popish Babylon, been too often celebrated before the
time, by sanguine and catholic men.   It is now nearly a century
since Whitefield said that it was fallen.   Good man ! he thought
the whole wall had surely given way, whenever he found an unexpected breach in it, at which he could enter with the gospel,
even if he was pelted with the broken fragments.   So other
good men thought and said, during the *novelty* of Bible and
Missionary Societies.   Then, not only was the partition wall
declared to be fallen, but bigotry was registered in the bills of
mortality, and said to be buried for ever.   And yet, even now
that there is a far nobler spirit of reformation gone forth in the
church, than ever Whitefield saw, or than the first friends of our
great societies anticipated, the wall is higher than ever, and has,
of late, had a *copping* of broken glass and rusty spikes laid upon
it.   There is, indeed, a sense in which, like Babylon, it is somewhat fallen ; but the great and final " fall thereof " is yet to
come in the case of both.   Neither will fall, however, like the
walls of Jericho, at one crash, nor by one crisis ; although both
will be overthrown by one process—by bearing around them the
ark of the covenant, with the sound of its own trumpets.

It is when such men as George Whitefield and Howel Harris meet and blend their hallowed fires, to set a "whole principality in a blaze," that the wall of bigotry is shaken, by the numbers which climb over from both sides, to hear the gospel. From the moment these champions of the cross joined issue in Cardiff, Wales began to be evangelized. In 1715, the number of dissenting chapels was only 35; in 1810, it amounted to 954; in 1832, to more than 1400. They are still multiplying; and, lately, the debt upon them, so far as they are independent, has been wiped off by a burst of "the voluntary principle." What then must have been the spiritual state of Wales, at the beginning of the last century? In 1715, there were only 35 dissenting chapels, and about 850 churches, in all the principality!

Whitefield says of his first interview with Howel Harris, "I doubt not but Satan envied our happiness; but I hope, by the help of God, we shall make his kingdom shake. God loves to do great things by weak instruments, that the power may be of God, and not of man."

Before leaving Cardiff, Whitefield preached again in the town-hall, to a large assembly. "My dear brother Harris sat close by me. I did not observe any scoffers within; but without, some were pleased to honour me so far, as to trail a dead fox, and hunt it about the hall. But blessed be God, my voice prevailed. This being done, I went with many of my hearers, amongst whom were two worthy dissenting ministers, to public worship; and in the second lesson were these remarkable words, 'The high priests, and the scribes, and the chief of the people sought to destroy him; but they could not find what they might do to him; for all the people were attentive to him.'

"In the afternoon, I preached again without any disturbance or scoffing. In the evening, I talked for above an hour and a half with the religious society, and never did I see a congregation more melted down. The love of Jesus touched them to the quick. Most of them were dissolved in tears. They came to me after, weeping, bidding me farewell, and wishing I could continue with them longer. Thanks be to God, for such an entrance into Wales! I wrestled with God for them in prayer, and blessed His holy name for sending me into Wales. I hope these are the first-fruits of a greater harvest, if ever it should please God to bring me back from Georgia. Father, thy will be done!"

"Friday, March 9. Left Cardiff about six in the morning, and reached Newport about ten, where many came from Pontypool and other parts to hear me. The minister being asked, and readily granting us the pulpit, I preached with great power to about a thousand people. I think Wales is excellently well prepared for the gospel of Christ. They have, I hear, many burning and shining lights both among the dissenting and church ministers; amongst whom Mr. Griffith Jones shines in particular. No less than fifty charity schools have been erected by his means, without any settled visible fund; and fresh ones are setting up every day. People make nothing of coming twenty miles to hear a sermon. Even so, Lord Jesus. Amen!"

On the following day Whitefield returned from this short excursion to Bristol again, "baptized with" Welch "fire," and renewed his labours amongst the Kingswood colliers, with extraordinary power and success. He could not, however, forget the Welch tears, which had entreated him to stay longer. Accordingly, on the 4th of April he visited Husk and Pontypool, and was met by Howel Harris again. At Husk, "The pulpit being denied, I preached upon a table, under a large tree, to some hundreds, and God was with us of a truth. On my way to Pontypool, I was informed by a man that heard it, that Counsellor H. did me the honour to make a public motion to Judge P. to stop me and brother Howel Harris from going about teaching the people. Poor man, he put me in mind of Tertullus, in the Acts; but my hour is not yet come. I have scarce begun my testimony. For my finishing it, my enemies must have power over me from above. Lord, prepare me for that hour."

This report did not prevent the curate of Pontypool from welcoming Whitefield to his pulpit. He also read prayers for him. After the sermon, it was found that so many had come to hear, who could not find room in the church, that another sermon was loudly called for. "I went," he says, "and preach-

ed to all the people in the field. I always find I have most
power when I speak in the open air; a proof to me—that God
is pleased with this way of preaching. I betook myself to rest,
full of such unutterable peace as no one can conceive but those
who *feel* it ! "

" April 5th. All the way from Pontypool to Abergavenny, I
could think of nothing so much as Joshua going from city to
city, and subduing the devoted nations. Here I expected much
opposition, having been informed that many intended to disturb
me. But God impressed an awe upon all; so that although
there were many opposers, no one dared to utter a word. I did
not spare the scoffers. Afterwards we retired and sung a
hymn; and some ladies having the curiosity to hear us, I took
that opportunity of dissuading them against balls and assemblies. Afterwards I learnt that they were the mistresses of
the assemblies in Abergavenny. I hope God intended them
good."

" April 6th. Reached Carleon, a town famous for having
thirty British kings buried in it, and producing three martyrs.
I chose particularly to come hither, because when Howel Harris
was here last, some of the baser sort beat a drum, and huzzaed
around him, to disturb him. Many thousands came to hear;
but God suffered them not to move a tongue, although from the
very same place, and I prayed for Howel Harris by name—as I
do in every place where I have preached in Wales. I believe
the scoffers *felt* me, to some purpose. I was carried out
beyond myself. Oh that the love of Christ would melt them
down ! "

" In the afternoon we set out for Trelek, ten miles from Carleon; but the Welch miles being very long, we could not reach
it till almost dark; so that many of the people who had been
waiting for me were returned home. The church being denied,
I stood on a horse-block before the inn, and preached to those
who were left behind; but I could not speak with such freedom
as usual; for my body was weak, through the fatigue of the
past day."

At the close of this second short excursion into Wales,
Whitefield exclaims, " Oh how swiftly this week has glided

away! To me, it has been but as one day. How do I pity those who complain that time hangs on their hands! Let them but love Christ, and spend their whole time in his service, and they will find but few melancholy hours."

Dr. Gillies says that in these tours Howel Harris preached after Whitefield, in Welch. He does not mean, of course, in the churches; and Whitefield does not mention any Welch sermons. Harris followed up, however, the labours of his new friend with great power. "I thank God for his goodness to brother Howel Harris. I thank you for informing me of it;" says Whitefield in a letter written whilst he was on his way to America. In another, from Philadelphia, to Harris himself, he writes thus: "I congratulate you on your success at Monmouth. By divine permission, in about a twelvemonth, I hope to make a second use of your *field* pulpits. Our principles agree, as face answers to face in the water. Since I saw you, God has been pleased to enlighten me more in that comfortable doctrine of election. At my return, I hope to be more explicit than I have been. God forbid that we should shun to declare the whole counsel of God."

"The people of Wales are much upon my heart. I long to hear how the gospel flourishes among you. How prospers your 'inward man?' Being always doing—no doubt you grow in grace. May you increase with all the increase of God!—As fast as I can, our Welch friends shall hear from me.—Salute them most affectionately in my name. Put them in mind of the freeness and eternity of God's electing love, and be instant with them to lay hold on the perfect righteousness of Christ by faith.—Talk to them, O talk to them, even till midnight, of the riches of His all-sufficient grace. Tell them, O tell them, what he has done for their souls, and how earnestly he is now interceding for them in heaven. Show them, in the *map* of the word, the kingdoms of the upper world and the transcendent glories of them; and assure them all shall be theirs, if they believe on Jesus Christ with their whole heart. Press them to believe on Him immediately. Intersperse prayers with your exhortations, and thereby call down fire from heaven, even the fire of the Holy Ghost,

K 2

> To soften, sweeten, and refine,
> And melt them into love !

Speak every time, my dear brother, as if it were your last ;—
weep out, if possible, every argument, and compel them to cry,
' Behold how he loveth us.'   Remember me—remember me
in your prayers, as being ever, ever yours."

Thus Whitefield fanned the " Welch fire" from time to
time.   In another letter, from Boston, he says, " And is dear
brother Howel Harris yet alive in body and soul?   I rejoice
in your success.   May you mount with wings like eagles!   You
shall not be taken nor hurt, till the appointed hour be come.   I
hope your conversation was blessed to dear Mr. Wesley.   Oh that
the Lord may batter down his free-will (scheme,) and compel
him to own His sovereignty and everlasting love.   God is
working powerfully in America.   He fills me with His presence.
Grace, grace !   Dear brother H.—yours eternally."

In another, from Philadelphia, he says, " Your letter, written
nearly a twelvemonth ago, came to my hand this afternoon.
My soul is knit to you.   We both speak and think the same
things.   The Lord be with your spirit.—Jesus manifests forth
his glory daily in these parts.   His word is like a fire and a
hammer.   Last week I saw many quite struck down.   America,
ere long, will be famous for christians.   Little did I think that
I should preach in all the chief places of America ; but that is
now done !   Glory be to rich, free, and sovereign grace.—The
Lord vouchsafe to us a happy meeting.   O Wales, thou art
dear to my soul !   Expect another journal shortly.   But wait
till we come to glory,—fully to see and hear what God has done
for your affectionate brother."

When Whitefield returned to England, he continued to urge
on Howel Harris to " abound in the work of the Lord," by
every event that encouraged himself.   " I want to see you face
to face.   I wish you could come up to London immediately, and
stay whilst I am in the country.   Or rather—go and preach at
Bristol, Gloucester, and Wiltshire, for about a fortnight, and
then come up to London.—Our congregations are large and solemn.   I never had greater freedom in preaching.   I am glad

brother Rowland is with you. Go on in the strength of our dear Lord, and you shall see Satan like lightning fall from heaven. May the Lord hide your precious soul under the shadow of his Almighty wings!—You need not fear my believing any reports to your disadvantage. Cease not to pray for yours, eternally."

In the same spirit, he wrote to him from Edinburgh, the moment that the fire began to kindle in Scotland. "My very dear brother Harris, though my eyes be dim, and my body calls for rest, I would fain send you a line before I go (to rest). I hope God is beginning such a work here, as he is now carrying on in New England. Night and day, Jesus fills me with his love.—I have preached twice, and talked and walked much to day.—My dear man, good night!"

He did not conceal from his friend the results of his interviews with the Associate Presbytery, nor his opinion of their spirit. "My heart is much united to you. I utterly disapprove of some persons' separating principles. Satan now turns himself into an angel of light, and stirs up God's children to tempt me to come over to some particular party. The Associate Presbytery have been hard upon me: but I find no freedom any longer than I continue just as I am, and evangelize to all. I know not that I differ from you in one thing. God is doing great things here!—It would make your heart leap for joy, to be now in Edinburgh. I question if there be not upwards of 300 in this city seeking after Jesus. Every morning, I have a constant levee—of wounded souls. I am quite amazed when I think what God hath done here in a fortnight. I am only afraid lest the people should idolize the instrument, and not look enough to the glorious Jesus, in whom alone I desire to glory. Congregations consist of many thousands. Never did I see so many Bibles, nor people look into them with such attention, when I am expounding. Plenty of tears flow from the hearers' eyes. The love of Christ quite strikes me dumb. O grace, grace! Let that be my song. I must away (to preach)."

As might be expected, Whitefield did not fail to appeal to Howel Harris from the vantage ground of *Cambuslang*. Along with a copy of his journal of that memorable awakening,

he wrote thus : " The account sent with this will show you how
often I have been enabled to preach ; but with what efficacy
and success—pen cannot describe. The glorious Redeemer
seems advancing from congregation to congregation, carrying
all before him. The Messrs. Erskine's people have kept a fast
for me ; and give out that all the work, now in Scotland, is
only delusion, and by the agency of the devil. O my dear
brother, to what lengths in bigotry and prejudice may good
men run ! I bless God, I can see the differences between God's
children, and yet love them from my heart.—What you say
about poor Wales, affected me. I am sorry to hear there have
been such divisions. But dividing times generally precede settling times. I should be glad to help the brethren in Wales
My brother, my heart is full ! "

Whitefield's letters on these subjects were not confined to
Howel Harris. Both from America and Scotland, he wrote to
other Welch friends in the church and amongst the dissenters ;
and thus spread the tidings of the revivals, and of their reaction.
The following extract from a letter to a clergyman in Wales, is
highly characteristic of Whitefield. " God is on my side—I will
not fear what men nor devils say of, or do unto, me. The dear
Erskines have dressed me in very black colours. Mr. Gibbs's
pamphlet will show you how black. Dear men, I pity them.
Writing, I fear, will be in vain. Oh for a mind divested of all
sects, names, and parties. I think it is my one simple aim, to
promote the kingdom of Jesus, without partiality or hypocrisy,
indefinitely amongst all. I care not if the name of George
Whitefield be banished out of the world, so that Jesus be exalted in it. Glory to His great name, we have seen much of
his power and greatness in Scotland. Last sabbath and Monday, great things—greater than ever, were seen at Kilsyth ! I
preach twice every day with great power, and walk in liberty
and love. At the same time, I see and feel my vileness,—and
take the blessed Jesus to be my righteousness and my all."

To another clergyman in Wales, he wrote from Philadelphia
thus : " When I first saw you at Cardiff, my heart rejoiced to
hear what God had done for your soul. You were then under
some displeasure from your rector (if I mistake not) for speak-

ing the truth as it is in Jesus. Ere now I hope you have had the honour of being—quite thrust out. Rejoice, my dear brother, and be exceeding glad; for thus was our Lord and Saviour served before you. Naked, therefore—follow a naked Christ. Freely you have received, freely give. If you preach the gospel, you shall live of the gospel. Though you go out without scrip or shoe, yet shall you lack nothing. Rather than you shall want,—ravens, those birds of prey, shall be commanded to feed you. If we go forth in the spirit of apostles, we shall meet with apostolical success. Stir up, then, the gift of God which is within you. Be instant in season and out of season. Debase man, and exalt Jesus. Self-righteousness overturn—overturn! The people of Wales (at least the common people) will receive you gladly."

Whitefield not only stirred up labourers thus, in Wales; he also watched over their safety, when their labours brought them into trouble. Accordingly, when some of the fellowship meetings were indicted as conventicles, he appealed at once to the candour and justice of the bishop of Bangor. " I assure your Lordship, it is a critical time for Wales. Hundreds, if not thousands, will go in a body from the church, if such proceedings are countenanced. I lately wrote them a letter, dissuading them from separating from the church; and I write thus freely to your Lordship, because of the excellent spirit of moderation discernible in your Lordship."

Some of these details violate the order of time; but they preserve what is better—a connected view of the *impulses* which Whitefield got and gave in Wales; and will enable the reader to appreciate their influence upon future movements and events in the principality

CHAPTER VII.

WHEN this continent was discovered by the English, it lay within the limits of that vast territory which the pope, although himself ignorant of its existence, conferred on Spain:—and, in these times, papal grants were "holy ground." Accordingly, Henry VII. was afraid to colonize it. Henry VIII. had not time. Edward VI. had not power. Queen Mary had not inclination. Elizabeth had not spirit. She sanctioned, but never seconded, the attempt of Raleigh in Virginia. The credit of colonizing North America belongs to James I. He had before tried the experiment of colonial towns in the highlands of Scotland, in order to improve the clans; and although it did not answer all his expectations, it confirmed him in the policy of the system. Unhappily, his ecclesiastical policy was not equally wise. He derided and denounced the puritans and nonconformists. And, alas, bishops ascribed this to *inspiration;* and even Lord Bacon justified it!

Amongst many who fled from this tyranny to the continent, for refuge, was the congregational church of the great and good John Robinson. In 1609, they settled in Leyden, and remained for some years. But the unhealthy climate, and especially the unhallowed sabbaths of the city, determined them to emigrate to America.

This resolution was not adopted hastily, nor without much prayer. The exiles felt for their children; and shrunk from the danger of their being absorbed in the mass, or assimilated to the morals, of a foreign nation. And, what gave irresistible effect to all their ordinary motives was,—they felt it to be their supreme duty to spread the gospel amongst the heathen, and to perpetuate the Scriptural system of christian churches.

It is not to the credit of Dr. Robertson, that he withheld the fact of their missionary spirit. He says, with an ill-concealed sneer, " They began to be afraid that all their high attainments in spiritual knowledge would be lost; and that the perfect fabric of policy which they had erected would dissolve, and be consigned to oblivion, if they remained longer in a strange land." The historian understood the character of Charles V.; but he was incapable of appreciating the character of John Robinson and his church, even although the Scotch martyrs furnished a clue to it. It requires, however, more than philosophical discrimination, to discern mental or moral greatness in the zeal of poor men for unpopular truth. The character of the first nonconformists must remain a mystery to mere philosophers, until the New Testament become " The Book of the Church."

A brief sketch of the character and principles of the founders of the first American churches, will justify this remark. Now, that Hume, and writers of his stamp, should designate the Plymouth pilgrims, weak or wild fanatics, is only what might be expected. Nor is it at all surprising, that even Robertson should call them enthusiasts and Brownists. It is, however, a matter both of surprise and regret, that such an historian as Grahame should have called them *Brownists,* in the face of a solemn injunction which he himself transcribes, and in which Robinson disavows the name, as " a brand for making religion odious." Even Baylie, the bitter enemy of the first dissenters, declares that " Robinson was the principal overthrower of the Brownists, and became the father of independency." Hornius also distinguishes the independents from the Brownists, and calls them Robinsonians. Governor Winslow also, in his " Grounds of planting New England," says,that "the Brownists were settled in Amsterdam, and would hardly hold communion with the people of Leyden." Besides, there is a work of Robinson's, which bears the following title : " A Just and Necessary Apology for certain Christians, no less *contumeliously* than commonly called Brownists or Barrowists."

The fact seems to be,—that Robinson had been, at first, a stricter dissenter than the generality of the nonconformists; and, by publishing his "Justification of Separation from the Church of England," in answer to Bernard's "Separatists' Schism," which was chiefly directed against the Brownists, he thus subjected himself to the charge of being one of them. But both his spirit and his system were of a far higher order. He was, in the best sense of the name, an independent, or congregationalist.

What he was as a scholar and a divine, may be judged from his masterly answer to Bernard, and from his signal triumph over the successor of Arminius at Leyden. The university of Leyden prevailed on Robinson to accept the challenge of Episcopius; and he silenced the impugner of Calvinism. In such estimation was he held at Leyden, that all the rank and talent of the city attended his funeral, and agreed to his interment in the chancel of their principal church.

Such was the man who formed the sentiments and the character of the men who formed the first church in New England. He himself was prevented from joining them there, by the intrigues of a faction in the Virginian company in this country; but his mantle and spirit were carried there by his elder and members. And nobly did they exemplify the principles of their pastor!

What these principles were, is not matter of conjecture. As to faith, the pilgrims held the doctrinal articles of the reformed churches; and, accordingly, admitted to communion in their own church the pious members of all protestant churches who chose to unite with them.

This open communion, and unshackled freedom of conscience, were, however, peculiar to the independents. The puritans who colonized Massachusetts Bay, availed themselves, at first, of these privileges; but they did not extend them so freely when they settled their own churches.

Agreeably to the spirit of the church in which they were educated, they soon began to govern religion, instead of submitting to be governed by it; and thus practical intolerance was grafted upon speculative liberty, as slavery still is, on American republicanism. The puritans were much upbraided for this by the church of England, whilst her own offsets in the southern provinces of America could hardly subsist; but, when they obtained a legal settlement, she soon fenced them by a sacramental test.

Even-handed justice, however, has not yet been rendered to the American puritans. Both eulogy and censure are still too unqualified. Their errors were the universal errors of their age; whereas their virtues were peculiar to themselves. God, indeed, " sifted three nations, that he might sow New England with the finest wheat." *Magnalia*.

A sketch of the rise and progress of religion in America will illustrate this. Its origin, although of recent date, was coeval with the discovery of the rock of Plymouth. The pilgrims had formed themselves, by covenant, into a church and a state, even before they landed; and thus Plymouth became a settlement and a sanctuary on the same day. The voice of praise and prayer first awoke the echoes of its forests; and before a tree was cut for fuel, or climbed for food, tears of gratitude had anointed the rock as an EBENEZER.

Webster, a member of congress, has depicted this scene with great power and pathos. " The morning that beamed on the first night of their repose, saw the pilgrims already established in their country. There were political institutions, and civil liberty, and religious worship.

" Poetry has fancied nothing in the wanderings of heroes, so distinct and characteristic. Here was man, indeed, unprotected, and unprovided for, on the shore of a rude and fearful wilderness; but it was politic, intelligent, and educated man. Every thing was civilized but the physical world. Institutions, containing in substance all that ages had done for human government, were established in a forest. Cultivated mind was to act on uncultivated nature; and, more than all, a government and a country were to commence, with the very first foundations laid under the divine light of the christian religion. Happy auspices of a happy futurity! Who could wish that his country's existence had otherwise begun? Who would desire to go back to the ages of fable? Who would wish for an origin ob-

scured in the darkness of antiquity ?   Who would wish for other
emblazoning of his country's heraldry, or other ornaments of
her genealogy, than to be able to say, that her first existence
was with intelligence ; her first breath, the inspiration of liberty;
her first principle, the truth of divine religion ? "

In a similar spirit, WHELPLEY, of New York, says, " On the
day they felt the firm earth, for weal or for woe, they adopted it
as their country; they looked off to the surrounding hills and
snow-clad ranges, and felt that these must henceforth be their
horizon; they surveyed the deep and frowning forest, with its
savage tenantry, and resolved to subdue and make it the abode
of pure religion; they looked along the far-sounding shore, and
resolved to explore its depths and islands, and point out to their
children the places of cities, and the marts of commerce; they
looked up to the broad heavens, where dwelt their covenant
God, and, in prayer, resolved to build Him a house for his worship, wherever under these heavens, like Jacob, they rested on
their pilgrimage."

Vivid and touching as these pictures are, they are, perhaps,
surpassed, as to effect, by the simple journals of the pilgrims
themselves ; from which PRINCE drew the materials, and, in a
great measure, the language, of his " Annals ;"—a book almost
unknown now in this country.

" 1620. Dec. 20.   This morning, after calling on Heaven for
guidance, they go ashore again, to pitch on some place for immediate settlement.   After viewing the country, they conclude
to settle on the main, on a high ground facing the bay ; a sweet
brook running under the hill, with many delicate springs.   On
a great hill they intend to fortify, which will command all
round ; whence they may see across from the bay to Cape Cod.
And here, being twenty in number, they rendezvous this evening ; but a storm rising, it blows and rains hard all night ; continues so tempestuous for two days, that they cannot get aboard,
and have nothing to shelter them.

" 21st.   Dies Richard Bretterige, the first who dies in this
harbour.

" 23d.   As many go ashore as can ; cut and carry timber for
a common building.

" 24th. Lord's day. Our people ashore are alarmed with the cry of savages ; expect an assault, but continue quiet. And this day, dies Solomon Martin, the sixth and last who dies this month.

" 25th. Monday. They go ashore again, felling timber, sawing, riving, carrying. Begin to erect their first house, about twenty foot square, for their common use, to receive them and their goods. Leaving twenty to keep a court of guard, the rest return aboard at evening. But in the night and next day, another sore storm of wind and rain.

" 28th. Thursday. They go to work on the hill ; reduce themselves to nineteen families ; measure out their lots, and draw for them. Many grow ill of grievous colds, from the great and many hardships they had endured. They see great smokes of fires made by Indians, about six or seven miles off.

" 31st. Lord's day. The generality remain aboard the ship, almost a mile and a half off. Some keep the sabbath, for the first time, in the place of their building.

" 1621. Jan. 9th. We labour in building our town in two rows of houses for greater safety : divide by lot the ground we build on : agree that every man builds his own house, that they may make more haste.

" 13th. Saturday. Having the major part of our people ashore, we purpose there to keep the public worship to-morrow.

" 14th. Lord's day morning at six o'clock, the wind being very high, we, on shipboard, see our rendezvous in flames, and fear the savages had fired it ; nor can we come to help, for want of the tide, till seven o'clock : at landing, find that the house was fired by a spark in the thatch."

" 31st. The people aboard see two savages, but cannot come to speak with them.

" Feb. 9th. This afternoon our house for sick people is set on fire by a spark lighting on the roof.

" About this time the Indians get all the *pawaws* (magicians) of the country together for three days, in a horrid and devilish manner to curse and execrate us with their conjurations : which assembly they hold in a dark and dismal swamp."

Such was their first winter ; and, before the return of spring,

disease or famine had swept off one half of them. The sur-
vivors, too, instead of being able to devote themselves to planting and building, had to spend the greater part of their time
in defending their persons and property from the savages.
Still, the pilgrims neither repented nor repined. "*Spring*,"
they say, "*puts new life into us.*" "*All the summer, no want.
We fit our houses against winter; are in health, and have all
things in plenty.*" *Prince's Annals.*

At this time, they had no minister. Mr. Brewster, the elder
of the church, conducted their worship, until Mr. Robinson
should be able to join them. But, whilst they were looking
and longing for his arrival, a faction in the Plymouth company
at home were intriguing to prevent him from leaving Leyden.
This faction seem to have had for their object the introduction
of episcopal forms into the worship of the colony. Accordingly,
in 1624, they sent out, as their tool, Lyford, a minister who had
lost his character in Ireland. On his arrival, the pilgrims say,
" He appears exceedingly complaisant and humble; sheds many
tears; blesses God, that had brought him to see our faces. We
give him the best entertainment we can. We make him larger
allowance than any others. At his desire, we receive him into
our church; when he blesses God for the opportunity and
freedom of enjoying his ordinances in purity." That purity
Lyford soon tampered with. He *insisted* upon administering
the sacrament in the episcopal form, and on using the liturgy.
Nor was this the worst part of his conduct. He caballed with
some unprincipled adventurers, who had come out, to betray the
colony, and usurp its government. The plot was, however, detected. The governor pursued the ship which brought Lyford
out, and arrested his letters. On his return, the governor summoned a general court, and charged Lyford and his party with
the plot. They denied it. He then produced Lyford's letters,
and confounded the traitors before all the assembly.

Incredible as it may seem, such was the leniency of the court,
that Lyford was even restored to his office, upon a profession of
repentance, " made with tears," before the church. But these
tears, like the former, were hypocritical; for, in less than a
month, he wrote another letter to betray the government; and

was detect ?d again. Cotton Mather says of Lyford, " On this he was banished from the plantation, and went into Virginia, where he shortly after ended his own life." Soon after this, the pilgrims say, " *We hear sad news; our dear pastor, Mr. Robinson, is dead; which strikes us with great sorrow. These things could not but cast us into great perplexity; yet, being stript of all human hopes and help, when we are now at the lowest, the Lord so helps us, as that we are not only upheld, but begin to rise.*" This " rise " was not, however, great nor rapid; for, at the end of ten years, the population of Plymouth was only three hundred persons.

Such was the rise of religion in America. Its progress, at this early period, was, of course, by the accession of pious settlers from Europe, and by the influence of the first churches upon the worldly settlers. In the former case, the progress was great. Charles I. was then upon the throne, and Laud *behind* it ; and their well-known measures compelled the puritans and nonconformists to choose between exile and chains. Many of them preferred the former. Aware of this, the Rev. Mr. White of Dorchester organized a colony for Massachusetts Bay, which obtained a royal charter. Neale, by a strange mistake, says, that " free liberty of conscience was granted by this charter." An improbable gift, from the iron hand of Charles ! The deed itself contains no permission of the kind. Such as it was, however, it soon drew into the colony eighteen hundred persons ; many of whom were wealthy, and most of them respectable. Several eminent ministers also accompanied them. These emigrants laid the foundations of Boston, Charlestown, Dorchester, and other towns ; in each of which a church was formed. And such was their prosperity and peace, that crowds continued to pour into the country.

Whilst this influx was proceeding, the small-pox broke out amongst the Indians, and swept off such multitudes, that whole tribes were annihilated. Providence, by thus evacuating the country, was supposed to indicate his appropriation of it to the English. The vacated space proved, however, a temptation ; because its best districts being far asunder, they drew the settlers too far off from each other. It was, however, this dispersion that led to the adoption of a representative system of government in New England.

It cannot surprise any one to hear that, amongst so many emigrants, so suddenly thrown together, and all passing at once from bondage to full liberty of conscience, there should have been some differences of religious opinion. There were, however, far fewer than could be expected; and these were confined, in every instance, to very few persons. The celebrated Roger Williams was the chief disturber of the harmony of the infant churches; but, with all his singularities, he was a noble-minded and right-hearted man. He understood religious liberty better than the puritans; and, to his spirit and firmness in resisting the jurisdiction of magistrates in religion, New England is chiefly indebted for her charter of conscience.

Whilst the Massachusetts' colony was thus advancing, similar motives and causes led to the settlement of Connecticut and Newhaven; in both of which the Scriptures were adopted as the *sole* code of law and religion. A colony was also planted in New Hampshire and Main; but by men of another spirit. It made no progress for some years, until it came under the jurisdiction of the Massachusetts' colony. Indeed, all the colonies, about this time, retrograded during a disastrous war with the Indians. Charles had also forbidden further emigration from England, without permission. He had even decided on taking away the Massachusetts' charter, and on remodelling the government agreeably to his own mind. The meeting of the long parliament, however, furnished him with other work. But, whilst this event saved their charter at the time, it likewise put a stop to emigration; there being then no intolerable pressure upon conscience. Whilst that pressure lasted, however, two hundred thousand British subjects had settled in New England; and £200,000 had been expended upon it: " a sum," says Robertson, " which no principles, inferior in force to those wherewith the puritans were animated, could have persuaded men to lay out on the uncertain prospect of finding subsistence and enjoying freedom."

During the Protectorate, although no great accession was made to the population of New England, great favour was shown to the colonies; or rather, they were allowed to take great liberties beyond their charter. They formed the confederacy of the States, and struck a coinage of their own. Whether these steps were approved, or overlooked amidst the crowd of nearer events, is not known. Cromwell, however, formed a plan for the colonists, which, happily, was plausible only to himself. When he had conquered Jamaica, he offered to transport to it the churches of New England, that they might resist popery in the centre of the new world. In this enterprise, so characteristic of its author, Cromwell pledged himself to support them with the whole weight of his authority and influence. They had, however, the wisdom to decline his proposals, without incurring his displeasure.

About this time, a better direction was given to their zeal, and new energy infused into their Indian missions, by the spirit with which parliament incorporated the Society for propagating the Gospel in New England; and, especially, by the success of Eliot. No great accession of numbers or strength was made to the infant churches, however, until the restoration of Charles II. restored the old system at home. Then the Act of Uniformity threw into their arms another large group of pilgrims, in " the spirit and power" of the Plymouth fathers. They knew, also, how to avail themselves of the crisis created by the Bartholomew bushel at home; and promptly invited some of the brightest stars which it had covered, to " arise and shine " in the western hemisphere. And many of them obeyed the summons. Even Dr. Owen was likely to have accepted a call to be pastor of the first church in Boston, had not the king laid an embargo upon him.

However much, therefore, we may deplore the Act of Uniformity, it became the axe which cut down the *principle* of uniformity in this country. What the cause of religious liberty lost here for a time, it more than regained in America.

When these victims of the Act of Uniformity arrived in America, there were forty flourishing churches in New England. The emigrants, however, had hardly time to become incorporated with them, or to taste the cup of their sweet fellowship, when the fatal Indian war broke out. And such were its ra-

vages, that nearly six hundred men, who were the strength both
of the churches and of the colony, were cut off. And even this
overwhelming loss was aggravated by a succession of harassing
measures from home, which almost ruined the trade of the colony,
until the Revolution.

The Revolution in England forms an epoch in the ecclesiastical, as well as the civil, history of America. From that time,
the churches of New England began to provide for the spiritual
wants of the southern provinces; and thus stirred up the bishop
of London to send a commissary into Maryland, who obtained
an act of the provincial legislature for a legal establishment
of episcopacy there.

There was, however, at this time, a blot upon the character
of New England, which, if it had not been copied from Old
England, would call for severe animadversion. The imputation
of witchcraft was accompanied by the prevalent belief of its
reality; and the lives of many weak persons were sacrificed to
a blind zeal and a superstitious credulity. Still, more persons
have been put to death for witchcraft in a single county of
England, than all who suffered in America. Besides, the chief
judge, Sewall, with more wisdom than our Hale, confessed, soon
after, the sin of these sentences, in a penitential paper, which
he gave in to his minister to be read publicly, on a fast day.
His diary also deplores and condemns them.

Nothing very memorable occurs in the history of religion,
from this time, until the revival at Northampton; except its
steady progress amongst some of the Indian tribes, and the
noble, though abortive, effort of Berkley to provide for them all,
by his projected college at Bermuda.

The remarkable revival of religion under the ministry of
Jonathan Edwards, was as *timely* as it was signal. He himself,
in narrating it, has said as little as possible of the long and deep
decay of vital godliness, which preceded it. That sad decay
has, however, but too many vouchers. " It began to appear,"
says Prince, " in 1660: in 1670, it was visible and threatening:
in 1680, it was bewailed bitterly by the few of the first generation who remained."

Governor Stoughton, in a sermon which he preached at Boston, before he resigned the pulpit for the bench, proclaimed it in the presence of the ministry and the magistracy, that, since the death of the Massachusetts' fathers, many had become like Joash after the death of Jehoiada, rotten, hypocritical—and a *lie!* In 1683, the venerable Torrey, of Weymouth, also preached a sermon before the legislature, and which he entitled "*A Plea for the Life of dying Religion.*" "There is," says he, "already a great death upon religion; little more left than a name to live. It is dying as to the BEING of it, by the general failure of the work of *conversion.*" In 1700, Mather published his "Vindication of the Order of the Gospel in New England;" in which he solemnly affirms, "that if the begun apostasy should proceed as fast the next thirty years, as it has done these last, it will come to that in New England, (except the gospel itself depart with the order of it,) that churches must be gather·· ed out of churches." President Willard, also, (the eloquent denouncer of the prosecutions for witchcraft,) published in the same year his searching sermon, "*The Perils of the Times displayed.*" "Whence," he asks, "is there such a prevalency of so many immoralities amongst professors? Why so little success of the gospel? How few thorough conversions to be observed; how scarce and seldom!" "It hath been," he adds, "a frequent observation, that if one generation begins to decline, the next that follows usually grows worse; and so on, until God pours out his Spirit again upon them."

Such was the melancholy state of things which followed the death of the first puritans and nonconformists in New England. The second generation grew up, not indeed in ignorance nor in avowed unbelief, but in a heartless formality which, itself, relaxed more and more, as their fathers went down to the grave. Nor was this falling off confined to the large towns. It took place even in such remote and obscure towns as Northampton. There, after the death of the celebrated Stoddard, who had, during his ministry, five signal revivals, or, as he called them, "five harvests," an extraordinary deadness in religion crept in. Politics divided the people, and pleasure absorbed the young. Family discipline was generally neglected, and licentiousness

rapidly spreading.   The sabbath evening became the chief season of mirth and dissipation.

This last circumstance led Edwards to preach a very solemn
sermon on the subject; not, however, that he held the *evening*
of the Lord's day sacred. They began their sabbath on the
Saturday evening, and closed it with the afternoon of Sunday.
It was, therefore, the "evil tendency" of passing from the sanctuary to the tavern and the dancing green, that led him to remonstrate.   He saw how the custom was defeating all his own
labours, and defying parental authority to check it; and he
singled it out, and threw all his soul into the assault against it.
He had also planned with the better disposed parents of his
flock, to take private measures for suppressing the evil. But
such was the effect of the sermon on the young themselves, that
they anticipated the wish both of their parents and pastor,
and abandoned at once and entirely their amusements on the
sabbath evening.

This was the first step towards the great revival at Northampton.   Edwards then persuaded the young people to spend
these evenings in little meetings for social prayer and reading.
In this also he succeeded.   These meetings began too at a time,
when some sudden and awful deaths had made a deep and
solemn impression in the town.   But still, he seems to have
expected nothing extraordinary to evolve from these symptoms.
The Arminian controversy was raging around him at the time,
and he, in common with his pious friends, was more afraid of
its influence, than encouraged by these "tokens for good."
Indeed, Edwards, instead of expecting or attempting to produce a signal revival of religion, seems to have thought only of
defending its great foundations. He began to preach boldly
the sovereignty and freeness of grace, more with a view to keep
error out of his church, than with the hope of "winning souls"
by the truth.   Accordingly he himself was as much, if not
more surprised than any one, when the great awakening began.
He, however, preached the truth from *love* to it, and not for
victory; and the Eternal Spirit wrought mightily by it.

This series of simple facts has been too much overlooked in
various accounts of "The work of God in Northampton."   It

was in nowise " got up," on the part of Edwards, as its enemies
have insinuated; nor was it so separated from rational means,
as some of its rash friends pretended. It certainly well deserves to be called wonderful—even miraculous, because the
same truth had never triumphed so gloriously in America before; but the means which the Spirit thus blessed, were as natural and orderly as philosophy herself could select or arrange,
whilst she kept the Bible open. Accordingly Dr. Watts and
Dr. Guyse did not hesitate to call it " *The renewal of the miracle of Gideon's fleece.*"

The chief characteristics of this work, at its commencement, were,—a melting down of all classes and ages in overwhelming solicitude about salvation ; an absorbing sense of
eternal realities, which banished all vain and useless conversation ; a self-abasement and self-condemnation, which acquitted
God of all severity, whatever he might do ; a spirit of secret
and social prayer, which redeemed time for itself under all circumstances ; and a concern for the souls of others, which
watched for all opportunities of doing good. It can only surprise sciolists, that this awakening, so sudden and solemn,
should have agitated the body, whilst thus agonizing the mind.
It produced in many instances loud outcries, and in some instances convulsions. The loudest cries were not, however, so
loud as the shrieks of Voltaire or Volney, when the prospect of
eternity unmanned them. What Edwards said of those who,
in his time, resolved the physical effect into mental delusion,
may be applied to all who echo their opinion, " I question if
they would behave themselves *better*, if they were equally
sensible of their guilt and danger, as sinners." Not that Edwards was the advocate of these things ; but he was too good
a philosopher to consider them incompatible with sense or sincerity ; and too honest, to allow them to be called " a distemper caught from Whitefield and Tennent," as some insinuated.
He candidly acknowledges they had appeared before Whitefield arrived. Indeed, they did not appear under his ministry at all.

" *But, what is the chaff to the wheat, saith the Lord?* "
Whatever were the accidental extravagances which marked this

work at any period of its progress, its permanent results were " Holiness to the Lord."

Perhaps a better proof of the substantial character of these conversions cannot be given, than the single fact that most of them stood the severe test of Edwards's " Treatise on Religious Affections :" a work which, if as generally read here as it was there, would tempt a large portion of our acknowledged converts to unchristianize themselves. There was noise in the new stream of religious feeling, which broke out at Northampton ; and noisy streams are said to be shallow ; but this one must have been an exception to the proverb, seeing it sustained that weighty book upon its bosom.

Besides, whoever will duly examine Edwards's " Narrative," will find, to his surprise and pleasure, all the usual varieties of experience, which show themselves in our own churches, in the succession of single converts. He was honoured to gather at once, what we collect slowly. But with this exception, and its natural consequences, the history of any hundred of true converts, won at wide intervals, will present almost all the varieties of case, which were crowded into the first year of the revival.

Wide and great as this revival was, however, it did not penetrate New England at large, until Whitefield and Tennent spread it. In many leading places the necessity, or the genuineness of such a work was doubted and denied. The churches, in general, were still in a Sardian or Laodicean state.

Dr. Holmes says, in his " American Annals," that " the zeal which had characterized the churches in New England at an earlier period, had, previous to Whitefield's arrival, subsided, and a calm, perhaps lethargic, state ensued. The discourses from the desk, though evangelical, were not impassioned." Shurtleff, of New Hampshire, in his defence of Whitefield, says of the state of the churches at this time, " No serious christian could behold it without a heavy heart, and scarce without a weeping eye ; to see the solid, substantial piety, for which our ancestors were justly renowned, having long languished under sore decays, brought so low, and seemingly just ready to give up the ghost." Edwards says of the colleges, " It certainly has sometimes been so with our colleges that, instead of being places of the greatest advantage for true piety, one cannot send a child thither, without great danger of his being infected as to his morals." Dr. Chauncy denies this charge, in unqualified terms ; but when he proceeds to disprove it, the only argument he adduces is, that, during twenty years, he had never known Harvard College " under *better* circumstances, in point of religion, good order, and learning, than at this day." What it really was, may, perhaps, be gathered from the fact, that Whitefield in his Letter to the students, when they became serious, says, " It was no small grief to me, that I was obliged to say of your college, that '*your light was darkness ;* ' yet are ye now become light in the Lord. Now we may expect a reformation indeed, since it is beginning at the house of God."

In regard to the general state of the churches, even Dr. Chauncy cannot effectually conceal the low ebb of spiritual religion at this time. In spite of all his special pleading, it betrays itself throughout the whole series of his " Seasonable Thoughts on the State of Religion in New England." At the close of that strange book he acknowledges, " that *disorderly walkers* have been suffered to take their course, without the administration of those censures which are proper to the kingdom of Jesus Christ. Have they not been left to themselves to act as they please, without public notice, any more than if they sustained no relation to the church of God ? "

It is equally painful to review or record these melancholy facts. It is, however, necessary to do both, in order to form a just estimate of the spirit, the character, and effects, of Whitefield's preaching in New England. He went there, not to spy out the nakedness of the land, nor to search for declensions ; but to be " refreshed amongst the descendants of the good old puritans." It was, therefore, with as much surprise as regret, that he found " the fine gold " of puritanism " dim." Indeed, it was not until Dr. Chauncy and others began to caricature the revivals, that Whitefield began to suspect the spirituality of the ministry. His correspondence with Dr. Colman and Mr. Cooper of Boston, and his recorded memorials of all the devoted ministers he met with, prove that he was inclined, and even solicitous, to be pleased with New England.

Whitefield had, however, seen enough, in Philadelphia, to convince him, that both the matter and spirit of his preaching in England were equally wanted in America. He accordingly wielded in New York and Boston all the spiritual and splendid weapons which he had employed at London and Bristol. The effect at Boston was amazing. Old Mr. Walter, the successor of Eliot, the apostle of the Indians, said, "It was puritanism revived." Such was the interest excited by his preaching, that his farewell sermon was attended by 20,000 persons. And, during his visit, it was testified by the first authorities in the city, that many of the careless were awakened, and more of the lukewarm quickened. "Such a power and presence of God with a preacher, and in religious assemblies," says Dr. Colman, "I never saw before." "Every day gives me fresh proofs of Christ speaking in him. A small set of gentlemen amongst us, when they saw the affections of the people so moved under his preaching, would attribute it only to the force of sound and gestures. But the impressions on many were so lasting, and have been so transforming, as to carry plain signatures of a divine hand going along with him." All this was, if possible, exceeded at Northampton, when Whitefield visited Jonathan Edwards, and reminded his people of "the days of old." "It was," says Gillies, "like putting fire to tinder." Similar success attended his ministry in the town and college of Newhaven. In the latter, it overthrew the self-righteousness of the celebrated Hopkins, and fanned into a flame the zeal of DAVID BRAINERD—a name that needs no epithet.

In like manner, at Harvard College the effect was great. The honourable Secretary Willard says, in a letter to Whitefield, "That which forebodes the most lasting advantage is, the new state of things in the college, where the impressions of religion have been, and still are, very general; and many, in a judgment of charity, brought home to Christ. Divers gentlemen's sons, that were sent there only for a more polite education, are now so full of zeal for the cause of Christ, and of love to souls, as to devote themselves entirely to the studies of divinity." Dr. Colman also informed Whitefield of this fact. "At Cambridge, the college is entirely changed; the students are full of God, and will, I hope, come out blessings in their generation; and, I trust, are so now to each other. Many of them are now, we think, truly born again, and several of them happy instruments of conversion to their fellows. The voice of prayer and praise fills their chambers; and sincerity, fervency, and joy, with seriousness of heart, sit visibly on their faces. I was told yesterday, that not *seven* of a hundred remain unaffected. I know how the good tidings will affect you. God give you like joy every where in the fruit of your labours." Thus Whitefield was then to the churches and colleges, what Washington was afterwards to the states.

Such were the results of his first visit to New England. And it deserves special notice that they were accompanied with none of the *extravagances* which marked the revival soon after. Much has been written on the subject of the subsequent effects of this mighty impulse; but, after deliberately weighing the works on both sides, I am fully persuaded that Whitefield himself has given the most judicious view of the whole matter. On his return to Boston, in 1745, he writes thus: "Some occasions of offence had, undoubtedly, been given whilst I was here, (before,) and preached up and down the country. Nothing, however, appeared but a pure divine power, working upon, converting, and transforming people's hearts, of all ranks,—without any extraordinary phenomena attending it. Good Mr. Tennent succeeded me: numbers succeeded him. Lecture upon lecture was set up in various places. One minister called to another to help to drag the gospel net. And, by all the accounts I can have from private information, or good Mr. Prince's weekly history, one would have imagined the millennium was coming indeed. But in this mixed state of things, wildfire will necessarily blend itself with the pure fire that comes from God's altar. This the enemy long waited for. At last, it broke out and spread itself. And, it must be confessed, by the instrumentality of many good souls, both among clergy and laity; who, mistaking fancy for faith, and imagination for revelation, were guilty of great imprudence. All is laid to me, as being the *primum mobile;* though there was not so much as the appearance of any thing of this nature, when

I left New England last. But, maugre all, my poor labours are yet attended with the usual blessings."

That Whitefield has fairly characterized the *first* aspect of this work, will be seen from the following public testimony, by three of the principal ministers in Boston; Prince, Webb, Cooper. It came out the year after his first visit.

" The wondrous work of God, at this day, making its triumphant progress through the land, has forced many men of clear minds, strong powers, considerable knowledge, and firmly rivetted in Arminian and Socinian tenets, to give them all up at once, and yield to the adorable sovereignty and irresistibility of the divine Spirit, in his saving operations on the souls of men. For, to see such men as these, some of them of licentious lives, long inured in a course of vices, and of high spirits, coming to the preaching of the word ; some only out of curiosity, and mere design to get matter of cavilling and banter ; all at once, in opposition to their inward enmity, resolutions, and resistances, to fall under an unexpected and hated power ; to have all the strength of their resolution and resistance taken away ; to have such inward views of the horrid wickedness, not only of their lives but of their hearts, with their exceeding great and immediate danger of eternal misery, as has amazed their souls, and thrown them into distress unutterable, yea, forced them to cry out in the assemblies with the greatest agonies : and then, in two or three days, and sometimes sooner, to have such unexpected and raised views of the infinite grace and love of God in Christ, as have enabled them to believe in him; lifted them at once out of their distresses ; filled their hearts with admiration ; and joy unspeakable and full of glory breaking forth in their shining countenances and transporting voices, to the surprise of those about them :—and to see them kindling up at once, into a flame of love to God, an utter detestation of their former courses and vicious habits ; yea, by such a detestation, that the very power of these habits receive at once a mortal wound : in short, to see their high spirits, on a sudden, humbled ; their hard hearts made tender ; their aversion to the Holy Ghost, now turned into a powerful and prevailing bent to contemplate Him as revealed in Christ ; to labour to be like Him in holi-

ness; to please and honour him by a universal and glad conformity to his will and nature ; and to promote his holy kingdom in all about them—loving them, forgiving them, asking
forgiveness of them ; abounding in acts of justice and charity,
in a meek and condescending carriage towards the meanest, and
aspiring after higher sanctity.

" And to see other gentlemen, of the like parts, knowledge,
and principles ; and of sober, just, and religious lives, as far as
mere reason, with outward revelation, is able to carry them ;
and prepossessed against this work as imagined enthusiasm ;
yet, at once, surprised to find themselves entirely destitute of
that inward sanctity, and supreme love to God, which the gospel teaches as absolutely needful ; to find themselves no more
than conceited Pharisees, who had been working out a righteousness for their own justification ; and to have a clear discovery
of their inward enmity to Christ, and to the nature and way of
redemption by him ; with the vileness of their hearts and lives,
which they had never seen before : in short, to find themselves
yet unrenewed in the spirit of their minds, and under the heavy
wrath and curse of God; to lose all their former confidence ;
give up their beloved schemes ; to see themselves undone and
helpless, and sink into great distress : and then, condemning
themselves as guilty wretches, humbly lying at the foot of absolute and sovereign grace, looking up to Christ, as the only Mediator, to reconcile them to God, to justify them wholly by his
own righteousness, and to enlighten, sanctify, and govern them
by his Holy Spirit ; and there to wait, till they find a new and
mighty life and power come into their souls, enabling them to
embrace, trust in, and love this divine Redeemer ; rejoice
with satisfaction in him ; and perform every kind of duty, both
to God and man, with pleasure, and with quite another spirit
than before."

Whilst such were the moral effects of this American Pentecost, well might the eloquent Parsons, of Byfield, say to the
mockers and opposers, " Whilst you stand amazed at the rings
of the wheel, as things too high and dreadful for you ; whilst you
know not what to make of the effusions of the Holy Spirit, but
are stumbling at every thing amiss ; beware, lest that come upon

you, which is spoken of by the prophets, ' Behold, ye despisers, and wonder, and perish.'   Dear, immortal souls ! I beseech and persuade you, by the mercies of God, and the astonishing love of the Lord Jesus Christ, that you would not sacrifice the operations of the blessed Spirit to your own prejudice, by means of our imperfections."

When Whitefield saw the first-fruits of this harvest, he wisely pressed into the field, as his successor, Gilbert Tennent.   The American Biographical Dictionary says of Tennent, " He was born in Ireland, and brought to this country by his father ; by whom also he was educated for the ministry.   As a preacher, he was, in his vigorous days, equalled by but few.   His reasoning powers were strong ; his language forcible and often sublime ; and his manner of address warm and earnest.   His eloquence was, however, rather bold and awful than soft and persuasive.   He was most pungent in his addresses to the conscience.   When he wished to alarm the sinner, he could represent in the most awful manner the terrors of the Lord.   With admirable dexterity he exposed the false hope of the hypocrite, and searched the corrupt heart to the bottom."   Such was the man whom Whitefield chose to take his place in the American valley of vision, when the " dry bones " began to shake.   And he entered on his new sphere with almost rustic simplicity ; wearing his hair undressed, and a large great coat girt with a leathern girdle.   But his " lofty stature and grave aspect dignified " the whole.   He had been remarkably useful in his former station in New Jersey ; and now, in New England, his ministry was hardly less successful than Whitefield's had been.   Much of the happy change which we have just reviewed, is ascribed by Whitefield himself to the instrumentality of Tennent.   He actually shook the country, as with an earthquake.   Wherever he came, hypocrisy and pharisaism either fell before him, or gnashed their teeth against him.   Cold orthodoxy also started from her downy cushion to imitate or to denounce him.   For, like Elijah on Carmel, he made neutrality an impossibility.   Accordingly, the attack upon him soon began, in the true spirit of mortified pride, by arraigning his *motives*.   It commenced in the Boston newspaper, in the form of a letter ;—of which Dr.

Chauncy, who was then the American *Sacheverell,* was, no doubt, the author. At least, he has made it his own, by republishing it, without note or comment. " Pray, Sir, let me put it to your conscience ; was not the reason of your travelling so many miles (300) to preach the gospel in this place, founded on the insufficiency of the ministers here for their office ? Had you not some suspicion, that they were not converted ? Perhaps you only thought that you might do a deal more good ? Is not this too near to vanity ? " This is a specimen of the letter to Tennent ; and, in the same spirit, Chauncy assailed the character and motives of Whitefield, and criticized the " Narrative and Vindication of the Work of God," by Edwards. By his own confession, he travelled farther to collect the materials of his book against, what he called, " the new light," than Tennent did to guard that light. The book itself was answered by various writers ; but the best reproof it called forth, was administered by a venerable lady, who had been converted under the ministry of Flavel. " New light ! " she exclaimed ; " it may be new to such as never saw it before ; but it is what I saw fifty years ago, from good Mr. Flavel."

Chauncy's principal charge against Whitefield is,—" that he seldom preached without saying something against unconverted ministers." " The first error I would take notice of," he says, " is that which supposes ministers, if not converted, incapable of being instruments of spiritual good to men's souls. Mr. Whitefield very freely vented this error. He said, the reason why congregations have been so dead, is, because they have dead men preaching to them." " But conversion," says Chauncy, " does not appear to be *alike* necessary for ministers, in their *public* capacity as *officers* of the church, as it is in their private capacity." If this was untenable ground, the Doctor was still more unfortunate, when he attempted to vindicate his brethren by quoting from Cotton Mather. Mather says, " No man becomes a minister, or a communicant, in our churches, until he hath been severely examined about his *regeneration,* as well as conversation." BACKUS, in his " History of the American Baptists," answers this appeal in a few words. " *When* was it so ? This testimony was given in 1696. How does it prove that their practice remained the *same* in 1740 ? "

These animadversions upon the conduct and writings of Dr. Chauncy are necessary, because his influence was great, and eventually beneficial. For, whilst his work on " The State of Religion," is contemptible in many respects, and especially in all that regards Whitefield and Tennent, it is invaluable as an antidote to the extravagances of conduct and sentiment which, in seasons of high and general excitement, the weak and the ignorant are so prone to fall into. It is only bare justice to make this acknowledgment; for Dr. Chauncy has embodied in the work the best sentiments of our best divines, upon the subject of the operations and fruits of the Holy Spirit. And these well-selected extracts are such an antidote to his own poison, that they could not have failed to correct the rashness and folly of others.

It was, however, the poison which operated first. The representations of the party, of which the Doctor was the champion, produced edicts of synod and assembly, which made the Say-brook platform all but a scaffold. Ministers who should preach out of their own parishes without permission, were subject to be treated as " vagrants," and to be " banished from the colony;" and if they returned, to " pay the expenses of their transportation ; besides being imprisoned until they should give a bond of £100, not to offend again." BACKUS. The full force of these sad measures was confined chiefly to Connecticut : and there Dr. Finlay, the successor of President Davies, was *thus* treated.

Such was the state of things in New England, on Whitefield's *second* visit. But neither the acts of assembly, nor the example of the leading ministers, could prevent the people from welcoming him with acclamation. They voted him into some of the churches, which would otherwise have been shut against him ; and prevailed on him to preach early in the morning, as he had done in Scotland. These morning lectures were soon so popular, that it became proverbial in Boston, that, between early rising to hear Whitefield, and the use of *tar-water*, the physicians would have no practice. During this visit, he made an extensive tour in New England, with great success. At the close of it, he says in his journal, " We saw great things. The flocking and power that attended the word, was like unto that seven years ago. Weak as I was and have been, I was enabled to travel eleven hundred miles, and to preach daily. I am now going to Georgia to winter."

This preliminary sketch of American ecclesiastical history, although it anticipates not a few of Whitefield's movements in the western world, will enable the reader to appreciate both their wisdom and necessity, when they are recorded at length, and in their order, from his journals.

The question, Why did Whitefield go to America in the first instance ? has never been satisfactorily answered. I have recorded, in his early life, some of his views and feelings on the subject, without attempting to account for them, or to explain them. They are remarkable. He uniformly speaks of his object as " a great work ;" and represents himself as " a stripling going forth like David against Goliath." He prays most fervently for " such a deep humility, well-guided zeal, and burning love," as should enable him to defy " men and devils," even if they did " their worst." Now all this is rather too much to be applied exclusively to the claims of an infant colony ; except, indeed, he foresaw what it would become eventually. Foresight of this kind, however, was not natural to him. Whitefield did not " see afar off," into the progress of society, or the bearings of colonization. He opened no long nor current accounts with Time, but only with Eternity. How his doings would tell upon future ages and generations—he seems never to have calculated. His immediate object was to win souls, and his final object, to present them before the throne " with exceeding joy."

Such being the cast of Whitefield's mind, as well as of his spirit, a new and destitute colony could absorb him, as fully as the hope of being another " apostle of the Indians," or another ELIOT, did Wesley. That brilliant hope does not seem to have dazzled Whitefield at all. At least, I have searched in vain for any distinct proof, that the example of Eliot inspired him, or that the sanguine expectations of the Wesleys were shared by him. No where does he express hopes of great success, nor explain his errand (as they did) by a desire to " save his soul." Whatever he anticipated or intended in reference to the Indians on the banks of the Savannah, he said but little ; and that little

only to an Indian trader in confidence. 182 *Let.* He may, however, have cherished fond expectations, although he did not
utter them as the Wesleys did. Not that he was more prudent
than his friends. In general, Whitefield thought *aloud.* It is
possible, however, that his reference to the prophecy, " I will
make thee the head of the heathen," may mean more than meets
the eye. I am not making a mystery of his silence. It is easily
explained by the single fact, that he went out, intending to
return to England in the course of the year, to " take priest's
orders." He could not, therefore, anticipate much success from
so short a visit to America. Besides, his silence is only too
easily accounted for, by the *oracular* summons to return immediately, which Wesley addressed to him, as their vessels met
and passed in the Channel. What I mean to say, therefore, is,
that nothing but the future results of his American enterprise
can explain its origin. It was " the burden of the Lord " upon
his spirit ; deeply felt, but not fully understood by himself at
the time, nor ever perhaps in this world. Only He, who " seeth
the end from the beginning," foresaw the bearings of Whitefield's
mission to Georgia, upon America. We can now see many of
the reasons why " the Spirit did not suffer " him to remain in
England: America needed him, in a sense he did not suppose, and
to an extent she herself did not suspect; and the reasons of his
mission are not all unfolded yet. It had much influence upon
the recent revivals in that country, when they began ; and is
likely to have still more as they proceed. In the mean time,
by a curious coincidence, the new revivals in America are assailed under the shelter of high-sounding compliments to the
old. What Dr. Chauncy denounced as wild extravagance, in
the times of Whitefield, Calvin Colton eulogizes as prudent
zeal, in his " Reasons for preferring Episcopacy." The truth
or the merits of Colton's parting charges against his former
connexions, I am unable to appreciate ; but it is pleasing to find,
that the episcopal church allows a new champion to compliment
old revivals. She ought not, however, to plume herself on the
compliments paid to her " ORDERS," at the expense of the English independents, by Colton. By what infatuation could he
have so forgotten all he saw and heard of us, as to tell Ame-

rica that we prefer *recognition* to ordination? It is the very *sacredness* in which we hold the latter, that leads to the distinction.

Whitefield, as we have seen, arrived at Georgia in 1738. " When able to look about him," says Dr. Gillies, " he found every thing bore the aspect of an infant colony ; and, what was more discouraging still, he saw it was likely to continue so, by the nature of its constitution. The people were denied the use of both rum and slaves!" This Whitefield wrote, and this Gillies recorded, without any comment. Indeed, Whitefield considered the denial of rum and slaves, as more than a misfortune to the colony. Hence he adds, (after stating that female heirs were not allowed to inherit lands,) " so that, in reality, to place a people there on such a footing, was little better than to tie their legs and bid them walk. The scheme was well meant at home; but, as too many years' experience evidently proved, it was absolutely impracticable in so hot a country abroad."

How differently would Whitefield write, if alive, now ! But then, he was not wiser than his times, on the subject of slavery. Indeed, he soon became a slave owner, when he founded his orphan-house at Georgia. I have seen the inventory, in his own hand-writing, of the dead and live stock belonging to that establishment. In that document, carts, cattle, and slaves are described and valued with equal formality and *nonchalance !*

I might have concealed this fact, now that there are Americans who may employ it in their own justification : but I have not hid it; because even they cannot hide from themselves the fact, that Whitefield ought never to have held a slave. It was not like himself—it was unworthy of him, to do so ! So it is of every American christian. " I wot that through ignorance " he did it, as did their and our fathers. He would not do it now. Who does not, instinctively, feel this ? How difficult it is to believe that ever George Whitefield could have written the following words ! In his memorial to the governor of Georgia, for a grant of lands to found a college, he urges his request by stating, that " a considerable sum of money is intended speedily to be laid out in purchasing a large number of negroes." In his memorial to the king, praying for a charter to the intended college, he pledges himself to " give up his trust, and make a free gift of all lands, negroes, goods, and chattels, which he now stands possessed of in the province of Georgia, for the present founding, and towards the future support, of a college, to be called Bethesda." He makes a similar appeal to the archbishop of Canterbury; informing him that " the number of negroes, young and old, is about thirty ;" and proving to him, that by " laying out only a thousand pounds in purchasing an additional number of negroes," the income of the college would be " easily and speedily augmented." In his own printed account of the state of the orphan-house in 1770, he thus classes the negroes ; men 24, women 11, children 15. In the college rules, drawn up by himself, although not unmindful of the coloured branches of his family, he makes a strange distinction: " The young negro boys to be baptized and taught to read. The young negro girls to be taught to work with the needle." " *Lord, what is man !* "

Whitefield did not, however, forget the negroes in his preaching. It was not uncommon for him to close his sermons thus : " I must not forget the poor negroes ; no, I must not ! Jesus Christ died for them as well as for others. Nor do I mention *you* last, because I despise your souls ; but because I would have what I shall say make the deeper impression on your hearts. Oh that you would seek the Lord to be your righteousness ! Who knows but he may be found of you ? For in Christ Jesus there is neither male nor female, bond nor free ; even you may be the children of God, if you believe in Jesus. Did you never read of the eunuch belonging to the queen of Candace ?—a negro like yourselves. He believed. The Lord was his righteousness. He was baptized. Do you also believe—and you shall be saved. Christ Jesus is the same now as he was yesterday, and will wash you in his own blood. Go home, then—and turn the words into a prayer, and entreat the Lord to be *your* righteousness. Even so, come, Lord Jesus, come quickly, into all our souls ! Amen, Lord Jesus, Amen and Amen ! " *Serm.* 14.

Whitefield embarked for Philadelphia, with a family consisting of eight men, one boy, and two children, besides his zealous and munificent friend Mr. Seward ; leaving the bishop of London, and whoever else it might concern, to digest as they could the blunt and bold answer to the "Pastoral Letter;" a Letter which Gibson ought not to have written, and Watts never to have sanctioned: for its moral excellences and just discriminations, however well meant, were mixed up with maxims *subversive* of the gospel of the grace of God. This conviction Whitefield proclaimed before 20,000 people at Blackheath, on the day the letter appeared; and he wrote in his diary that night, after going on board, the following note: "I felt great freedom in myself, and could not but take notice of a mistake his Lordship of London was guilty of;—for he exhorts his clergy, *so* to explain the doctrine of justification by faith alone, as to make our good works a *necessary condition of it.* St. Paul pronounces a dreadful anathema against those who join faith and works together, in order to their being justified in the sight of God.· I pray God, that all preachers may be freed from so tremendous a sentence! And let all the people say, Amen and Amen."

I mention this fact again, because it gave Whitefield a *new* point to contend for, which much improved his views of the point he began with; for at first, he almost put regeneration in the room of justification; as well as preached too little of the truth, by which the Spirit regenerates the soul.

The delay of the vessel in the river enabled him to answer the bishop before sailing; and the new question absorbed him in thought and reading, throughout the voyage. Not, however, so as to divert him from the duties of a ship chaplain. These he discharged with the same fidelity as formerly; but as they did not make so much demand upon his time, he gave himself "to reading."

Amongst the books which helped him mightily at this time, were Jonathan Warne's "*Church of England Man turned Dissenter,*" and "*Arminianism the back-door to Popery.*" I have not been able to obtain these two; but as they are chiefly composed of extracts from Dr. Edwards' *Preacher*, their character is no secret; and it loses nothing of its point in the hands of Warne, if I may judge from his pamphlet entitled, "The dreadful Degeneracy of the Clergy, the means to promote Irreligion, Atheism, and Popery," which he drew from Edwards, and dedicated to Whitefield.

Warne was thus the *first* dissenter who wrote on Whitefield's behalf. The compliment also was well timed, and well judged; for it sustained him against the bishop, by the testimony of the fathers and martyrs of the church; and brought the puritans under his notice. Warne tells Whitefield, to "go on in the name of the Lord;" for the truths submitted him (with which his own preaching is delicately identified) "are to be found sparkling up and down in the labours of our godly reformers and holy martyrs, like so many diamonds of the greatest lustre, and are the bases of all sound religion both in heart and life."

It was well for Whitefield that he had studied Warne's specimens of the reformers and puritans, before he reached New England : they enabled him to adjust his phraseology in the pulpit to "the form of sound words" in the States; and prepared him to retract and explain expressions in his printed sermons, which the descendants of the puritans were not slow, nor ceremonious, nor wrong, in condemning.

Another thing which helped to clear and simplify his own views of the gospel, during the voyage, was, the discussion he carried on with a quaker, who preached occasionally in the cabin, and always against the *outward* Christ. His doctrine of the *inward* Christ, and his confounding of the inward light with the Spirit, led Whitefield to confess and contend, that "the outward righteousness of Christ imputed to us, is the sole fountain and cause of all the inward communications received from the Spirit."

In other respects his voyage had not much interest. It was, however, so useful to himself, that he said on reviewing the knowledge he had acquired during it, "I would not but have come this voyage for a thousand worlds." One of the fruits of it was his "Letter to the Religious Societies in England and Wales, lately set on foot ;" a pamphlet which had no ordinary influence upon their faith and patience. It is founded upon Heb. x. 23, which he translates thus : "Having been washed in the body with pure water, let us hold fast the mutual and uniform profession of the hope, without wavering; for He is faithful that hath promised."

The letter bears date Sept. 22; and presents a remarkable contrast to his own hopes on that day, as these appear in his diary:—not that he himself was in despair; but he felt, he says, " something of that which Adam felt when he was turned out of Paradise, ate but little, and went mourning all the day long." Accordingly, he does not mention the letter, nor intimate that he had done any thing but " weep bitterly."

This arose from the overwhelming discoveries he had made of the plagues of his own heart, and of the depths of Satan. It happily reminded him, however, of Luther's experience,— " that he never undertook any fresh work, but he was visited either with a fit of sickness, or with some strong temptation." " May I follow him," he says, " as he did Christ." Thus humbled, improved, and encouraged to persevere in his work, he arrived at Philadelphia, after a passage of nine weeks; and after having had, he says, " a legion of devils cast out of his heart by the power of Christ."

His welcome at Philadelphia was cordial. Both ministers and laymen of all denominations visited him, and invited him to preach. He was especially pleased to find that they preferred sermons when " not delivered within the church walls." It was well they did; for his fame had reached the city before he arrived, and thus collected crowds which no church could contain. " The court-steps" became his pulpit; and neither he nor the people wearied, although the cold winds of November blew upon them night after night.

Old Mr. Tennent, of Neshaminy, (the father of the Tennents,) came to visit and hear him; and thus paved his way to New Brunswick, where he became acquainted with Gilbert, the oldest son " of the good old man," as Whitefield always called him. Gilbert Tennent and George Whitefield were just the men to meet at this time. Both were popular, and both had been persecuted. Accordingly, they understood and appreciated each other at once. Tennent readily entered into Whitefield's views; and Whitefield, nobly despising all the abominable imputations which the world cast upon Tennent, identified himself with him in America; and told England that he was "a son of thunder, whose preaching must either convert or enrage hypocrites." *Journals.*

This was no ordinary magnanimity; for, at the time, Tennent's name was loaded with reproach, and the grossest immoralities were attributed to him. *American Biog. Dict.* He outlived them all, however, and closed a life of signal usefulness by a death of signal peace.

How much Whitefield was both struck and humbled by his preaching, will be seen from the following record:—" Never before heard I such a searching sermon. He went to the bottom indeed, and did not daub with untempered mortar. He convinced me more and more, that we can preach the gospel of Christ no further than we have experienced the power of it in our hearts. I found what a *babe* and *novice* I was in the things of God." *Diary.*

After preaching together in various places, they went to Neshaminy, to visit the good old patriarch; and to see the log-house, (so like "the schools of the ancient prophets!") where Mr. Tennent had by himself trained for the ministry, Rowland, Campbell, Lawrence, Beatty, Robinson, and Samuel Blair, besides his own four sons. Whitefield was delighted with the scene, and predicted the result of the patriarch's enterprise: "The devil will certainly rage against the work, but I am persuaded it will not come to nought." It did not. It became Princetown College.

At New York Whitefield was refused the use of both the church and the court-house. The commissary of the bishop, he says, was "full of anger and resentment, and denied me the use of his pulpit before I asked for it. He said, they did not want my assistance. I replied, If they preach the gospel, I wish them good luck: I will preach in the fields; for all places are alike to me." So they were: for in the afternoon he preached in the fields, and in the evening in Mr. (afterwards Dr.) Pemberton's meeting-house. (Dr. Pemberton published a funeral sermon on the death of Whitefield. He was then at Boston, having been dismissed from New York by a cabal of ignorance and bigotry.)

Whitefield did not excite much public attention in New York, at this time, nor, indeed, on any subsequent visit, until 1764, when he preached there seven weeks, with great acceptance and success. Still, even his first labours were not in vain. Pemberton wrote to him at Philadelphia, that "many were deeply affected; and some who had been loose and profligate, were ashamed, and set upon thorough reformation." The printers also, at both places, applied to him for sermons to publish; assuring him that hundreds had called for them, and that thousands would purchase them. This request he complied with, and "gave out" (I use his own expression, without knowing its meaning) "two *extempore* discourses to be published."

His own opinions of this tour, of which New York and Philadelphia were the centres, are expressed in stronger language than I can illustrate from my documents, ample as they are. "It is unknown," he says, "what deep impressions have been wrought upon the hearts of hundreds. Many poor sinners have, I trust, been called home, and great numbers are under strong convictions. An opposer told me, I had unhinged many *good sort* of people. I believe it."

One proof of the impression he made, was given in the presents he received for his orphan family. "They sent me butter, sugar, chocolate, pickles, cheese, and flour, for my orphans; and, indeed, I could almost say, they would pluck out their own eyes and give me. Oh that what God says of the church of Philadelphia, may now be fulfilled in the city called after her name—' *I know thy works.*'"

This readiness to aid him in his favourite enterprise, determined him to go to Georgia by land, that he might collect by the way. Several entered heartily into this plan, and purchased a sloop (which he called the Savannah) to send on the family by sea.

On leaving Philadelphia, with Seward, nearly twenty gentlemen on horseback accompanied him; and before they reached Chester, two hundred more had come to meet him. On his arrival, the judges sent him word, that they would defer their meeting until his sermon was over; and the clergyman, finding the church would be too small, (for nearly a thousand people had come from Philadelphia,) prepared a platform for him, from which he addressed an immense assembly.

Amongst other places which he visited on this tour, was Whitely Creek, where he became acquainted with William Tennent; and met with what hardly gratified him less, a Welch family who had heard him at Cardiff and Kingswood, before they emigrated. In vain any one else begged of him to be their guest; he would go no where but to the *Howels*. The name accounts for their fascination; it was associated with Wales, Bristol, and Howel Harris.

Whitefield became much attached to William Tennent. It was from him he received the well-known reproof against impatience for heaven. They were dining with Governor Livingston one day, and Whitefield being much exhausted by severe labour, expressed a hope that he should soon enter into his rest. He appealed also to Tennent, if that was not *his* comfort? Tennent replied, " What do you think I should say, if I were to send my man Tom into the field to plough, and at noon should find him lounging under a tree, complaining of the heat, and begging to be discharged from his hard service? What should I say? Why, that he was an idle, lazy fellow, and that his business was to do the work I had appointed him." This would have been a powerful rebuke from any one. It was *peculiar* from William Tennent. In early life he had lain in a trance, which was so like death, that his funeral was prepared, and with difficulty prevented. The physician having heard that the flesh under the arm had quivered, when the body was laid out, insisted upon a delay of three days. At the close of that time, no change had taken place; and, therefore, the family resolved to inter the corpse. But still the physician hesitated. He begged for another hour; then for half an hour; then for a quarter of an hour: and just as this last period was expiring, whilst he was moistening the swollen tongue, the eyes opened, and a groan was uttered. He persevered; and in the course of a few hours, Tennent revived, but with the loss of all his former ideas. His mind was a *blank* for nearly a year, in reference to all his past life. He had, however, a vivid impression of having been in heaven during his trance; and, for three years after, the sounds he seemed to have heard in glory were never out of his ears. Indeed, all through his future life he was a heavenly-minded christian. This was the man who reproved Whitefield; and the effect was increased by the fact, that Tennent was a champion for civil and religious liberty, as well as a conscious heir of glory. *American Biog. Dict.*

In the course of this tour towards Georgia, Whitefield had to endure considerable privations and peril in riding through the woods. On one occasion, he heard the wolves "howling like a kennel of hounds," near to the road. On another, he had a narrow escape in trying to cross the Potomac in a storm. He had also to swim his horse once, owing to the floods; for it was now the depth of winter. One night Seward and he lost themselves in the woods of South Carolina, and were much alarmed at seeing groups of negroes dancing around great fires. No real injury, however, was sustained from the journey, notwithstanding all its hardships.

He arrived at Charleston in good health and high spirits. "Here," says Gillies, "he soon found that, by field preaching, he had lost his old friend the commissary, who once promised to defend him with life and fortune." The commissary had shame enough to keep out of the way, whilst Whitefield staid; and the curate said, he could not admit him into the pulpit whilst Garden was absent. The people, however, had not forgotten him. All the town were clamorous for him to preach some where. Accordingly, he accepted invitations to both the French church and the independent chapel.

The congregations were large and polite; but presented "an affected finery and gaiety of dress and deportment, which," he says, "I question if the court-end of London could exceed." Before he left, however, there was what he calls "a glorious alteration in the audience." Many wept; and the light and airy had a visible concern in their faces. Such was their urgency to hear more, that they won him back from the boat, after he had gone to the shore to sail for Georgia, and prevailed on him to preach again.

Here he formed an intimate friendship with the independent minister, Josiah Smith; the first native of South Carolina, who

received a literary degree. *Miller's Retrospect.* Smith published a remarkable sermon soon after, entitled, " *The Character and Preaching of Whitefield, impartially represented and
supported.*" Strange as this title is, both Dr. Colman and Mr.
Cooper of Boston united in writing a recommendatory preface
to it. And no wonder; it was worthy of their sanction. I do
not know of any thing written since, which defines and defends
the character of Whitefield better. The text is, Job xxxii.
17, " I said, I will answer also my part, I also will show mine
opinion." He begins by saying, " My design from this text
is, to show my impartial opinion of that son of thunder, who
lately graced and warmed this desk; and would have been an
ornament, I think, to the best pulpit in the province." (This was
a hit as well as a hint to Commissary Garden.) The plan of the
sermon is stated thus : " The scheme I propose is, First, To
give my opinion of the *doctrines* he insisted on, and so well
established. Second, To speak something of the *manner* of his
preaching. Third, To offer my sentiments upon his personal
character. Lastly, To give you my thoughts, what Providence
seems to have in its view, in raising up men of this STAMP in
our day; almost every where spoken against, yet crowded after
and justly admired."

Smith's defence of Whitefield's doctrine is masterly. His
account of his *manner* is the best I have ever met with. " He
is certainly a finished preacher. A noble negligence ran through
his style. The passion and flame of his expressions will, I trust,
be long felt by many. My pen cannot describe his action and
gestures, in all their strength and decencies.

" He appeared to me, in all his discourses, very deeply affected
and impressed in his own heart. How did *that* burn and boil
within him, when he spake of the things he had made ' touching the King!' How was his tongue like the pen of a ready
writer, touched as with a coal from the altar! With what a flow
of words—what a ready profusion of language, did he speak to
us upon the great concerns of our souls! In what a flaming light
did he set *our* eternity before us! How earnestly he pressed
Christ upon us! How did he move our passions with the con-
straining love of *such* a Redeemer! The awe—the silence—the

attention which sat upon the face of the great audience, was an argument how he could reign over all their powers. Many thought he spake as never man spake before him. So charmed were the people with his manner of address, that they shut up their shops, forgot their secular business, and laid aside their schemes for the world ; and the oftener he preached, the keener edge he seemed to put upon their desires to hear him again.

" How awfully—with what thunder and sound—did he dis-charge the artillery of heaven upon us ! And yet, how could he soften and melt even a soldier of *Ulysses,* with the mercy of God! How close, strong, and pungent were his application to the con-science ; mingling light and heat ; pointing the arrows of the Almighty at the hearts of sinners, while he poured in the balm upon the wounds of the contrite, and made broken bones re-joice. Eternal themes, the tremendous solemnities of our reli-gion, were all *alive* upon his tongue ! So, methinks, (if you will forgive the figure,) St. Paul would *look* and speak in a pulpit. In some such manner, I am tempted to conceive of a seraph, were he sent down to preach among us, and to tell us what things he had seen and heard above.

" How bold and courageous did he look ! He was no flatterer ; would not suffer men to settle on their lees ; did not prophesy smooth things, nor sew pillows. He taught the way of God in truth, and regarded not the person of men. He struck at the politest and most modish of our vices, and at the most fashion-able entertainments, regardless of every one's presence, but His in whose name he spake with this authority. And I dare war-rant, if none should go to these diversions, until they have an-swered the solemn questions he put to their consciences, our theatre would soon sink and perish. I freely own he has taken my heart ! "

In a note to this sermon, Smith states that £600 were con-tributed in Charleston to the orphan-house, when Whitefield returned.

He left Charleston in an open canoe, with five negro rowers, and reached Savannah in safety. " In their way," says Gillies, " they lay, for the first time, in the woods, upon the ground,

near a large fire, which keeps off the wild beasts:" " An em-
blem," says Whitefield, " of the divine love and presence keep
ing off evils and corruptions from the soul." He found Georgia
much deserted and depressed; but was much pleased with the
tract of land, which Habersham had selected as the site of the
orphan-house. It was about ten miles distant from Savannah,
and included five hundred acres. On the 24th of January, 1740,
he took formal " possession of his lot, and called it Bethesda,
the House of Mercy." Next week, he laid out the ground-plan
of the building; and employed many workmen, who would otherwise have left the colony. In the mean time, he hired a large
house, and took in twenty-four orphans. Thus he incurred at
once the heavy responsibility of a large family and a larger institution; " encouraged," he says, " by the example of Professor
Franck." Many years after, on reverting to this undertaking,
he said, " I forgot to recollect, that Professor Franck built in
Glaucha, in a populous country, and that I was building at the
very *tail* of the world, where I could expect the least supply,
and which the badness of the constitution (of the colony) which
I expected every day to be altered, rendered it by far the most
expensive part of all his Majesty's dominions. But had I received more and ventured less, I should have suffered less, and
others more." It was well for the colony, however, and better
for the world, that he did " forget to recollect " all this. By
committing himself upon Bethesda, he was compelled, like Paul
when he espoused the cause of the poor saints in Jerusalem, to
visit the churches every where.

Having laid the foundation of the orphan-house, he left Savannah, to provide as he could for forty orphans, and about
sixty servants and workmen; for such was the number dependent on him. He, however, had no fears nor misgivings of heart.
" Near a hundred mouths," he writes at the time, " are daily to
be supplied with food; the expense is great; but our great and
good God will, I am persuaded, enable me to defray it. As yet, I
am kept from the least doubting. The more my family increases,
the more enlargement and comfort I feel. Set thy almighty
fiat to it, O gracious Father, and for thine own name's sake
convince us more and more, that thou never wilt forsake those

who put their trust in thee." On reviewing this passage fifteen years after, he wrote, " Hitherto, blessed be God, I have not been disappointed of my hope." *Rev. Journ.*

Philadelphia was the first place where he pleaded the cause of the orphan-house, after having commenced the work : and he succeeded, although not in the churches. The commissary told him, that he would lend the church no more to him. *" The fields are open,"* was his laconic answer ; and eight thousand people replied to his call that night, and ten thousand next day. On the sabbath morning he collected £110 for his " poor orphans ;" and then went to church, where the commissary preached a sermon on justification by works. Whitefield had been recognised at church ; and, accordingly, was expected to answer the sermon in the evening. He did ; and collected £80 more for Bethesda.

Money was, however, the least part of his success. Many souls were both awakened and won. Negroes came to him, asking, " Have I a soul ?" Societies for prayer and mutual edification were set up in various parts of the city. Scoffers were silent, or only muttered their curses over the punch-bowl in taverns, " because," says he, " I did not preach up more morality !" *Seward* relates an anecdote in his journal, at this time, which deserves to be extracted. " A drinking club, whereof a clergyman was a member, had a negro boy attending them, who used to mimic people for their diversion. The gentlemen had him mimic our brother Whitefield ; which he was very unwilling to do (Whitefield had just published an appeal on behalf of the negroes) ; but they insisting upon it, he stood up and said, ' I speak the truth in Christ, I lie not ; unless you repent, you will all be damned.' This unexpected speech broke up the club, which has never met since." *Seward's Journal.*

At this time Whitefield and Seward became acquainted with Anthony Benezett, the philanthropist. He was a quaker : but he confessed to them with tears, that the society, in general, were in a state of carnal security. This led Whitefield to " be very plain and powerful " in exposing their errors. The consequence was, that many of them forsook him. Benezett evidently caught something of Whitefield's spirit, if I may judge from his subsequent history. It was at this amiable philanthropist's funeral, when hundreds of weeping negroes stood round, that an American officer said, " I would rather be Anthony Benezett in that coffin, than George Washington with all his fame." *Amer. Biog.*

The simplicity of Seward, at this time, is amusing. He was not only Whitefield's Boswell, but also his trumpeter. And he makes no secret of his being the writer of the paragraphs and advertisements which then appeared in the newspapers. One of them, which he sent from Philadelphia to the New York paper, is worth quoting, for the facts it contains. " We hear from Philadelphia, that since Mr. Whitefield's preaching there, the dancing school and concert room have been shut up, as inconsistent with the doctrines of the gospel ; at which some gentlemen were so enraged, that they broke open the door. It is most extraordinary that such devilish diversions should be supported in that city, and by some of that very sect, whose first principles are an utter detestation of them ; as appears from William Penn's ' No Cross, no Crown ;' in which he says, ' Every step in a dance is a step to hell.' "

It was Seward himself who had taken away the keys of the assembly rooms, that all the people might come to hear Whitefield. He obtained the keys from the keeper, on promising to meet all consequences. Accordingly, he was threatened with a *caning*, and got well abused ; which quite delighted him. It ought, however, to be known, that Seward was hurried away into rash zeal on this occasion, by finding a son of PENN one of the proprietors of the assembly house. This would have provoked even an English quaker, as well as a methodist. *Journal*, p. 6. He had, however, to provide for the dancing master's family. He did also a better thing at this time : " Agreed with Mr. Allen for five thousand acres of land, on the forks of the Delaware ; the conveyance to be made to Mr. Whitefield, and after that assigned to me as security for my money, £2200." This purchase was chiefly made for the benevolent design of a negro school, similar to the orphan-house. Seward, however, did not live to carry his design into effect. He died before Whitefield returned to England.

After visiting various places, and producing every where a great impression, Whitefield arrived at New York, where he was met by William Tennent. He had, however, overtaxed his strength by labour, and lost his appetite. He did not, therefore, create a great sensation there at this time; at least, not equal to that in other places. His audiences, however, were never under seven or eight thousand persons, and he obtained £300 for Bethesda.

It is very affecting to read his diary at this time: he was so unwilling to give way to his sufferings, and so unable to do justice to his burning zeal. He made a desperate effort at Long Island to reach his usual pitch; but almost sunk under it, as he turned to the ministers, exclaiming, " *Oh that we were all a flame of fire !* "

On his way to Philadelphia again, he revived; having had the assistance and society of the Tennents, and some refreshing sleep, which, he says, " my body much wanted." This rally was opportune; for the whole city was moved at his coming. He, too, was moved with indignation, on hearing that *antinomianism* had been charged against the tendency of his doctrine. Accordingly, he " cleared himself from the aspersion with great spirit," in his first sermon. " I *abhor* the thoughts of it," he said ; " and whosoever entertains the doctrines of free grace in an honest heart, will find them cause him to be fruitful in every good word and work." In this loathing abhorrence of antinomianism, Rowland Hill always appeared to me to inherit the mantle and spirit of Whitefield, and to remember that he inherited them. His well-known sarcasm, " It is a *nasty* religion," did more execution upon that monster of the mire, than any weapon I have seen wielded. The look and the tone, in which this was uttered, justified as they were by his own holy character, were irresistible. The *hit* struck as wit, and stuck as wisdom. Whitefield having repelled the charge of antinomianism in Philadelphia, had next to justify his zeal. That was attacked on the following sabbath in church, whilst he himself was present. The clergyman took for his text, " I bear them record, they have a zeal for God, but not according to knowledge." It was an unfortunate selection for the accuser ; and Whitefield turned the context upon him with tremendous point and power, in the evening, before an audience of twenty thousand. " I could have wished he had considered the next words—' for they being ignorant of God's righteousness, and going about to establish their *own* righteousness, have not submitted themselves to the righteousness of God. For Christ is the end of the law for righteousness to every one that believeth,' " Rom. x. 3, 4. That night *fifty negroes,* besides many other converts, came to tell him " what God had done for their souls."

Next day he set out for Derby, and found, when he came to the ferry, that " people had been crossing over, as fast as two boats could carry them, ever since *three* o'clock in the morning." Many of them followed him to Chester and Wellington also, and almost wore him out by their claims upon his time and strength. They were not, however, inconsiderate of his object : they gave him much, and promised him more, for his orphans.

Whilst in " Chester county," a *new* feature was added to the effects of his ministry. It had often been accompanied by the deep silence of awe, and the silent tears of penitence, both in England and America : but it never produced paroxysms of crying or conviction. Something of this kind certainly happened at Bristol ; for Wesley appeals with triumph to " outward signs," similar to those produced there by himself, although Whitefield says nothing about them in his journals ; " which," says Southey, " assuredly he would have done, had he been convinced, with Wesley, that these fits were the immediate work of God." The only thing of the kind, however, which Whitefield mentions before the scenes at Nottingham and Fog's Manor, occurred at Philadelphia, whilst he was " settling " one of his societies, but not preaching. It was a female society, composed of many who had just been awakened by his preaching. When, therefore, he met them, and proceeded to organize and exhort them, their unexpected number and new position overcame them. " Their cries might be heard at a great distance." Still this was all. And it took only a *devotional* form : for he adds, " When I had done prayer, I thought proper—to leave them at their devotions." But this was far exceeded at Nottingham. " I had not spoke long, when I perceived numbers melting. As

I proceeded, the influence increased, till at last, both in the morning and afternoon, thousands cried out so that they almost drowned my voice. Oh what strong cryings and tears were shed and poured forth after the dear Lord Jesus! Some fainted; and, when they got a little strength, would hear and faint again. Others cried out in a manner almost as if they were in the sharpest agonies of death. And after I had finished my last discourse, I myself was so overpowered with a sense of God's love —that it almost took away my life."

Next day, even this commotion was exceeded at Fog's Manor. " Look where I would, most were drowned in tears. The word was sharper than a two-edged sword. Their bitter cries and tears were enough to pierce the hardest heart. Oh what different visages were then to be seen! Some were struck pale as death, others lying on the ground, others wringing their hands, others sinking into the arms of their friends, and most lifting up their eyes to heaven, and crying out to God for mercy. I could think of nothing, when I looked at them, so much as the great day! They seemed like persons awakened by the last trump, and coming out of their graves to judgment!"

Remarkable as all this is, it admits of some explanation, although Gillies passed it over. Now, in both instances, Whitefield, accompanied by Tennent and Blair, rode away from the scene, to the distance of *twenty* miles, immediately after these sermons and sensations : a self-evident proof, that they apprehended no danger from the paroxysms. They rode, too, " singing psalms and hymns by the way." Now they were not men who would have abandoned the conscience-struck, nor sung as they left them, had there been any symptoms of bodily or mental disease, at all ominous. Both W. Tennent and Blair were emphatically " nursing fathers," and Whitefield's heart was made of tenderness. It is thus evident, that he did not consider the people to be unnaturally nor unduly excited.

Besides, they were not altogether unprepared for the appeals of Whitefield. Blair, who was the minister at Fog's Manor, was himself a powerful preacher, and had been creating a strong impression throughout the county, for some time. The Tennents also had co-operated in preparing the way of the Lord.

N

Whitefield went to their field of labour, because " a good work had begun " in it by their labours. He had, therefore, " good ground " to sow in: and he felt this, when he saw twelve thousand people assembled " in a desert place," where he did not expect so many hundreds. " I was surprised," he says, " to see such a great multitude gathered together, at so short warning." And they themselves must have been surprised at their own numbers. These facts lessen the mystery of the commotion, without diminishing its real interest. It was, as at Pentecost, men who had come from all quarters " *to worship*," that were cut to the heart; and many of whom had " smote on their breasts," before they heard the *Peter*—of England's Pentecost.

Whilst Whitefield was thus moving about from place to place, he wrote the following letters, in order to obtain a wife; and it will not be wondered at *now*, that they defeated their own wise purpose by their unwise form.

TO MR. AND MRS. D.

" On board the Savannah, bound to Philadelphia
from Georgia, April 4th, 1740.

" My dear Friends,

I find by experience, that a mistress is absolutely necessary for the due management of my increasing family, and to take off some of that care which at present lies upon me. Besides, I shall in all probability, at my next return from *England*, bring more women with me; and I find, unless they are all truly gracious, (or indeed if they are,) without a superior, matters cannot be carried on as becometh the gospel of Jesus Christ. It hath been therefore much impressed upon my heart, that I should marry, in order to have a help meet for me in the work whereunto our dear Lord Jesus hath called me. This comes (like *Abraham's* servant to *Rebekah's* relations) to know whether you think your daughter, *Miss E——*, is a proper person to engage in such an undertaking? If so; whether you will be pleased to give me leave to propose marriage unto her? You need not be afraid of sending me a refusal. For, I bless

God, if I know any thing of my own heart, I am free from that foolish passion which the world calls love. I write only because I believe it is the will of God that I should alter my state; but your denial will fully convince me that your daughter is not the person appointed by God for me. He knows my heart; I would not marry but for him, and in him, for ten thousand worlds.—But I have sometimes thought *Miss E——* would be my help-mate; for she has often been impressed on my heart. I should think myself safer in your family, because so many of you love the Lord Jesus, and consequently would be more watchful over my precious and immortal soul. After strong crying and tears at the throne of grace for direction, and after unspeakable troubles with my own heart, I write this. Be pleased to spread the letter before the Lord; and if you think this motion to be of him, be pleased to deliver the enclosed to your daughter;—if not, say nothing, only let me know you disapprove of it, and that shall satisfy, dear Sir and Madam,

Your obliged friend and servant in Christ,

G. W."

TO MISS E——.

" On board the Savannah, April 4th, 1740.

" Be not surprised at the contents of this :—the letter sent to your honoured father and mother will acquaint you with the reasons. Do you think you could undergo the fatigues that must necessarily attend being joined to one, who is every day liable to be called out to suffer for the sake of Jesus Christ? Can you bear to leave your father and kindred's house, and to trust on him (who feedeth the young ravens that call upon him) for your own and children's support, supposing it should please him to bless you with any? Can you bear the inclemencies of the air, both as to cold and heat, in a foreign climate? Can you, when you have a husband, be as though you had none, and willingly part with him, even for a long season, when his Lord and Master shall call him forth to preach the gospel, and command him to leave you behind? If after seeking to God for direction, and searching your heart, you can say, ' I can do all

N 2

those things through Christ strengthening me,' what if you and I were joined together in the Lord, and you came with me at my return from *England*, to be a help meet for me in the management of the orphan-house? I have great reason to believe it is the divine will that I should alter my condition, and have often thought you were the person appointed for me. I shall still wait on God for direction, and heartily entreat him, that if this motion be not of him, it may come to nought.—I write thus plainly, because I trust I write not from any other principles but the love of God.—I shall make it my business to call on the Lord Jesus, and would advise you to consult both him and your friends—for in order to attain a blessing, we should call both the Lord Jesus and his disciples to the marriage.—I much like the manner of *Isaac's* marrying with *Rebekah;* and think no marriage can succeed well, unless both parties concerned are like-minded with *Tobias* and his wife.—I think I can call the God of *Abraham, Isaac,* and *Jacob* to witness, that I desire ' to take you my sister to wife, not for lust, but uprightly ;' and therefore I hope he will mercifully ordain, if it be his blessed will we should be joined together, that we may walk as *Zachary* and *Elisabeth* did, in all the ordinances of the Lord blameless. I make no great profession to you, because I believe you think me sincere. The passionate expressions which carnal courtiers use, I think ought to be avoided by those who marry in the Lord. I can only promise by the help of God, ' to keep my matrimonial vow, and to do what I can towards helping you forward in the great work of your salvation.' If you think marriage will be any way prejudicial to your better part, be so kind as to send me a denial. I would not be a snare to you for the world. You need not be afraid of speaking your mind,—I trust I love you only for God, and desire to be joined to you only by his command and for his sake. With fear and much trembling I write, and shall patiently tarry the Lord's leisure, till he is pleased to incline you, dear Miss E——, to send an answer to,

Your affectionate brother, friend,
and servant in Christ,
G. W."

Whitefield returned to Savannah, with collections for Bethes-da, to the amount of £500, in money and goods. On his way he preached at Lewis Town, to what he calls " as unaffected a congregation" as he had seen in America. Next day, however, he compelled the *politest* of them to weep, whilst he pictured the trial of Abraham's faith ;—a favourite and efficient sermon with him : but he adds, (what other ministers have found only too true,) " Alas, when I came to turn from the creature to the Creator, and to talk of God's love in sacrificing his only begot-ten Son, their tears, I observed, dried up. I told them of it ;— and could not but hence infer the dreadful depravity of human nature, that we can weep at the sufferings of a martyr, a mere man like ourselves ; but when are we affected at the relation of the sufferings of the Son of God ? "

His reception at Savannah, on this occasion, deserves parti-cular attention. It engraved the orphan-house upon his heart, as with the pen of a diamond ; and was for ever vividly present to him, wherever he went afterwards. " And no wonder !"—it will be said, after reading his own account of this welcome. " Oh what a sweet meeting I had with my dear friends! What God has prepared for me—I know not : but surely I cannot well expect a greater happiness, till I embrace the saints in glory ! When I parted, my heart was ready to break with sor-row ;—but now it almost burst with joy. Oh how did each, in turn, hang upon my neck, kiss and weep over me with tears of joy ! And my own soul was so full of a sense of God's love, when I embraced one friend in particular, that I thought I should have expired in the place. I felt my soul so full of a sense of the divine goodness, that I wanted words to express myself. Why me, Lord—why me ?

" When we came to public worship, young and old were all dissolved in tears. After service, several of my parishioners, all my family, and the little children, returned home, crying along the street, and some could not avoid praying very loud.

" Being very weak in body, I laid myself upon a bed ; but finding so many in weeping condition, I rose and betook my-self to prayer again. But had I not lifted up my voice very high—the groans and cries of the children would have prevented

my being heard.   This continued for near an hour; till at last,
finding their concern rather increase than abate, I desired all to
retire.   Then some or other might be heard praying earnestly,
in every corner of the house.

" It happened at this time to thunder and lighten, which
added very much to the solemnity of the night.   Next day the
concern still continued, especially among the girls.   I mention
the orphans in particular, that their benefactors may rejoice in
what God is doing for their souls."

This was just the scene to inspire and determine Whitefield
to live or die for the orphan-house.   Accordingly, the memory
of it followed him like his shadow, wherever he went.

His family had now increased to a hundred and fifty persons.
He therefore visited Charleston again, to plead their cause
anew.   But by this time Commissary Garden was ready to
stake his " fortune and life " against him.   He began by abusing Whitefield and the methodists, in their presence, by a sermon " as virulent, unorthodox, and inconsistent as ever was delivered;" and ended by refusing him the sacrament.

This insult had its natural effect.   It so disgusted several of
Whitefield's friends, that they would not receive the sacrament
from Garden.   This led to sacraments in a private house; and
there, " Baptists, church folks, and presbyterians, all joined together, and received according to the church of England; ex-
cepting *two*, who desired to have it sitting."   Garden then
cited Whitefield to appear in an ecclesiastical court, for not
reading the Common Prayer in the presbyterian meeting-house,
at Charleston.   He accordingly did appear, and appealed according to law, to his Majesty's commissioners for reviewing
appeals.   He wrote also to the bishop of London, inquiring
" Whether the commissary of South Carolina had power to
exercise any judicial authority over him or any other clergyman,
not belonging to the province."   Garden had, in fact, suspended him from the ministry.   He had, therefore, no alternative
but to submit, or to lay his case before the high court of chan-
cery; which he did.   Strange to say, this suspension, and his
appeal against it, were afterwards pleaded against him in the
synod of Glasgow, when they met " anent employing Mr.

Whitefield" in the pulpits of the church of Scotland. One member of the synod, however, (probably Dr. Erskine,) asked indignantly, " For what was Whitefield suspended ? Why, for no other crime than omitting to use a form of prayer prescribed in the communion-book, when officiating in a *presbyterian* congregation ! And shall a meeting of presbyterian ministers pay any regard to a sentence which had such a foundation ? "

Notwithstanding this suspension, he continued preaching, wherever he could, in the province, until the excessive heat of the season compelled him to sail for New England. He embarked for Rhode Island, intending to go by land to Boston ; and such was the *spring* of his constitution, that the short voyage completely restored him, although he had often been all but *dead* before he left.

On his arrival at Newport, he met with a new friend, Mr. Clap, whom he describes thus : " An aged dissenting minister ; *but* the most venerable man I ever saw in my life. He looked like a good old puritan, and gave me an idea of what *stamp* those men were, who first settled in New England. His countenance was very heavenly ! He rejoiced much to see me, and prayed most affectionately for a blessing on my coming to Rhode Island. Whilst at his table, I could not but think that I was sitting with one of the patriarchs." Whitefield has not over-rated nor over-coloured the patriarch of Rhode Island. Clap " had some singularities ; but his zeal to promote the knowledge of Christ and the interests of the gospel, cast a lustre over all his character." *American Biog.* Children, servants, and slaves, were objects of his special care ; and, being a bachelor, he gave away all his income to the poor and the perishing. I mention this, to distinguish him (in this country) from Clap, the president of Yale College, who opposed Whitefield.

After preaching with great success on Rhode Island, he rode on to Boston, and was met by the governor's son, and other gentlemen, four miles (not *ten,* as Gillies says) from the city. At this time, Jonathan Belcher was governor of Massachusetts ; a man equally distinguished for piety and polish. He owed his honours to the favourable impression made by his high charac-

ter and address, upon the Princess Sophia and her son, (afterwards George II.) when in England; and he regained them,
when they were lost through calumny, by vindicating himself
before the throne, where they had been conferred. Princetown
College owes much to Belcher; and he was much indebted to
Whitefield for the impulse, which made him its "chief patron
and benefactor." His splendid hospitalities and style were in
their palmy state, when Whitefield first visited Boston. Willard, also, the secretary of Massachusetts, was a man of high and
holy character. He was the son of Vice-President Willard, of
Harvard College; the author of the first theological *folio* printed in America, and one of the chief opponents of trial for witchcraft. The son inherited the father's spirit.

Such were the statesmen who welcomed Whitefield to Boston. Some of the ministers also were not less eminent. Dr.
Colman, his first friend, had been, when in England, the friend
of Howe, Calamy, Burkitt, and Mrs. Rowe, then Miss Singer.
Indeed, he had a *caste* of Howe in his demeanour and spirit.
Cooper, also, his colleague, was a man who wanted only the
visit of Whitefield, in order to be a Whitefield; which, as a
revivalist, he soon became. Webb, too, was no ordinary man.
Dr. Eliot, who was his colleague for eight years, said of him,
that "he was one of the best of christians, and one of the best
of ministers." Foxcroft, also, deserves a high place in the religious annals of Boston, and in the list of Whitefield's American
friends;—Dr. Chauncy, his colleague, being witness. He published "An Apology for Whitefield," in 1745, as well as a sermon on his "Labours," in 1740. Dr. Chauncy says of Foxcroft, "His writings bear testimony to his unfeigned piety, and
evince clearness of conception, copiousness of invention, liveli-
ness of imagination, and soundness of judgment." *Funeral
Sermon.*

Prince, the annalist, was another of the Boston stars, which
"fought in their courses," for Whitefield and revivals: a somewhat eccentric star, indeed, when judged of by the plan of his
"Chronological History of New England," which begins at the
creation of the world, and ends with the arrival of Governor
Belcher! Still, he was evidently a man of great research and

erudition, as well as of ardent piety.   Dr. Chauncy (no mean
judge in the matter) regarded him as next to Cotton Mather
in learning.   By the way, what became of the MSS. and books
which Prince left to the old south church, as " The New England Library ? "   The collection was great and valuable.   Can
it be true, that the MSS. were destroyed by the British,
except by accident?   I ask this question, because I find " No,"
in pencil-mark, on the margin of my copy of *Amer. Biog.*

Gee, also, deserves honourable mention amongst the friends
of Whitefield.   He had been, in early life, the colleague of Dr.
Cotton Mather.   After the Doctor's death, his son Samuel became the colleague of Gee, and continued so until they differed
on the subject of revivals ; of which Gee was both a wise and
warm advocate.   He seems to have had, with some of Coleridge's genius, all his indolence and love of talking.   The judicious and cautious Dr. Sewall, also, was one of the first to welcome Whitefield to his pulpit and his confidence.

Thus Whitefield fell into the best hands at Boston.   Nothing
gratified him more, however, than his interviews with old Mr.
Walter, the colleague and successor of the apostolic Eliot, at
Roxbury.   The pastorship of that church had been confined to
these two patriarchs a hundred and six years at this time.
Whitefield says of Walter, " he was a good old puritan."   He
returned Whitefield the compliment on hearing him preach at
the governor's table ; saying of the sermon, " It was puritanism
revived."   Dr. Colman said of this interview, that " it was the
happiest day he ever saw in his life."   One remark of Walter's
pleased Whitefield very much : " I am glad to hear," said the
old apostle, " that you call man half devil half beast."

Neither the governor nor the doctors of Boston, however,
could get Whitefield into the church.   The commissary treated
him politely, and introduced him to his clergy, but would not
admit him into the pulpit ; he therefore preached in all the
large chapels, and when they became too small for the audiences,
he betook himself to the Common, and there renewed the scenes
of Moorfields and Blackheath.

A melancholy catastrophe arose from fright, at one of the
chapels.   The place was crowded to excess, but there had been

nothing to create alarm : " yet, on a sudden, all the people were in an uproar; and so unaccountably surprised, that some threw themselves out of the windows; others out of the galleries; others trampled on one another : so that *five* were actually killed, and many dangerously wounded." This awful uproar was at its height when Whitefield reached the chapel : and although he saw some the victims of it, he had presence of mind enough to call off the people to hear him on the Common. This restored confidence. Thousands followed him to the fields, and listened with deep attention, whilst he improved this " humbling providence." It did humble *him*. I have no doubt of its being the chief consideration, which made him write in his journal, on leaving Boston, " I had such a sense of my own vileness upon my soul, that I wondered people did not stone me." Not that he could blame himself at all for the catastrophe : but it made him feel his own *nothingness* before God, and thus before man also. Accordingly, in a letter to Howel Harris, at this time, he predicted with great accuracy the reverses of his own popularity in London : " My coming to England will try my fidelity to my Master. Those that before, I suppose, would have plucked out their eyes for me, now, I suspect, will be very shy, and avoid me." This had no reference to the calamity at Boston ; but that had opened his eyes to the precariousness of popularity. He saw how any token of judgment, in connexion with his ministry, might be turned into an objection against his doctrines, now that he had assailed Wesley.

The calamity did not affect his popularity at Boston. On the day after, he preached twice in Mr. Gee's chapel, to immense audiences. He then visited Cambridge College, and preached before the professors and students, and a great number of the neighbouring ministers. What was " the *close* application " he made of the sermon to " the tutors and students," may be easily judged from the horror he felt at an unconverted ministry. It was, however, too unqualified, bad as the spiritual state of Cambridge was at the time. Accordingly, he afterwards begged pardon for his rashness in taking things upon " hearsay." But, whilst some took offence, his Boston friends, including the governor, seem to have taken the warning well. They all met him next day at the governor's table. Before dinner, his Excellency thanked him privately with tears, and, after dinner, sent him in the state-carriage through the city to the place where he had to preach. On the following sabbath he collected, in two of the chapels, upwards of £1000 currency for his orphan-house.

In the excursions he make through Massachusetts, Whitefield met, at Ipswich, with a venerable descendant of Rogers of Dedham, who himself was a descendant of Rogers the martyr. The hallowed associations which enshrined this hoary head were not lost upon him. " Happy lot !" he exclaimed, as he looked back to the old man's ancestors, and around upon his promising sons. Whitefield inherited the spirit of the Rogers's ; but he felt that he had not their mantle.

On his return to Boston, the public interest was higher than ever. A report that he had been poisoned, filled the city. Twenty thousand people, therefore, attended his first sermon. And both in the fields and in the chapels, all seemed melted, and many acknowledged themselves won, by the gospel. One of his most effectual sermons at Webb's chapel, was occasioned by the touching remark of a dying boy, who had heard him the day before. The boy was taken ill after the sermon, and said, " I want to go to Mr. Whitefield's God ;"—and expired. This touched "the secret place" of both the thunder and the tears of Whitefield. " It encouraged me to speak to little ones : but oh, how were the old people affected, when I said, ' Little children, if your parents *will not* come to Christ, do you come, and go to heaven without them.' " After this awful appeal, no wonder that " there were but few dry eyes." Only a Whitefield, however, could have drawn *tears* by it. In the generality of lips, it would harden, not soften, worldly parents ; and only shock affectionate children.

In this state of mind Whitefield set out to visit Jonathan Edwards, at Northampton. He was not allowed to quit Boston privately. The governor took him in the state-carriage to the ferry ; and, as he entered the boat, embraced him, and bade him farewell, with many tears. Belcher could not be satisfied with even this courtesy. He crossed the country, and met him again at Marlborough, Worcester, and Leicester. On parting finally, his Excellency said to him in private, " Mr. Whitefield, go on in stirring up the ministers; for reformation must begin at the house of God. And do not spare rulers, no not the *chief* of them, any more than ministers."

I have often thought, whilst reviewing the sweeping and severe invectives, which Whitefield so bitterly repented, that no small part of the blame lay at the governor's door. A charge like this, uttered with tears and entreaties, was enough to mislead a cooler man than George Whitefield. I must, therefore, say of it, what he said of his own conduct, " It was well meant, but it did hurt." To his credit for impartiality, however, he did not spare the governor himself; but, before leaving New England, wrote to him thus faithfully : " I thought your Excellency wanted a more clear view of your own vileness, and of the all-sufficiency of Jesus Christ. I mean a more experimental view : for what is all head-knowledge without that of the heart? It only settles people more upon their lees. May God give you to see and to follow the simplicity of the blessed Jesus ! Honoured Sir, I make no apology for this freedom ; your Excellency *bade* me not spare rulers—no not the chief of them." Whitefield has often been charged with flattering himself upon the attentions paid to him by the great : this is one instance in which he did not flatter the great in return.

On his arrival at Northampton, that cradle of revivals, he was at home at once with Jonathan Edwards. Their meeting, as Gillies says, " was like putting fire to tinder." So it was, in the best sense. Edwards's family and flock soon glowed with the warmth of their first love, and melted to their first penitence. But whilst these two eminent ministers esteemed, and even loved each other, as servants of God, Edwards did not think that Whitefield regarded him as a *confidential* friend exactly. The fact is, Edwards had cautioned him upon the subject of impulses, and guarded him against the practice of judging others to be unconverted. This was touching sore places, at the time. Whitefield seems to have winced a little, with impatience, under the metaphysical probe of Edwards ; but to have conceded nothing then. They parted, however, with mutual love ; and whatever difference existed between their theories of impulses, both soon rejoiced equally in " a glorious progress of the work of God," at Northampton, that year. *Sereno Dwight's Life of Edwards.*

On the way from Northampton to Windsor, Whitefield had a narrow escape : his horse shrunk back at a broken bridge; and when urged forward, threw him over it. He fell upon his face ; but providentially in the sand, not in the water. He was stunned for a time, and bled a little ; but next day he preached twice. His evening service was at East Windsor, where Jonathan Edwards's venerable father was minister. He was much pleased with this family. " Mr. Edwards's wife was as aged, I believe, as himself; so that I fancied I was sitting in the house of Zacharias and Elizabeth."

His visit to Newhaven, also, deserves to be recorded. It had not a little to do with the conversion of the celebrated Dr. Samuel Hopkins, then a student; although not so much connected with it as the subsequent appeals of Brainerd to him. Hopkins says, that he was " somewhat impressed " by what Whitefield said, both in public and private : and that he " justified him ". in his own mind, whilst many " condemned him " for his severe attacks upon the " mixed dancing and frolicking," then so prevalent in New England. *Hopkins's Memoirs.* Would that all the Hopkinsians in America were *Hopkinsian* in that article of their father's creed, " that it is both the duty and interest of the American State to emancipate all their African slaves."

Whilst at Newhaven, Whitefield dined at the college with Principal Clap ;—afterwards his opponent. Clap's dislike to him seems to have begun with their first interview. At table, Whitefield attacked the scheme of " an unconverted ministry," and showed its " ill consequences," without ceremony. He appears also to have hinted at his own scheme of supplying " faithful men " to the American churches, from Britain, to be ordained by the Tennents.

This was certainly the subject then discussed at Newhaven Hall ; and the spirit of the discussion, on the part of Whitefield, may be conjectured from the evening note in his diary : " Oh that God may quicken ministers ! Oh that the Lord may make

us all flames of holy fire! Come, Lord Jesus; come quickly.
Amen and Amen."

In general, Whitefield's evening reflections embody the spirit
of the day : and on this day, his spirit was too warm for Clap's
temperament.   Clap, although a good man, would have sympathized more with a Newton or a Paley, than with a flaming
evangelist.   He could construct an *orrery* for America ; but he
could not elevate the stars of her churches.   He could refute
infidels and heretics ; but he could not revive formalists.

The governor, although very old, sympathized, more than the
professor, with Whitefield's zeal.   He said to him, after sermon,
" I am glad, Sir, to see you, and heartily glad to hear you."
" His heart was so full, that he could not speak much.   The tears
trickled down his aged cheeks, like drops of rain."   " He was
thankful to God," he said, " for such refreshings on the way to
our rest : food does us good, when we eat it with an appetite."

On leaving Newhaven, he thundered out at Stamford and
Rye, the opinions against unconverted ministers, which he had
broached at college : and the effect was tremendous.   " All
hearers were ready to cry out."   At dinner, two ministers, with
tears in their eyes, publicly confessed that they had laid hands
on two young men, without so much as asking whether they
were born again of God, or not ?"   One aged minister confessed
in private, that he had " never felt the power of the doctrines
of grace on his soul, although he had preached them long."

What Whitefield himself thought of the attacks he thus made
upon an unregenerate ministry, during his tour in New England,
is but too evident from a letter to his friend Habersham, dated
on the very day he was with Clap at Newhaven : " I am glad
God is scourging out the children of Belial.   You often heard
me say, He would do so."   All were not the children of Belial
whom Whitefield scourged at this time ; but still, it is as impossible to doubt the need of the scourge, as it is to approve of
its sweeping strokes.   Those who did not deserve them, would
not have got them, had every converted minister been faithful
to his unconverted brother.   Had all the spiritual men done
their duty to the formalists, Whitefield would have been the
first to honour them.

He now directed his steps again towards New York. His former visit to that city disappointed him. He could not forget this by the way. " My heart was somewhat dejected. I told Mr. Noble (his companion) I expected but little movings in New York; but Mr. Noble bid me expect great things from God; and told me of several who were, as he hoped, savingly wrought upon by my ministry, when there last." Accordingly, the impression was great *for* New York—then. It made him cry out in his chamber, " Lord, why did I doubt?" Under his first sermon, a few cried out; and even his friend Noble could hardly refrain.

On the sabbath, however, he was much dejected, before the evening sermon. " For near half an hour, I could only lay before the Lord, saying,—I was a miserable sinner, and wondered that Christ would be gracious to such a wretch. As I went to meeting, I grew weaker; and when I came into the pulpit, I could have chosen to be silent, rather than speak."

As might be expected, this self-emptying was followed by a rich unction from on high. " After I was begun, the whole congregation was alarmed. Crying, weeping, and wailing, were to be heard in every corner; and many seen falling into the arms of their friends. My own soul was carried out, till I could scarce speak any more." Still, the *Common* was not needed at New York.

Next day he went to Staten Island, on his way back to Philadelphia; preaching by turns with Gilbert Tennent. At Baskerredge, a poor negro woman, who had been converted under his sermon, somewhat embarrassed, as well as pleased him, by her gratitude. She insisted upon going along with him, (to Savannah, I suppose,) and told him that her master had consented to let her go. He says, " I bid her go home, and with a thankful heart serve her present master."

At New Brunswick he found, if not a warmer, a more influential, friend in Aaron Burr, afterwards the president of New Jersey College; one of the master-spirits of his age and country. Whitefield owed much to this friendship, besides the degree of A. M. in 1754. It was mainly through Burr's influence that

Gilbert Tennent was induced to go to Boston, to water the seed Whitefield had sown there.

As they drew nearer Philadelphia, they had a most providential escape. " There were two creeks in the way, much swollen with rain. In one of them, two of my fellow-travellers, in all probability, must have perished, had not a woman cried out, and bid us stop. A man (as I afterwards found) who had been touched by my ministry, hearing my voice, came and swam our horses over the other creek, and conducted us safe over a very narrow bridge."

On his arrival at Philadelphia, he found a house, 100 feet long and 70 broad, building for him to preach in. He *opened* it, although the roof was not on ; and continued to preach in it every day, until the snow (it was now the middle of November) drove him to the chapels again. One afternoon, whilst preaching against " reasoning unbelievers," his sermon made but little impression on the people. An infidel caught at this failure of effect ; and said to one of Whitefield's friends, " What! Mr. W. could not make the people cry this afternoon ? " " A good reason for it," (said his friend,) " he was preaching against deists, and *you* know they are a hardened generation." He was not, however, always so unsuccessful amongst the Philadelphian infidels. Brockden, the recorder, who had long been almost an atheist, was induced to steal into the crowd at night, to hear him for once. The sermon was on Nicodemus's visit to Christ. Brockden's visit to Whitefield had a similar motive. He saw, as he afterwards confessed, that " the doctrine did people good." When he came home, his wife (not knowing where he had been) wished that he had heard what she had been hearing. He said nothing. Another and another of his family came in, and made the same remark. He burst into tears, and said, " I have been hearing him, and approve of his sermon." Whitefield afterwards knew him as a christian with the spirit of a " martyr."

His tour was now closing. On reviewing it, before he sailed for Charleston, he says,—" Stop, O my soul, and look back with gratitude on what the Lord hath done for thee, during this excursion. It is now, I think, the seventy-fifth day since I arrived at Rhode Island. My body was then weak ; but the

Lord has renewed its strength. I have been enabled to preach, I think, a hundred and seventy-five times in public, besides exhorting frequently in private. I have travelled upwards of eight hundred miles, and gotten upwards of £700 sterling, in money, &c. for the Georgia orphans. Never did God vouchsafe me greater comforts. Never did I perform my journeys with so little fatigue, nor see so much of the divine presence in the congregations."

In this spirit he arrived at Bethesda, and found all his family well. For some time he was much occupied with making his arrangements for sailing to England; and having completed them, and taken "a sorrowful and affectionate leave" of his family, he went to Savannah to take leave there also. On the way, he narrowly escaped being shot by a labourer, who was walking with a gun under his arm, only two yards behind him. The gun went off unawares; but its mouth was towards the ground. "Otherwise," he says, "in all probability, I and one of my friends must have been killed."

Whilst at Charleston, waiting for a vessel, he received many inspiring letters from his Boston friends, informing him of the amazing progress of conversion in the city and throughout the province. He received also a copy of the following letter.

"To all and singular, the *constables* of Charleston.—WHEREAS I have received information on oath, that George Whitefield, clerk, hath made and composed a *false, malicious, scandalous,* and *infamous* LIBEL against the *clergy* of this province, in contempt of his Majesty and his laws, and against the king's peace:—THESE are therefore, in his Majesty's name, to charge and command you and each of you forthwith, to apprehend the said George Whitefield, and bring him before me, &c. &c. &c. Given under my hand and seal, B. W."

This mandate referred to a Letter, which Whitefield had only *revised* for the press. It was written by one of his friends, and had just come out on his arrival at Charleston. The writer was apprehended, and meanly (Whitefield says "frankly") confessed that "corrections and alterations" had been made by Whitefield.

I have not seen the Letter. Whitefield's account of it is,

that "it *hinted* that the clergy break the canons." If this was all, he might well write with emphasis in his diary, "I think *this* may be called PERSECUTION! I think it is for righteousness' sake."

He went before the magistrate at once, and gave security for appearing by attorney, under a penalty of £100, proclamation money. He became his own attorney, however, before he left. Even next day, he preached in the morning upon Herod's stratagem to kill Christ : in the afternoon on the murder of Naboth. That he did not spare the persecutors, is evident. " My hearers," he says, " as well as myself, made application. It was pretty close. I especially directed my discourse to men in authority, and showed them the heinous sin of abusing their power." Neither the commissary, nor the magistrate, slept on a bed of roses that night. Public opinion was against them. The people so overloaded him with sea-stores for his voyage, that he had to send much of the stock to Savannah. Next day, January 15th, he embarked for England, on board the Minerva, and arrived at Falmouth early in March. On the sabbath following he was again on Kennington Common—but with "not above a hundred" to hear him.

CHAPTER VIII.

WHITEFIELD'S absence from London extended from August, 1739, to March, 1741; during which, as we have seen, he founded his orphan-house, traversed America with varied success, and revived the revivalists of Northampton, as well as caught the spirit of Jonathan Edwards and the old puritans of New England.

On his return, he soon found occasion for all the faith and patience he had acquired in America. They were both tried to the utmost, for a time. His own account of the new and unexpected situation he found himself in, is very touching. "What a trying scene appeared here! In my zeal, during my journey through America, I had written two well-meant, though ill-judged, letters, against England's two great favourites, ' The whole Duty of Man,' and Archbishop Tillotson, who, I said, knew no more about religion than Mahomet. The Moravians had made inroads on our societies. Mr. John Wesley, some way or other, had been prevailed on to preach and print in favour of perfection and universal redemption; and against election, a doctrine which, I then thought, and do now believe, was taught me of God; and therefore could not possibly recede from.

"Thinking it my duty so to do, I had written an answer at the orphan-house, which, though revised and much approved by some good divines, had I think some too strong expressions about absolute reprobation, which the apostle leaves rather to be inferred than expressed. The world was angry at me for the former, and numbers of my own spiritual children for the latter."

" One that got some hundreds of pounds by my sermons, refused to print for me any more.   And others wrote to me, that
God would destroy me in a fortnight, and that my fall was as
great as Peter's.   Instead of having thousands to attend me,
scarce one of my spiritual children came to see me from morning to night.   Once on Kennington Common I had not above
a hundred to hear me.

" At the same time, I was much embarrassed in my outward
circumstances.   A thousand pounds I owed for the orphan-
house.   Two hundred and fifty pounds bills drawn on Mr.
Seward, were returned upon me.   I was also threatened to be
arrested for two hundred pounds more.   My travelling expenses
also to be defrayed.   A family of a hundred to be daily maintained, four thousand miles off, in the dearest place of the king's
dominions.

" Ten thousand times would I rather have died than part
with my old friends.   It would have melted any heart, to have
heard Mr. Charles Wesley and me weeping, after prayer, that,
if possible, the breach might be prevented.   Once, but no
more, I preached in the FOUNDERY, a place which Mr. John
Wesley had procured in my absence.   All my work was to *begin*
again.

" Never had I preached in Moorfields on a week day: but
in the strength of God, I began on Good Friday, and continued
twice a day, walking backward and forward from Leadenhall,
for some time preaching under one of the trees ; and had the
mortification to see numbers of my spiritual children, who but
a twelvemonth ago would have plucked out their eyes for me,
running by me whilst preaching, disdaining so much as to look
at me ; and some of them putting their fingers in their ears,
that they might not hear one word I said.

" A like scene opened at Bristol, where I was denied preaching in the house I had founded.

" Busybodies on both sides blew up the coals.   A breach
ensued.   But as both sides differed in judgment, not in affection, and aimed at the glory of our common Lord, (though we
hearkened too much to tale-bearers on both sides,) we were kept
from anathematizing each other, and went on in our usual way ;

being agreed in one point, endeavouring to convert souls to the ever-blessed Mediator."

Gillies records all this without comment or explanation. Watson, in his " Life of Wesley," sums up the whole history of the breach in a single paragraph. Southey explains the real grounds of the rupture, but with equal contempt for Wesley's doctrine of perfection, and for Whitefield's doctrine of election. The separation of Whitefield and Wesley led, however, to results too momentous to be thus treated. Whilst, therefore, I have no inclination to revive controversies, which time has laid asleep, nor to perpetuate painful recollections of good men, I must register *instructive* facts, however offensive they may be to the adherents of Calvinistic or Wesleyan methodism. The breach between their founders may well teach a solemn lesson to both.

Neither Whitefield nor Wesley appears to have understood Calvinism, when they began to preach, the one for and the other against it. Indeed, Whitefield assured Wesley, when they began to differ, that he had never read a page of Calvin ; and if Wesley read him through the same spectacles he wore when reading the works of Calvinists,—of whom he wrote thus to Whitefield, " No baptist or presbyterian writer, I have read, knew any thing of the liberties of Christ,"—his knowledge of the question may well be doubted. Whitefield's retort on this occasion, although sharp, was not uncourteous : " What ! neither Bunyan, Henry, Flavel, Halyburton, nor any of the New England and Scots divines, (know any thing of the liberties of Christ ?) See, dear Sir, what narrow-spiritedness and want of charity arise out of your principles ; and then do not cry out against election any more, on account of its being destructive of meekness and love." *Answer to Wesley's Sermon on Free Grace.*

The sermon which led to this controversy, had a curious origin. The Wesleys had threatened (perhaps playfully at first) to " drive John Calvin out of Bristol." This led some one to charge Wesley, in a letter, with not preaching the gospel—because he did not preach up election ; a charge which, at the time, was equally applicable to Whitefield : for although his

creed was somewhat Calvinistic from the first, he did not
preach up election, until Wesley began to preach it down. This
is no conjecture. He appeals to Wesley himself thus,—"For
Christ's sake, if possible, dear Sir, never speak against election
in your sermons; no one can say—that I *ever* mentioned it in
public discourses, whatever my private sentiments may be.
For Christ's sake, let us not be divided amongst ourselves.
Nothing will so much prevent a division, as your being silent
on *that* head."

Wesley met this solemn adjuration, and many like it, by the
mock solemnity of "drawing lots," to determine the question
of silence or assault. The *lot* was, "preach and print;" and
he did both forthwith. He did not publish, however, until
Whitefield had gone to America. So far he yielded to his
friend's remonstrances, contenting himself, for a time, with calling election a "doctrine of devils."

This sortilege was practised at Bristol; and it reminded
Whitefield of "the wrong lot," which Wesley had formerly
drawn, when their vessels were in sight in the Channel. Accordingly, in answering the lot-sermon, Whitefield told the
story of the lot-letter. He has been much blamed for publishing this private transaction. Indeed, he blames himself heavily.
It was done with compunction at the time; and afterwards, he
thus deplored it: "My mentioning Mr. Wesley's casting a lot
on a private occasion, known only to God and ourselves, has
put me to great pain. It was wrong in me to publish a private
transaction to the world; and very ill-judged to think the glory
of God could be promoted by exposing my friend unnecessarily.
For this I have asked both God and him pardon, years ago.
And though I believe both have forgiven me, yet I believe I
shall never be able to forgive myself. As it was a public fault,
I think it should be publicly acknowledged; and I thank a kind
Providence for giving me this opportunity of doing it." *Answer
to Lavington*. Dr. Southey says truly, that this manner of referring to the subject does Whitefield "honour." I feel this:
and yet, unless Wesley's feelings were very much *wounded* by
the disclosure, I do not see the necessity of so much self-condemnation and self-abasement. For my own part, at least, I

should have preferred either *more*, or *less*, confession on the occasion. Whitefield played at sortilege as well as Wesley, although in another way. His Letter was not like the sermon, written in obedience to a *drawn* lot; but still, it was determined by a *mystic* reason. He says, "I am apt to think one reason why God should so suffer you to be deceived was, that hereby a *special* obligation should be laid on me, faithfully to declare the Scriptural doctrine of election." What is this, but impulse *versus* lot? For, at the time, Whitefield was incapable of declaring that doctrine faithfully, if he mean by faithfully, Scripturally. This he proved, by declaring in his Letter, that "without doubt, the doctrine of election and reprobation must stand or fall together:" a fallacy he soon saw through. A lot to preach against election could not be a greater fallacy, than a "special" call to contend for reprobation. Well might Wesley, if he had understood the sovereignty of grace, have retorted on Whitefield: he contented himself, however, with tearing the Letter before his congregation. "'I will just do what I believe Mr. Whitefield would, were he here himself:' he tore it in pieces. Every person present followed his example." *Southey's Wesley.*

Who else believes—that Whitefield would have thus torn his own Letter? None but those who believe that Wesley would have torn his "lot," when he drew it. Whitefield might, indeed, have torn the printed copy, because it was printed without his consent, and published in his absence, by officious friends; but, in the sense of retracting it, he would no more have torn it than he would have torn the Thirty-nine Articles. It was a pitiful pretence, although a dexterous shift, to say that he would have been his own executioner. He was quite capable of tearing Wesley's "lot," had that been surreptitiously thrust upon his friends, to bias their judgment; for he was as *off-hand* as he was warm and honest, whenever he deemed the honour of God at stake.

It is because I never heard that Wesley humbled himself at all for this summary and insulting treatment of the Letter, that I think Whitefield too humble for his treatment of the lot. I think with Dr. Southey, that it "does him honour;" but as

Wesley was evidently more mortified than hurt by the disclosure, and as he amply retaliated, I do not see where the *dishonour* would have been, had the humiliation been less. Whitefield had not published the Letter, nor was he aware of its publication. Dr. Southey is quite correct in saying, that, although it was certainly intended for publication, yet "there seems to have been a hope in Whitefield's mind, that the effect which its perusal would produce might render publication needless." Thus Wesley might have taken the *sting* out of it, by humbling himself for drawing lots ; but as he did not tear his lot along with the Letter, it was not very unfair to let the world know something of the *secret* of his attack on Calvinism. Indeed, I doubt if it would have been honest to the public, or fair to the cause of truth, to have concealed this process of sortilege altogether. I do not even see how Whitefield could have dealt so gently with Wesley, as by simply stating the facts. He could not forget, in answering the sermon, that the author of it believed himself *divinely* warranted to publish it. That supposed warrant had to be invalidated. By what? If not by facts, who does not see that *arguments* would have implied heavier reflections upon Wesley's judgment, and subjected him to the suspicion of a presumption worse than that of the old lottery?

This transaction was made so much of at the time, that I could not, as an historian, hush it up ; nor, as an umpire, treat it as Whitefield has done. It roused, as may be supposed, the partisans of the two creeds ; and created that alienation which Whitefield has so feelingly described, in his account of the reception he met with on his return from America.

Some of the Calvinistic party were very imprudent. Acourt, of London, thrust himself and his high Calvinism upon the Wesleys' meetings ; demanding the opportunity of setting them right on the subject of election; and prophesying, when refused, that his proclamation of them as false prophets, would throw them all into confusion. At Kingswood also, Cennick divided the society, and headed the Calvinists against the Wesleys. Dr. Southey calls him "a certain John Cennick," "who had great talents for popular speaking ;" and gives only Charles

Wesley's picture of him. Cennick was both a wiser and a better man than the Wesleys painted him, when he withstood them to the face at Kingswood. Until then, John Wesley held him a friend, as his "own soul," and one who "lay in his bosom." Charles Wesley confirms this by an appeal to Cennick's knowledge of it: "I need not say how well he loved you." It was not because this love was too hot, that it did not last. Charles upbraided him for ingratitude and treachery, and John excommunicated him, with others, for lying and slandering, thus:—"I, John Wesley, by the consent and approbation of the Band Society in Kingswood, do declare the persons above mentioned to be no longer members thereof. Neither will they be so accounted until they shall openly confess their fault," &c. &c. What was this tremendous fault? "Dissembling, lying, and slandering," says the excommunicator. "Ingratitude and treachery," says his brother. Heavy charges, it must be allowed; and, if true, well deserving all the chastisement they met with.

The truth of the charges, as they affect Cennick, the friend and fellow-labourer of Whitefield, must be examined. Happily, this is easily done; for Wesley rested the proof of "private accusations" upon the copy of a letter from Cennick to Whitefield. When Cennick denied that he had "ever privately accused him," Wesley produced the letter in the society, and said, "Judge, brethren!" So say I. Here is the letter.—"I sit solitary like Eli, waiting what will become of the ark: and while I wail and fear the carrying of it away from among my people, my trouble increases daily. How glorious did the gospel seem once to flourish at Kingswood! I spake of the everlasting love of Christ with sweet power. But now, brother Charles is suffered to open his mouth against this truth, while the frighted sheep gaze and fly, as if no shepherd was amongst them. It is just as if Satan was now making war on the saints, in a more than common way. O, pray for the distressed lambs yet left in this place, that they faint not. Surely they would, for they have nothing whereon to rest but their own faithfulness, who now attend on sermons. With universal redemption, brother Charles now pleases the world. Brother

John follows him in every thing. I believe no atheist can more
preach against predestination than they : and all who believe
election are counted enemies to God, and called so. Fly, dear
brother !—I am as alone.—I am in the midst of the plague.
If God give thee leave—make haste ! "

Now, where is the lie, or the slander, in all this ?   No where,
except it be in the charge, that " all who believe election are
counted enemies to God, and called so."   And even this charge,
although not literally, is substantially, true.   For although neither John nor Charles would have called any good man, who let
them alone, an enemy of God, for believing election, both would
and must have counted the very best man such, so far as he
tried to spread the doctrine of election at the Foundery, or at
Kingswood. How could they reckon otherwise, whilst they
held themselves to be the *friends* of God, by enmity to Calvinism?
Their forbearance with the *silent* Calvinists in the society, was
because they were silent.

I am no admirer of Cennick's letter. I think the style and
spirit of it quite as bad as Wesley's sermon ; which affirms, that
the doctrine in question " directly tends to destroy that holiness
which is the end of all the ordinances of God ;" and has " a
direct and manifest tendency to overthrow the whole christian
religion."   The only difference between this railing and that of
Cennick, is, that Cennick's is applied to two men by name, and
Wesley's is an attack upon all men who preached the doctrine.

This is not, however, the whole case.   The chief charge
against Cennick is, that he " supplanted " Wesley " in his own
house ; stealing the hearts of the people " from him.   This asserted betrayal of trust, Charles depicted in the darkest colours.
Now it is true, that Wesley placed Cennick as one of the masters in the Kingswood school ; and true, that the school was
Wesley's " own house," in the sense of its being chiefly built
and furnished by him. On the other hand, it is equally true,
that Whitefield originated the school ; obtained the gift of " a
piece of ground for it ;" laid the foundation-stone of it ; and collected so much money for it, that " the roof was ready to be
put up " before he left England. However truly, therefore, in
a legal sense, it was Wesley's " own house," inasmuch as he

alone was responsible for all the debt upon it, and thus the possessor of the deeds; it was morally Whitefield's own house too. Accordingly, Wesley bequeathed it to his brother and Whitefield by will, the moment the responsibility devolved the property on him.

Cennick was not ignorant of these facts, and ought not to have been uninfluenced by them. He was, indeed, Wesley's servant; but he was also a conscientious Calvinist. "Why, then, did he not resign," says Charles, "rather than gainsay" his employer? Why, I ask, did his employer undertake the completion of Whitefield's school, and then turn it into an Arminian nursery, in Whitefield's absence? The servant did all he could to sustain the views of its founder, in the absence of its finisher; and the finisher did all he could to supplant the Calvinistic views of its absent founder. Whitefield never would have left it to Wesley to carry forward, had this design been avowed. Cennick knew this; and therefore he was just as conscientious in opposing Arminianism in the place, as Wesley in opposing Calvinism in it. In a word, if the one alienated some hearts from Wesley, the other alienated *many* hearts from Whitefield. " I was denied preaching in the house I had founded at Bristol," says Whitefield.

These are, indeed, pitiful transactions on both sides : but they were the transactions which brought on the rupture of the societies; and are thus essential to its explanation. Cennick also, as the chosen coadjutor of Whitefield afterwards, deserved vindication from the bitter invectives and aspersions of Charles Wesley's letter, and from the ecclesiastical *ban* of John Wesley and the " Band Society in Kingswood." On reviewing his character and career, the late Mr. Wilks, of the Tabernacle, exclaimed, " O my soul, come thou into his secret; into his assembly, mine honour, be thou united!" He says of Cennick, " As to success in his labours, perhaps there was not one in his day, except Whitefield, more highly honoured in this particular. His language was not with the enticing words of men's wisdom; yet his doctrine and address were powerful, and found access to the hearts of thousands. His career was short; but if life may be estimated by the comparative quantity of good produced in it, then this truly active, spiritual, and useful man, may be said to have lived to a good old age. A good understanding, an open temper, and tender heart, characterized the man. His christian qualities were not less distinguishable. If unaffected humility, deadness to the world, a life of communion with God, and a cheerful reliance on a crucified Saviour, constitute the real christian,—he was one in an eminent degree. He possessed a sweet simplicity of spirit, with an ardent zeal in the cause of his divine Master." *Preface to Cennick's Sermons, 2 vols. by Matthew Wilks.*

Cennick's own account of his expulsion by the Wesleys, is highly creditable to his heart; and as it palliates very much the conduct of Mr. Wesley, and is not much known, (the pamphlet being rare,) I gladly insert it. It is the 44th Section of a Life of Cennick, written by himself, 4th Edition. " About Christmas, 1740, a difference in doctrine broke out between the Mr. Wesleys and me; they believed and taught many things which I thought not according to the gospel, neither to mine own experience : and in a very little time, while I was preaching in several parts of Wiltshire, Mr. John Wesley took the entire possession of Kingswood school, and I was forbid to preach there any more ; neither from that time did I. And not long after, when I and some of the colliers had met apart to consider on these things, and to lay them before the Lord, the rest of the society, who held Mr. Wesley's doctrines, were so offended— that they would not let Mr. Wesley *rest*, till he put me, and those few who believed my word, out of the society ;—though, I believe, *against* his will. When we separated, we were in number twelve men and twelve women. In a short time, we so increased our company, that we were about a hundred and twenty. In many villages of Wiltshire, the word was received gladly." To them " the differences were never once known, till Mr. Whitefield came from America, and joined the brethren with me ; neither after they knew it, (the difference,) did it make any stir, as it were, in all that country."

The breach between Whitefield and Wesley led, soon, to the erection of a new house at Kingswood, and of " a large temporary shed," called a Tabernacle, in London. The latter was built by " certain *free-grace* dissenters," as Gillies calls them. This phrase does not enable us to identify them with any of the three denominations. Perhaps it refers to Whitefield's definition of " free grace indeed," in his Letter to Wesley :— " free, because not free to *all;* but free, because God may withhold or give it to whom, and when, he pleases." But whoever the dissenters thus characterized were, their timely help soon enabled him to turn the tide, which had set in against him. It realized for him, what had much refreshed him, when all his work was to " begin again,"—Beza's hint in the life of Calvin ; " Calvin is turned out of Geneva ; but, behold, a new church arises ! " Dr. Gillies says, " A fresh awakening immediately began. Congregations grew exceedingly large : and, at the *people's* desire, he sent for Messrs. Cennick, Harris, Seagrave, Humphries, &c. to assist." In the country also, and especially in Essex, (first at Braintree,) the old scene of " multitudes, multitudes in the valley of decision," began to be renewed. And it was with no ordinary pleasure he then visited the many towns in Essex and Suffolk, such as Dedham, Halstead, Ipswich, &c., from which the pilgrim fathers of New England came ; and the counterparts of which he had found in America, perpetuating there the names and recollections of the mother country.

I know of few studies so fraught and fragrant with delight, now that we know New England, as tracing in Mather's " Magnalia," upon his old maps, the first American *edition* of Old England. I shall never forget how sacred I felt that line of English towns to be, when I visited them, as the antitypes of the Magnalian maps ; nor the interest taken by the old families of the district, whilst I pointed out to them the coincidences, and congratulated them on the connexion. I myself, indeed, would not pass over Runnymede, to visit the cradles of the pilgrim fathers ; but no American christian ought to visit Runnymede, until he has been at Dedham, if he love his country.

Whitefield's momentary reverses in London did not, as may be supposed, at all lessen his fame in Scotland, nor prevent the Erskines from urging upon him his promise to visit that country. There, the Wesleys were considered as sadly " left to themselves," (E. Erskine,) if not as somewhat *demented,* when they quarrelled with Whitefield's Calvinism, and avowed themselves Arminians. There was also more than enough in Scotland then, of an Arminianism not redeemed, like that of the Wesleys, by holy zeal or sterling piety, to render an eloquent Calvinist a welcome visitor to the godly ministers of both the kirk and the secession. Had Whitefield, therefore, wanted other letters of commendation to them, than his own character and fame; or needed any thing to confirm the confidence he had won by his own letters and journals; his rejection at the Foundery would have secured him a welcome both at Dunfermline and in Edinburgh.

This he found on his arrival: but, lest his old and still dear friend, Wesley, should suspect him of accepting any honour at *his* expense, he renewed his correspondence with him, when his honours in Scotland were at their height. The following letter from Aberdeen is delightful: " Reverend and dear brother, I have for a long time expected that you would have sent an answer to my last; but I suppose you are afraid to correspond with me, because I revealed your secret about the lot. Though much might be said *for* my doing it, yet I am sorry now, that any such thing dropped from my pen,—*and I humbly ask pardon.* I find I love you as much as ever; and pray God, if it be his blessed will, that we may all be united together.

" It hath been for some days upon my *heart* to write to you. May God remove all obstacles that now prevent our union! Though I hold particular election—yet I offer Jesus freely to every individual soul. You may carry sanctification to whatever degrees you will; only I cannot agree, that the in-being of sin is to be destroyed in this life.

" O my dear brother, the Lord has been much with me in Scotland, In about three weeks I hope to be at Bristol. May all disputings cease, and each of us talk of nothing but Jesus, and Him crucified! *This is my resolution.* The Lord be with your spirit. I am, without dissimulation, ever yours." *Lett.* 363.

The only letter of Wesley's on this subject, that I know of, is not like the above. It concludes thus : " The general tenor both of my public and private exhortations, when I touch thereon at all, as even my enemies know, if they would testify, is,—

'Spare the young man, even Absalom, for my sake.'" *Southey's Wesley.* This is David's language, but not David's spirit. It is sarcasm, more than sympathy; as the whole strain of the letter shows. Dr. Southey justly says, " Wesley felt more resentment than he here thought proper to express." *Ibid.* Whitefield had, however, been as *dictatorial* in some of his remonstrances, at the beginning of the controversy, as Wesley was sarcastic at the close. On one occasion he wrote thus : " Dear brother Wesley, what mean you by disputing in all your letters ? May God give you to know yourself,—and then you will not plead for absolute perfection, nor call election a doctrine of devils. My dear brother, take heed ! See that you are in Christ a new creature. Beware of a false peace. Remember you are but a *babe* in Christ—if so much. Be humble. Talk little. Pray much. If you will dispute, stay till you are master of the subject; otherwise you will hurt the cause you would defend." Whatever truth there may be in this tirade, it is more than defeated by its unhallowed form. Such an appeal could only exasperate. Not, however, in this style generally, did Whitefield appeal to his brother and friend. It was more usual with him to write thus : " Why will you dispute ? I am willing to go with you to prison and death ;—but I am not willing to oppose you." " Do not oblige me to preach against you : I had rather die." " Dear, dear Sir, O be not offended ! For Christ's sake be not rash. Give yourself to reading. Study the covenant of grace. Down with your carnal reasoning. Be a little child ; and then, instead of *pawning* your salvation, as you have done, in a late Hymn Book, if the doctrine of universal redemption be not true, you will compose a hymn in praise of sovereign, distinguishing love.

" I love and honour you for Christ's sake ; and when I come to judgment—will thank you before men and angels for what you have, under God, done for my soul. There, I am persuaded, I shall see dear Mr. Wesley convinced of election and everlasting love. And it often fills me with pleasure, to think how I shall behold you casting your crown at the feet of the Lamb— and, as it were, filled with a holy blushing for opposing the divine sovereignty as you have done. But I hope the Lord will show you this, before you go hence. Oh how do I long for that day ! ". (It is somewhat amusing to find this passage, the first one quoted by Dr. Southey, just after his declaration, that Whitefield's " written compositions are nearly worthless.")

Having given these specimens of the spirit of both parties in this breach, it is only bare justice to Whitefield, to state strongly the trying circumstances he was in, when Wesley *cut* with him. Southey truly and tenderly says, " Many things combined to sour him at this time." Seward, on whose life and fortune he had calculated for the sake of Georgia, was just dead, and had left him nothing. He was deeply in debt for the orphan-house, and more deeply pledged. He was in danger of being arrested every day for £450, whilst he had not twenty pounds in the world, and hardly a friend to help him. He was all but hissed by the multitude, who formerly were almost ready to cry, " Hosanna," when they saw him in the streets. His heart was *torn* by the pressure of strife at home, and by the prospect of distress abroad.

Is it any wonder that he should have been betrayed into hasty, and even some harsh, reflections upon Wesley ? Could he think well of the doctrine of " *perfection*," whilst its champion and adherents were so *imperfect*, as to leave him to sink or swim, as it might happen ? True ; he had given his old friend great pro-vocation, by turning the laugh against his lottery ; and all men resent an exposure of their weakness, more than an injury to their property : but still, Wesley could have afforded to wait, whilst Whitefield was in danger of imprisonment for debt, and well nigh overwhelmed with disappointments. This was just the time for a perfectionist to " heap coals of fire " upon the head of an enemy ; and to *pawn* something upon the truth of universal love, as well as his " salvation upon the truth of uni-versal redemption." Whitefield would have pawned the FOUN-DERY, had it been his, to save and soothe Wesley, had he come from America, embarrassed and bowed down with care. Who does not see and feel this ?

It is painful, but it is very necessary, to place the matter in this light ; for if the faults of such men are hushed up, such faults will be repeated and perpetuated by men who have fewer redeeming qualities. Future quarrels are not to be prevented by forgetting the past. It is by seeing how *unseemly* strife between great brethren is, that little brethren learn to dread its beginnings. He is throwing back the progress of brotherly love in the church, who would bury in oblivion, or veil in vague generalities, the " sharp contention " between Whitefield and Wesley. Like Paul and Barnabas, they can afford to have it all told, without sustaining any material loss of fame or influence. They are just the men whose faults should be transmitted to posterity, that posterity may not glory in men, nor think more highly of them than they ought to think; and that similar men, of like passions, may not run into like extremes. He is not, therefore, the best friend of " peace on earth," whatever be his love for Whitefield or Wesley, who would throw a veil over the rashness of the former, or over the selfishness of the latter, on this occasion.

Whitefield was rash. He listened to tale-bearers, who put the worst construction upon Wesley's hard words against Calvinism, and harsh treatment of the Kingswood Calvinists. He rashly promised not to preach against him, and as rashly threatened to oppose him every where. He wept with Charles, and scolded John. In a word, they were, as he says, only " kept from anathematizing each other," for a time ; so divided were they in judgment, although not exactly alienated in affection.

This is, indeed, a humiliating exhibition : but how full of warning it is ! The oracle, " ye are brethren," which had so often fallen upon their ear and their heart, like music from heaven, fell unheeded on both for a time, although both were absorbed with equal zeal for the glory of God and the salvation of souls. But whilst the *spirit* of their breach was thus deplorable, it is impossible to deplore the breach itself. It fell out to " the furtherance of the gospel." Wesley *foresaw* this, as well as prayed for it : " The case is quite plain. There are bigots both for and against predestination. God is sending a message to those on *either* side : but neither will receive it, unless from one who is of their *own* opinion. Therefore, for a time, you are suffered to be of one opinion, and I of another." Whitefield's *heart* responded to this, although his acuteness did not discern it so fully : " The great day will discover, why the Lord per-

P

mits dear Mr. Wesley and me to be of a different way of thinking.   At present, I shall make no inquiry into that matter, beyond the account he has given of it.   I heartily pray God to
hasten the time, when we shall be closely united in principle
and judgment, as well as in heart and affection : and then,
should the Lord call to it,—I care not if I go with him to prison
or to death.   For, like Paul and Silas, I hope we shall sing
praises to God, and count it our highest honour to suffer for
Christ's sake, and to lay down our lives for the brethren."
Preface to " A Letter to Wesley."

An earlier day than " the great day" discovered why Whitefield and Wesley were permitted both to differ and divide.   It
was a happy thing for the world and the church that they were
not of one opinion : for had they been united in either extreme,
truth would have made less progress.   As joint Arminians, they
would have spread Pelagianism ; and as joint Calvinists, they
would have been *hyper,* though not antinomian.   It was well,
therefore, that they modified each other : for they were "two
suns," which could not have fixed in

" one meridian,"

without setting on fire the whole course of sound theology.   In
their respective spheres, however, they were equally blessed,
notwithstanding the difference of their creeds on some points.
This is not inexplicable, when it is remembered that they agreed
thoroughly in exalting the Saviour, and in honouring the Eternal Spirit.   And their *mode* of honouring the Spirit deserves
particular attention.   They sought and cherished His *unction*
for themselves, as well as enforced the necessity of His operations upon others.   And until preaching be, itself, a " *demonstration* of the Spirit and of power," as well as in humble dependence upon the Spirit, its effects will not be very great, nor
remarkably good.   It will win but few souls to Christ, and even
their character will not, in general, rise high in the beauty of
holiness, nor in the zeal of love.   They may just keep their name
and their place in the church of the living God ; but they will
not be to Him, nor to his church, " for a name and an everlasting sign."

There is much more connexion between the piety of a church, and the spirituality of its minister, than appears at first sight; and between his preaching, and the conversion of sinners, than is usually kept in view. A minister not spiritually-minded, both " quenches the Spirit " on the altar of renewed hearts, and prevents the sacred fire from reaching the altar of unregenerated hearts. He who is not " a sweet savour of Christ," *makes himself* " a savour of death unto death," inevitably :—of the second death to the undecided; and of spiritual deadness to the church.

It was not in this sense, that Paul was a savour of both life and death, during his ministry. The lost *made* him, what he became to them; by turning into death the very truth which quickened the saved: for it was the same fragrance of " the knowledge of Christ," which proved the savour of death unto death to the former, that proved the savour of life unto life to the latter. Paul did as much, and said as much, and prayed as much, and all in the same spirit too, for the impenitent, as for the considerate ; for despisers, as for penitents. Both saw and heard in his preaching, the *same* " demonstration of the Spirit and of power." He stood before each class, equally the ambassador of Christ, and beseeching both alike to be reconciled unto God. So did Baxter, Edwards, Whitefield, and the Wesleys. Whenever they were the savour of death unto death, they were *made* so by those who perished under their ministry. Such men might, therefore, without presumption or imprudence, apply to themselves the apostolic maxim, " We are unto God—a sweet savour of Christ, in them that are saved, and in them that perish." Such ministers would not, indeed, say this without adding, " Who is sufficient for these things ?" nor without weeping whilst they said, " to the other we are a savour of death unto death;" but they could not blame themselves with the blood of souls. It was not their fault, that any were lost, who heard them ; for they extended the golden sceptre of mercy as freely, and frequently, and fervently, to the heedless and the hardened, as to the thoughtful or the timid.

This is a very different case from that of a minister, who preaches the gospel without the demonstration of the Spirit, or power. He makes himself the savour of death unto death to

others, even when he teaches " the knowledge of Christ ;" because he breathes not the fragrance of that knowledge. He,
therefore, has no right to throw himself upon the apostolic
maxim, when his ministry is unsuccessful. It is unsuccessful,
because it is *unsavoury*. It brings no sinners to life, because it
is lifeless : for it is the " *savour* " of the knowledge of Christ,
that God " maketh manifest in every place," 2 Cor. ii. 14;
and that savour cannot breathe from the lips or looks of a
minister, unless his heart *burn* with love to Christ and immortal souls.

It is high time that the church of Christ should consider, not
only the duty of depending on the Spirit, but also the import
and the importance of the " demonstration of the Spirit," in
preaching. That is more—than the demonstration of orthodoxy.
It is more than the demonstration of either sound scholarship or
hard study. It is even more than the demonstration of mere
sincerity and fidelity. Sincerity may be cold, and fidelity harsh.
Even zeal may be party rivalship, or personal vanity; whilst
it seems holy fire searching only for incense to the glory of
God and the Lamb. To preach in demonstration of the Spirit,
is even more than bringing out " the mind of the Spirit," faithfully and fully. The real meaning of His oracles may be honestly
given, and yet their true spirit neither caught nor conveyed.
" What the Spirit saith unto the churches," may be repeated to
the churches without evasion or faltering; but it will not be
heard as His counsel or consolation, unless it is spoken with
something of his own love and solemnity. He is the Spirit of
power, and of grace, and of love, as well as the Spirit of truth
and wisdom; and therefore He is but half copied in preaching, when only his *meaning* is given. That meaning lies in His
mind, not merely as truth, nor as law, nor as wisdom, but also
as sympathy, solicitude, and love for the souls it is addressed
unto. The words of the Spirit are spirit and life; and therefore the *soul*, as well as the substance, of their meaning is essential to faithful preaching. They can hardly be said to be the
words of the Holy Ghost, when they are uttered in a spiritless
or lifeless mood.

This will be more obvious by looking at " the truth, as it is in Jesus." In Him it is *grace* as well as truth. All his heart, and soul, and strength, breathes and burns in his words. His *motives* are part of his meaning. He explains the great salvation, that he may endear and enforce its claims at the same time. He makes us feel, that he feels more for our souls than words can express. He compels us to see a beaming of earnestness in his eye, and to hear a beating of intense solicitude in his heart, and to recognise a fixedness of purpose in all his manner, unspeakably beyond all he says. The real pleading of the Saviour with sinners begins where his words end. His *weeping silence*, after speaking as never man spake, tells more of his love to souls than all his gracious words. We feel that he feels he has gained nothing by his preaching, unless he has won souls. He leaves upon every mind the conviction, that nothing can please him but the *heart;* and that nothing would please him so much as giving him the heart. No man ever rose, or can rise, from reading the entreaties of Christ, without feeling that Christ is in earnest—is intent—is absorbed, to seek and save the lost.

The apostles evidently marked this with great attention, and copied it with much success, when they became ambassadors *"for* Christ," by the ministry of reconciliation. Then, they did more than deliver the truth He taught. They tried to utter it with His solemnity, tenderness, and unction. They tried to put themselves in " Christ's stead," when Christ was no longer on earth to beseech men to be reconciled unto God. This was " the demonstration of the Spirit ! " Saying what Christ did, was not enough for them: they laboured to say it *as* he did ; or in the spirit, and for the purpose, he had preached the gospel. Thus the truth was in them as it was " in Jesus ;" not merely as true, but also as impressive, persuasive, and absorbing. They spoke the truth, as he had done, " in the love of it," and with love to the souls it was able to make wise unto salvation.

And this is not impossible even now, although apostolic inspiration be at an end. The best part of the Spirit's influences—*love* to the gospel and immortal souls—is yet attainable, and as easily attained as any other ministerial qualification. A minister ought to be as much ashamed, and more afraid, of being *unbaptized* with the Holy Ghost and fire, as of being ignorant of the original languages of the Holy Scriptures. Men who can demonstrate the problems of Euclid, or the import of Greek or Hebrew idioms, have no excuse if they are unable to preach with the demonstration of the Spirit and power. The same attention to the latter demonstration, which they gave to the former, would fill them with the Holy Ghost, and fire them with holy zeal.

Nothing is so *simple*, although nothing be so sublime, as preaching " the gospel with the Holy Ghost sent down from heaven." Any prayerful and thoughtful minister may preach in this spirit ; for it neither includes, nor excludes, great talents, learning, or ingenuity. " An unction from the Holy One " can subordinate the mightiest and wealthiest minds to the one grand object—watching for souls ; and it can render subservient and successful the most ordinary powers of mind. The acute reasonings of Wesley, and the warm-hearted remonstrances and beseechings of Whitefield, were equally useful, because equally demonstrations of the Spirit. In like manner, many of their uneducated colleagues " turned many to righteousness ;" and are themselves, now, turned into stars which shall shine for ever in the firmament of the church in both worlds. The *secret* of this success in winning souls was the same in both classes of preachers ;—their heart, their soul, their all, was in their work. Truth had the force of divine truth, the fire of eternal truth, and the glory of saving truth, upon their minds. Their hearts were *full* (whether holding much or little) of heavenly treasure ; and they held it as *heavenly* treasure, and poured it out as stewards who had to account for it in heaven, and to review their stewardship of it through eternity. Accordingly, both regular congregations and promiscuous mobs, whatever they thought of the office or the talents of these itinerants, felt that they were on *fire* to watch for and win souls ; and were compelled to acknowledge, that even men who had never been at the University, " had been with Jesus," and were, indeed, " moved by the Holy Ghost." Another way in which the apostles caught and kept up the demonstration of the Spirit in their preaching, was, by trying to beseech men to be reconciled unto God, just as God himself might be supposed to plead with them, were He to bow the heavens and come down as a minister of reconciliation. This was a bold attempt! Even its sublimity and benevolence cannot hide its boldness, however they may excuse it. "As though God did *beseech* you, we pray you in Christ's stead, be ye reconciled unto God." Archangels would hardly have ventured to go so far as the apostles, in thus trying to *represent* both God and the Lamb, as reconcilers. It was, however, an attempt to win souls, as wise and humble, as it was sublime or bold. There was no presumption, nor ostentation, nor pretence in it. They magnified their office, only that they might humble themselves the more deeply, and discharge its duties the more faithfully. The attempt to copy God was, also, the best way of relieving themselves from the fear of man, and their best security against all trifling, temporizing, and display in the work of God. As his representatives, there would, of course, be no airs nor affectation in their manner of preaching; no parade of novelty or learning in their matter; no taint of bitterness or harshness in their spirit. Thus, by adopting Him as their model, they were sure to preach better than any other example could have taught them; for, whilst it bound them to soberness and solemnity, it left them free to speak in thunder when the conscience was to be roused; and in metaphor when attention was to be won or relieved; and with all the forms of eloquence whenever their subject inspired

" Thoughts which breathe, or words that burn."

Yes; this divine standard, equally lofty and lovely, left them at full liberty to ransack creation for figures; time for facts; heaven for motives; hell for warnings; and eternity for arguments: binding them only to make the whole bear directly, consistently, and supremely, upon their one grand object—reconciling the world unto God by the blood of the cross: for whilst that was " all and all" as the final end of their ministry, they might warrantably and legitimately employ in the pursuit of it, every tone and term, image and emotion, in which God himself had ever appealed to the hopes or fears of man. Accordingly, there was much that was *godlike* in their preaching. They could not, of course, realize fully, nor imitate far, the manner or the spirit in which God would plead his own cause, were He to preach his own gospel : but still, their reasonings were not unlike His manifold wisdom ; nor their appeals unworthy of His paternal tenderness ; nor their remonstrances inconsistent with His judicial authority.   There was a fine demonstration° of the Spirit in the boldness of Peter, in the sublimity of Paul, and in the heavenliness of John.

It was to this beseeching as in the " stead of Christ and God," that Paul referred, when he besought the Ephesians to pray for him, " that utterance might be given him, to speak boldly " as an ambassador, though in bonds, " ought to speak." He meant more than not being silent or ashamed ; more than rising superior to circumstances and danger.   He meant also, speaking with equal demonstration of the Spirit and power, in peril as in peace ; in Rome as in Jerusalem ; before Cæsar as before the sanhedrim.

In nothing, perhaps, did Whitefield keep Paul more before him, than in this strong solicitude to " speak as he ought to speak."   No phrase occurs so often in his journals as, " preached with much power ; with some power."   He does not venture to call even his greatest efforts a " demonstration of the Spirit ;" but the word " power " occurs so uniformly, that it tells plainly what he was thinking about, after all sermons which produced a visible effect.   His enemies said he was complimenting his own sermons.   They little knew his heart, and still less the *humility* which springs from " an unction " of the Spirit !   To prevent unnecessary misunderstanding, however, he explained his meaning thus, in a note to his revised journals : " By the word power, I mean, all along, no more, nor no less, than enlargement of heart, and a comfortable frame, given me from above ; by which I was enabled to speak with freedom and clearness, and the people were impressed and affected thereby." This is only explaining—not retracting nor qualifying.   He knew, and tens of thousands felt, that God was with him of a truth, making the gospel rebound from his heart to their hearts ;

melting them by warming him ; winning their souls, by absorbing his soul with the glories of salvation.

Happily, this spirit cannot be *imitated* in preaching. It may be imbibed and breathed by any devotional and devoted minister ; but it cannot be copied. No tones, looks, nor tears, can demonstrate the presence of the Spirit in a sermon, if the preacher has not been " *in the Spirit,*" before coming to the pulpit. Neither the melting nor the kindling of men but half devoted, or but half-hearted in devotion, can melt down or wield an audience, by the gospel ; because the Holy Spirit will not honour fits and starts of fidelity. The minister must be a holy temple unto the Holy Ghost, who would have that Spirit speak to the hearts of men by him. Never does a preacher dupe himself, or endanger others, more, than when he imagines that the Spirit will give power to the gospel amongst his people, whilst it has not power upon himself. God makes ministers a blessing to others, by blessing themselves first. He works *in* them, in order to work by them.

I throw out these hints, not to ministers, but to private christians, who know what it is to pray in the Spirit, and what it is to see divine things in the light of eternity. Preaching with the Holy Ghost sent down from heaven, is just what praying in the Holy Ghost is ; not form, nor forcing, nor copying ; but the *outpouring* of a heart penetrated with the greatness of the great salvation, and absorbed with the solemn responsibilities involved in the hope of salvation. Did such hearers sustain such preachers, by prayer, and esteem, and co-operation, there would be far more demonstration of the Spirit in the evangelical pulpits of the land : and many who now content themselves with *depending* on the Holy Spirit, would be compelled to cultivate the *fellowship* of that Spirit, instead of merely complimenting his power.

CHAPTER IX.

1741.

THE state of religion in Scotland at this time will be best understood, as well as most fairly represented, by a brief view of the rise and progress of the Secession. That *second* Reformation in Scotland brought into full light and play all the good and evil of the national church. I shall, therefore, state the facts, just as they now challenge and defy investigation. I have never seen the *final* appeals of the Associate Synod invalidated; and therefore I employ their own words.

" The Secession is regarded both by its friends and its enemies as a highly important event in the history of the church of Scotland. However slight and accidental the circumstances by which it was immediately occasioned may appear, it unquestionably arose from a general state of matters in the church, naturally tending towards such a crisis. Divine Providence, whose operations are often apparently slow, but always sure and progressive, had been gradually paving the way for an open division, calculated, notwithstanding all its accompanying evils, to prevent the utter extinction of religious principle and freedom in the land, and to advance the interests of truth and piety. A torrent of corruption, which threatened the overthrow of every thing sacred in doctrine and valuable in privilege, was proceeding to so great a height, that enlightened and conscientious men were impressed with the necessity of bold and decisive steps.

" The prevalence of those erroneous tenets and oppressive

measures, which gave rise to the Secession, may be traced back to the defects attending the settlement of ecclesiastical affairs at the era of the Revolution 1688. That era was truly glorious; and in no quarter of the British empire were its blessings more necessary, or more sensibly experienced, than in Scotland. Religious as well as civil rights and liberties were then restored to a nation, which, under the tyrannical sway of Charles II. and James VII. had been most cruelly degraded and oppressed. Episcopacy was abolished; the presbyterian worship and government re-established; pastors who had been ejected from their churches in 1661, were replaced; and the law of patronage, though not absolutely annulled, was so modified, and, in consequence, so gently administered, that it was scarcely felt as a grievance.

"But while the Scottish presbyterians had much cause for gratitude and joy, they had at the same time several sources of regret. The omission of an act formally asserting Christ's sole headship over the church, and expressly condemning the royal supremacy which had been assumed under the two preceding reigns, was deeply lamented. Nor was it an inconsiderable evil, that, in compliance with the wishes of the court, about three hundred of the prelatical incumbents, some of whom had even been active agents in the work of persecution, were, ' upon easy terms,' permitted to retain their stations in the parishes of Scotland, and to sit in the ecclesiastical courts. Attached, in many instances, to unscriptural doctrines, no less than to episcopalian forms of worship and discipline, these men could not fail to obstruct the efforts of those faithful ministers who attempted to promote the cause of evangelical truth and practical religion. Among those ministers themselves, there were comparatively few who displayed all that magnanimity and zeal which the interests of the Redeemer's kingdom required; and the exercise of which, on that momentous occasion, might have proved incalculably advantageous to vital christianity in their own days, and in succeeding ages. Owing to the pusillanimity of some clergymen, and the waywardness of others, lamentable symptoms of degeneracy in principle and practice were discernible within a short period after the happy Revolution. The worthy Halyburton accordingly, amid the triumphant expressions of christian faith and hope, which he uttered on his death-bed, in 1712, deplored in the strongest terms 'the growing apostasy' of the times, and, in particular, that indifference to the peculiarities of the gospel and to the power of godliness, which prevailed among a great proportion of the clergy. He exclaimed, for example, ' Oh that the ministry of Scotland may be kept from destroying the church of Scotland. Oh that I could obtain it of them with tears of blood, to be concerned for the church! Shall we be drawn away from the precious gospel, and from Christ.' *Fraser's Erskines.*

" The Secession did not originate in any dissatisfaction with the professed principles of the church of Scotland, which seceders venerate as a precious summary of divine truths— the most valuable inheritance they have received from their fathers—and which they are anxious to transmit in purity to their children. But for some time before they were expelled from the communion of the national church, a tide of defection had been flowing in from the prevailing party in her judicatories, which, while it spared the erroneous in doctrine, and the irregular in conduct, bore down the christian people contending for their religious privileges, and those ministers who testified faithfully against ecclesiastical misconduct.

" A professor of divinity, in one of the Universities, taught that the souls of children are as pure and holy as the soul of Adam was in his original condition, being inferior to him only as he was formed in a state of maturity; and that the light of nature, including tradition, is sufficient to teach men the way of salvation. For these doctrines, subversive of the first principles of christianity, a process was instituted against him, in which it was clearly proved that he was chargeable with teaching publicly these and other errors. But so far from being subjected to the censure he deserved, he was permitted to retain his place in the University and the church; and the General Assembly were satisfied with declaring that some of his opinions were not evidently founded on the word of God, nor necessary to be taught in divinity, and prohibiting him from publishing such sentiments in future.

" The ' Marrow of Modern Divinity' teaches, ' that God in the gospel makes a gift of the Saviour to mankind as sinners, warranting every one who hears the gospel to believe in him for salvation ; that believers are entirely freed from the law as a covenant of works ; that good works are not to be performed by believers that they may obtain salvation by them.' In the unqualified condemnation of these principles, the General Assembly materially condemned some of the most important doctrines of the gospel, such as the unlimited extent of the gospel call, and the free grace of God in the salvation of sinners.

" For a short time after the revival of the law of patronage, in 1712, such as received presentations were backward to accept of them, and the church courts were unwilling to proceed to their settlement, where opposition was made by the people of the vacant charge. But presentees and judicatories became gradually less scrupulous, and several settlements afterwards took place in reclaiming congregations, which gave plain evidence that the rights of the members of the church would be no longer regarded. The little influence which might occasionally be left to the people in the choice of their ministers, was destroyed by an act of the General Assembly, passed immediately before the commencement of the Secession. This act, providing that where patrons might neglect, or decline to exercise, their rights, the minister should be chosen by a majority of the elders and heritors, if protestant, was unconstitutionally passed by the Assembly, as a great majority of the presbyteries, who gave their opinions upon the subject, were decidedly hostile to the measure.

" Many pious and faithful ministers were grieved by these defections ; but being deprived, by the prevailing party in the Assembly, of the liberty of marking their disapprobation in the minutes of the court, no method of maintaining a good conscience remained, except testifying against defection, in their public ministrations. This method was adopted ; and for a public condemnation of these corruptions by the Rev. Ebenezer Erskine, 1732, a process was instituted against him, which terminated, 1733, in first suspending him and three of his brethren, the Rev. Messrs. William Wilson, Alexander Moncrieff, and

James Fisher, who had joined him, from the exercise of the ministerial office, and afterwards, 1740, dissolving their relation to their congregations and the national church." *Dr. Waugh's Life.*

" The valuable order of husbandmen, who constituted a very considerable portion " of the Secession, " were, at this period, of the third generation in descent from the covenanters, who lived towards the latter end of the seventeenth century ; to whom their country owes a deep debt of gratitude, for their pious zeal, their patient sufferings, and their severe, long-protracted, and ultimately successful struggle with a despotic and persecuting government. Like their ancestors, whose memory for the most part they warmly cherished and venerated, besides being zealous presbyterians, they were distinguished by frugal habits, simple manners, and an ardent regard for evangelical doctrines. In addition to a regular and exemplary attendance on the public ordinances of divine worship, they faithfully performed the exercises of devotion in their families, and laboured, with patriarchal diligence, to instil into the minds of their children and domestics the principles of sound doctrine and a holy life. The strict and regular observance of the duties of family religion, appears to have been one chief cause of the high eminence in Scriptural knowledge, in sobriety of manners, as well as in every domestic virtue, for which the northern part of Great Britain was then justly celebrated. The patriarchal simplicity of manners which, about the middle of the last century, so especially characterized Scottish husbandmen, was calculated, in a high degree, to foster deep affections, and a sober but manly earnestness both of principle and deportment ; and it may be fairly stated, as one of the happy privileges of the Secession church, that so large a number of its ministers have sprung from this virtuous and valuable order of men.

" But the religious order of the family was the distinguishing trait. The whole household assembled in the hall (or kitchen) in the morning before breakfast, for family worship, and in the evening before supper. The goodman, of course, led their devotions, every one having his Bible in his hand. This was the stated course even in seed-time and harvest : between five

and six in the morning was the hour of prayer in these busy
seasons.

" On sabbath all went to church, however great the distance,
except one person in turn, to take care of the house or younger
children, and others to tend the cattle.   After a late dinner, on
their return, the family assembled around the master, who first
catechised the children and then the servants.   Each was required to tell what he remembered of the religious services they
had joined in at the house of God ; each repeated a portion of
the Shorter Catechism ; and all were then examined on heads of
divinity, from the mouth of the master.   Throughout the whole
of the sabbath, all worldly concerns, except such as necessity or
mercy required to be attended to, were strictly laid aside ; and
nothing was allowed to enter into conversation, save subjects of
religion." *Dr. Waugh's Life.*   Such were the principles and
character of the Seceders : and they were common in the kirks
which possessed evangelical ministers.

Amongst other steps taken by the Erskines, in order to
strengthen the Secession, was their overture to Whitefield.
Fraser's account of this negociation is, upon the whole, the most
candid and complete that we possess.   It hardly shows, however,
all the urgency of the Erskines to secure a *monopoly* of Whitefield's influence.   Ralph's letter to him, of April 10, 1741, contains more than Fraser has quoted.   The following appeals are
omitted : " Come, if possible, dear Whitefield, come, and *come
to us also*.   There is no face on earth I would desire more
earnestly to see.   Yet I would desire it *only* in a way that, I
think, would tend most to the advancing of our Lord's kingdom,
and the reformation work, among *our* hands.   Such is the situation of affairs among us, that unless you came with a design to
meet and abide with us, particularly of the Associate Presbytery,
and to make your public appearances in the places especially of
their concern,—I would *dread* the consequences of your coming,
lest it should seem equally to countenance our persecutors.
Your fame would occasion a flocking to you, to whatever side
you turn ; and if it should be in their pulpits, as no doubt some
of them would urge, we know how it would be improven against
us.—I know not with whom you could *safely* join yourself, if not

with us." *Oliphant's Whitefield, Edin.* 1826. To all such appeals, Whitefield's answer was, " I come only as an occasional preacher, to preach the simple gospel to all that are willing to hear me, of whatever denomination. I write this, that there may be no misunderstanding between us." *Letters.* With this *key*, the following documents from Fraser will be as intelligible as they are interesting.

Mr. Erskine sustained a heavy disappointment when White-field refused to co-operate with him in the manner asked and expected. " Having received favourable accounts respecting the character and doctrine of this celebrated man, and the ex-traordinary success of his ministry in England and America, he affectionately invited him to make a visit to Scotland, and to unite his efforts with those of the Associate Presbytery, in pro-moting the interests of truth and godliness. A letter from Mr. Erskine to Mr. Whitefield, a short-hand copy of which we have discovered in his 38th Note-book, throws some light on the views and motives which influenced him and his brethren in giving him that invitation. Several expressions are illegible. We give the following extracts :" *Fraser's Life of Erskine.*

" Hilldown, near Dunbar, June, 1741.

" Rev. and very dear brother,

I inclined much to have written you as soon as I heard of your return to England; but I was at a loss for want of a direc-tion, till I received yours from Bristol, of the 16th of May, which was very acceptable. Though I have not yet seen your last journal, yet I have heard of it, and of the great things God has done for you and by you in the American world, and at home also, in this island of the sea ; which brings that doxology to mind—' Thanks be unto God, who always causeth us to triumph in Christ, and maketh manifest the savour of his knowledge by us in every place.' May you be enabled more and more to be joyful in his salvation, and in the name of your God to set up your banner. The banner which God has given you to display, because of truth, is far more glorious than that of (Admiral) Ver-non. But I know that you are disposed to say, ' Not I, but the grace of God in me ;' ' Not unto us, but unto thy name be the glory.'

" How desirable would it be to all the sincere lovers of Jesus Christ in Scotland, to see him ' travelling in the greatness of his strength ' among us also in your ministrations ! Truth falls in our streets. Equity cannot enter into our ecclesiastical courts. As our Assembly did last year eject us from our churches, and exclude us from our ministry and legal maintenance, for lifting up our reformation testimony ; so, from all I can hear, they have this year, in May last, appointed several violent intrusions to be made upon christian congregations ; whereby the flock of Christ is scattered more and more upon the mountains ; for a stranger will they not follow, who know the Shepherd's voice. The wandering sheep come with their bleatings to the Associate Presbytery ; whereby our work is daily increasing, in feeding and rallying our Master's flock, scattered and offended by the established church.

" From this short glimpse of the state of matters among us, you will easily see what reason the Associate Presbytery have to say, Come over to Scotland and help us ; come up to the help of the Lord against the mighty ; for the enemy comes in like a flood, but I hope the Spirit of the Lord will lift up a standard against him. We hear that God is with you of a truth, and therefore we wish for as intimate a connexion with you in the Lord as possible, for building up the fallen tabernacle of David in Britain ; and particularly in Scotland, when you shall be sent to us. This, dear brother, and no party views, is at the bottom of any proposal made by my brother Ralph, in his own name, and in the name of his associate brethren. It would be very unreasonable to propose or urge that you should incorporate as a member of our Presbytery, and wholly embark in every branch of our reformation, unless the Father of lights were clearing your way thereunto ; which we pray he may enlighten in his time, so as you and we may see eye to eye. All intended by us at present is, that, when you come to Scotland, your way may be such as not to strengthen the hands of our corrupt clergy and judicatories, who are carrying on a course of defection, worrying out a faithful ministry from the land, and the power of religion

with it. * * * *   Far be it from us to limit your great
Master's commission to preach the gospel to every creature.
We ourselves preach the gospel to all promiscuously who are
willing to hear us.   But we preach not upon the call and invitation of the ministers, but of the people, which, I suppose, is
your own practice now in England ; and should this also be
your way when you come to Scotland, it could do the Associate
Presbytery no manner of harm.   But if, besides, you could find
freedom to company with us, to preach with us and for us, and
to accept of our advices in your work, while in this country, it
might contribute much to weaken the enemy's hand, and to
strengthen ours in the work of the Lord, when the strength of
the battle is against us.

" These things I only propose with all submission.   The Lord
himself, I pray and hope, will direct you to such a course and
conduct as shall be for his own glory, and the edification of his
church every where, and particularly among us in Scotland.
We, in this country, are generally a lifeless, lukewarm, and up-
sitten generation.   What a blessing would it be to us, if your
visit should be attended with such fruits and effects as at Boston ; an account of which I have read in your last to my brother
Ralph—which yields great matter of thanksgiving.

" I am truly sorry for the Wesleyans—to see them so far left
to themselves.   I have seen your letter to them, and praise the
Lord on your behalf, who enables you to stand up so valiantly
for the truth, and with so much light and energy.   May his
truth be more and more your shield and buckler.

I am, your unworthy and affectionate brother,

EBENEZER ERSKINE."

This letter had been preceded by one from Ralph Erskine,
the brother and coadjutor of Ebenezer.

" Dunfermline, Aug. 21, 1739.

" Reverend and very dear Sir,

Yours, dated July 23rd, was most acceptable; and I would
have answered it by the first post, as you propose, but that, as
it lay about eight days in my house before I was at home to

receive it, so I delayed a few days thereafter, as I was to meet with my brethren of the Associate Presbytery, to whom I communicated your line, and Mr. William Seward's, and at the same time gave to each of them a copy of your last journal, as a present from you. I received nine of them at Burntisland, where we then were. I received also, much about the same time, six of your last sermon, on John vii. 37 ; some of which, with some of the former, I also gave to some of the brethren. And as I return you hearty thanks for these presents, so my brethren received them as tokens of that love and kindness which you express in such affectionate terms, in the close of your letter to me, as gave them very much pleasure and satisfaction, and tended to increase and inflame their love more and more to you. Your being opposed for owning us, and your maintaining such a regard for us, give ground to hope and expect that you will receive no information about us to our disadvantage, unless or until you have account thereof from ourselves, since you have laid such a foundation of kindly correspondence with us.

" I have some acquaintance with Mr. Davidson in Edinburgh, whom you mention, and was glad to hear he had sent you Mr. Boston's books. However, he has not had so much communication with us, as I hear he has with you, since he began to sway towards the independent or congregational way, which he has for some time been active to promote, though otherwise, I hope, a good and well-disposed man. Meantime, by whatever hand you please to send any print, (expecting, by the first occasion, to see the appendix, if published,) it can scarce fail to come safe, if but directed as your letters are. I have given orders to send you the prints relating to our public affairs in the Associate Presbytery ; and in case of your absence, they are to come to Mr. Seward or Mr. John Wesley.

" I have now read your journals and sermons ; and I can assure you, with reference to the whole work in general, and the main scope of it, my soul has been made to magnify the Lord for the very great things he has done for you and by you ; and I rejoice to see you ascribe all to the free grace of God in Christ, and that he has so remarkably raised you up to testify against the errors and corruptions of the times, to rouse and awaken a secure gene-

ration, and to bring such a number of sinners from darkness to
light, and from the power of Satan unto God.   If I shall speak
of any particulars wherein we differ, it shall only be to show
the greatness of my love to you, by the greatness of the freedom
I use with you ; also to prevent after-mistakes, and to promote
unfeigned love, which can both cover a multitude of infirmities,
and overlook a number of differences—not by quite concealing
them, which might bring love under a suspicion, but by a
friendly mentioning of them, which may prove it to be without
dissimulation.

   " Though we desire to cover with the mantle of love all the
differences betwixt you and us that flow from your education in
the church of England, and adore the merciful providence of
God, who has so far enlightened and qualified you and your
brethren to be witnesses for him and instruments of reformation, yet we hope the more this work is of God, the more will
it tend to bring about a happy union in the Lord betwixt you
and us, not only in a private and personal, but even in a more
public and general way.   My brethren and I, that have had
occasion here to confer about you, see a beauty in the providence of your being in communion with the English church.
Otherwise such great confluences from among them had not
attended your ministry, nor consequently received the benefit
or reaped the advantage which so many of them have done.
And though infinite wisdom has made, and may yet make, this
an alluring bait to draw them forth, yet as England's reformation at first, (from popery and its superstitious and ceremonial
services,) however great and glorious, was far from being so
full as that of some other protestant churches, particularly that
of Scotland ; so we would fain hope that when a new and general
reformation shall be set on foot, some more at least of the rags
of that Romish church shall be dropt, such as (abstracting at
present from the subject of church government) many useless
rites and customs relating to worship, which have no Scriptural
foundation.   This is what some of the most pious and learned
divines of your communion have wished to see reformed, knowing that many of these were retained at first, only under the
view of reforming gradually and from some prudential consider-

ations ; and knowing also that the continued retaining of these things, which the reforming fathers designed gradually to cast off, has been more stumbling to the friends, than ever it was gaining to the enemies, of the Reformation. Therefore, though Providence at present be making a good use of your being, according to your light, of that way, yet when you are beginning, as it were, to lay a new foundation, may the Lord, in due time, enable you to guard against such things as may afterwards prove a hinderance to a multitude of tender christians, their holding communion with you, as has been the case formerly. *Principiis obsta,* is a caution most necessary in many cases. What the great and famous reformer Luther retained from his original Romish education, proved a sad dividing snare among the protestant churches ; and since, by the good hand of God upon you, you are so well occupied in dashing down bigotry and party zeal, I hope the hint I here give you on this head will be the more agreeable. The first and main business, no doubt, is to lay the foundation of saving faith by preaching the pure truths and precious doctrines of the everlasting gospel, which (glory to God) you are so busy about, and we, I hope, are joining heart and hand with you.

" Very dear Sir, if you and your brethren, whom I honour and esteem in the Lord as his eminent witnesses, shall judge the freedom I have here used already to be rash or unseasonable, the least challenge of this sort from you shall be to me as excellent oil which shall not break my head ; for I think I would choose to suffer many miseries rather than choose to offend you. But, hoping my freedom shall rather be taken as a mark of that kindness of which my heart is full, I proceed to tell you what may be reckoned exceptionable in the last journal, though, at the same time, the wonders of divine grace therein recorded were most savoury to me, and to all I have spoken with upon it, and will, I hope, stir up many to prayer and praise. Your opinion about the business of the attorney has I hear been written of to you already, and therefore I shall say nothing of it. The correction you gave to your opinion of its unlawfulness by adding "at least exceedingly dangerous," satisfied me. Some have thought your love and charity extended a little too far beyond the Scripture rule in some instances ; such as Journal last, page 59th, where you say the quakers' notions about walking and being led by the Spirit, you think are right and good. Unless they be quakers of another stamp than the rest, whose dangerous tenets are inconsistent with the right notion of being led by the Spirit, while, beside other things, they deny justification by the imputed righteousness of Christ, or his active and passive obedience received by faith, to be the only ground of justification before God ; and while thus they cannot receive Jesus Christ, they consequently cannot walk in him, nor be led by his Spirit, who is the Spirit of truth, testifying of Christ according to the revelation made of him in the word, which they contradict. Whatever duties of love you perform towards these men, I will never believe you mean or intend to justify their principles and delusive notions.

" There is a passage in the same book, page 83d, that has been improven against us and our secession from the judicatories ; which yet, when I read it over again, seems to show to me how much you are of our mind, and that you would take the same course had you been in the same situation. You very justly, I think, express your dissatisfaction with three of your brethren that were driven to deny Christ's visible church upon earth, and show that needless separation from the established church would no doubt be attended with ill consequences ; and you judge of the state of a church, not from the practice of its members, but from its primitive and public constitution. Hence to me it would seem that if even the plurality of its members meeting judicially should contradict its primitive and public constitution, you would see fit to leave them and cleave to the said constitution ; which is the case with us in our secession from the present judicatories of the established church of Scotland. Such seem to be the defects, it is true, of your ecclesiastical government in England, that, unless in the case of a convocation, you can never boast of an ecclesiastical and judicial cleaving unto, nor complain of a judicial seceding from, the primitive public constitution. But as I make no question but, in that case, you would find (as matters are at present stated in England) there would be defections of the same sort

with you as there are with us, and consequently that you would
see need to take the same course that we of the Associate Presbytery do; so while you want the same advantages for seeing
clearly when it is that defections are become national and judicial, and when there is a universal practical departure from
the Scriptural principles of the church you profess yourselves to
be of, it is a question how far it is consonant with the word of
God to maintain close communion with those of that church
who are either subverting its primitive public constitution, or
openly and avowedly denying the foresaid principles.

"Since right communion is founded on union in the truth,
at least by some open profession of it, which most of your
clergy seem to have little of, while they excommunicate you
and your brethren from the use of their churches; however well
ordered this also is in providence for good, yet it discovers
them to be what they are. You likewise add that so long as
the Articles of the church of England are agreeable to Scripture, you resolve to preach them up, without either bigotry or
party zeal. This I heartily approve of, and this is the case with
us also. We preach up and defend, doctrinally and judicially,
those articles of the church of Scotland agreeable to the Scriptures, which the judicatories are letting go. Hence, I conclude,
you seem to be just of our mind as to separation from an
established church. We never declared a secession from the
church of Scotland, but, on the contrary, only a secession from
the judicatories, in their course of defection from the primitive
and covenanted constitution, to which we stood also bound by
our ordination engagements. And hence, to this day, we never
did quit our charges or congregations, to which we were ordained by the imposition of the hands of our several respective presbyteries, nor did we ever design, unless we were obliged by violence or compulsion, so to do.

"As to your sermons, dear Sir, I am ashamed you should
mention my approbation of them, as if it were of any signi-
ficancy. The general strain of your doctrine I love, admire,
and relish, with all my soul, and hope, through the blessing of
God, it will do much service. And, as to some particular expressions which I myself could not have used, my love to you,

and my view of the countenance of Heaven with you, made me to put such a favourable gloss upon them as to discern no odds betwixt you and us. But since I am using all the kind freedom I can, I shall give you some instances :

" ' Almost Christian,' penult page.—' We shall then look back on our past sincere and hearty services which have procured us so valuable a reward.' This I could by no means interpret, as if you meant it to the detriment of the doctrine of heaven's being a reward of grace in Christ Jesus, and not of debt to our services, or of eternal life its being the gift of God through Jesus Christ our Lord.

" ' Sermon on Justification by Christ,' at the close.—' Do but labour to attain that holiness, without which no man shall see the Lord, and then, though your sins be as scarlet, they shall be white as snow.'——I could by no means think that this was intended any way to thwart the doctrine of free remission of sins by the blood and righteousness of Christ only, which is the subject of the preceding sermon ; or to make sanctification or labouring after holiness, which is the fruit and evidence, to be the root, ground, cause, or condition of forgiveness. No ; I take your view to be, that in this way of labouring to attain holiness, people would evidence to themselves and others, that they were pardoned persons in Christ, or that they could not maintain the knowledge or assurance of it but in this way of holiness.

" ' Sermon on Phil. iii. 10,' page 14.—' He has passed from death to life, and shall never, if he stir up the gift of God that is in him, fall into condemnation.' This ' *if* ' here, I did not interpret as favouring the Arminian error against the certainty of the perseverance of saints that are once savingly united to Christ by faith of the operation of God, and passed from death to life ; but rather viewed it as favouring the gospel doctrine concerning the connexion betwixt the means and the end, and the necessity of the one in order to the other, though both are secured by promise to a believer in Christ.

" I was told by one, that in some part of your works you speak of justification by the act of believing ; but as I noticed nothing of this in the prints, so I affirmed that you had not so learned Christ, as to put the Arminian το *credere*, or any thing done by us, or wrought in us, in the room of Christ and his righteousness, or of his obedience and satisfaction, which alone received by faith, I was sure, from your writings, you would own to be the only matter and ground of justification.

" Again, though I could not use the English of your *Bone Deus*, because profane persons here sometimes swear in these terms, yet, as I know it is common among your writers, so I judge nothing is intended by it but a note of astonishment.

" Though some of these remarks are perhaps but trifling, and not so material as others of them, I have noted all down, that I may keep nothing back from you that in the least occurred to my mind of any seeming dissonancy betwixt us in words. Yet I judged, that, under various ways of speaking, we meant the same thing, and point at the same end; and I can say before the Lord, I not only approve of your sermons and journals, but see much matter of praise to God for them. I see much of the glory and majesty of God, and many of the stately steps and goings of our mighty King Jesus in them, and have at times, with tears of joy, adored his name for what he is doing for you and by you, and I pray for the continuance and advancement of that work of God. I rejoice that the Lord's work is going on with you, and that days of power continue. May it do so till all the powers of darkness give way to it, and till every Dagon fall before the ark of God!

" Your way of arguing against the apostatizing clergy of your church in your last sermon, even from the instances drawn out of your service-book, may be to them, I think, arguments *ad hominem*. May the Lord bless it for their conviction, and for awakening them out of their spiritual lethargy.

" When I consider how you and your brethren are stirred up of God to such a remarkable way of witnessing for him in England against the corruptions and defections of that church, and when we of the Associate Presbytery have been called forth in a judicial way to witness against the corruptions and defections of the church of Scotland, and both at a juncture when popish powers are combining together against us, and desolating judgments are justly threatened from Heaven,—there is perhaps more in the womb of providence relating to our several situations and successes therein than we are aware of. What he doth we know not now, but we may know hereafter. If he be gathering his birds together before a storm, according to the call, Zeph. i. 1—3, and Isa. xxvi. 20, 21, glory to him who doth all things well.

"We have lately been attending several sacramental solemnities in our brethren's congregations, where vast multitudes of people were assembled at the tents without doors as well as in the church, and I never found more of the presence of God than at some of these occasions. The Spirit of God was sometimes remarkably poured out, and I hope the power of the Lord was present to heal many souls. Enemies gnash with their teeth, as they do with you, but the Lord carries on his work. My brethren salute you most affectionately, they love and respect you in the Lord. Now, very dear Sir, I have in this long letter opened my very heart unto you, and told you the very worst thought that ever entered into it concerning you; which I could not have done, if it were not filled with love to you. And it loves you because you love Christ, and he loves you and honours you; and I hope he will spare and honour you more and more, to be a happy instrument in his hand for advancing his kingdom, and pulling down the throne of iniquity. May the weapons of your warfare be more and more mighty through God for that end.

I am, Rev. and dear Sir,
Yours, most affectionately in our blessed Immanuel,
RALPH ERSKINE.

"I salute the worthy Sewards and Wesleys in the Lord."

This long and open-hearted epistle afforded great satisfaction to Whitefield; as appears from the following extract of his reply :—

REV. G. WHITEFIELD, TO MR. RALPH ERSKINE.

"Savannah, Jan. 16th, 1740.

"Rev. and dear Sir,

With much pleasure, though not till last week, I received your kind, affectionate letter. I thank you for it with all my soul, and pray God to reward you for this, and all other your works of faith and labours of love. You may depend on my not being prejudiced against you or your brethren by any evil report. They only endear you to me more and more; and were your enemies to represent you as black as hell, I should think you were the more glorious in the sight of Heaven. Your sweet criticisms and remarks on my journal and sermons were exceedingly acceptable and very just. I assure you, dear Sir, I am fully convinced of the doctrine of election, free justification, and final perseverance. My observations on the quakers were only intended for those particular persons with whom I then conversed. The tenets of the quakers, in general, about *justification*, I take to be false and unscriptural. Your adversaries need take no advantage against you by any thing I have written, for I think it every minister's duty to declare against the corruptions of that church to which they belong, and not to look upon those as true members of their communion, who deny its public constitutions. This is your case in Scotland and ours in England. I see no other way for us to act at present than to go on preaching the truth as it is in Jesus; and then, if our brethren cast us out, God will direct us to that course which is most conducive to his glory and his people's good. I think I have but one objection against your proceedings—your insisting only on presbyterian government, exclusive of all other ways of worshipping God.——Your welfare is much upon my heart; and, as I am enabled, I make mention of you in my prayers.

Your weak unworthy brother,
and fellow-labourer in Christ,
GEORGE WHITEFIELD."

In a letter of nearly the same date, addressed to Mr. Gilbert Tennent, Whitefield, alluding to the above communication, says, " Since my arrival here, I have received a sweet, endearing, and instructive letter from Mr. Ralph Erskine."

About two months, however, prior to the receipt of this " endearing " letter, Whitefield had despatched three letters from Philadelphia ; one to the Associate Presbytery, a second to

Ebenezer Erskine, and a third to Ralph; in all of which he solicits information about the constitution and covenants of the Scotch kirk, and especially about the *Cameronians:* a bishop having called the seceders by that name, and thus made him somewhat jealous of their spirit. In subsequent letters, also, he repeats his determination to be " *quite neuter* " on the subject of church government and reform in Scotland.

Thus, never were men more prepared to love and welcome each other, than Whitefield and the Erskines. He thought the Associate Presbytery " a little too hard upon " him, and Ralph too much on their side, in pressing him to " join *them* wholly ;" but, otherwise, he had great confidence in both brothers, and they in him. On his arrival in Edinburgh, he accordingly resisted all applications made to him to preach there before he went to Dunfermline, although they were made to him by persons of the first distinction in the city. In a letter to a friend, he says, " I determined to give the Erskines the *first* offer of my poor ministrations, as they gave me the first invitation to Scotland." *Lett.* 337, vol. 1. Ralph says of him, " he came to me over the belly of *vast* opposition." Whitefield says, " I was received very *lovingly* at Dunfermline."

So far the interview was mutually gratifying. Whitefield was surprised and delighted when he preached in the meeting-house, to an immense assembly, by the rustling of a host of Bibles all at once, as he gave out his text: " a scene," he says, " I never was witness to before ! " and Ralph was equally pleased with the sermon and the preacher. He wrote next day to Ebenezer thus ; " The Lord is evidently with him ;" and to Adam Gibb, (whose spirit seems to have been suspicious of Whitefield from the first,) " I have many pleasant things to say of him :" " I see the Lord is with him."

Indeed, Ralph did every thing, wise and kind, in order to bring on a happy meeting between Whitefield and the Presbytery. He prepared Ebenezer for this by informing him, that Whitefield had " owned" to him, on the subject of his ordination, " that he would not have it again in *that* way for a thousand worlds; but, then, he knew no other way." *Fraser's Life of R. Erskine,* p. 326. To Gibb he wrote, " He designs and *desires* to meet with the brethren. I expect he will call for you." Whilst Ralph thus conciliated the brethren, he was equally candid in telling them what they had to expect: " As to his preaching, he declares he can refuse no c ll to preach, *whoever* gives it: were it a Jesuit or a Mahometan, he would embrace it for testifying *against* them."—" I find " (to Gibb) " his *light* leads him to preach, even at the call of those against whom he can freely testify. I hope you will inform Mair and Hutton." *Fraser*, 327.

Such were the preliminary steps to an interview and negociation, which Dr. Gillies (himself of the church party) has abruptly introduced, and hastily dismissed, " as a conference to set Whitefield right about church government, and the solemn league and covenant." It certainly was about these points; but as certainly not for the *sake* of these points, apart from the spiritual purposes they were intended to answer. Besides, neither the church government, nor the solemn league and covenant, were the inventions or the peculiarities of the Secession. Whether good, bad, or indifferent things, they were the *platform* of the kirk of Scotland. Willison of Dundee, sustained by a number of the clergy, testified as loudly at the time against " denying the lawfulness or obligation of our national covenant engagements," as Erskine and his brethren. *Struthers's Hist. Scotland.* And who does not see, that Dr. Gillies and his party, had they been negociating with Whitefield to join them, would just have begun as the Associate Presbytery did, by setting him " right, about the same points?" Indeed, Willison of Dundee did press the same points upon Whitefield, by letter; and received from him much the same answer he gave to the seceders: " I wish you would not trouble yourself or me, in writing about the corruptions of the church of England. You seem not satisfied, methinks, unless I openly renounce the church of England, and declare myself a presbyterian. Your letter gave me some little concern. I thought it breathed a sectarian spirit, to which I hoped dear Mr. W. was quite averse. I have shown my freedom in communicating with the church of Scotland, and in baptizing children in their own way. *I can go no further."* *Lett.* p. 429.

Thus the Secession were not the only sticklers for presbyterianism. They made it, however, what the clergy did not, the *condition* of employing Whitefield. His own account of the negociation with the Presbytery, although graphic, is rather too humoursome for the gravity of history, when the facts affect a body of christians. Whilst, therefore, I admire the candour of Fraser in giving Whitefield's half-playful letter first, I prefer to give the Presbytery's own narrative first; because the transaction involves their character most, and because their subsequent attacks on Whitefield were far more inexcusable than their treatment of him at Dunfermline.

The official minutes of this conference are, I am afraid, irrecoverably lost. That they did exist is, however, evident from a letter to Gibb, from Ralph Erskine, requesting a copy of them. " I expected before this time a copy of the conversation we had with Mr. Whitefield in this place. I have some occasions that require my having it. Therefore, please send me, if you can, a copy with this post." *Fraser's Life.*

This letter makes it highly probable, that the following original memorandum, written about the time by Ebenezer Erskine, is substantially correct, so far as it goes. It was copied verbatim from the short-hand characters of Erskine, in a note-book recently discovered by Fraser. " *Here follows an account of a conversation held with Mr. Whitefield at Dunfermline, Wednesday, Aug. 5th,* 1741. *The ministers of the Presbytery present were Messrs. Ralph and Ebenezer Erskine, Mr. Moncrieff, Mr. Gibb, Messrs. Thomas and James Mair, Mr. Clarkson; and two elders, namely, Mr. James Wardlaw, and Mr. John Mowbray.*"

" We, being advertised to be here this day, by a letter from Mr. Ralph Erskine, who had formed the *tryst* with Mr. Whitefield; Mr. Ralph's letter bearing, that Mr. Whitefield desired the conference, &c. and that he had yielded so far to him, as to his episcopal ordination, that he would not take it again for a thousand worlds; but at the time he knew no better.

" Upon Tuesday night, when we arrived at the place, we waited upon Mr. W. at Mr. Erskine's house; where and when we had some conversation about several things relating to the state of affairs in the church.

" Wednesday forenoon, the ministers and elders above men-

tioned, met with Mr. Whitefield, in consequence of a letter from
Mr. Ralph Erskine, desiring they would have a conference with
him: and they having met as above, a motion was made that
Mr. Ebenezer Erskine pray before they entered upon conversation.   As Mr. Whitefield showed an inclination to proceed to a
conference about toleration for a time, it was proposed, that,
seeing toleration of all sects by a church is an opinion of his, as
supported by some scriptures,—it was thought fit to consider,
what is that form of government Christ has laid down in his
word ?   And, agreeably to this, Mr. Whitefield put the question,
Whether presbyterian government be that which is agreeable to
the pattern shown in the mount ?   And supposing that it is,—
if it excluded a toleration of such as independents, anabaptists,
and episcopalians, among whom are good men ?

" Mr. Ebenezer Erskine said to him, ' Sir, God has made you
an instrument of gathering a great multitude of souls to the
faith and profession of the gospel of Christ, throughout England
and in foreign parts : and now it is fit—that you should be considering how that body is to be organized and preserved ; which
cannot be done without following the example of Paul and Barnabas, who, when they had gathered churches by preaching the
gospel, visited them again, and ordained over them elders in
every city ; which you cannot do *alone*, without some two or
three met together in a judicative capacity, in the name of the
Lord.'

" Unto all which Mr. Whitefield replied, (how like him !)
that he reckoned it his present duty to go on in preaching the
gospel, without proceeding to any *such* work.

" It was urged, that it might please the Lord to call him (by
death); and in that case, there being none other, the flock might
be scattered, and fall into the hands of grievous wolves, without
any to care for them.   He said, that he being of the communion
of the church of England, had none to join him in that work ;
and that he had no freedom to separate from the church of
England, until they did cast him out or excommunicate him."

Here, unhappily, Erskine's memorandum closes ; and, to his
honour, it contains no reflections upon the spirit of Whitefield,
although he said some sharp things, which must have been not

a little trying to the patience of stanch presbyterians. Neither
Whitefield nor the Presbytery, however, were so calm as they
appear in this still-life picture ; Dr. Jamieson himself being the
judge. When he animadverted upon Rowland Hill's " Journal
of a Tour in Scotland," he said, " That, after a good deal of reasoning (there was some *railing* too) as to a particular form of
church government being prescribed in Scripture, Mr. Whitefield, laying his hand on his *heart*, said, ' I do not find it here.'
Mr. A. Moncrieff, who was of a warm temper, giving a *rap* on
the Bible, which was lying on the table, said, ' But I find it
here.' " The Doctor adds, " On this, if I mistake not, the conversation terminated; and it has still been asserted, that the
proper ground of their giving up any connexion with Mr. Whitefield was—his denial that any particular form of church government was of divine authority ; and declaring his resolution to
maintain this in his public ministrations." So thought and
wrote Dr. Jamieson, who was not there : not so, however, did
Whitefield think or write. I keep out of the question still, his
playful letter, as it is called, because Fraser says, that " it has
been eagerly appealed to by writers, who wished to expose the
Associate Presbytery to ridicule and contempt." Besides, it
was a letter to Noble of New York, in answer to one about a new
synod by the Tennents ; and thus had a *purpose* to answer in
America, which warranted, what Fraser calls, " its indications "
of Whitefield's " constitutional vein for humour." None of
these objections, if they be such, lie against the following letters ;
which were written " weeping," and to men who knew the facts
of the Dunfermline conference. Now, on the *eighth* day after it,
Whitefield wrote thus to one of the sons of Ebenezer Erskine,
at Stirling : " The treatment I met with from the Associate
Presbytery was not altogether such as I expected. It grieved
me, as much as it did you. I could scarce refrain from bursting
into a flood of tears. I wish all were like-minded with your
honoured father and uncle : matters would not then be carried
on with so high a hand. Such violent methods—such a narrow
way of acting—can never be the way to promote and enlarge
the kingdom of our blessed Jesus.

" It surely must be wrong to forbid even our *hearing*—those who love our Lord Jesus in sincerity, and have also been owned of him. Christ would not have done so.

" Supposing the scheme of government for which the Associate Presbytery contend to be Scriptural ; yet, forbearance and long-suffering is to be exercised towards such as may differ from them. I am verily persuaded there is no such form of government prescribed in the book of God, as excludes a toleration of all other forms whatsoever. Were the Associate Presbytery scheme to take effect, they must, out of conscience, if they acted consistently, restrain and grieve, if not persecute, many of God's children, who could not possibly come in to their measures ; and I doubt not but their present violent methods, together with the corruptions of the Assembly, will cause many to become independents, and set up particular churches of their own. This was the effect of Archbishop Laud's acting with so high a hand : and whether it be presbytery or episcopacy, if managed in the same manner, it will be productive of the same effects. Blessed be God, I have not so learned Christ ! " *Lett.* 347. Would any man in his senses have written thus to David Erskine, had there been nothing more violent at Dunfermline than Moncrieff's *rap* on the table ; or had nothing been insisted upon but the divine authority of presbytery ? This letter both implies and asserts the avowal of intolerance, on the part of all but the Erskines : and even they wanted to shackle Whitefield with all the links of their own chain of exclusiveness. Ralph forgot himself so far, as to suspect and insinuate, in a letter, that Whitefield *temporized* for the sake of the orphans. This fact does not appear in the " previous *jottings,* which show the scope of that letter ;" (Fraser ;) but it appears in the dignified and indignant answer : " Indeed, dear Sir, you mistake if you think I temporize on account of the orphans. Be it far from me ! I *abhor* the very thought of it. I proceed now,—just as I have done, ever since I came out in the ministry." *Lett.* 350.

Even the "*jottings*" charge Whitefield (in " sorrow " indeed) with " coming *harnessed* with a resolution, to stand out against every thing that might be said against ———— ;" and with not " lying open to light," but " declining conversation on that head." Now, whatever this mean, the answer is unequivocal :

R

" I thank you for your kind letter. I believe it proceeded from love; but, as yet, I cannot think the solemn league and covenant any way binding upon me. You seem to think, I am not open to light. That I may give you satisfaction on that head, I am willing to confer with Mr. W———— at Perth, on Thursday, Sept. 3rd." *Ibid.* Whitefield takes no notice of the charge of " coming harnessed " to the conference. Perhaps Erskine softened it in the letter. If this was not the case, then Whitefield did not condescend to notice it. Something equivalent, however, was in the letter. Erskine says of it, to Gibb, " I have sent Mr. Whitefield this day a letter, wherein I used much plainness with him, on account of his declining conversation with us upon church government, and upon the *influence* I dreaded he is now under;—although all my plainness was in the most kindly way." *Fraser,* p. 335.

Fraser refers this " influence and harnessing " to " prejudices infused into Whitefield's mind against the ministers of the Secession, and the cause in which they had embarked, at the very moment of his first landing in Scotland." In proof of this, he quotes the fact, that Whitefield was " met and entertained at Edinburgh, by Dr. Webster and some of his brethren; from whom he learned the state of church prejudices and parties in Scotland." There can be no doubt of the truth of this. It is, however, equally true, that he found the Associate Presbytery to be as *intolerant* as their enemies had represented them : and if any thing worse was said against them, in his hearing, it did not prevent him from visiting them, nor from treating them as brethren in Christ. Even in his playful letter (which I now subjoin) there is as much kindliness as humour.

TO MR. THOMAS NOBLE, AT NEW YORK.

" Edinburgh, Aug. 8th, 1741.

" My dear brother,

I have written you several letters; and I rejoice to hear that the work of the Lord prospers in the hands of Messrs. Tennents, &c.; am glad they intend to meet in a synod by themselves. Their catholic spirit will do good. The *Associate Presbytery* here are so confined, that they will not so much as

hear me preach, unless I only will join with them. Mr. Ralph
E———, indeed, did hear me, and went up with me into the
pulpit of the *Canongate* church. The people were ready to
shout for joy ; but, I believe, it gave offence to his associates.
I met most of them, according to appointment, on *Wednesday*
last—a set of grave, venerable men ! They soon agreed to form
themselves into a presbytery, and were proceeding to choose a
moderator.—I asked them for what purpose ? They answered,
to discourse, and set me right, about the matter of church government, and the solemn league and covenant. I replied, they
might save themselves that trouble, for I had no scruples about
it ; and that settling church government, and preaching about
the solemn league and covenant, was not my plan. I then told
them something of my experience, and how I was led out into
my present way of acting. One in particular said, he was deeply
affected ; and the dear Mr. E——— desired they would have
patience with me, for that, having been born and bred in *England,* and never studied the point, I could not be supposed to be
so perfectly acquainted with the nature of their covenants. One,
much warmer than the rest, immediately replied, ' that no indulgence was to be shown me ; that *England* had revolted most
with respect to church government ; and that I, born and educated there, could not but be acquainted with the matter now
in debate.' I told him, I had never yet made the solemn league
and covenant the object of my study, being too busy about matters, as I judged, of greater importance. Several replied, that
every pin of the tabernacle was precious.—I said, that in
every building there were outside and inside workmen ; that
the latter, at present, was my province ; that if they thought
themselves called to the former, they might proceed in their own
way, and I should proceed in mine. I then asked them seriously,
what they would have me to do ; the answer was, that I was not
desired to subscribe immediately to the solemn league and covenant ; but to preach only for them till I had further light.
I asked, why only for them ? Mr. Ralph E——— said, ' they
were the Lord's people.' I then asked, whether there were no
other Lord's people but themselves ? and supposing all others
were the devil's people, they certainly had more need to be

preached to, and therefore I was more and-more determined to
go out into the highways and hedges; and that if the pope himself would lend me his pulpit, I would gladly proclaim the righteousness of Jesus Christ therein.   Soon after this, the company
broke up; and one of these, otherwise venerable men, immediately went into the meeting-house, and preached upon these
words, ' Watchman, what of the night? Watchman, what of the
night? The watchman said, The morning cometh, and also the
night, if ye will inquire, inquire ye; return, come.'   I attended;
but the good man so spent himself in the former part of his sermon, in talking against prelacy, the common-prayer book, the
surplice, the rose in the hat, and such like externals, that when
he came to the latter part of his text, to invite poor sinners to
Jesus Christ, his breath was so gone, that he could scarce be
heard.   What a pity that the last was not first, and the first
last!   The consequence of all this was, an open breach.   I retired, I wept, I prayed, and after preaching in the fields, sat
down and dined with them, and then took a final leave.   At
table, a gentlewoman said, she had heard that I had told some
people, that the Associate Presbytery were building a *Babel*.
I said, ' Madam, it is quite true; and I believe the *Babel* will
soon fall down about their ears:' but enough of this.   Lord,
what is man, what the best of men, but men at the best?   I
think I have now seen an end of all perfection.   Our brethren
in *America*, blessed be God, have not so learned Christ.   Be
pleased to inform them of this letter."

Now, certainly, had it not been for the use made of this letter
by the enemies of the Secession,—who interpreted the prophecy,
and wielded the wit of it wantonly,—it requires no apology.   It
is as true as it is graphic; not, perhaps, to the very letter of the
scene, but to the spirit of it.   It just embodies, in lively forms,
the very ideas suggested by the preceding details.   Even the
prophecy in it was sufficiently fulfilled, to accredit the foresight
of Whitefield.   Enough of what was " Babel" in the synod,
soon fell down " about their ears."   The division of the Secession, in 1747, into burghers and antiburghers, with the bitter
controversy it originated, was more than enough to justify the

prediction. Even Fraser applies to that sharp contention father Paul's proverb, that " In verbal contentions, the smallness of the difference often nourishes the obstinacy of the parties." It was not, therefore, necessary to rebut Whitefield's prophecy, even if it was uttered with " oracular solemnity," by the fact, that the edifice of the Secession " has now lasted for almost a century," and was not " so obnoxious to the frowns of Heaven, as that *good man* imagined." *Fraser's E. Erskine.* Had that " good man " seen it as it now subsists, he would have been as ready as Fraser or Jamieson to say, " the Secession church has become a fair, strong, and extensive fabric,—in no great danger of soon tumbling into ruins." *Ibid.*

The bad use made of this far-famed letter, by Sir Harry Moncrieff and others, in order to ridicule the Secession, and caricature its venerable founders, has tempted Fraser to find more fault with the letter than it is really chargeable with, or than he could justify. Hence he has quoted from a Review of Sir Harry's Life in " The Christian Repository," the unchristian assertion, that " no one, who knew any thing of Ralph Erskine, will for a moment *believe* that he would have said of the Seceders, ' we are the Lord's people.' " It is believed by many who know and believe that Ralph Erskine, a year *before* this time, and many times in later years, said, " We are far from thinking all are Christ's friends that join with us, or that all are His enemies that do not. No, indeed ! This would be to cast off all that have Christ's imâge—unless they have *our* image too." *Fraser.*

There is so much candour characterizes Fraser's version of these transactions, that I am unwilling to criticize his narrative. It is, however, impossible to agree with him in his conclusion— " that considerate and unbiassed judges will see cause, on the whole, to conclude that Mr. Whitefield and the Associate Presbytery parted in a manner, which has left no credit to *either* party." Neither the manner nor the spirit of Whitefield's parting reflects any discredit upon him.

In Edinburgh the issue of this negociation was waited for with more than curiosity. The clergy welcomed Whitefield's return to their pulpits in the city as a triumph to the kirk : and it was a triumph at the time. As such, however, he cared nothing about it. He forgot, equally, the joy of the kirk, and the mortification of the chapel, in seeking the triumphs of the cross. Whilst churchmen were pluming themselves on their gain, and seceders trying to despise their loss, he was singing with Paul, " Now thanks be unto God, who always causeth us to triumph in Christ, and maketh manifest by us the savour of His knowledge in every place." It was manifested in Edinburgh, and became " the savour of life unto life " to very many in all ranks. For some weeks he preached twice or thrice every day in the churches, and renewed in the orphan-house park the scenes of Moorfields and Blackheath. He obtained also £500 for his orphans, in money or goods.

The latter was a timely help to him. How much he felt this will be best told by himself. In a letter to Mr. Habersham, he says, " O my dear friend, how faithful is the Lord Jesus! He has enabled me to pay my brother, and Mr. Noble's bill of £300. I have sent you £70 worth of different sorts of goods to be disposed of, and the money applied to the orphan-house. I have sent also six hundred yards of cloth, a present of my own, to make the boys and girls gowns and coats. You will find some *damask table cloths*, which I desire you will sell, they being too good, in my opinion, for our use."

Whitefield could not appreciate the *moral* value of this last gift; but all Scotchmen well understand the sacrifice made by Scotchwomen, in thus contributing damask *nappery!* It was next to parting with their wedding ring. Had he known this, he would not have sold the table cloths!

Such presents in money or goods were new things in Edinburgh then, and, of course, misrepresented by many. Some were alarmed, lest he should " impoverish the country! " His answer to all insinuations of this kind was, " I value them not in the least. My largest donations are from the rich and substantial. The mites which the lower sort of the people have given, will not prevent them from paying their debts, nor impoverish their families." When, however, it was proposed to make a contribution in Edinburgh for himself, although *privately*, he changed his tone, and said,—" I know nothing of—and will not admit of any such thing! I make no purse. What I have I give away. ' *Poor, yet making many rich,*' shall be my motto still." *Letter.*

Whitefield's own accounts of the success of the gospel in Edinburgh at this time, although *flaming*, are not exaggerated. Dr. Muir, who witnessed the effect, says, " Upon the whole, we hope there is such a flame kindled, as shall never be extinguished. The ministers are learning to speak with new tongues." *Edin. Memoir.* The only drawback upon the following accounts is, an appearance of vanity, when the nobility are mentioned; and of flattery, when they are addressed. Dr. Southey says truly, that " Wesley would not have written in this strain:" but it is equally true, that Jeremy Taylor, and Dr. Donne, wrote both letters and dedications quite as fulsome, and more servile; and which " might well provoke disgust and indignation, were not the real genius and piety of the writers beyond all doubt." *Southey's Wesley,* p. 360, vol. 2.

To Habersham, Whitefield writes from Edinburgh thus, " God is pleased to bless my ministrations here in an abundant manner. The little children in the hospitals are much wrought upon. Saints have been stirred up and edified, and many others, I believe, translated from darkness to light. The good that has been done is inexpressible. I am intimate with three noblemen, and several ladies of quality, who have a great liking for the things of God. I am now writing in an earl's house, (Melville,) surrounded by fine furniture; but, glory be to free grace, my soul is in love only with Jesus."

To Cennick he wrote, " This day Jesus enabled me to preach *seven* times; notwithstanding, I am as fresh as when I arose in the morning. Both in the church and park the Lord was with us. The girls in the hospital were exceedingly affected. One of the mistresses told me, that she is now awakened in the morning by the voice of prayer and praise; and the master of the boys says, that they meet together every night to sing and pray. The presence of God at the *old* people's hospital was really very wonderful. The Holy Spirit seemed to come down like a rushing mighty wind. The mourning of the people was like the weeping in the valley of Hadadrimmon. Every day I

hear of some fresh good wrought by the power of God. I scarce
know how to leave Scotland."

Thus the rich and the poor, the young and the old, not only
heard him gladly, but melted down alike under his preaching;
and that—in Scotland, where the melting mood is not predominant. And then, Whitefield's doctrine was not *new* to them
as a people, as it was to the English. Why, therefore, do we
see nothing of this kind now, upon a large scale, in either England or Scotland? The gospel is widely and faithfully preached in both; but not with remarkable success in either. This
is not satisfactorily explained by saying, that a greater blessing
attended Whitefield's ministry than follows ours. The fact
is, that the outpouring of the Spirit on his audiences was *preceded* by an unction of the Spirit on his own soul, which we
hardly understand, and still less cultivate. What a *heart* he
had in Edinburgh! He does not, indeed, always describe its
emotions in good taste; but, alas for the man, and especially
the minister, who can read the bursts and outpourings of George
Whitefield's heart, without shame, or without feeling his own
heart *burn* to share them! " Night and day Jesus fills me
with his love."—" The love of Christ strikes me quite dumb."
—" I walk continually in the comforts of the Holy Ghost."—
" My heart is melted down with the love of Jesus."—" I despair not of seeing Scotland like New England."—" I want a
thousand tongues to set off the great Redeemer's praise."—" I
am daily waiting for the coming of the Son of God."—" I every
morning feel my fellowship with Christ, and he gives me all joy
and peace in believing."—" The sight I have of God by faith
ravishes my soul: how I shall be ravished when I see him face
to face!"—" I would *leap* my seventy years, and fly into His
presence." All this is as burning as abrupt. He lived, and
moved, and had his being, in this warm and pure element; and
thus preached, not only in dependence on the Holy Spirit, but
" in *demonstration* of the Spirit and in power." Thus the holy
oil which anointed so many under him, had first been poured on
his own head. I have endeavoured to illustrate this fact in
another part of the volume. In the mean time, however, I cannot quit this hint, without solemnly reminding myself and

others, that we can be Whitefields in *unction,* although not in energy or eloquence ; we can walk with God as he did, although unable to " go about " doing good upon his scale.

The results of his first visit to Edinburgh are thus summed up by himself : " Glory be to God; he is doing great things here. I walk in the continual sunshine of his countenance. Never did I see so many Bibles, nor people look into them with such attention, when I am expounding. Plenty of tears flow from hearers' eyes. I preach twice daily, and expound at private houses at night ; and am employed in speaking to souls under distress great part of the day. Every morning I have a constant *levee* of wounded souls, many of whom are quite slain by the law. I have a lecture in the fields, attended not only by the common people, but persons of great rank. I have reason to think some of the latter sort are coming to Jesus. I am only afraid, lest people should idolize the instrument, and not look enough to Jesus, in whom alone I desire to glory."

Scotland, and especially Edinburgh, owes much to this visit. Any check it gave to the Secession for a time, was more than counterbalanced by the impulse it gave to the establishment. The evangelical clergy had as much need of a commanding ally, as the Associate Presbytery ; and, in general, as well deserved the weight and fame of Whitefield's name. That name drew on their side some of the peerage, who would never have followed him into a chapel ; and thus strengthened the hands of " *the wild men,*" (as the evangelical party were called,) when they were but weak. Edinburgh should never forget this. Next to Knox, Whitefield deserves a monument on the Calton Hill, as the *second* reformer of the metropolis. But for him, the moderate party would have held the ascendant in it. I do therefore hope that, at least, no Scottish champion of the gospel will imitate some in England, by trying to prove that Whitefield had little or no influence upon the revival of evangelical preaching in the establishment. If any do try there, I can only say, as I do here,—their *fathers* knew better, and posterity will *laugh* at them. *Venn's Life of Venn.*

As a counterpart to the sermon against Whitefield in the meeting-house, by one of the Associate Presbytery, the following scene in the kirk at Aberdeen may instruct as well as amuse. Dr. Southey has told the story well; but Whitefield tells it better. " *Aberdeen,* Oct. 9, 1741. At my first coming here, things looked a little gloomy; for the magistrates had been so prejudiced against me by one Mr. Bisset, that when applied to, they refused me the use of the kirk-yard to preach in. This Mr. Bisset is colleague with one Mr. O. at whose repeated invitation I came hither. Though colleagues of the same congregation, they are very different in their natural tempers. The one is, what they call in Scotland, of a *sweet-blooded,* the other of a choleric, disposition. Mr. B. is neither a seceder, nor quite a kirk-man; having great fault to find with both.

" Soon after my arrival, dear Mr. O. took me to pay my respects to him. He was prepared for it; and immediately pulled out a paper, containing a number of insignificant questions, which I had neither time nor inclination to answer. The next morning, it being Mr. O.'s turn, I lectured and preached. The magistrates were present. The congregation was very large, and *light and life fled all around.*

" In the afternoon, Mr. B. officiated. I attended. He begun his prayers as usual; but in the midst of them, naming me by name, he entreated the Lord to forgive the dishonour that had been put upon him, by my being suffered to preach in that pulpit. And that all might know what reason he had to put up such a petition,—about the middle of his sermon, he not only urged that I was a curate of the church of England, (had Whitefield been an archbishop or bishop, Bisset would have *begun* his prayers against him,) but also quoted a passage or two out of my first printed sermons, which he said were grossly Arminian.

" Most of the congregation seemed surprised and chagrined, especially his good-natured colleague, Mr. O.; who, immediately after sermon, and without consulting me in the least, stood up, and gave notice that Mr. Whitefield would preach in about half an hour. The interval being so short, the magistrates returned into the sessions-house, and the congregation patiently waited —big with expectation of hearing my resentment.

" At the time appointed I went up, and took no other notice

of the good man's ill-timed zeal, than to observe in some part of my discourse, that if the good old gentleman had seen some of my later writings, wherein I had corrected several of my former mistakes, he would not have expressed himself in such strong terms.

" The people being thus diverted from controversy with man, were deeply impressed with what they heard from the word of God. All was hushed, and more than solemn ! On the morrow, the magistrates sent for me, expressed themselves quite concerned at the treatment I had met with, and begged me to accept the freedom of the city. But of this enough." Dr. Southey justly says, " this triumph Whitefield obtained, as much by that perfect self-command which he always possessed in public, as by his surpassing oratory."

Bisset's hostility did not end here, nor confine itself to Whitefield. Next year he assailed the Scotch clergymen, who had employed the English *curate ;* and charged them with caressing Whitefield, " as it would seem, to *break* the seceders." *Bisset's Letter on Communion with a Priest of the Church of England.* Thus it was not the Associate Synod alone who attributed the friendship of the kirk for Whitefield to selfish motives.

One thing occurred in Edinburgh which pleased Whitefield very much. After preaching in the orphan-house park, a large company came to salute him. Amongst the rest a fine portly quaker took him by the hand, and said, " Friend George, I am as thou art. I am for bringing all to the life and power of the ever-living God ; and, therefore, if thou wilt not quarrel with me about my *hat,* I will not quarrel with thee about thy gown." I know some ex-quakers who would say, that Whitefield would not have been so much pleased, if he had known the *mystery* of the hat in quakerism.

CHAPTER X.

NEITHER the revivals in Scotland, nor the riots in England, won for Whitefield the sympathy of the London ministers. Bradbury lampooned him ; Barker sneered at him ; Dr. Watts was silent; and Coward's trustees were *insolent* to Dr. Doddridge, because he gave him some countenance at Northampton. There was a deeper cause for all this than their dread of his enthusiasm. They were then in treaty with some of the bishops, in order to revive that scheme of COMPREHENSION, which Bates, Manton, and Baxter tried to negociate with Stillingfleet ; but which Clarendon, even whilst in banishment, had influence enough at home to defeat, although the bill in favour of it was drawn up by Lord Chief Baron Hale. *Tillotson's Life.*

The *Clarendon* party were not dead nor idle, when the subject of the comprehension was revived by Chandler and Doddridge with Archbishop Herring. Warburton, who knew them well, foretold the issue thus, even when the prospect was brightest *before* curtain ; " I can tell you of *certain science*, that not the *least* alteration will be made in the ecclesiastical system." *Letter to Doddridge.* The progress of this affair will explain both the shyness and the sharpness of the London ministers towards Whitefield. They could not have negociated with him and the archbishop at the same time. Indeed, they had no wish to be identified with any of his measures.

It belongs to history to tell this matter gravely : I prefer the *graphic* sketch of its origin and progress, given in the following letters. The first letter is from Barker to Doddridge. " As for the comprehension, so much talked of in town and country, the utmost of the matter is this :—Mr. Chandler, while his meeting-place was shut up, made a visit to his friends at Norwich ; and there happened to hear the bishop give a charge to his clergy, which he thought not very candid. One expression appeared to him invidious, viz. that the heads of the rebellion were presbyterians ; as appeared by those lords in the Tower sending for presbyterian *confessors.* Upon Mr. Chandler's return to London, he wrote a letter to Dr. Gooch, complaining of his charge, and particularly of that expression. This letter was written very handsomely, and it brought a very civil, respectful answer. After Gooch came to town, Chandler, at his desire, made him a visit, in which they had much discourse ; and amongst other things, there was talk of a comprehension. This visit was followed, at Gooch's desire, with another, when the bishop of Salisbury was present, who soon discovered his shrewdness, but said, ' Our church, Mr. Chandler, consists of three parts,—doctrine, discipline, and ceremonies : as to the last, they should be left indifferent, as they are agreed on all hands to be : as to the second, our discipline,' said he, ' is so bad, that no one knows how, or where, to mend it : and as to the first, what is your objection ? ' He answered, ' Your Articles, my Lord, must be expressed in Scripture words, and the Athanasian creed be discarded.' Both the bishops answered, they wished they were rid of that creed, and had no objection to restoring the Articles into Scripture words ; ' but what shall we do about reordination ? " To this Mr. Chandler made such a reply as he judged proper ; but, I think, granted more than he ought : he said none of us would renounce his presbyterian ordination ; but if their Lordships meant only to impose their hands on us, and by that rite recommend us to public service in their society or constitution, that, perhaps, might be submitted to : but when he told me this, I said, ' perhaps not—no, by no means ; that being, in my opinion, a virtual renunciation of our ordination, which I apprehend not only as good but better than theirs.' The two bishops, at the conclusion of the visit, requested Mr. Chandler to wait on the archbishop, which he did, and met Gooch there by accident. The archbishop received him well, and being told by Gooch

what Chandler and he had been talking on, viz. a comprehension, said, A very good thing; he wished it with all his heart;
and the rather, because this was a time which called upon all
good men to unite against infidelity and immorality, which
threatened universal ruin; and added, he was encouraged to
hope, from the piety, learning, and moderation of many dissenters, that this was a proper time to make the attempt. But,
may it please your Grace, said Gooch, Mr. Chandler says the
Articles must be altered into the words of Scripture. And why
not? replied the archbishop; it is the impertinences of men,
thrusting their words into articles instead of the words of God,
that have occasioned most of the divisions in the christian
church, from the beginning of it to this day. The archbishop
added, that the bench of bishops seemed to be of his mind; that
he should be glad to see Mr. Chandler again, but was then obliged to go to court. And this is all. I have smiled at some who
seem mightily frighted at this affair, are very angry with Mr.
Chandler, and cry out, ' We won't be comprehended—we won't
be *comprehended*.' One would think, they imagined it was like
being electrified, or inoculated for the small pox. But most of
your fault-finders, I apprehend, are angry with Mr. Chandler, for
an expression he used in the second visit. When urging the ex-
pediency of expressing the Articles in Scripture words, he said, it
was for others, not himself, he suggested this, his conscience not
being disturbed by them as they now stood, for he freely owned
himself a *moderate Calvinist*."

Six months after this, Doddridge himself had an interview
with Herring, and found, at first, that although the archbishop
had " most candid sentiments of his dissenting brethren, he had
no great *zeal* for attempting any thing in order to introduce
them into the church; wisely foreseeing the difficulties with
which it might be attended." *Doddridge's Letters.* He was not
likely to have zeal for it. He had not zeal even for the *orthodox*
of his own church. Jortin concludes his formal and inflated
sketch of him thus; " he was willing to think the *best* of other
people's principles." What this means, may, perhaps, be guessed
from the primate's letters to Duncombe; of which, the following is one specimen : " I *abhor* every tendency to the TRINITY

controversy. The manner in which it is always conducted is the disgrace and ruin of christianity."

When Doddridge saw that the comprehension scheme, as proposed by Chandler, did not suit Herring, he suggested " a sort of medium between our present state, and that of a *perfect* coalition." " I mentioned," he says, " acknowledging our churches as *unschismatical;* by permitting their clergy to officiate amongst us, if desired, and dissenting ministers to officiate in churches. It struck him as a new and important thought. He told me, more than once, that I had suggested—what he should lay up in his mind for further consideration."

Next year, however, Doddridge learned from Sir Thomas Birch, that, although " several of the bishops endeavoured to have White's Third Letter (see Towgood) suppressed, as unfriendly to comprehension, Sherlock insisted upon having *all* objections brought out at once." Good Doddridge, however, still cherished hopes for his own plan ; and, accordingly, cultivated intimacy with the heads of the church so closely, that the very men who censured him for risking the comprehension, at first, by countenancing Whitefield, came at last to insinuate that he paid more court " to eminent members of the establishment," than was prudent. However this may be, he rejoiced with Lady Huntingdon, at the *same* time, that " the mighty, the noble, the wise, and the rich," assembled at her house, " to hear Whitefield."

How Doddridge acted and was censured, in reference to Whitefield, when the vision of a comprehension dawned upon some of the leading dissenters of 1743, will be best told by the secretary of Coward's trustees, Nathaniel Neal, Esq. of Million Bank.

" It was with the utmost concern that I received the information of Mr. Whitefield's having preached last week in your pulpit, and that I attended the meeting of Coward's trustees this day, when that matter was canvassed, and that I now find myself obliged to apprize you of the very great uneasiness which your conduct herein has occasioned them.

" The many characters you sustain with so much honour, and in which I reverence you so highly, make me ashamed, and the character I sustain, of your friend, makes it extremely irksome for me, to express any sentiments as mine, which may seem to arraign your conduct; but when I reflect in how disadvantageous a light your regard to the methodists has for some considerable time placed you in the opinion of many, whom I have reason to believe you esteem amongst your most judicious and hearty friends, and what an advantage it has given against you to your secret and avowed enemies, of either of which facts I believe you are not in any just degree sensible, I could run any hazard of your censure rather than that you should remain unapprized of these facts.

" You cannot be ignorant, how obnoxious the imprudences committed, or alleged to be committed, by some of the methodists, have rendered them to great numbers of people; and though, indeed, supposing they have a spirit of religion amongst them to be found no where else, so that a man would, for his own sake, and at any temporal hazard, take his lot amongst them; yet if, besides their reputation for a forward and indiscreet zeal, and an unsettled, injudicious way of thinking and behaving, they have nothing to distinguish them from other serious and devout christians, surely every man would choose to have as little concern with them as possible.

" But in the case of such a public character, and so extensive a province for the service of religion, as yours, it seems to me a point well worth considering, whether, supposing even the ill opinion the world entertains of them to be groundless, it is a right thing to risk such a prospect as Providence has opened before you, of eminent and distinguished usefulness, for the sake of any good you are likely to do amongst these people.

" For my own part, I have had the misfortune of observing, and I must not conceal it from you, that wherever I have heard it mentioned, that Dr. Doddridge countenanced the methodists, and it has been the subject of conversation much oftener than I could have wished, I have heard it constantly spoken of by his friends with concern, as threatening a great diminution of his usefulness, and by his adversaries with a sneer of triumph.

" The trustees are particularly in pain for it, with regard to your academy; as they know it is an objection made to it, by some persons in all appearance seriously, and by others craftily; and yet they are almost afraid of giving their thoughts even in the most private manner concerning it, lest it should be made an occasion of drawing them into a public opposition to the methodists, as they are likely to be in some measure by your letter to Mr. Mason, (excusing your prefixing a recommendation of a book of theirs, without the advice of the trustees,) which letter they have desired me to inform you has given them great offence.

" What weight these considerations will or ought to have with you, I cannot determine; as I have thrown them together in a good deal of haste, I am afraid lest I should have said any thing in such a manner as may justly give you offence: this, however, I am sure of, that you will not read any such line with more pain than that in which I wrote it. If I have used any assuming language, my heart did not dictate it; if I have betrayed any earnestness or warmth unbecoming the deference due to your superior judgment, impute it to the passionate regard I bear to so great and so valuable a character: if, on the other hand, I have said any thing worthy your consideration, I am persuaded it will have its weight, notwithstanding any disadvantage from the mode of saying it, and the person who says it, especially when I assure you, that that alone which you may find in it becoming the sincerity and affection of a friend, and the respect and veneration due to a man of eminent learning and piety, has the approbation of,

Reverend and dear Sir,
Your most affectionate and faithful, humble servant,
NATHANIEL NEAL."

The answer to this first letter from the *Coward* trust, Doddridge himself did not trouble himself to preserve. A second came.

" The candid reception you gave my last of the 11th instant, I impute principally to your own condescending and friendly disposition, and next, to the credit you gave to that simplicity of intention with which it was written, and wherein alone I can in any way be sure that it was not defective.

S

" I am not insensible, Sir, that the respect many of your people bore to Mr. Whitefield, and your own acquaintance with him, must have made it a matter of difficulty for you entirely to have avoided showing him some polite regards on his coming to Northampton ; and I greatly rejoice in being furnished with so particular an account of the circumstances attending his visit, that may enable me to say, you were so far, at that time, from seeking his preaching in your pulpit, that you took several steps, and indeed all that you thought you could prudently venture on, and such as might, if they had succeeded, have been sufficient to have prevented it ; which I doubt not will, and I am sure ought, to have some weight with those who censure this step on the ground of imprudence. I could only wish that I were able to make these circumstances known as far as that censure is likely to extend.

I should be very sorry, Sir, if you had any just reason to apprehend, that what has been written to you on this subject by any of your friends was intended to have any weight on the footing of authority. They ought to be ashamed of wishing for any greater influence over you than what their arguments, backed by the affection which all who deserve the name of your friends so justly entertain, will give them. And it is in that confidence that you will not think me vain, or so weak as to wish any greater for myself, that I venture to write another word to you on this subject.

" And there is one thing wh ch your letter gives me an occasion to suggest for your present consideration, with regard to your apprehensions of the growth of infidelity, which I am abundantly satisfied are too well founded ; and that is, whether the enthusiasm and extravagances of *weak* christians have not furnished out some of the most specious pleas, as well as splendid triumphs, of infidelity ? The pamphlet of " Christianity not founded on Argument " alone, sufficiently convinces me that they have ; inasmuch as that pamphlet was calculated to serve the interests both of enthusiasm and deism ; actually made both enthusiasts and deists ; and raised a doubt, not yet, as I apprehend, fully cleared, whether the world was obliged to the one or other of these parties for that *excellent* performance. If enthusiasts, therefore, by their principles, are laying a foundation of deism, however they may abhor it in their intentions, it surely behoves us to see to it, that we give them no assistance in that work ; and the rather, as deists are watching for every possible advantage of this kind. A remarkable instance of which was accidentally mentioned to me very lately. In a late conversation in a mixed company of deists, the countenance which a *certain* eminent divine had given to some reputed enthusiasts was mentioned by one of the deists in support of this position,—that the most learned and considerable among christian divines, who were really honest men, were enthusiasts. You may certainly depend on the truth of this relation."

The answer to this also is not preserved. A *third* came.

" Million Bank, Dec. 10th, 1743.

" I am sorry you appear so apprehensive in your last letter, lest I should interpret what you said in your first too unfavourably of the methodists and Mr. Whitefield, as it confirms me in my fears of your attachment to them ; but, whatever my wishes were in that respect, you may be assured I could never venture to represent you as indifferent to them, when I read your commendation of his sermon for its excellence and oratory, and remember the low, incoherent stuff I used to hear him utter at Kennington Common.

" Whilst I continued oppressed and hurt with these reflections, your excellent sermon for the County Hospital came in to my relief. The piety, the justness of the sentiments and arguments, the manly, graceful diction, and the benevolent spirit that runs through the whole of it, both amazed and charmed me. It must have extorted from any heart less acquainted with your disposition for public usefulness than I am, a devout ejaculation, that God would never permit such talents to come under a wrong direction, or suffer the disadvantages they must necessarily submit to, if engaged amongst men of weak heads and narrow, gloomy sentiments, who may and ought to be pitied and prayed for, and better informed, as opportunity allows, but whom no rules of piety or prudence will oblige us to make our friends and confidants.

" There are letters shown about town, from several ministers
in the west, which make heavy complaints of the disorders occasioned by Whitefield and Wesley in those parts.   One of them,
speaking of Mr. Whitefield, calls him ' *honest, crazy, confident*
Whitefield.'   These letters likewise mention, that some ministers there, who were your pupils, have given them countenance ;
and you can hardly conceive the disrespect this has occasioned
several ministers and other persons in town to speak of you with.
Whether you are aware of this I know not ; and I am sure, if I
did not esteem it a mark of sincere friendship, I would not give
you the uneasiness of hearing it."

The answer to this letter Doddridge preserved, and I would
perpetuate.

TO NATHANIEL NEAL, ESQ.

" I am truly sorry that the manner in which I spoke of Mr.
Whitefield in my last should give you uneasiness.   I hope I did
not assert his sermon to have been free from its defects ; but I
must be extremely prejudiced indeed, if it were such ' wild, incoherent stuff,' as you heard on Kennington Common.   Nor does
it seem at all difficult to account for this ; for that preached
here, which, I believe, was one of his more elaborate and, perhaps, favourite discourses, might deserve to be spoken of in a
different manner.   What I then said, proceeded from a principle which I am sure you will not despise : I mean a certain
frankness of heart, which would not allow me to seem to think
more meanly of a man to whom I once professed some friendship,
than I really did.   I must, indeed, look upon it as an unhappy
circumstance, that he came to Northampton just when he did,
as I perceive, that, in concurrence with other circumstances, it
has filled town and country with astonishment and indignation.
Nor did I, indeed, imagine my character to have been of such
great importance in the world, as that this little incident should
have been taken so much notice of.   I believe the true reason
is, that for no other fault than my not being able to go so far as
some of my brethren into the new ways of thinking and speaking, I have long had a multitude of enemies, who have been

watching for some occasion against me ; and I thank God, that they have hitherto, with all that malignity of heart which some of them have expressed, been able to find no greater !

" As for you, dear Sir, I must always number you among my most affectionate and faithful friends ; and though the human heart is not so formed that it is agreeable to hear ourselves spoken of with disrespect, yet I am well assured that the writing the information you gave me was among the instances of your greatest kindness. You know, Sir, that a fear to offend God, by doing as most *self*-prudent people do, has generally been esteemed a weakness : and my conscience testifies that those actions of mine which have been most reproached, have proceeded from that principle. It is impossible to represent to you the reason, at least the excuse, I have had, and esteemed a reason, unless I could give you an account of the several circumstances in which I have successively been placed for these few past years. If I could, I believe you would be less inclined to blame me than you are ; though I am sensible your censures are very moderate, when compared with those of many others.

" I had, indeed, great expectations from the methodists and Moravians. I am grieved, from my very heart, that so many things have occurred among them which have been quite unjustifiable : and I assure you faithfully, they are such as would have occasioned me to have dropped that intimacy of correspondence which I once had with them. And I suppose they have also produced the same sentiments in the archbishop of Canterbury, who, to my certain knowledge, received Count Zinzendorf with open arms, and wrote of his being chosen the Moravian bishop, as what was done ' plaudente toto cœlesti choro.' I shall always be ready to weigh whatever can be said against Mr. Whitefield, as well as against any of the rest : and, though I must have actual demonstration before I can admit him to be a dishonest man, and though I shall never be able to think all he has written, and all I have heard from him, nonsense, yet I am not so zealously attached to him as to be disposed to celebrate him as one of the greatest men of the age, or to think that he is the pillar that bears up the whole interest of religion among us. And if this moderation of sentiment towards him will not

appease my angry brethren, as I am sensible it will not abate
the enmity which some have, for many years, entertained towards me, I must acquiesce, and be patient till the day of the
Lord, when the secrets of all hearts shall be made manifest; in
which, I do from my heart believe, that with respect to the part
I have acted in this affair, I shall not be ashamed.

" I had before heard from some of my worthy friends in the
west of the offence which had been taken at two of my pupils
there, for the respect they showed to Mr. Whitefield; and yet
they are both persons of eminent piety. He whose name is
chiefly in question, I mean Mr. Darracott, is one of the most
devout and extraordinary men I ever sent out; and a person
who has, within these few years, been highly useful to numbers
of his hearers. Some of these, who were the most abandoned
characters in the place, are now become serious and useful christians; and he himself has honoured his profession, when to all
around him he seemed on the borders of eternity, by a behaviour
which, in such awful circumstances, the best of men might wish
to be their own. Mr. Fawcett labours likewise at Taunton;
and his zeal, so far as I can judge, is inspired both with love
and prudence. Yet I hear these men are reproached because
they have treated Mr. Whitefield respectfully; and that one of
them, after having had a correspondence with him for many years,
admitted him into his pulpit. I own I am very thoughtful when
these things will end: in the mean time, I am as silent as I can
be! I commit the matter to God in prayer, and earnestly beg
his direction, that he would lead me in a plain path. Sometimes
I think the storm will soon blow over, and that things will return again to their natural course. I am sure I see no danger
that any of my pupils will prove methodists: I wish many of
them may not run into the contrary extreme. It is really, Sir,
with some confusion that I read your encomium upon my sermon: I am sensible it is some consolation to me, amidst the
uneasiness which, as you conclude, other things must give me.
I hope our design will go on, though it has not at present the
success I could have wished. The dissenters do their part, but
I am sorry to say the neighbouring clergy are exceedingly defi-
cient in theirs." *Doddridge.*

Neal was not the only person of influence amongst the dissenters who was alarmed at Doddridge's liberality. Dr. Jennings assailed him for prefacing a book of Mason's; by which " his friends were given by name," he says, " to be *baited* by the methodists,—as their opposers." At the same time, also, Mr. Blair wrote to him, begging his opinion of Whitefield—" a man," he says, " more railed at by some, and idolized by others, than any person I ever knew in my life." His friend Barker also told him, that he had thought it " needful to warn his hearers to avoid the errors " of Whitefield and his followers. So little did good men appreciate or understand Whitefield at this time!

CHAPTER XI.

WHITEFIELD'S DOMESTIC LIFE.

It is, indeed, almost a *misnomer*, to call Whitefield's conjugal life, domestic. His engagements, like Wesley's, were incompatible with domestic happiness,—as that is understood by domestic men. Accordingly, their kind and degree of home enjoyment he neither expected nor proposed to himself. All that he wanted was, a help meet, who could sympathize in his absorbing public enterprises, as well as in his personal joys and sorrows; and a home, where he might recruit after labour and exhaustion. And such a wife and a home he deserved, as well as needed. He mistook sadly, however, when he sought for such a wife in the ranks of widowhood, then. There were no *missionaries'* widows "in these days." A young female, of eminent piety and zeal, might have fallen in with his habits and plans, and even found her chief happiness in sustaining his mighty and manifold undertakings, like Paul's Phœbe: but a widow, who had been "a housekeeper" (her own) "many years," and that in the retirement of Abergavenny, in Wales, could hardly be expected to unlearn the domestic system of the country, nor to become a heroine for the world. Both Whitefield and Wesley forgot this obvious truth, and married widows.

How much Wesley smarted for this oversight, is as proverbial as it is painful. Mrs. Whitefield had none of Mrs. Wesley's faults. She had, however, no commanding virtues, running in grand parallel with any of the noble features of her husband's character; and thus, because she was not prominently a help to him, she seems to have been reckoned a hinderance, by the gossips and busybodies who watched Mrs. Wesley. These, in their fears for their own "*dear* minister's comfort," watched Mrs. Whitefield also, lest he should be made as unhappy as his old friend!

The tattle of such spies is beneath contempt. It has, however, found some countenance from a quarter which no impartial judge can overlook or underrate. Cornelius Winter, in the letters which form the substance of his "Life," by Jay of Bath, has said expressly, that Whitefield "was not happy in his wife;" that "she certainly did not behave as she ought;" and that "her death set his mind much at rest." Now, whatever this sweeping charge means, it came from a man of the highest character. Of Cornelius Winter, Matthew Wilks used to say, "I am never in this man's company without being reminded of *Paradisaical* innocence." Rowland Hill also, although he did not give Winter credit for all the candour Jay has done, did not hesitate to say of him, that "he would make the worst *devil* of any man in the world;" meaning, that he was the most *unlike* the devil. All this is so true,—that Winter's account of Mrs. Whitefield has acquired currency, although it is neither confirmed nor illustrated by a single document or line from any other writer, so far as I can learn. It will, no doubt, surprise some, however, who have formed their opinion of her from this single source, to be informed that Winter's opportunity of knowing her, from personal observation, was very short. Whitefield was married to her before Winter was born. She died in 1768. Now Winter says, that Berridge introduced him to Whitefield by letter, in February, 1767. *Jay's Life of Winter.* And even then, he did not become "one of the family" until his "fidelity was proved." Thus he had not two years to judge; and even this brief space occurred when Mrs. Whitefield was breaking down. Unless, therefore, he received his information from Whitefield himself, (and he does not say so,) Winter must be deemed, for once, rash, at least.

This is a painful conclusion; but it is inevitable, except on the supposition that the sweeping charge was made against her by her husband. But his first report of her is, that "Mrs. James," although "once gay, is now a despised follower of the

Lamb." *Gillies.* In like manner, throughout a long series of his letters, he uniformly styles her his "dear partner," or "dear fellow-pilgrim," or "dear yoke-fellow," or "dear wife." He also tells with evident delight, how she assisted the sailors to make *cartridges,* when their vessel was preparing for battle, on the voyage to America. He also praises her as his "tender nurse," whilst he was ill at Toronto. He often joins her name with his own, in sending salutations to Lady Huntingdon, Mr. Hervey, and other dear friends. In July, 1768, he writes thus from Edinburgh, "tender love to all, particularly to my dear wife." In the same month (she died in August) he writes to another friend, "My wife is as well as can be expected. Both of us descending, in order to *ascend,*

> ' Where sin, and pain, and sorrow cease,
> And all is calm, and joy, and peace.' "

Is it likely that the man who wrote thus of his wife, from first to last, would have said of her afterwards to Winter, a comparative stranger, what would have warranted Winter to throw so dark a cloud over her memory?

I have given Winter credit for a longer opportunity of observing her, than he himself pretends to have had. "Thrice," he says, "it pleased the Lord to lay him upon a bed of sickness," after he became one of the family. Then, "eight months" of his short opportunity were spent in Bristol, for the recovery of his health. This is not all the subtraction to be made from the time. "A second visit to Bristol held four months." Besides, when he returned to London, he had to "bury the dead at Tottenham Court chapel." *Jay's Life.* Now certainly, whatever may be thought of Winter's high character, it is impossible to attach much importance to his facilities for observation: they were both few and small; and he ought to have said so, instead of leaving the fact to be thus found out by comparing scattered dates, and calculating long intervals of absence.

A great deal, indeed, may be learnt in a short time, in any family, where all is not right between husband and wife; and if Winter, whilst a bachelor, had all those delicate and noble perceptions of conjugal love, which he exemplified when he became a husband, long observation was not necessary in order to enable his fine eye to see exactly how matters stood between Mr. and Mrs. Whitefield.

I have felt it to be my duty to scrutinize this only recorded stigma upon Mrs. Whitefield;—not because I question the general truth of it, so far as Winter was a witness,—but because it passes for more than I think he ever intended. The Whitefields, so far as I can judge, neither lived nor loved like Mr. and Mrs. Winter. They were not unhappy in the sense Mr. and Mrs. Wesley were so; but still their communion of spirit, or oneness of soul, was not what Cornelius Winter nor I could conscientiously call domestic happiness.

I say this, because I cannot forget the *strangeness*, to say the least, of Whitefield's text, when he preached his wife's funeral sermon. It was,—" For the creature was made subject to vanity; not willingly, but by reason of Him who hath subjected the same in hope," Rom. viii. 20. *Gillies*. Now, even if he dwelt upon the context, there was still an implication, anything but complimentary to her memory. In like manner, his letter to Torial Joss on her death, is more pious than tender:—" The late very unexpected breach is a fresh proof that the night soon cometh when no man can work. Pray, where may I *find* that great promise made to Abraham, after Sarah's death? May it be fulfilled in you, whilst your Sarah is yet *alive!* Sweet bereavements, when God himself fills up the void. I find it so." *Letters*. There was no promise, great or small, given on that occasion.

On the other hand, I find a letter a year after her death, in which he says to a friend, " I feel the loss of my ' right hand' daily; but right hands and right eyes must be parted with for Him, who doeth all things well." *Letter* 1406. This acknowledgment Winter had access to when he said that her death set Whitefield's " mind much at rest." He might also have read, as well as myself, the following references to the early and middle parts of their domestic history. Whitefield wrote thus from on board the Wilmington, in 1744: " All except myself seem ready for fire and smoke. My wife, after having dressed

herself to prepare for all events, set about making cartridges,—
whilst the husband wanted to go into the *holes* of the ship,
hearing that was the chaplain's usual place." After recovering
from an attack of colic, which seemed likely to terminate in
mortal convulsions, at York, in the same year, he sang with
gratitude,

> " My wife and friends stood weeping by,
> In tears resolved to *see* me die."

In a subsequent letter, he bears testimony to her usefulness
and zeal : " My dear wife is fully employed in copying my letters. We do not, however, forget our dear London and English friends. We pray for them often, and cannot help wishing
some may come over into this delightful wilderness (Pisca-
taqua); it is a fruitful field." In 1747, he wrote from Charleston to Wales, " My dear yoke-fellow is in Georgia. Blessed be
God, she is well, and prospers in soul and body. We hope to
live and have our hearts warmed with our Welch friends ere
we go hence and be no more." In the same year he wrote thus
of her to a friend, " We lead a moving life, but I trust we move
heavenward." " We are more than happy." " We go on like
two happy pilgrims, leaning on our Beloved." In 1748, when
he sailed from Bermudas to England, he wrote, " I intend to
return to beloved America next year, which is one reason why
I leave my dear yoke-fellow behind. Oh that I knew how it was
with her ! But I see God will make those he loves to live by
faith and not by sense." In 1749 he says, " We are both well,
and surrounded with mercies on every side :—only ungrateful,
ill, and hell-deserving I, want a grateful and humble heart ! "

At a later period, 1754, I find him writing from Lisbon thus :
" You will not forget to visit my *widow-wife !* Blessed be God,
her Maker is her Husband ; and ere long we shall sit down together, at the marriage-supper of the Lamb." In 1756, he
says, " I have no thoughts at present of her ever seeing the
orphan-house again. We shall ere long see heaven. Some ante-
pasts of it we are favoured with already." *Letters.*

But enough, more than enough, is now presented, to prove
that Winter's unqualified statements were unwarranted. I

must, however, add, that they are to me unaccountable, unless he meant only the period whilst he was a witness of the White-field family, and unless he made his *own* experience the standard by which he tried their conjugal love ; and this he has not said. I must, therefore, leave the case of Whitefield *versus* Winter to the verdict of time.

Whitefield's marriage did not interrupt his work, nor damp his ardour. In a few days after, his success in Wales made him exclaim, " God has been pleased to work by my hands since I have been here. O stupendous love. O infinitely con-descending God! " He was married on the 11th of November, 1741, and before the end of the month he was electrifying Bris-tol, as in the days of old. " We have a growing church " here again. It had been checked for a time by the breach between Wesley and Cennick. " Yesterday, and several other times, the Lord hath filled many as with new wine. Sometimes I have scarce known whether I have been in the body or out of the body. It is a good thing to know how to manage a *manifesta-tion* aright; nature so frequently and artfully blends with grace! The more grace I receive, the more I desire to lie as a poor, very poor sinner at the feet of the wounded Lamb."

In this spirit he came to Gloucester, " where, by a particular providence," one of the churches was again opened to him ; St. John's. The old incumbent, who had been his " grand op-poser " formerly, was dead ; and the new minister had not taken possession of the pulpit ; and, therefore, the churchwardens paid their townsman the compliment of a church to preach in, be-cause he was newly married. He preached twice on the sab-bath " with unspeakable power ;" and then upon " a *hill* six miles off," and at night at Stroud. There was, he says, " a new awakening, and revival of the work of God." " We shall never know," he exclaims, " what good field preaching has done, till we come to judgment."

At Stroud and Painswick he flew as on eagles' wings, he says, " with wondrous power, and every sermon was blessed." Whilst thus darting off every now and then from his home, he sent word to Gilbert Tennent, that Mrs. Whitefield, although neither " rich in fortune, nor beautiful in person, was a true

child of God," who would not "for the world hinder him in
God's work." "The Lord hath given me a daughter of Abraham," he says to another American friend.

In February, 1742, Whitefield returned to London, where
"life and power soon flew all around" him again; "the Redeemer getting himself victory daily in many hearts." The
renewed progress of the gospel at this time in London, he calls
emphatically, "the Redeemer's *stately steps*." Well he might;
for during the Easter holidays, "Satan's booths" in Moorfields poured out their thousands to hear him. This determined him to dare all hazards on Whit-Monday, the great gala-
day of vanity and vice there. Gillies' account of this enterprise,
although not incorrect nor uninteresting, is very incomplete,
considering the fame of the feat at the time. The following
account is from the pen of Whitefield himself; and written
whilst he was reporting, at home and abroad, his marriage.

"For many years, from one end of Moorfields to the other,
booths of all kinds have been erected for mountebanks, players,
puppet-shows, and such like. With a heart bleeding with compassion for so many thousands led captive by the devil at his
will, on *Whit-Monday*, at six o'clock in the morning, attended
by a large congregation of praying people, I ventured to lift up
a standard amongst them in the name of Jesus of *Nazareth*.
Perhaps there were about ten thousand in waiting, not for me,
but for Satan's instruments to amuse them.—Glad was I to find,
that I had for once as it were got the start of the devil. I
mounted my field pulpit; almost all flocked immediately around
it. I preached on these words, ' As *Moses* lifted up the serpent
in the wilderness, so shall the Son of man be lifted up,' &c.
They gazed, they listened, they wept; and I believe that many
felt themselves stung with deep conviction for their past sins.
All was hushed and solemn. Being thus encouraged, I ventured out again at noon; but what a scene! The fields, the
whole fields seemed, in a bad sense of the word, all white, ready
not for the Redeemer's, but Beelzebub's harvest. All his
agents were in full motion, drummers, trumpeters, merry-andrews, masters of puppet-shows, exhibiters of wild beasts,
players, &c. &c. all busy in entertaining their respective audi-

tories. I suppose there could not be less than twenty or thirty thousand people. My pulpit was fixed on the opposite side, and immediately, to their great mortification, they found the number of their attendants sadly lessened. Judging that, like Saint Paul, I should now be called as it were to fight with beasts at *Ephesus*, I preached from these words : 'Great is *Diana* of the *Ephesians.*' You may easily guess, that there was some noise among the craftsmen, and that I was honoured with having a few stones, dirt, rotten eggs, and pieces of dead cats thrown at me, whilst engaged in calling them from their favourite but lying vanities. My soul was indeed among lions ; but far the greatest part of my congregation, which was very large, seemed for a while to be turned into lambs. This encouraged me to give notice that I would preach again at six o'clock in the evening. I came, I saw, but what—thousands and thousands more than before, if possible, still more deeply engaged in their unhappy diversions ; but some thousands amongst them waiting as earnestly to hear the gospel.

This Satan could not brook. One of his choicest servants was exhibiting, trumpeting on a large stage ; but as soon as the people saw me in my black robes and my pulpit, I think all to a man left him and ran to me. For a while I was enabled to lift up my voice like a trumpet, and many heard the joyful sound. God's people kept praying, and the enemy's agents made a kind of a roaring at some distance from our camp. At length they approached nearer, and the merry-andrew (attended by others, who complained that they had taken many pounds less that day on account of my preaching) got up upon a man's shoulders, and advancing near the pulpit attempted to slash me with a long heavy whip several times, but always with the violence of his motion tumbled down. Soon afterwards they got a recruiting serjeant with his drum, &c. to pass through the congregation. I gave the word of command, and ordered that way might be made for the king's officer. The ranks opened, while all marched quietly through, and then closed again. Finding those efforts to fail, a large body quite on the opposite side assembled together, and having got a large pole for their standard, advanced towards us with steady and formidable steps, till they came very near the skirts of our hearing, praying, and almost undaunted congregation. I saw, gave warning, and prayed to the Captain of our salvation for present support and deliverance. He heard and answered; for just as they approached us with looks full of resentment, I know not by what accident, they quarrelled among themselves, threw down their staff and went their way, leaving, however, many of their company behind, who, before we had done, I trust were brought over to join the besieged party. I think I continued in praying, preaching, and singing (for the noise was too great at times to preach) about three hours.

" We then retired to the Tabernacle, with my pockets full of notes from persons brought under concern, and read them amidst the praises and spiritual acclamations of thousands, who joined with the holy angels in rejoicing that so many sinners were snatched, in such an unexpected, unlikely place and manner, out of the very jaws of the devil. This was the beginning of the Tabernacle society.—Three hundred and fifty awakened souls were received in one day, and I believe the number of notes exceeded a thousand; but I must have done, believing you want to retire to join in mutual praise and thanksgiving to God and the Lamb.

" Fresh matter of praise; bless ye the Lord, for he hath triumphed gloriously. The battle that was begun on *Monday,* was not quite over till Wednesday evening, though the scene of action was a little shifted. Being strongly invited, and a pulpit being prepared for me by an honest quaker, a coal merchant, I ventured on *Tuesday* evening to preach at *Mary le Bow Fields,* a place almost as much frequented by boxers, gamesters, and such like, as *Moorfields.* A vast concourse was assembled together, and as soon as I got into the field pulpit, their countenances bespoke the enmity of their hearts against the preacher. I opened with these words—' I am not ashamed of the gospel of Christ, for it is the power of God unto salvation to every one that believeth.' I preached in great jeopardy; for the pulpit being high, and the supports not well fixed in the ground, it tottered every time I moved, and numbers of enemies strove to push my friends against the supporters, in order to throw me down. But the Redeemer stayed my soul on himself, therefore I was not much moved, unless with compassion for those to whom I was delivering my Master's message, which I had reason to think, by the strong impressions that were made, was welcome to many. But Satan did not like thus to be attacked in his strong holds, and I narrowly escaped with my life : for as I was passing from the pulpit to the coach, I felt my wig and hat to be almost off. I turned about, and observed a sword just touching my temples. A young rake, as I afterwards found, was determined to stab me, but a gentleman, seeing the sword thrusting near me, struck it up with his cane, and so the destined victim providentially escaped. Such an attempt excited abhorrence ; the enraged multitude soon seized him, and had it not been for one of my friends, who received him into his house, he must have undergone a severe discipline. The next day, I renewed my attack in *Moorfields;* but, would you think it? after they found that pelting, noise, and threatenings would not do, one of the *merry-andrews* got up into a tree very near the pulpit, and shamefully exposed himself before all the people. Such a beastly action quite abashed the serious part of my auditory ; whilst hundreds of another stamp, instead of rising to pull down the unhappy wretch, expressed their approbation by repeated laughs. I must own that, at first, it gave me a shock. I thought Satan had outdone himself. But, recovering my spirits, I appealed to all, since they had now such a spectacle before them, whether I had wronged human nature, in saying, after pious Bishop Hall, ' that man, when left to himself, was half a beast and half a devil;' or, as the great Mr. Law expressed himself, ' a motley mixture of beast and devil.'

" Silence and attention being thus gained, I concluded with a warm exhortation, and closed our festival enterprises in reading fresh notes that were put up, praising and blessing God, amidst thousands at the Tabernacle, for what he had done for precious souls, and on account of the deliverances he had wrought out for me and his people. I could enlarge ; but being about to embark in the *Mary and Ann* for *Scotland,* I must hasten to a close : but I cannot help adding, that several little boys and girls who were fond of sitting round me on the pulpit, while I preached, and handing to me people's notes, though they were often pelted with eggs, dirt, &c. thrown at me, never once gave way; but, on the contrary, every time I was struck, turned up their little weeping eyes, and seemed to wish they could receive the blows for me. God make them in their growing years great and living martyrs for him, who out of the mouths of babes and sucklings perfects praise!" *Letters.*

In this way Whitefield signalized his marriage ; verifying to his wife the assurance he had given her, that he would not preach a sermon less, nor travel a mile fewer, than formerly. And she had no occasion to regret, that he did not take her with him in his short excursions around London ; for, however good a rider he was, he was a bad driver. The first time he took her out in a chaise, he drove into a ditch. " My wife," he says to a friend, " has been in trying circumstances, partly through the unskilfulness of a chaise-driver ;—I mean *myself.* Being advised to take her out into the air, I drove her, as well as myself, through inadvertency, into a ditch. Finding that we were falling—she put her hand across the chaise, and thereby preserved us both from being thrown out. The ditch might be about fourteen feet deep ; but, blessed be God, though all that saw us falling, cried out, They are killed, yet, through infinite mercy, we received no great hurt. The place was very narrow near the bottom, and yet the horse went down, as though let down by a pulley. A stander-by ran down and catched hold of its head, to prevent its going forwards. I got upon its back, and was drawn out by a long whip, whilst my wife, hanging between the chaise and the bank, was pulled up on the other side by two or three kind assistants. Being both in a comfortable frame, I must own, to my shame, that I felt rather regret than thankfulness in escaping what I thought would be a kind of a *translation* to our wished-for haven. But, O amazing love ! we were so strengthened, that the chaise and horse being taken up, and our bruises being washed with vinegar in a neighbouring house, we went on our intended way, and came home rejoicing in God our Saviour. Not expecting my wife's confinement for some time, I intend making a short excursion, and then you may expect further news."

It must not be supposed that the chaise was his own. He was so poor, at this time, that he had to *borrow* furniture for his house. This may surprise some; but it is only too true. " I thank you a thousand times for your great generosity," he writes to a friend, " in lending me some furniture;—having little of my own. I know who will repay you." *Lett.* 546.

Even this is not all the fact concerning his poverty. Almost immediately after the baptism of his son, he wrote to the same friend, " My dear wife and little one will come to Gloucester, for I find it *beyond* my circumstances to maintain them here. But why talk of wife and little one? Let all be absorbed in the thoughts of the love, sufferings, free and full salvation of the infinitely great and glorious Emmanuel. In respect to other things, at present, this is the habitual language of my heart,

> ' Thy gifts, if called for, I resign;
> Pleased to receive, pleased to restore.
> Gifts are thy work. It shall be mine,
> The Giver only to adore.' "

It was well he was thus minded; for he had soon to give up his Isaac. The journey to Gloucester proved fatal to the child: and yet, how *slightly* he refers to the poverty which rendered that journey necessary! His narrative of the event is very touching, in all respects.

" Who knows what a day may bring forth? Last night I was called to sacrifice my Isaac; I mean to bury my only child and son, about four months old. Many things occurred to make me believe he was not only to be continued to me, but to be a preacher of the everlasting gospel. Pleased with the thought, and ambitious of having a son of my own so divinely employed, Satan was permitted to give me some wrong impressions, whereby, as I now find, I misapplied several texts of Scripture. Upon these grounds I made no scruple of declaring ' that I should have a son, and that his name was to be *John.*' I mentioned the very time of his birth, and fondly hoped that he was to be great in the sight of the Lord. Every thing happened according to the predictions; and my wife having had

several narrow escapes while pregnant, especially by her falling
from a high horse, and my driving her into a deep ditch in a
one-horse chaise a little before the time of her confinement, and
from which we received little or no hurt, confirmed me in my
expectation, that God would grant me my heart's desire. I
would observe to you, that the child was even born in a room,
which the master of the house had prepared as a prison for his
wife for coming to hear me. With joy would she often look
upon the bars, and staples, and chains which were fixed in
order to keep her in. About a week after his birth, I publicly
baptized him in the Tabernacle, and in the company of thousands
solemnly gave him up to that God who gave him to me. A
hymn, too fondly composed by an aged widow, as suitable to
the occasion, was sung, and all went away big with hopes of the
child's being hereafter to be employed in the work of God;
but how soon, are all their fond, and, as the event hath proved,
their ill-grounded expectations blasted as well as mine! House-
keeping being expensive in London, I thought it best to send
both parent and child to Abergavenny, where my wife had a little house of my own, the furniture of which, as I thought of soon
embarking for Georgia, I had partly sold, and partly given
away. In their journey thither, they stopped at Gloucester, at
the Bell Inn, which my brother now keeps, and in which I was
born. There my beloved was cut off with a stroke. Upon my
coming here, without knowing what had happened, I inquired
concerning the welfare of parent and child; and by the answer
found that the flower was cut down. I immediately called all to
join in prayer, in which I blessed the Father of mercies for
giving me a son, continuing it to me so long, and taking it from
me so soon. All joined in desiring that I would decline preaching till the child was buried; but I remembered a saying of
good Mr. Henry, ' that weeping must not hinder sowing,' and
therefore preached twice the next day, and also the day following; on the evening of which, just as I was closing my sermon,
the bell struck out for the funeral. At first, I must acknowledge, it gave nature a little shake, but looking up I recovered
strength, and then concluded with saying, that this text on
which I had been preaching, namely, ' All things worked toge-

ther for good to them that love God,' made me as willing to go out to my son's funeral, as to hear of his birth.   Our parting from him was solemn.   We kneeled down, prayed, and shed many tears, but I hope tears of resignation : and then, as he died in the house wherein I was born, he was taken and laid in the church where I was baptized, first communicated, and first preached.   All this you may easily guess threw me into very solemn and deep reflection, and I hope deep humiliation ; but I was comforted from that passage in the book of Kings, where is recorded the death of the Shunammite's child, which the pro phet said, ' the Lord had hid from him ;' and the woman's answer likewise to the prophet when he asked, ' Is it well with thee ? Is it well with thy husband ? Is it well with thy child ? ' And she answered, ' *It is well.*'   This gave me no small satisfaction.   I immediately preached upon the text the day following at Gloucester, and then hastened up to London, preached upon the same there ; and though disappointed of a *living* preacher by the death of my son, yet I hope what happened before his birth, and since at his death, hath taught me such lessons, as, if duly improved, may render his mistaken parent more cautious, more sober-minded, more experienced in Satan's devices, and consequently more useful in his future labours to the church of God.   Thus, ' out of the eater comes forth sweetness.'   Not doubting but our future life will be one continued explanation of this *blessed riddle*, I commend myself and you to the unerring guidance of God's word and Spirit."

Happily for himself, Whitefield had the prosecution of the Hampton rioters to provide for at this time.   This compelled him to bestir himself in visiting and corresponding, in order to obtain money to meet the expenses of the trial.   He took a right view of that outrage when he said, " much depends on our getting the victory."   Colonel Gardiner (now his friend) entered into this view of the case, and sustained him.   So did many other influential men.   A lady, also, in Wales, subscribed five pounds towards the expenses.   The Welch Association were " very generous, according to their circumstances;" and the Tabernacle friends had " a glorious fast, at which they collected above sixty pounds " for the assistance of their suffering brethren

at Hampton.   The following is his own account of " The Occasion, Process, and Issue of the Trial at Gloucester, March
3, 1743."

" On Thursday evening I came hither from the Gloucester
assizes, where I have been engaged in a trial between some of
those who are called methodists, and some violent rioters.
Perhaps this news may a little startle you, and put you upon
inquiry (as it hath done some others) ' How we came to go to
law with our adversaries, when it is our avowed principle to
suffer patiently for the truth's sake ?'   I will tell you, my dear
friend : though perhaps there is nothing in the world more
abused than the law, and there are very few that go to law out
of a proper principle ; yet we hold that there is a proper use of
it, and the law is good when used lawfully.   Whether or no we
have used it lawfully in the present case, I shall leave my
friend to judge, after I have told him the motives that induced
us to engage in it.—The methodists, you know, are every where
accounted enthusiasts, in the worst sense of the word ; but
though they are accounted such, yet they would not be enthusiasts in reality.   Now we look upon it to be one species of enthusiasm, to expect to attain an end without making use of
proper means.   We also think that believers should be very
careful not to be fond of suffering persecution, when they may
avoid it by making application to the high powers.   We are
likewise of opinion, that good christians will be good subjects,
and consequently it is their duty, as much as in them lies, to
put a stop to every thing in a rightful way, that may prove destructive to the king or the government under which they live.
Christian ministers, in particular, we think, ought to consider
the weakness of people's grace, and, in pity to precious souls,
do what they can to remove every thing out of the way that
may discourage or prevent poor people's hearing the everlasting
gospel.   These considerations, my dear friend, for some time
past, have led me to examine whether the *methodists* in general
(and I myself in particular) have acted the part of good subjects, and judicious christian ministers, in so long neglecting to
make an application to the superior courts, and putting in execution the wholesome laws of the land, in order to prevent those

many dreadful outrages which have been committed against us. I need not descend to particulars. Our *Weekly History* is full of them; and before that came out, several of our brethren, both in England and Wales, have received much damage from time to time, and been frequently in great hazard of their lives. Wiltshire has been very remarkable for mobbing and abusing the methodists; and, for about ten months last past, it has also prevailed very much in Gloucestershire, especially at Hampton, where our friend Mr. Adams has a dwelling-house, and has been much blessed to many people. This displeased the grand enemy of souls, who stirred up many of the baser sort, privately encouraged by some of a higher rank, to. come from time to time, in great numbers, with a low-bell and horn, to beset the house, and beat and abuse the people.

" About the beginning of July last, their opposition seemed to rise to the highest. For several days they assembled in great bodies, broke the windows, and mobbed the people to such a degree, that many expected to be murdered, and hid themselves in holes and corners, to avoid the rage of their adversaries. Once, when I was there, they continued from four in the afternoon till midnight, rioting, giving loud huzzas, casting dirt upon the hearers, and making proclamations, ' That no anabaptists, presbyterians, &c. should preach there, upon pain of being first put into a tan-pit, and afterwards into a brook.' At another time they pulled one or two women down the stairs by the hair of their heads. And on the 10th of July they came, to the number of near a hundred, in their usual way, with a low-bell and horn, about five in the afternoon, forced into Mr. Adams's house, and demanded him down the stairs whereon he was preaching, took him out of his house, and threw him into a tan-pit full of noisome things and stagnated water. One of our friends named Williams asking them, ' If they were not ashamed to serve an innocent man so ? ' they put him into the same pit twice, and afterwards beat him, and dragged him along the kennel. Mr. Adams quietly returned home, and betook himself to prayer, and exhorted the people to rejoice in suffering for the sake of the gospel. In about half an hour they came to the house again, dragged him down the stairs, and led him away a mile and a half to a place called Bourn Brook, and then threw him in. A stander-by, fearing he might be drowned, jumped in and pulled him out; whereupon another of the rioters immediately pushed him into the pool a second time, and cut his leg against a stone, so that he went lame for near a fortnight. Both the constable and justices were applied to, but refused to act, and seemed rather to countenance the mobbing, hoping thereby *methodism* (as they called it) would be put a stop to, at least at Hampton. For a season they gained their end. There was no preaching for some time, the people fearing to assemble on account of the violence of the mob.

" Upon my return to town, I advised with my friends what to do. We knew we wanted to exercise no revenge against the rioters, and yet we thought it wrong that the gospel should be stopped by such persons, when the government under which we lived countenanced no such thing; and also that it was absurd to thank God for wholesome laws, if they were not to be made use of. We knew very well, that an apostle had told us, that magistrates were ordained for the punishment of evil-doers; and that they bear not the sword in vain. We were also fearful that if any of our brethren should be murdered by future riotings, (as in all probability they might,) we should be accessary to their death, if we neglected to tie up the rioters' hands, which was all we desired to do. Besides, we could not look upon this as allowed persecution, since it was not countenanced by the laws of the land, and we might have redress from these rioters and inferior magistrates, by appealing to Cæsar, whose real friends and loyal subjects we judged ourselves not to be, if we suffered his laws to be publicly trampled under foot by such notorious rioting; and which, though begun against the methodists, might terminate in open rebellion against King George. For these and such like reasons, we thought it our duty to move for an information in the King's Bench against five of the ringleaders, and fixed upon the riot which they made on Sunday, July 10th, when they put Mr. Adams and Williams into the tan-pit and brook. But before this was done, I wrote a letter to one whom they called Captain, desiring him to inform his associates, ' That if they would acknowledge their fault, pay for curing a boy's arm, which was broken the night I was there, and mend the windows of Mr. Adams's house, we would readily pass all by; but if they persisted in their resolutions to riot, we thought it our duty to prevent their doing, and others receiving, further damage, by moving for an information against them in the King's Bench.' I also sent a copy of this letter to a minister of the town, and to a justice of the peace, with a letter to each from myself: but all in vain. The rioters sent me a most insolent answer, wrote me word, 'They were in high spirits, and were resolved there should be no more preaching in Hampton.' Finding them *irreclaimable*, we moved the next term for a rule of court in the King's Bench, to lodge an information against five of the ringleaders, for the outrage committed, violence offered, and damage done to Mr. Adams and Williams, on Sunday, July 10th. The rioters were apprized of it, appeared by their counsel, and prayed the rule might be enlarged till the next term. It was granted. In the mean while they continued mobbing, broke into Mr. Adams's house one Saturday night at eleven o'clock, when there was no preaching, made those that were in bed get up, and searched the oven, cellar, and every corner of the house, to see whether they could find any methodists. Some time after, they threw another young man into a mud pit three times successively, and abused the people in a dreadful manner.

" The next term came on. We proved our accusations by twenty-six affidavits; and the defendants making no reply, the rule was made absolute, and an information filed against them. To this they pleaded *not guilty;* and, according to the method in the Crown Office, the cause was referred to the assize held at Gloucester, March 3d. Thither I went, and on Tuesday morning last the trial came on. It was given out by some, that the methodists were to lose the cause, whether right or wrong. · And I believe the defendants depended much on a supposition that the gentlemen and jury would be prejudiced against us. We were easy, knowing that our Saviour had the hearts of all in his hands. Being aware of the great consequences of gaining or losing this trial, both in respect to us and the nation, we kept a day of fasting and prayer through all the

societies both in England and Wales.   Our Scotch friends also
joined with us, and cheerfully committed our cause into His
hands by whom kings reign and princes decree justice.   We
had about thirty witnesses to prove the riot and facts laid down
in the information.   Our counsel opened the cause (as I heard,
being not present when the trial begun) with much solidity and
sound reasoning: they showed, that rioters were not to be
reformers; and that his Majesty had no where put the reins of
government into the hands of mobbers, or made them judge or
jury.   One of them in particular, with great gravity, reminded
the gentlemen on the jury of the advice of Gamaliel, a doctor
of the law, recorded Acts v. 38, 39, " Refrain from these men,
and let them alone; for if this counsel, or this work, be of men,
it will come to nought; but if it be of God, ye cannot overthrow it, lest haply ye be found even to fight against God.'
Our witnesses were then called.   I came into court when the
second witness was examining.   Mr. Adams and four more
(three of which were not called methodists) so clearly proved both
the riot and the facts laid to the charge of the defendants, that
the judge was of opinion there needed no other evidence.   The
counsel for the defendants then rose and exerted a good deal of
oratory, and I think said all that could well be said, to make
the best of a bad matter.   One urged, that we were enthusiasts, and our principles and practices had such a tendency to
infect and hurt the people, that it was right, in his opinion, for
any private person to stand up and put a stop to us; and whoever did so, was a friend to his country.   He strove to influence the jury, by telling them, that if a verdict was given
against the defendants, it would cost them two hundred pounds;
that the defendants' rioting was not premeditated; but, that
coming to hear Mr. Adams, and being offended at his doctrine,
a sudden quarrel arose, and thereby the unhappy men were led
into the present fray, which he could have wished had not happened; but however it did not amount to a riot, but only an *assault*.   Their other counsel then informed the jury, that they
would undertake to prove that the methodists began the tumults
first.   He was pleased also to mention me by name, and acquainted the court, that Mr. Whitefield had been travelling

from common to common, making the people cry, and then picking their pockets, under pretence of collecting money for the colony of Georgia; and knowing that Gloucestershire was a populous country, he at last came there. That he had now several curates, of which Mr. Adams was one, who in his preaching had found fault with the proceedings of the clergy, and said if the people went to hear them, they would be damned. He added, that there had lately been such a mobbing in Staffordshire, that a regiment of soldiers was sent down to suppress them; insinuating that the methodists were the authors; that we had now another cause of a like nature depending in Wiltshire; and that we were not of that mild, pacific spirit as we would pretend to be.—This, and much more to the same purpose, though foreign to the matter in hand, pleased many of the auditors, who expressed their satisfaction in hearing the methodists in general, and me in particular, thus lashed, by frequent laughing. The eyes of all were upon me. Our Saviour kept me quite easy. I thought of that verse of Horace,

'——Hic murus aheneus esto,
Nil conscire sibi, nulla pallescere culpa.'

Tertullus's accusing Paul came also to my mind, and I looked upon myself as highly honoured in having such things spoken against me falsely for Christ's great name's sake. To prove what the defendants' counsel had insinuated, they called up a young man, who was brother to one of the defendants, and one of the mob. He swore point blank, that Mr. Adams said, if people went to church they would be damned; and if they would come to him, he would carry them to Jesus Christ. He swore also, that the pool into which Mr. Adams was thrown, was no deeper than half way up his legs. He said first, that there were about ten of them that came to the house of Mr. Adams; and then he swore that there were about threescore. He said, there was a low-bell, and that one of the defendants did ask Mr. Adams to come down off the stairs, but that none of them went up to him; upon which Mr. Adams willingly obeyed, went with them briskly along the street, and, as he would have represented it, put himself into the tan-pit and pool, and so came out again. He said also some other things; but throughout his whole evidence appeared so flagrantly false, that one of the counsellors said, it was enough to make his hair stand on end. The judge himself wished he had had so much religion as to fear an oath. So he went down in disgrace. Their second evidence was an aged woman, mother to one of the defendants. She swore that her son did go up the stairs to Mr. Adams, and that Mr. Adams tore her son's coat, and would have broken his neck down-stairs. But she talked so fast, and her evidence was so palpably false, that she was sent away in as much disgrace as the other. Their third and last evidence was father to one who was in the mob, though not one of the defendants. The chief he had to say was, that when Mr. Adams was coming from the pool, one met him, and said, 'Brother, how do you do?' Upon which he answered, that he had received no damage, but had been in the pool, and came out again. So that all their evidences, however contrary to one another, yet corroborated ours, and proved the riot out of their own mouths. The book was then given to a justice of the peace, who had formerly taken up Mr. Cennick for preaching near Stroud, and had lately given many signal proofs that he was no friend to the methodists. But he intending to speak only about their characters, and the counsel and judge looking upon that as quite impertinent to the matter in hand, he was not admitted as an evidence. Upon this, his Lordship, with great candour and impartiality, summed up the evidence, and told the jury, that he thought they should bring all the defendants in guilty; for our evidences had sufficiently proved the whole of the information, and also that the riot was premeditated. He said, that, in his opinion, the chief of the defendants' evidence was incredible; and that, supposing the methodists were heterodox, (as perhaps they might be,) it belonged to the ecclesiastical government to call them to an account; that they were subjects, and riotous men were not to be their reformers. He also reminded them of the dreadful ill consequences of rioting at any time, much more at such a critical time as this; that rioting was the forerunner of, and might end in, rebellion; that it was felony, without benefit of clergy, to pull down a meeting-house; and, for all he knew, it was high treason to pull down even a brothel. That this information came from the King's Bench; that his Majesty's justices there thought they had sufficient reason to grant it; that the matters contained in it had been evidently proved before them, and consequently they should bring all the defendants in guilty. Upon this the jury were desired to consider of their verdict. There seemed to be some little demur amongst them. His Lordship perceiving it, informed them, They had nothing to do with the damages, (that was to be referred to the King's Bench,) they were only to consider whether the defendants were guilty or not.

" Whereupon, in a few minutes, they gave a verdict for the prosecutors, and brought in all the defendants, ' guilty of the whole information lodged against them.' I then retired to my lodgings, kneeled down, and gave thanks with some friends to our all-conquering *Emmanuel.* Afterwards I went to the inn, prayed, and returned thanks with the witnesses, exhorted them to behave with meekness and humility to their adversaries, and after they had taken proper refreshment sent them home rejoicing. In the evening I preached on those words of the psalmist, ' By this I know that thou favourest me, since thou hast not suffered mine enemy to triumph over me.' God was pleased to enlarge my heart much. I was very happy with my friends afterwards, and the next morning set out for London, where we have had a blessed thanksgiving season, and from whence I take the first opportunity of sending you as many particulars of the occasion, progress, and issue of our trial, as I can well recollect. What report his Lordship will be pleased to make of the case, and how the defendants will be dealt with, cannot be known till next term; when I know I shall apprize you of it, as also of our behaviour towards them.—In the mean while let me entreat you to give thanks to the blessed Jesus in our behalf, and to pray that his word may have free course, may run and be glorified, and a stop be put to all such rebellious proceedings." *The Trial, in a Letter to a Friend.*

Whitefield had also at this time to put some *writers* as well as rioters upon their defence. An anonymous pamphlet, " On

the Conduct and Behaviour of the Methodists," had obtained
no small sanction from the bishops.   Indeed, the bishop of London was reported to be the author of it.   The object of it was,
to prove the methodists to be dangerous to both church and
state, and to obtain an Act of Parliament against them, which
would stop their field preaching and conventicles, or compel
them "to secure themselves by turning dissenters."   The Toleration Act, it argued, did not permit their irregularities : and
besides, they were *enthusiasts !* Parts of this pamphlet seem
to have been printed and handed about secretly at first, as
feelers of the pulse of the religious societies.   Strict injunctions
were given to every one who was intrusted with any of them,
" not to lend them, nor let them go out of his hands."   Whitefield, however, obtained a sight of them ; and finding that they
contained not only charges against himself, but a deep design
against religious liberty, he *advertised* in the newspapers, and
demanded their speedy publication, that he might answer them
before he went to America.   He followed up this advertisement
by a private letter to the bishop of London.   " My Lord, simplicity becomes the followers of Jesus Christ, and therefore I
think it my duty to trouble your Lordship with a few lines, concerning the anonymous papers which have been handed about
in the societies.   As I think it my duty to answer them, I should
be glad to be informed whether the report be true, that your
Lordship composed them, that I may the better know how to answer them.   A sight also of one of the copies, if in your Lordship's
keeping, would much oblige."   His Lordship sent word by the
bearer, that Whitefield should " hear from him ;" but he forgot
his promise.   Whitefield heard from the printer, not from the
prelate.   " Sir, my name is Owen.   I am a printer in Amen
Corner.   I have had orders from several of the bishops to print
for their use, such numbers of the ' Observations ' (with some few
additions) as they have respectively bespoken.   I will not fail
to wait on you with *one* copy, as soon as the impression is
finished."   Owen kept his word.   He did not venture, however, to put his name on the title page of the pamphlet, " to let
the world know where, or by whom, it was printed."   " It came
into the world," says Whitefield in a letter to the bishop, " like

a dropt child, that nobody cares to own.   And, indeed, who can
be blamed for disowning such a libel ?   A more notorious libel
has not been published."   *Lett.*

Whitefield was fully justified in branding the pamphlet thus.
It charged the methodists with making "open inroads on the
national constitution ;" with *pretending* to be "members of the
national church ;" with being "open defiers of government,"
as well as breakers of "the canons and rubrics."   His answer
to this, Whitefield addressed, very properly, to "The bishop
of London, and the other bishops concerned in the publication" of such charges ; taking for his motto the appropriate
words, "*False witnesses did rise up : they laid to my charge
things I knew not.*"   They did not sit down so easily as they
rose up !   They told the religious societies, clandestinely, that
methodism was unlawful ; and Whitefield told the world, openly,
that this mode of attack was "like *Nero* setting fire to Rome,
and then charging it on the christians."   "I cannot think," he
says, "that such a way of proceeding will gain your Lordships
any credit from the public—or any thanks from the *other*
bishops who have not interested themselves in this affair, and
who, I believe, are more NOBLE than to countenance the publication of any such performance."

This bold retort upon anonymous slanderers, astounded both
the slaves and the sycophants of "superiors."   Prebendary
Church, the vicar of Battersea, was *horrified* to find the heads
of the church made accountable for a libel they had adopted,
if not indorsed.   This is the worthy to whom Bolingbroke said,
"Let me tell you seriously, that the greatest miracle in the
world is, the subsistence of christianity, and its preservation as
a religion, when the preaching of it is committed to the care of
such unchristian wretches as you."   This tremendous rebuke
does not, I think, imply all that the word *wretch* means.   It
refers to principles, not to morals.   I am led to this conclusion,
because Whitefield treats Church respectfully, in answering his
pamphlet, and because the following is the true account of the
prebendary's interview with the peer.   Church found Bolingbroke reading Calvin's Institutes, one day, and was surprised.
"You have caught me," said the viscount, "reading John Cal-

vin. He was, indeed, a man of great parts, profound sense, and vast learning. He handles the doctrines of grace in a very masterly manner." (Strange language from Bolingbroke! But he had been hearing Whitefield at Lady Huntingdon's the week before.) "Doctrines of grace!" exclaimed Church, "the doctrines of grace have set all mankind by the ears." "I am surprised," said Bolingbroke, "to hear you say so, who profess to believe and preach christianity. Those doctrines are certainly the doctrines of the Bible; and if I believe the Bible I must believe them." Then came the well known rebuke I have quoted. This is the anecdote, as the Countess of Huntingdon was wont to tell it; and she had it from the lips of Bolingbroke. *Toplady*.

I would not have referred to the prebendary or his pamphlet, had he not become the *scape-goat* for the bishops he vindicated. There is quite as much of the gospel in his letter to Whitefield, as in their charges to their clergy. The only thing amusing in Church's letter is its conclusion. He charges Whitefield with glaring inconsistency, in blaming the clergy for non-residence. "You have been *more* culpable than any of them," he says, in reference to Whitefield's residence at Georgia. He then proceeds to count the times, and the length of each time, that Whitefield was at his post. This was pitiful; knowing as he did *why* the chaplain of the colony travelled. Well might Whitefield say, in answer to this charge, "I wish every non-resident could give as good an account of his non-residence, as I can give of mine. When I was absent from my parishioners, I was not loitering nor living at ease, but *begging* for them and theirs; and when I returned, it was not to fleece my flock, and then go and spend it upon my lusts, or to lay up a fortune for myself and my relations." *Letter to Church*.

Whitefield's letter to the bishops called forth another champion of the clandestine papers; a Pembroke College man, who called himself "a gentleman," although he took a motto from that vilest of all vulgar books, "The Scotch Presbyterian Eloquence." He did not fail in imitating his original. He finds in Whitefield's letter, instead of "the arguing of the true saint, the *wheedling* of the woman; the daring of the *rebel*; the pertness of the *coxcomb;* the evasions of the *jesuit;* and the bitter maliciousness of the *bigot.* He classes him with Bonner and Gardiner, as " a fire-brand minister of wrath ;" and with Cromwell, whom he calls " the *Whitefield* of the last century." Why? Because he "artfully compounded churchmen and dissenters." " It will be an eternal monument of your disgrace," he says, "that dissenters lived peaceably, according to the national constitution, and preached in licensed places, until *you* poisoned and corrupted them, by your evil communications." Would he had! But unfortunately for the dissenters then, Whitefield's influence had brought only *two* into the fields, as fellow-helpers with him in the gospel.

He does not appear to have noticed this Pembroke gentleman; but he renewed his attack upon the bishops, when he went to sea. On his voyage, he wrote a second letter to them. They had made the anonymous pamphlet their own, by printing and circulating it at their own expense ; and he held them accountable for its *doctrines,* as well as its politics. It had impugned justification by faith, and he stretched them on Luther's rack ; and on what must have been more annoying to their Lordships, the fact, that this doctrine was *singled out* by Edward VI. and Elizabeth, to be *principally* taught to the people ; " First, because it is the chiefest cause and means of our peace with God ; second, that ministers might go with a *right-foot* (ορθοποδεῖν) to the gospel ; third, because it is the best way ' to discover and suppress Romish antichrist ;' and fourth, because ' such bishops as do, by terms of error, schism, or heresy, hinder this *main light* of God's word from the people, are the *chiefest traitors* in the land ; traitors to God, traitors to their king, traitors to their own souls and bodies, and traitors to the whole country." *Homily.* Gibson remembered this homily when he said, " Justification by faith alone is asserted in the strongest manner by our church :" but he forgot it when he added, " I hope our clergy explain it in such a manner, as to leave no doubt whether good works are a necessary *condition* of being justified in the sight of God." *Pastoral Letter.*

From this vantage ground, Whitefield assailed both Chillingworth and the author of " The Whole Duty of Man," as

U

traitors to this *" articulus stantis aut caudentis ecclesiæ."* The latter, he said, had shown only *" Half the Duty of Man;"* and the former had made " universal obedience" a necessary condition of justification. In like manner, whilst be begged pardon of the public for saying that Tillotson knew no more of the gospel than Mahomet, (a comparison, by the way, which he had borrowed,) he repeated, that "the good archbishop, in turning people's minds to moral duties, without turning them to the doctrine of justification by faith," erred from the faith.

" Incidit in Scyllam, qui vult vitare Charibdin."

He did not embarrass their Lordships less on the subject of regeneration. Their adopted champion had said, " If there be such a thing—as a sudden, instantaneous change." " If there be," says Whitefield ; " does he not lay an axe to the very root of the baptismal office ? If the child be actually regenerated, when the minister sprinkles it, the change must be instantaneous and sudden. If there *be* any such thing ! Do your Lordships assent thereto ? An instantaneous change is the very essence of baptismal regeneration,—that DIANA of the present clergy."

He concludes this bold appeal thus, " If the whole bench of bishops command us to speak no more of this doctrine, we take it to be an *ungodly* admonition. Whether it be right in the sight of God, to obey man rather than God,—judge ye ! " *Second Letter.*

These were the public affairs which diverted Whitefield from his private sorrows. The *off-hand* and unceremonious style in which they are told, can only offend those who venerate *titles* more than truth. It may be vastly unpolite to treat bishops in this straightforward way, when they pervert the gospel : it is, however, *apostolical* to pay neither deference nor respect to an angel, if he preach " another gospel " than Paul's. This *Gathercole* affair of the bishop of London cannot be too bluntly told, if such affairs are to be put down. Binney told the *last* one so well, that there will be fewer Gathercoles patronized in the next century.

CHAPTER XII.

WHITEFIELD went in the power of the Spirit from the Pentecost at Moorfields, to the Pentecost at Cambuslang and Kilsyth, in Scotland. His return to the north was, however, wormwood and gall to some of the Associate Presbytery. Adam Gibb, especially, signalized himself on the first sabbath of Whitefield's labours in Edinburgh, by publishing a "WARNING against countenancing his ministrations." This pamphlet is so strange, and now so rare, that I must preserve some specimens of it, as memorials of the provocation as well as opposition given to Whitefield by the seceders of that day. Most cheerfully, however, do I preface them with Fraser's declaration, that "the violence then discovered by individual members of the Presbytery, has not only been sincerely deplored by their successors in office; but that they themselves lived to repent of the rancour into which the heat of controversy had at first betrayed them." Even Gibb, it is said, wished, on his death-bed, that no copies of his pamphlet were on the face of the earth; and said, if he could recall every copy he would burn them. My copy was presented by Dr. Erskine to Dr. Ryland, who wrote the following note upon it,—" A Bitter Warning against Mr. Whitefield, by Mr. Gibbs, the Seceder. He became more moderate afterwards, and spoke respectfully of Mr. Hervey's writings, and Mr. Walker's of Truro." I am quite willing that these facts should be borne in mind, whilst the following astounding charges are read.

" This man (' Mr. George Whitefield') I have no scruple to

look upon as one of the *false Christs,* of whom the church is
forewarned, Matt. xxiv. 24. It is no unusual thing with him,
in his journals, to apply unto himself things said of and by the
Christ of God."—" I look upon him, in his public ministrations,
to be one of the most *fatal* rocks whereon many are now split-
ting."—" That he is no minister of Christ, appears from the
manner wherein that office he bears is conveyed to him. He
derives it from a diocesan bishop, who derives his office from the
king, and the king professes not to be a church officer."—" Mr.
Whitefield, in swearing the oath of supremacy, has sworn that
Christ is not supreme and sole Head of the church. He will not
allege that he hath yet vomited that spiritual poison."—" His *universal* love proceeds on the erroneous and horrid principle, that
God is the lover of all souls, and the God of all churches."—" The
horror of this is still more awful, because he hales in our Lord
and his apostles to patronize this catholic spirit."—" He breaks
off a piece of the glass of truth, and turns his back on the remainder : thus, though he hold up that piece of the glass, I say,
before his face, he cannot see the *true* Christ, because his back
is toward Him. So then, the doctrine of grace Mr. Whitefield
retains, cannot possibly discover the true Christ, because his
back is toward him, in *flouting* away the doctrine that discovers
Christ a King of a visible kingdom."—" The doctrine of grace,"
he publishes, " is carried off from its true posture, connexion,
and use, and applied to a *diabolical* purpose ; viz. to create a
Christ in people's imaginations, as a competition with the true
Christ."—" The horror of this scene strikes me almost dumb.
I must halt, and give way to some awful ideas that I cannot
vent in language.

> ' Obstupui, steteruntque comæ, et
> Vox faucibus hæsit ! ' "—

" The proper and designing author of his scheme, is not Mr.
Whitefield, but Satan : and thus our contendings against Mr. W.
must be proportioned, not to his design, but Satan's ; while
hereof he is an effectual though blinded tool."—" As for the
gentleman himself, while he is under a very ruinous delusion,
and thereby gathering upon him his own blood, and the blood

of multitudes, this his condition loudly requires the pity of all that know him. And I know of no way wherein this can be rightly exercised, without avoiding company with him, that he may be *ashamed,* 2 Thess. iii. 14. In this manner it is, that we are called to exercise *love* to his person, and desire of his recovery : for as his unwarrantable and woeful ministrations must be idolatrous, so idolaters *(Whitefield's !)* slay their own children."—" The complex scheme of Mr. W.'s doctrine is diabolical, as proceeding through diabolical influence, and applied to a diabolical use, against the Mediator's glory and the salvation of men."—" What shall be the procedure of God in such a dismal case ? Can His justice *sleep* now ? No !"—" Forasmuch as Mr. Whitefield's followers do, as such, seek after a Christ, convictions, and conversions, that are really idols, it is therefore to be fearfully expected, that God will, in judgment, answer them accordingly, and send them an *idol* Christ, and *idol* conversions, according to their lust. God's great executioner, Satan, must be employed in the producing of such effects. He will *ape* the work of God's Spirit."—" The doctrine of *impressions,* which Mr. W. is at pains to teach, is a very *necessary* part of Satan's doctrine."—" Hence Satan, while kindling men's fancies, must carry them out under strong and blind impulses, frights, freaks, raptures, visions, boastings, blunders, &c."

All this, as it stands here, seems mere rant and raving. In the pamphlet, however, it is blended with much acute reasoning upon the subject of the *Kingship* of Christ. Gibb's grave charge against Whitefield was, that he preached Christ only as a *Saviour :* not meaning, however, that he did not enforce holiness of life ; but that he taught a latitudinarian scheme of church polity, the tendency of which was, to " make men *sceptics* as to the discipline and government of the house of God." And there is some truth in this. Whitefield knew little and cared less about the *visible* form of the kingdom of Christ in the world. All his concern was, to see His spiritual kingdom set up in the hearts of individuals. But whilst it is well that this was *his* chief object, it was well too that others laid more stress than himself upon church government. Gibb laid too much ; but Whitefield went to an equally unscriptural extreme. Accordingly, Whitefield's societies, in general, subsided into other churches; especially in America.

It must not be supposed, that Gibb *predicted* the scenes of Cambuslang or Kilsyth. It was *cheap* prophesying on July 23rd, 1742, that a lying spirit, working by " the *foreigner*," (Whitefield,) would produce " strong impulses, frights, freaks, and visions." The effects, thus exaggerated, had begun at Cambuslang in the winter of 1741, under the ministry of M'Cullock, the pastor of the parish. " His hearers, in considerable numbers, were on different occasions so violently agitated, while he preached regeneration, as to fall down under visible paroxysms of bodily agony. But nothing can be more certain, than that the unusual events had been a subject of general observation and inquiry, for many months before Whitefield had ever been at Cambuslang. It is impossible to identify their commencement with his labours, by any fair examination of the facts as they occurred." *Sir Henry Moncrieff Welwood's Life of Dr. Erskine.*

Whitefield did not lessen the effect, however, when he went; and thus Gibb's tirade, being well timed to Whitefield's visit, seemed prophecy; for the WARNING and the WORK came before the public at large together. It was this coincidence that gave so much point and currency amongst the seceders, to the proverbial maxim, that " the wark *at Caumuslang was a wark o' the deevil.*" Seceders were not the only persons, however, that said that Whitefield cast out devils by the power of Beelzebub. Bishop Lavington concludes his examination of the enthusiasm of methodists thus: " If there be any thing in it exceeding the powers of nature; any thing beyond the force of distemper, or of imagination and enthusiasm artfully worked up; any thing beyong the reach of juggle and imposture; (which I take not upon me to affirm or deny ;) in that case, I see *no* reason against concluding, that it is the work of some evil spirit; a sort of magical operation, or other *diabolical* illusion." *Lavington,* p. 398. *Polwhele's Ed.* Again: " We know that in the latter days, *demons* should be the authors of many surprising things; God permitting Satan to work upon the affections of false prophets and evil men." *Ibid.* 217. Thus prelate and presbyter were equally vulgar and virulent upon this subject; and, therefore, ought to be placed together at the bar of posterity.

Thus caricatured and denounced, Whitefield came to Cambuslang; a parish four miles distant from Glasgow. He came by the special invitation of Mr. M'Cullock, the minister of the parish, to " assist at the sacramental occasion, with several worthy ministers of the church of Scotland." Gillies says, " he preached no less than three times upon the very day of his arrival, to a vast body of people, although he had preached that same morning at Glasgow. The last of these exercises he began at nine at night, continuing until eleven, when he said he had observed such a commotion among the people, as he had never seen in America. Mr. M'Cullock preached after him, till past one in the morning; and even then they could hardly persuade the people to depart. All night in the fields might be heard the voice of praise and prayer."

Whitefield said to a friend, before going to this sacramental service, " I am persuaded I shall have more *power*—since dear Mr. Gibb hath printed such a bitter pamphlet." He did not miscalculate. " On Saturday," he says, " I preached to above twenty thousand people. In my prayer the power of God came down and was greatly felt. In my two sermons, there was yet more power. On sabbath, scarce ever was such a sight seen in Scotland. There were undoubtedly upwards of twenty thousand people. A brae, or hill, near the manse of Cambuslang, seemed formed by Providence for containing a large congregation. Two tents were set up, and the holy sacrament was administered in the fields. The communion table was in the field. Many ministers attended to preach and assist, all enlivening and enlivened by one another.

" When I began to serve a table, the power of God was felt by numbers; but the people crowded so upon me, that I was obliged to desist, and go to preach at one of the tents, whilst the ministers served the rest of the tables. God was with them and with his people. On Monday morning I preached to near as many as before: but such a universal stir I never saw before! The motion fled as swift as lightning, from one end of the auditory to another. You might have seen thousands bathed in tears. Some at the same time wringing their hands, others almost swooning, and others crying out, and mourning over a pierced Saviour.

" But I must not attempt to describe it. In the afternoon the concern again was very great. Much prayer had been previously put up to the Lord. All night, in different companies, you might have heard persons praying to and praising God. The children of God came from all quarters. It was like the passover in Josiah's time. We are to have another sacrament, in imitation of Hezekiah's passover, in about two or three months. The Messrs. Erskines and their adherents (would you have thought it?) have appointed a public *fast*, to humble themselves, among other things, for my being received in Scotland, and for the *delusion*, as they term it, at Cambuslang and other places; and all this, because I would not consent to preach only for them, till I had light into, and could take, the solemn league and covenant. To what lengths may prejudice carry even good men!" *Letters.*

Before the next sacrament he was suddenly taken ill. The efforts and the excitement overcame him for a short time. " My friends thought I was going off: but how did Jesus fill my heart! To-day I am, as they call it, much better. In the pulpit, the Lord out of weakness makes me wax strong, and causes me to triumph more and more."—" I feel the power of His precious, live-giving, all-atoning blood more and more every day. I was happy when in London. I am *ten* times happier now. The Lord hath done great things for us, whereof we are glad."

When the second sacrament came, the scenes of the first were renewed. " Mr. Whitefield's sermons," says Mr. M'Cullock, " were attended with much power; particularly on sabbath night about ten. A very great but decent weeping and mourning was observable throughout the auditory. While serving some tables, he appeared to be so filled with the love of God, as to be in a kind of transport. This second occasion did, indeed, much excel the former, not only in the number of ministers and people, but, which is the main thing, in a much greater increase of the power and special presence of God. The lowest estimate of numbers, with which Mr. Whitefield agrees, and he has been used to great multitudes, makes them upwards of thirty thousand. The number of communicants appears to have been about three thousand. Some worthy of credit, and that had opportunities to know, give it as their opinion, that such a blessed frame fell upon the people, that, had they possessed means to obtain *tokens*, (tickets of admission to the sacrament,) there would have been a thousand more." *Robe's Narrative.* " Some who attended, declared they would not for a world have been absent from this solemnity. Others cried, ' Now let thy servants depart in peace, since our eyes have seen salvation here.' Others wishing, if it were the will of God, to die where they were attending God in his ordinances, without ever returning to the world." *Ibid.*

It will be seen from these extracts that Whitefield did not exaggerate the *power* under which he spoke, although he states it in strong terms. Again, therefore, let him bear witness. " Such a commotion, surely, was never heard of, especially at eleven at night. For about an hour and a half, there was such weeping, so many falling into deep distress, as is inexpressible. The people seem to be slain by scores. They are carried off, and come into the house, like soldiers wounded and carried off a field of battle. Their cries and agonies are exceedingly affecting." This occurred at the first sacrament. Of the second he says, " People sat unwearied till two in the morning. You could scarce walk a yard, without treading on some, either rejoicing in God for mercies received, or crying out for more. Thousands and thousands have I seen, before it was possible to catch it by sympathy, melted down under the word and power of God." *Letters.*

Sir Henry Moncrieff Welwood, in his Life of Dr. Erskine, says, " From this time (Whitefield's visit) the multitudes who assembled were more numerous than they ever had been, or perhaps than any congregation ever before assembled in Scotland. The religious impressions made on the people were apparently much greater, and more general."

These were engrossing scenes. They did not, however, divert Whitefield from any of the ordinary duties of life or godliness at the time. Some *spy* did, indeed, insinuate that he gave but little time to secret devotion at night, after preaching. In answer to this charge, he said, " I think not my spirit in bondage, if through weakness of body, or frequency of preaching, I cannot go to God at my usual set times. It is not for me to tell how often I use secret prayer. If I did not use it,—if in one sense I did not pray without ceasing, it would be difficult for me to keep up that frame of mind, which by the divine blessing I daily enjoy. God knows my heart : I would do every thing I could to satisfy all men, and give a reason of the hope that is in me with meekness and fear ; but I cannot satisfy all that are waiting for an occasion to find fault. Let my Master speak for me." *Letters.*

He redeemed time to write the following letter to his mother, also, from Cambuslang :—" Honoured mother, I rejoice to hear that you have been so long under my roof. Blessed be God, that I have a house for my honoured mother to come to ! You are heartily welcome to any thing my house affords, as long as you please. If need was, indeed, these hands should administer to your necessities. I had rather want myself, than you should : I shall be highly pleased when I come to Bristol, and find you sitting in your youngest son's house. Oh may I sit with you in the house not made with hands, eternal in the heavens ! Ere long your doom, honoured mother, will be fixed. You must shortly go hence and be no more. Your only daughter, I trust, is now in the paradise of God. Methinks I hear her say, ' Come up hither.' I am sure Jesus calls you by his word. May His Spirit enable you to say, ' Lo, I come.'—Oh that my dear mother may be made an everlasting monument of free and sovereign grace ! How does my heart *burn* with love and duty to you ? Gladly would I wash your aged feet, and lean on your neck, and weep, and pray until I could pray no more."

Besides this, and many other private letters, he wrote frequently to his coadjutors at the Tabernacle, and to his managers at Georgia. Indeed, at this time, his responsibilities for the orphan-house pressed heavily upon his spirits. " I yet owe upwards of £250 in England, and have nothing towards it. How is the world mistaken about my circumstances ! Worth nothing myself,—embarrassed for others,— and yet looked upon to flow in riches ! Our extremity is God's opportunity." So it was !

Before he left Scotland he could say, "Blessed be God, I owe nothing now in England on the orphan-house account. What is due is abroad. At Edinburgh I collected £128; at Glasgow £128; in all about £300. Since I have been in England, we have got near £1500. The Lord will raise up what we further need."

Thus no relative duty was neglected, notwithstanding the multiplicity of his public engagements. He even found time at Cambuslang (just the spot for the task!) to write his letter, entitled "*A Vindication and Confirmation of the Remarkable Work of God in New England;* being remarks on a late pamphlet, entitled, The State of Religion in New England, since the Rev. G. Whitefield's arrival there; in a Letter to a Minister of the Church of Scotland." This pamphlet, like Gibb's "Warning," was intended to depreciate both Whitefield and his work in Scotland. In answering it, however, he wisely left the work at Cambuslang to vindicate itself, and confined his explanations to New England; that the revivals there might in nowise depend upon those in Scotland for their justification. He also proved pretty fully, although without bringing home the fact to any one, that the pamphlet was *altered* in Scotland, to suit a purpose. And there are dates of Scotch publications in it, which could not have been known in Boston, when it was written. Hence he asks, "How could that gentleman (the author) see at Boston on May 24th, that Edwards' Sermon was reprinted in Scotland; which was not done till June following? I myself was chiefly concerned in publishing it."

Besides the great awakening at Cambuslang at this time, there was another similar at Kilsyth, which Whitefield visited also. As might be expected, both were misrepresented by formalists and bigots. The seceders, Whitefield says, "Taking it for granted that God had left the Scotch established church long ago, and that he would not work by the hands of a curate of the church of England, condemned the whole work as the work of the devil; and kept a fast throughout all Scotland to humble themselves, because the devil was come down in great wrath; and to pray that the Lord would rebuke the destroyer— for *that* was my title." *Oliphant's Memoirs.*

The Associate Presbytery, in their hot zeal to depreciate the conversions, confounded them, like Lavington, with the extravagance of fanatics and impostors, Camizars, and the first quakers. They issued from Dunfermline an Act of Presbytery *anent* a public fast, of which Mr. Robe of Kilsyth says, " It is the most *heaven-daring* paper that hath been published by any set of men in Britain these three hundred years past." This is a bold charge. It was not, however, advanced in a bad spirit ; as the following appeals and explanations abundantly show, " My dear brethren, (of the Secession,) my heart's desire and prayer to God for you is, that he may open your eyes to see the many mistakes you labour under. Whatever bitter names you give us, and however you magnify yourselves against us, we take all patiently ; and there are thousands of witnesses that we return you blessing for cursing. We would lay our bodies as the ground, and as the street, for you to go over, if it could in the least contribute to remove your prejudices, and advance the kingdom of our dear Redeemer."

This is humble and earnest pleading ; and so far as the word *" we "* includes Mr. Robe and the leaders of the revival, the pleading is honest. It must not, however, be considered as a specimen of the spirit of the clergy, in general, towards the seceders. This being understood, I proceed with the appeal.— " You declare the work of God to be a delusion, and the work of the grand deceiver. Now, my dear brethren, for whom I tremble, have you been at due pains to know the nature and circumstances of this work ? " (Their Act was issued whilst the work was going on.) " Have you taken the trouble to go to any of these places, where the Lord has appeared in his glory and majesty ? Have you so much as written to any of the ministers to receive information of it ? Is it not amazing *rashness*, without inquiry or trial, to pronounce that a work of the devil, which, for any thing *you* know, may be the work of the infinitely good and holy Spirit ? "

" My dear brethren, can you find in your hearts, after all the prayers you have put up in public and private for the outpouring of the Spirit upon this poor church and land, to deny that it *is* He, when he is come ?—Will ye be so fearless, can you be so cruel to thousands of perishing sinners, who begin to fly to Jesus Christ as a cloud and as doves to their windows; as in the most solemn manner, with lifted up eyes and hands, to pray that there may be a restraint upon the influences of the Holy Spirit, and that this outpouring of His grace may be withdrawn, and not spread over the length and breadth of the land?" *Robe's Preface.*

It is impossible not to ask, and that with strong emotion too, after reading such remonstrances,—how could such good men as the Erskines withstand these appeals? Now it is not easy to explain this anomaly, without seeming to palliate its enormity. It admits, however, of some explanation. The Erskines, on raising the standard of Reformation in Scotland, planted it upon the mount of the solemn league and covenant; arguing, that God would carry on his work only " in a way of solemn covenanting," as in the days of their "reforming forefathers." *R. Erskine, on Witnessing for God.* With this principle, Whitefield had no sympathy; for, whether right or wrong, he did not understand it. He would not therefore submit to it. The reformers also laid it down as a maxim, "that little truths" (at such a time) were " like the little *pinnings* of a wall, as necessary as the great stones ;" that it was " a false conversion," which " draws men off from *any* of the ways of God ;" that "aversion from, and opposition to, the testimony of the *time,*" was opposing God. *Ralph Erskine's Sermons, 2nd vol. folio.* All this, as they understood it, Whitefield rejected; and therefore they rejected him, and defamed his principles, in order to defend their own. " I shall show you, in eight or ten particulars," said Ralph in a sermon, " what another God, and what another Christ, is appearing in the delusive spirit of this time, brought in by the instrumentality of the *foreigner* (Whitefield); of whom we had some grounds for very favourable thoughts and expectations, till we understood him more fully, and found him in several respects a *stranger* to our God, and setting up *another* God." *Sermons, folio.*

The chief ground of this charge, however hollow, is plausible. The Associate Presbytery were asserting the legislative supremacy of Christ, as King of Zion. The evils they were con-

tending against in the kirk, had grown out of a long disregard
to this sacred principle. Now Whitefield *sided* with the ministers who, however good in other respects, did not "testify"
against the violations of this principle ; but against the Secession who avowed and advocated it. Hence, he was identified
and denounced with the enemies of church reform. He had
joined their ranks, and therefore he had to share in their rebuke, as well as to suffer for mortifying the Presbytery. It was
thus the Erskines were tempted to oppose and impugn the revivals at Cambuslang and Kilsyth. These revivals checked
the *kind* of reformation, which the Erskines were chiefly pleading for. They saw and felt this, and hence they said, " Satan
seems content that Christ should preach, providing He do not
reign nor rule ; knowing that his doctrine will not be long uncorrupted, if His *government* can be overturned." *Sermons.*
" The power and policy of hell is at work, to bring any attempt
at reformation under contempt." *Ibid.* Thus the seceders
could not imagine that any thing could be another work of
God, which was visibly and virtually hindering that work of
God which they had so solemnly espoused, and which was so
much needed at the time. It became, therefore, a solemn duty,
as they supposed, to pour contempt and obloquy upon conversions, which were pouring doubt upon the necessity and value
of church reform. " That must be a wrong conversion," says
Ralph, " that hath no tendency to the *public* good, but a tendency to oppose a public reformation." *Sermons.*

The *depicting* power also of Whitefield's oratory, so unlike
Scotch reasonings, gave the Erskines another handle against
him. Cornelius Winter says of him, " It was not without great
pathos, you may be sure, he treated upon the sufferings of the
Saviour. He was very ready at that kind of painting,—which
frequently answered the end of *real* scenery. As though Geth-
semane were within sight, he would say, stretching out his
hand,—' Look yonder ! What is it I see ? It is my agonizing
Lord !' And, as though it were no difficult matter to catch
the *sound* of the Saviour praying, he would exclaim, ' Hark,
hark !—do you not hear ?' You may suppose that as this occurred frequently, the efficacy of it was destroyed :—but, no ;

though we often knew what was coming, it was as new to us as though we had never heard it before." *Jay's Life of Winter.* Such painting Ralph Erskine had witnessed, and the effect of it upon the people led him to say, " They see a beautiful and glorious person presented to their imagination, or to their bodily eye. What a *devil*, instead of Christ, is this!" " Never, I think, did Satan appear as an angel of light, so evidently, as in the delusive spirit now spreading." *Sermons.*

On the other hand, Robe and some of his brethren founded a theory upon the vivid images thus produced; and argued that " imaginary ideas of Christ as man, belonged to saving faith; or at least, were helpful to the faith of His being God-man." *Fraser.* Ralph Erskine replied to this theory, in a work, entitled, " Faith no Fancy, or a Treatise of Mental Images." Well might Fraser say of this book, " it is not every where level to mere ordinary capacities." It is not, indeed! It proves, however, that the author was a man of extraordinary capacity; and could be as much at home amongst the depths of metaphysics as amongst the heights of poetry or devotion. It is said, that Reid found in this work the principles on which he afterwards built his System of the Philosophy of the Human Mind. If he did, happily he did not draw the *spirit* of his philosophy from it. The treatise certainly displays " an extraordinary degree of metaphysical acuteness :" but if it prove any thing against such mental images as Whitefield created, and Robe commended, it stultifies the author's " GOSPEL SONNETS ;" for they are " chambers of imagery." It is not necessary to illustrate this *retort*, to those who have read both the poetry and the philosophy of Ralph Erskine; and the point of it could not be explained to those who have not read both. Suffice it to say, that his sonnets refute his system, and have survived it, although they are often as *fantastical* as they are devotional.

It is amusing to read the charges and disclaimers of the parties in Scotland, upon the subject of religious liberty. The Associate Presbytery gravely charged the revivalists in the kirk " with pleading for a boundless toleration and liberty of conscience :" no great crime, as we now judge. Not so, however, did the revivalists of that day deem it. The imputation roused then, however, the Scotch blood of even the kind-hearted and liberal Robe. " Where and when did we that ? " he exclaims. " I know none of my brethren ever did it : and I am so far conscious of my innocence, that I insist upon your making your charge good. If you do not, as I am sure you cannot, it is no pleasure to me, that you give reason to the world to reckon you *slanderers.*" How true it is, that nations are

> " slowly wise, and meanly just;"

and that even good men are seldom wiser than their times! Whitefield's visits would have been a blessing to Scotland, had they led to nothing but a canvassing of the rights of conscience ; for he was far *ahead* of both parties on the subject of religious liberty.

Another handle against the Cambuslang and Kilsyth revivals, was, the physical effects of the awakening. " We have *convulsions* instead of convictions," said Erskine. He might and ought to have known, that this was not true of one in *six* of the converts. " They are greatly mistaken, who imagine, that all those who have been observably awakened, have come under faintings, tremblings, or other bodily distresses. These have been by far the *fewest* number." *Robe.* Notwithstanding this assurance from the principal witness, the Erskines went on to confound the exceptions with the rule, in these conversions. Even in 1765, the editor of Ralph's Sermons kept up this misrepresentation, and said, in a note, " the subjects of the extraordinary work" were " strangely agitated by strong convulsions, fearful distortions, foamings, and faintings." This is caricature, not history. In 1742, the instances of " conversion carried on in a calm, silent, quiet manner, for six months, are the more numerous and unquestionable." *Robe.* Whitefield's visit occurred in this period. Besides, even Ralph Erskine himself could not always prevent, though he reproved, " clamorous noise," under his own ministry. FAITH NO FANCY. *Appendix to Preface.* But these effects have been sufficiently explained in the American department of this volume.

It would be wrong, after having quoted so often from Ralph Erskine's Sermons, were I not to say even of the sermons which

WHITEFIELD'S LIFE AND TIMES.

are most disfigured with tirades against Whitefield and the revivals, that they are full of evangelical truth, and flaming with
love to immortal souls, and as faithful to the conscience, as any
that Whitefield preached at Cambuslang. Indeed, had they
been preached on the *brae-head*, at the great sacrament there,
Erskine would as surely have " slain his hundreds," as Whitefield did " his thousands."

CHAPTER XIII.

WHITEFIELD ITINERATING.

On returning from Cambuslang to London, Whitefield found, says Gillies, " the Tabernacle enlarged, and a new awakening" begun. As might be expected, he was just in the right spirit for turning both facilities to the best account. Remembering the *unction* he enjoyed in Scotland, he wrote to a friend on arriving at London, " I *feel* it—I feel it *now,* and long to preach again ! " When he did, he soon had occasion to inform one of his Cambuslang companions, " Our glorious Emmanuel blesses me in like manner, now he has brought me to England."

This flourishing state of the Tabernacle society, now equally large and harmonious, enabled him to forget all his old griev-ances, and to renew his wonted spirit towards the Wesleys. They were then triumphing gloriously at Newcastle, and he " heartily rejoiced" in their success. He wrote to one of their friends thus :—" I am dead to *parties* now, and freed from the pain which, on that account, once disturbed the peace of my soul. I redeem time from *sleep* rather than your letter should not be answered."

His letters at this time are full of a holy impatience to get out of his " winter-quarters," pleasant as they were, and to en-ter upon a " fresh campaign." His old friends in the country, and especially in Wales, were crying out for him, to do there what he had done in Scotland. He could not, however, gratify them at once. Persecution had begun to harass some of his coadjutors in Wales and Wiltshire ; and therefore he kept upon his vantage ground in London, to expose and defeat it. Ac-cordingly, he appealed thus to the bishop of Bangor, on behalf

of Cennick, who had been " shamefully used" in that diocese :
" In Wales they have little fellowship meetings, where some
well-meaning people meet together, simply to tell what God
hath done for their souls. In some of these meetings, I believe,
Mr. C. used to tell his experience, and to invite his companions
to come and be happy in Jesus Christ. He is, therefore, indicted
as holding a conventicle ; and this, I find, is the case of one if
not two more. Now, my Lord, these persons, thus indicted,
as far as I can judge, are loyal subjects to his Majesty, and true
friends to, and attendants upon, the church of England service.
You will see by the letters (I send with this) how unwilling
they are to leave her. And yet, if all those acts against persons meeting to plot against church and state, were put in execution against *them*, what must they do ? They must be
obliged to declare themselves dissenters. I assure your Lordship it is a *critical* time for Wales. Hundreds, if not thousands,
will go in a body from the church, if such proceedings are countenanced. I lately wrote them a letter, dissuading them from
separating from the church ; and I write thus freely to your
Lordship, because I would not have such a fire kindled *in* or
from your Lordship's diocese." To this letter the bishop returned a prompt and polite answer, promising to hear both sides.
What he *did* eventually, I know not. However, six months
afterwards, Whitefield found some difficulty, though he carried
his point, in preventing a separation from the church in Wales ;
as we shall soon see.

The next case of persecution which he had to resist, came
to him from Wiltshire. It was of a kind not altogether cured
by another century of " the march of intellect." It was this :
"The ministers of Bramble, Segery, Langley, and many others,
have strictly forbidden the overseers and churchwardens to let
any of the C——s (Cennickites ?) have any thing out of the
parish ; and they obey them, and tell the poor, if they cannot
stop them from following any other way (than the church !)
they will *famish* them. Several of the poor, having large families, have already been denied any help. Some, out of fear, denied they ever came, (to the conventicle,) and others have been
made to promise they will come no more ; whilst the most part

come at the loss of friends and all they have. When the officers threatened some to take away their pay, they answered, "If
you *starve* us we will go; and rather than forbear, we will live
on *grass* like kine."

These facts, in this form, Whitefield submitted to the bishop
of *Old* Sarum; telling his Lordship plainly, that if C—— left the
church, "hundreds would leave it with him." The effect, as
usual, is not known. The only thing certain is, that both persecution and petty annoyance went on in most quarters.

Whitefield having done what he could by letters, left London to visit these disturbed districts, and attend the associations of the Welch methodists. On his way he preached at
Hampton Common, to about "twelve thousand." Gillies does
not mention the occasion. It was this. "A man was hung in
chains" there, that day. "A more miserable spectacle," says
Whitefield, "I have not seen. I preached in the morning to a
great auditory, about a mile off from the place of execution. I
intended doing the same after the criminal was turned off; but
the weather was very violent. Thousands and thousands came
and staid to hear; but through misinformation, kept on the *top*
of the hill while I preached at the bottom."

From this he went to Dursley, one of the seats of persecution, to dare the consequences; but although the mob had
taken down an itinerant on the sabbath before, "no one was
permitted to touch or molest" him. "The word came (upon
them) with a most gloriously convincing power." He then
went to his TUMP again at Hampton. "I cannot tell you," he
says, "what a *solemn* occasion that was! They do, indeed,
hang on me to hear the word. It ran, and was glorified.
Preaching in Gloucestershire now, is like preaching at the
Tabernacle."   ↴

After preaching at Bristol and Bath, he went to Waterford
in South Wales, and there presided at the *first* Association of
the Welch Calvinistic Methodists. All who know how much
Wales owes to the meetings of this union, and how often and
signally they have been Pentecostal scenes, well accounting for,
if not excusing, the shouts of " *Gogunnyant, bendyitti*," will
learn with pleasure that Whitefield " opened the Association."

Gillies. " I opened, with a close and solemn discourse on walking with God.   Afterwards we betook ourselves to business; settling the affairs of the societies, till about two in the morning."   Next day, they sat till midnight.   " All acknowledged God was with them."   Thus began that which eventually immortalized *Bala* (bach!) and sainted *Charles.*

In the spirit of this meeting he went to Cardiff, and again made " the greatest scoffers quiet."   But at Swansea, the effect was so great, that he wrote off to a friend after preaching, " Swansea is *taken!*   I never preached with a more convincing power.   Free grace for ever!"   From this he went to Caermarthen, and preached from " the *top* of the CROSS."   The great sessions were then sitting.   " The justices," he says, " desired I would stay till they rose, and they would come.   Accordingly, they did, and many thousands more, and several people of quality."   He was still more pleased, however, with an audience " of several thousand souls at Jefferson," because they were " very like the *Kingswood* colliers ; and at Llassivran, because he had, " as it were, a *Moorfields* congregation," and chiefly, because "*Jerusalem* sinners bring most glory to Christ."

Whilst thus in what he calls " a new and very unthought-of world," a clergyman in the neighbourhood of Larn preached against him by name on the sabbath day, much and violently. This defeated its own purpose.   To his surprise, on crossing the ferry at Larn, one vessel fired a salute, and several hoisted their flags as tokens of respect and welcome.

During this itinerancy in Wales he travelled, he says, " four hundred miles in three weeks, spent three days in attending two associations, preached about forty times, visited about thirteen towns, and passed through seven counties." *Lett.* 514.   At the close of this tour, his first question to himself was, " Where shall I go next ? "   He was at a loss to determine.   " A visit to Yorkshire would be very agreeable.   Perhaps Exeter and Cornwall may be the next places.   That is *dry* ground.   I love to range in such places."   He determined, however, to make, first, one more attack upon the prince of darkness in Moorfields.   This he did ; and one of its effects was, that he was enabled to remit £25 to Georgia, in addition to £100 sent out by his brother's ship a lit-

tle before. " Grace, grace," he exclaims in his letter to Habersham, " I have paid all that is due in England, and have sent you
£25 by the bearer. God willing, I will remit you more soon."

After a few weeks, he left London again for Gloucestershire,
to " strengthen the persecuted," or to share the *brunt* with Cennick, of whom he was very fond. He thus describes him at this
time : " He is truly a great soul! one of those weak things,
which God has chosen to confound the strong. Such a hardy
worker with his hands, and hearty preacher at the same time, I
have scarce known. All call him a second Bunyan." Having
countenanced and consoled Cennick, he went to Bristol. On
his arrival he learnt that the king had fought and conquered in
Germany. Whitefield did not know before, that GEORGE had
joined the army. He, therefore, said, with his characteristic
simplicity and loyalty, " I had observed for some time past, when
praying for him, that, whether I would or not, *out* came this
petition,—Lord, cover thou his head in the day of battle. While
praying, I wondered why I prayed so; not knowing he was gone
to fight. This gave me confidence." *Lett.* 124. He had need
of it ; for his own day of battle was at hand. A letter came to
him from his itinerant at Hampton, urging him to place himself
in the breach. The appeal, as will be seen, was not likely to be
lost on Whitefield. " On sabbath morning," says the writer,
" about twenty of the society met. In the afternoon, the mob
came to my house, demanding me to come down. I asked, by
what authority they did so ? They swore they would have me.
Then said I, you shall, so they took me to the *lime-pit*, (for
skins,) and threw me in. But oh, what a power of God was on
my soul ! I thought, with Stephen, the heavens opened to my
sight, and the Lord Jesus was ready to receive me. I believe
my undaunted courage shook some of them. I told them, I
should meet them at the judgment-seat, and then their faces
would gather paleness. They let me out,—and I came home
and prayed with the people who were there. After that, I exhorted. And when I was concluding, the mob came again, and
took me to a *brook* to throw me in there. They told me, they
would let me go, if I would forbear preaching for a month. I
would make no such promise. So forward I went. One of them

threw me in, and I went to the bottom, but came up again, with my hands *clasped* together. I did not desire to come out until they fetched me. Accordingly, in jumped one or two of them, and took me out. But then, one maliciously and cowardly pushed me in again, and much cut and bruised one of my legs against a stone. Some of the others were going to throw *him* in for doing so. I came home talking with them. Many seemed to repent of what they had done, and promised to molest me no more. The *chief* says, he will in nowise touch me again. Many advise us to prosecute them: but if they are quiet, I am content, and can say from the heart, ' Father, forgive them.' I should be glad if *you* would be here next Sunday." *Thomas Adams.*

Whitefield was soon on the spot! " On Thursday I came here, and expected to be attacked; because I had heard that the mob had threatened that, if ever I came there again, they would have a piece of my black gown to make *aprons* with. No sooner had I entered the town, but I heard and saw the signals; such as blowing of *horns,* and ringing of *bells,* for gathering the mob. My soul was kept quite easy. I preached on a large glass-plat. I finished just as the ringleader of the mob broke in upon us. One of them called me *coward.* I then went to the house and preached on the stair-case, to a large number of serious souls: but the troublers in Israel soon came in to mock and mob us. But, feeling what I never felt before, as I have very little natural courage,—strength and power from above,—I leaped down-stairs; and all ran away before me. However, they continued making a noise about the house till midnight; abusing the poor people as they went home, and, as we hear, they broke one young lady's arm in two places.

" Hearing that two or three clergymen were in the town, one of whom was a justice of the peace, (query, of the *war ?*) I went to them: but, alas,—they laid the cause of all the grievance at *my* door; but, by the help of my God, I shall persist in preaching, and in encouraging those to do so, who are moved by the Holy Ghost. As I came out from the clergymen, two of the unhappy mobbers were particularly insolent, and huzzaed us out of town. Let us ' rejoice and be exceeding glad,' for now, I humbly hope, I begin to be a disciple of Jesus Christ, since to *suffer* for Him is given unto me."

Whitefield had to " appeal unto Cæsar" for justice, in this case. The trial of the Hampton rioters came on very soon after the sudden death of his only son; and as the preparation and bustle of the affair diverted him somewhat from brooding upon his loss, I have connected the report with his domestic life.

About this time, a motion was made at one of the associations in Wales, whilst Whitefield was present, to separate from the established church. This grieved him much, although it was made only by " a few contracted spirits," as he calls them. " By far the greater part most strenuously opposed it," and agreed to go on as usual, because they enjoyed such " great liberty under the mild and paternal government of his Majesty." Thus, with all his attachment to the church, Whitefield was too honest to ascribe any of his liberty to her government. His definition of liberty, at this association, is characteristic of himself and his coadjutors ;—" the privilege of ranging up and down, preaching repentance to those multitudes, who come neither to church nor meeting, but who are led from curiosity to follow us into the fields ;"—a privilege, which very few *exercise* now, however many would contend for it. The crushing of Sidmouth's bill was not followed by much field preaching.

In the course of his itineracy this year, Whitefield visited Exeter twice, and created a stir which turned the bishop into a *pamphleteer*. Lavington had heard of the " enthusiasm of the methodists," and now he saw it. It drew ten thousand of his flock out to Southern Bay, and several of his clergy out of their stalls into the fields, to hear Whitefield. Some of the latter, however, " went off," when " the Lord made way for himself into the hearts of the people." Having introduced this leaven into the city, Whitefield left it to ferment for two months, and then returned, determined to be " all heart and all humility, at the same time." The result was, " the common people began to feel, and even some of the *polite* were much affected," although in the fields. This will account for Lavington's tirades against itinerant preaching. The bishop had the insolence to insinuate, though not the boldness to say, that the methodist preachers,

" as well as *St. Anthony*, were attended with a sturdy set of followers, as their guards, armed with clubs *under* their clothes,
menacing and threatening such as should dare to speak lightly
of their apostle. I have often *heard* it affirmed." In the same
mean spirit Lavington chose to forget, that itineracy had been
practised by other churches than St. Anthony's. Knox provided
for it in Scotland, in his " First Book of Discipline." Queen
Elizabeth appointed twelve, to travel continually. By the way,
who pockets the *salary* of the church-itineracy now; for the
work is neglected ? Whitefield knew both the legitimacy of
his office and the need of it; and therefore persisted in Exeter,
until the bishop saw nearly " a third part of the city " attending
on " the word preached" in the fields; and until he himself
could say, " I am here, as in Scotland and New England. Praise
to free grace ! Here is work enough for months. The weather
is favourable : *range*, therefore, I must and will ! " *Lett.*

On the morning of the last day of his visit, he went to Ottery
to preach in the market-place : but just as he named his text,
the *bells* rang. He then went to the fields, and the people ran
after him " in droves." On his way, one of the clergymen, with
the same zeal as the bell-ringers, questioned his authority, and
denounced the meeting as illegal and as a riot. " I answered
him pertinently, as I thought, and showed my authority by
preaching from these words, ' GO ye into all the world, and
preach the gospel to every creature.' "

Next day he went to Biddeford, and was much pleased to
find there a clergyman, nearly eighty years of age, who had lately
preached three times in one day, and rode forty miles: but says
Whitefield, "he is not above *one* year old in the school of Christ."
" Dear Hervey," he says, " laid the blessed foundation, whilst a
curate here." Such was the " Edinburgh-like " effect of a sermon
in the dissenting chapel, that he wrote off to the Tabernacle,
" I cannot think of *nestling* in London. I am more and more
convinced, that I should go from place to place." Accordingly,
instead of nestling, he flew into Cornwall, and alighted once again
in a *church*, at St. Gennis. " Many, many prayers," it seems,
" had been put up by the good rector and others, for an outpouring of God's blessed Spirit."—" They were answered.

Arrows of conviction fled so thick and fast, and such a universal weeping prevailed from one end of the congregation to the other, that good Mr. J—— could not help going from seat to seat to comfort the wounded souls." After preaching some time in Cornwall thus, he said, " But I must away to Biddeford, just to give Satan *another* stroke, and then return the way I came to the great metropolis."

It was now winter ; " but the Lord," he says, " warms my heart." In this spirit he came to Birmingham. There he heard of the mobs which had been stirred up at Wednesbury, against the Wesleyans, by a sermon in the church; of which Wesley says, " I never heard so wicked a sermon, delivered with such bitterness of voice and manner." Its effect, as is well known, was almost murder. Ill as Adams was treated at Hampton, it was mercifully, compared with the fiend-like assault upon Wesley. Whitefield went to Wednesbury, and was well received. " I cannot tell you," he says, " what a sweet melting time there was. Many were in tears." Next day, however, whilst preaching at Mare Green, in the neighbourhood, " several clods were thrown," one of which fell on his head, and another struck his fingers, whilst he was praying. He then returned to Birmingham, and preached to many thousands on a common, with great effect. When he went on the ground, a regiment of soldiers were exercising ; but the officers, when they saw him, dismissed them, and promised that there should be no disturbance.

Whitefield closed this itineracy by a visit to his old friend Mr. Williams of Kidderminster. In his house, he recognised " a sweet savour," amongst the visitors, " of good Baxter's doctrine, works, and discipline, remaining until this day." That savour he did not find in Baxter's church; its bells were rung whilst he was preaching ; and that by men who " had promised not to do so."

On his return to London, Whitefield had to sustain the loss of his child, to prosecute the Hampton rioters, and to answer some pamphlets, as well as to prepare for revisiting America. In June, 1744, he engaged his passage from Portsmouth ; but the captain of the vessel refused to let him on board, when the time to sail came, lest he should " spoil the sailors." He had, therefore, to go to Plymouth for a vessel.

Whilst at Plymouth, he had a very narrow escape from being *murdered.* On the night of his arrival, a *bear* and *drum* were paraded on the ground where he was expected to preach. He did not, therefore, preach that night. Next night he did; and after returning to his inn, some ruffians, under the pretence of a " hue-and-cry " warrant, broke into his room, and insulted him. This led him to remove to private lodgings. Again he preached and visited the French prisoners, without any thing happening to awaken fear or suspicion. That night, however, his landlady informed him, that " a well-dressed gentleman desired to speak with him."—" Imagining," he says, " that it was some *Nicodemite,* I desired him to be brought up. He came, and sat down by my bedside; told me he was a lieutenant of a man of war; congratulated me on the success of my ministry, and expressed himself much concerned from being detained from hearing me. He then asked me if I knew him? I answered, no. He replied, his name was *Cadogan.* I rejoined, I had seen one Mr. Cadogan, formerly an officer at Georgia, about a fortnight ago at Bristol. Upon this, he immediately rose up, uttering the most abusive language; calling me dog, rogue, villain; and beat me most unmercifully with his gold-headed cane. As you know I have not much natural courage, guess how surprised I was! Being apprehensive that he intended to shoot or stab me, I underwent all the fears of a sudden, violent death.

" It providentially happened, that my hostess and her daughter, hearing me cry ' *murder,*' rushed into the room, and seized him by the collar. However, he immediately disengaged himself from them, and repeated his blows upon me. The cry of ' murder' was repeated; which putting him in some terror, he made towards the chamber-door, from whence the good woman pushed him down-stairs.

" At the bottom, a *second* cried out, ' Take courage, I am ready to help you.' Accordingly, whilst the other was escaping, he rushed up; and, finding one of the women coming down, he took her by the heels, and threw her upon the stairs, by which her back was almost broken. By this time, the neighbourhood was alarmed. Unwilling to add to it, I desired the doors to be shut, and retired to rest."

This mysterious affair Whitefield did not prosecute for, although much urged to do so. "I am better employed," he says, "being greatly blessed in preaching the gospel. I was well paid for what I had suffered; curiosity having led, perhaps, two thousand more than ordinary to see and hear a man that had like to have been murdered in his bed. Thus all things work for the furtherance of the gospel.

      ' Thus Satan thwarts, and men object,
         And yet the thing they thwart, effect.' "

The only explanation of this outrage that I know of, only rendered it more mysterious. "I had," he says, "some particular information about the late *odd* adventure. It seems, four gentlemen came to the house of one of my friends, kindly inquiring for me; and desiring to know where I lodged, that they might come and pay their respects. He directed them. Some time afterwards, I received a letter, informing me that the writer was a nephew to Mr. S——, an eminent attorney at New York; that he had the pleasure of supping with me at his uncle's house; and desired my company to sup with him and a few more friends at a tavern. I sent him word, that it was not customary for me to sup out at taverns; but should be glad of his company, out of respect to his uncle, to eat a morsel with him at my lodgings. He came. We supped; and I observed that he looked around him frequently, and seemed very *absent*. But having no suspicion, I continued in conversation with him and my other friends, until we parted.

"THIS, I now find, was to have been the *assassin*. On being interrogated by his companions, on his return to the tavern, about what he had done, he answered, that being so civilly used he had not the *heart* to touch me. Upon which, as I am informed, the person who assaulted me laid a wager of *ten guineas* that he would do my business for me. Some say, that they took his *sword* from him;—which I suppose they did, for I saw and felt only the weight of his cane."

The deserved odium of this dastardly attack must be equally

WHITEFIELD'S LIFE AND TIMES. 317

divided between England and America. That the volunteer assassin was an American, there can be no more doubt, than that the bravo was an Englishman. Whitefield could not have mistaken the former. Indeed, it was " out of respect " to the uncle in New York, that he welcomed the nephew without hesitation.

He availed himself adroitly of the notoriety thus given to him in Plymouth, to divide public attention with the bishop of the diocese, who was there at the time confirming. " Could you think it," he says, " I have been preaching a confirmation sermon? Do you ask me where? In a *quaker's* field. As I saw thousands flocked to the church to have the bishop's hand imposed upon them, I thought it not improper to let them have a word of exhortation suitable to the occasion."

This confirmation sermon produced one good effect, equal at least to any that resulted from the confirmation itself. The late Rev. Henry Tanner, then a young man, and a ship-builder, had just come to Plymouth, in search of employment at the dock. Whitefield's powerful voice from the field arrested his attention, and that of his fellow-workmen. They deemed him mad, and determined to *capsize* him from his block. Nor was this all: they went, not only to throw him down from his stand, but with their pockets full of stones, " to injure the mad parson." *Dr. Hawker's Life of Tanner.*

Tanner's resolution failed him, when he saw Whitefield with open arms and gushing tears, entreating " poor, lost sinners " to come to Christ. He went home much impressed, and resolved to hear the preacher again next evening. He did. The text was, " Beginning at Jerusalem." Whitefield " *depicted* the cruel murder of the Lord of life " there. Then, turning to the spot where Tanner stood, he said, " You are reflecting on the cruelty of these inhuman butchers, who imbrued their hands in innocent blood." At this moment his eye fell upon Tanner, and his lips said, " *Thou* art the man." The convicted sinner was forced to cry, " God be merciful to me." Whitefield saw the effect, and met the emotion with a burst of tenderness which cheered the penitent. Another sermon, on Jacob's vision of the Bethel ladder, led Tanner *up* to the Lamb slain in the midst of the throne, and thus gave him both joy and peace in believing.

The advances he made, from this time, in religious knowledge and experience, were great and rapid. They eventually encouraged and enabled him to preach the everlasting gospel to others. This he did with such success, that even Dr. Hawker (that strange compound of spirituality and absurdity) acknowledges, that Tanner seldom preached " one sermon in vain." Tanner's frequent prayer was, that he might die in his Master's work. His petition was granted. He broke down in the pulpit, before he could finish his sermon; and soon fell asleep in Jesus. *Life by Hawker.*

This was not the only good effect of Whitefield's detention at Plymouth. Some of the very persons who opposed him at first, offered him " a piece of ground, surrounded with walls, for a society house." No wonder: for he came from the docks every evening, " with great companies, singing and praising God." *Letters.* As he was now about to leave for America, he communicated the glad tidings of this new opening to Cennick; and wrote to those who had most influence over him—" Brother Cennick *must* come to these parts soon." One thing he wrote for his encouragement was, that the ferrymen, who were like Levi at the receipt of custom, would take nothing of the multitude who came to hear him preach. They said, " God forbid that we should *sell* the word of God." Thus preserved and blessed, he embarked for America with two New England friends.

CHAPTER XIV.

1744.

" In the beginning of August, 1744, Whitefield embarked, though in a poor state of health ; and after a tedious passage of eleven weeks, arrived at York." *Gillies.* He sailed from Plymouth, with nearly a hundred and fifty ships, under several convoys. It was, however, " full six weeks " before they reached the Western islands. This was owing to the want of wind. When the wind did spring up, one of the vessels, which missed stays, drove right upon his ship ; striking her mainsail into the bowsprit. Whitefield's vessel, being large, sustained little damage ; but the other received a blow, which disabled and well nigh sunk her. The cries and groans of her crew, he says, " were *awful !* "

He had been singing a hymn on deck when the concussion took place. This fact, with the news of the concussion, was communicated to the convoy. It drew out, he says, the remark, " This is your praying, and be damned ! with many sayings of the like nature." He adds, " this, I must own, shocked me more than the striking of the ship." It did not, however, stop nor intimidate him. " I called my friends together, and broke *out* into these words in prayer ; God of the sea, and God of the dry land, this is a night of rebuke and blasphemy. Show thyself, O God, and take us under thine own immediate protection. Be thou our Convoy, and make a difference between those who fear thee, and those that fear thee not."

Providence soon made a difference ! Next day, a " violent

Euroclydon arose," which " battered and sent away our convoy, so that we saw him no more all the voyage." *Letters*. White- field, at first, thought this " no loss:" but when two strange sail appeared in the distance, and preparation was made for action, by mounting guns, slinging hammocks on the sides of the ship, and encircling the masts with chains, he (being " naturally a coward," as he says) found it " formidable " to have no convoy. The vessels were, however, only part of their own fleet. This was a pleasant discovery to more than the skulking chaplain in the *holes* of the ship. " The captain, on clearing the cabin, said, ' After all, this is the best fighting.' You may be sure I con- curred, praying that all our conflicts with spiritual enemies might, at last, terminate in a thorough cleansing, and an eternal purification of the defiled *cabin* of our hearts." *Letters*.

No other accident occurred during the voyage. Its tedious- ness overcame his patience, however, when he saw the port. In order to land a few hours sooner than the vessel, he went on board a smack in the bay; but darkness coming on, she missed her course, and was tossed about all night. Unfortunately, too, she had no provisions, and he was so hungry that he " could have gnawed the very boards." Besides this, he was suffering from " nervous cholic." Altogether he was thoroughly morti- fied, until a man, lying at his elbow in the cabin, began to talk of " one Mr. Whitefield, for whose arrival the *new lights* in New England " were watching and praying. " This," he says, " made me take courage. I continued undiscovered; and in a few hours, in answer, I trust, to new-light prayers, we arrived safe."

He was received at York by a physician, once a notorious deist, who had been converted under his ministry. This was a signal providence: for in about half an hour after he entered the doctor's house, he became racked with cholic, and convulsed from the " waist to the toes." A " total convulsion " was appre- hended by the physician. He himself dreaded *delirium*, and implored his weeping wife and friends not to be " surprised if he uttered any thing wrong." Both fears, however, were soon allayed: but he was brought so low, that he could not " bear the sound of the tread of a foot, or the voice of friends." Four days elapsed before nature could be relieved; and for weeks he had to be carried like a child. The fact is, he had eaten "eagerly" of some *potatoes*, during his gnawing hunger on board the smack, and they had remained on the stomach undigested. They were not even "discoloured" when they were removed.

When Whitefield recovered, the excellent though eccentric Moody, the minister of York, called upon him, and accosted him thus: "Sir, you are first welcome to America; secondly, to New England; thirdly, to all faithful ministers in New England; fourthly, to all the good people in New England; fifthly, to all the good people of York; and sixthly and lastly, to me, dear Sir, less than the least of all." This welcome was followed by an urgent request for a sermon. Whitefield hesitated for a time; but " good old Mr. Moody " did not give him the benefit of his own favourite maxim, " When you know not what to do, —you must *not* do you know not what." This, however, he did. He preached, and immediately after went over the ferry to Portsmouth. As might be expected, he caught cold, and was again brought to the gates of death. Three physicians attended him during the night.

With his usual simplicity, he says, " My pains returned; but what gave me most concern was, that notice had been given of my being to preach next evening. I felt a divine life *distinct* from my animal life, which made me, as it were, laugh at my pains, though every one thought I was 'taken with death. My dear York physician was then about to administer a medicine. I, on a sudden, cried out, Doctor, my pains are suspended: by the help of God, I'll go and preach,—and then come home and die! With some difficulty I reached the pulpit. All looked quite surprised, as though they saw one risen from the dead. Indeed, I was as pale as death, and told them they must look upon me as a dying man, come to bear my dying testimony to the truths I had formerly preached to them. All seemed melted, and were drowned in tears. The cry after me, when I left the pulpit, was like the cry of sincere mourners when attending the funeral of a dear departed friend. Upon my coming home, I was laid on a bed upon the ground, near the fire, and

Y

I heard them say, ' *He is gone !* ' But God was pleased to order it otherwise. I gradually recovered."

Gillies has added to this account an interesting anecdote, from some of Whitefield's papers. " A poor negro woman insisted upon seeing the invalid, when he began to recover. She came in, and sat down on the ground, and looked earnestly in his face. She then said, in broken accents, ' Massa, you just go to heaven's gate. But Jesus Christ said, Get you down, get you down, you must not come here yet : go first, and call some more poor negroes.' I prayed to the Lord that, if I was to live, this might be the event." *Gillies.*

He thought himself " dying indeed," when he was laid near the fire, after preaching. But when he recollected " the life and power which spread all around," whilst " expecting to stretch into eternity," he said, " I thought it was worth dying for a *thousand* times ! " In three weeks after, he was able to go to Boston, though still very weak. His arrival was announced thus in Prince's Christian History : " The Rev. George White-field was so far revived, as to be able to set out from Portsmouth to Boston, whither he came in a very feeble state, the Monday evening after : since which he has been able to preach in several of our largest houses of public worship, with great and growing success. He comes with the same extraordinary spirit of meek-ness, sweetness, and universal benevolence, as before. In oppo-sition to the spirit of separation and *bigotry*, he is still for hold-ing communion with all protestant churches. In opposition to *enthusiasm*, he preaches a close adherence to the Scriptures, and the necessity of trying all impressions by them, and of rejecting as delusions whatever is not agreeable to them. In opposition to *antinomianism*, he preaches up all kinds of relative and religious duties—though to be performed in the strength of Christ ; and in short, the doctrines of the church of England, and of the first fathers of this country. As before, he applies himself to the *understanding* of his hearers, and then to their affections. And the more he preaches, the more he convinces people of their mistakes about him, and increases their satisfaction." *Prince.*

This defence was not needless at the time. Both calumny and caricature had been busy at Boston against Whitefield. Harvard College, and *half-penny* squibs, called "testimonies," united against him. A good old puritan of the city said of the testimonies, " they do not *weigh* much :" this was equally true of the more learned charges from the college. Accordingly neither *weighed* with the public. They soon offered to build for Whitefield " the *largest* place of worship that was ever seen in America." This he declined. He did not decline, however, when the people *voted* him into the pulpits of their " shy pastors." This led him to say, in reference to the old joke, " that the lord brethren of *New* England could tyrannize as well as the lord bishops of *Old* England,"—" Well is it at present, that the people are lord brethren ; for they have passed votes of invitation to me to preach in the pulpits !" Had he been *himself* at the time, however, he would have gone into the fields.

The coolness and shyness of many ministers did not surprise him now. When he was the guest of Governor Belcher, on his former visit to Boston, he quite understood the " *civil nod* " of the clergy, at table ; and said, at the time, " many who are now extremely civil, will turn out my open and avowed enemies." They did ; and he said now, " I have been no false prophet." Still he *felt* the difference, when the clergy, " freed from restraints, appeared *in puris naturalibus.*" *Letters.* He found that " the good old man (Moody) judged too much by his own honest feelings," when he welcomed him " to *all* the faithful ministers of New England." But Whitefield soon forgot all who forgot him at Boston, when the high sheriff, who was once the leader of the persecution, began to hear him, and especially when his " spiritual levees," for the awakened, became crowded. At one of them, a very singular Bostonian visited him ;—a man of ready wit and racy humour, who delighted in preaching over a *bottle* to his boon companions. He had gone to hear Whitefield, in order to get up a new " tavern harangue :" but when he had caught enough of the sermon for his purpose, and thus wanted to quit the church for the inn, " he found his endeavours to get out fruitless, he was so pent up." Whilst thus fixed, and waiting for " fresh matter of ridicule," he was arrested by the gospel. That night he went to Prince, full of horror, and longing to beg pardon of Whitefield. Prince encouraged him to visit the preacher. Whitefield says of him, " by the paleness, pensiveness, and horror of his countenance, I guessed he was the man of whom I had been apprized. ' Sir, can you forgive me?' he cried, in a low but plaintive voice. I smiled, and said, ' Yes, Sir, very readily.' ' Indeed you cannot,' he said, ' when I tell you all.' I then asked him to sit down; and judging that he had sufficiently felt the lash of the law, I preached the gospel unto him." This, with other remarkable conversions, gave increased energy and influence to his preaching in Boston. "My bodily strength," he says, " is recovered, and my soul more than *ever* in love with a crucified Jesus ! "

At this time, the Cape Breton expedition was committed to his friend Colonel Pepperell; the first and last native of New England created a baronet of Great Britain. For his success at the siege of Louisburgh, which led to this unusual honour, Pepperell was not a little indebted to Whitefield. He gave him a rallying motto for his flag, and preached to his soldiers before they embarked. It is painful to recollect this patronage of war by a minister of peace ! He himself did not easily get over his scruples of conscience. His friend Sherbourne, the commissary of the war, had to tell him, that if he refused men would not enlist. This made him " sleep and pray " on the subject. It was, however, Lady Pepperell who vanquished him, by assuring him, that " God enabled her to give up the general to the expedition, for His glory, and the good of the country." He preached on the surrender of Louisburgh. So also did Mr. Prince. The latter published his sermon. Alas, both have had too many imitators !

Whitefield was now *himself* again, and began to move southward, hunting for souls. On his way to Philadelphia, he had the privilege (to him unspeakable!) of preaching by an interpreter " to some converted Indians, and of seeing nearly fifty young ones in one school, learning the Assembly's Catechism." This was at one of Brainerd's stations ; and thus doubly interesting to him.

His reception at Philadelphia was very flattering. The place erected for him on his former visit was flourishing, and its managers offered him £800 a year, with liberty to travel six months a year wherever he chose, if he would become their pastor. This pleased him, although he declined the offer at once. He was more pleased, however, to learn, that after his former visit there were so many under " soul-sickness," that even Gilbert Tennent's feet were *blistered* with walking from place to place to see them.

When he went into Virginia, he was agreeably surprised to find " a fire kindled " there, by a volume of his sermons, which had been brought from Glasgow to Hanover. " It fell into the hands of Samuel Morris," says Whitefield : " he read and found benefit. He then read them to others. They were awakened and convinced. Other labourers were sent for, and many, both whites and negroes, were converted to the Lord." *Gillies.* Whitefield's version of this event is too brief. The following version is from the lips of Morris himself, in 1751. It was taken down by Mr. Davies of Hanover, his minister. " In 1740, Whitefield preached at Williamsburgh ; but, we being sixty miles distant, he left the colony before we could hear him. I invited my neighbours, in *forty-three,* to hear a book of his sermons. A considerable number met to hear, every sabbath, and on week days. My dwelling-house soon became too small to contain the people ; whereupon we determined to build a meeting-house, merely for *reading ;* for, having never been accustomed to social extempore prayer, none of us durst attempt it. Many were convinced of their undone condition, and could not help crying out and weeping bitterly.

" When the report was spread abroad, I was invited to several places, at a distance, to read these sermons ; and by this means the concern was propagated. About this time, our absenting ourselves from the established church, contrary, it was said, to the laws of the land, was taken notice of, and we were called upon to say what *denomination* we belonged to ? We knew but little of any, except quakers, and were at a loss what name to assume. At length, recollecting that Luther was a noted reformer, and that his *books* had been of special service to us, we called ourselves *Lutherans ;* and thus we continued till Providence sent us that zealous and laborious minister, Mr. Robinson. Afterwards Mr. Roan came, speaking pretty freely about the

degeneracy of the clergy. I was tried for letting him preach in
my house. Afterwards, I was repeatedly fined in court for absenting myself from church. Messrs. Tennent and Blair then
visited us. When they were gone, Mr. Whitefield came and
preached four or five days, which was the happy means of giving
us further encouragement, and of engaging others to the Lord,
—especially among *church* people, who received the gospel more
readily from him, than from ministers of the presbyterian denomination." *Morris's Narrative.* In 1747, there were four
chapels in and around Hanover, which had sprung from the
"*mustard seed*" of sermons taken in short-hand from Whitefield's lips at Glasgow.

Amongst the converts in this quarter, who *saw* Whitefield,
was deaf and dumb Isaac Oliver. He had been so from his
birth. And yet he could represent the crucifixion with such *significant* signs, that any one could understand his meaning. He
could also converse in *signs* at home, about the love of Christ,
until he was transported to rapture, and dissolved in tears.
Many incredible things are told of Oliver. It is evident, however, that he was, what he was called, "a miraculous monument
of Almighty grace." It is enough to say, in proof of this, that
Blair, of Fog's Manor, thought him " truly gracious." Robinson, the first minister of the Hanover *Lutherans,* (as they called
themselves,) seems unknown by American biography. And yet
his success in Kent county, and Queen Anne's, was astonishing.
" Oh, he did much in a little time," says Davies to Bellamy ;
" and who would not choose such an expeditious pilgrimage
through the world?" In Maryland also, about Somerset county, there was " a most glorious display of grace " under his
ministry.

Many instances of his former usefulness came under Whitefield's notice in New England. He was much pleased with a
negro, who had been his chaise-driver, when he first visited
Cambridge. The negro had been *allowed* to hear him in the
college! The sermon was an invitation to the " weary and
heavy laden." It took such a hold upon poor *Sambo,* that he
repeated it in the kitchen, when he came home. Cooper, of
Boston, was so satisfied with his conversion, and Whitefield so

pleased with it, that Sambo was soon admitted to the Lord's table.

Another " brand plucked from the burning " ought not to be forgotten. A son of Mackintosh, the rebel consigned to perpetual imprisonment by George I. had settled in New England. One of his daughters, a lady of fortune, heard Whitefield at Prince's meeting in Boston. She was arrested and won. She was soon ripe for heaven. On her death-bed, she cried out for her *soul-friend*, Mr. Whitefield ; but soon stopped, saying, " Why should I do so ? He is gone about his Master's work, and in a little time we shall meet to part no more." Whitefield had a high opinion of her piety ; and his interest in her was enhanced by a signal escape from some bribed ruffians, who attempted to transport her and her sister to Scotland, that their uncle might seize on an estate of a thousand a year. *Hist. Coll.*

There were at this time not less than twenty ministers, in the neighbourhood of Boston, who did not hesitate to call Whitefield their spiritual father; thus tracing their conversion to his ministry. One of them, who went merely to " pick a hole in his coat," (to find fault,) said, " God picked a *hole* in my heart, and afterwards healed it by the blood of sprinkling."

Although Whitefield travelled eleven hundred miles during this itineracy in America, I have found it impossible to trace him much, except by letters, which merely state his health or his happiness : and even his letters, at this time, are both few and brief. They leave, however, a conviction, that he was inclined, as Gillies says, " to return no more to his native country." New England had evidently won his heart, and for a time almost weaned him from Old England and Scotland too. When he left it for North Carolina, he said, " God only knows what a cross it was to me to leave dear New England so soon. I hope death will not be *so* bitter to me, as was parting with my friends. Glad shall I be to be *prayed* thither again, before I see my native land ! But future things belong to God. I would just be where He would have me, although in the uttermost parts of the earth. I am now hunting for poor lost sinners in these *ungospelized* wilds."

This expression, " hunting for souls," occurs so often in

Whitefield's American letters, that I long thought it was his
own, from his fondness of it.   I am now inclined to think that
he borrowed it from Brainerd's converted Indians; some of
whom were very zealous to win the souls of other *red* men.
But however this may be, the expression is common still amongst
the Indians.   An old hunter once said to me, " When my
soul was caught by Jesus Christ, I gave up the chase of beasts
to hunt for more souls to Jesus.   The old traders called me an
idle fellow ; but I knew better, and hunted for my new Master."
This was Whitefield's favourite work.   " I would not but be
thus employed," he says, " for millions of worlds ! "

He did not, however, forget Bethesda.   When he had pleaded
its cause over New England, he visited it, and added a *Latin*
school to the orphan-house.   His South Carolina friends also
enabled him to purchase a plantation in aid of it, " of six hundred and forty acres of excellent land, with a good house, barn
and out-houses, and sixty acres of ground ready cleared, fenced,
and fit for corn, rice, and every thing necessary for provisions,"
—except *slaves* ! They gave him only one.

Having found Bethesda prosperous, he started for Maryland,
where he found " thousands who had never heard of redeeming
grace."   This roused him anew.   " The heat tries my wasting
tabernacle," he said, " but, through Christ strengthening me, I
intend persisting until I drop."   He did persist, although some
discouraged him ; and he had soon to say, in answer to their
question,—" Have *Marylanders* also received the grace of God ?"
—" Amazing love, Maryland is yielding converts to Jesus.   The
gospel is moving southward.   The harvest is promising.   The
time of singing of birds is come."   His circuit in this quarter
extended over three hundred miles, besides some visits in Pennsylvania.   The *secret* of this mighty effort was this—" thousands
and thousands are ready to hear the gospel, and nobody goes
out scarcely but myself.   Now is the time for stirring.   The
time for *sitting* is coming ; in no meaner place (O amazing love !)
than at the right hand of the Lamb of God.   Let us see what
we can do for precious and immortal souls."   It was such considerations as these, that inspired Whitefield, and determined
him " to die fighting."

After this tour he went to Philadelphia, much exhausted. But still he preached, although his convulsions returned, and the "whole frame" of his "nature seemed to be shocked." "I have," he says, "almost always a continual burning fever. With great regret I have omitted preaching *one* night, (to oblige my friends,) and purpose to do so once more, that they may not charge me with murdering myself. But I hope yet to die in the *pulpit*, or soon after I come out of it. Next Monday I purpose to set out for New York, to see if I can gain strength. It is hard work to be silent: but I must be tried every way."

On his arrival at New York, he said, "I am as willing to hunt for souls as ever. I am not weary of my work." Next day he was at his work again! "I have preached to a very large auditory, and do not find myself much worse for it." He did so again with success. Then he said, "I shall go to Boston like an *arrow* out of a bow, if Jesus strengthen me. I am resolved to preach and work for Him until I can preach and work no more. I have been upon the water three or four days, and now eat like a *sailor*." He went to Boston, and there congregations were larger than ever; and what was better, "arrows of conviction fled and stuck fast, and opposers' mouths were stopped." This good news he sent to Tennent, in order to tempt him to make "another trip" there; adding, "I am determined to die fighting, though it be on my *stumps*." He had just heard of the sudden, but happy, death of his aged and excellent friend Dr. Colman.

In these journeyings and vicissitudes, Whitefield never forgot the Wesleys. They had sent him word, that they were "more moderate with respect to *sinless* perfection," than when he left England; and he returned the compliment by assuring them, that he would "never preach for or against reprobation." Some one had written to him charges against Charles Wesley. He immediately sent word to him of them; adding, "I do not believe them. Love thinks no evil of a friend. Such are you to me. I love you most dearly."

He returned again to Maryland; and as his New York friends were anxious about his health, he wrote to them from Bohemia. In one of these letters, to an aged veteran whom he could not expect to see again, he says, (referring to the Jewish tradition,) "Honoured Sir, may He who *kissed away* the soul of his beloved Moses, appoint a Joshua to succeed you, when He calls you up into the mount to die." His own health was still very fluctuating, even when he reached North Carolina. "I am here," he says, "hunting in the woods, these ungospelized wilds, for sinners. It is pleasant work, though my body is weak and crazy. But after a short *fermentation* in the grave, it will be fashioned like unto Christ's glorious body. The thought of this rejoices my soul, and makes me long to *leap* my seventy years! I sometimes think *all* will go to heaven before me. Pray for me as a dying man; but oh pray that I may not go off as a *snuff.* I would fain die *blazing*—not with human glory, but with the love of Jesus." At this time, a very little riding fatigued him much, and thus his progress was both slow and painful. He preached, however, with great power; cheered from stage to stage by the hope that the conversion of "North Carolina sinners would be glad news in heaven."

In the autumn of 1747, he sailed again for Georgia. From this time, until he went to Bermudas for a change of climate, in 1748, I am unable to trace him.

The only thing melancholy in this sketch of Whitefield's history in New England, during his visit, is, the conduct of the president and professors of Harvard College; and that was worse than it appears from the anecdotes I have told. They published a testimony against him, in which they said, "We look upon Mr. Whitefield as an uncharitable, censorious, and slanderous man." In proof of this, they refer to his *monstrous* reflections on Archbishop Tillotson; whom, they say, Dr. Increase Mather called "great and good." They forgot to say, that Mather, whilst he spoke highly of Tillotson's character and spirit, "constantly warned the students against his books." They testified against his extempore preaching also, "because it is impossible any man can manage an argument instructive to the mind, or cogent to the reasonable powers," thus. He meekly said, "Indeed, gentlemen, I love study, and delight to meditate. Preaching without notes costs as much, if not more, close and solemn thought, as well as confidence in God, than with notes." They had also the audacity to say, "that it is not unlikely, indeed to be suspected, that he is an antinomian;" yea, "stronger in the antinomian scheme than most of the professors of that heresy." In answer to this charge he appealed, as he well might, to the tenor and tendency of his preaching, and reminded them that the *lapsus linguæ* from which they argued had been retracted publicly before they wrote.

His "itinerant way of preaching" comes in, as might be expected, to be testified against in the "strongest" language of the learned doctors. They define an itinerant to be "one that stands ready to preach the gospel to any congregation that may call him." Whitefield says at once,—"*I own the charge.* Were not Knox, Welch, Wishart, and several of the good old puritans, itinerant preachers?"

They also repeated the charge of Clap, of Yale College, that he came into New England "to turn out the generality of their ministers, and to replace them with ministers from England, Ireland, and Scotland." "Such a thought," Whitefield says, "never entered my heart; neither, as I know of, has my preaching any such tendency." This *solemn* denial ought to be held decisive on this point. I did not know of it when I wrote the account of his interviews with Jonathan Edwards.

Their closing charge against Whitefield was, that "the coming in of *hot men*, disturbing the churches, was wholly owing to his influence and example." This refers, of course, to the Tennents,—and the heat of their memory is not yet exhausted in America! Gilbert Tennent will be remembered and revered, long after all the *cold men* of Harvard are forgotten. As Whitefield said, "thousands will thank him for coming into New England, through all the ages of eternity." Having said this, he left the cold men in his *own* way:—"if pulpits should be shut, the fields are open, and I can go without the camp. This I am used to, and glory in. If I have done your society any wrong in my journal, I ask forgiveness. If you have injured me in the testimony you published against me, (as I really think you have,) it is forgiven already, without asking." *Letter to Harvard College, Cambridge.*

Whilst in New England, Whitefield wrote his letter on the

bishop of Litchfield's charge to his clergy. This charge was delivered in 1741, but not published until 1744. It was, therefore, a *deliberate* attack on methodism. Indeed, in a subsequent charge, printed in 1746, now before me, his Lordship refers his clergy to it; assuring them, that "if the false doctrines of the methodists prevail, they must unavoidably create a general disorder in our constitution; and if so, favour the return of popery itself." The bishop, Dr. Smalbroke, was a better scholar than this *prophecy* indicates. He had grappled with Whiston, on Arianism; with Bentley, on the authority of the primitive Complutensian; and with Woolston, on miracles. It was not, however, a very formidable matter to grapple with him, when the subject was the *grace* of the Holy Spirit. Smalbroke certainly believed that there is a Holy Ghost; but no one could well believe less about His work and witness.

It will hardly be credited now, but it is only too true, that a bishop preached, and his clergy called for, the publication of the following sentiments :—" The indwelling and inward witnessing of the Spirit, are all extraordinary gifts, belonging *only* to apostolical and primitive times; and consequently all pretensions to such favours in these last days, are vain and enthusiastical." The Spirit spoken of as helping our infirmities in prayer, " was the Spirit acting in the *inspired* person, who had the gift of prayer, and who in that capacity prayed for the whole assembly. It is *he* (not the Holy Spirit) that maketh intercession with God for private christians" with groanings which cannot be uttered! The Searcher of hearts " knowing the mind of the Spirit," means that " God knows the *intentions* of the inspired" prayer-leader! Preaching in "the demonstration of the Spirit," means no more than proving " Jesus to be the Messiah, by proofs out of the Old Testament," and by miracles!

No wonder Whitefield could not forget these perversions of truth and soberness in America. They haunted him on his voyages, and whilst he was hunting in the woods. He sent over an answer to the charge, addressed to the clergy who called for its publication; not to the bishop, " because I hear," he says, " that he is very aged."

I wish I could say, that either the episcopal *bench*, or the dissenting *board*, had answered it also.   They knew better than Whitefield, that Smalbroke, although an old man, was a sturdy polemic, and in no danger of death or illness from hard blows. But the bench slumbered.   They could *worry* Whitefield or Wesley for an extravagant word; but they would not even bark when a bishop sapped the very vitals of christianity.   Pope certainly knew his men when he said,

> " A saint in crape, is twice a saint in lawn."

A man in *lawn* then, might say almost any thing with impunity, if it was only well said, or argued with a show of learning. Happily, it is not so now.   Such a theologian as Smalbroke would not be left to the lash of methodists or dissenters; he would be chastised by some of his own clergy, or rebuked by some of the bench.   It is needless to analyze or characterize Whitefield's answer to the bishop.   It is enough to say, that it is full of the great doctrines of the Reformation.   Even where it pleads for too much of the direct witness of the Spirit, it is more than excusable; for had not Whitefield and the Wesleys said both strong and startling things on this subject, when both the work and witness of the Spirit were denied and denounced from " high places," those in *low* places would not have listened, or not brought " a pressure from without " upon the hierarchy.

CHAPTER XV.

THE isles of Bermuda are more associated in the public mind with the memory of good Bishop Berkeley, and the poetry of Waller, than with Whitefield. They were probably indebted to Berkeley's example for Whitefield's visit.

In 1721, the " *Vanessa* " of Swift bequeathed her fortune to Berkeley. This was soon followed by his deserved elevation to the deanery of Derry—worth eleven hundred pounds per annum. Never was preferment better bestowed. He had long cherished the design of evangelizing the American Indians, by means of a college in the Bermudas. Now, he issued proposals for it in London ; offering to resign his preferment, and to devote his life to the instruction of young Americans, and stipulating for only a hundred a year to himself. This noble disinterestedness won patronage at first. Government gave him a grant of £10,000 ; and he sailed to carry his plans into effect. He was not sustained by the ministry, however, in the way he expected. He, therefore, made presents of his library to the clergy of Rhode Island, and to Yale College. To the latter, although not at all episcopalian, he gave a thousand volumes, besides his estate at Newport, where he wrote his " Minute Philosopher."

Berkeley then returned to Ireland, and in 1773 was made bishop of Cloyne. It is almost impossible, in the presence of these facts, to remember either his Platonism or his idealism. He was a great and a good man. Atterbury might well say of him, " So much understanding, so much knowledge, so much innocence, and such humility,—I did not think had been the portion of any but *angels*, till I saw this gentleman."

These facts, as well as the climate, drew Whitefield to Bermudas, where he met with the kindest reception, and for about a month preached generally twice a day, traversing the island from one end to the other. His activity, treatment, and success, will best appear from the following extracts from his manuscript journal of that period.

" The simplicity and plainness of the people, together with the pleasant situation of the island, much delighted me. The Rev. Mr. Holiday, minister of Spanish Point, received me in a most affectionate christian manner; and begged I would make his house my home. In the evening I expounded at the house of Mr. Savage, at Port Royal, which was very commodious; and which also he would have me make my home. I went with Mr. Savage, in a boat lent us by Captain ——, to the town of St. George, in order to pay our respects to the governor. All along we had a most pleasant prospect of the other part of the island, but a more pleasant one I never saw. One Mrs. Smith, of St. George's, for whom I had a letter of recommendation from my dear old friend, Mr. Smith of Charlestown, received me into her house. About noon, with one of the council, and Mr. Savage, I waited upon the governor. He received us courteously, and invited us to dine with him and the council at a tavern. We accepted the invitation, and all behaved with great civility and respect. After the governor rose from table, he desired, if I stayed in town on the Sunday, that I would dine with him at his own house.

" Sunday, March 20. Read prayers and preached twice this day, to what were esteemed here large auditories,—in the morning at Spanish Point church, and in the evening at Brackish Pond church, about two miles distant from each other. In the afternoon I spoke with greater freedom than in the morning; and I trust not altogether in vain. All were attentive—some wept. I dined with Colonel Butterfield, one of the council; and received several invitations to other gentlemen's houses. May God bless and reward them, and incline them to open their hearts to receive the Lord Jesus! Amen and Amen!

" Wednesday, March 23. Dined with Captain Gibbs, and went from thence and expounded at the house of Captain

F——le, at Hunbay, about two miles distant. The company was here also large, attentive, and affected. Our Lord gave me utterance. I expounded on the first part of the 8th chapter of Jeremiah. After lecture, Mr. Riddle, a counsellor, invited me to his house; as did Mr. Paul, an aged presbyterian minister, to his pulpit; which I complied with, upon condition the report was true, that the governor had served the ministers with an injunction that I should not preach in the churches.

" Friday, March 25. Was prevented preaching yesterday by the rain, which continued from morning till night; but this afternoon, God gave me another opportunity of declaring his eternal truths to a large company at the house of one Mr. B——s, who last night sent me a letter of invitation.

" Sunday, March 27. Glory be to God! I hope this has been a profitable sabbath to many souls; it has been a pleasant one to mine. Both morning and afternoon I preached to a large auditory, for Bermudas, in Mr. Paul's meeting-house, which I suppose contains about four hundred. Abundance of negroes, and many others, were in the vestry, porch, and about the house. The word seemed to be clothed with a convicting power, and to make its way into the hearts of the hearers. Between sermons, I was entertained very civilly in a neighbouring house. Judge Bascom, and three more of the council, came thither, and each gave me an invitation to his house. How does the Lord make way for a poor stranger in a strange land!—After the second sermon, I dined with Mr. Paul; and in the evening expounded to a very large company at Counsellor Riddle's. My body was somewhat weak; but the Lord carried me through, and caused me to go to rest rejoicing.—May I thus go to my grave, when my ceaseless, uninterrupted rest shall begin!

" Monday, March 28. Dined this day at Mrs. Dorrel's, mother-in-law to my dear friend the Rev. Mr. Smith; and afterwards preached to more than a large house full of people, on Matthew ix. 12. Towards the conclusion of the sermon, the hearers began to be more affected than I have yet seen them. Surely the Lord Jesus will give me some seals in this island! Grant this, O Redeemer, for thy infinite mercy sake!

" Thursday, March 31. Dined on Tuesday, at Colonel Corbusiers, and on Wednesday, at Colonel Gilbert's, both of the council; and found, by what I could hear, that some good had been done, and many prejudices removed. Who shall hinder, if God will work? Went to an island this afternoon, called Ireland, upon which live a few families; and to my surprise, found a great many gentlemen, and other people, with my friend Mr. Holiday, who came from different quarters to hear me. Before I began preaching, I went round to see a most remarkable cave, which very much displayed the exquisite workmanship of Him, who in his strength setteth fast the mountains, and is girded about with power.—Whilst I was in the cave, quite unexpectedly I turned and saw Counsellor Riddle, who, with his son, came to hear me; and whilst we were in the boat, told me that he had been with the governor, who declared he had no personal prejudices against me—and wondered I did not come to town, and preach there, for it was the desire of the people; and that any house in the town, the court-house not excepted, should be at my service. Thanks be to God for so much favour! If his cause requires it, I shall have more. He knows my heart; I value the favour of man no further than as it makes room for the gospel, and gives me a larger scope to promote the glory of God. There being no capacious house upon the island, I preached for the first time here in the open air. All heard very attentive; and it was very pleasant after sermon to see so many boats full of people returning from the worship of God. I talked seriously to some in our own boat, and sung a psalm, in which they readily joined.

" Sunday, April 3. Preached twice this day at Mr. Paul's meeting-house, as on the sabbath, but with greater freedom and power, especially in the morning; and I think to as great, if not greater, auditories. Dined with Colonel Harvy, another of the council—visited a sick woman, where many came to hear—and expounded afterwards to a great company, at Captain John Dorrel's, Mrs. Dorrel's son, who, with his wife, courteously entertained me, and desired me to make his house my home.—So true is that promise of our Lord's, ' that whosoever leaves father and mother, house or lands, shall have in this life a hundredfold, with persecution, and in the world to come, life

z

everlasting.' Lord, I have experienced the one: in thy good
time grant that I may experience the other also !

" Wednesday, April 6. Preached yesterday at the house of
Mr. Anthony Smith, of Baylis Bay, with a considerable degree
of warmth ; and rode afterwards to St. George's, the only town
on the island. The gentlemen of the town had sent me an invitation by Judge Bascom ; and he, with several others, came
to visit me at my lodgings, and informed me that the governor
desired to see me. About ten I waited upon his Excellency,
who received me with great civility, and told me he had no objection against my person, or my principles, having never yet
heard me ; and he knew nothing in respect to my conduct in
moral life, that might prejudice him against me ; but his instructions were, to let none preach in the island, unless he had
a written license to preach some where in America, or the West
Indies ; at the same time he acknowledged that it was but a
matter of mere form. I informed his Excellency that I had
been regularly inducted to the parish of Savannah ; that I was
ordained priest by letters dimissory from my lord of London,
and under no church censure from his Lordship ; and would
always read the church prayers, if the clergy would give me the
use of their churches.—I added further, that a minister's pulpit
was looked upon as his freehold, and that I knew one clergyman who had denied his own diocesan the use of his pulpit.
But I told his Excellency, I was satisfied with the liberty he
allowed me, and would not act contrary to his injunction. I
then begged leave to be dismissed, because I was obliged to
preach at eleven o'clock. His Excellency said he intended to
do himself the pleasure to hear me. At eleven the church bell
rung. The church Bible, prayer book, and cushion, were sent
to the town-house. The governor, several of the council, the
minister of the parish, and assembly-men, with a great number
of the town's people, assembled in great order. I was very
sick, through a cold I caught last night ; but read the church
prayers. The first lesson was the 15th chapter of the 1st book
of Samuel. I preached on those words, " Righteousness ex-
alteth a nation." Being weak and faint, and afflicted much
with the head-ache, I did not do that justice to my subject I

sometimes am enabled to do ; but the Lord so helped me, that, as I found afterwards, the governor and the other gentlemen expressed their approbation, and acknowledged they did not expect to be so well entertained. Not unto me, Lord! not unto me, but unto thy free grace be all the glory!

" After sermon, Dr. F——bs, and Mr. P——t, the collector, came to me, and desired me to favour them and the gentlemen of the town with my company to dinner. I accepted the invitation. The governor, and the president, and Judge Bascom were there. All wondered at my speaking so freely and fluently, without notes. The governor asked, whether I used minutes? I answered, No. He said it was a great gift. At table, his Excellency introduced something of religion, by asking me the meaning of the word HADES? Several other things were started about free will, Adam's fall, predestination, &c. to all which God enabled me to answer so pertinently, and taught me to mix the *utile* and *dulce* so together, that all at table seemed highly pleased, shook me by the hand, and invited me to their respective houses. The governor, in particular, asked me to dine with him on the morrow; and Dr. F——bs, one of his particular intimates, invited me to drink tea in the afternoon. I thanked all, returned proper respects, and went to my lodgings with some degree of thankfulness for the assistance vouchsafed me, and abased before God at the consideration of my unspeakable unworthiness. In the afternoon, about five o'clock, I expounded the parable of the prodigal son to many people at a private house ; and in the evening had liberty to speak freely and closely to those that supped with me. Oh that this may be the beginning of good gospel times to the inhabitants of this town! Lord, teach me to deal prudently with them, and cause them to melt under thy word!

" Friday, April 8. Preached yesterday with great clearness and freedom, to about fourscore people, at a house on David's Island, over against St. George's Town—went and lay at Mr. Holiday's, who came in a boat to fetch me—and this day I heard him preach and read prayers ; after which I took the sacrament from him. Honest man! he would have made me administer and officiate ; but I chose not to do it, lest I should bring him into trouble after my departure. However, in the afternoon, I preached at Mr. Todd's, in the same parish, to a very large company indeed. The Lord was with me. My heart was warm—and what went from the heart, I trust went to the heart; for many were affected. Oh that they may be converted also! Then will it be a good Friday, indeed, to their souls.

" Sunday, April 10. Dined and conversed yesterday very agreeably with Judge Bascom, who seems to have the greatest insight into the difference between Arminian and Calvinistical schemes, of any one I have met with upon the island.—In the afternoon, I visited a paralytic; and this day preached twice again at Mr. Paul's meeting-house. The congregations were rather larger than ever, and the power of God seemed to be more amongst them. I think I see a visible alteration for the better every Lord's day. Blessed be God!—In the evening I expounded at Mr. Joseph Dorrell's, where I dined, to a very large company; then went to his kinsman's, my usual lodging on Saturday and Sunday evenings; who with his wife and other friends, seemed kinder and kinder daily. Good measure, pressed down, and running over, may the Lord, both as to spirituals and temporals, return into all their bosoms!

" Saturday, April 16. Preached since Lord's day at five different houses, to concerned and affected congregations, at different parts of the island; but was more indisposed one night after going to bed, than I had been for some time. On two of the days of this week, I dined with the president, and Captain Spafford, one of the council, both of whom entertained me with the utmost civility.

" Sunday, April 17. Still God magnifies his power and goodness more and more. This morning we had a pleasing sight at Mr. Paul's meeting-house. I began to preach, and the people to hear and be affected as in days of old at home. Indeed, the prospect is encouraging. Praise the Lord, O my soul!— After preaching twice to a large congregation in the meeting-house, I, at the desire of the parents, preached in the evening a sermon at the funeral of a little boy, about five years of age. A great number of people attended, and the Lord enabled me so to speak, as to affect many of the hearers. Blessed be the

Lord for this day's work ! Not unto me, O Lord ! not unto me, but unto thy free grace be all the glory !

" Sunday, April 24. The last week being rainy, I preached only five times in private houses ; and this day but once in the meeting-house ; but I hope neither times without effect. This evening expounded at Counsellor Riddle's, who, with the other gentlemen, treat me with greater respect every day. Colonel Gilbert, one of the council, has lent me his horse, during my stay ; and Mr. Dorrell, this morning, informed me of a design the gentlemen had, to raise a contribution to help me to discharge my arrears, and support my orphan family. Thanks be given to thy name, O God ! Thou knowest all things ; thou knowest that I want to owe no man any thing, but love ; and provide for Bethesda, after my decease. Thou hast promised thou wilt fulfil the desire of them that fear thee. I believe, Lord, help my unbelief, that thou wilt fulfil this desire of my soul. Even so. Amen.

" Saturday, April 30. Preached since Lord's day two funeral sermons, and at five different houses in different parts of the island, to still larger and larger auditories, and perceived the people to be affected more and more. Twice or thrice I preached without doors. Riding in the sun, and preaching very earnestly, a little fatigued one ; so that this evening I was obliged to lie down for some time. Faint, yet pursuing, must be my motto still.

" Sunday, May 1. This morning, was a little sick ; but I trust God gave us a happy beginning of the new month. I preached twice with power, especially in the morning, to a very great congregation in the meeting-house ; and in the evening, having given previous notice, I preached about four miles distant, in the fields, to a large company of negroes, and a number of white people who came to hear what I had to say to them. I believe, in all, near fifteen hundred people. As the sermon was intended for the negroes, I gave the auditory warning, that my discourse would be chiefly directed to them, and that I should endeavour to imitate the example of Elijah, who, when he was about to raise the child, contracted himself to its length. The negroes seemed very sensible and attentive. When I asked, if they all did not desire to go to heaven? one of them, with a very audible voice, said, 'Yes, sir.' This caused a little smiling; but, in general, every thing was carried on with great decency; and I believe the Lord enabled me so to discourse, as to touch the negroes, and yet not to give them the least umbrage to slight or behave imperiously to their masters. If ever a minister, in preaching, need the wisdom of the serpent to be joined with the harmlessness of the dove, it must be when discoursing to negroes. Vouchsafe me this favour, O God, for thy dear Son's sake!

" Monday, May 2. Upon inquiry, I found that some of the negroes did not like my preaching, because I told them of their cursing, swearing, thieving, and lying. One or two of the worst of them, as I was informed, went away. Some said, they would not go any more. They liked Mr. M——r better, for he never told them of these things; and I said, their hearts were as black as their faces. They expected, they said, to hear me speak against their masters. Blessed be God, that I was directed not to say any thing, this first time, to the masters at all, though my text led me to it. It might have been of bad consequences, to tell them their duty, or charge them too roundly with the neglect of it, before their slaves. They would mind all I said to their masters, and, perhaps, nothing that I said to them. Every thing is beautiful in its season. Lord, teach me always that due season, wherever I am called, to give either black or white a portion of thy word! However, others of the poor creatures, I hear, were very thankful, and came home to their masters' houses, saying, that they would strive to sin no more. Poor hearts! These different accounts affected me; and upon the whole, I could not help rejoicing, to find that their consciences were so far awake.

" Saturday, May 7. In my conversation these two days, with some of my friends, I was diverted much, in hearing several things that passed among the poor negroes, since my preaching to them last Sunday. One of the women, it seems, said, 'that if the book I preached out of was the best book that was ever bought at London, she was sure it had never all that in it which I spoke to the negroes.' The old man, who spoke out loud last Sunday, and said, 'yes,' when I asked them whether all the negroes would not go to heaven? being questioned by somebody, why he spoke out so? answered, 'That the gentleman put the question once or twice to them, and the other fools had not the manners to make me any answer; till, at last, I seemed to point at him, and he was ashamed that nobody should answer me, and therefore he did.' Another, wondering why I said negroes had black hearts; was answered by his black brother thus; 'Ah, thou fool! dost thou not understand it? He means black with sin.' Two more girls were overheard by their mistress talking about religion: and they said, 'They knew, if they did not repent, they must be damned.' From all which I infer, that these Bermudas negroes are more knowing than I supposed; that their consciences are awake, and consequently prepared, in a good measure, for hearing the gospel preached unto them.

"Sunday, May 8. This also, I trust, has been a good sabbath. In the morning I was helped to preach powerfully to a melting, and rather a larger congregation than ever, in Mr. Paul's meeting-house; and in the evening, to almost as large a congregation of black and white as last Sunday in the fields, near my hearty friend, Mr. Holiday's house. To see so many black faces was affecting. They heard very attentively, and some of them now began to weep. May God grant them a godly sorrow, that worketh repentance not to be repented of!

"Friday, May 13. This afternoon preached over the corpse of Mr. Paul's eldest son, about twenty-four years of age; and by all I could hear, and judge of by conversing with him, he did indeed die in the Lord. I visited him twice last Lord's day, and was quite satisfied with what he said, though he had not much of the sensible presence of God. I find he was a preacher upon his death-bed: for he exhorted all his companions to love Christ in sincerity; and blessed his brother and sister, and, I think, his father and mother, just before his departure. A great many people attended the funeral. I preached on Luke viii. 13, 'And when the Lord saw her, he had compassion on her, and said unto her, Weep not.' Many were affected in the application of my discourse; and, I trust, some will be in-

duced, by this young man's good example, to remember their
Redeemer in the days of their youth.   Grant it, O Lord, for
thy dear Son's sake.

" Sunday, May 15.   Praise the Lord, O my soul, and all that
is within me, praise his holy name !   This morning I preached
my farewell sermon at Mr. Paul's meeting-house—it was quite
full ; and, as the president said, above one hundred and fifty
whites, besides blacks, were round the house.   Attention sat
on every face ; and when I came to take my leave, oh ! what a
sweet, unaffected weeping was there to be seen every where ! I
believe there were few dry eyes.   The negroes, likewise, without
doors, I heard weep plentifully.   My own heart was affected ;
and though I have parted with friends so often, yet I find every
fresh parting almost unmans me, and very much affects my
heart.   Surely, a great work is begun in some souls at Bermudas.
Carry it on, O Lord ! and if it be thy will, send me to this dear
people again.   Even so, Lord Jesus.   Amen !

" After sermon, I dined with three of the council, and other
gentlemen and ladies, at Captain Bascom's ; and from thence
we went to a funeral, at which Mr. M——r preached ; and after
that, I expounded on our Lord's transfiguration, at the house of
one Mrs. Harvey, sister to dear Mr. Smith, of Charlestown.
The house was exceeding full, and it was supposed above three
hundred stood in the yard.   The Lord enabled me to lift
up my voice like a trumpet.   Many wept.   Mr. M——r returned from the funeral with me, and attended the lecture ; as
did the three councillors, with whom I conversed freely.   May
God reward them, and all the dear people of the island, for those
many favours conferred on me, who am the chief of sinners, and
less than the least of all saints !

" Sunday, May 22.   Blessed be God ! the little leaven thrown
into the three measures of meal, begins to ferment, and work
almost every day for the week past.   I have conversed with
souls loaded with a sense of their sins ; and, as far as I can judge,
really pricked to the heart.   I preached only three times, but
to almost three times larger auditories than usual.   Indeed the
fields are white ready unto harvest.   God has been pleased to
bless private visits.   Go where I will, upon the least notice,

houses are crowded, and the poor souls that follow, are soon drenched in tears. This day I took, as it were, another fare-well. As the ship did not sail, I preached at Somerset in the morning to a large congregation in the fields; and expounded in the evening at Mr. Harvey's house, round which stood many hundreds of people. But in the morning and evening, how did the poor souls weep! Abundance of prayers and blessings were put up for my safe passage to England, and speedy return to Bermudas again. May they enter into the ears of the Lord of Sabaoth! With all humility and thankfulness of heart, will I here, O Lord, set up my *Ebenezer;* for hitherto surely thou hast helped me! Thanks be to the Lord for sending me hither. I have been received in a manner I dared not expect; and have met with little, very little opposition, indeed. The inhabitants seem to be plain and open-hearted. They have loaded me with provisions for my sea-store; and in the several parishes, by a private voluntary contribution, have raised me upwards of ONE HUNDRED POUNDS sterling. This will pay a little of Bethesda's debt, and enable me to make such a remittance to my *dear* yoke-fellow, as may keep her from being embarrassed, or too much beholden, in my absence. Blessed be God, for bringing me out of my embarrassment by degrees! May the Lord reward all my benefactors a thousandfold! I hear that what was given, was given exceedingly heartily; and people only lamented that they could do no more."

Transmitting to Georgia the contributions he had received, and fearing a relapse if he had returned to America in the heat of the summer; and also being much pressed to return to Eng-land, Mr. Whitefield took his passage in a brig, and arrived safe in twenty-eight days at Deal; and the next evening, July 6, he came to London, having been absent near four years.

CHAPTER XVI.

WHITEFIELD RANGING.

In 1748, after an absence of four years, Whitefield returned to his native land; not exactly from choice, but because he was afraid to risk his restored health in America again, during the heat of July. He embarked at Bermudas in June, on board the Betsey; and lived, as he expresses it, "like people that came from the continent, not from an island—so bountiful were his friends." His appetite was, however, somewhat spoiled one day. The Betsey was chased by a large French vessel, and shot at thrice. "We gave up all for lost! We were almost defenceless. I was dressing myself to receive our *visitors*. In the mean time our captain cried, 'The danger is over.' The Frenchman turned about and left us. In the Channel we expect such alarms daily."

During the voyage he abridged, and endeavoured to *gospelize*, Law's "Serious Call;" and finished a revisal of his own journals: but he was not allowed to preach on board. This, he says, "may spare my lungs, but it grieves my heart." It seems he could not write with much composure. The reason he assigns for this is, "We have four *gentlewomen* on board; so you may guess how it is!"

His own private review of his sayings, doings, and writings, up to this time, I have recorded in "The Specimens of Whitefield," at the close of this volume. It is equally humble and honest; and it led to many *improvements* in his conduct and spirit towards the opponents of truth and godliness.

The prospect of home led him naturally to anticipate the pleasure of seeing his aged and beloved mother. He had been so long absent, and she was so poor, that he did not know, when he wrote, where she resided. He added to the prayer for her, " Oh that I may see you laden with holiness, and bearing fruit in old age," the request, " Let me know whether you stand in *need* of any thing." There was a contemporary clergyman of notoriety, *Sterne*, who could weep over a dead ass, and a caged starling, who neither prayed nor felt for his aged mother, although she was in distress : but Sterne was a *wit*, not a methodist !

On his arrival in London, Whitefield was welcomed by thousands, with a joy which well nigh overcame them and himself too. One cause of this joy was, that a large *church* was open to him on his return. It was St. Bartholomew's, where he had a *thousand* communicants on the first sabbath, besides " multitudes flocking to hear." How different from the reception he met with on his former return from America. The fact is, both he and the Wesleys were now wiser men.

He was not, however, without his cares on this occasion. His outward affairs were " far behindhand." Antinomianism had " made sad havoc " in the religious societies, during his absence. " I came," he says, " at a *critical* juncture." One of the *hyper* party threatened to rival him in Moorfields—a sphere which these zealots have seldom coveted. Whitefield sent him word,—" The fields are no doubt as free to you as to another. God send you a clear head and a *clean* heart. I intend preaching there on Sunday evening." He did ; and found " Moorfields as white to harvest as ever." In other respects, also, he had soon the satisfaction of seeing " things take a good turn " in London.

At this time he renewed his intimacy with Hervey, who was now popular as a writer ; and that not undeservedly. It has been fashionable, of late, to denounce his *florid* style : and, so far as this prevents Hervey from becoming a *model* to young preachers or imaginative writers, it is a good fashion. It is, however, bad, so far as it prevents the young from reading his works, or from yielding to their inspiration. They cannot be read without interest by the young. Both the " Meditations " and " Theron and Aspasio " have an irresistible charm to them. They lay hold upon the heart at once, and are never forgotten.

The secret of this fascination is, their sympathy with visible nature, as *young* eyes see it, and young hearts enjoy it. Hervey *reflects* the heavens and the earth to them, in the broad and brilliant forms which haunt their own dreams. Who does not remember this ? True ; we cease to read Hervey, and learn to find fault with his style : but, which of us would have relished or read, in early life, the *chaster* works on piety, which now charm us ? Even our taste for the *simple,* is the reaction of the gorgeous. I owe this passing tribute to Hervey. My love of nature was made religious by him. And, had I never tried to imitate him, I should never have formed a puritanical style for myself.

The *second* reformation in this country owes much to Hervey. He was the Melancthon of it, by his writings. They suited, as Whitefield says of them, " the taste of the polite world." They refined the taste of the methodists also. The former read them, because they were flowery ; the latter, because they were savoury. The one looked at grace, through their medium, with less prejudice ; the other at nature, with more delight than formerly. Whitefield saw this twofold influence of Hervey's works, and wisely said nothing against their style, when they were submitted to his revision.

Amongst all Whitefield's converts, no one has been more useful than Hervey, as a writer. That he was one of them is certain, although seldom remembered. In a letter to Whitefield, he says, " Your journals and sermons, and especially that sweet sermon, on ' What think ye of Christ ? ' were a mean of bringing me to the knowledge of the truth." *Brown's Memoirs of Hervey.* This will account for the deference he paid to his spiritual father, and for the eulogium he pronounced on him at Doddridge's : " I never beheld," he said, " so fair a copy of our Lord ; such a living image of the Saviour ; such exalted delight in God ; such unbounded benevolence to man ; such steady faith in the divine promises ; such fervent zeal for the divine glory ; and all this, without the least moroseness of humour, or extravagances of behaviour ; but sweetened with the most engaging cheerfulness of temper, and regulated by all the sobriety of reason and wisdom of Scripture : insomuch, that I cannot forbear applying the wise man's encomium on an illustrious woman, to this eminent minister of the everlasting gospel—'Many sons have done virtuously, but thou excellest them all.'"

It was not in return for this compliment, but before it, that Whitefield introduced Hervey's works into America, and rejoiced in their popularity. "The author," he said, "is my old friend; a most heavenly-minded creature; one of the first methodists, who is contented with a small *cure*, and gives all he has to the poor. We correspond with, though we cannot see, each other." Gillies says, that Whitefield left a blank in his manuscripts thus,—" Here a character of Hervey;" and adds, " What a pity he did not write it down!" Doddridge also was not ashamed to preface a work of Hervey's, although Warburton called it a weak rhapsody, and said it would degrade the Doctor.

At this time his acquaintance with the Countess of Huntingdon commenced. She had engaged Howel Harris to bring him to Chelsea, " as soon as he came ashore." He went and preached twice in her drawing-room, in a manner that determined her to invite some of the nobility to hear him.

As she had, from this time, much influence upon his future movements, the following masterly sketch of her history and character will tell best here. It is by a descendant of Doddridge, who *hates* Calvinism.

" The Right Honourable Selina Countess Dowager of Huntingdon, second daughter, and one of the coheiresses of Washington, second Earl of Ferrars, was born August 13th, 1707, and married in the year 1728, to Theophilus Earl of Huntingdon, by whom she had issue four sons and three daughters: of these, only one, the Countess of Moira, survived their mother, whose death occurred in 1791, at the age of eighty-four, and after a widowhood of forty-five years.

" Upon the decease of her mother, the Countess of Moira received an accession to her income of fifteen hundred pounds per annum, and her son, Lord Rawden, a bequest of two thousand two hundred pounds. Lady Huntingdon also left an annuity of a hundred a year to her friend Lady Ann Erskine, and the sum of four thousand pounds to be disposed of in charitable gifts, at the direction of the Earl of Dartmouth, Sir Richard Hill, and her chaplain, Mr. Haws. The residue of her fortune was bequeathed for the support of sixty-four chapels, which she had contributed to establish throughout the kingdom.

" Few characters have been more erroneously estimated by the world than that of Lady Huntingdon. She was, in fact, neither the gloomy fanatic, the weak visionary, nor the abstracted devotee, which different parties have delighted to paint her.

" The circumstance of her having forbade the publication of her papers, and her retired mode of life, for even her charities were principally distributed through the medium of her chaplains, were the causes which baffled the curiosity of those who felt desirous of discovering the motives which could tempt a woman to resign the allurements of station, and to devote, in addition to what is mentioned in her will, at least a hundred thousand pounds, given during her life, for the extension of peculiar religious opinions, without any view towards that personal distinction which has been too often a leading inducement with the founders of new sects.

" In the absence of circumstantial detail, all that remains is to collect the few personal traits which are here and there accidentally mentioned, and to unite them with facts of public notoriety. Having thus combined these scattered rays, their condensed light at once reveals the actual character of this remarkable woman; and we perceive her peculiarities to have arisen from the blight of domestic sorrow, acting upon a mind swayed to a great extent by the imagination, and, therefore, highly susceptible of religious impressions.

" In the spring day of her life, there was little to distinguish Lady Huntingdon from the many charming and intelligent young women who ever grace the courtly circle in which she moved. She was naturally gay, and the quickness of her disposition rendered her sprightly and amusing; but it does not appear that her gaiety tended towards dissipation, or that her conversational talents amounted to wit. How far her religious education had been attended to is not indicated, but there is no reason to surmise that it was defective; and had not her maternal and conjugal affections suffered from the shock of family bereavements, her character would probably have remained not less worthy, but far less remarkable, than it is at present.

" The loss of children, and the death of her lord, which occurred before the charms of existence had with her been subdued by the lapse of time, gave a blow to the elasticity of her mind from which it never recovered. When the first paroxysm of grief had subsided, her exhausted feelings naturally sought a refuge in devotion; and it is only to be regretted that under the melancholy impressions of the period, her mind the more deeply imbibed the Calvinistic tenets." *(Not exactly!)*

" An affecting incident shows that at this time she still retained the fond recollections of human regard in all their wonted intensity. Lady Huntingdon had a fine bust of herself placed upon the tomb of her deceased husband; and it is but justice to observe, that the widowed bosom in which his memory was enshrined ever remained as cold to earthly passion, as the insensible marble, whose gentle smile, amid the symbols of death, seemed eloquent with immortality.

" For some years the religious views of Lady Huntingdon were those of the church of England; she was pious and benevolent in an eminent degree, as her letters in this work evince, but her sentiments were unmarked by peculiarity. As might, however, have been expected, the spirit-stirring eloquence of Whitefield caught her attention, and she became one of his most determined proselytes; and, doubtless, felt delighted to obtain so important a witness to a reality of her *election*. Be this as it may, under his influence, although she never renounced the doctrines of episcopacy, yet she embraced sectarian views incompatible with its practice and well-being; she endowed chapels, and sanctioned an independent *form* of worship.

" Of the results to which her conduct, in such respects, was likely to lead, she was doubtless unconscious, and, in fact, acted from the impressions produced upon her mind by the interested parties around her. She was, indeed, so much the child of emotion, that she is related to have described herself 'as like a ship before the wind, carried on by an impulse she could not resist or describe.'

" The influence of Whitefield and his friends over the mind

of Lady Huntingdon, was most apparent from the year 1748, when he became her chaplain. That influence was, however, so guardedly employed, that the natural vigilance of her character was fully exercised in plans for the propagation of the highly Calvinistic ideas she had espoused. It was not until the year 1768, that she opened her ' college' near Talgarth, in South Wales, ' for the education of serious and godly young men, and such as she believed had a *divine call.*' Besides this academy, the whole expense of which she defrayed, she was deeply interested in the missionary schemes then in motion; and that she might the better uphold the *cause*, reduced her style of living far below what her station in society demanded; and even exhausted her income to such an extent, that she was not able to afford charitable relief in some cases of the utmost necessity, that were brought under her notice.

" Her death occurred on the 17th of June, 1791, and was marked with the serenity of the christian, and the humble confidence of a saint. As the awful moment was approaching, she said, ' My work is done ; and I have nothing to do but to go to my Father.' (This was *her* Calvinism !)

" The romantic turn of her feelings was as strongly marked during her last illness, as in any former period of her life. She desired that her remains might be dressed in the suit of white silk which she wore at the opening of the chapel in Goodman's Fields ; and in speaking of death, said, ' It was like putting off her cloak.' When the blood-vessel burst, which was the commencement of her illness, on being asked how she did, by Lady Ann Erskine, she observed, ' I am well—all is well—well for ever ! I see, wherever I turn my eyes, whether I live or die, nothing but victory.' And a day or so before her decease, she remarked, ' The Lord has been present with my spirit this morning in a remarkable manner : what He means to convey to my mind, I know not ; it may be my approaching departure. My soul is filled with glory ; I am in the element of heaven.' " *Humphries.*

Such was Lady Huntingdon. She soon brought around Whitefield some of the stars of the court. Chesterfield and a whole circle of them attended, and having heard once, desired they might hear him again. " I, therefore, preached again," he says, " in the evening, and went home, never more surprised at any thing in my life. All behaved quite well, and were in some degree affected. The Earl of Chesterfield thanked me, and said, ' Sir, I shall not tell you what I shall tell others, how I approve of you ;' or words to this purpose. At last Lord Bolingbroke came to hear; sat like an *archbishop*, and was pleased to say, I had done great justice to the divine attributes in my discourse. (Hume also was present.) Soon afterwards, her Ladyship removed to town, where I generally preached twice a week, to very brilliant auditories. Blessed be God, not without effectual success on some." *Gillies.* Bolingbroke invited Whitefield to visit him; which he did, and found him both candid and frank. And the impression made upon him, may be judged by his saying to the Countess, " You may command my pen when you will. It shall be drawn in your service. For, admitting the Bible to be true, I shall have little apprehension of maintaining the doctrines of predestination and grace, against all your revilers." All the nobility also accepted, with pleasure and surprise, copies of Whitefield's sermons. On recording this, he says, " Thus the world turns round ! In all time of wealth, good Lord, deliver me." Lord Bath and others had given him money for the orphan-house. One of the Prince of Wales's favourites, a privy counsellor of the king of Denmark, and several persons of rank, dined and drank tea with him.

The manner in which he refers to this introduction amongst the great, has been quoted against him as a proof of vanity. Why should it ? True ; he says in his letters to Wesley, and other private friends, " the noble, the mighty, the wise, have been to hear me." These are also the very words which Lady Huntingdon employed in her letters to Doddridge, at the time. Was *she vain* or flattered, because she rejoiced that a door was opening for " the nobility to hear the gospel ? " Besides, this new sphere did not divert him from any of his old work, nor at all change his spirit or purposes. At the very crisis of this elevation, he said to Wesley, " My attachment to America will not permit me to abide long in England. If I formed societies, I should but weave a *Penelope's* web. I intend, therefore, to go about preaching the gospel to every

2 A

creature." Accordingly, he was off to Scotland in a few days.

On his arrival at Edinburgh, he found a *Moorfields* congregation, as to numbers, to welcome him. At Glasgow also, the prospects were still more encouraging. Many at both places came to inform him of their conversion, on his former visits. Cambuslang also kindled again. All this was too much for some of the kirk folks, now that the Seceders were quarrelling amongst themselves. The synod of Glasgow and Ayr debated a motion, "tending to prohibit ministers from employing Whitefield;"—because he was a *priest* of the church of England; because he had not subscribed the *formula;* because the scheme of the orphan-house was chimerical, and the *money* collected for it not fully accounted for ! The first count in the indictment is not so heavy now. Dr. Chalmers is the champion of the English priesthood. The charge was better met, however, by the clergyman who said at the synod, " If Bishop Butler, Sherlock, or Secker, were in Scotland, I should welcome them to my pulpit ; and in this, I should imitate Rutherford, as firm a presbyterian as any of us, who employed Usher. There is no law of Christ, and no act of assembly, prohibiting me to give my pulpit to any episcopal, or anabaptist, or independent minister, if of sound principles in the fundamentals of religion. Our church expressly enjoins, Art. 13, that great tenderness is to be used to foreign protestants." *Gillies.*

Whitefield's personal character was nobly and indignantly vindicated by Dr. Erskine. He appealed to the *affidavit* of the magistrates of Georgia, in the Philadelphia Gazette, in proof of the honest application of the money collected for the orphan-house ; and cried *shame* upon presbyterians, who could object to Whitefield as a " suspended minister," whilst his only fault was, refusing to " use the communion-book in a presbyterian chapel." The result of the debate was, " the decent burial of the motion." It was, however, supported by thirteen. Twenty-seven voted for employing Whitefield in the pulpits of the kirk. Gillies says truly, " Upon the whole, the attacks informed the synod of the falsehood of many aspersions thrown out against him : and thus what was intended for his reproach, turned out to his honour."

Whitefield himself says of these conclaves, " Two synods and one presbytery brought me upon the carpet; but all has worked for good. The more I was *blackened,* the more the Redeemer comforted me. If my enemies show themselves, I am persuaded Jesus will bless me to his people more and more." Amongst the charges then advanced against him, in order to injure him in the estimation of the poor, one was, that he was sent and paid by government to preach against the *Pretender !* This charge came with an ill grace from both the Kirk and the Secession. Both preached against the Pretender, as much as he did ; with only this difference, that the former had pay and the latter thanks, while he had neither.

It was, I think, about this time, that Whitefield had another interview with Ralph Erskine. Their *last* was in 1750. It was short, but affecting. On parting, Erskine embraced him and said, " We have seen strange things." They had both seen *strange* things ! Whitefield had seen himself traduced by ministers of a kirk, which had gladly played him off against the Secession : and Erskine had seen himself excluded by the presbytery of Dunfermline, whilst his own *son,* John, sat in judgment upon him. It is not true that John pronounced the sentence of ex-communication on his father. Gibb did that. It is, however, true, that the good old man said, " It was a sword piercing my heart, to see *Johnny* sitting with them." Erskine and Whitefield might well embrace as brethren after these strange things. *Erskine's Life.* This reconciliation went no further. The other Seceders kept up the old clamour against him, be-cause he did not " preach up the covenant ;" and he gave his old answer, " I preach up the covenant of grace."

Notwithstanding all these attempts to lower him in public estimation, his old friends in Scotland stood by him. The godly ministers not only encouraged his attempts to serve the New Jersey college ; but also entered into his spirited (though im-prudent) design of turning the orphan-house into a college.

On his return to London, he resumed his lectures at Lady Huntingdon's to the " great ones," as he calls them. Thirty, and sometimes sixty, persons of rank attended, although the newspapers were full of " strange lying accounts " of his recep-

tion in Scotland. He availed himself of this influence, to forward his intended college : for which his plea was,—" If some
such thing be not done, I cannot see how the southern parts will
be provided with ministers ; for all are afraid to go over." On
this ground he appealed to the trustees of Georgia ; reminding
them that he had expended £5000 upon the orphan-house ; begging them to relieve it, as a charitable institution, from all quit-
rent and taxes ; and especially to allow him slaves. " *White
hands*," he said, had left his tract of land uncultivated.

Whilst thus pleading for his own seminary, he did not forget
New Jersey. He wrote to Mr. Pemberton, " If you or some
other popular minister come over, and make an application in
person, a collection might be recommended by the general assembly, and large contributions be raised from private persons.
If one of the *Indians* was brought over,—and a proposal made to
educate some of the converted Indians in the college,—it would
certainly be of service." Thus he had our best missionary *plans*,
as well as spirit, a century ago.

Having set these schemes on foot, he went to Bristol ; and
attended the sacrament at the cathedral next day. The bishop,
he says, " behaved respectfully " to him. He visited also his
old tutor, now one of the prebendaries, and met with the old
kindness of Oxford. Those who have had a kind tutor will quite
understand the following account of the interview. " I told him,
that my judgment (as I trust) was a little more ripened than it
was some years ago ; and that as fast as I found out my faults,
I should be glad to acknowledge them. He said, the offence of
the governors of the church would lessen and wear off, as I grew
moderate." Whitefield did not tell the Doctor how little he
cared for such moderation as the governors of that day required :
but he wrote to Lady Huntingdon, on the subject of *their* favour,—" I am pretty easy about that ! If I can but act an honest
part, and be kept from *trimming*, I leave all consequences to
Him who orders all things well."

On his return to London, he found his assemblies at the
Countess's " brilliant indeed," and Bolingbroke still one in
them. It was now winter, and some of his noble friends from
Scotland joined them. He felt not only deep interest in Boling-

broke, but had much hope of him at one time ; owing to his declared satisfaction with the doctrines of grace. "Who knows," he says, " what God may do ?" If Bolingbroke was *hoaxing* Whitefield, it is to his everlasting disgrace. If he was not, it was no small item in his advantages, that God gave him a place in Whitefield's heart and prayers. The place *he* held there, had proved the means of salvation to many. Two or three of the nobility were won to Christ at this time.

Still, they could not keep him from itinerating. In a few weeks he was at Bristol again. " I long to take the *field*," he said to the Countess ; and he did not take it in vain. "There was a great stirring among the dry bones at Kingswood and Bristol. Many new converts were won. One of them was a counsellor, who was so much affected, that his style of counselling others to hear Whitefield, led his wife to suspect him of madness.

At Plymouth also, where he had so many enemies formerly, he found a Tabernacle had been built in his absence, to which he was welcomed. He became the guest of a married couple, who claimed him as their spiritual father. Plymouth, he says, " seems quite a *new* place to me." He was much amused there to learn, that he had been called a Roman catholic. " If I am a Roman catholic," he said, " the pope must have given me a *large* dispensation."

The " married couple" were the *Kinsmans;* soon the useful, as well as the intimate, friends of Whitefield. Mr. Kinsman became a popular preacher at the Tabernacle in London. He preached the *first* sermon in the present Tabernacle. His fame and success at Bristol were such that Whitefield was in the habit of calling Bristol, " Kinsman's *America;*" in allusion to his own foreign labours. His eloquence also must have been considerable ; for *Shuter*, the comedian, was fond of hearing him. Poor Shuter once told Kinsman a sad story. He had been acting *Falstaff* in London so often, that the physicians ordered him to Plymouth for change of air. Kinsman too had been sent home, after a hard campaign at the Tabernacle. Both had been wrought out. "Had you died," said Shuter, " it would have been in the service of the best of masters ; but had

I, it would have been in the service of the devil. O Sir, do
you think I shall ever be *called* again? I certainly was—whilst
studying my part in the park; and had Mr. Whitefield let me
come to the sacrament with him, I never should have gone back
again. But the caresses of the great are insnaring. Poor
things! they are unhappy, and they want Shuter to make them
laugh. O Sir, for such a life as yours! But when I have you
I shall be Richard the Third again. That is what they call a
good play; as good as some sermons. And there are some
striking moral things in it. But, after it, I shall come in again
with my farce, 'A Dish of all Sorts,' and knock all that on the
head. Fine *reformers* we are!"

It was on Shuter, as *Ramble*, that Whitefield fixed his eye
one morning at Tottenham Court, while inviting sinners of all
classes to Christ, and said,—"And thou, poor Ramble, who
hast long rambled from Him, come thou also. Oh, end thy
ramblings, and come to Jesus." Cornelius Winter says,
" Shuter was exceedingly struck, and coming unto Whitefield
said,—' I thought I should have fainted; how could you serve
me so?'" At Plymouth also, when asked if he was a methodist,
he said, " Mine is a fine *method*, is it not? A methodist! no;
I wish I was. If any are right, they are."

Whitefield found in Plymouth and its neighbourhood many
proofs, that his former visit had been very useful. Next to the
conversion of Kinsman, no case pleased him so much as that of
a young man, "now a preacher," who had then ascended a tree,
to hear and mock. His levity had drawn the notice of Whitefield, who exclaimed, " Come down, Zaccheus, come down, and
receive the Lord Jesus Christ. The word was backed with
power. He heard, came down, believed, and now adorns the
gospel." *Letter to Lady Huntingdon.*

He had also the pleasure, at this time, to administer the sacrament to a whole family, " who had no pastor." " It was an
affecting sight," he says;—"two parents presenting two daughters and a son, in the most solemn manner, for the first time,
to be communicants. I received them with all joy."

It was not all sunshine, however, in Devonshire. He was
rudely treated at Tavistock. The rabble brought a bull and

dogs, and created much disturbance whilst he was praying. He managed, however, to preach down the uproar. At Exeter, also, a man came prepared to knock him on the head with a stone, whenever the sermon should furnish an offensive expression. He stood with the stone in his hand. He could find no fault. The sermon soon interested him so, that the stone dropped from his hand. Then his heart melted. After the service he went to Whitefield, and said with tears, " Sir, I came to break your head; but God has given me a broken heart."

Whitefield now returned to London in high health, after an itineracy in the west of 600 miles. He came back, however, " with a kind of fear and trembling," lest his health should break down in the city, and thus unfit him " to speak to the great and the noble, so as to win them to Jesus." But he soon rid himself of this fear, by his old maxim, " I throw myself *blindfold* into my Master's hands." The bishop of Exeter's *pamphlet* also, " The Enthusiasm of the Methodists and Papists compared," came out at this time, and created a stir, which helped him to forget his fears. He began immediately to answer it, and made greater efforts than ever to ingratiate the truth with the aristocracy. But this kind of work did not suit him.

He was equally out of his element at his own desk, and in Lady Huntingdon's drawing-room. Accordingly, in a month, he was too ill to hold a pen. He therefore started off on a new itineracy; and by the time he reached Portsmouth, he was himself again. The night after his arrival, he preached to many thousands; and with such power, in spite of disturbance, that the chief opposer was conquered, and received him into his house with tears of shame and joy. Indeed, many who, a few days before, had been speaking all manner of evil of him, were soon urgent with him to prolong his visit. But Wales was waiting for him, and he could not stay long.

In the Principality he had soon the pleasure, as in the days of old, to see " Jesus riding *on* in the chariot of the everlasting gospel." He now found all towns open, and all justices and magistrates civil. On some occasions his audience amounted to twenty

thousand persons. He himself computed the whole number he
addressed, in eight Welch counties, at more than a hundred
thousand; and adds, " I think we have not had one *dry* meeting." So complete was his ascendancy in Wales now, that
" not a dog stirred a tongue," during his circuit of eight hundred miles. From this vantage ground, he made a powerful
appeal to Hervey, in the hope of drawing him into the fields.
" Had you seen the simplicity of so many dear souls, I am persuaded you would have said, *Sit anima mea cum methodistis.*"
But Hervey was too weak for field work. Whitefield himself
broke down after this mighty effort, and was for some days at
" the gates of the grave."

He returned to London to welcome his wife home from Bermudas. On her arrival he learned that his character had been
aspersed in the island by one of the clergy. But whilst he did
not overlook this calumny altogether, he merely sent out the
following answer; " I am content to wait until the day of judgment for the clearing up of my character; and after I am dead,
I desire no other *epitaph* than this,—*Here lies George Whitefield. What sort of a man he was, the great day will discover.*"
He then arranged his London affairs, and started again for the
fields.

On his arrival at Bristol, he was told that the bishop of W.
(Wells?) had charged him with *perjury* at the pump-rooms.
The bishop had not, however, used the word perjury. He had
only left others to give a name to his picture of violated ordination vows. Indeed, the question had a *parliamentary* settlement on both sides. Whitefield said, that he vowed to obey
only " *godly* admonitions." And the bishop meant " nothing
personal."

In a few days after, Whitefield set out for Exeter, by way of
Wellington. At this time he does not appear to have known
Darracott, whom he afterward designated,—" *The Star of the
West;*" transferring the title from its first owner, Hieron. Indeed, he would have rode through Wellington without stopping,
had not a woman recognised him in the street. She implored
him to alight, and give the people a sermon. When he complied, she soon spread the news, and " a great company" came

to hear him. He was so pleased, that he preached next day to a still larger audience. It does not appear that Darracott attended either sermon. He made ample amends, however, afterwards.

One reason of Whitefield's visit to the west, at this time, was (although perhaps he hardly acknowledged it to himself) to see how his letter to the bishop of Exeter had been received. He found, in his own circle there, that it had been " much blest." He learnt, also, that " my lord of Exeter had said, he wrote like an honest man, and has recanted several things ;" but, added Lavington, " he *goes on* in the same way yet." He did. He went to Exeter, and appeared in the *fields* again. The bishop, therefore, threatened another pamphlet. Lavington could do more against methodists than write. About this time, he threatened to strip the gown from one of his own clergy, who was methodistical, and countenanced Whitefield. The bishop was saved the trouble. That moment the clergyman stripped himself, saying, " I can preach the gospel without a gown ;" and retired. Lavington was then glad to " send for him, and soothe him :" but he indemnified himself for this condescension, by publishing immediately the second part of his " Enthusiasm compared." Whitefield had good reason, as well as great provocation, to say of both parts, " The bishop has served the methodists, as the bishop of Constance served *John Huss*, when he ordered painted devils to be put round his head, before burning him." He did not answer him. He did better. He went to Exeter, accompanied by a rural dean, to preach the gospel as usual ; and divine influence accompanied the word. " This," he says, " is, I think, the best way to answer those who oppose themselves." He preached there twice on the same day. In the evening, the bishop and several of his clergy stood near to him, and saw ten thousand people awe-struck by his appeals. They saw also three large stones thrown at his head in succession, by a furious drunkard,—one of which cut him deeply ; but neither the high priest nor his Levites interfered, although one of their own parishioners also was felled to the ground at the same time. *Letter to Lady H.*

Next week he returned to London, and found some of the

pious peeresses waiting to receive the sacrament from him. He
spent a few days at home, and then started off for Yorkshire.
There he visited *Grimshaw*, at Haworth, and administered the
sacrament to above a thousand communicants in the church.
When he preached, the churchyard was crowded. On a future
occasion, when preaching in the church, he had such a high
opinion of the pastor, that he took for granted the piety of the
flock. " No, no, Sir," said good Grimshaw aloud, " the half of
them are not converted by the grace of God. Speak to them
faithfully." It is easy to conceive the effect of such an appeal
on Whitefield. It was just the kind and manner of appeal, to
set him on fire. It would have disconcerted almost any other
man ; but it was vantage ground to him.

He went from Haworth to Leeds, at the invitation, he says,
" of one of Mr. Wesley's preachers, and by all his people." He
was also introduced into their pulpit at Newcastle, by Charles
Wesley, who, meeting him by the way, turned back to accompany him. This gratified him so much, that he preached *four*
times in their rooms at Newcastle ; but he was obliged, at last,
to go into the open air, to meet the crowds. At Leeds both
the crowds and the commotion were immense. . So much so,
that he returned back upon it, after visiting some other parts of
Yorkshire and Lancashire.

During this tour, he won to Christ many of the men, who
laid the foundations of not a few of the flourishing churches in
these counties. He met, however, with as much " rude treatment," here and there in both, as sent him home praying, " Lord,
give me a pilgrim heart, for my pilgrim life."

On his arrival in London, he found many urgent invitations
awaiting him from Ireland ; and the Cork riots had awakened
his sympathies for the sufferers ; but although he used his influence on their behalf with the great, and sent them word of this,
he was afraid lest a visit might be deemed an intrusion upon the
Wesleyan sphere. Besides, the PRIMATE of Ireland wished to
give him preferment ; a thing he did not wish for.

He was now " in winter quarters ;" but he was not idle nor
useless. To use his own words, " the glory of the Lord filled
the tabernacle, and the shout of a King was in the camp," from

week to week. " Thousands, thousands crowded to hear." Every day, also, he heard of instances of conversion. One instance pleased him very much. It was that of a boatswain, who before hearing him, knew no more about divine truth, "than the *whistle* he blew on board." He particularizes also a boy of *eleven* years of age, a woman of *eighty*, and a baker, who had been " a *Jerusalem* sinner."

At this time, his intended college occupied much of his attention. He wrote in all directions, in order to make friends to the plan. His usual appeal was, " We propose having an academy or college at the orphan-house. The house is large ; it will hold a hundred. My *heart*, I trust, is larger, and will hold ten thousand."

Still, his heart was in America. London did not, he says, " agree with his outward man." " RANGING seems my province ; and methinks I hear a voice behind me saying, *This* is the way, walk in it. My heart echoes back, Lord, let thy presence go along with me, and then send me where thou pleasest." That America would have pleased *himself* best, is evident from the following apostrophe, " In the midst of all, America, *dear* America ! is not forgotten. I begin to count the days, and to say to the months, ' Fly fast away, that I may spread the gospel net once more in dear America !' " This is delightful. It must be gratifying to American christians to be thus reminded of the place which their country held in Whitefield's heart a century ago. It is gratifying to me to tell them, that we did not learn from Whitefield, but from the revivals and missionary spirit in their *own* churches, to say, " America, *dear* America." When will they *fulfil* our joy, and be likeminded with us on the subject of slavery ? Surely no one will quote Whitefield against us !

Another object lay near to Whitefield's heart. It was during this winter's quarters, that he formed the design of identifying Lady Huntingdon with his societies—the *only* plan he ever laid for perpetuating them. He saw her a *Dorcas*, at " that dead place "—Ashby Place, and felt that she might and ought to be a Phœbe. She had used her influence, at his solicitation, with the court and the government, on behalf of the sufferers in the Cork riots ; and had readily patronized such poor or persecuted

ministers, as he brought under her notice. All this, and the
want of a leader, led him to seek her patronage, especially for
his societies in the west end of the town.

How he *opened* the subject to her, I have been unable to discover. It does not seem, however, to have been ill received :
for she desired the public prayers of the Tabernacle for herself
at the time ;—(not, of course, in reference to this matter ;)—and
Whitefield read that part of her letter to the people, and informed her, that " thousands heartily joined in singing the following verses for her Ladyship : "

> " Gladly we join to pray for those
> Who rich with worldly honour shine,
> Who dare to own a Saviour's cause,
> And in that hated cause to join :
> Yes, we would praise Thee, that a few
> Love Thee, though rich and noble too.

> " Uphold this star in thy right hand,
> Crown her endeavours with success ;
> Among the great ones may she stand,
> A witness of thy righteousness,
> Till many nobles join thy train,
> And triumph in the Lamb that 's slain."

All this was in bad taste on both sides, however well meant
or meekly taken.   In the same letter, he said to her, " A *leader*
is wanting.   This honour hath been put upon your Ladyship
by the great Head of the church : an honour conferred on few ;
but an earnest of one to be put on your Ladyship before men
and angels, when time shall be no more.   That you may every
day add to the splendour of your future crown, by always abounding in the work of the Lord, is the fervent prayer of ——."

How much " leader " means, in this document, or how far, if
at all, it refers to the Tabernacle, I cannot judge.

In the midst of all these attentions from and to nobility,
Whitefield did not forget nor overlook his aged mother. A
woman had neglected to procure for him some things he had
ordered for her. A week's delay was thus occasioned. The
moment he discovered this, he wrote, " I should never forgive

myself, was I, by negligence or any wrong conduct, to give you a moment's needless pain. Alas, how little I have done for you! Christ's care for his mother excites me to wish I could do any thing for you. If you would have any thing more brought, pray write, honoured mother!"

On this occasion he reminded her of his age. "To-morrow, it will be *thirty-five* years since you brought unworthy me into the world. Oh that my head were waters, and mine eyes fountains of tears, that I might bewail my barrenness and unfruitfulness in the church of God." About the same time he wrote thus to Lady Huntingdon, " Next Saturday I am thirty-five years old: I am ashamed to think how little I do or suffer for Christ. *Fye* upon me, *fye* upon me!"

These anecdotes are, I know, *little;* but they reveal much of Whitefield's real character: and surely his deep self-abasement before God, may be allowed to balance his self-complacency in the patronage of the countess and her " elect ladies." His compliments to them admit of no excuse. They are almost as many and fulsome, as the flatteries which used to be addressed to the royal and noble patrons of Bible Societies. Those who remember that incense, and the assemblies which offered it, will hardly wonder, however much they deplore, that a poor methodist burnt more incense to rank, than was wise or seemly. Whitefield was not *constitutionally* humble, bold, or unambitious. It took " twice seven years " of " pretty close intimacy with *contempt*," he says, to make contempt an " agreeable companion " to him. Like Paul, he had to *learn* contentment. " I did not like to part with my pretty character at first. It was death to be despised; and worse than death to think of being laughed at by all. God knows how to train us up *gradually* for the war. He often makes me bold as a lion; but I believe there is not a person living more timorous by nature. I find, a love of power sometimes intoxicates even God's dear children. It is much easier for me to obey than govern. This makes me fly from that which, at our first setting out, we are too apt to court. I cannot well buy humility at too dear a rate." *Letters.*

At this time, Whitefield was not unknown at court, nor his elect ladies unnoticed by the king. On one occasion, Lady

Chesterfield appeared in a dress, "with a brown ground and silver flowers," of foreign manufacture. The king came up to her, smiling significantly. He then laughed *aloud*, and said,—" I know who chose that gown for you,—Mr. Whitefield : I hear you have attended on him for a year and a half." Her Ladyship confessed she had, and avowed her approbation of him. She also regretted deeply afterwards, that she had not said more whilst she had such an opportunity. The secretary of state also assured him, that " no hurt was designed by the state " to the methodists. He had gone to the secretary, accompanied by a *dissenting* minister, Mr. G. (query Dr. Gifford?) to " open the case " of the Irish brethren. The outrages committed upon them, brought him nearer to the dissenters and the Wesleyans. They had now a common cause. Accordingly, he was invited to preach in the Wesleyan chapel. Mr. Wesley read the prayers for him ; and next time Whitefield read them, before Mr. Wesley preached, and then united with him in administering the sacrament. This delighted him much. " Oh for love and gratitude ! " he exclaims,—" I have now preached thrice in Mr. Wesley's chapel, and God was with us of a truth."

He was now tired of London, and relapsing into his old complaints. The fact is, he had grown *field-sick ;* for that was *his* home-sickness. Accordingly, he started for the west of England again, and although rain and hail pelted him in his field pulpits, he preached " about twenty times in eight or nine days." The moment he was in his own element, he saw every thing in his old lights. Hence he says, " Every thing I meet with seems to carry this voice with it,—' Go thou and preach the gospel ; be a pilgrim on earth ; have no party or certain dwelling-place.' My heart echoes back, Lord Jesus, help me to do or suffer thy will. When thou seest me in danger of *nestling*,—in pity—in tender pity,—put a *thorn* in my nest, to prevent me from it."

Whilst at Bristol, Charles Wesley talked with him *about* preaching in the new Wesleyan room ; but it does not appear to have been much desired. Accordingly, Whitefield says, " *I said but little.*" He found, however, a larger sphere. He was allowed to preach from the window of Smith's Hall, and thus many thousands heard him.

From Bristol he went to Wellington, and became the welcome guest of Darracott, whom he calls " a flaming and successful preacher of the gospel." Good Darracott had just lost three lovely children. Two of them had died on " the Saturday evening before the sacrament : but," says Whitefield, " weeping did not prevent sowing. He preached the next day, and administered as usual. Our Lord strengthened him; and, for his three natural, gave him above *thirty* spiritual, children; and he is likely to have many more. He has ventured his little all for Christ: and, last week, a saint died who left him and his heirs £200 in land. Did ever any one trust in God, and was forsaken ? "

This interview with Darracott, who had also suffered much *reproach* in the service of Christ, and an interview with Pearsall of Taunton, who had been a preacher of righteousness before Whitefield was born, had an inspiring influence upon him. " I *began* to take the field again at *his* dwelling," he says, " for the spring! I begin to *begin* to spend and be spent for Him who shed his own dear heart's blood for me. He makes *ranging* exceedingly pleasant. I want more tongues, more bodies, more souls, for the Lord Jesus. Had I ten thousand,—He should have them all." In this state of mind he visited many parts of Devonshire and Cornwall. At Gwinnop, he preached to a large audience, although the clergyman had preached a virulent sermon against him in the morning. This worthy had said on Saturday, " Now Whitefield is coming—I must put on my old armour." He did. Whitefield says, " It did but little execution, because not *Scripture-proof;* consequently, not out of God's armoury. I preached to many thousands. The rain dropped gently upon our bodies, and the grace of God seemed to fall like a gentle dew, sprinkling rain upon our souls." Thus in Cornwall, " an unthought-of and unexpectedly wide door " was opened. He preached in many churches, and the power of God came down so, that even the ministers were overcome. Such was the flying of doves to their windows there, that he ceased for a time to long for the wings of a dove to flee away to America.

He returned to London much improved in health and spirits; and, having rested a few days, he visited Doddridge and Hervey, in order to promote a public subscription for the New

Jersey college. Doddridge entered warmly into the plan; nobly hazarding all the consequences of associating with the man whom the Coward trust despised. Whitefield appreciated his kindness : " I thank you a thousand times," he says, " for your kindness, and assure you it is reciprocal. Gladly shall I call upon you again at Northampton." In this letter, he informed the Doctor, that Lady Huntingdon was to write to him that night, and thus playfully prepared him for her news: " She is *strangely* employed now. Can you guess? The *kind* people of Ashby stirred up some of the baser sort to riot before her Ladyship's door, whilst the gospel was preaching. Some of the people narrowly escaped being murdered, in their way home. The justice has ordered to bring the offenders before him." To her Ladyship he said on this occasion, " I trust you will live to see many of these *Ashby stones* become children to Abraham."

Soon after this he went again into Yorkshire. At Rotherham, he says, " Satan rallied his forces. The crier was employed to give notice of a bear-baiting. You may guess who was the *bear!* However, I preached twice. The drum was heard, and several watermen attended with great staves. The constable was struck, and two of the mobbers apprehended, but rescued afterwards. But all this does not come up to the *kind* usage of the people of Ashby!" Sheffield and Leeds, he found to be a new and warmer climate. Lancashire, however, he still found to be but *cold* to him. All was quiet at Manchester, and he humbly hoped " some had enlisted;" but no great impression was made, although thousands attended. Liverpool he did not visit, at this time. At Bolton, a drunkard stood up to preach behind him ; and the wife of the person who lent him the field, twice attempted to *stab* the workman who put up the stand for him. This roused him, and he bore down all opposition by a torrent of eloquence, which quite exhausted him. In the night, however, some of the *Boltoners* got into the barn and stables where his chaise and horses were put up, and cut both shamefully. This he called, "Satan showing his teeth."

From this quarter, he went into Cumberland ; new ground to him. At Kendal, " such entrance was made as could not have been expected." The impression was so great under his first sermon, that he could not forget it when he left, and therefore he returned to confirm " the souls of the disciples." At Ulverston, also, much good was done. " There," he says, " Satan made some small resistance : a clergyman, who looked more like a *butcher* than a minister, came with two others, and charged a constable with me. But I never saw a poor creature sent off in such disgrace."

Further particulars of this northern itineracy would only present similar alternations of insult and success. He preached " above ninety times, and to a hundred and forty thousand people," on this route from London to Edinburgh, where he arrived in the beginning of July.

" He was received," says Gillies, " as usual, in the most tender and loving manner; preaching generally twice a day to great multitudes, whose seriousness and earnest desire to hear him, made him exert himself beyond his strength." " By preaching always twice," (he says,) " and once thrice, and once *four* times, in a day, I am quite weakened; but I hope to recruit again. I am burning with a fever, and have a violent cold : but Christ's presence makes me smile at pain, and the fire of His love burns up all *fevers* whatsoever."

Whitefield's own estimate of this visit to Scotland, was very high. He says, " I shall have reason to all eternity to bless God for it. I *have* reason to think that many are under convictions, and am *assured* of hundreds having received great benefit and consolation. Not a dog moved his tongue all the while I was there, and many enemies were *glad* to be at peace with me. Oh that I may spring afresh ! "

On his return to London, he was received with great joy both at the Tabernacle and West-Street. During his stay, Hervey came up on a visit, and resided with him, and Wesley met with them occasionally. As may be supposed, they had much " sweet fellowship." But even that could not divert him from the fields long. It was now autumn ; and, therefore, he resolved to work hard before going into winter quarters. Chatham owes much to this resolution ! The awakening produced by his visit he calls " as promising a work as in almost any part of England." It re-acted also upon Sheerness. There a few pious people won the confidence of good *Shrubsole*, and drew him on step by step to read and pray amongst them, until he became a minister, although without relinquishing his office in the dock-yard. In reference to this, he said, " I am accounted a phenomenon, there never having been a preaching master mast-maker before. However, I know there has been a preaching *Carpenter*, of the most exalted rank, and this blessed person I am resolved, by the grace of God, to imitate while I live." He did. Mr. Shrubsole wrote a " Pilgrim's Progress," in which he has drawn the character of Whitefield with great accuracy, and sustained it with much effect, under the name, *Fervidus*. He wrote also an elegy on Whitefield's death, quite equal to any thing of the kind which appeared on that occasion. His " Pilgrim, or Christian Memoirs," presents, perhaps, a fairer and fuller view of the state of religion in England at this time, than any other contemporary book. I hope it is not out of print ! It was the first book which drew my attention to the *Times* of Whitefield. It was lent to me, whilst a student at Hoxton College, by the late W. Shrubsole, Esq. of the Bank of England ; the son of the author, in every sense, and one of my earliest and kindest friends, when I was " a stranger in a strange land." I never enter the Bank of England, without remembering with a thrill of grateful emotion, the sweet evenings I spent there in his chambers, and in his family circle ! There I obtained my first glimpses of English society, (and I shall never forget them,) on my arrival in the metropolis from the mountains and solitudes of Aberdeenshire. I feel *young* again in recording this fact. There I heard, for the first time, *instrumental* music and musical science combined with divine worship ; and now I never hear them, without remembering how all my Scotch prejudices against this combination were charmed away at the Bank chambers of Mr. Shrubsole.

CHAPTER XVII.

WHITEFIELD's connexion with Ireland was too slight to impress any character upon the religion of the country, or even to give an impulse to it. His preaching won souls; but it set in motion no evangelizing enterprise, except the itineracy of the celebrated John Cennick, who obtained for the methodists in Ireland the nick-name of *swaddlers*, by a Christmas sermon. His text was, "Ye shall find the babe, wrapped in swaddling clothes, lying in a manger." A catholic who was present, and to whom the language of Scripture was a novelty, says Dr. Southey, "thought this so ludicrous, that he called the preacher a swaddler, in derision; and this unmeaning word became the nick-name of the methodists, and had all the effect of the most opprobrious appellation." It had indeed! When persecution arose against the Wesleys and their adherents, the watchword of the mob was, "Five pounds for a swaddler's head!" "Anti-swaddlers" was a name chosen for themselves, by the popish party, and even avowed by them at the trial of the rioters. A public notice was posted up at the Exchange, with the writer's name affixed to it, in which he offered to head any mob that would pull down any house that should harbour a swaddler. And houses were demolished, and much furniture destroyed. Nor was this all. In Cork, Butler's mob fell upon men and women, old and young, with clubs and swords, and beat and wounded them in a dreadful manner. Even the mayor told one of the complainants, whose house was beset and about to be pulled down, that if he would not "turn the preachers out," he must take whatever he might get. The sheriff also sent a poor woman to Bridewell, for expressing regret at seeing the vagabond ballad-singer, Butler, going about in the dress of a clergyman, with the Bible in one hand, and ballads in the other. *Moore's Life of Wesley.* Mr. Wesley himself describes, what he calls, "Cork persecution," thus;—"breaking the houses of his Majesty's protestant subjects, destroying their goods, spoiling or tearing the very clothes from their backs; striking, bruising, wounding, murdering them in the streets; dragging them through the mire, without any regard to age or sex; not sparing even those of tender years; no, nor women, though great with child; but, with more than pagan or Turkish barbarity, destroying infants that were yet unborn."

These enormities were well nigh over before Whitefield visited Ireland. The higher powers had interfered, when they found that the *lower* were nearly as low as Butler. Whitefield found the benefit of the shield which Wesley so much needed, and so nobly won. He had, however, preached in Ireland before Wesley visited it; which was in 1747. In 1738, Whitefield touched there, on his return from America, weak and weary, after a tedious and famishing voyage. When he landed from the vessel, " we had," he says, " but half a pint of water left, and my stomach was exceeding weak through long abstinence. Most of us begin to be weak, and look hollow-eyed. My clothes have not been off, except to change, all the passage. Part of the time I lay on open deck, part on a chest, and the remainder on a bedstead covered with my buffalo's skin." He was welcomed at a " strong castle," where, he says, " I asked the servant for water, and she gave me milk, and brought forth butter in a lordly dish. And never—did I make a more comfortable meal !"

After resting for a day or two at Kilrush to renew his strength, he went to Limerick, where the bishop, Dr. Burscough, received him with much hospitality and candour. His Lordship requested him to preach in the cathedral on Sunday, and on parting with him *kissed* him, and said, " Mr. Whitefield, God bless you; I wish you success abroad; had you staid in town, this house should have been your home." This welcome was the more gratifying, because his sermon had agitated the people. In walking about the town next day, "all the inhabitants,", he says, "seemed alarmed, and looked most wishfully at me as I passed along." The contrast in his circumstances, also, affected him very deeply. "Good God!" he exclaims, "where was I on Saturday last? In hunger, cold, and thirsting; but now I enjoy fulness of bread, and all things convenient for me. God grant I may not, Jeshurun-like, wax fat, and kick! Perhaps it is more difficult to know how to abound, than how to want."

From Limerick he went to Dublin, where he preached twice in the churches; the second time to such a rivetted crowd, that he calls it, "like a London congregation." Here also the bishops were neither afraid nor ashamed of him. The primate of all Ireland invited him to dinner, and told him that he heard of him from Gibraltar. The bishop of Londonderry also was equally kind. Whitefield felt all this deeply, and rejoiced with trembling. "Dearest Jesus," he exclaims, "grant me humility; so shall thy favours not prove my ruin."

Such was his first reception in Ireland. His second, in 1751, although upon the whole favourable, was not "like unto it." He was now a field preacher, and just hot from Wales, where he had been preaching twice a day, over a space of 500 miles. He began his labour in Dublin, and found at once large congregations hearing, "as for eternity." In Limerick and Cork, also, his commanding eloquence overawed the old persecutors. The public cry was, "Methodism is revived again;" but it was the signal of welcome, not of war, as formerly. At this time he was both very weak in body, and subject to daily vomiting. During this visit, he preached eighty times, and with great success. "Providence," says he, "has wonderfully prepared my way, and overruled every thing for my greater acceptance. Every where there seems a shaking among the dry bones, and the trembling lamps of God's people have been supplied with fresh oil. The word ran and was glorified." "Hundreds," says Dr. Southey, "prayed for him when he left Cork; and many of the catholics said, that, if he would stay, they would leave their priests."

One cause of Whitefield's popularity at this time was, that

he meddled not with Irish politics. " He condemned all politics," says Dr. Southey, " as below the children of God :" but
why did the Doctor add, " alluding, apparently, to the decided
manner in which Wesley always inculcated obedience to government as one of the duties of a christian ; making it his boast,
that whoever became a good methodist, became at the same
time a good subject."   Was Whitefield less loyal than Wesley ?
When ? Where ? Not in Ireland certainly.   I have now before me the letter which justifies the Doctor in hinting that
Whitefield " seems to have regarded the conduct of Wesley and
his lay-preachers," in Ireland, " with no favourable eye."   But
why should this be interpreted to mean their politics chiefly, or
at all ?   Dr. Southey quotes from Whitefield, as if he had said
that " some *dreadful* offences had been given" by the Wesleyans ; and argues as if they had been political offences.
Whitefield himself says, " I find, through the *many* offences
that have lately been given, matters (among the methodists)
were brought to a low ebb ; but now the cry is, ' Methodism is
revived again.'   Thanks be to God, that I have an opportunity
of showing my disinterestedness, and that I preach not for a
party of my own, but for the common interest of my blessed
Master.   Your Ladyship" (the letter is to Lady Huntingdon)
" would smile to see how the wise have been catched in their
own craftiness."   Now this justifies the hint, that Whitefield
" seems to have regarded their conduct with no favourable eye."
Indeed, it is the severest thing I know of, that he says in connexion with Wesley's name,—for that he meant him, by " the
wise caught in their own craftiness," is obvious.   It is not " apparent," however, that he alluded to " the decided manner in
which Wesley inculcated obedience to government."   That, in
fact, was not a matter of policy, but of vital *principle*, with
Wesley and Whitefield too.   Wesley had, however, lines of
policy, which Whitefield was jealous of, and opposed to, not
without reason.

Whitefield's last visit to Ireland was in 1757, when he nearly
lost his life, after preaching at Oxminton Green.   This was
popish outrage.   The church was not unfriendly to him.   Indeed, one of the bishops said to a nobleman, who told White-

field, " I am glad he is come to rouse the people." Even the primate solicited him to " accept of some considerable church preferment, which he declined." *De Courcy.*

> " Preferments, honours, ease, he deemed but loss,
> Vile and contemptible, for Jesus' cross:
> Inur'd to scandal, injuries, and pain,
> To him to live was Christ; to die was gain."
> *De Courcy's Elegy.*

His own narrative of the outrage is as interesting as it is circumstantial.—" Many attacks have I had from Satan's children, but yesterday you would have thought he had been permitted to give me an effectual *parting* blow. I had once or twice ventured out to Oxminton Green, a large place like Moorfields, situated very near the barracks, where the Ormond and Liberty boys, that is, the high and low party boys, generally assemble every Sunday, to fight each other. When I was here *last,* the congregations were very numerous, and the word seemed to come with power, and no noise nor disturbance ensued. This encouraged me to give notice, that I would preach there again. I went through the barracks, the door of which opens into the Green, and pitched my tent near the barrack walls—not doubting of the protection, or at least interposition, of the officers and soldiery, if there should be occasion. But how vain is the help of man! Vast was the multitude that attended. We sang, prayed, and preached without molestation ; only now and then a few stones and clods of dirt were thrown at me.

" It being war time, I exhorted, as is my usual practice, my hearers, not only to fear God, but to honour the best of kings ; and after sermon, I prayed for success to the *Prussian* arms. All being over, I thought to return home the way I came ; but, to my great surprise, access was denied, so that I had to go near half a mile from one end of the Green to the other, through hundreds and hundreds of *papists*, &c. Finding me unattended, (for a soldier and four methodist preachers, who came with me, had forsook me and fled,) I was left to their mercy. But their mercy, as you may easily guess, was perfect cruelty. Volleys of hard stones came from all quarters, and every step I took a fresh stone made me *reel* backwards and forwards, till I was almost breathless, and all over a *gore* of blood. My strong beaver hat served me as it were for a *scull cap* for a while; but at last it was knocked off, and my head left quite defenceless. I received many blows and wounds; one was particularly large, and near my temples. I thought of Stephen, and as I believed that I received more blows, I was in great hopes that like him I should be despatched, and go off in this bloody triumph to the immediate presence of my Master. But providentially a minister's house lay next door to the Green; with great difficulty I staggered to the door, which was kindly opened to, and shut upon, me. Some of the mob in the mean time having broke part of the boards of the pulpit into large splinters, they beat and wounded my servant grievously in his head and arms, and then came and drove him from the door. For a while I continued speechless, panting for, and expecting every breath to be my last. Two or three of the hearers, my friends, by some means or other, got admission, and kindly with weeping eyes washed my bloody wounds, and gave me something to smell to and to drink. I gradually revived, but soon found the lady of the house desired my absence, for fear the house should be pulled down. What to do I knew not, being near two miles from Mr. W——'s place; some advised one thing, and some another. At length, a carpenter, one of the friends that came in, offered me his wig and coat, that I might go off in disguise. I accepted of and put them on, but was soon ashamed of not trusting my Master to secure me in my proper habit, and threw them off with disdain. I determined to go out (since I found my presence was so troublesome) in my proper habit; immediately deliverance came. A methodist preacher, with two friends, brought a coach; I leaped into it, and rode in gospel triumph through the oaths, curses, and imprecations of whole streets of papists unhurt, though threatened every step of the ground. None but those who were spectators of the scene, can form an idea of the affection with which I was received by the weeping, mourning, but now joyful methodists. A christian surgeon was ready to dress our wounds, which being done, I went into the preaching-place, and after giving a word of exhortation, joined in a hymn of praise and thanksgiving to Him who makes our extremity his opportunity, who stills the noise of the waves, and the madness of the most malignant people. The next morning I set out for Port Arlington, and left my persecutors to His mercy, who out of persecutors hath often made preachers. That I may be thus revenged of them, is my hearty prayer."

CHAPTER XVIII.

CONTENTMENT. "I find all uneasiness arises from having a will of my *own ;* therefore I would desire to will only what God wills."

CONDITION. "Alas! that any one should inquire after such a wretch as I am. As for my quality; I was a poor, mean drawer (tapster); but, by the grace of God, I am now intended for the ministry. As for my estate; I am a servitor. And as to my condition and circumstances; I have not (of my own) where to lay my head. But my friends, by God's providence, minister daily to me: and, in return for such unmerited, unspeakable blessings, I trust the same good Being will give me grace to dedicate myself without reserve to his service—to spend and be spent for the welfare of my fellow-creatures, and in endeavouring to promote the gospel of his Son as much as lieth in my poor power." Whitefield's early purpose turned out an accurate prophecy! He became what he wished to be, and did what he designed.

HUMILITY. "Catch an old christian without humility—if you can! It is nothing but this flesh of ours, and those cursed seeds of the proud apostate, which lie lurking within us, that make us think ourselves worthy of the air we breathe. When our eyes are opened by the influence of divine grace, we then shall begin to think of ourselves 'as we ought to think ;' even that Christ is all in all, and we less than nothing."

INEXPERIENCE. "Oh let us young, inexperienced soldiers, be always upon our guard. The moment we desert our post, the enemy rushes in : and if he can but so divert our eyes from looking heavenward, (often,) he will soon so blind us, that we shall not look towards it at all. A great deal may be learnt from a little fall."

EXAMPLE. " The degeneracy of the age is not the least objection against advances in piety. It is true, indeed, that instances of exalted piety are rarely to be met with in the present age: one would think, if we were to take an estimate of our religion from the lives of most of its professors, that christianity was nothing but a dead letter. But then—it is not our religion but ourselves that is to blame for this."

Such were some of Whitefield's " first principles," when he began to study at Oxford. How well they lasted, and how much they influenced him, all through life, will appear equally from his history, and from their frequent recurrence in other and more powerful forms, in this sketch of his governing maxims. The sketch itself I have made with some care, in order to illustrate both his talents and piety ; that those who speak of him, may judge of him from his " sayings," as well as from his " doings." Had Dr. Doddridge reviewed the following Miscellany of Whitefield's maxims, he would have retracted the charge of " weakness " he made against him, and heightened all his eulogiums on the piety and zeal of his friend. But Doddridge saw Whitefield chiefly, if not only, when Whitefield had preached away all his strength and spirits, in " the great congregations," and could speak only of his work and warfare. Thus he judged of his talents, as a Scotch minister did of his devotion, when he was jaded by hard labour. Posterity will now judge of both for themselves,—from the following specimens of both.

SELF-RENUNCIATION. " What is there so monstrously terrible in a doctrine, that is the constant subject of our prayers, whenever we put up that petition, ' Thy will be done on earth as it is in heaven ? ' The import of which seems to be this,—that we do every thing God wills, and nothing but what he willeth ; that we do those things he willeth, only because he willeth. This cannot, indeed, be done in a day. We have not only a *new* house to build up, but also an *old* one to pull down."

TEMPTATION. " We find our Saviour was led into the wilderness before he entered upon his public ministry: and so must we too, if we would tread in his steps."

PRAYERS REQUESTED. " If Pauncefort's petitions for me should run in this manner, I should be thankful :—That God should finish the good work he has begun in me ; that I may never seek nor be fond of worldly preferment; but may employ every mite of those talents it shall please God to intrust me with, to His glory and the church's good; and likewise, that the endeavours of my friends to revive pure religion in the world, may meet with proper success."

CONSECRATION. " I can call heaven and earth to witness, that when the bishop laid his hand upon me, I gave myself up a martyr to him who hung upon the cross for me.   Known unto him are all future events and contingencies : I have thrown myself *blindfold*, and I trust without reserve, into His almighty hands."

FIRST SERMON. " It was my intention to have at least a hundred sermons with which to begin my ministry : I have not a single one by me, except one which I sent to a neighbouring clergyman—to convince him how unfit I was to take upon me the important work of preaching.   He kept it a fortnight, and then sent it back with a guinea for the loan ; telling me he had preached it morning and evening to his congregation, by dividing it."

REPROACH. " Strange, that any one should let a little reproach deprive them of an eternal crown !   Lord, what is man !   In a short time we shall have praise enough.   Heaven will echo with the applause given to the true followers of the Lamb."

A WIFE'S PORTRAIT. " I live in hopes of seeing you and your wife again (growing in grace) in England.   You told me, she desired I would draw her picture ; but, alas ! she has applied to an improper limner.   However, though I cannot describe what she is, I can tell what she ought to be:—Meek, patient, long-suffering, obedient in all things, not self-willed, not soon angry, no brawler, swift to hear, slow to speak, and ready to every good word and work.   But I can no more ; I dare not go on in telling another what she ought to be, when I want so much myself; only this I know, when possessed of those good qualities before-mentioned, she will then be as happy as her heart can wish."

MIRACLES. " What need is there for them, now that we see greater miracles every day done by the power of God's word? Do not the spiritually blind now see? Are not the spiritually dead now raised, and the leprous souls now cleansed, and have not the poor the gospel preached unto them? And if we have the thing already, which such miracles were only intended to introduce, why should we tempt God in requiring further signs? He that hath ears to hear, let him hear."

WARNING. " God forbid I should be called, at the great day, to say, that my dear Mr. ———— put his hand to the plough and turned back unto perdition. Good God! the thought strikes me as though a dart was shot through my liver. Return, return. My dear friend, I cannot part from you for ever. Do not speak peace to your soul, when there is no peace. Do not turn factor for the devil. Do not prejudice or hurt my brother, and thereby add to the grief you have already occasioned."

ZEAL. " I love those that thunder out the word. The christian world is in a deep sleep. Nothing but a loud voice can awaken them out of it."

ZEAL AND PRUDENCE. " Had we a thousand hands and tongues, there is employment enough for them all : people are every where ready to perish for lack of knowledge. As the Lord has been pleased to reveal his dear Son in us, oh let us stir up that gift of God, and with all boldness preach him to others. Freely we have received, freely let us give : what Christ tells us by his Spirit in our closets, that let us proclaim on the house-top. He who sends will protect us. All the devils in hell shall not hurt us, till we have finished our testimony. And then if we should seal it with imprisonment or death, well will it be with us, and happy shall we be evermore! But the proof of our sincerity will be when we come to the trial. I fear for no one so much as myself."

IMPATIENCE. " I want to leap my seventy years. I long to be dissolved, to be with Christ. Sometimes it arises from a fear of falling, knowing what a body of sin I carry about me! Sometimes from a prospect of future labours and sufferings, I am out of humour, and wish for death as Elijah did. At others, I am tempted, and then I long to be freed from temptations. But it

is not thus always: there are times when my soul hath such
foretastes of God, that I long more eagerly to be with him ; and
the frequent prospect of the happiness which the spirits of just
men made perfect now enjoy, often carries me, as it were, into
another world."

BUNYAN. " And oh what sweet communion did he enjoy in
Bedford gaol! I really believe a minister will learn more by
one month's confinement, than by a year's study."

BLASTS. " The light that has been given us, is not to be put
under a bushel, but on a candlestick. Satan, indeed, by blasts
of persecution, will do all he can to put it out. If our light be the
light of Christ, those blasts will only cause it to shine the brighter."

FRIENDS. " Nothing gives me more comfort, next to the
assurance of the eternal continuance of God's love, than the pleasing reflection of having so many christian friends to watch with
my soul. I wish they would smite me friendly, and reprove me
oftener than they do ; I would force my proud heart to thank
them."

CANDOUR. " Success I fear elated my mind. I did not behave towards you, and other ministers of Christ, with that humility which became me. I freely confess my fault ; I own myself to be but a novice. Your charity, dear Sir, will excite you
to pray that I may not through pride fall into the condemnation
of the devil. Dear Sir, shall I come out into the world again
or not ? Must I venture myself once more among firebrands,
arrows, and death ? Methinks I hear you reply, ' Yes, if you
come forth in the strength of the Lord God, and make mention
of his righteousness only.' It is my desire so to do. I would
have Jesus all in all. Like a pure crystal I would transmit all
the light he poureth upon me."

HUMILITY. " If possible, Satan will make us to think more
highly of ourselves than we ought to think. I can tell this by
fatal experience. It is not sudden flashes of joy, but having
the humility of Christ Jesus, that must denominate us christians. If we hate reproof, we are so far from being true followers of the Lamb of God, that in the opinion of the wisest of
men, we are brutish."

INGENIOUS FIDELITY. " The principles which I maintain,

are purely Scriptural, and every way agreeable to the Church of *England* Articles. What I have been chiefly concerned about is, lest any should rest in the bare speculative knowledge, and not experience the power of them in their own hearts. What avails it, Sir, if I am a patron for the righteousness of Jesus Christ in behalf of another, if at the same time I am self-righteous myself? I am thus jealous, I trust with a godly jealousy, because I see so many self-deceivers among my acquaintance. There is one in particular, (whom I love, and for whom I most heartily pray,) who approves of my doctrine, and hath heard it preached many years past, but I could never hear him tell of his experiences, or of what God has done for his soul. He hath excellent good desires and intentions, but I think he wants something more : Lord, for thy infinite mercy's sake, grant he may know himself even as he is known! I need not tell Mr. D—— who this dear friend is—you are intimately acquainted with him ; you love him as you do your own heart ; you are never out of his company. O dear Sir, be not angry. Methinks I hear you, by this time, making an application, and saying, ' Then I am the man.' True, dear Sir, I confess you are. But love, love for your better part, your soul, your precious soul, this love constrains me to use this freedom. You are more noble than to take it ill at my hands : I could not bear even to suspect that you deceived yourself, dear Sir, and not tell you such a suspicion was in my heart. That God may powerfully convince you of self-righteousness, and clothe you with the righteousness of his dear Son ; that he may fill you with his grace, and thereby fit you for, and at last translate you to, his glory, is the hearty prayer of,

dear Sir,

your most obliged and affectionate friend,

and humble servant,

G. W."

CATHOLICITY. " I wish all names among the saints of God were swallowed up in that one of *christian.* I long for professors to leave off placing religion in saying, ' I am a church man,' ' I am a dissenter.' My language to such is, ' Are you of Christ ? If so, I love you with all my heart.' "

SELF-KNOWLEDGE. " My heart is like Ezekiel's temple, the further I search into it, the greater abominations I discover; but there is a fountain opened for sin and all uncleanness."

GODLY JEALOUSY. " There is nothing I dread more than having my heart drawn away by earthly objects.—When that time comes, it will be over with me indeed; I must then bid adieu to zeal and fervency of spirit, and in effect bid the Lord Jesus to depart from me. For alas, what room can there be for God, when a rival hath taken possession of the heart? My blood runs cold at the very thought thereof. I cannot, indeed I cannot away with it."

WONDER. " As for my own part, I often stand astonished at the riches of free distinguishing grace, and I often feel myself so great a sinner, that I am tempted to think nothing can be blessed which comes from such unhallowed hands and lips; but yet the Lord is with me, and attends his word with mighty power."

ASSURANCE. " The root of the matter is twisted round every faculty of the soul, which daily is supported with this assurance, that Christ can no more forsake the soul he loves, than he can forsake himself."

CONFESSION. " All that people do say of me, affects me but little; because I know worse of myself than they can say concerning me. My heart is desperately wicked. Was God to leave me I should be a remarkable sinner."

ZEAL. " Nature would sometimes cry out, 'Spare thyself;' but when I am offering Jesus to poor sinners, I cannot forbear exerting all my powers. Oh that I had a thousand lives; my dear Lord Jesus should have them all."

AFFLICTION. " Well may God afflict me; I richly deserve it; and when he brings me low, nothing grieves me so much, as to think that I should be so froward, as to oblige the God of love to strike me with his rod. But, oh the goodness of the Lord! His rod, as well as staff, do comfort and build up my soul. I would not but be tried for ten thousand worlds. Blessed be God, I am enabled to clasp the cross, and desire to glory in nothing more."

LUTHER. " I find Luther's observation to be true: ' Times

of reformation are times of confusion;' as yet the churches in America are quiet, but I expect a sifting time ere long."

AMERICA. " I am more and more in love with the good old puritans; I am pleased at the thoughts of sitting down hereafter with the venerable Cotton, Norton, Elliot, and that great cloud of witnesses, which first crossed the western ocean for the sake of the gospel, and the faith once delivered to the saints. At present, my soul is so filled, that I can scarce proceed."

PARLIAMENT. "Though I scarce know an oak from a hickory, or one kind of land from another, I am subpœnaed to appear before parliament, to give an account of the condition of the province of Georgia, when I left it."

ASSURANCE. " As for assurance, I cannot but think all who are truly converted must know that there was a time in which they closed with Christ: but then, as so many have died only with an humble hope, and have been even under doubts and fears, though they could not but be looked upon as christians, I am less positive than once I was, lest haply I should condemn some of God's dear children. The farther we go in the spiritual life, the more cool and rational shall we be, and yet more truly zealous. I speak this by experience."

HOLY FIRE. "I desire that none of my wildfire may be mixed with the pure fire of holy zeal coming from God's altar. I think it my duty to wait, to go on simply in preaching the everlasting gospel, and I believe we shall yet see the salvation of God."

FIELD PREACHING. " Every one hath his proper gift. Field preaching is my plan. In this I am carried as on eagles' wings."

PHARISEES. " I find no such enemies to the cross of Christ, as those who keep up the form of religion, and are orthodox in their notions, but are ignorant of an experimental acquaintance with Jesus."

PUNNING. " Once in my sermon I said, 'Oh that New England was full of new creatures!'"

CATHOLIC SPIRIT. "I talk freely with the Messrs. Wesley, though we widely differ in a certain point. Most talk of a catholic spirit; but it is only till they have brought people

2 c

into the pale of their own church. This is downright secta-
rianism, not catholicism. How can I act consistently, unless I
receive and love all the children of God, whom I esteem to be
such, of whatever denomination they may be? Why should we
dispute when there is no probability of convincing? I think
this is not giving up the faith, but fulfilling our Lord's new
command, 'Love one another;' and our love is but feigned,
unless it produces proper effects. I am persuaded, the more
the love of God is shed abroad in our hearts, the more all nar-
rowness of spirit will subside and give way: besides, so far as
we are narrow-spirited, we are uneasy. Prejudices, jealousies,
and suspicions make the soul miserable, so far as they are entertained."

ZEAL. " Those who are not solidly established in the love
of God, will fall too much in love with the outward form of their
particular church, be it what it will. But as the love of God
gets the ascendency, the more they will be like him and his
holy angels, and consequently rejoice when souls are brought to
Jesus, whatever instruments may be made use of for that purpose. If therefore some that you and I know, are too confined
(as I believe is too much the case); if they do not preach more
frequently, and abound more in good works; I think it is for
want of having their hearts more inflamed with the love of God,
and their graces kept in more constant exercise. To stir up
the gift of God that is in us, is an apostolical injunction; and
if we do not keep upon our watch, we shall fall into a false still-
ness. Nature loves ease; and as a blind zeal often prompts us
to speak too much, so tepidity and lukewarmness often cause us
to speak too little. Divine wisdom alone is profitable to direct;
and I would be very cautious how I speak, lest I should take
too much upon me."

BIGOTRY. " Disputing with bigots and narrow-spirited people
will not do. I intend henceforward to say less to them, and
pray more and more to our Lord for them. 'Lord, enlarge
their hearts,' is my continual prayer for such, who are so straitened in their own bowels. Blessed be God, this partition-wall
is breaking down daily in some of our old friends' hearts in
London. I exhort all to go where they can profit most. I

preach what I believe to be the truth, and then leave it to the Spirit of God to make the application. When we have done this, I think we have gone to the utmost bounds of our commission."

LIFE AND DEATH. "'Why are you reconciled to life?' Because I can do that for Jesus on earth, which I cannot do in heaven: I mean, be made instrumental in bringing some poor, weary, heavy laden sinners to find rest in his blood and righteousness; and, indeed, if our Saviour was to offer either to take me now, or to stay only to take one sinner more, I would desire to stay to take him with me."

DEVOTION. "Morning and evening retirement is certainly exceeding good; but if through weakness of body, or frequency of preaching, I cannot go to God in my usual set times, I think my spirit is not in bondage. It is not for me to tell how often I use secret prayer; if I did not use it, nay, if in one sense I did not pray without ceasing, it would be difficult for me to keep up that frame of soul, which by the divine blessing I daily enjoy. If the work of God prosper, and your hands become more full, you will then, dear Sir, know better what I mean. But enough of this. God knows my heart; I would do every thing I possibly could to satisfy all men, and give a reason of the hope that is in me with meekness and fear; but I cannot satisfy all that are waiting for an occasion to find fault: our Lord could not; I therefore despair of doing it."

BUT A SINNER. "You are but a sinner, and Jesus died for sinners. Come and welcome to Jesus Christ."

GOD'S WORK. "I have been faulty in looking too much to foreign help, and despising that which God had given me. When our Lord was to feed the multitude, he would not create new bread, but multiplied the loaves that were already at hand. 'Ye need not send them away, give ye them to eat,' said he: so say I to my dear brethren at the Tabernacle. Work with the materials you have. In doing the work, God will teach you how to do it. Experience will grow up with the work itself. Thus God hath dealt with me, and so he continues to deal."

LUTHER AND CALVIN. "Mr. Wesley I think is wrong in

2 c 2

some things, and Mr. Law wrong also; yet I believe that both
Mr. Law and Mr. Wesley, and others, with whom we do not
agree in all things, will shine bright in glory. It is best therefore for a gospel minister, simply and powerfully to preach those
truths he has been taught of God, and to meddle as little as
possible with those who are children of God, though they should
differ in many things. This would keep the heart *sweet*, and at
the same time not betray the truths of Jesus. I have tried both
the disputing and the quiet way, and find the latter far prefer-
able to the former. I have not given way to the Moravian
brethren, or Mr. Wesley, or to any, whom I thought in an
error, no not for an hour. But I think it best not to dispute,
when there is no probability of convincing. I pray you, for
Christ's sake, to take heed lest your spirit should be imbittered, when you are speaking or writing for God. This will give
your adversaries advantage over you, and make people think
your passion is the effect of your principles. Since I have been
in England this time, Calvin's example has been very much
pressed upon me. You know how Luther abused him. As we
are of Calvinistical principles, I trust we shall, in this respect,
imitate Calvin's practice, and show all meekness to those who
may oppose."

POVERTY. "How is the world mistaken about my circumstances: worth nothing myself, embarrassed for others, and yet
looked upon to flow in riches! Our extremity is God's opportunity."

HEAD AND HEART. "Though principles are not to be rested
in, yet it is a good thing to have a clear head as well as a clean
heart. Some people make nothing of principles; but why are
they so zealous in propagating their own."

JUDGING. "Do not think that all things the most refined
christian in the world does, is right; or that all principles are
wrong, because some that hold them are too imbittered in their
spirits. It is hard for good men, when the truths of God are
opposed, to keep their temper, especially at the first attack.
Nothing but the all-conquering blood of the dear Redeemer
can destroy the wildfire in the heart."

USEFULNESS. "I have the pleasure often to go without the

camp, and to bear a little of his sacred reproach, and I prefer it to all the treasures in the world. Weak as I am, my Jesus makes me more than conqueror through his love. He has brought mighty things to pass here, and gotten himself the victory in many hearts. I trust there is not a *day* passes but some poor creature or another is plucked as a brand out of the burning. I wish I could hear God was more in the camp."

PERSECUTION. "I had once the honour of being publicly arraigned, for not reading the Common Prayer in a meeting-house. At another time, I was taken up by a warrant for correcting a letter wherein were these words, 'Shall our clergy break the canons?' The prosecutions were unjust; but there is our glory. I remember when Socrates was about to suffer, his friends grieved that he suffered unjustly. What! says he, would you have me suffer justly? 'If we are buffetted for our faults, and take it patiently,' says a greater than Socrates, 'we are not to glory; but if we are reproached for Christ, and suffer as christians, happy are we.' I think our present sufferings are for him."

SELF-KNOWLEDGE. "I know what a dreadful thing it is, to carry much sail without proper ballast, and to rejoice in a false liberty. Joy floating upon the surface of an unmortified heart, is but of short continuance. It puffs up, but doth not edify. I thank our Saviour that he is showing us here more of our hearts, and more of his love."

CHRIST'S LIBRARY. "Oh that I could lie lower! then should I rise higher. Could I take deeper root downwards, then should I bear more fruit upwards. I want to be poor in spirit. I want to be meek and lowly in heart. I want to have the whole mind that was in Christ Jesus. Blessed be his name for what he has given me already. Blessed be his name, that out of his fulness I receive grace for grace. Oh that my heart was Christ's library! I would not have one thief to lodge in my Redeemer's temple. 'Lord, scourge out every thief,' is the daily language of my heart. The Lord will hear my prayer, and let my cry come unto him."

MAXIM. "When I discover a new corruption, I am as thankful as a sentinel keeping watch in a garrison, would be at spying a straggling enemy come near him. I stand not fighting with it myself in my own strength, but run immediately and tell the Captain of my salvation. By the sword of his Spirit, he soon destroys it, and makes me exceeding happy. This is what I call a simple looking to Christ. I know of no other effectual way of keeping the old man down, after he has gotten his deadly blow."

MELANCTHON. " As Luther said to Melancthon, ' *Nimis es nullus.*' You are kept in bondage by a false humility. It is good to see ourselves poor, and exceeding vile ; but if that sight and feeling prevent our looking up to, and exerting ourselves for, our dear Saviour ; it becomes criminal, and robs the soul of much comfort. I can speak this by dear-bought experience. How often have I been kept from speaking and acting for God, by a sight of my own unworthiness ! but now I see that the more unworthy I am, the more fit to work for Jesus, because he will get much glory in working by such mean instruments ; and the more he has forgiven me, the more I ought to love and serve him. Fired with a sense of his unspeakable loving-kindness, I dare to go out and tell poor sinners that a Lamb was slain for them ; and that he will have mercy on sinners as such, of whom indeed I am chief."

WHITEFIELD'S TUMP. " I preached to about ten thousand on Hampton Common, at what the people now call Whitefield's Tump, because I preached there first. I cannot tell you what a solemn occasion that was. I perceive a great alteration in the people since I was in these parts last. They did indeed hang on me to hear the word. It ran and was glorified."

RAMS' HORNS. " The rams' horns are sounding about Jericho ; surely the towering walls will at length fall down. But we must have patience. He that believeth, doth not make haste. The rams' horns must go round seven times."

JERUSALEM SINNERS. " I purpose once more to attack the prince of darkness in Moorfields, when the holidays come. Many precious souls have been captivated with Christ's love in that wicked place. Jerusalem sinners bring most glory to the Redeemer."

ORPHAN SCHOOL. " I think I could be sold a *slave* to serve

at the galleys, rather than you and my dear orphan family should want."

OLD COLE. " I must acquaint you of the following anecdote of the old Mr. Cole, a most venerable dissenting minister, whom I was always taught to ridicule, and (with shame I write it) used, when a boy, to run into his meeting house, and cry, Old Cole ! old Cole ! old Cole ! Being asked once by one of his congregation, what business I would be of ? I said, ' A minister, but I would take care never to tell stories in the pulpit, like the old Cole.' About twelve years afterwards, the old man heard me preach in one of the churches at Gloucester ; and on my telling some story to illustrate the subject I was upon, having been informed what I had before said, made this remark to one of his elders, ' I find that young Whitefield can now tell stories, as well as old Cole.' Being affected much with my preaching, he was as it were become young again ; and used to say, when coming to and returning from Barn, ' These are days of the Son of man indeed ! ' Nay, he was so animated, and so humbled, that he used to subscribe himself, *my curate*, and went about preaching after me in the country, from place to place. But one evening, whilst preaching, he was struck with death, and then asked for a chair to lean on till he concluded his sermon, when he was carried up-stairs and died. O blessed God ! if it be thy holy will, may my exit be like his !" The Tump at Hampton had been Cole's stand before it was called Whitefield's Tump.

PARTY. " Those who think I want to make a party, or to disturb churches, do not know me. I am willing to hunt in the woods after sinners ; and, according to the present temper of my mind, could be content that the name of George Whitefield should die, if thereby the name of my dear Redeemer could be exalted. Indeed, I am amazed that he employs me at all. But what shall we say ? He hateth putting away, therefore I am not consumed. Grace, sovereign, free grace ! shall be all my song."

BEHIND THE CURTAIN. " Satan hath desired to have you, that he may sift you as wheat ; but surely Jesus prays for you, though as it were behind the curtain."

THE ROD.   " O happy rod,
                   That brought me nearer to my God.

I think I can say, it is good to bear the yoke of affliction in
youth. It teaches one to keep silence, and weans us from a too
great attachment to all sublunary enjoyments. I have a few
strokes of my Father's rod from time to time, as well as you.
But I find that his rod as well as his staff do comfort. I am a
naughty child, and want much correction; but he that wounds,
heals also, and in glory we shall find, that his loving correction
hath made us great. O glory! It is yonder in view; Jesus
stands at the top of the ladder to receive us into it."

COLONEL GARDINER. " The noble Colonel Gardiner once
wished me ' a thriving soul in a healthy body.' Or however
it may be with the one, I earnestly pray that the other may
prosper. Sickness is often made use of as a means, in the hands
of an all-gracious Father, to ripen our graces and fit us for heaven. Through grace, I can say it is good for me to be sick,
though I am afraid I am too impatient to be gone. Well! He
that cometh, will come, and cannot tarry long : till then may I
be resigned, and work the works of him that sent me whilst it
is day, before the night cometh when no man can work."

RESIGNATION. " My schemes are so frequently disconcerted,
that I would willingly put a blank into his hands, to be filled up
just as he pleases. But this stubborn will would fain avoid
swallowing some wholesome bitter-sweets, which the all-gracious
Physician reaches out unto me. Nevertheless, through grace,
the prevailing language of my heart is, ' Not my will, but thine
be done.' "

CANDOUR. " Alas! alas! in how many things have I judged
and acted wrong.—I have been too rash and hasty in giving
characters, both of places and persons. Being fond of Scripture
language, I have often used a style too apostolical, and at the same
time I have been too bitter in my zeal. Wildfire has been mixed
with it, and I find that I frequently wrote and spoke in my own
spirit, when I thought I was writing and speaking by the assistance of the Spirit of God. I have likewise too much made inward impressions my rule of acting, and too soon and too ex-

plicitly published what had been better kept in longer, or told after my death. By these things I have given some wrong touches to God's ark, and hurt the blessed cause I would defend, and also stirred up needless opposition. This has humbled me much since I have been on board, and made me think of a saying of Mr. Henry's, ' Joseph had more *honesty* than he had *policy*, or he never would have told his dreams.' At the same time, I cannot but bless, and praise, and magnify that good and gracious God, who filled me with so much of his holy fire, and carried me, a poor, weak youth, through such a torrent both of popularity and contempt, and set so many seals to my unworthy ministrations. I bless him for ripening my judgment a little more, for giving me to see and confess, and I hope in some degree to correct and amend, some of my mistakes."

POPULARITY. " It is too much for one man, to be received as I have been by thousands. The thoughts of it lay me low, but I cannot get low enough. I would willingly sink into nothing before the blessed Jesus, my All in All."

NOBILITY. " Paul preached privately to those that were of reputation. This must be the way I presume of dealing with the nobility, who yet know not the Lord. Oh that I may be enabled, when called to preach to any of them, so to preach as to win their souls to the blessed Jesus."

TO DR. DODDRIDGE. " The Moravians first divided my family, then my parish at Georgia, and after that the societies which, under God, I was an instrument of gathering. I suppose not less than four hundred, through their practices, have left the Tabernacle. But I have been forsaken otherwise. I have not had above a hundred to hear me, where I had twenty thousand; and hundreds now assemble within a quarter of a mile of me, who never come to see or speak to me, though they must own at the great day that I was their spiritual father. All this I find but little enough to teach me to cease from man, and to wean me from that too great fondness which spiritual fathers are apt to have for their spiritual children. Thus blessed Paul was served; thus must all expect to be treated who are of Paul's spirit, and are honoured with any considerable degree of Paul's success. But I have generally observed, that when one door of usefulness is shut, another opens."

SAMUEL. " ' Surely ' (says the prophet that was sent to anoint one of Jesse's sons) ' the Lord's anointed is before me.' He guessed several times ; but always guessed wrong, till little David was sent for, who was thought nothing of. And if a prophet was mistaken, when thus sent in a peculiar manner, and, no doubt, particularly engaged in prayer for direction, is it any wonder, that we should find ourselves mistaken in many things, even when we have been most earnest with God for guidance and direction ? God often guides us by disappointments."

SECRETS. " You know me too well to judge I have many secrets. May the secret of the Lord be with me ! and then I care not if there were a window in my heart, for all mankind to see the uprightness of my intentions."

MAXIM. " Like a pure crystal, I would transmit all the glory God is pleased to pour upon me, and never claim as my own what is his sole property."

ANGELS. " As we advance in the divine life, we shall be more and more conformed to those ministering spirits, who, though waiting on us below, do always behold the face of our heavenly Father above."

LUTHER. " How was Paul humbled and struck down before he was sent forth to preach the everlasting gospel ! Prayer, temptation, and meditation, says Luther, are necessary ingredients for a minister. If God teach us humility, it must be as Gideon taught the men of Succoth, by thorns."

BLOSSOMS. " I have always found awakening times like spring times ; many blossoms, but not always so much fruit."

POPULARITY. " You judge right, when you say, ' It is your opinion, that I do not want to make a sect, or set myself at the head of a party.' No, let the name of *Whitefield* die, so that the cause of Jesus Christ may live. I have seen enough of popularity to be sick of it, and, did not the interest of my blessed Master require my appearing in public, the world should hear but little of me henceforward. But who can desert such a cause ? Who, for fear of a little contempt and suffering, would decline the service of such a Master ? Oh that the Lord Jesus may thrust out many, many labourers into his harvest ! Surely the time must come, when many of the priests also shall be obedient to the word. I wait for thy salvation, O Lord ! "

COMPLIMENT. " Luther observed, that ' he was never employed in any new thing, but he was beset with some temptations, or visited with a fit of sickness.' I only wish I could bear it for your Ladyship; but then your crown would not be so bright, nor the inward purity of your heart so great."

NATURE. " Nature is a mere Proteus, and till renewed by the Spirit of God, though it may shift its scene, will be only nature still."

A PRETTY CHARACTER. " I wish the beloved physician was more reconciled to the cross. I am persuaded, let him say what he pleases, that a too great attachment to the world makes him reason as he does in many things. Well,—he is in good hands. He must either come or be dragged to the cross. That pretty character of his must be crucified and slain; and, as well as others, he must be content (as Mr. Gurnall expresses it) ' to go to heaven in a fool's coat.' "

THE KING. " Lately his Majesty, seeing Lady Chesterfield at court with a grave gown, pleasantly asked her, ' whether Mr. Whitefield advised her to that colour.' Oh that all were clothed in the bright and spotless robe of the Redeemer's righteousness! How beautiful would they then appear in the sight of the King of kings!"

SELF-KNOWLEDGE. " Oh that I may learn from all I see, to desire to be nothing; and to think it my highest privilege to be an assistant to all, but the head of none! I find a love of power sometimes intoxicates even God's own dear children, and makes them to mistake passion for zeal, and an overbearing spirit for an authority given them from above. For my own part, I find it much easier to obey than govern, and that it is much safer to be trodden underfoot, than to have it in one's power to serve others so. This makes me fly from that which, at our first setting out, we are too apt to court. Thanks be to the Lord of all lords for taking any pains with ill and hell-deserving me! I cannot well buy humility at too dear a rate."

THE HOLLOW SQUARE. " As long as we are below, if we have not one thing to exercise us, we shall have another. Our trials will not be removed, but only changed. Sometimes troubles come from without, sometimes from within, and sometimes

from both together. Sometimes professed enemies, and sometimes nearest and dearest friends, are suffered to attack us.
But Christ is the believer's *hollow square;* and if we keep
close in that, we are impregnable. Here only I find my refuge.
Garrisoned in this, I can bid defiance to men and devils. Let
who will thwart, desert, or overreach, whilst I am in this strong
hold, all their efforts, joined with the prince of darkness, to disturb or molest me, are only like the throwing chaff against a
brass wall."

A GOOD SOLDIER. " I am called forth to battle ; remember
a poor cowardly soldier, and beg the Captain of our salvation,
that I may have the honour to die fighting. I would have all
my scars in my breast. Methinks, I would not be wounded
running away, or skulking into a hiding-place. It is not for
ministers of Christ to flee or be afraid.—And yet, alas !—Well
—*nil desperandum Christo duci.*"

PREACHERS. " It has long since been my judgment, that it
would be best for many of the present preachers to have a tutor,
and retire for a while, and be content with preaching now and
then, till they were a little more improved. Otherwise, I fear
many who now make a temporary figure, for want of a proper
foundation, will run themselves out of breath, will grow weary
of the work, and leave it."

HEAVEN. " Oh what amazing mysteries will be unfolded,
when each link in the golden chain of providence and grace
shall be seen and scanned by beatified spirits in the kingdom of
heaven ! Then all will appear symmetry and harmony, and
even the most intricate and seemingly most contrary dispensa-
tions, will be evidenced to be the result of infinite and consummate wisdom, power, and love. Above all, there the believer
will see the infinite depths of that mystery of godliness, ' God
manifested in the flesh ;' and join with that blessed choir, who,
with a restless unweariedness, are ever singing the song of Moses
and the Lamb."

THE SCOTCH. " Though I preached near eighty times in
Ireland, and God was pleased to bless his word, yet Scotland
seems to be a new world to me. To see the people bring so
many Bibles, turn to every passage when I am expounding,

and hang as it were upon me, to hear every word, is very encouraging."

LETTERS. " I must have *aliquid Christi* in all my letters."

UPRIGHTNESS. " I am easy, having no scheme, no design of supplanting or resenting, but, I trust, a single eye to promote the common salvation, without so much as attempting to set up a party for myself. This is what my soul abhors. Being thus minded, I have peace ; peace which the world knows nothing of, and which all must necessarily be strangers to, who are fond either of power or numbers. God be praised for the many strippings I have met with : it is good for me that I have been supplanted, despised, censured, maligned, judged by, and separated from, my nearest, dearest friends. By this I have found the faithfulness of him, who is the Friend of friends ; by this I have been taught to wrap myself in the glorious Emmanuel's everlasting righteousness, and to be content that He, to whom all hearts are open, and all desires are known, now sees, and will let all see hereafter, the uprightness of my intentions towards all mankind."

UNBELIEF. " Unbelief is the womb of misery, and the grave of comfort. Had we faith but as a grain of mustard seed, how should we trample the world, the flesh, the devil, death, and hell under foot ! Lord, increase our faith ! I know you say, Amen. Even so, Lord Jesus, Amen and Amen ! "

POLICY. " Worldly wise men, serpent like, so turn and wind, that they have many ways to slip through and creep out at, which simple-hearted, single-eyed souls know nothing of, and if they did, could not follow after them. Honesty is the best policy, and will in the end (whether we seek it or not) get the better of all."

Such was the progress of Whitefield's opinions and maxims, during the first *ten* years of his ministerial life. I need not say, that these samples are not from his sermons. They are all specimens of the spirited hints he was scattering over the world by his letters and conversation.

CHAPTER XIX.

It was a maxim with Whitefield to return back in a few days, if possible, upon new spots where his first or second sermon had made a visible impression. On the same principle, he often revisited the chief scenes of his early labours; "confirming the souls of the disciples," and confronting his enemies. In reference to his avowed converts, he cherished much godly jealousy as well as brotherly love. He did not, like one of his friends, pretend to "know when persons are justified." "It is a lesson," he says, "I have not yet learnt. There are so many stony-ground hearers which receive the word with joy, that I have determined to suspend my judgment, till I know the tree by its fruits." In like manner, when he reports *individual* cases of sudden arrest under the gospel, it is common for him to say, "I shall wait, until we see how the physic works."

Thus whilst he had *other* reasons which compelled him to travel and revisit much, he was also impelled by solicitude for the stedfastness and consistency of his widely scattered converts. He would have looked well to the state of his herds and flocks, (although perhaps not so well,) had he had no orphanhouse to sustain, and no college in contemplation. Witness his countless letters! What are they in general, but the overflowing of his *pastoral* love and watchfulness for and over the souls whom he deemed committed to his charge?

In this spirit he left Ireland to revisit Scotland in 1751, to talk "with the *winter* as well as with the *summer* saints." He landed at Irvine, where he preached before the magistrates, at their own request. Next day the whole city of Glasgow was moved at his coming. "Thousands attend every morning and evening. They seem never to be weary. I am followed more than ever. Scotland seems (still) to be a *new* world to me. To see the people bring so many Bibles, and turn to every passage as I am expounding, and hang upon me to hear every word, is very encouraging." He abruptly breaks off this letter to the Countess by saying, "I could enlarge, but am straitened. Some ministers wait for me." These were *Mac Laurin*, Scott, Mac Culloch, &c. who delighted to visit him at his friend *Niven's*, near the Cross, after the labours of the day. Mac Laurin was both the guardian and champion of his reputation, in public and private ; and therefore gave Whitefield no rest, nor himself either, until he cleared up all flying reports. He would get at the facts of the case, even if he tried his friend's patience. Whitefield often smiled at the *Scotch* scrutiny of this great and good man. It left no stone unturned, when there was a calumny to overturn, or a mistake to rectify.

It was not, however, for this purpose chiefly that these good men sought his company. They admired and enjoyed his conversational talents. These were sprightly, and could be humoursome ; and as he thought aloud, and had seen much of real life, his company was equally instructive and enlivening, especially over his *light* supper. He then unbent the bow of his spirit, until it cooled from the friction of the burning arrows he shot during the day. A seat at Niven's table was then an honour, as well as a privilege. Gillies says truly, "One might challenge the sons of pleasure, with all their wit, good humour, and gaiety, to furnish entertainment so agreeable. At the same time every part of it was not more agreeable than it was useful and edifying."

He was much pleased to find, while at Glasgow, that Dinwiddie, the brother-in-law of Mac Culloch of Cambuslang, had been appointed governor of Virginia. This had an important bearing on the work Whitefield began there. He himself states it thus. "In that province, there has been for some years past a great awakening, especially in Hanover county, and the counties adjacent. As the ministers of the establishment did not favour the work, and the first awakened persons put themselves under the care of the New York synod, the poor people were from time to time fined, and very much harassed, for not attending on the church service : and as the awakening was supposed to be begun by the reading of my books, at the instigation of the council a proclamation was issued out to prohibit itinerant preaching. However, before I left Virginia, one Mr. Davies (afterwards President) was licensed, and settled over a congregation. Since that the awakening has increased, so that Mr. D—— writes, " that one congregation is multiplied to seven." He desires liberty to license more houses, and to preach occasionally to all, as there is no minister but himself. This, though allowed of in England, is denied in Virginia, which grieves the people very much. The commissary is one of the council, and with the rest of his brethren, I believe no friend to the dissenters. The late lieutenant-governor was like-minded. I therefore think that Mr. D—— is raised up to succeed him, in order to befriend the church of God, and the interest of Christ's people. They desire no other privileges than what dissenting protestants enjoy in our native country. This I am persuaded your brother-in-law will be glad to secure them."

On revisiting Edinburgh, the only thing he *did* deplore was, that Mr. Wesley intended to " set up societies" in Scotland, upon his own plan. This he thought " imprudent ;" and he said so. He had before warned Wesley, that the Scotch did not want him ; that neither his sentiments nor his system would suit the north, even if he preached " like an angel." Wesley would not believe this, and tried both ; but the experiment, for *him*, was a complete failure. And it deserved to be so, so far as he conducted it ; for he *libelled* and *caricatured* the people. True ; they heard him coldly : not more so, however, than his own people at the Foundery would have listened to one of the Cambuslang Calvinists. Besides, his very resolution to avoid all controversial points, was, however well meant, unwise, in a country where he was so well known to be an Arminian. It created suspicion, if not disgust, when they found that he kept back his notorious peculiarities. The people would have listened to them, and disputed them one by one with him, and counted him a " *pawky chiel* " had he come off with the best of the argument. But he was silent, and they suspected him of blinking the questions at issue between them. This is the real secret of Wesley's failure. His very candour seemed artifice to the Scotch.

So far, they misunderstood him, and thus did him injustice. He also misunderstood and misrepresented them. They were not "unfeeling multitudes," because *he* could not move them. The same multitudes had wept and rejoiced under Whitefield's preaching. He could bring them out on week days, as well as on sabbath, although Wesley found his congregation "miserably small," and said it verified what he had often heard, "that the Scotch dearly love the word of the Lord on the Lord's day." For, what did Whitefield's week-day congregations *verify?* At this time, as well as formerly, he had to say, "I now preach twice daily to many thousands. Many of the best rank attend. O Edinburgh, Edinburgh, surely thou wilt never be forgotten by me! The longer I stay, the more eagerly both rich and poor attend on the word preached. Perhaps, for near twenty-eight days together, in Glasgow and Edinburgh, I preached to near 10,000 saints every day." In like manner, when he took his leave at Glasgow, "numbers set out from the country, by two or three o'clock in the morning."

Whitefield left Scotland in the autumn, to revisit Georgia; becoming again, as he calls himself, "a *floating pilgrim.*" Indeed, he was fit for nothing but floating at the time. He had been much reduced at Edinburgh by vomitings of blood; and though his journey to London recruited him somewhat, he went on board the Antelope very weak. His voyage was, however, short and easy; and he arrived at Georgia in good health. His spirit also was much cheered by the flourishing condition of the orphan-house, and the flattering prospect of a college, now made plausible by the grant of a tract of excellent land. But whilst enjoying all this, he heard of the death of Dr. Doddridge at Lisbon, and started off to his old work with new diligence. He says, "Dr. Doddridge I find is gone. Lord Jesus, prepare me to follow after! I intend to *begin;* for as yet I have done nothing. Oh that I may begin in earnest. It is a new year. God quicken my tardy pace, and help me to do *much* work in a little

2 D

time. This is my highest ambition." Under this impulse he
revisited South Carolina. He durst not, however, risk the heat
of the summer in America, and therefore he returned to England
in the spring.

Whilst resting for a little in London, he revised some of
Hervey's manuscripts. This he called, on his own part, "holding up a candle to the sun." With his usual tact, however, he
foretold their fate. "Nothing but your *scenery* can screen you.
SELF will never bear to die, though slain in so *genteel* a manner, without showing some resentment against its *artful* mur-
derer." But reviewing did not suit him : he rose up from his
desk, exclaiming, "Oh that I could fly from pole to pole, publishing the everlasting gospel!" Even the transfer of Georgia
from trustees into the hands of government, at this time, and
all the prospects which the change opened for the colony, could
not detain him in London.

He was invited to revisit Ireland; but as it was for the purpose of organizing the Calvinistic methodists, he refused. "I
hate to head a party. It is absolutely inconsistent with my
other business to take upon me the care of societies in various
parts." He, therefore, revisited Bristol, where he preached
nine times in four days, to congregations almost equal in numbers to his Moorfields audiences. "Old times revived again.
Much good was done. The last evening it rained a little, but
none moved. I was *wet*, and contracted a cold and hoarseness;
but I trust preaching will cure me again." It did. In the
course of the next fortnight, he preached twenty times, and travelled three hundred miles on horseback, in Wales. He also
attended an association, at which nine clergymen, and nearly
forty other labourers, were present. His interview with these
brethren was inspiring as well as refreshing to him. "All was
harmony and love." He left them, more resolved than ever, to
"expose the wine and milk of the gospel to sale," and to ex-
postulate with sinners to "come *down* to the price, and be willing
to be saved by grace."

On his return to London he wrote, amongst many other letters, one to *Dr. Franklin*. Franklin, as well as Hume, admired
him; and for much the same reason,—his genius and power as

an orator. They cared about equally little for the grand TRUTH which fired his eloquence, and made him *wise* to win souls. It is painful to state this, but it is only too true. Franklin was, indeed, friendly to the moral and philanthropic tendency of Whitefield's doctrine, and had abandoned the rabid infidelity of Shaftesbury and Collins : but still, all the christianity he put into his own epitaph, was only the hope of a resurrection ; and all he put into his confession, a few weeks before his death, in answer to President Stiles, was, that he had doubts as to the divinity of Jesus of Nazareth, and thought his system of religion, although the best, not free from "various corrupting changes." In this opinion, he claimed kindred with *most* of the dissenters in England! To the credit of Dr. Priestley, he contradicted Franklin, and set the Americans right on this point.

Whitefield tried to set Franklin right upon a more important point ; that divine change of heart, without which no man can enter heaven. "I find," he says, "that you grow more and more famous in the learned world. As you have made a pretty considerable progress in the mysteries of electricity, I would now humbly recommend to your diligent, unprejudiced pursuit and study, the mystery of the new birth. It is a most important and interesting study, and when mastered will richly answer and repay you for all your pains. One at whose bar we are shortly to appear, hath solemnly declared that without it we cannot enter the kingdom of heaven. You will excuse this freedom. I must have *aliquid Christi* in all my letters. I am yet a willing pilgrim for his great name's sake." This honest letter ought to have delighted the philosopher in his closet, even more than the eulogium he heard whilst standing behind the bar of the House of Lords, when CHATHAM said of him, "Franklin is one whom Europe holds in high estimation, for his knowledge and wisdom ; one who is an honour, not to the English nation only, but to human nature."

The American Biographical Dictionary has done all it honestly could, to rescue the memory of this great patriot from the charge of being "friendly to infidelity." It quotes an instance in which he rebuked a youth, who was treating religion

2 D 2

as a vulgar prejudice, and who had appealed to him for countenance. Franklin said emphatically, " Young man, it is *best* to believe." Hume once said to La Roche, " Oh that I had never doubted." Such expressions prove nothing, but the suspicions of the sceptical. Besides, there could have been no religious *tone* about Franklin, if a raw witling could thus have dared to appeal to him against religion.

The most ingenious vindication of him I have ever seen, is in the sketch of his history in the American National Portrait Gallery :—" With such a *life* as Franklin led, we should, perhaps, offer an injury to religion, in supposing him, as some have done, an enemy to its prevalence, or a stranger to its benign influence." This is plausible, but hollow. His *life* in Paris will not sustain the argument. True ; he said there, that his success as a negociator would have convinced him of the being and government of a Deity, had he ever before been an atheist. Equally true it is, however, that, as a philosopher, he was often the companion of both atheists and infidels. Besides, what was he upon his death-bed? The best said of him then is, " that he was afraid he did not bear his pains as he ought," and was grateful for the many blessings he had received from the Supreme Being, who had raised him from " a humble origin to *such consideration among men*." In a word, he was not so unchristian in his creed as unitarians : he only *doubted*, what they deny, the divinity of the Saviour.

Franklin died in 1790. Whitefield's letter to him was in 1752. Their acquaintanceship seems to have commenced when the claims of the orphan-house were first pleaded in Philadelphia. Then Franklin, although he approved of the object, refused to contribute to it, when applied to in private, because he disapproved of the situation. He went to hear Whitefield, therefore, resolved to give nothing. He had, however, in his pocket, a handful of copper, three or four dollars, and five pistoles in gold. As the sermon began to kindle, Franklin began to soften, and was willing to give the copper. The next stroke won the silver ; and the finishing stroke was so admirable, he says, " that I emptied my pocket wholly into the collector's *dish* —gold and all." This is a good story ; but he tells a still bet ter one of his friend Hopkinson. He had gone empty-handed, that he might be sure to give nothing. But he was melted too, and tried to borrow money of a quaker. The quaker's answer was, " At any other time, friend, I would lend thee freely: but not now; for thee seems to me to be out of thy right senses." This is *unlike* a quaker! And it was unlike a christian, for Franklin to say, " The request was *fortunately* made to perhaps the only man in the company, who had the *firmness* not to be affected by the preacher."

It is no pleasure to me to write thus. Franklin was White-field's friend, and the friend of liberty and humanity; but his *half-homage* to christianity should be rejected by her friends. She needs not the compliments of *almost* christians. Indeed, they only tend to prevent inquirers from becoming *altogether* like Paul. It is all very well, when infidelity is to be put down, to appeal to the great cloud of scientific, philosophical, and poetical witnesses, who have complimented Revelation; but when christianity is to be enforced, it is worse than useless to appeal to great names who only believed the half of it. What minister would tell young men, that they might safely stop at the points where such doubters as Franklin stood still? Not any " able minister of the New Testament." Let Unitarianism take (and welcome!) all the philosophers and poets she can prove to have been Arians.

With what satisfaction the mind turns from such men, to follow Whitefield to Lutterworth, where he was drawn by the *magnetic* memory of Wycliffe, on his way from London to visit Scotland again! There, a protestant is at home. The interest of this hallowed spot was, if possible, enhanced to Whitefield—at least he was prepared to enjoy it—by meeting on the way to it one of Doddridge's students, who had been converted at Olney, four years before, from a " bitter scoffer," to be a young evangelist. He felt this to be a call to " go forward " in his work. He did; and preached " twice in the famous Wycliffe's parish" with such effect, that, before he reached Scotland, he received a letter, informing him that he had won souls in the reformer's parish. How enviable his associations with Lutterworth! My own were sadly disturbed, when I passed through it. I had watched the *morning-star* from the window of the mail, as it lingered and smiled over the tower of the church; and had pleased myself all night long with the hope of being able to "drink of the brook" into which Wycliffe's ashes were thrown. The guard, however, would not allow me to run down the hill, whilst the horses were changing. I was more than mortified; but he was inexorable. When, lo, he discovered that one of the fresh horses wanted a shoe; and there was no other horse in the stable. " Call the blacksmith," he cried in thunder. Off I ran that moment, down the hill, rejoicing in the accident. I leaped the hedge, and reached the brook. Alas, it was covered with *yeasty* scum from the dye-houses, or manu-factories, upon its banks. I could not drink! It was then only three o'clock in the morning. I tasted the water, however, by laving up a handful where the slime was least offensive. My reader will pardon this digression, when he remembers *old* FUL-LER's climax. This brook conveyed the *ashes* of Wycliffe into the Avon; the Avon into the Severn; and the Severn into the main sea; and thus the reformer's ashes became emblems of his doctrine, which shall spread from the rivers to the ends of the earth.

Whitefield's associations were less sublime at Leicester. He had *turnips* thrown at him, whilst preaching his first sermon. At his second, however, "all was hushed," and he "heard afterwards that good was done." Then he revisited Newcas-tle; and there he was, " as it were, *arrested* to stay." Accord-ingly, he preached four times, and " a whole shower of blessings descended from heaven on the great congregation." This led to a *second* arrest, and the shower was repeated. I use his own strong language concerning Leicester and Newcastle, because he afterwards told Lady Huntingdon that he had received "brave news" from both places.

These arrests by the way, made him *due* in Scotland. His invitations to revisit Edinburgh and Glasgow, had been very strong; and he was nothing loth to comply. " I love *state* too well, especially in Scotland, not to take it upon me as often as possible," by mounting " my despised throne." There is *truth* as well as playfulness in this confession. Whitefield did love a little *state* now and then ;—who does not ? Edinburgh *was* his throne, and coronets graced it. None of these things, however, estranged or diverted him from humbler spheres, or lessened his interest in " men of low estate." Accordingly, his letters to the Countess at this time, whilst they report briefly the " abundance of the better sort," who came out to hear him twice a day, in common with the multitude, dwell chiefly upon the case of a poor *highland* schoolmaster, who had been very useful amongst the young Gaels ; and upon the claims of a poor student, who had not the means of finishing his ministerial education. In none of his letters at this time, is there any reference to the personal honours paid to him, although they were neither few nor small. What he mentions with most complacency, is, an account he had received of " a *dozen* young men, that were awakened" under his ministry, " ten years ago," and who were now useful preachers. This was emphatically good news to Whitefield; for although he was not far-sighted, he saw clearly all the bearings of his own favourite maxim, that " every student's name is *legion ;*" " catching him is catching thousands ; helping him, helping many."

This maxim (in a better *form*) deserves the consideration and adoption of both ministers and wealthy christians. Who can calculate how many souls have been won, or what trains of good have been set in *perpetual* motion, by the young men, whom the Thorntons, and especially the Simeons and Wilsons, of England, the Haldanes of Scotland, and the Bethunes of America, took by the hand, and sustained at college ? The *reflection* of that good is already bright upon " the sea of glass before the throne," and it will increase in space and splendour there until the end of time, and then " shine as the stars for ever and ever." Go *thou*, and do likewise ! Or if unable to bear the entire expense of a student, unite some of your friends with you. In like manner, each of the voluntary churches in large towns should sustain a young evangelist. I have tried the experiment, and my little flock have always come to my help.

To the poor student who applied to him for advice, Whitefield wrote, " God willing, I shall not be unmindful of you."

Like myself, he had neither silver nor gold enough of his own;
but he had *friends*, and he pleaded the case with them. He seems
also, whilst in Edinburgh, at this time, to have aimed much to
catch students; many of whom from the classes, as well as from
the divinity hall, came daily to hear him. This was the case at
Glasgow, when he revisited it. There, indeed, his audiences
were even greater than at Edinburgh.

An event had occurred at the General Assembly this year,
which called forth Whitefield's characteristic vein of humour.
The assembly had deposed Gillespie, the founder of the RELIEF
Presbytery. "I wish Mr. Gillespie joy," he said: "the POPE
is turned *presbyterian*. How blind is Satan! What does he
get by casting out Christ's servants? I expect great good will
come out of these confusions. Mr. Gillespie will do more good
in a week now, than before in a year." Whitefield's jokes are
not two-edged swords, which cut both ways at once: but if his
sarcasm against the Secession cut deep, this one against the
Kirk cut deeper. The *Babel* story, and the *Babylon* story,
therefore, if told at all again, should be told together, in justice
to Whitefield's impartiality. Both, however, had better be
dropped, when the Assembly and the Synod contend at all.

On leaving Scotland, Whitefield revisited several of his old
stations in Yorkshire, Lancashire, and Cheshire, in a state of
mind so heavenly and absorbed, that he scarcely knew at times,
he says, "whether he had been in heaven or on earth." During
three weeks of such preaching, he " never had more encouragement, since the Lord of the harvest sent him out. A gale of
divine influence every where attended it." This does not rest
on his own testimony only. His Leeds friends brought him
back from Sheffield again, " to make hay while the sun shone."

It was now November: but the weather was "uncommonly
favourable;" and, therefore, he thought it "a pity to go into
winter quarters, whilst work could be done in the fields." He
was, however, *driven* in soon by rain and sickness. He expected death in the coach, between Northampton and London.
When he reached home, he found his wife had almost as much
need of a nurse as himself. Next day, however, he set himself
to reconsider the claims of Ireland, and again refused to go over

to head a party. In a few days, also, he resumed his correspondence with Hervey; and in a week, he was absorbed with the affairs of Georgia; writing now a short letter to a manager of the orphan-house, and anon a long one to "*dear Nat.*" one of the orphans. By December, he was "longing to range Yorkshire again, and to revisit Leeds." Night nor day, he could not forget the scenes he witnessed there, although he was now hearing "every day of fresh awakenings" in the Tabernacle.

At this time, Charles Wesley consulted him on a delicate subject—separation from John; some of whose measures he could not fall in with. His letter I have never seen. It embarrassed Whitefield. He knew not what to say. Something, however, rendered it necessary for him to say, that he thought John "still jealous" of him and his proceedings. But lest this should injure John with Charles, he said also, "The connexion between you and your brother hath been so close,—and your attachment to him so necessary to *keep up* his interest,—that I would not willingly, for the world, do or say any thing that may separate such friends. I have seen an end of all *perfection!* More might be said were we face to face." Wesley was somewhat jealous of Whitefield at this time. A *new* Tabernacle was now on the carpet; and for a long time the nobility had smiled on Whitefield. Wesley felt this. He could have taken their smiles more coolly than Whitefield; but he could not sustain their neglect philosophically. It was, however, the *contrast*, not the loss, that mortified him.

When Whitefield agreed to the plan of a new Tabernacle, he resolved, he says, "on the principle that burnt children dread the fire, not to begin till he had £1000 in hand, and then to contract at a certain sum for the whole." His fingers had been burnt at Bethesda; and he told his friends so. They took the hint, and soon raised upwards of £900; and by the time the foundation-stone was laid, the contributions amounted to £1100. Whitefield himself laid the stone, 1st March, 1753, on the old spot, and preached from Exod. xx. 24.

To the credit of the Wesleys, his kind but honest letter to Charles not only prevented their rupture, but also led to a loan of their Spitalfields' chapel, when the old Tabernacle was pulled down. Whitefield returned this compliment, by remonstrating with one of his preachers against giving offence or creating jealousies amongst the friends of Wesley.

When the time of the year came, that he could sing, " Lo, the winter is past," he quitted winter quarters. " The time of the singing of birds and the voice of the turtle in the land," called *forth* his voice too. He revisited Norwich for a few days in April. He says, that he " triumphed there in spite of all opposition." What the opposition was I do not know. One part of the triumph Whitefield did not know on earth. The late FULLER of Kettering was wont to tell the following anecdote, which he had from the lips of the person. A young man who had gone out in the morning on a frolic, with a party of his companions, would have his *fortune* told by a gipsy they met. She predicted for him a good old age, and lots of children and grandchildren. He believed the prophecy, and resolved to store his mind with such knowledge as would make young folks *like* an old man. " Let me see," he said, " what I can acquire first ? O, here is the famous methodist preacher, Whitefield; he is to preach to-night, they say ; I will go and hear him." From these strange motives, he really went to hear. The sermon was on John's appeal to the Sadducees and Pharisees, to " flee from the wrath to come." " Whitefield," said he, " described the *Sadducean* character : but that did not touch me. Then the *Pharisaic :* that shook me a little. At length he abruptly broke off —then burst into a flood of tears—then lifting up his hands, he cried with a loud voice, O my HEARERS ! the wrath is to *come* —the *wrath* is to come ! These words sunk into my heart like lead in the waters. I wept. I went alone. These words followed me wherever I went. For days and weeks I could think of little else but the awful words, ' The wrath is to come—is to come.' " Fuller said, the young man became " a considerable preacher."

Whitefield's work and reward during his revisits in 1753, were much as usual for him ;—like that of nobody else. I can scarcely believe my own eyes, as I read the distances, dates, and numbers of his audiences, in his memoranda ; connected as these are with frequent and even startling attacks of sickness. If he had not eagle's wings, his strength was certainly renewed like the eagle's, even in a physical sense.

Having opened the new Tabernacle, and preached in it for a short time, ("weeping in secret," however, to get back to Yorkshire,) he set out again for the north. Some of his Leeds converts met him by the way, to hurry him off from Sheffield. He *would* stop at Rotherham, however, because the insults he had formerly received there, had tempted him to return no more. Then, he thought no good was done. Now, he found the chief family of his " bitter persecutors " converted to God, and ready to welcome him under their roof. He became their guest. Rotherham had signalized itself by hostility to Whitefield. Both his person and character had been assailed there; and by none more than the late Thorpe of Masborough, then a young man. He was in the habit of meeting his boon companions in the alehouse, to mimic Whitefield, and turn religion into mockery. One evening Thorpe and three others laid a wager, which of them could imitate him in the highest style, at an off-hand sermon, from the first text which should turn up on opening the Bible. The buffoonery of the three soon failed, and Thorpe sprung on the table, saying, " I shall beat you all hollow." The Bible was handed to him. He opened it at random. His eye fell on the words, " Except ye repent, ye shall all likewise perish." He uttered them without fear or hesitation. But that moment his conscience smote him. It burst into flames. It compelled him to preach repentance to himself and all the club. He went on in spite of himself, until his own hair stood on end with horror, and all the bacchanals were blanched with terror. Not a word was said of the *wager* when he came down. He walked out in awful silence. Soon after this he joined the Wesleyans, and was sent out by Wesley himself as a preacher, who wisely stationed him at Rotherham. He afterwards became an independent.

When Whitefield arrived at Leeds, he found that neither reports, nor his own hopes of his past success, were exaggerated. Twenty thousand assembled to hear him on the sabbath, and many fruits of his former ministry were presented to him. Such was his *elevation* of soul now, that he saw nothing impossible, which it was proper to attempt by the preaching of the gospel; for even *York* could not resist the fascination of *his* field preaching. The methodist thinned out the Minster, and overawed the mob. Indeed, so great was his success at this time in Yorkshire, that he exceedingly regretted his engagement to visit Scotland. He had heard that " poor Scotland was *dead* " again, notwithstanding the power of the revivals; and, therefore, he was afraid to breathe a cold atmosphere, now that he was on fire amidst " a people full of fire," and enjoying " perpetual *Cambuslang* seasons." He kept his promise, however; and found Scotland not so dead as it was reported. Both the rich and the poor thronged to hear him twice every day at Edinburgh. " Attention sat upon all faces, and friends came round like *bees,* importuning him to stay another week." It was the same at Glasgow. There, the *owner* of the play-house was made so uneasy by a sermon against theatrical amusements, that he pulled the roof off the building, to put an end to them so far as he was concerned. This was laid hold of by Whitefield's enemies, and held up as the act of his mobs. He says, " The devil owed me a *grudge* for speaking against the play-house." That grudge appeared in the following form, in the Newcastle Journal : " We are informed, that Mr. Whitefield, the itinerant, being at Glasgow, and preaching near the play-house *lately built,* influenced the mob so much against it, that they ran directly from before him, and pulled it down to the ground. Several of the rioters are since taken up, and committed to gaol." This was all a lie. The " lately built " house was only a temporary booth, supported by the old walls of the *bishop's* palace ;—a strange spot, it will be said, for a theatre. Perhaps not, in Scotland ! I recollect, however, to feel it more than strange at Chester, to find that part of the abbey had been turned into a theatre ! I shrunk from the *desecration,* notwithstanding all my Scotch prejudices.

Whitefield came back upon York and Leeds, on leaving Scotland; and again what he saw and felt " was inexpressible." The parting at Leeds was so overpowering, that he did not recover the shock for some time. At Haworth also, they had a sacrament at which *thirty-five* bottles of wine were used. What a day for good Grimshaw ! I say *good;* for with all his eccen-

tricities, he was a noble-minded man. He made the wilderness
blossom as the rose around him. And God did not forget his
labours of love. His *prodigal* son was restored to him in heaven.
This young man was reclaimed; and said on his death-bed,
" What will my father say, when he sees *me* in heaven? "

Altogether, this was, perhaps, Whitefield's most successful
campaign in England, although I am unable to illustrate it by
a detail of facts. In the space of three months, he travelled
about " twelve hundred miles, and preached a hundred and
eighty sermons, to many, very many thousands of souls."

" The partings " in Yorkshire, he says, " nearly *killed* me."
He does not write thus, except when parting from those he
hoped to meet in heaven. Whenever he speaks strongly of success, I have found that he had strong reasons. Ordinary success never inflames nor inflates his language.

Having rested a few days in London, he started again, to make
the most of the autumn, whilst it lasted. He went first into
Northamptonshire, where " a new scene of usefulness opened"
to him. It was the season of their *feasts* in that county. He
says, in his own off-hand style, " If I mistake not, some of their
feasting was spoiled." He did not mistake. I once saw a venerable patriarch there, sitting smoking his evening pipe under
a hoary sycamore, who remembered having seen Whitefield at
this time. He had no recollection of the sermon; but his eye
brightened, when he told me, how the people made him and the
other boys keep quiet. My friend, George Bennet, Esq. the
missionary traveller, will recollect this scene under the sycamore
tree, near Long Buckbey. We must, however, have loved the
old man, even if he had not seen Whitefield; for, like Simeon,
he had seen Jesus.

On leaving Northamptonshire, Whitefield revisited Birmingham; and there " souls fled to the gospel like doves to their
windows." At Gornall, (a place I have already described,) he
heard of " a whole company," who had been " awakened by
reading his sermons." But *conversions* were not his only reward
in this quarter. Many aged believers blessed him. One said
to him, " I was comforted when you were here last, and now I
can go more *cheerful* to heaven." Another, who had been long

a pilgrim, said, on first hearing him, " Why, this is just the *old* story of fifty-five years ago." Upon the whole, he was much cheered by his success in Staffordshire. He would not, however, give his judgment upon it, until he came, as he expresses it, " to *cross-plough* the ground again."

He now went into Cheshire, where his " way was prepared " by the usefulness which had sprung from his books. Accordingly, at Chester a great concourse, together with some of the clergy, attended ; and the most " noted rebel in the town " was so alarmed under the sermon, that he could not sleep night or day for some time afterwards. At Wrexham, however, and at Nantwich, he was stoned whilst preaching ; but, providentially, he " got off pretty free," although some of his friends were " much pelted." " I met," he says, " with a little rough treatment " (he calls it *apostolic* treatment in one letter) ; "but what have *pilgrims* to expect better in the wilderness." He found better at Liverpool. There another convert, won by his printed sermons, met him on landing, and took him home, and convened great numbers to hear him.

It was now November, and he returned to London ; but not for winter quarters. In a few days, he was in his " native county," at the house of a "nineteen years' friend," one of the aldermen of Gloucester. That house, he says, was made a *Bethel* to him ; and never before had he such " freedom " in preaching to his townsmen. Altogether, this new freedom was " so pleasant " to him, that he resolved to take Gloucestershire again on his way home. On his arrival in Bristol, he found his usual welcome, and what surprised him more—that not a few of " the quality, and one of Cæsar's household, wished to hear him at his brother's great house." He preached to them twice. On the sabbath following, he opened the new Tabernacle at Bristol. " It is large," he says, " but not half large enough. Would the place contain them, I believe as many would attend as in London."

It was now cold weather ; but he was unwilling to return to his metropolitan nest. " Winter quarters ! "—he says, " the word *winter* almost shocks me." He, therefore, went into Somersetshire. How much he enjoyed this detention from London, and the work that detained him, let the following fine memorial tell: "At seven in the evening I preached in the open air, to a great multitude. All was hushed, and exceedingly solemn. The stars shone exceedingly bright. Then, if ever, I saw by the eye of faith, Him who calleth them all by their names. My soul was filled with a holy ambition, and I longed to be one of those, who shall shine as the stars for ever and ever. My hands and my body were cold; but what are outward things, when the soul within is warmed by the love of God. Oh that I may die in the field." The scene of this apostrophe I once visited. The air was equally cold—the stars equally bright—all nature the same; but there was no *Whitefield!* I had only *fifty* persons to preach to. However, my "soul within" was not cold.

Whilst thus reluctant to give in, Whitefield heard of the illness of Wesley, and forgot every thing but his dying friend. The disease was said to be "galloping consumption," and he threw up all his engagements, and hastened to London. He also wrote to both brothers, before he could set out. To "poor Mr. Charles," he wrote thus: "The Lord help and support you. A wife, a friend, a brother, all ill together! Well, this is our comfort—all things shall work together for good to them that love God. May a double spirit of the *ascending* Elijah descend and rest upon the *surviving* Elisha! To-morrow I leave Bristol."

The letter from which these lines are transcribed, enclosed one to Wesley himself, written, as Whitefield says, out of the fulness of his heart. "The news and prospect of your approaching dissolution hath quite weighed me down. I pity myself and the church;—but not you. A radiant throne awaits you, and ere long you will enter into your Master's joy. Yonder He stands with a massy crown, ready to put on your head, amidst an admiring throng of saints and angels. But I—poor I, who have been waiting for my dissolution these nineteen years, must be left behind to 'grovel here below.' Well, this is my comfort—it cannot be long until the chariots will be sent even for worthless me. If prayers can detain *you*—even you shall not leave us yet. But if the decree is gone forth, that you must now fall asleep in Jesus—may He kiss your soul away, and give you to die in the embraces of triumphant love. If in the

land of the living, I hope to pay my last respects to you next
week. If not—farewell! My heart is too big. Tears trickle
down too fast. And I fear you are too weak for me to enlarge.
May underneath you be Christ's everlasting arms. I commend
you to his never-failing mercy, and am your most affectionate,
sympathizing, and afflicted younger brother in the gospel."
Well might, and well did, Wesley say, in his funeral sermon
for Whitefield, " He had a heart susceptible of the most
generous and the most tender friendship : I have frequently
thought, that this, of all others, was the *distinguishing* part of
his character." *Funeral Sermon.*

Whilst Wesley continued in danger, Whitefield remained in
almost agonizing suspense ; "praying and inquiring, inquiring
and praying again, and always dreading to hear the worst." It
was, however, his friend's *usefulness* to the church and the
world, which made him thus solicitous ; for when he heard that
his lungs were injured, he said to Lady Huntingdon, " I cannot
wish him to survive his usefulness. It is *poor* living to be
nursed." At this time a *storm* of persecution broke upon some
quarter of his vineyard, and an appeal was made to his sympathy by the sufferers. He did sympathize with them ; but told
them, " should the present illness of dear Mr. Wesley issue in
his death, that will be a storm of a far more *threatening* nature." Happily for the world and the church, Wesley was
spared nearly forty years longer.

Whitefield was cheered in his winter quarters this year, by
the visit of his friends Tennent and Davies of America, who
had come over to collect for the college of New Jersey. He
entered with all his soul into their object, and threw all his influence upon their side. He also obtained, in prospect of his
return to Georgia, " *twenty-two prizes*," as he calls the orphans,
whom he had selected to go with him. He then prepared to sail.
The next chapter contains his *own* account of Lisbon ; and is
worthy of deep notice at this time, whilst popery is softened by one
class of politicians, and libelled (if that be possible) by another.

It is curious, that *living* popery made Whitefield forget,
during his visit, *dead* Doddridge, at Lisbon : at least, I have
found no letter yet that shows any visit to his tomb.

CHAPTER XX.

1754.

" The following letters were written about a twelvemonth ago, and are now sent into the world at the earnest desire of many. If an infinitely condescending God shall vouchsafe to bless the perusal of them, to excite in any, either at home or abroad, a more obediential and zealous thankfulness for the civil and religious liberties we enjoy ; or make them any way instrumental in stirring up my fellow-protestants and dear countrymen to exert themselves more vigorously, at this critical juncture, against those who, if conquerors, would quickly rob us of those invaluable blessings, I shall not repent that the publication of them was consented to by, courteous reader, thy willing servant, for Christ's sake, G. W.

" By this time, I suppose, you have heard of my having been at Lisbon, and are wondering what led me thither, especially since my last informed you of my intention to go to Georgia by way of New York. This was really my design at the time of my writing ; but being afterward called by Providence to take with me several orphan children, I thought it most advisable to go and settle them, and my other domestic affairs, at the orphan-house first ; that I might visit the northern parts of America with more ease and freedom in my own mind.—It happened that the Success, Captain Thompson, bound for Port Royal, South Carolina, (which is not very far from Georgia,) was then almost ready to sail. I sent for the owner, and finding that the ship was to touch at Lisbon to unload some wheat, it occasioned a little demur ; but, upon second thoughts, believing it might be serviceable to me, as a preacher and protestant, to see something

2 E

of the superstitions of the church of Rome, I took my passage
and embarked in the Success the 7th of March.   On the 14th
we reached Cape Finisterre ; on the 15th came in sight of the
Burlings ; and on the 16th anchored safe before Bellem, about
four miles distant from Lisbon city, the metropolis of Portugal.
As I knew nobody there, and had formed but an indifferent idea
of the inhabitants, from the account that had been given me of
them, I had purposed within myself to keep on board, and go
ashore only now and then in the day-time.   But Providence so
ordered it, that a gentleman of the factory, who had heard me
himself, and whose brother had been awakened under my ministry several years ago, immediately, upon hearing of my arrival, sent me an offer of his house during my stay.   I thankfully accepted it ; and special leave being procured for my going
ashore, I was carried in a chaise and pair from Bellem to Lisbon.   A new scene, both in respect to the situation of the place,
the fashion of the buildings, and the dress of the inhabitants,
presented itself all the way.   But what engaged my attention
most, was the frequency of crucifixes and little images of the
Virgin Mary, and other real or reputed saints, which were placed
almost in every street, or fixed against the walls of the houses
almost at every turning, with lamps hanging before them.   To
these I observed the people bow as they passed along; and near
some of them stood several little companies, singing with great
earnestness.   This seemed to me very odd, and gave me an idea
of what further ecclesiastical curiosities would probably fall in
my way, if I should be detained any time here.   These expectations were quickly raised ; for, not long after my arrival at my
new lodgings, (where I was received and entertained with great
gentility, hospitality, and friendliness,) upon looking out of the
window, I saw a company of priests and friars bearing lighted
wax tapers, and attended by various sorts of people, some of
which had bags and baskets of victuals in their hands, and
others carried provisions upon their shoulders on sticks between
two.   After these followed a mixed multitude, singing with a
very audible voice, and addressing the Virgin Mary in their
usual strain, ' *Ora pro nobis.*'   In this manner they proceeded
to the prison, where all was deposited for the use of the poor

persons confined therein. But a far more pompous procession
of the like nature (as a stander-by informed me) passed by a few
days after. In this there were near three hundred Franciscan
friars, many of which (besides porters hired for the purpose)
were loaded with a variety of food ; and those who bore no burden, carried either ladles or spoons in their hands. Sights of
this nature being quite a novelty to me, I was fond of attending
as many of them as I could. Two things concurred to make
them more frequent at this juncture, viz. the season of Lent,
and an excessive drought, which threatened the total destruction of the fruits of the earth. For the averting so great a judgment, and for the imploring the much-longed-for blessing of
rain, daily processions had been made from one convent or another for a considerable time. One of these I saw. It was
looked upon as a pretty grand one, being made up of the Car-
melite friars, the parish priests, and a great number of what they
call the brothers of the order, who walked two by two in divers
habits, holding a long and very large lighted wax taper in their
right hands. Amidst these was carried, upon eight or ten men's
shoulders, a tall image of the Virgin Mary, in a kind of man's
attire; for I think she had a very fine white wig on her head,
(a dress she often appears in,) and was much adorned with jewels
and glittering stones. At some distance from the lady, under a
large canopy of state, and supported likewise by six or eight
persons, came a priest, holding in his hand some noted relic.
After him followed several thousands of people, joining with the
friars in singing, ' *Eandem cantilenam, ora pro nobis,*' all the
way. Still rain was denied, and still processions were continued. At length the clouds began to gather, and the mercury
in the barometer fell very much. Then was brought out a
wooden image, which they say never failed. It was the figure
of our blessed Lord, clothed with purple robes, and crowned with
thorns. I think they call him the LORD OF THE PASSION. Upon
his shoulders he bore a large cross, under the weight of which
he was represented as stooping, till his body bent almost double.
He was brought from the Le Grass convent in very great pomp,
and placed in a large cathedral church. Being on board at that
time, I lost this sight; but, the subsequent evening, I beheld the

Seigneur fixed on an eminence in a large cathedral church, near the altar, surrounded with wax tapers of a prodigious size. He was attended by many noblemen, and thousands of spectators of all ranks and stations, who crowded from every quarter, and, in their turns, were admitted by the guards to come within the rails and perform their devotions. This they expressed by kneeling, and kissing the Seigneur's heel, by putting their left and right eye to it, and then touching it with their beads, which a gentleman in waiting received from them, and then returned again. This scene was repeated for three days successively; and, during all this time, the church and space before it was so thronged with carriages and people, that there was scarce any passing. The music on this occasion was extremely soft, and the church was illuminated in a very striking manner. The third day in the forenoon it rained, and soon after the Seigneur was conducted home in as great splendour, and much greater rejoicing, than when he was brought forth. As my situation was very commodious, I saw the whole; and afterwards went and heard part of the sermon, which was delivered before him in the church to which the Seigneur belonged. The preacher was full of action; and in some part of his discourse, (as one who understood Portuguese informed me,) pointing to the image, he said, ' Now he is at rest. He went out in justice, but is returned in mercy.' And towards the conclusion, he called upon the people to join with him in an extempore prayer. This they did with great fervency, which was expressed not only by repeating it aloud, but by beating their breasts, and clapping their cheeks, and weeping heartily. To complete the solemnity, immediately after the delivery of the blessing, all on a sudden, from the place near which the image stood, there was heard a most soft and soothing symphony of music; which being ended, the assembly broke up, and I returned to my lodgings, not a little affected to see so many thousands led away from the simplicity of the gospel, by such a mixture of human artifice and blind superstition, of which indeed I could have formed no idea, had I not been an eye-witness of it myself. This concern was still increased by what I heard from some of my fellow-passengers, who informed me, that about eleven one night, after I came aboard, they not only heard a friar preaching most fervently before the Seigneur, but also saw several companies of penitents brought in, lashing and whipping themselves severely. How little unlike this to those who cut themselves with knives and lancets, and cried out from morning till night, ' O Baal, hear us!' Methinks I hear you say, And, had I been present, I should have wished for the spirit of an Elijah to—Hush, my friend—I am content to guess at the rest till we meet. In the mean while, let us comfort ourselves with this thought, that there is a season approaching, when the Lord God of Elijah will himself come, and destroy this and every other species of antichrist, ' by the breath of his mouth, and the brightness of his appearing,' even by the all-conquering manifestations of his eternal Spirit. Whether as men, christians, and protestants, we have not more and more reason to pray, night and day, for the hastening on of that glorious and long wished-for period, you will be better able to judge, when I send you (as I purpose to do, if I have time) a further account of a Lent procession or two, of which I was also a spectator. At present I can only beg a continual remembrance at a throne of grace, as being, my dear friend, ———.

" Though some other business demands my attention, yet I must not forget the promise made you of a further account of the processions I saw at Lisbon. Some of those already mentioned were *extraordinary*, by reason of the great drought ; but that which is to be the subject of my present letter was an *annual* one ; it being always customary at Lisbon to exhibit some procession or another every Friday in Lent. An intelligent protestant who stood near me, was so good as to be my interpreter of the dumb show as it passed along—I say dumb show —for you must know it was chiefly made up of waxen or wooden images, and carried on men's shoulders through the streets, intending to represent the life and death of St. Francis, the founder of one of their religious orders. They were brought out from the Franciscan convent, and were preceded by three persons in scarlet habits with baskets in their hands, in which they received the alms of the spectators, for the benefit of the poor prisoners. After these came two little boys in parti-coloured clothes, with wings fixed on their shoulders, in imitation of little angels. Then appeared the figure of St. Francis, very gay and beau-like, as he used to be before his conversion. In the next, he was introduced under conviction, and consequently stripped of his finery. Soon after this was exhibited an image of our blessed Lord himself, in a purple gown with long black hair, with St. Francis lying before him, to receive his immediate orders. Then came the Virgin Mother, *(horresco referens,)* with Christ her Son at her left hand, and St. Francis making his obeisance to both. Here, if I remember aright, he made his first appearance in his friar's habit with his hair cut short, but not as yet shaved in the crown of his head. After a little space followed a mitred cardinal gaudily attired, and before him lay St. Francis almost prostrate, in order to be confirmed in his office. Soon after this he appears quite metamorphosed into a monk, his crown shorn, his habit black, and his loins girt with a knotted cord. Here he prays to our Saviour hanging on a cross, that the marks of the wounds in his hands, feet, and side, might be impressed on the same parts of his body. The prayer is granted; blood comes from the hands, feet, and side, and the saint with great devotion receives the impressions. This was represented by red waxen strings, reaching from those parts of the image to the corresponding parts of St. Francis's body. Upon this he begins to do wonders; and therefore in a little while he was carried along, holding up a house which was just falling. This miracle they say was performed (if my information be true) at Madrid, but the particulars of its history I have forgotten. At length the father dies, and is brought forth lying in his grave. But lo! the briers and nettles under which he lay are turned into fine and fragrant flowers. After this he is borne along upon a bier covered with a silver pall, and four friars lamenting over him. He then appears for the last time, but with an increase of power; for he was represented as drawing tormented people out of purgatory with his knotted cord, which, as you may well imagine, the poor souls catched at and took hold of very eagerly. At length came a gorgeous friar under a splendid canopy, bearing in his hand a piece of the holy cross. After him followed two more little winged boys, and then a long train of fat and well-favoured Franciscans, with their *calceis fenestratis*, as Erasmus calls them; and so the procession ended. Methinks I hear you say, It is full time. And so say I—for as the sight itself disgusted me, so I am persuaded the bare narration of it, though ever so short, cannot be very pleasant to you, who I know abhor every thing that savours of superstition and idolatry. We will therefore take our leave of St. Francis, whose procession was in the day-time; but I must tell you it is only to inform you of another of a much more awful and shocking nature, which I saw afterwards by night. It was about ten o'clock, when being deeply engaged in conversation with my kind host, in came an Englishman, and told me in all haste, that he had seen a train of near two hundred penitents passing along, and that in all probability I might be gratified with the same sight, if I hastened to a place whither he would conduct me. I very readily obeyed the summons, and, as curiosity quickened my pace, we soon came up with some of those poor creatures, who were then making a halt, and kneeling in the street, whilst a friar from a high cross, with an image of our Lord crucified in his hand, was preaching to them and the populace, with great vehemence. Sermon being ended, the penitents who had already been preached to, went forwards, and several companies followed after with their respective preaching friars at their head bearing crucifixes. These they pointed to and brandished frequently, and the hearers as frequently beat their breasts and clapped their cheeks. At proper pauses they stopped and prayed; and one of them, more zealous than the rest, before the king's palace, sounded out the word *penitentia* through a speaking trumpet. The penitents themselves were clothed and covered all over with white linen vestments, only holes were made for their eyes to peep out at. All were barefooted, and all had long heavy chains fastened to their ancles, which, when dragged along the street, made a dismal rattling: but though alike in dress, yet in other respects there was great variety amongst them; for some carried great stones on their backs, and others dead men's bones and sculls in their hands. Some bore large and seemingly very heavy crosses upon their shoulders, whilst others had their arms extended quite wide, or carried a bow full of swords with the points downwards. Most of them whipped and lashed themselves, some with cords, and others with flat bits of iron. It being a moonshine night I could see them quite well; and, indeed, some of them struck so hard that I perceived that their backs (left bare on purpose to be slashed) were quite red, and swollen very much by the violence and repetition of the blows. Had my dear friend been there, he would have joined with me in saying, that the whole scene was horrible—so horrible, that, being informed it was to be continued till morning, I was glad to return from whence I came, about midnight. Had you been with me, I know you would have joined in praising and gratefully adoring the Lord of all lords, not only for the great wonder of the Reformation, but also for that glorious deliverance wrought out for us in stopping of our late unnatural rebellion. Oh with what a mighty Spirit and power from on high, must Luther, Calvin, Melancthon, Zuinglius, and those glorious Reformers, be necessarily endued, who dared first openly to oppose and stem such a torrent of superstition and spiritual tyranny!— And what gratitude owe we to him, who, under God, was instrumental in saving us from the return of such spiritual slavery, and such blind obedience to a papal power! To have had a cardinal for our king—a cardinal, if not born, yet from his infancy nursed up, at Rome—a cardinal, one of whose sons is advanced to the same ecclesiastical dignity, and both under the strongest obligations to support the interest of that church whose superstitions, as well as political state principles, they have sucked in and imbibed even from their infancy. But, blessed be God, the snare is broken, and we are delivered. Oh for protestant practices to be added to protestant principles! Oh for an obediential acknowledgment to the ever blessed God for our repeated deliverances! But alas! pardon me, my dear friend, I stop to weep—adieu—I cannot enlarge, but leaving you to guess from what source my tears flow, I must hasten to subscribe myself, ———.

" Providence still detains us at Lisbon, and therefore I know you will be inquiring what more news from thence? Truly, as extraordinary as ever—for I have now seen the solemnities of a Holy Thursday, which is a very high day in this metropolis,

and particularly remarkable for the grand illuminations of the
churches, and the king's washing twelve poor men's feet.—
Through the interest of a friend I got admittance into the gallery where the ceremony was performed. It was large, and
hung with tapestry; one piece of which represented the humble
Jesus washing the feet of his disciples. Before this, upon a
small eminence, sat twelve men in black. At the upper end,
and several other parts of the gallery, were sideboards with gold
and silver large basons and ewers most curiously wrought; and
near these a large table covered with a variety of dishes, all
cold, set off and garnished after the Portuguese fashion. Public
high mass being over, his Majesty came in attended with his
nobles, who seemed to me to look like so many Roman senators.
The very act of washing the feet I did not get in time enough
to see; but that being ended, several of the young noblemen
served up the dishes to the king's brother and uncles; these
again handed them to his Majesty, who gave (I think) twelve of
them in all to each poor man. Every thing was carried on with
a great deal of decency and good humour. The young noblemen served very cheerfully, their seniors looked quite pleased,
and the king and his royal relations behaved in a very polite,
easy manner. Upon the whole, though, as you may easily guess,
it was not an exact copy of the tapestry, yet as the poor men's
clothes and food, when sold, came to about ten moidores, and as
there was little mixture of superstition in it, I cannot say but I
was as well pleased with my morning's entertainment as with
any thing I had met with since my arrival. I believe the whole
took up near two hours. After dinner we went to see the
churches, but the magnificence and sumptuousness of the furniture, on this occasion, cannot well be expressed. Many of them
were hung with purple damask trimmed with gold. In one of
them there was a solid silver altar of several yards circum-
ference, and near twelve steps high; and in another a gold one,
still more magnificent, of about the same dimensions. Its basis
was studded with many precious stones, and near the top were
placed silver images in representation of angels. Each step
was filled with large silver candlesticks, with wax tapers in
them, which, going up by a regular ascent till they formed them-

selves into a pyramid, made a most glittering and splendid
blaze. The great altars also of the other churches were illuminated most profusely, and silver pots of artificial flowers with
a large wax taper between each, were fixed all round several of
them. Between these were large paintings in black and white,
representing the different parts of our Saviour's passion. And,
in short, all was so magnificently, so superstitiously grand, that
I am persuaded several thousands of pounds would not defray
the expenses of this one day. Go which way you would, nothing was to be seen but illuminations within and hurry without. For all persons, the crowned heads themselves not excepted, are obliged on this day to visit seven churches or altars,
in imitation, as is supposed, of our Lord's being hurried from
one tribunal to another before he was condemned to be hung
upon the cross. I saw the queen pass by in great state to visit
three of them. Velvet cushions were carried before her Majesty, and boards laid along the streets for herself and retinue
to walk upon. Guards attended before and behind, and thousands of spectators stood on each side to gaze at them as they
passed along. Being desirous of seeing the manner of their entrance, we got into the last church before they came. It was
that of St. Domingo, where was the gold altar before mentioned,
and at which her Majesty and train knelt about a quarter of an
hour. All the while the Dominican friars sung most sur-
prisingly sweet. But as I stood near the altar over against the
great door, I must confess my very inmost soul was struck with
a secret horror, when, upon looking up, I saw over the front of
the great window of the church the heads of many hundred
Jews, painted on canvass, who had been condemned (by what
they call the Holy Inquisition) and carried out from that church
to be burnt. Strange way this of compelling people to come
in ! Such was not thy method, O meek and compassionate
Lamb of God ! Thou camest not to destroy men's lives, but
to save them. But bigotry is as cruel as the grave. It knows
no remorse. From all its bitter and dire effects, good Lord, deliver us. But to return to the queen—having performed her
devotions she departed, and went in a coach of state, I believe,
directly from the church to her palace, and without doubt suffi-

ciently fatigued. For, besides walking through the streets to the several churches, her Majesty also, and the princesses, had been engaged in waiting upon and washing the feet of twelve poor women, in as public a manner as the king. In our walk home we met his Majesty with his brother and two uncles, attended only with a few noblemen in black velvet, and a few guards without halberts. I suppose he was returning from his last church, and, as one may well imagine, equally fatigued with his royal consort and daughters. When church and state thus combine to be nursing fathers and nursing mothers to superstition, is it any wonder that its credit and influence is so diffusive among the populace? O Britain! Britain! hadst thou but zeal proportionable to thy knowledge, and inward purity adequate to the simplicity of thy external worship, in what a happy and god-like situation wouldst thou be! Here I could weep again. Again I leave you to guess the cause; and if I can send you one more letter of a like nature, before we leave this place, it is all you must expect from, ———.

" After the news sent you in my last, I thought our Lisbon correspondence would entirely have been put a stop to. For upon returning to my lodgings, (as weary, I believe, as others that had been running from church to church all day,) word was sent me, that our ship would certainly sail next morning. This news, I own, was not altogether agreeable to me, because I wanted to see the conclusion of the Lent solemnities. However, I made ready; and having despatched my private affairs the over-night, was conducted very early in the morning, by my kind host, down to Bellem, where the ship lay. We parted. The wind promised to be fair; but dying away, I very eagerly went ashore once more. But how was the scene changed! Before, all used to be noise and hurry: now, all was hushed and shut up in the most awful and profound silence. No clock or bell had been heard since yesterday noon, and scarce a person was to be seen in the street all the way to Lisbon. About two in the afternoon we got to the place where (I had heard some days ago) an extraordinary scene was to be exhibited. Can you guess what it was? Perhaps not. Why, then, I will tell you. ' It was the crucifixion of the Son of God, represented partly by dumb im-

ages, and partly by living persons, in a large church belonging
to the convent of St. De Beato.' Several thousands crowded
into it; some of which, as I was told, had been waiting there
ever since six in the morning. Through the kind interposition
and assistance of a protestant or two, I was not only admitted
into the church, but was very commodiously situated to view
the whole performance. We had not waited long before the
curtain was drawn up. Immediately, upon a high scaffold, hung
in the front with black baize, and behind with silk purple damask laced with gold, was exhibited to our view an image of the
Lord Jesus at full length, crowned with thorns, and nailed on a
cross, between two figures of like dimensions, representing the
two thieves. At a little distance, on the right hand, was placed
an image of the Virgin Mary, in plain long ruffles, and a kind
of widow-weeds. Her veil was purple silk, and she had a wire
glory round her head. At the foot of the cross lay, in a mournful, pensive posture, a living man, dressed in woman's clothes,
who personated Mary Magdalene; and not far off stood a young
man, in imitation of the beloved disciple. He was dressed in a
loose green silk vesture, and bob-wig. His eyes were fixed on
the cross, and his two hands a little extended. On each side,
near the front of the stage, stood two sentinels in buff, with
formidable caps and long beards; and directly in the front stood
another yet more formidable, with a large target in his hand.
We may suppose him to be the Roman centurion. To complete
the scene, from behind the purple hangings came out about
twenty little purple-vested winged boys, two by two, each bearing a lighted wax taper in his hand, and a crimson and gold cap
on his head. At their entrance upon the stage they gently
bowed their heads to the spectators, then kneeled and made
obeisance, first to the image on the cross, and then to that of
the Virgin Mary. When risen, they bowed to each other, and
then took their respective places over against one another, on
steps assigned for them at the front of the stage. Opposite to
this, at a few yards' distance, stood a black friar, in a pulpit hung
in mourning. For a while he paused, and then, breaking silence, gradually lifted up his voice, till it was extended to a
pretty high pitch, though, I think, scarce high enough for so

large an auditory. After he had proceeded in his discourse about a quarter of an hour, a confused noise was heard near the front great door; and, upon turning my head, I saw four long-bearded men, two of which carried a ladder on their shoulders, and after them followed two more with large gilt dishes in their hands, full of linen, spices, &c.   These (as I imagined) were the representatives of Nicodemus and Joseph of Arimathea. On a signal given from the pulpit, they advanced towards the steps of the scaffold.   But upon their very first attempting to mount it, at the watchful centurion's nod, the observant soldiers made a pass at them, and presented the points of their javelins directly to their breasts.   They are repulsed.   Upon this a letter from Pilate is produced.   The centurion reads it, shakes his head, and, with looks that bespoke a forced compliance, beckons to the sentinels to withdraw their arms.   Leave being thus obtained, they ascend; and having paid their homage, by kneeling first to the image on the cross, and then to the Virgin Mary, they retired to the back of the stage.   Still the preacher continued declaiming, or rather (as was said) explaining the mournful scene.   Magdalene persists in wringing her hands, and variously expressing her personated sorrow; whilst John (seemingly regardless of all besides) stood gazing on the crucified figure. By this time it was near three o'clock, and therefore proper for the scene to begin to close.   The ladders are ascended, the superscription and crown of thorns taken off, long white rollers put round the arms of the image, and then the nails knocked out which fastened the hands and feet.   Here Mary Magdalene looks most languishing, and John, if possible, stands more thunder-struck than before.   The orator lifts up his voice, and almost all the hearers expressed concern by weeping, beating their breasts, and smiting their cheeks.   At length the body is gently let down.   Magdalene eyes it, and, gradually rising, receives the feet into her wide-spread handkerchief; whilst John, (who hitherto stood motionless like a statue,) as the body came nearer the ground, with an eagerness that bespoke the intense affection of a sympathizing friend, runs towards the cross, seizes the upper part of it into his clasping arms, and, with his disguised fellow-mourner, helps to bear it away.   And here the play should end,

was I not afraid you would be angry with me if I did not give
you an account of the last act, by telling you what became of the
corpse after it was taken down.   Great preparations were made
for its interment.   It was wrapped in linen, and spices, &c. and
being laid upon a bier richly hung, was afterwards carried round
the churchyard in grand procession.   The image of the Virgin
Mary was chief mourner, and John and Magdalene, with a whole
troop of friars with wax tapers in their hands, followed after.
Determined to see the whole, I waited its return; and in about
a quarter of an hour the corpse was brought in, and deposited
in an open sepulchre prepared for the purpose; but not before
a priest, accompanied by several of the same order in splendid
vestments, had perfumed it with incense, sung to and kneeled
before it.   John and Magdalene attended the obsequies; but the
image of the Virgin Mary was carried away and placed upon the
front of the stage, in order to be kissed, adored, and worshipped
by the people.   This I saw them do with the utmost eagerness
and reverence.   And thus ended this Good Friday's tragi-
comical, superstitious, idolatrous droll.   A droll which, whilst
I saw, as well as now whilst I am describing it, excited in me a
high indignation.   Surely, thought I, whilst attending on such
a scene of mock devotion, if ever, now is the dear Lord Jesus
crucified afresh; and I could then, and even now, think of no
other plea for the poor beguiled devotees, than that which suffering Innocence put up himself for his enemies, when actually
hanging upon the cross, viz. ' Father, forgive them, for they
know not what they do.'   There was but one thing wanting to
raise one's resentment to the highest pitch, and that was for
one of the soldiers to have pierced the side of the image upon
the cross.   This, in all probability, you have heard hath actually
been done in other places, and, with a little more art, might, I
think, have been performed here.   Doubtless it would have
afforded the preacher as good, if not a better, opportunity of
working upon the passions of his auditory, than the taking down
the superscription and the crown of thorns, and wiping the head
with a blooded cloth, and afterwards exposing it to the view of
the people; all which I saw done before the body was let down.
But alas! my dear friend, how mean is that eloquence, and how

entirely destitute of the demonstration of the Spirit, and of a divine power, must that oratory necessarily be, that stands in need of such a train of superstitious pageantry to render it impressive! Think you, my dear friend, that the apostle Paul used or needed any such artifices to excite the passions of the people of Galatia, amongst whom, as he himself informs us, 'Jesus Christ was crucified, and evidently set forth?' But thus it is, and thus it will be, when simplicity and spirituality are banished from our religious offices, and artifice and idolatry seated in their room. I am well aware that the Romanists deny the charge of idolatry; but after having seen what I have seen this day, as well as at sundry other times since my arrival here, I cannot help thinking but a person must be capable of making more than metaphysical distinctions, and deal in very abstract ideas indeed, fairly to evade the charge. If 'weighed in the balances of the sanctuary,' I am positive the scale must turn on the protestant side. But such a balance these poor people are not permitted to make use of! Doth not your heart bleed for them? Mine doth, I am sure; and I believe would do so more and more, was I to stay longer, and see what they call their hallelujah and grand devotions on Easter day. But that scene is denied me. The wind is fair, and I must away. Follow me with your prayers, and believe me to be, ————."

CHAPTER XXI.

ALTHOUGH Whitefield derived neither the good nor the evil from the Moravians that Wesley did, his personal history would be incomplete, and his Times would lack a slight feature of their true character, were I to pass over his connexion with that singular people,—then so *ill* represented, in some respects, in London. It is, however, with great reluctance I touch the subject. I am dissolving (so far) a *charm,* which has often soothed and cheered me, when I have been soured or saddened by looking too closely at human nature. Oh, what have the tyrants of conscience to answer for! Truly " oppression makes a wise man mad." Had the first quakers been free to follow the Lamb by the lamp of the New Testament, and to reject " *Roman* candles," they and their posterity might have been as useful to the church as they have been to the world. In like manner, had the Bohemian church not been deprived of Huss and Jerome, nor denounced for reading Wycliffe, the descendants of her martyrs might have had no startling singularities of sentiment or ceremony. The Moravians were drawn into both, because their fathers were driven into unnatural and trying positions, which inevitably created fancies, and called forth rhapsodies.

Time, happily, has so pruned both the wild luxuriance and the worldly policy of Moravianism, that it is almost impossible to believe now, that Molther ever taught the doctrines, or Nitschmann ever sung the hymns, or Zinzendorff ever sanctioned the practices in London, which Whitefield and Wesley exposed. These things, however, ought not to be forgotten. Their memory is the safeguard against their recurrence. It is wanted too as *ballast*, by the Moravian church; just as all churches need to remember the blots upon their escutcheon. Dr. Southey says, " few religious communities may look back upon their history with so much satisfaction as the united brethren." This is true of their general history; but it is equally true that their *vagaries* in London did them no credit. These first alarmed, and then alienated, both Watts and Doddridge, as well as Whitefield and Wesley. Doddridge was right too in supposing, that " they produced the same sentiments in the archbishop of Canterbury." Potter could forgive much to a people whom he recognised as an " apostolical and episcopal church;" but he seems to have doubted eventually, whether Zinzendorff was elected their bishop, "*plaudente toto cœlesti choro.*" At least his arms were not so "open" to him as at first. And it was well for the Moravians, that good men both took and sounded an alarm, from the exposures made by Rimius. It taught them, as Dr. Southey well says, " to correct their perilous error in time;" and since, " they have continued not merely to live without reproach, but to enjoy in a greater degree than any other sect, the general good opinion of every other religious community." Both Wesley and Whitefield contributed not a little to this improvement by the influence they had over Ingham, Dellamotte, and Gambold, and by their writings. The manner in which Whitefield dealt with the subject will be best seen in his own letter to Zinzendorff.

He remonstrated thus with the Count, as the lord advocate of the UNITAS FRATRUM. " For these many years past I have been a silent, and I trust I can say, an impartial, observer of the progress and effects of Moravianism, both in England and America; but such shocking things have been lately brought to our ears, and offences have swelled to such an enormous bulk, that a real regard for my king and my country, and, if I am not greatly mistaken, a disinterested love for the ever-blessed Jesus, that King of kings, and the church which he hath purchased with his own blood, will not suffer me to be silent any longer.

" Pardon me, therefore, my Lord, if at length, though with great regret, as the Searcher of hearts knows, I am constrained to inform your Lordship, that *you*, together with some of your *leading brethren*, have been unhappily instrumental in misguiding many real, simple, honest-hearted christians; of distressing, if not totally ruining, numerous families; and introducing a whole farrago of superstitious, not to say idolatrous, fopperies into the English nation.

" For my own part, my Lord, notwithstanding the folio that was published (I presume under your Lordship's direction) about three years ago, I am as much at a loss as ever, to know what were the principles and usages of the ancient Moravian church; but if she was originally attired in the same garb, in which she hath appeared of late amongst many true-hearted, though deluded protestants, she is not that simple, apostolical church the English brethren were made to believe about twelve years ago. Sure I am, that we can find no traces of many of her present practices in the yet more ancient, I mean the primitive churches, and which we all know were really under an immediate and truly apostolical inspection.

" Will your Lordship be pleased to give me leave to descend to a few particulars? Pray, my Lord, what instances have we of the first christians walking round the graves of their deceased friends on Easter-day, attended with hautboys, trumpets, French horns, violins, and other kinds of musical instruments? Or where have we the least mention made of pictures of particular persons being brought into the first christian assemblies, and of candles being placed behind them, in order to give a transparent view of the figures? Where was it ever known, that the picture of the apostle Paul, representing him handing a gentleman and lady up to the side of Jesus Christ, was ever introduced into the primitive love-feasts?

" Or do we ever hear, my Lord, of incense, or something like it, being burnt for Paul, in order to perfume the room before he made his entrance among the brethren? Or can it be supposed that he, who, together with Barnabas, so eagerly repelled the Lycaonians, when they brought oxen and garlands, in order to sacrifice unto them, would ever have suffered such things to be done for him, without expressing his abhorrence and detestation of them? And yet your Lordship knows both these have been done for *you*, and suffered by *you*, without your having shown, as far as I can hear, the least dislike.

" Again, my Lord, I beg leave to inquire, whether we hear any thing in Scripture of elderesses or deaconesses of the apostolical churches seating themselves before a table, covered with artificial flowers, and against that a little altar surrounded with wax tapers, on which stood a cross, composed either of mock or real diamonds, or other glittering stones ?   And yet your Lordship must be sensible this was done in Fetter Lane chapel, for Mrs. Hannah Nitschman, the present general elderess of your congregation, with this addition, that all the sisters were seated, clothed in white, and with German caps ; the organ also illuminated with three pyramids of wax tapers, each of which was tied with a red riband ; and over the head of the general elderess, was placed her own picture, and over that *(horresco referens)* the picture of the Son of God.   A goodly sight, this, my Lord, for a company of English protestants to behold ! Alas ! to what a long series of childish and superstitious devotions, and unscriptural impositions, must they have been habituated, before they could sit silent and tame spectators of such an antichristian scene.   Surely, had Gideon, though but an Old Testament saint, been present, he would have risen and pulled down this, as he formerly did his father's altar.   Or had even that meek man Moses been there, I cannot help thinking, but he would have addressed your Lordship, partly at least, in the words with which he addressed his brother Aaron, ' What did this people unto thee, that thou hast introduced such superstitious customs among them ? '

" A like scene to this was exhibited by the single brethren, in a room of their house at Hatton Garden.   One of them, who helped to furnish it, gave me the following account.   The floor was covered with sand and moss, and in the middle of it was paved a star of different coloured pebbles, upon that was placed a gilded dove, which spouted water out of its mouth into a vessel prepared for its reception, which was curiously decked with artificial leaves and flags ; the room was hung with moss and shells.   The Count, his son, and son-in-law, in honour of whom all this was done, with Mrs. Hannah Nitschman, and Mr. Peter

Boehler, and some other labourers, were present. These were
seated under an alcove, supported by columns made of paste-
board, and over their heads was painted an oval, in imitation of
marble, containing the ciphers of Count Zinzendorff's family.
Upon a side table, was a little altar covered with shells, and on
each side of the altar was a bloody heart, out of or near which
proceeded flames. The room was illuminated with wax tapers,
and musicians placed in an adjacent apartment, while the company performed their devotions, and regaled themselves with
sweetmeats, coffee, tea, and wine. After this the labourers departed, and the single brethren were admitted in. I am told,
that most, if not all, of these leading persons were present also
at the celebration of Mrs. Hannah Nitschman's birth-day.

" But this is not all ; I have another question to propose to
your Lordship. Pray, my Lord, did any of the apostles or
leaders of the primitive churches, ever usurp an authority, not
only over people's consciences, but their properties also ? Or
draw in the members of their respective congregations to dispose of whole patrimonies at once, or to be bound for thousands
of pounds more than they well knew they were worth ? And
yet your Lordship knows this has been done again and again, in
order to serve the purposes of the brethren for several years
last past ; and that too, at, or very near the time, when, in order
to procure an act in their favour to go abroad, (which now appears to be rather a scheme to settle at home,) they boasted to
an English parliament, how immensely rich they were.

" Your Lordship cannot but be sensible, that at this present
time you stand indebted to sundry persons to the value of forty
thousand pounds sterling ; and unless some of your brethren
had agreed to stay six years for about twenty thousand pounds,
due to them ; (though after the expiration of that term, as they
have no security, in all probability they will be just where they
are now ;) and if the other creditors also, upon consideration of
some bonds given, and mortgages made for principal and interest, had not agreed to stay four years, for twenty-one thousand pounds more, many of the English brethren, who, out of I
know not what kind of infatuation, have not only given their all,
but have been bound for thousands more than they are able to

pay, must either have immediately become bankrupts, and thereby the creditors perhaps not have had a shilling in the pound, or have been obliged to shut up their shops, go to prison, or be turned out into the wide world, to the utter ruin of themselves and families.

" I have been told of a very singular expedient made use of by Mr. Peter Boehler, one of the brethren's bishops, in order to strengthen the faith and to raise the drooping spirits of Mr. William Bell, who hath been unhappily drawn in (with several others) to be one of their agents. It was this : It being Mr. Bell's birth-day, he was sent for from his house in Nevil's Alley, Fetter Lane ; but for a while, having had some words with Mr. Boehler, he refused to come : at length he complied, and was introduced into a hall, in the same alley, where was placed an artificial mountain, which, upon singing a particular verse, was made to fall down, and then behind it was discovered an illumination, representing Jesus Christ and Mr. Bell, sitting very near, or embracing each other ; and out of the clouds was also represented plenty of money falling round Mr. Bell and the Saviour. This story appeared to me so incredible at the first hearing, that, though I could not doubt the veracity of the relater, yet fearing he might be misinformed, I sent for him again, and he assured me, that Mr. Bell told this story himself some time ago in company, and a person of good reputation of that company related it to an acquaintance of mine. May God grant him and all others who have been undesignedly concerned, a more sure and stable prop for their faith, even his own word, in which he causes his people to trust ! Then, and not till then, even upon the greatest emergency, they may without any fanciful representations, boldly say, ' Who art thou, O great mountain ? before the Lord Jesus, our all-conquering Zerubbabel, thou shalt become a plain.'

" The distress and anguish of mind that hundreds have been involved in upon this very account, is, I believe, unspeakable. And the bare reflection upon it, whilst I am writing, makes my heart almost to bleed within me. Who, who, but themselves, my Lord, can tell the late perplexity of their minds, who have been already arrested, or obliged to break off their respective partnerships? Or what words can express the great concern which Mr. Freeman and Mr. Thomas Grace must have been necessarily under, when they found that bills had been drawn in their name, unknown to them, to the value of forty-eight thousand pounds? And how pitiable, my Lord, must the present circumstances of young Mr. Rhodes be, who, to stop a little of the above-mentioned gap, was prevailed on, (your Lordship knows by whom,) about eighteen months ago, to sell his estate of above four hundred pounds a year, and went or was sent off very lately, as I am assured, to France, (leaving a destitute mother behind him,) and only with twenty-five pounds, for the payment of which he left his watch, bureau, horse, and saddle!

" These are but a few instances, my Lord, amongst many, indeed, too, too many, that might be given. The brethren's agents, and those concerned with them, can best tell what horrid equivocations, untruths, and low artifices have been used, to procure money, at high interest, wherever it was to be had, in order to keep up the brethren's credit; and in that poor, lame manner, it hath been kept up for a considerable time. Was the whole scene to be opened, I believe every one would be of opinion, that such an ecclesiastical project never was heard of before in any part of his Majesty's dominions.

" Of this, my Lord, the Royal Exchange hath long since rung; and if the same part hath been acted abroad, how many families must have been ruined there, and how many more may yet be ruined, in order to fill up the present English chasm; and consequently, what loads of guilt must needs lie at the door of somebody! Surely, the Lord of all lords, whose eyes are like a flame of fire, and who requires truth in the inward parts, will one day or other visit for these things, by bringing to light the hidden things of darkness, and thereby making manifest the counsels of the heart!

" I need not inform your Lordship, that Babels are generally suffered to be built pretty high, before God comes down to confound the language of the builders. If knaves are employed, (as commonly they are,) God's honour is concerned to discover them. And if any of his own children are undesignedly drawn in, (which is frequently the case,) he, who hath promised not to suffer them to be tempted above what they are able to bear, will in mercy, some way or other, rebuke the tempter, and make a way for them to escape. It is true, this, in public concerns, may sometimes expose them to a little worldly contempt, and for a while they may seemingly be crushed under the rubbish of the fallen fabric, but even this shall work together for their good; and happy will it be for them, if, after all, they at length learn this important lesson, ' That it is dangerous, upon any pretence whatsoever, to go from the written word, or give up their consciences to the guidance of any man, or body of men, under heaven.' This, your Lordship well knows, is what weak and unstable souls are too apt to do; and artful and designing men, who are fond of power, especially if naturally they are of an ambitious turn of mind, easily catch at the pleasing bait. But honesty, my Lord, will be found to be the best policy after all; and therefore, God forbid that any who call themselves the followers of the Lamb, should glory in any thing save the cross of Christ.

"At present, I shall add no more, but earnestly say Amen, to that part of the brethren's litany, however exceptionable in other respects, ' From untimely projects, and from unhappily becoming great, keep us, our good Lord and God!'"

This controversy had one effect, which Whitefield did not anticipate, nor can I fully explain; it led Cennick to quit him, and to go over to the Moravians : a proof, however, that the Moravians as a body were not perverted by their leaders. A large party went over with Cennick on this occasion; amongst whom was Mrs. Greenfield, one of Queen Caroline's ladies. She is the person called in Whitefield's Letters, " one of Cæsar's household." He visited her at St. James's Palace, and found her " *ready to show out.*" Indeed, she had ; for the palace was then *ringing* about her. But whilst he thought she would make a glorious martyr, if she stood firm, he saw the peril of her position, and said to her friend Lady Huntingdon, " Till Mrs. Greenfield can meet with company really in earnest, the closer she keeps to her God and her book the better." She retired from the court on a pension ; and though she joined the Moravians, she continued to correspond with Whitefield, and to hear him at the house of the Countess. She also parted with her favourite servant, to furnish the Tabernacle house in Bristol with a suitable housekeeper. I ought to add, that Whitefield's letter to Zinzendorff " cured many of the fopperies and faults it exposed."

CHAPTER XXII.

WHITEFIELD's former visits to America, although not unwelcome to her spiritual churches, were, in some measure, unsought for by them, as churches. I mean, he consulted his own sense of duty, and the interest of his orphan-house, and the urgency of private friends, rather than public opinion, on either side of the Atlantic. On the present occasion, besides his ordinary reasons for ranging America, he had many pressing invitations " to cross-plough " his old grounds, and to water where he had planted. He had also a *home* reason. He wished to come back upon England and Scotland again, in the power of an *American* unction; a savour he had found to be " of life unto life," in all his movements through his native land. Hence he said on his voyage, " After a short tour through America, I hope to see my native country, and begin to *begin* to ramble after poor sinners again." It was there he learnt to range, and there he discovered how much he *could* range, as well as how much good ranging did; and therefore he was unwilling to forget the lesson. And no wonder. Had he not hunted in the American woods and wilds, he would not have done nor dared what he attempted at home. Indeed, every foreign place was a school, where he studied for home. And he was an *apt* scholar. It must have been a strange place indeed, where Whitefield could pick up nothing useful. Every where his maxim was, " I would fain be one of Christ's *bees,* and learn to extract honey from every flower ;"—whilst every where his feeling was, " Alas, I am a *drone,* and deserve to be stung out of God's hive."

He arrived in safety with his orphans at Bethesda, after an
easy voyage; and found himself at the head of a family of a
hundred and six members, "black and white," all dependent
upon his personal efforts and influence. But he had no fears.
He regarded his charge as a stewardship of Providence, and
hoped and begged accordingly, nothing doubting. Having
arranged his household, he started to his work, and traversed
Carolina. It was now high summer; and besides the oppressive
heat, "great thunders, violent lightnings, and heavy rains,"
frequently beat upon him as he journeyed from town to town;
but his health improved and his spirits rose, as he advanced.
One reason of this was that he chiefly travelled by night. " In
spite of thunder, lightning, rain, and heat, God is pleased," he
says, " to hold my soul in life, and to let me see his glorious
work prosper in my unworthy hands." One part of this prosperity was, the conversion of a clergyman, and the prospect of
a faithful successor to Smith at Charleston—from *Bethesda!*
This was the first student sent forth from the orphan-house.
I can give no account of him : but he must have had considerable ministerial talent, to commend himself to Josiah Smith's
flock. The reader remembers *his* sermon on Whitefield's
character.

Having " fully preached the gospel " in the regions of Carolina, he went to New York and Philadelphia, and found at both
" prejudices removed, and a more effectual door than ever," for
labour. At this time, however, he seems to have lost his *horse;*
and thus to have been dependent upon his friends for convey-
ances. He had been so before, and remembered that neither
all horses nor all drivers were alike. To one of his former *whips*
he wrote, " You must bring a chaise ;—I have no horse ;—I will
once more venture your throwing me down." This was on the
way to Philadelphia. There he was thrown down suddenly, but
not from a chaise. He was seized " with a violent *cholera mor-
bus*," and soon brought to the gates of death. He had, he said,
" all his cables out, ready to cast *anchor* within the port " of
eternity: but he was soon " at sea again ;" although only able to
preach once a day, for some time. When he was himself again,
and looked at the " glorious range for hunting in the American
woods," he was at a loss what hand to go to : " Affection, in-

tense affection, cries aloud, Away to New England, *dear* New England, directly.   Providence, and the circumstances of the southern provinces, point directly to Virginia."   Whilst thus undecided, he visited his old friend Governor Belcher, and found him an improved and ripening pilgrim, now willing to depart and be with Christ.   The venerable governor enjoyed this visit much ; and found it as conducive to his own peace, as his patronage and *state-coach* had formerly been to Whitefield's popularity. It was now the New Jersey *commencement,* and the president and trustees of the college presented Whitefield with the degree of M. A.   He was pleased with this mark of their respect from the senate : but much more pleased with the synod of ministers.   " I was much refreshed," he says, " with the company of the whole synod : such a number of simple-hearted, united ministers, I never saw before.   I preached to them several times, and the great Master of assemblies was in the midst of us."

By their counsel he determined to visit New England first, and to return through Virginia to Georgia ; a circuit of about " two thousand miles ;" but not at all intimidating to him.   On looking at it he said, " The Redeemer's strength will be *more* than sufficient."   President Burr accompanied him to New England, and saw at Boston, morning after morning, three or four thousand people hanging in breathless silence on the lips of the preacher, and weeping silent tears.   Whitefield himself calls it " a lovely scene," and says, he " *never* saw a more effectual door opened for the gospel."   " Sinners have been awakened, saints quickened, and enemies made at peace with me. Grace, grace !   Surely my coming here was of God !   Convictions *do* fasten, and many souls are comforted."   Such was the crowd at the early sermons, that he had to get in at the *windows* of the chapels, in order to reach the pulpit.   In a letter to the Countess, he says, " At Boston the tide ran full as high as ever your Ladyship knew it at Edinburgh, or in any part of Scotland."

Before leaving Boston he heard with unspeakable satisfaction, that his friend Habersham was appointed secretary to the new governor of Georgia.   " I wish you joy," he wrote to him, " of your new honour.   May the King of kings enable you to discharge your trust as becomes a good patriot, subject, and christian. You have now a call, I think, to retire from business, and to give up your time to the public." His complete triumph in Boston, opened for him " a wider and wider door " all around. He hardly knew where to go first, or how to go fast enough, in order to meet the public demand. He seems on one occasion to have let down, or over-ridden his horse, in his haste ; but he knew the owner ; obtained another; and sent word, " I left the horse a little lame at Long Island, with one who is called *Saint* Dick. All hail such reproach."

On his journey northward, he was able to preach twice or thrice every day : and his success will be best judged from his own account, for he never speaks strongly without strong reason. " What have I seen? Dagon falling every where before the ark ; enemies silenced, or made to own the finger of God; and the friends of Jesus triumphing in his glorious conquests. A *hundredth* part cannot be told. We had scarce one *dry* meeting." When he came near to Portsmouth, the end of his northern boundary, he was overwhelmed with humility as well as joy, by the cavalcade which came out to meet and welcome him. He says of them, they " were too many ;" and of the whole expedition so far, " It seems to me the *most* important one I was ever engaged in."

He now turned back, " to preach all the way to Georgia ;" a journey of sixteen hundred miles. This had no terrors to him. He called it " a ride," and said, " *Nil desperandum, Christo duce, auspice Christo.*" Little, I regret to say, is to be found in either his memoranda or letters to illustrate this ride, except proofs that many of his hearers must have ridden forty or fifty miles, in order to reach the line of his itineracy. From the manner also in which he was received at every town, and from the multitudes who assembled, it is evident that great exertions had been made to prepare them for his coming, and to enable him to keep his appointments. This throws no small light upon the influence he now had in America. It was felt to be a privilege every where, to forward him on his mission, " after a godly sort," and to *telegraph* the wilderness before him : and rich and poor answered the signals ; churches and chapels opened to them.

When he reached Charleston, he had the pleasure of seeing the student from Bethesda ordained there. It does not appear whether he took any part in the ordination, or not. He merely says, that it was solemn. He was not less pleased, however, on this occasion, to find that one of the *players* of Charleston had been " snatched as a brand from the burning."

His health failed again now. His old vomitings returned with violence, and his spirits sunk with his strength. He, therefore, embarked for England, in the fond hope that the voyage would recruit him for his " Father's business ;"—for which, he says, " I am a poor pilgrim, willing to give up all that is near and dear to me on this side eternity ! "

This brief chapter is merely preparatory to one on the same subject. Whitefield's influence in America would, however, fill a volume ; were it traced in all its bearings and on-goings, from the first rousing of her churches, down through the progress of her revivals. This cannot, perhaps, be done by any British writer. Indeed, it would be imprudent to attempt the task on this side of the Atlantic. We do not know enough of the men who caught and carried on the influence which Whitefield's ministry had upon the public mind ; to tell where their influence began, or where his ended. We should thus be for ever in danger of ascribing too much to him, and too little to them. We see only the mighty impulses which he gave ; and not the men nor the measures by which they were turned to immediate account, or transmitted to posterity. For, after all, they were but *impulses* on the public mind. They were, indeed, many, and mighty, and good, and unparalleled : and just because they were all this, there must have been *much* of this goodness and greatness about the agency which wrought with them and by them. The " *action* taken upon them," (to use an Americanism,) was one chief cause of their extensive and enduring usefulness. I have not dared, therefore, to bring together the proofs of Whitefield's influence in America, which might be collected and embodied from the results of all his visits : but have simply given illustrations of it from *two* of them ; and these, perhaps, not the most influential.

CHAPTER XXIII.

" On his return from America, the first thing he took notice of," says Gillies, "was the success of religion in his native country." He was delighted to find " the poor methodists as lively as ever; the gospel preached with power in many churches; some fresh ministers almost every week determining to know nothing but Jesus Christ, and him crucified; and many at *Oxford* awakened to the knowledge of the truth."

Almost the first thing he did on his arrival, was, to use his influence with the Marquis of Lothian, for a *diploma* to his friend President Burr of New Jersey. His Lordship applied to the university of Edinburgh; and the senate consented at once; requiring only " an account of Mr. Burr's literature." This Whitefield sent to the Marquis; assuring him, that the favour done to the president would " endear " his Lordship to " the good people in America." I suppose the degree of D. D. was sent, seeing it was thus readily promised: it is not noticed, however, in the " American Biographical Dictionary." There, the president is styled *Mr.* Burr, to the end of the chapter. How is this? Was the diploma lost, or not sent out? Or, was the president too modest to adopt the title? I put this question, because all the American diplomas, which are not acknowledged in this country, are neither lost nor unappreciated. They are not all used; but none of them are lightly esteemed by their possessors. They never can be so, unless the future issue of degrees becomes promiscuous: and America will surely respect herself too much to permit this.

Whitefield had at the Tabernacle, on his return, what he

calls "*golden seasons :*" but by this time there were other clergymen in London, who preached the gospel faithfully ; and as that was the only thing he cared for, it made, he says, his " call to go *abroad* still more clear." Indeed, so little did he like London as a sphere of labour, and so much did he judge of spheres by their destitution, that he wished to return to America this year, without ranging England or Scotland. Hence he says, " Methinks I could set out for America to-morrow, though I have not yet entered upon my country range." *Lett.* 1534.

But if he loved America most, England loved herself more, and drew him with " the cords of love," into Gloucestershire and Bristol again. He went also to open the Norwich Tabernacle, at the request of the Countess ; and there he so turned the tide out of the Wesleyan channels, that he deemed it necessary to apprize his friend Wesley of the fact, and to assure him that there were no *party* designs on foot. At first, and for a long time, the Norwich Tabernacle was distinguished amongst the Countess's chapels, as one of the most promising. In 1777, the Hon. Walter Shirley spent some time at it, and had eight hundred communicants in fellowship. He said of them, " Their experience, lives, and conversation are so excellent, that there is nothing like it in the whole kingdom." This once flourishing place the *trustees* have managed to break up. In 1836, the great body of the congregation retired to another sanctuary.

When Whitefield returned to London, he was *goaded* by not a few, to engage in controversy with the Wesleys again. His measures at Norwich seem to have been misrepresented to them. Instead, however, he preferred to wait until he could converse with Wesley " face to face." " I have no time for controversy," he says. He redeemed time, however, at this crisis, to write a grateful letter to his old tutor at Oxford ; begging his prayers, and blessing him for his instructions and counsels.

At this time, the encroachments of the French upon the British colonies in America, awakened his jealousy. He saw more than civil liberty at stake. He trembled for the ark of God. Accordingly, when he heard that his old friend Colonel Pepperell was in the field again to resist the enemy, he wrote to Lady P. an inspiring letter ; and one to the colonel, challenging

him to meet him often at the throne of grace, in prayer for success against " popish tyranny and arbitrary power." In like
manner, when he set out on his northern tour, he carried this
subject with him, like his shadow, through Yorkshire and Lancashire. "At this time," he says, " next to Jesus, my king and
country were upon my heart. I hope I shall always think it my
bounden duty, next to inviting sinners to the blessed Jesus, to
exhort my hearers to exert themselves against the first ap-
proaches of popish tyranny. Oh that we may be enabled to pray
and watch against antichrist in our *hearts;* for there, after all,
lies the most dangerous man of sin."

With all his partiality, indeed love, to Leeds, Whitefield was
sadly disconcerted there, when he found that his friends, without his knowledge, had built a large chapel. He saw at a
glance that it would create an " awful separation amongst the
societies ;" and lost no time in writing off to Wesley, that they
might try to prevent a breach. Both the plan and the spirit
of this undertaking so vexed him, that he exclaimed, " Oh
this self-love—this self-will—*is the devil of devils.*" This he
wrote to Lady Huntingdon; a proof that *party* was not their
object.

During two months, he preached twice or thrice a day, to
still greater numbers than before; inviting them to Christ, and
" exhorting them to pray for King George, and the dear friends
in America." On his return to London, he heard that the
American ladies were making the soldiers' *coats;* and he wrote
off immediately to urge his own female friends there, to be
" some of the most active in this labour of love."

Notwithstanding his immense labours on this tour, he grew
fat: but it was disease, not strength. Sore throat set in, and
was followed by an inflammatory quinsey, which assumed almost
a fatal aspect. One physician prescribed " silence and warmth ;"
and he promised to be " very obedient." He was so for a few
days. Then another physician prescribed a " *perpetual* blister ;"
this proposal roused him, and he *soon* tried his old remedy,—
" perpetual preaching." It was, of course, painful; but he said,
" When this grand catholicon fails, it is all over with me." In
this, he judged aright of his own constitution.

Whilst compelled to take *" the medicine of silence,"* the sad news of the earthquake at Lisbon arrived. At the time, it was doubtful whether death or life would be the issue of the quinsy: but he forgot his own sufferings, when told of the public calamity: " Blessed be God," he said, " I am ready ; I know that my Redeemer liveth. Oh that all in Portugal had *known* this! Then, an earthquake would only be a *rumbling* chariot, to carry the soul to God. Poor Lisbon! how soon are thy riches and superstitious pageantry swallowed up!" One almost regrets that Whitefield was unable to preach on this catastrophe. His vivid recollections of Lisbon, with his deep sense of its superstitions, would have enabled him to render the scene visible to the eye, as well as overpowering to the heart and conscience. This reflection just reminds me, that I have seen nothing in all his memoranda or letters, of his own well-known *heroism* at the time of the earthquake in London. He preached then in the parks at midnight to trembling thousands; and presented to them, in his own composure, a sublime illustration of " the peace which passeth all understanding." So did Charles Wesley at the Foundery. I quite agree with Watson, that it is difficult to say which was the nobler spectacle, Charles Wesley in the chapel, or Whitefield in the open air, at *midnight;* and both triumphing in God, whilst the earth shook and trembled! How could methodism fail to commend itself then to the public mind? Doddridge also signalized himself in London, by a sermon on the earthquake, which produced a *thrilling* effect amongst the dissenters. One of its fruits was, the formation of " The London Religious Book Society," by Benjamin Forfitt, Esq.; then a *British* though not a Foreign Bible Society; for its object was " to distribute Bibles, Testaments, and other books, *gratis,* among the poor, and particularly to send such books to the country." That this society originated from the sermon is evident from Forfitt's letter to the preacher : " If the world receives any advantage from this design, I think it is indebted, under God, to Dr. Doddridge for it; as the sacred fervour which animated your addresses from the pulpit, when last in town, kindled a spark of the same benevolence to the souls of men, in the breast of one, who could no longer retain his desires

2 G

of usefulness within the compass of his own small abilities, without exciting others to the same views." *Doddridge's Diary*, vol. iv. 192.

In the winter of 1755, Whitefield was applied to by his friends, who resided near the theatres, to preach regularly at a chapel they had licensed in Long Acre. It was hazardous ground ; but he did not hesitate a moment. He engaged to " preach twice a week, and read prayers." On the first night the chapel was overflowing. Hundreds went away, who could not get in. But he was soon disturbed. " The sons of Tubal and Cain," as he called the rioters, *serenaded* him every night with " bells, drums, clappers, and a *copper-furnace*," as a kettle-*drum*. These men were hired by subscription, although some of them were *soldiers*, to annoy and insult him. It became, therefore, necessary to arrest some of them as rioters. These the bishop of B—— sent for, and inquired of them, *where* Whitefield lived ? This surprised him ; for he thought his " *house pretty public*." This bishop, however, neither knew it, nor the law of the land ; for he sent him a *prohibition*, although the chapel was duly licensed, and unconsecrated.

Whitefield took the episcopal " bull by the horns at once ;" but with the greatest courtesy. He began by telling the bishop, " I thought I might *innocently* preach the love of a crucified Redeemer,—and, for His sake, loyalty to the best of princes, our dread sovereign King George, without giving any just offence to Jew or gentile,—much less to any bishop or overseer of the church of God." He ended by telling his Lordship, " I hope you will not look upon it as *contumacy*, if I persist in prosecuting my design, till I am more particularly apprized wherein I have erred. I trust the irregularity I am charged with (if called to answer for it) will appear justifiable to every lover of *English* liberty ;—and, what is *all* to me, be approved at the awful and impartial tribunal of the great Shepherd and Bishop of souls." Whilst waiting for an answer to this letter, Whitefield took up the case of the persecuted French protestants, and collected £80 for them at the Tabernacle. He had likewise the gratification of finding that one of the *subscribers* to the riots had been arrested by the gospel at Long Acre, and was now

weeping to see him. A once " confirmed deist," also, had become " as a little child."

The next time Whitefield preached in Long Acre, " all was
hushed ;" and he publicly ascribed the peace to the bishop's
intervention. It was only a pause in the storm. The rioters
contented themselves with making " odd noises " in an adjoining house, whilst a *scaffold* was preparing for the full flourish
and chorus of " such instruments of *reformation* " as " a copper-
furnace, bells, drums, clappers, marrow-bones and cleavers, and
large stones of a pound weight to break the windows." This
volley was planted and played off against the chapel, in the yard
of his Lordship's overseer, by some of his Lordship's vestry and
parishioners. This fact Whitefield told him, *Lett.* 1122, 1124 ;
and added, " C., one of your Lordship's *relations*, can acquaint
you with many more particulars ; and if you would be so good
as ride to C.'s house, you would see such a scaffold, (if not taken
down,) and such costly preparations for a noise upon it, that
must make the ears of all that shall hear it to tingle. I have
only one favour to beg of your Lordship, that you will send to
the gentlemen, as they are your parishioners, and desire them
henceforward to desist from such riotous and dangerous proceedings."—" Indeed, my Lord, it is more than noise. It deserves no milder a name than premeditated rioting."

His Lordship's answer to these appeals seems to have been
respectful to Whitefield, but useless to the occasion. He quoted
canons, instead of quelling the riots ; and threw doubts upon
the lease and license of the chapel, instead of displacing the
overseer of the parish. He had admonished some of the rioters,
whilst they merely *serenaded* the congregation ; but when they
" sadly wounded " some of the hearers, he sailed out of the difficulty upon a raft of canonical technicalities. But he mistook
his man, when he quoted canons and Scripture to stop Whitefield from preaching the gospel. He told him at once, that the
former were mere " *bruta fulmina*," which ought to be set at
defiance, like the *withs* of the Philistines, whenever they stood
in the way of " preaching against sin, the pope, and the devil."
That, he declared he would do, at all hazards of pains and penalties. And as to the apostolical canon against trenching on

2 G 2

another man's line of things, Whitefield reminded him of the welcome Philip Henry had from the vicar at Broad Oaks, to " throw a handful of seed," now and then, into his field ; " there is work enough for us both :" " this I humbly conceive is the case, not only of your Lordship, but of every minister's parish in London, and every bishop's diocess in England."

This faithful appeal to principle and conscience, did not prevent Whitefield from clearing up to his Lordship the legal claims of the chapel to protection. It had been regularly licensed in the Commons for a dissenting minister, Barnard ; and the certificate was in the hands of Culverwell. To these men he referred the bishop. The " unhallowed noises " went on, however, and lives were endangered by the stones thrown in at the windows ; one òf which nearly struck Whitefield himself. He now felt that private letters were merely *child's play*, when public liberty and safety were thus outraged ; and therefore he apprized the bishop, that he would throw the whole affair before the world. His Lordship thought, that this implied the pub-lication of his letters ; and claimed his privilege as a *peer*, to prevent it. He had no occasion. Whitefield was a *gentleman*, as well as a christian. He therefore made a final appeal to the bishop for protection, and told him he would trouble him no more.

The outrages went on, and became so flagrant, that *prosecution* seemed inevitable, and was contemplated. When the rioters heard of this, they threatened his life. One man went up to him in the Tabernacle pulpit ; and others sent him menacing letters, " denouncing a certain, sudden, unavoidable *stroke*, unless he desisted from preaching, and from pursuing the offenders by law." One of these letters he sent to the government ; who at once offered a reward and his Majesty's pardon to any one who would discover the writer. This pleased him of course ; but it also embarrassed him. " My greatest distress is," he said to Lady Huntingdon, " to act so as to avoid rashness on the one hand, and timidity on the other." For his *own* sake, he would not have stirred in it ; but viewing it as " the cause of civil and religious liberty," he wisely let the law take its course, at the hazard of his own life by assassination.

The preparations for bringing the matter into the King's Bench seem, however, to have stopped the evil.

The annoyances at Long Acre led him to plan Tottenham Court chapel. The sabbath after he had taken the ground, he obtained nearly £600 towards the building. He intended to put it under the protection of Lady Huntingdon; but found, on consulting Doctors' Commons, that "no nobleman could license a chapel" for himself, if the public were to be admitted to it. It was begun in May, and opened in November, 1756, and licensed "as the other houses" of prayer.

Having laid the foundation of Tottenham Court, and shown himself again at Long Acre to the enemy, Whitefield went to Bristol; but not to rest, although the cares and labours of the winter and spring had nearly worn out both his strength and spirits. Still he preached as usual in that quarter, and then returned to London "to keep *Pentecost* at Long Acre;" that no one might suspect him of having been "frightened away." After visiting Kent, he set out again for Scotland, preaching by the way to still greater audiences than ever. At Leeds and York, he found "many trophies of redeeming love," which had been won at former visits. Such was the effect of two sermons he now preached at Burstall, that "several hundreds rode eight miles" with him in the evening, "*singing* and praising God." *Lett.* 1146.

At Edinburgh, Whitefield received more than his usual welcome. Politicians now thronged to hear him, and the newspapers lauded him, for his spirit-stirring exposures of "popish tyranny and arbitrary power." He preached twice every day in the Orphan Hospital Park, and blended with almost every sermon rousing appeals to the protestantism, courage, and loyalty of the Scotch. He also pleaded the cause of the poor Highlanders at the close of one sermon, and collected £60 for them.

On his way back to London, he had at Leeds what he calls "the *Welch* night;" a meeting peculiarly solemn and refreshing. After it, he braced his nerves by a tour of *mountain-preaching*, in company with his friend Grimshaw. But it was now late in October, and as he found "these cold countries

bringing on his last year's disorder," and being (he says significantly) "grown *very* prudent," he came to London to open
Tottenham Court chapel. He had, however, another errand to
London. The new governor of Georgia had sent for him from
the north, to consult with him before sailing. He met him,
and was so much delighted, that he wrote off to Bethesda to
prepare them for a *state* visit. "Waited upon his Excellency,
and gave him, and all whom he pleases to bring, an invitation
to Bethesda. Dear Mrs. C. will make proper provision." This
was not all. He wanted to have *military* honours paid to the
governor. "Have you persons enough to *exercise* before him?
Can they receive him under *arms?*" Whitefield was thinking
of his intended COLLEGE, whilst thus ingratiating himself with
the governor.

At this time Cudworth, (no *antinomian,* as Moore ignorantly
calls him in his "Life of Wesley,") having embroiled Hervey
with Wesley, wrote a pamphlet against what he calls, "Some
Fundamental Mistakes in Whitefield's Sermons;" and as Hervey had allowed him "to put out and put in" whatever he
pleased in his letters to Wesley, he seems to have sought his
sanction to this attack on Whitefield also. Mason charged
him with saying, that Hervey offered to *preface* the pamphlet.
"This," Whitefield wrote to Hervey, "I as much believe, as
that I am at *Rome.*" Perhaps he was wrong! The pamphlet
sustained Hervey's own theory of *appropriating* faith, and set
Marshall against Whitefield; and so far Hervey may have
countenanced Cudworth, who was now the champion of "Theron
and Aspasio." Hervey's posthumous letters do not clear up this
fact. Indeed, Cudworth had too much to do with their publication to leave any light on the subject! It is, however,
curious, that from this time there is no letter of Whitefield to
Hervey, that I can find; nor any notice in others, of Hervey's
death. But the series of Whitefield's letters, about this time,
is very incomplete. He was now preaching *fifteen* times a week
in London, and daily occupied with the converts caught in his
"SOUL TRAP," as some Doctor designated the new chapel. He
welcomed the nickname, and prayed that "Whitefield's Soul
Trap" might catch many wanderers. It nearly caught poor

Shuter, the player. He always attended at this time, and brought many with him. Some of the nobility also became stated hearers, and took seats in the chapel.

In 1757, Whitefield planned his visit to Scotland to fall at the time of the General Assembly. But before leaving London, he placed the scheme of his college in the hands of Lord Halifax. He seems, on his arrival, to have attended the sittings of the Assembly; and Gillies says, " Perhaps a hundred ministers at a time attended his sermons." Thirty of the ministers honoured him with a *public* entertainment, and Lord Cathcart, his Majesty's commissioner, invited him to his own table. This was wormwood and gall to the high churchmen. Some of them had the insolence to remonstrate with Cathcart, on the impropriety of inviting Whitefield to meet the clergy! " It would give *offence*" to the church, they said! His Lordship spurned their paltry "overture with indignation." *Gillies.* Whitefield preached, he says, "just *fifty* times," on this visit: that was about as much in a month, as some of these clergymen did in a year! Such a *contrast* could hardly endear his company to half-day labourers.

At Glasgow, Whitefield preached in the High Church yard with equal success, and collected money for the poor. He then went to Ireland, and was stoned (as we have seen) on Oxmantown Green; not, he says, " for speaking against the papists in particular, but for exciting all ranks to be faithful to King Jesus, and to our dread sovereign King George ;" and because he prayed for the King of Prussia. In the other parts of Ireland he found hunting for souls to be " delightful sport when the heart is in it." The well-known *Edwards* of Leeds was converted under the sermon at Oxmantown Green. The Irish Liberty Boys used to call him " their *swaddling* John."

On his return to London, he found that the governor of Georgia had visited Bethesda, and promised to communicate his sentiments to Lord Halifax, " concerning its being enlarged into a college :" but the pressure of public affairs deterred him from applying to the government. There were bad news from America " about the fleet," and therefore he kept a fast day at his chapels.

His health now failed sadly. He was brought to live on the
" short allowance of preaching but once a day, and thrice on the
Sunday :" very short allowance for *him!* Once, however, he
broke through the restraint, and preached three times on the
success of the King of Prussia ; which, he says, " somewhat *recovered*" him, after he had been for a week at the gates of the
grave ! He was not able to attempt great things this winter.
Tottenham Court was, however, his *Bethel,* as he calls it ; and
as it was then surrounded by a " beautiful piece of ground," he
formed the plan of an almshouse for twelve "godly widows ;"
as " a standing monument that the methodists were not against
good works." This charity he soon carried into effect. His
thoughts, however, were not confined to home. Although
broken down in health and spirits by weakness and want of
rest, he watched the affairs of Prussia with intense interest, and
assured the German protestants, through Professor Franck, that
" we looked on their distresses as our own."

In the spring of 1758, he went into the west of England, and
visited Wales ; but he was so feeble, that he could not bear to
drive nor ride in a one-horse chaise. He was obliged to give
it up. The roads shook it, and it shook him nearly to pieces.
" Every thing," he says, " wearies this shattered bark now ! "
A friend interfered, and purchased a " close chaise" for him,
advancing the money until he could conveniently repay it. He
felt this kindness deeply, because by no other means could he
have itinerated. " I would not," he says, " lay out a single
farthing but for my blessed Master : but it is inconceivable
what I have undergone these three weeks. *I never was so before !* Oh for a *hearse* to carry my weary carcass to the wished-
for grave !" During all this tour, he was unable to sit up in
company even once ; yet he often preached to ten or fifteen
thousand people, and made their " tears flow like water from the
rock." His views of himself at this time were more than
usually humble ; and that is saying a great deal, to those who
have read his letters before this time. He said to Lady Huntingdon, " Oh I am sick—I am sick—sick in body ; but infinitely more so in mind, to see so much *dross* in my soul. Blessed be God, there is One who will sit as a refiner's fire, to purify

the sons of *Levi*. I write out of the *burning* bush.   Christ is
there! Christ is there!"

In the summer, he went north again; but was often ready
to turn back, through extreme weakness, even before he reached Northampton.   There, however, he "took the field" again.
Preaching in "*Bishop Bunyan's*" pulpit at Bedford, had rallied his spirits.   My eye rests at this moment upon a fragment
of that hallowed pulpit; and I hardly know whether it is most
associated in my mind with *Bunyan* in his strength, or with
Whitefield in his weakness.   This I know—I often see them
both leaning over it, and *reproving* me!

This year, Whitefield lost by death some of his earliest and
dearest friends; Hervey, President Burr, Governor Belcher,
and Jonathan Edwards.   Their death, and his own dying life,
made him long "to depart."   When he reached Edinburgh, he
expected death after "every sermon."   Yet he preached twice
a day in general, and that to immense auditories.   On one occasion he collected upwards of £200 for the orphan hospital.
He also preached thanksgiving sermons for the victories at
Crevelt, Cape Breton, and on the defeat of the Russians.   He
allowed nothing to escape him unimproved.   The *races* came on
at Edinburgh, and he consented to preach to the people, to "run
the race set before" them.

Well might he say, " This preaching is a *strange* restorative."
Still, it did restore him.   He was unable to visit private friends,
and was *adjourning* to see them until they met in heaven :
"but," he says, "*it will not do!*"   His health was, in fact, im-
proving by hard labour.   He therefore went to Glasgow, and
laboured harder than ever.   "I am put out to sea again," he
said; " and if to take some more *prizes*, I shall rejoice."   There
is good reason to believe that he took many in Scotland on this
occasion.   One thing which gave him additional influence
amongst the poor in Glasgow, was the zeal with which he pleaded the cause of the Highland families, whose fathers were serving
the king in America.

Whitefield never, perhaps, was more *overcome* than now in
parting from his friends.   He called the day of his farewell to
Scotland, the " *execution day;* " not, however, that he despaired

of seeing it again; but that his friends were like Paul's at
Miletus. In fact, he was almost *himself* again, for a little,
when he got into Yorkshire. Then, the idea of winter-
quarters was as painful as ever. He resolved, that nothing
but "change of weather should drive" him into them. He
could not help feeling, however, that he must soon retire
from the fields; and, therefore, he prayed, " Lord, prepare
me for winter trials : they are preparatives for an *eternal*
summer."

In 1759, Whitefield had the satisfaction to clear off all his
debts for the orphan-house. "Bethesda's God," he said, "lives
for ever, and is faithful and all-sufficient." He, therefore,
wished much to visit America; but he could not find supplies
to relieve him from his chapels in London. This pained him.
"Strange!" he says, "that nobody will relieve me, that I may
once more flee to America." No one did, and he returned to
Scotland. He became *fat* by the way, and his friends congratulated him on the prospect of a new lease of life; but he did
not flatter himself on becoming corpulent : "so did Darracott
a little before he died," he said. It is much to be regretted,
that *paintings* of Whitefield multiplied at this time. It cannot
be wondered at, because his friends could not but feel that his
life was precarious. Still, these portraits convey no idea of the
man who awed the multitude in Moorfields, and electrified the
nobility at Lady Huntingdon's. Some of them, especially Nathaniel Hone's, are faithful likenesses of Whitefield, when disease made him corpulent; and thus they are the Whitefield
our grandfathers knew : but not the Whitefield of *their* fathers.
I defy any one to associate the *emotions* of the old or of the new
world with the *pursy* parson of these figures ;—all of them
"born out of due season!" Whitefield was "*slender* in person," until he began to sink in strength. Indeed, were there not
reason to suppose that the *first* portrait of him was transmuted
by the trade into a *Hervey,* when "Theron and Aspasio" became
popular, I should have made it the frontispiece to this volume.
It, and the one I have adopted as the *medium* between the first
and last, are the portraits which Whitefield himself presented
to his friends. In regard to the others he said, he should *hate*

himself, if he were " the *sour*-looking creature" they represented him to be. *Jay's Life of Winter.*

I mention this here, because on his visit to Edinburgh this
year, (I think,) the governors of the orphan hospital had his
likeness taken, and hung up in the hall, as a mark of their
respect and gratitude to him, for the collections he made for
the charity. On this occasion, he collected £215 for the orphan
hospital.

What was thought of his *political* influence, at this time,
may be best told, perhaps, in the language of the newspapers.
One of them says, " The Rev. Mr. Whitefield has been preaching here and at Glasgow. He has preached nearly a *hundred*
times ; and yet his congregations were always increasing.
Whatever this be owing to—every body must judge for themselves : but it is certain that he continually exerted all his rhe-
toric in stirring up zeal for his God, his king, and his country,
in this time of danger ; and he seemed particularly pleased, as
were thousands more, that he had an opportunity of preaching
a thanksgiving sermon to a most thronged auditory, on account
of the glorious victory lately vouchsafed to Prince Ferdinand
over the French." *Edin. Aug.* 1759.

During this visit to the north, he had an opportunity of de-
monstrating his disinterestedness. A Miss Hunter, " a young
lady of considerable fortune, made a *full* offer of her estate,
both money and lands, amounting to about £7000." This gift
he promptly refused. Even when it was offered, not for his
own use, but for his orphan-house, he " absolutely refused" it.
Gillies says, he himself had the facts " from undoubted authority." There is a similar anecdote of Wesley, and it is
equally authentic. Indeed, they resembled each other very
much in their disinterestedness ; and left all their enemies as
silent on this subject, as Wesley did the Cumberland guide,
who asked him, what he *made* a year by so many preachings ?

Whitefield was not much pleased with the state of religion in
Scotland, on this visit. " It is a dead time indeed," here, he
says ; " little or no stirring among the dry bones. I preach—
and people flock—as usual : but Scotland is not London. The
Redeemer is doing wonders there. Every post brings fresh

good news." He solved this difference to himself by saying, " God's Spirit blows when and where it listeth ;" forgetting that his own spirit was a little too political, at the time. He did not suspect this ; but he felt that the " *languor* " of the north was infectious, and hastened back to London, lest it should " take hold " on his own " already too languid heart."

Much of this languor arose from sudden corpulency. That broke in upon him, he says, " like an *armed* man." Labour could not keep it down, nor abstinence check it. This both pained and alarmed him. " I dread a corpulent body. Oh that my heart may not wax gross at the same time ! I would fain not flag ; but rather begin to begin in the *latter* stages of my road." In this spirit he entered upon his winter campaign in London ; during which, he edited a new edition of Samuel Clarke's Bible, which, next to " holy Henry's," was his favourite Commentary. It well deserved to be so. It had the joint sanction of Owen, Baxter, Bates, and Howe. Calamy says, that the most eminent divines of the church of England also used it, and that " one of the highest rank recommended it to young divines at their ordination."

The care and commendation bestowed on Clarke's Commentary, by Whitefield, and the heartiness with which he identified himself in the preface, as " a small cedar," with " the tall cedars of our Lebanon," conciliated the dissenters. I mean,—they now saw that he had " one faith " with themselves and their fathers : and thus their fears of novelty and fanaticism were allayed. They now began to read and hear him by the light of a *Bartholomew* candlestick. This, and the intimacy he had formed with Dr. Gifford, whilst memorializing government on behalf of religious liberty in Ireland, gave him his *first* hold upon the confidence of the regular dissenters ; and it became a strong hold, and is likely to be lasting. The manner in which it became *strong*, is interesting. Whitefield made no advances to the dissenters, nor they to him. He was no dissenter in theory ; and, in practice, he set Lady Huntingdon against all proposals for dissenting chapels. But he did not set his *converts* against dissent. They were numerous in all quarters of England ; and thus many of them became *his* " epistles," in dissenting churches :

for, having to apply for sacramental fellowship, to pastors who examined both the creed and experience, as well as the moral character, of communicants, they revealed Whitefield's principles while stating their own; and thus brought *home* to the orthodox pastors and churches the fact, that God had delighted to honour Whitefield beyond all men. This truth had the *force* of truth, amongst all the evangelical nonconformists. Their churches were strengthened, and their hearts cheered, by the fruits of his ministry. The consequence has been, that, for half a century, his name has been associated and enshrined with the names of their real fathers, as if he had been *one* of them. No one would call him a dissenter; but all pious dissenters *feel* that he belonged to them : so much ascendency has love to the *image* of Christ, above party zeal, in their churches! And this feeling is the same towards the *catholic* stars of the establishment. It is not dissenters who distinguish, because of *rituals*, between Owen and Hughes, of the Bible Society; Carey and Heber, of India; Wilberforce and Philip, of Africa; Simeon of Cambridge and Morrison of China. The church herself, being the judge, must allow, that her best ministers never live unloved, nor die unwept, by the evangelical dissenters. What bishop, who loves the truth as it is in Jesus, is not as much loved for the truth's sake, by pious nonconformists, as by pious churchmen?

In the spring of 1760, Whitefield enlarged his new chapel, and celebrated the event by collecting upwards of £400 for the Prussian protestants, who had been stripped and peeled by the Russians at Costein and Niewmark. Two hundred of this sum he remitted to Franck; and part of it he kept, until he should hear "from the Professor himself," how it could be best applied. There is good reason to suppose, as Gillies says, that Whitefield received the thanks of the king of Prussia for this act. And yet this was the time chosen by the London stage, to caricature and insult him! I will not condescend to characterize "The MINOR." It is enough to say, that it was written by the miscreant Foote. He had mimicked Whitefield, and been applauded for it by the Long Acre rioters; and, therefore, Drury Lane employed him to bring out "The Minor." Madan remonstrated with Garrick against

the outrage ; but in vain. The fact is, " Whitefield's Soul Trap "
was thinning old Drury. The experiment was tried at Edinburgh also, to counteract his influence there. But there it failed.
On the second night of the performance, only ten women were
present. On the following sabbath, the principal clergyman
denounced the outrage on truth and decency. " How base and
ungrateful," said Baines, " is such treatment of the dead !
(Whitefield was then dead ;)—and that too, so very nigh to a
family of orphans, the *records* of whose hospital will transmit
Mr. Whitefield's name to posterity with honour, when the
memory of others will rot." The " *Hypocrite*," by Isaac Bicker-
steth, was an experiment of the same kind. Cantwell was *intended* to burlesque Whitefield. If George IV. did not know
this, when he commanded the comedy, and " roared and rolled
with immoderate laughter," at Liston in Mawworm, the public
knew it. *Preface to Cumberland's edition.* The play, however, can neither be acted nor published now, without disclaim-
ing, as " an absurd notion, that Cantwell was intended for Mr.
Whitefield,—that eloquent, pious, though eccentric man."
This sounds well : but the critic forgot, that both his author
and himself connect Cantwell and Mawworm with the Tabernacle and Tottenham Court. Whitefield himself cared very
little about the attacks of the theatre. When they began,
he merely said, " Satan is angry. All hail such contempt ! "

His autumnal tour in Yorkshire this year brought on a
severe cold, which hung upon him through the winter. At
times he was unable to write a letter. But a destructive fire at
Boston, and the increasing distress of the German protestants,
roused him, and he collected for them in one day nearly £600
in his own chapels. The effort was too much for his strength.
Gillies says, " he grew worse and worse, so that in April 1761,
he was brought to the gates of death." One cause of this was,
that he was much *shaken*, although not much hurt, on a journey
from Bristol, whilst thus weak. He was returning " post-haste "
to London, and once the chaise was overturned, and once he had
to leap out " though going very fast."

In the midst of these troubles, *Berridge* of Everton came to
his help : no acquisition, if Dr. Southey be the judge. He says,

" Berridge was buffoon as well as fanatic." The late Simeon of Cambridge did not think so, when he preached his funeral sermon. Clare Hall did not think him either, when it presented him to the vicarage of Everton. What is meant by his having been " lately *Moderator* of Cambridge," (as Whitefield calls him,) I do not know ; but the office is surely proof, that the officer was neither buffoon nor fanatic. One thing I do know ;—that the memory of Berridge is *fragrant* throughout and around Cambridgeshire. That would have been a *dark* district but for him, until Simeon arose, so far as the church was concerned. Even the dissenters in that quarter owe much of their increase and energy to the influence of Berridge. I, who care nothing about either church or dissent, any further than they care for the *souls* of men, and the *supremacy* of Christ, shall never forget the churches or the chapels which owed to him—the former, their possession of the glorious gospel ; and the latter, their origin and the gospel too. I traced both with equal patience, and remember them with equal pleasure.

I am not evading the charge of buffoonery, which Southey has advanced. Berridge was such another *wag* as Rowland Hill. He was not, however, such a buffoon as South, nor such a punster as Dr. Donne, nor such a satirist as Lavington. His wit never wounded a penitent, nor hardened a sinner. It disturbed many a solemn drone, and mortified the self-righteous ; but it never intimidated the humble, nor led the weak to confound methodism with hypocrisy. It was, indeed, unmerciful to Arminianism, and thus unjust to Wesley. There I *loathe* as well as lament it. It is not so inexplicable, however, as it is unpardonable. Fletcher and Wesley libelled Calvinism, as heartily as Berridge and Toplady caricatured Arminianism. The style differs, but the *sting* is the same. The " Mr. *Frybabe* " of the Arminian Magazine is just as vile and vulgar a caricature, as the " old Fox " of the Gospel Magazine. Fletcher's Royal Proclamation of " free *grace* and free *wrath*," dated from Geneva, and signed by his Majesty's secretaries for the " *predestinarian* department, Calvin, Crisp, and Rowland Hill, is quite as indefensible as Toplady's *genealogy* of atheism. Indeed, they are equally disgraceful. Apart, however, from its

occasional personalities, the wit of Berridge, as a preacher, deserves all the benefit of Southey's generous concessions on
Whitefield's occasional playfulness:—" Minds of a *certain* power
will sometimes express their strongest feelings with a levity,
at which *formalists* are shocked, and which *dull* men are wholly
unable to understand. But language which, when coldly repeated, might seem to border upon irreverence and burlesque, has its
effect in popular preaching, when the intention of the speaker is
perfectly understood: it is suited to the great mass of the people;
it is *felt* by them when better things would have produced no
impression, and it is borne away when wiser arguments would
have been forgotten." *Southey's Wesley.*

Berridge's was just a mind of this " certain " order. Few
men had more right to say to those who did not understand his
vein,—had you been born a wit, you must have borne with
it. He was constitutionally *mercurial,* and his perfect scholarship as a *classic,* enabled him to give *point* to piquant thoughts:
for he was equally familiar with Aristotelian and Aristophanic
Greek ; and there will be some buffoonery, whenever the latter
is understood. He did not, however,

" Woo a grin, where he should win a soul."

He often caused a smile, that he might create a tear : a hazardous, if not an unwarrantable, experiment in the pulpit. Rowland Hill often ventured upon it; but he did not approve of it.
Indeed, he was often surprised, as well as grieved, that he had
created a laugh. He did not suspect, that many of his phrases
were ludicrous. I recollect once, when travelling with him, to
inquire into the truth of certain *sallies,* I had heard ascribed to
him. He denied the whole of them: but, at the same time, he
told me some that " were true," which, to my Scotch taste, were
even more *extravagant* than those he disclaimed. But enough
of this : had Berridge been either fanatic or buffoon, Whitefield
would not have called him " an angel of the churches indeed,"
much less employed him as his own substitute at Tottenham
Court, where so many persons of both rank and talent attended.

At this time, Whitefield wished much to go into Scotland

again; not that he had much hope of recovery, but he thought that a "desirable place to go to *heaven* from." He was not able to undertake the journey: he therefore tried the effect of bathing at Plymouth, and then of the air at Bristol. These recruited him a little, and " stirred up an ambition to be employed again;" but his first sermon on his return to London threw him back. He became exceedingly *nervous;* a kind of suffering to which he had formerly been a stranger. Alas, how many, like myself, will see unutterable emphasis in his simple account of this: " I now *know* what nervous disorders are!" Happy those who can say with him, " Blessed be God, they were contracted in His service ; and I do not repent."

In the autumn he went into Yorkshire, by gentle stages ; not preaching, but " travelling in order to preach ;" and his Yorkshire friends were considerate enough not to tempt him into the pulpit often. By the end of October, therefore, he could bear to ride " sixty miles a day, in a post-chaise, quite well." On reaching Edinburgh, however, he became much worse. Silence, " the bitter cup of continued silence," as he calls the medical prohibition against preaching, was now forced upon him ; but with the assurance, from four of the principal physicians of the city, that it would recover him. Accordingly, he drunk it for a month, and then preached once on new-year's day. This encouraged him. His nerves also began to brace again by riding; although he fell off one day, and pitched on his head. He merely says of this accident, "I had a violent fall upon my head ; but was neither surprised nor hurt."

Having thus preached once without injury, and not being interdicted from preaching again in a week after, at Edinburgh, he caught at the prospect of resuming his " delightful work" with rapture. " Who knows,—who knows ? " he exclaims, " I may again see Plymouth ! " He was able to return to London, and his first work there was to read all his letters from the German protestants, and to consult with Ziegenhagan for their further relief. But whilst planning for that, he had to bestir himself again for Georgia. One of his agents had drawn upon him ; and he was now pennyless, and very unequal to the task of begging. " How could you," he says to the agent, " draw

2 H

on *me* for so large a sum as £147? Lord, help me." The Bristol friends had not collected for the German sufferers, and he carried his case there. Its urgency roused him, and he preached four or five times a week "without hurt," and with great success. This wound up his spirit to its old pitch, and led him to look at the *fields* again, as his proper sphere. "How gladly," he exclaims, "would I bid adieu to ceiled houses and vaulted roofs? Mounts are the best pulpits, and the heavens the best sounding-boards. Oh for power equal to my will! I would fly from pole to pole, publishing the glorious gospel."

On his return to London he was soon overcome by cares and labour, and obliged to spend the month of June in Holland, in order to prepare himself for the *dog-days* at home. The visit had the desired effect. All his "old times revived again," on his return to England. But *new* troubles awaited him. Travelling was essential to his health, and injurious to his chapels: he had, therefore, to devolve the management of them upon trustees, and to make the best arrangements he could for their supply. This he accomplished with great difficulty, and then started for Scotland; intending to sail from Greenock to Virginia.

On his way to the north, he wrote, in the intervals of public labour, his answer to Warburton's attack on methodism;—an account of which will be found in the chapter "Whitefield and the Bishops." He intended it to be, in the event of his not seeing England again, "a *parting* testimony for the good old puritans and the free-grace dissenters;" because the bishop had "sadly maligned them." At Edinburgh he soon broke down again, and had to drink anew the bitter cup of silence for six weeks. It restored him, however; and he went in "brisk spirits" to embark for America.

CHAPTER XXIV.

In June, 1763, Whitefield sailed from Scotland for Rapanach, in Virginia. The voyage was pleasant, but tedious. He was *twelve* weeks on the passage; but it did him good. The length of time wore out the painful impressions which had been created by his solicitude for the Tabernacle and Tottenham Court. The order and harmony on board, also, added to the bracing and tranquillizing effect of the voyage. " I enjoyed," he says, " that quietness which I have in vain sought after for some years on shore." He had sailed " with but little hopes of further public usefulness," owing to his *asthma:* but after being six weeks at sea, he wrote to a friend, " Who knows but our latter end may *yet* increase ? " He was, however, afraid of presuming, and added—" If not in public usefulness, Lord Jesus, let it be in heart-holiness ! I know who says, Amen. I add, Amen and Amen."

On his arrival, he found many Christian friends, of whom he had " never heard before," waiting to welcome him. They were the fruits of his former visit to Virginia; and the more welcome to him, because he was not very sure that he had won any souls upon the voyage. It was with great difficulty, however, that he preached to them ; his breathing was so bad, although his general health was better. At Philadelphia, also, a still higher gratification awaited him : not less than " forty *new-creature* ministers, of various denominations," visited him ; some of them " young and bright witnesses " for Christ. He heard, also, that sixteen students had been converted last year, at New Jersey college. This was medicine to him for every thing but his asthma; and even that he tried to forget : for now the *Lutherans* in Philadelphia thronged to hear the friend of the German protestants. Accordingly, he preached twice a week, and with " remarkable " success amongst all ranks.

He wanted much to go to Georgia ; but the physicians absolutely prohibited him, until he should gain strength. He therefore went to New Jersey college, to fan the flame he had kindled amongst the students; and had " four sweet seasons " there, which resembled old times. His spirits rose at the sight of the *young* soldiers, who were to fight when he fell. Thus cheered he went on to New York. It was now winter; and " cold weather and a warm heart " always suited him best. He therefore was able to preach thrice a week, for seven weeks. " Such a flocking of all ranks," he says, " I never saw before at New York." This flocking was not confined to the sanctuary. Many of the most respectable gentlemen and merchants went home with him after his sermons, to " hear something more of the kingdom of Christ." Such was his influence as a philanthropist also, that, although prejudices ran high against the Indians, because of a threatened insurrection in the south, he collected £120 for the Indian school at Lebanon. This, with the numerous conversions under his sermons, made him say, " We are trying to echo back from America the *Gogunniant* " of Wales. Thus he found " New York *new* York indeed " to him.

Soon after, he visited the Indian school at Lebanon, then under Dr. Wheelock. The sight of this " promising nursery for future missionaries," inspired him. All his old plans for its extension expanded. I am inclined to think, from a full comparison of dates, that he arranged on the *spot* with Wheelock or Whitaker, the mission of Occum to Britain, on behalf of the Indian seminary. It was certainly Whitefield's plans and pledges which brought Whitaker and Occum here ; and it was his influence which won Lord Dartmouth to be the patron of the college at Hanover, which Wheelock very properly called " Dartmouth." But this subject will come up again.

In 1764, Whitefield came to Boston, and was " received with

the usual warmth of affection." Again he saw there "the Redeemer's *stately* steps in the great congregation." Small-pox were, however, raging so in the city, that he deemed it prudent to move about in the adjacent towns. The Bostonians bore with this for some weeks : but when they heard that he was likely to slip off to the south, they brought him back by force. "They sent," he says, "a gospel hue-and-cry after me, and really *brought* me back." It was not so much to their credit, that they "begged earnestly for a six o'clock morning lecture," when they got him back. He seems to have been unable to comply with their cruel request : but he declined with reluctance. He preached for them, however, thrice a week for some time ; and such was the number of converts discovered after his farewell sermon, that his friends actually proposed to send after him a book, *full* of names of the multitude who were clamorous for his return, although he was fleeing for his life. The *heat* alone had compelled him to leave. It was now summer, and he began to sink again. What could he do but fly ? The good Bostonians assured him, that their summers had lately become much *cooler* than formerly, and that he might safely risk *their* dog-days now ! He tried to believe them, until he had hardly *breath* enough to say farewell. His parting with them tried him much. "It has been heart-breaking," he says, "I cannot *stand* it !" They acted more considerately when his visit commenced. Then, "at a meeting of the freeholders and other inhabitants of the town of Boston, it was unanimously voted, that the thanks of the town be given to the Rev. George Whitefield, for his charitable care and pains in collecting a considerable sum of money in Great Britain, for the distressed sufferers by the great fire in Boston, 1760. A respectable committee was appointed to wait on Mr. Whitefield, to inform him of the vote, and present him with a copy thereof." *Boston Gazette, February,* 1764.

Urgency, like that at Boston, was employed with him at New Haven college. He had preached to the students, and taken his leave : but such was the impression, that they sent the president after him, to entreat for another "*quarter* of an hour's exhortation." He complied, of course : and the effect was

what he called, " the *crown* of the expedition." *Letters.* He
spent the summer in and around New York, without suffering
much from the heat.   Often, a *hundred* carriages might be seen
in the streets, around whatever chapel he preached in.   This
pleased him : but twice he got into the *fields* again ; and then
he exclaims, " We sat under the Redeemer's shadow with great
delight."

In September, he went to Philadelphia again ; and the effect,
he says, " was great indeed."   It made him exclaim, " Grace,
grace ! "   He was also much gratified at Nassau Hall, where
he preached at Commencement.   Both the governor and ex-
governor of the state, with the principal gentlemen of the city,
attended, and the *provost* of the college read prayers for him.
The trustees also sent him a vote of thanks for his services and
the countenance he gave to the institution.   About this time, a
picture of him was taken by an American artist, who could not
finish the drapery, owing to an attack of ague.   Whitefield must
have been pleased with it ; for he sent it to England to be finished,
and then " hung up in the Tabernacle parlour."   There is a
painting there, imperfect in its drapery, which has often astounded me ; the figure is so *unwieldy*, and so unlike all my *old*
prints.   Until this moment, I could not account for its enormous
obesity.   It is, I now suspect, the original he sent from Philadelphia ; for he was then much swollen.   He calls it, in his
letter, " *my shadow:*"   I should like to have seen his *smile*, when
he used these words !   He must have been very ill, if he was
grave then.

He was well enough, however, to cross-plough Virginia again.
During this itineracy, he found here and there, in places as
" unlikely as ROME itself," groups of new lights, formed and led
on by a wealthy planter in the state.   This he calls " grace
indeed."   They also met him in a body, to identify themselves
publicly with him.   The character and result of this camp-
meeting at Lockwoods, I do not know : but such was his own
opinion of the prospects in Virginia at large, that he wrote home
thus : " Surely the *Londoners,* who are fed to the full, will not
envy the poor souls in these parts.   I almost determine to come
back in the spring " to them, from Georgia.

He spent the winter at Bethesda. How flourishing he found it, will be best told in his own words. "Peace and plenty reign at Bethesda. All things go on successfully. God hath given me great favour in the sight of the governor, council, and assembly. A memorial was presented for an additional grant of lands, consisting of two thousand acres. It was immediately complied with. Both houses addressed the governor in behalf of the intended college. A *warm* answer was given; and I am now putting all in repair, and getting every thing ready for that purpose. Every heart seems to *leap* for joy, at the prospect of its future utility to this and the neighbouring colonies. He that holdeth the stars in his right hand, will direct in due time, whether I shall directly embark for England, or take one tour more to the northward. I am in delightful winter-quarters (for *once !*) His EXCELLENCY dined with me yesterday, and expressed his satisfaction in the warmest terms. Who knows—how many youths may be trained up for the service of the ever-loving and altogether lovely Jesus? Thus far, however, we may set up our Ebenezer. Hitherto the bush hath been burning, but not consumed."

On transcribing this sentence, I was about to say, "Alas, the *consuming* fire is kindling ;"—when the recollection of Berridge's opinion on the eventual fate of Bethesda, checked me. He thought it a good thing that that bush was consumed, and thus prevented from becoming a nursery for unconverted ministers. But this subject will occur again.

In the spring of 1765, Whitefield began to prepare again for his "wilderness range." He was tired of "ceiled houses and crowded tables." These, he says, "I leave to others: a morsel of bread, and a little bit of cold meat, in a wood, is a most luxurious repast" to me. He left Georgia, however, with great regret, on some accounts. It was all *alive* to hear him. It was, in his opinion, "such a scene of action" then, that "words could not express" the facilities for usefulness which it presented. But both Old and New England were clamorous for his return to them. All the way from Charleston to Philadelphia, the loud and piercing cry was,—"For Christ's sake, stay, and preach the gospel to us." Even in Charleston, of

which he often said, its motto is, " *Chastened* but not *changed*,"
(referring to its calamitous visitations by storms,) he was detained a week longer than he intended, by the urgency of the
mayor and the principal gentlemen of the town.   Indeed, he
calls his parting from it and Bethesda, " affecting, cutting,
and awful."   So it was to him every where : for he doubted
very much whether it was his *duty* to move homewards.   But
he had laid the foundation of his college, and the superstructure
depended upon his influence at home.   Besides, the *heat* soon
decided the question, when he reached Philadelphia.   In a few
days, he could scarcely move.   He even dreaded the motion of
a ship, when he was compelled to embark for England ; but he
said, " If it shake this tottering frame to pieces, it will be a
trading voyage indeed ! "   In this spirit he sailed, and reached
home so speedily, that he could hardly believe his own senses,
when he found himself there in twenty-eight days.

In this second illustration, as in the first, of Whitefield's influence in America, there is (it will be seen) no selection of
facts from any former or subsequent visits ; but merely the details of the moment.   I have already stated my reasons for not
going into the general estimate of his influence in the new
world.   Let some of my American friends show this out.   The
old world, instead of being jealous, will be thankful, to see
Whitefield, as we now see Luther, Knox, and Latimer, in his
own place, amidst the Aarons and Hurs who sustained his
hands, and the Joshuas who carried on his work and warfare.   It
is worthy of American christians, that whilst they would feel at
a loss between two of their patriarchs—one of whom had shaken
hands with George Washington, and the other with George
Whitefield—with which to shake hands first,—they would venerate most a veteran who had known both.   Again I tell them,
that I have not dared to do Whitefield full justice, in reference
to their father-land, because I was afraid of doing injustice to
their fathers, who acted with him, and followed after him.   I
devolve the duty, therefore, upon America.   Let her give
Britain the *Transatlantic* Life and Times of Whitefield !

CHAPTER XXV.

WHITEFIELD's deliberate and final opinion of the episcopate as an order, or as an office, is very doubtful. Until I read his solemn declaration to the Erskines, that he would not be episcopally ordained again for a thousand worlds, I had seen nothing to warrant even a suspicion of the kind. Even now I know of nothing to illustrate that declaration. It is not repeated in any of his letters. It is not reported in any popular anecdote of his preaching or conversation. The dissenters had no idea of his doubts on this head, and his episcopalian friends regarded him as a *sound*, although irregular, churchman upon the whole. It is thus evident that he was very silent upon the subject. Besides, although he was present at several ordinations of another kind, he took no part in any of them. He preached in the evening at Deal, *after* Dr. Gibbons and other ministers had ordained a pastor there. He also spent the afternoon with them, greatly to his own edification, he says. All this is proof that he did not doubt the validity of their ordination; but not proof that he *preferred* their way. The strongest thing I know him to have said of " that way " is,—" The prayer put up in the very act of laying on of hands, by Dr. Gibbons, was so affecting, and the looks and behaviour of those that joined so serious and solemn,—that I hardly know when I was more struck under any one's ministration. Several very important questions were asked and answered before, and a solemn charge given after imposition of hands." Thus he thought, felt, and wrote, on this subject, *thirty* years after what he said to the Erskines about his own ordination. He showed, however, no preference

during all that time to either presbyterian or congregational ordination. What, therefore, ought we to think of his strong language to the Erskines? Was it a hasty assertion never repeated? Did he repent of it as a rash saying? With my
knowledge of Whitefield, I cannot think that he kept silence
from either policy or repentance. He had, indeed, no policy
except that of trying to do the greatest sum of good.

My own conviction is, that he had neither fixed nor definite
opinions upon the subject of episcopacy. He was for it and
against it, just as it was for and against the work of evangelizing
the country. He thought highly of episcopal power, when it
aided or protected faithful preaching; and *meanly*, when it
hindered the gospel. If a bishop did good, or allowed good to
be done, Whitefield venerated him and his office too: but he
despised both, whenever they were hostile to truth or zeal;—I
have no objection to say, whenever they were hostile to his *own*
sentiments and measures. The question comes thus within a
narrow compass,—Were his measures and sentiments, or those
of the hostile bishops, the more apostolical? Gibson compro-
mised the apostolic doctrine of regeneration; Lavington caricatured it; Smallbroke all but denied the work of the Spirit;
and Warburton evaporated divine influence. Whitefield sustained the doctrine of the Reformation on the subject; and
however his modes of expression varied, his invariable meaning
was, that it is Christ *in* the heart, that is the hope of glory. It
was this apostolic maxim which made him at first, and kept
him to the end, a faithful echo of the supreme oracle,—" Mar-
vel not that I say unto you, Ye must be born again." They
may be prelates, but they are not *bishops* of the church of
Christ, who either oppose or explain away this oracle. To
honour such masters in Israel, is to dishonour Christ. And as
to respecting their *office*, notwithstanding their errors, that is
drawing a distinction equally unwise and unwarrantable. What
honest man would respect an unjust judge or an ignorant physician, because of their professional titles? It is high time to
put an end to this nonsense. Bishop is a name of office in the
Bible, because it is a name of creed and character; and therefore ought never to be conceded to any man whose creed and

character are not apostolical, whoever may confer it upon him. Ordination can no more make a worldly man a bishop, than a diploma can make an ignorant man a physician, or a theologian.

Whitefield's sentiments on this subject came out, most fully, in his exposure of Warburton. He did not spare him, as he did Smallbroke; for although no match for Warburton as a scholar or a reasoner, his *spirit* compelled the wrangler to calculate consequences. I have never seen the *original* form of the bishop's pamphlet on the grace of the Spirit; but as sermons, it is evidently softened and qualified in his works. The memory of Doddridge had, perhaps, some influence upon him. Not much, however. When I read his letters to Doddridge I can hardly believe my own recollections of his works; and when I read his works, I can hardly believe that he wrote the letters. I regret this discrepancy: for Warburton, if the most " impudent man of the age," was a mighty man of valour, and warred well against the twin-scepticism of Bolingbroke and Middleton. I select him, therefore, that the *point* of Whitefield's argument may be felt. It penetrates " the joints of *his* armour," even.

The following remonstrances are not addressed to the *leviathan* of the Legation himself. Whitefield was probably afraid to put " a hook in his jaws," by a direct effort; and therefore he caught him with holy guile, by addressing a private friend; probably *Keene*, one of the first managers of the Tabernacle.

" However profound and unintelligible our author's comments may be, yet, when he comes to show the reasonableness and fitness of an abatement or total withdrawment of divine influence in these last days, he speaks intelligibly enough. ' On the Spirit's first descent upon the apostles, he found their minds rude and uninformed, strangers to all celestial knowledge, prejudiced in favour of a carnal law, and utterly averse to the dictates of the everlasting gospel. The minds of these he illuminated, and, by degrees, led into all truths necessary for the professors of the faith to know, or for the propagators of it to teach.' *True!* ' Secondly, the nature and genius of the gospel were so averse to all the religious institutions of the world, that the whole strength of human prejudices was set in opposition to

it.   To overcome the obstinacy and violence of those prejudices,
nothing less than the power of the Holy One was sufficient.'
Good! 'And, thirdly and lastly, there was a time when the
powers of this world were combined together for its destruction.   At such a period, nothing but superior aid from above
could support humanity in sustaining so great a conflict as that
which the holy martyrs encountered with joy and rapture, the
horrors of death and torment.' *Excellent!* But what follows ?—
According to our author,

'Tempora mutantur, nos et mutamur in illis,'

' But now,' (a dreadful *but* it is!) 'the profession of christianity is attended with ease and honour;' and we are now, it
seems, so far from being 'rude and uninformed, and utterly
averse to the dictates of the everlasting gospel, that whatever
there may be of prejudice, it draws another way.   Consequently, a rule of faith being now established, the conviction
which the weight of human testimony, and the conclusions of
human reason, afford us of its truth, are abundantly sufficient to
support us in our religious perseverance ; and therefore it must
certainly be a great mark of fanaticism, to expect such divine
communications, as though no such rule of faith was established ; and also as highly presumptuous or fanatical to imagine,
that rule to be so obscure, as to need the further assistance of
the Holy Spirit to explain his own meaning.'

"This, you will say, my dear friend, is going pretty far ; and
indeed, supposing matters to be as this writer represents them,
I do not see what great need we have of any established rule
at all, at least in respect to practice, since corrupt nature is
abundantly sufficient of itself, to help us to persevere in a religion attended with ease and honour.   And I verily believe, that
the deists throw aside this rule of faith entirely, not barely on
account of a deficiency in argument to support its authenticity,
but because they daily see so many who profess to hold this
established, self-denying rule of faith with their lips, persevering all their lives long in nothing else but an endless and insa-
tiable pursuit after worldly ease and honour.   But what a total
ignorance of human nature, and of the true, unalterable genius

of the everlasting gospel, doth our author's arguing discover! For supposing, my dear friend, that this or any other writer should undertake to prove, that the ancient Greeks and Romans were born with sickly, disordered, and crazy bodies, but that we in modern days, being made of a firmer mould, and being blessed with the established rules of Galen and Hippocrates, need now no further assistance from any present physician, either to explain or apply those rules to our present ails and corporeal distresses, though we could not, without the help of some linguist superior to ourselves, so much as understand the language in which those authors wrote.—Supposing, I say, any one was to take it into his head to write in this manner, would he not be justly deemed a dreaming enthusiast or real fanatic? And yet this would be just as rational as to insinuate with our author, that we who are born in these last days, have less depravity in our natures, less enmity to, and less prejudice against, the Lord Jesus Christ, and less need of the divine teachings of the Blessed Spirit to help us to understand the true spiritual meaning of the holy Scriptures, than those who were born in the first ages of the gospel. For as it was former-ly, so it is now, the natural man discerneth not the things of the Spirit; and why? 'Because they can only be spiritually discerned.' But when is it that we must believe this author? for, p. 73, he talks of 'some of the first christians, who were in the happy circumstance of being found innocent, when they were led into the practice of all virtue by the Holy Spirit.' And what occasion for that, if found innocent? But how inno-cent did the Holy Spirit find them? Doubtless, just as innocent as it finds us, 'conceived and born in sin.'

" But, by this time, my dear friend, I imagine you would be glad to know against whom these *bruta fulmina*, this unscrip-tural artillery, is levelled. Our author shall inform you : " All modern pretenders to divine influence in general ;' and you may be assured, ' the *poor methodists* (those scourges and eye-sores of formal, self-righteous, letter-learned professors) in particu-lar.' To expose and set these off in a ridiculous light, (a method that Julian, after all his various tortures, found most effectual,) this writer runs from Dan to Beersheba ; gives us quotation upon quotation out of the Rev. Mr. John Wesley's journals; and to use his own simile upon another occasion, by a kind of Egyptian husbandry, draws together whole droves of obscene animals of his own formation, who rush in furiously, and then trample the journals, and this sect, already every where spoken against, under their feet. In reading this part of his work I could not help thinking of the papists dressing *John Huss* in a cap of painted devils, before they delivered him up to the secular arm. For our author calls the Rev. Mr. John Wesley 'paltry mimic, spiritual empiric, spiritual martialist, meek apostle, new adventurer.' The methodists, according to him, are 'modern apostles, the saints, new missionaries, illuminated doctors, this sect of fanatics. Methodism itself is modern saintship. Mr. Law begat it, and Count Zinzendorff rocked the cradle; and the devil himself is man-midwife to their new birth.' And yet this is the man, my dear friend, who in his preface to this very book, lays it down as an invariable maxim, 'That truth is never so grossly injured, or its advocates so dishonoured, as when they employ the foolish arts of sophistry, buffoonery, and personal abuse in its defence.' By thy own pen thou shalt be tried, thou hapless, mistaken advocate of the christian cause. Nay, not content with dressing up this meek apostle, this spiritual empiric, these new missionaries, in bear-skins, in order to throw them out to be baited by an ill-natured world, he proceeds to rake up the very ashes of the dead; and, like the witch of Endor, as far as in him lies, attempts to bring up and disquiet the ghosts of one of the most venerable sets of men that ever lived upon the earth; I mean, the good old puritans: 'For these,' (says our author,) 'who now go under the name of methodists, in the days of our forefathers, under the firm reign of Queen Elizabeth, were called precisians; but then, as a precious metal which had undergone its trial in the fire, and left all its dross, the sect, with great propriety, changed its name' (a very likely thing, to give themselves a nick-name, indeed) 'from precisian to puritan. Then in the weak and distracted times of Charles I. it ventured to throw off the mask, and under the new name of independent, became the chief agent of all the dreadful disorders which terminated that unhappy reign.' So that, according to this author's heraldic, genealogical fiction, 'methodism is the younger daughter to independency, and now a methodist is an apostolic independent,' (God grant he may always deserve such a glorious appellation,) 'but an independent was then a Mahometan methodist.' Pages 142—144. What! an independent a Mahometan methodist? What! the learned Dr. Owen, the great Dr. Goodwin, the amiable Mr. Howe, and those glorious worthies who first planted the New England churches, Mahometan methodists? Would to God, that not only this writer, but all who now profess to preach Christ in this land, were not only almost, but altogether such Mahometan methodists in respect to the doctrine of divine influence, as they were! For I will venture to affirm, that if it had not been for such Mahometan methodists, and their successors, the free-grace dissenters, we should some years ago have been in danger of sinking into Mahometan methodism indeed; I mean, into a christianity destitute of any divine influence manifesting itself in grace and knowledge, and void of any spiritual aid in spiritual distresses. But from such a christianity, good Lord, deliver this happy land! The design our author had in view in drawing such a parallel, is easily seen through. Doubtless, to expose the present methodists to the jealousy of the civil government. For, says he, p. 142, 'We see methodism at present under a well-established government, where it is obliged to wear a less audacious look. To know its true character, we should see it in all its fortunes.' And doth this writer then, in order to gratify a sinful curiosity of seeing methodism in all its fortunes, desire to have the pleasure of seeing the weak and distracted times of Charles I. brought back again? Or dares he insinuate, that because, as he immediately adds, our country hath been productive of every strange thing, 'that we are in the least danger now of any such distracting turn, since we have a king upon the throne who, in his first most gracious speech to both houses of parliament, declared he would preserve the Act of Toleration inviolable? And that being the case, blessed be God, we are in no danger of any return of such weak and distracted times, either from the apostolic independents, Maho-

metan methodists, or any religious sect or party whatsoever.'
My dear friend, ' if this is not gibbeting up names with unregenerate malice, to everlasting infamy,' I know not what is.   But
it happens in this, as in similar cases, whilst men are thus busy
in gibbeting up the names of others, they unwittingly, like
Haman, when preparing a gallows for that apostolic independent,
that Mahometan methodist, Mordecai, all the while are only
erecting a gibbet for their own.

   " But, methinks, I see you now begin to be impatient to know
(and indeed I have neither inclination nor leisure at present to
pursue our author any further) who this can be, that takes such
gigantic strides ?   I assure you he is a perfect Goliath in the
retinue of human learning.—Will you guess ?—Perhaps Dr.
Taylor of Norwich.—No—he is dead.   Certainly not a churchman ?   Yes ; a member, a minister, a dignitary, a bishop of the
church of England ;—and, to keep you no longer in suspense, it
is no less a man than Dr. Warburton, the author of " The
Divine Legation of Moses," and now William Lord Bishop of
Gloucester.   I know you are ready to say, ' Tell it not in Gath,
publish it not in the streets of Askelon.'   But, my dear friend,
what can be done ?   His Lordship hath published it himself:
nay, his book hath just gone through a second impression; and
that you may see and judge for yourself, whether I have wronged
his Lordship or not, (as it is not very weighty,) I have sent you
the book itself.   Upon the perusal, I am persuaded you will at
least be thus far of my opinion, that however *decus et tutamen*
is always the motto engraven upon a *bishop's mitre*, it is not
always most certain, though his Lordship says it is, p. 202,
that they are written on every *prelate's breast ?*   And how can
this prelate, in particular, be said to be the *ornament* and *safeguard* of the church of England, when his principles are as
directly contrary to the offices of that church, over which he is
by divine permission made overseer, as light is contrary to darkness ?   You know, my dear friend, what our ministers are taught
to say, when they baptize: ' I beseech you to call upon God
the Father, through our Lord Jesus Christ, that of his boun-
teous goodness he will grant to this child that thing which by
nature he cannot have.'   But what says his Lordship ? ' All

influence exceeding the *power of humanity,* is miraculous, and
therefore to abate or be totally withdrawn, now the church is
perfectly established.' What say they when they catechise?
' My good child, know this, that thou art not able to do these
things of thyself, nor to walk in the commands of God, and to
serve him, without *his special grace.*' But what says his Lordship? ' A rule of faith being now established, the conviction
which the weight of *human testimony,* and the conclusions of
human reason, afford, are abundantly sufficient to support us in
our religious perseverance.' What says his Lordship himself,
when he confirms children thus catechised? ' Strengthen them,
we beseech thee, O Lord, with the Holy Ghost, the Comforter,
and daily increase in them thy manifold gifts and grace, the
spirit of wisdom and understanding, the spirit of counsel and
ghostly strength.' But what says his Lordship, when he speaks
his own sentiments? ' All aids in spiritual distresses, as well
as those which administered help in corporeal diseases, are now
abated or totally withdrawn.' What says his Lordship when he
ordains? ' Dost thou trust that thou art inwardly moved by
the Holy Ghost? then, receive thou the Holy Ghost.'

" What says his Lordship, when pronouncing the blessing?
' The peace of God, which passeth all understanding, keep your
hearts and minds in the knowledge and love of God.' But
what says his Lordship when retired to his study? ' All supernatural influence, manifesting itself in grace and knowledge, is
miraculous, and therefore to cease under a perfect establishment.' What says——But I check myself; for the time would
fail me, was I to urge all those quotations that might be produced out of the articles, homilies, and public offices, to confront and invalidate the whole tenor and foundation of his Lordship's performance. But how it is consistent with that wisdom
which is from above, (and by which his Lordship attempts to
arraign, try, and condemn, the Reverend Mr. John Wesley,) to
subscribe to, and make use of, public offices in the church, and
then as publicly deny and contradict them in the press, I leave
to his Lordship's more calm and deliberate consideration. Sure
I am, if weighed in the same balance, his Lordship would be
found equally wanting, at least. Indeed, during the whole trial,

I could scarcely refrain breaking out into the language of the eunuch of Queen Candace to Philip the evangelist, ' Speaketh the prophet this of himself, or of some other man?' I hope, my dear friend, you know me better than to suspect I thus re- tort upon his Lordship, in order to throw dust in your eyes, to prevent your seeing what his Lordship may justly except against in the conduct of the methodists in general, or in the journals of the Reverend Mr. John Wesley in particular. Whatever that indefatigable labourer may think of his, you know I have long since publicly acknowledged, that there were, and doubtless, though now sent forth in a more correct attire, there are yet, many *exceptionable passages* in my journals. And I hope it will be one of the constant employments of my declining years, to humble myself daily before the most high God, for the innu- merable mixtures of corruption which have blended themselves with my feeble, but, I trust, sincere endeavours, whether from the press or pulpit, to promote the Redeemer's glory, and the eternal welfare of precious and immortal souls. And I assure you, that if his Lordship had contented himself with pointing out, or even ridiculing, any such blemishes or imprudences, or yet still more important mistakes, in my own, or any of the methodists' conduct or performances, I should have stood en- tirely silent. But when I observed his Lordship through almost his whole book, not only wantonly throwing about the arrows and firebrands of scurrility, buffoonery, and personal abuse, but, at the same time, on account of some unguarded expressions and indiscretions of a particular set of honest, though fallible, men, taking occasion to wound, vilify, and totally deny the all-pow- erful, standing operations of the blessed Spirit, by which alone his Lordship or any other man living can be sanctified and sealed to the day of eternal redemption, I must own that I was con- strained to vent myself to you, as a dear and intimate friend, in the manner I have done. Make what use of it you please; per- haps hereafter I may trouble you with some further remarks." *Letter.*

It was a significant " sign of the times," that Payne, the ac- comptant-general of the Bank of England, wrote an answer to Warburton. I ought also to add, that the bishop could *persecute* as well as rail. This ought to be known; because he appears somewhat *amiable* in his correspondence with Doddridge, and not a little faithful in exposing "the unclean beasts" in his own ark. Adams of Stinchcombe, near Gloucester, was the friend of Whitefield and Venn. He was an infirm man, but zealous. Warburton had been his patron; but when he began to itinerate, and to preach for Lady Huntingdon at Bath, the bishop insisted, in his *own* style, upon strict residence at home. "I shall insist," he says, "upon your constant residence in your parish,— not so much for the good you are likely to do there, as to prevent the *mischief* you may do by rambling about to other places. Your bishop and (though your fanatic conduct has almost made me ashamed to own it) your patron, W. GLOUCESTER."

Adams remonstrated, and proved that during three years he had only been three months non-resident. He argued also that he had accepted Stinchcombe, a living of £36 per annum, in preference to one of £80, because he was unable to give full service. All this was in vain. He was a methodist. Warburton, therefore, (without a *divine* legation,) replied, "If I indulged you in giving your parish only one service on Sunday, I hereby *revoke* that indulgence, and insist upon your giving them full service." *Nichols.*

It might have been unsafe then to defy such legates, when they interdicted itineracy; and even now an *infirm* man could do no good by rambling; but let some men of renown take the *field*, and their gowns are as safe as any mitre on the bench. Mitres must now lead *on* the evangelization of the country, or follow cardinal's hats to Rome.

CHAPTER XXVI.

WHITEFIELD'S LAST LABOURS AT HOME.

ALTHOUGH Whitefield's last days were not "his best days," either at home or abroad, they were both happy and useful days. The very *evening* of his life includes more labour and success than the *whole* day of ordinary men. After opening the Countess's chapel at Bath, the care of his own chapels in London quite absorbed him for some months. He could neither range nor revisit, because of the difficulty of supplying his pulpits. Besides, he was too weak " to do now as he had done." He thought himself fit only to " stand by an *old gun* or two in a garrison," instead of leading the battle. But such thoughts did not last long in his mind. His " old ambition" soon returned, whenever his strength or spirits rallied for a day. A very slight improvement in his health would make him exclaim, —" Who knows but this feeble arm may yet be strengthened to annoy the enemy ? "

In the spring of 1766, he was assisted by *Occum*, the Indian preacher, who came over with Whitaker, to collect for Dr. Wheelock's college. He was much pleased with Occum's spirit, and with his preaching ; for both the noble and the poor heard him gladly, and contributed liberally. Whitefield threw all his soul into this enterprise, and nearly a thousand pounds were soon raised for it. Even the king, through the influence of Lord Dartmouth, contributed to the fund. Occum, as well as his object, deserved this welcome. He was a superior man and a popular preacher in his own country, both in the woods and in the cities. He died in 1792, at New Stockbridge, and was followed to the grave by three hundred weeping Indians.

In the spring and summer of 1766, Whitefield paid some visits
to Bath and Bristol, for the benefit of the waters, and in the
hope of making excursions. But both the weather and his health
were bad, and he could seldom preach in these cities, except
at *six* in the morning. But even at that hour he had large
audiences.

Two things pleased him much at this time. He had got
Fletcher of Madely into his pulpits at London, and had formed
an acquaintance with *Rowland Hill*. Of the former he said,
" Dear Mr. Fletcher is become a *scandalous* Tottenham Court
preacher." " Were we more scandalous, more good would be
done." Still, " the shout of a King is yet heard in the methodist
camp." This was particularly the case in Bath, before Whitefield returned to winter quarters. The nobility crowded to hear
him; and whatever effect his sermons had upon them, many of
the poor were effectually called. Such was, however, the *apparent* impression on all ranks, that he left Bath, longing and praying that God would open his way again into *all* the towns in
England.

This prayer was not granted : but God enabled Whitefield to
quicken the zeal of stronger men. He heard of " four methodist
parsons " being the guests of one of his friends; and exclaimed,
" *Four* methodist parsons !—it is enough to set a whole kingdom on fire, when Jesus says,—Loose them, and let them *go !* "
This message was followed up by an appeal to them, which must
have been *felt:*—" Indeed and indeed, my dear and honoured
friends, I am ashamed of myself. I blush and am confounded,
so very little have I done or suffered for Jesus ! What a poor
figure shall I make amongst the saints, confessors, and martyrs
around His throne, without some deeper *signatures* of his divine
impress, without more *scars* of christian honour ! To-morrow
I intend to take the sacrament upon it, that I *will* begin to begin
to be a christian." It was appeals of this kind, which made the
Romaines and Venns (nothing loth !) bestir themselves; and
which brought around Whitefield the Shirleys and De Courcys
of the time. Another way in which he helped on, at this time,
the work he had begun, was by prefacing a new edition of Bunyan's Works; and thus reviving public attention to the old

puritans, by grouping their names with those of the reformers :
a process equally fair and wise ! They *libel* the reformers, who
think them at all lowered by identifying Owen, Baxter, or Bunyan with them. These men dwell in the *same* mansion in
heaven, with Latimer, Jewel, and Usher. Let, therefore, all
who believe their identity maintain it ! The conviction will soon
enthrone itself in the public mind, in spite of all the efforts
made to keep up a distinction. There is no real distinction.
They were only distinct billows of the *one* sea of protestant
reformation. Their differences were mere *foam*, which the hal-
cyon wings of time and truth will soon obliterate. Or, if there
be a bench in heaven, Bunyan is an archbishop !

In the spring of 1767, Whitefield visited Cambridge and
Norwich, and preached with something of his *old* power for
some time. He left London, intending a " *large* plan of operations ;" but his " inward fever " returned upon him, and checked him. Lady Huntingdon then took him to Rodborough by
easy stages, and he was soon in the *fields* again. This encouraged him to venture into Wales also : for he had great faith in
the " thirty-year-old methodistical medicine," of preaching in
the *open* air; and the Welch liked him best in that element.
" Thousands on thousands," therefore, now met him around his
"*field throne*," and light and life flew in all directions, as in
the days of old. This was, however, more than he could stand
long. Both the work and the reward were too much for his
strength to sustain. He was soon as thankful to be again on
" *this* side of the Welch mountains," as he had been to get to
" the *other* side " of them, although they *rung* with the cry,
" Evermore give this bread of life."

In the summer he returned to London, weak but lively; and
finding that some laymen had not been unacceptable nor unsuccessful in his pulpits, " the itch for itinerating " returned upon
him, he says, to a degree not curable " out of heaven;" and
therefore he prepared to go into Yorkshire again, upon " a
blessed methodist *field-street* preaching plan." He now preferred streets to fields ; I do not know why. Perhaps he was
afraid of sudden attacks of illness, and wished to be near medical help. However that may be, he had to exclaim at almost

every stage, " Old methodism is the thing. *Hallelujah !* Good old work—good old seasons." Both were improved at this time by the company and help of Captain *Scott,* who often preached for him.

This Yorkshire tour improved his health, notwithstanding all the fatigue he went through; because he travelled much, and always on horseback. He was, therefore, afraid of London, where he had much labour, and no riding. It tempted him to *nestle,* he said; and his favourite maxim was, " No nestling, no nestling, on *this* side Jordan." On his arrival at home, he preached for the Religious Book Society at the Tabernacle, and afterwards dined with them at Drapers' Hall. On this occasion (and it was both the first and the last) almost all the dissenting ministers of London heard him, and met him at dinner. He was pleased, and they seem to have been so too : for the collection amounted to £105, and eighty new subscribers were obtained. It is thus unity of heart is produced, by uniting hands in work which cannot be carried on without peace and goodwill. But for this society, Whitefield and the London ministers, as a body, would hardly have known each other, except by name. This fact should not be forgotten by the dissenters. It was at this *door* Whitefield and they entered into the fellowship and unity of the Spirit. And what has been the effect? His memory is an enshrined star, and his name a watch-word, in all their orthodox churches.

At this time, he had much labour and more care pressing upon him. The question of his college at Bethesda was coming to a crisis, and he had a " little college of *outcasts* " (as he calls some false and fickle brethren) to reclaim from error and apostasy. In regard to the former, he began by memorializing the king ; informing his Majesty, that there was no seminary for academical studies southward of Virginia, and thus no stimulus to improvement in Georgia ; that he had expended twelve thousand pounds upon Bethesda, and thus laid a foundation for a college, if a charter like that of New Jersey were granted. He then sent, through Lord Dartmouth, a draught of the charter to the archbishop of Canterbury. His Grace sent it to the premier ; and the premier sent it back, requiring that the head of the college should be an episcopalian, and its prayers established forms:—not very *modest* requisitions, in a case where the *money* came chiefly out of the pockets of American and British dissenters ! Whitefield explained and pleaded this fact, until his patience was worn out : he then, very properly, begged leave to inform his Grace, that he would " trouble him no more, but turn the charity into a more generous and useful channel." " Accordingly, he resolved," says Gillies, " in the mean time, to add a public academy to the orphan-house, and wait for a more favourable opportunity for making a fresh application for a charter upon a broad bottom." That opportunity he never found. His failure to obtain a charter, however pitiable or paltry in its causes, cannot surprise those who know the history of the charter of the London university. Nearly a century was required to make the state wiser than it was in the days of Whitefield ; and even that long period has not improved the liberality of the church much. Oxford still frowns, and Cambridge does not smile, upon the call for *open* doors. There are, however, men in both universities, who would be glad to see them open ; and men out of both, who will not stop their " Sesame," because a charter has been *won* for the London university. In the mean time, (and I record it with pleasure and gratitude,) a dissenter may find more than courtesy at the libraries, when he has occasion to visit them for literary purposes. I have found Oxford " more noble than " *Red-cross* Street.

Whitefield having failed to obtain a charter for a college abroad, opened an *unchartered* one at home,—Trevecca in Wales. This was a timely measure ; for Oxford had just expelled six *praying* students, and thus proved to Lady Huntingdon that it would be no nursery for the kind of ministers she wanted. Another *college* was, also, a practical comment upon Vice-Chancellor Durell's edict ; which was more intelligible to the heads of houses, than either Whitefield's solemn remonstrances or the Shaver's sarcastic rebukes. They could comprehend a methodist seminary better than methodistical defences of extempore prayer. Whilst, therefore, the spirit-stirring pamphlets of Whitefield and M'Gowan placed the heads of houses before the public, as the persecutors of godly students,

Trevecca placed before them a specimen of reaction which they had not foreseen.

I am not willing to enter at present upon the history of the Countess's college. There is *now* an opportunity of restoring it to its original purpose and spirit. It ought not to be the least amongst the schools of the prophets, nor the last in aggressive evangelization. It ought to have been to Whitefield and its founder, what Elisha was to Elijah, the heir of both their mantle and spirit; but it has long had neither. As the college of the existing " Connexion," it is, perhaps, all that could be fairly expected; but as the Whitefield seminary it is nothing. I could say much on this subject;—and I *will* say much, should I be spared to publish The History of Methodism as a Reformation,—if nothing is done to give efficiency to Cheshunt. In the mean time, I not only forbear, but fondly hope that I may have no occasion to remonstrate. There remains enough of the Whitefield leaven in the *lump*, to ferment the whole, if well managed; and there are some managers *Whitefieldian* in their spirit. I charge them, " before God, and the Lord Jesus Christ, and the elect angels, and many witnesses," to make Cheshunt what the Countess and Whitefield intended and anticipated! They expected to hear more of it in heaven—than they have heard. They ought to have heard more. They *shall* hear more. Let their joy be fulfilled soon! It has been too long postponed. Besides, Cheshunt needs only a *commanding* man in its theological chair, in order to renovate it: and if any *minutiæ* of its old rules stand in the way of such a man, or in the way of students, what is a departure from such *forms*, compared with a departure from its original spirit and design?

I have a right to be thus explicit on this subject. I am as responsible for the *facts*, concerning the original design of this college, as the trustees are for its funds; and I will deal as honestly with them. I know that the endowments of Trevecca died with the Countess. I refer only, therefore, to Cheshunt's inheritance of what can never die,—the *names* of Lady Huntingdon and George Whitefield. These are more precious than the gold of Ophir, and their possession involves higher and holier responsibilities than " much fine gold " could bring with it. This is my *sole* reason for speaking at all; and therefore I have spoken out.

Whilst engaged in maturing the college at Trevecca, and opening chapels for the Countess, Whitefield lost his wife. On this subject, I have nothing to add to a former chapter; except that his own health and spirits declined afterwards. Still he preached, although often bringing up blood when he came down from the pulpit.

It will be gratifying to the reader to learn, that Trevecca, so long holy ground, and so intimately associated with the name and labours of Howel Harris, is about to become a theological seminary for the Welsh Calvinistic methodists. Let them *realize* the designs of Whitefield!—and do *justice* to the memory of Harris! Some will watch vigilantly, and I for one, how *his* memory is treated, when Trevecca is again made a college. He belongs too much to the ecclesiastical history of his country, to be forgotten or misrepresented. This hint will be understood by my friend John Elias, and not lost, I hope, on some of his friends in the principality.

CHAPTER XXVII.

WHITEFIELD AND EDMUND-HALL.

THE well-known expulsion of six students from Oxford, in 1763, was thus announced in the St. James's Chronicle ;—" On Friday last, six students belonging to Edmund-Hall, were expelled the University, after a hearing of several hours, before Mr. Vice-Chancellor and some of the heads of houses, for holding methodistical tenets, and taking upon them to pray, read, and expound the Scriptures, and singing hymns in a private house. The (principal) of the college (Dr. Dixon) defended their doctrines from the Thirty-nine Articles of the established church, and spoke in the highest terms of the piety and exemplariness of their lives : but his motion was overruled, and sentence pronounced against them. One of the heads of houses present observed, that as these six gentlemen were expelled for having too *much* religion, it would be very proper to inquire into the conduct of some who had too *little.* Mr. (the Vice-Chancellor) Durell was heard to tell the chief accuser, that the UNIVERSITY was much *obliged* to him for his good work ! "

The *form,* as well as the facts, of this Oxford *bull,* deserves preservation, because it will be the *last* of its race : for now, public opinion would soon expel from the university of *christian* fellowship, any number of heads of houses, who should repeat this act of tyranny. That great tribunal has just pronounced the sentence of unqualified condemnation against the late *popish* " Oxford Tracts," and neither the chancellor, nor the vice-chancellor, could obtain, were they to try, any mitigation of the sentence. The tracts are *unprotestant,* and, therefore, unpopular.

The hisses and yells of the raw witlings of Oxford against

dissenters, at the late installation, were the mere ebullitions of
political folly, and prove nothing against the university but the
want of good manners on *gala* days : whereas the tracts prove
the want of good theology ; a defect not so easily remedied as
ill-breeding.

It is one way of remedying both to keep up for a time the
names and the acts of the conclave, who excluded six Oxonians
for extempore prayer, and kept in one who was proved guilty of
ridiculing the miracles of Moses and Christ. Another way
(which I prefer) is, to perpetuate the names of the wise and
good men who protested against these outrages on truth, decency, and consistency. Oxford was never without some *Ab-
diels*. Her cloud of witnesses is not great ; but it is splendid
enough to inspire both hallowed recollections and high anticipations. I have felt and enjoyed this whilst musing in her
cloisters and halls. Often have her *redeeming* spirits gathered
around my own spirit, in such numbers and radiance, that I
forgot every thing but the service she had rendered to the Reformation, and the power she could apply to the defence and
diffusion of the gospel. Oh that she were wise to win souls !
She has won all kinds of fame, but the immortality of leading on
the evangelization of the world. If I am not her enemy in
writing thus,—then she has no enemies amongst orthodox dissenters. Their eyes are upon both universities, not to divide
the popish spoil, nor to divert the national endowments into
sectarian channels or foreign enterprises ; but to secure for all
who can *pay* for it, free access to all the literature and science
of Cam and Isis.

The junto who expelled Matthews, Jones, Shipman, Kay,
Middleton, and Grove, were, Drs. Durell, Randolph, Fothergill,
Nowell, and the senior proctor, Atterbury. They evidently
feared a *new* edition of Whitefield and Wesley. These men,
who had "turned the world upside down," and the church inside out, had begun with reading, praying, and expounding in
private houses ; and, if two did so much damage to the old system, what might not *six* do ? To prevent this danger, "each
of them, for the *crimes* above mentioned," was deemed " worthy of being expelled the Hall :" " I, therefore, by my visitorial

power," said the vice-chancellor, " do hereby pronounce them expelled." This was the *form* of the bull!

Middleton, in his " Ecclesiastical Memoir," laments that " the archives" of Oxford should " preserve the entry of a record which seemed *unsuitable* to the character of a great protestant community in the eighteenth century:" but its unsuitableness is just the reason for its preservation. Were it not in the archives, it would hardly be credited now ; and the next century would deem it a mere calumny.

Amongst the writers who exposed the folly and infamy of this decree, was Dr. Horne, afterwards bishop of Norwich. He nobly defended the students, whilst Sir Richard Hill lashed, and M'Gowan *shaved,* their judges. But neither this defence, nor that volunteered at the trial by two heads of houses, prevented Dr. Nowell, the principal of St. Mary's Hall, from attempting to justify the expulsion. He had even the effrontery to plead *drunkenness* as Welling's excuse for ridiculing the miracles!

Whitefield rebuked this conclave with much severity ; but in a better spirit than the baronet or the Shaver. His letter to Durell, on the occasion, is scarce now, and as it is not likely to be reprinted, I subjoin some specimens of it. They are not, however, the best as remonstrance, although the best as history. Whitefield never wrote better than on this occasion.

" It hath gladdened the hearts of many, and afforded matter of uncommon joy and thanksgiving to the Father of mercies and God of all consolation, to hear, that for some time past there hath been a more than common religious concern and zeal for promoting their own and others' salvation among some of the *sons of the prophets.* What a pleasing prospect hath hereby been opened of a future blessing to the rising generation ! A blessing which we well hoped would be not less salutary and beneficial to the moral, than the new cruse of salt was to part of the natural, world, which the prophet Elisha, when complaint was made that the water was naught and the ground barren, cast into the spring of waters, with a ' Thus saith the Lord, There shall not be from thence any more dearth or barren land: so the waters were healed unto this day.'

" But alas ! how is this general joy damped, and the pleasing prospect almost totally eclipsed, by a late melancholy scene exhibited in that very place, from whence, as from a fountain, many of their preachers frequently and expressly pray that pure streams may for ever flow, to water the city of the living God. You need not be told, reverend Sir, what place I mean ; it was the famous university of *Oxford.* Nor need I mention the scene exhibited, it was a tribunal, a visitatorial tribunal, erected in *Edmund-Hall.* Six pious students, who promised to be the salt of the earth, and the lights of the world, entire friends to the doctrines and liturgy of our church, by a citation previously fixed upon the college door, were summoned to appear before this tribunal. They did appear ; and as some were pleased to term it, were tried, convicted, and to close the scene, in the chapel of the same hall, (consecrated and set apart for nobler purposes,) had the sentence of expulsion publicly read and pronounced against them.

" So severe a sentence, in an age when almost every kind of proper discipline is held with so lax a rein, hath naturally excited a curiosity in all that have heard of it, to inquire of what notable crime these delinquents may have been guilty, to deserve such uncommonly rigorous treatment. But how will their curiosity be turned into indignation, when they are told, that they were thus rigorously handled for doing no evil at all, and that 'no fault could be found in them, save in the law of their God ? '

" It is true, indeed, one article of impeachment was, ' that some of them were of *trades* before they entered into the university.' But what evil or crime worthy of expulsion can there be in that ? To be called from any, though the meanest mechanic employ, to the study of the liberal arts, where a natural genius hath been given, was never yet looked upon as a reproach to, or diminution of, any great and public character whatsoever. *Profane history* affords us a variety of examples of the greatest heroes, who have been fetched even from the plough to command armies, and who performed the greatest exploits for their country's good. And if we examine *sacred history,* we shall find that even David, after he was anointed king, looked back with sweet complacence to the rock from whence he was hewn, and is not ashamed to leave it upon record, that ' God took him away from the sheep-folds, as he was following the ewes great with young ones ;' and as though he loved to repeat it, ' he took him,' (says he,) ' that he might feed Jacob his people, and Israel his inheritance.'

" But why speak I of David? when Jesus of Nazareth, David's Lord and David's King, had for his reputed father a carpenter, and in all probability, as it was a common proverb among the Jews, that ' he who did not teach his son a trade, taught him to be a thief,' he worked at the trade of a carpenter himself. For this indeed he was reproached and maligned ; ' Is not this,' said they, ' the carpenter's son?' nay, ' Is not this the carpenter?' But who were these maligners? The greatest enemies to the power of godliness which the world ever saw, the scribes and Pharisees, that ' generation of vipers,' as John the Baptist calls them, who upon every occasion were spitting out their venom, and shooting forth their arrows, even bitter words, against that Son of man, even that Son of God, who, to display his sovereignty, and confound the wisdom of the worldly wise, chose poor fishermen to be his apostles; and whose chief of the apostles, though bred up at the feet of Gamaliel, both before and after his call to the apostleship, laboured with his own hands, and worked at the trade of a tent-maker.

" If from such exalted and more distant, we descend to more modern and inferior, characters, we shall find that very late, not to say our present, times furnish us with instances of some, even of our *dignitaries*, who have been called from trades that tended to help and feed the body, not only to higher employs of a spiritual nature, but even to preside over those that are intrusted with the care of souls. And who knows but some of these young students, though originally mechanics, if they had been suffered to have pursued their studies, might have either climbed after them to some preferment in the church, or been advanced to some office in that university from which they are now expelled? One of the present reverend and worthy proctors, we are told, was formerly a lieutenant in the army, and as such a military employ was no impediment to his being a minister or proctor, it may be presumed that being formerly of trades could have been no just impediment to these young men becoming, in process of time, true gospel ministers and good soldiers of Jesus Christ.

"Their being accustomed to prayer, whether with or without a form, would by no means disqualify them for the private or public discharge of their ministerial functions. For if it did, what sinners, what *great* sinners must they have been, who prayed in an extempore way before any forms of prayer could be printed! Why also are not some few others expelled for extempore *swearing?*" *Lett.*

Of the six exiles from Edmund-Hall, Erasmus Middleton was the most distinguished. He was sustained at Cambridge by Fuller the banker, a dissenter; and ordained in Ireland by the bishop of Downe. In Scotland, he married a branch of the ducal family of Gordon. In London, he became curate to Romaine and Cadogan, and compiled his well known "Biographia Evangelica." The Fuller family presented him, in his old age, with the living of *Turvey* in Bedfordshire.

CHAPTER XXVIII.

MANY things conspired to enable Whitefield to embark again for America, without suspecting that he was not likely to return. Both his health and spirits were unusually good. He had often raised his old *war-cry,* " Field preaching, field preaching for ever ! " and followed it up with the shout, " Ebenezer, Hallelujah, Pentecost ! " on the spots of his former triumphs. His chapels in London also were well provided with acceptable supplies, and his affairs at Georgia all prosperous. Indeed, he appears to have had nothing to vex him but the heavy expense incurred for *coach-hire,* in making his last excursions. It had " mounted very high," he says ; " and means must be found to save the late great expense." This proves that he *expected* to return ; and none of his letters at the time indicate any misgivings of heart, or breathe even his usual longing for heaven. " I am brave as to my bodily health, and have not been in better spirits for years," is his own account of himself, when he went on board the *Friendship ;* and of his prospects, he said, " I am persuaded this voyage will be for the Redeemer's glory, and the welfare of precious and immortal souls." It was—but not in the way he anticipated. Cornelius Winter's account of his general tone of mind and body agrees, on the whole, with Whitefield's own account of himself. He had occasional seasons of " remarkable lowness and languor," at sea ; but he was able to spend much of his time in close study of the History of England, and in preparing sermons ; and was in better health at the end of the voyage, than he had been after the generality of his former voyages.

2 K

Thus the only thing which really oppressed him, on leaving, was the pain of parting from his friends for a time. But this was nothing new with him. What he said now, he had said often; " Oh these partings! without a divine support they would be intolerable. Talk not of taking *personal* leave : you know my *make.* Paul could stand a *whipping*—but not a weeping farewell." *Letters.*

The parting scene at the Tabernacle and Tottenham Court was awful, and seems to have been repeated : for he says, in his own manuscript journal, that he preached on the vision of Jacob's ladder, at both places ; and Winter says, that " The Good Shepherd " was his farewell sermon. Indeed, Whitefield himself, in a letter, calls this his "last sermon." Thus there must have been " more last words " than his journal records. He himself was " disgusted " with the manner in which this farewell sermon was reported and printed. Well he might, as to the latter, if the first edition was like the second, which is now before me. Still, with all its faults, it is *characteristic ;* and, therefore, I will give some specimens of it, as few persons have ever seen it.

The text is, John x. 27, 28. These words, it will be recollected, were uttered by Christ, at the feast of dedication. " This festival," says Whitefield, " was of bare *human* invention; and yet I do not find that our Lord preached *against* it. And I believe, that when we see things as we ought, we shall not entertain our auditories about rites and ceremonies—but about the grand thing. It is the glory of *methodists,* that whilst they have been preaching forty years, there has not been (that I know of) one single pamphlet published by them about the non-essentials of religion."

On the words, " My sheep hear my voice, and they follow me," he says, " There are but *two* sorts of people. Christ does not say, Are you an independent, a baptist, a presbyterian, or are you a church of England man ? Nor did he ask, Are you a *methodist ?* The Lord divides the whole world into sheep and goats. O sinners, you are come to hear a poor creature take his last farewell : but I want you to forget the creature and his preaching. I want to lead *further* than the Tabernacle—even to mount Calvary, to see with what expense of blood, Jesus Christ purchased ' his own.' Now, before I go any further, will you be so good, before the *world* gets into your hearts, to inquire whether you belong to Christ or not ? Surely the world did not get into your hearts before you rose from your beds ! Many of you were up sooner than usual." (The sermon was preached at *seven* o'clock in the morning.) " I hope the world does not get into your hearts before *nine*. Man, woman, sinner ! put thy hand upon thy heart, and say, didst thou ever hear Christ's voice so as to follow him ? "

Speaking of the restoration of wandering sheep, he said, " I once heard Dr. Marryat—who was not ashamed of *market-lan-guage*—say at Pinner's Hall, ' God has a great dog to fetch his sheep back when they wander.' He sends the devil after them, to bark at them; but instead of barking them further off, he barks them *back* to the fold."

On the subject of the ministry, he said, " I am sure I never prayed so much against my infirmities, as against going into *holy* orders so soon. However some may come to preach here and there,—and I know not how much they are concerned,— but I am sure it concerned me greatly. I have prayed hundreds of times, that God would not let me go so soon. I remember once at Gloucester—I know the room—and I cannot help looking up at the window, whenever I am there, and going by : I know the bed-side—I know the floor, on which I have been prostrate for weeks together, crying, I cannot go ; I am a novice ; I shall fall into the condemnation of the devil. Yet I wanted to be at Oxford. I wanted to stay there three or four years, that I might make a hundred and fifty sermons at least, for I wished to set up with a stock in trade. I remember wrestling, praying, groaning, striving with God ; and said, I am un-done, unfit to speak in thy name ; my God, send me not. After I had written to all my friends, to pray against the bishop's solicitation, these words came into my mind,—' My sheep hear my voice, and none shall pluck them out of my hand,'—then I said, Lord, I will go ; send me *when* thou wilt."

The following remarks are very characteristic. " ' None shall pluck them out of my hand :' this implies that there is always

somebody *plucking* at Christ's sheep. The lust of the flesh is
plucking ; the pride of life is plucking ; and the devil is continually plucking at them : but nothing shall pluck them out of
my hands. I have bought them, and am gone to heaven to prepare a place for them." *Sermon.*

This sermon was preached at the Tabernacle on the morning
of the day he went to Gravesend to embark. The companions
of his voyage were Smith and Cornelius Winter. His own
account of their services to him during the voyage is, " Mr.
Smith hath really behaved very well, and been handy and attentive. The same may be said of Mr. Winter." This he said at
the end of the voyage. Whilst on board, he wrote to a friend,
concerning them, " I only want somebody about me that hath
a little more *brains ;* but we must have our *buts* in this trying,
imperfect state." This, I have no doubt, contains the real
secret of Rowland Hill's mode of explaining Winter's account of
Whitefield's temper ; as " the version of a worthy but weak
man." It is well known by many, that Rowland Hill empowered
me to contradict, with all the authority of his own name, Winter's picture of Whitefield's temper ; and to explain it by Winter's want of brains. I have done neither, because very little
historical importance belongs to the knowledge of either party.
Both knew Whitefield late in life, and not long, and only after
his nerves were shattered. Wesley's opinion is of more value
than that of both. He knew him from the *beginning,* and said
at the end, " How few have we known of so *kind* a temper ! "
Funeral Sermon. Whitefield's temper in his last days was not
so bland as Rowland Hill thought, nor so hasty as Cornelius
Winter said. The former had, therefore, no occasion to refer
the picture drawn by the latter, to mortification. Winter had
brains, as well as fine feelings, whatever might have been the
development of them at sea. The good man was too often *sick*
there, to be very clever : for it was his first voyage ; but Whitefield's thirteenth : a fact which quite explains the impatience of
the latter, and the opinions of the former.

I have touched this contested point, because more has been
made of it, on both sides, than was at all necessary. Neither
Hill nor Winter had any personal acquaintance with Whitefield

until 1767; and he died 1770. This fact should have moderated
the opinions of both. Wilberforce said, without knowing this
fact, " Even Winter's account detracts little from the sum of
Whitefield's excellences." Dr. Reed's epithet at his grave—
" *that seraphic man !* " will for ever absorb both the compliments of Hill and the complaints of Winter ; and just because
it is historically true, or borne out by the whole tenor of his life.

These dates give, however, great importance to Winter's
account of Whitefield's preaching : for if it was so commanding
and melting during the few years he heard him, what must it
have been when it awed Moorfields, and agitated Blackheath,
whilst they were thronged with tens of thousands ?

I feel reluctant, I confess, to enter upon this *last* voyage. I
have journeyed so long in vision with Whitefield, and so often
when I could enjoy little else, that I shrink from the near prospect of parting with him. Perhaps my readers share this feeling with me. If so, they will not regret to *linger* with me,
whilst he was detained on the coast. He was accompanied to
Gravesend by " a very large party, in coaches and chaises; and
next day preached two sermons " there. Not in the church,
however, as formerly. " That was refused to him." *Winter.*
This fact creates in my mind an association with that church,
which is any thing but what I enjoy, when I visit Gravesend.
This is not my fault ; nor can other visitors be blamed if they
feel as I do. True; I am thus teaching visitors to recollect the
pitiable fact. I avow the design. This is one way of bringing
into discredit the worse than *synagogue bigotry,* which excludes
from national churches men who are the glory of the nation.
Shame upon the folly and effrontery which can shut them upon
stars that Christ is not ashamed to hold in his " right hand ! "
And equal shame upon any chapel, if such there be, that would
not welcome an evangelical clergyman, even if he were a bishop
or an archbishop, into its pulpit, and at its communion table !
The tide of public opinion is setting in to this point, strongly
and directly ; and I, for one, both go with it, and try to help it
on. True ; many are trying to turn it. Well; they will only
strengthen it. The tide of public opinion is slow upon ecclesiastical channels ; but then it has no *reflux,* except to gather

strength. It can afford to be slow ; for it is sure. Let not the
spirit of these remarks be called *levelling:* it is *elevating,* if
there be no arbitrary nor unnatural distinctions in the church of
the first-born, in heaven.   Besides, who does not see, that the
first bishop who shall preach in a dissenting or methodist chapel, or preside at a missionary sacrament in Zion or Surrey, will
win more golden opinions for his church from all the good and
wise in the world, by that one act of duty, than by a thousand
acts of power ? It is in vain now to dream of uniting the three
kingdoms, or any one of them, in the fellowship of *one* church :
but all protestants may be gradually united in the fellowship of
the Spirit, if their leaders will only set the example.

A specimen of this catholicity occurred at Deal, whilst Whitefield's vessel was detained by contrary winds.   Dr. Gibbon of
London, and Mr. Bradbury of Ramsgate, had come there to
ordain a student.   The Doctor, on hearing that Whitefield was
in the bay, went on board, and spent a day with him.   Bradbury and the young minister also visited him, and urged him to
be present at the ordination, and to preach after it.   He did
both ; and as we have seen, with great delight to himself and
others.   Winter, who accompanied him, says, " I hope I shall
never forget the solemnities of that day."   What would have
been thought of Whitefield had he refused, or of Gibbon and
the dissenters had they not invited him, to be present ? Just so
is thought of the *exclusives,* by the thinkers who are destined to
pilot the church of Christ out of the narrow seas of party, into
the Pacific of catholic communion.   Whitefield tells an anecdote of Dr. Gibbon's " warm-hearted " visit to him on board,
which may be applied to good men who forget this.   The Doctor
became sea-sick, and was obliged to lie down, for some time, in
the state cabin.   " There," says Whitefield, " he learnt more
experimentally to *pray* for those who do business in the great
waters."   Like many others, the Doctor had cared less for
seamen than he ought: but sickness made him sympathizing.
So it is in this matter: something is always occurring in the
exclusive system to *sicken* good men, and thus to teach them to
pray with the understanding and the heart, " Thy will be done
on earth as it is in heaven."   Whoever regrets the frequency of

that prayer in the church service, I do not. It will pull down the middle wall of partition soon: and it is, in the mean time, the protest of the church (however unconsciously) against that wall. She thus denounces at the font, the altar, and the grave, her own bigotry.

During the month Whitefield was tossed about on the coast, he preached whenever he could land, and paid his usual attentions to all on board. The voyage was both long and dangerous; but not unpleasant. He arrived at Charleston in such health, that he preached on the very day he landed. The fact is, his spirits were elevated by the welcome he received, and especially by the good news which awaited him from Georgia. " The increase of the colony was incredible, and the governor, Wright, had laid the foundation of two wings to the orphanhouse, for the accommodation of students." All this wound up his hopes and spirits, until he forgot that he was in the body. And the impulse was both increased and prolonged, when he saw Bethesda in its glory. The governor, council, and assembly attended in a body at the academy chapel, to hear him preach for the college. They then surveyed and approved the new buildings; each of which was " a hundred and fifty feet long, and executed with taste, and in a masterly manner." Afterwards the whole party dined with him in the hall of the orphanhouse, " at a handsome and plentiful table ;" and testified both their gratitude and satisfaction. Nor was this all. The commons' house of assembly voted the warmest thanks to him for his " truly generous and disinterested benefactions to the province." *Georgia Gazette.* All this was done after a sermon, in which he avowed that, as far as lay in his power, " Bethesda should always be upon a *broad* bottom." " All denominations have freely given," he said ;—" all denominations—all the continent shall receive equal benefit from it." *Sermon.*

The inspiring effect of all this was, that his health was better than it had been for many years, and his strength equal to the task of every-day preaching. His *moral* strength was such, that he " annihilated his own name " in the deed of settlement for the college, that trustees might accept the office of wardens, " without suffering contempt for being connected with " him !

Thus it was not pretence, nor mere exclamation, when he said, years before this time, " Let the name of George Whitefield perish, if God be glorified." As I have often said, he only spoke strongly, when words could not fully express all he felt and meant. But his name will be imperishable, just by the little care he took to *make* it so : for he did imperishable work, without calculating upon any lasting reward in this world. No man, indeed, ever understood less, or proved more, the truth of the sacred oracle, " He that loseth his life for my sake shall save it."

Bethesda was now to him " a Goshen—a Bethel." He was almost tempted to say, " It is good to be here ;" but he said instead, " No *nestling* on this side eternity : all must give way to that divine employ—gospel ranging." This was his resolution, even while he could say, " Never did I enjoy such domestic peace, comfort, and joy during my whole pilgrimage. It is unspeakable and full of glory ! " Strong as this language is, he used still stronger on leaving the institution, although fondly and fully expecting to return to it : " O Bethesda, my Bethel, my Peniel ! My happiness is inconceivable. Hallelujah, Hallelujah ! Let chapel—tabernacle—earth—heaven, rebound with Hallelujah ! I can no more. My heart is too big to add more than my old name, ' Less than the least of all,' G. W." *Letters.*

The vigour and versatility of his mind, at this time, may be estimated by the *speech*, which he wrote for one of the orphans to deliver, after the sermon before the governor and council. I venture to ascribe the authorship of it to Whitefield, because the document was found in his own hand-writing, by Dr. Gillies. This assumption involves, I am aware, the awkward fact, that he paid some compliments to himself. But the speech would have been unnatural and unacceptable, if, while complimenting the patrons of the institution, it had passed by the founder. Had Whitefield not made the *orphan-boy* thank him, who else in the assembly would have accepted public thanks ? It is, however, for its beautiful simplicity I quote the document.

THE ORPHAN'S SPEECH. " When I consider where I stand, and before whom I am about to speak, no wonder that, previous to my rising, a trembling seized my limbs ; and now, when risen, a throbbing seizes my heart, and, as a consequence of both, shame and confusion cover my face. For what am I, (a poor *unlettered orphan,* unlearned almost in the very rudiments of my mother-tongue, and totally unskilled in the persuasive arts of speaking!) that I should be called to speak before such a venerable, august assembly, as is this day convened under Bethesda's roof? But when I reflect, that I stand up at your command, reverend Sir, to whom, under God, I owe my little all; and when I further reflect on the well-known candour of those that compose this venerable and august assembly,—my trembling begins to abate, my throbbing ceases, and a gleam of hope breaks in, that the tongue of the stammerer will, in some degree, be able to speak plainly.

" But where shall I begin, and how express the various emotions that, within the last hour, have alternately agitated and affected my soul? If the eye, as I have been taught to think, is the *looking-glass* of the soul; and if the outward gestures and earnest attention, are indications expressive of the inward commotions and dispositions of the human heart; then, a heartfelt complacency and joy hath possessed the souls of many in this assembly, whilst the reverend founder hath been giving from the pulpit such a clear, succinct, and yet withal affecting account of the rise and progress of this orphan-house academy, and of the low estate of this now flourishing colony, when the first brick of this edifice was laid. All hail, that happy day! which we now commemorate, when about thirty-two years ago, in faith and fervent prayer, the first brick of this edifice was laid. Many destitute orphans were soon taken in, and without any visible fund, in the dearest part of his Majesty's dominions, more than fifty labourers were employed, and honourably paid, and a large orphan-family, for these many years, hath been supported, clothed, and brought up in the nurture and admonition of the Lord. Oh, could these walls speak, could every chamber, every corner of this fabric speak, what agonizing supplications, what inwrought, energetic prayers would they tell us they had been witness to, and also of the blessed fruits of which we are now partakers! Behold! a once infant, deserted, despised colony, not only lifting up its drooping head, and, in some degree, overtopping, at least for trade, and increase, and extent of commerce, vying with some

of its neighbouring provinces. Behold the once despised institution ! (the very existence of which was for many years denied,)
through the indefatigable industry, unparalleled disinterestedness, and unwearied perseverance of its reverend founder, ex-
panding and stretching its wings, not only to receive a larger
number of helpless orphans like myself, but to nurse and cherish
many of the present rising generation, training them up to be
ornaments both in church and state. For ever adored be that
Providence, that power and goodness, which hath brought matters to such a desirable and long-expected issue ! Thanks,
thanks be rendered to your Excellency, for the countenance you
have always given to this beneficial plan, for laying the first
brick of yonder wings, this time twelvemonth, and for the favour
of your company on this our anniversary. Thanks to you, Mr.
President, who have long been a fellow-helper in this important
work, and have now the pleasure of seeing the fruit of all your
labours. Thanks to the gentlemen of his Majesty's honourable
council, and to the members of the general assembly, who so
warmly recommended the utility of this institution. Thanks to
you, Sir, who first opened it by preaching. Thanks to you, who
left your native country, and, without fee or reward, have for
many years laboured and watched over us in the Lord. Thanks
to all who have this day honoured us with your presence. And
above all, thanks, more than an orphan tongue can utter, or
orphan hearts conceive, be, under God, rendered unto you,
most honoured Sir, who have been so happily instrumental, in
the hands of a never-failing God, in spreading his everlasting
gospel."

CHAPTER XXIX.

WHITEFIELD never sought the patronage of the great, nor ever employed it for any personal end. To the credit of his first noble friends, Lothian, Leven, and Rae, they sought his friendship because they admired his talents, and appreciated his character. They were won by the preaching which won the multitude; and when they wrote to him, he answered them just as he did any one else, who sought his counsel or prayers, courteously and faithfully. He paid them, indeed, the current compliments of his times : and if these ever amount to flattery in appearance, they are followed by *warnings* which no real flatterer would have dared to whisper. In his first letters to the Marquis of Lothian, he said, " You do well, my Lord, to *fear*, lest your convictions should wear off.—Your Lordship is in a dangerous situation," in the world. " Come, then, and lay yourself at the *feet* of Jesus."—" As for praying in your *family*, I entreat you, my Lord, not to neglect it. You are *bound* to do it. Apply to Christ for strength to overcome your present fears. They are the effects of pride, or infidelity, or of both." These are not unfair specimens of Whitefield's correspondence with the Scotch nobles, who honoured him with their confidence. Upon some of the English noblemen, who were brought to hear him by Lady Huntingdon, his influence was equally great and good.

Amongst his friends were, also, " honourable women not a few." I wish I could say of his compliments to them, all that I have said of his general influence upon their " order :" but I cannot. I cannot even qualify, after long rejudging, the opinion I have given of his letters to them. True ; they needed and deserved

" strong consolation," in order to resist the strong temptations
presented by a frivolous court, a witty peerage, and a learned
bench, in favour of a formal religion. Nothing but " the joy of the
Lord " could have sustained them in such a sphere. Whitefield
judged well, therefore, in not plying the peeresses with the same
warnings he addressed to the peers. Happiness in religion was
the best security for their holiness. They could not be *laughed*
out of a good hope through grace. Wit and banter may make
the fear of perishing seem a weakness or a fancy; but they cannot make hope, peace, or joy, seem absurd. Neither the rough
jibes of Warburton, nor the polished sarcasms of Chesterfield
and Bolingbroke, could touch the *consciousness* of peace in believing, or of enjoyment in secret prayer, in the hearts of those
peeresses who had found, at the cross and the mercy-seat, the
happiness they had sought in vain from the world. Whitefield
knew this, and ministered to their comfort. What I regret,
therefore, is, that he mingled more compliment with consolation
than was wise or seemly. Each of " the twelve manner " of ripe
fruits on the tree of life, requires to be served up in its *own*
" leaves;" and needs no other garnishing.

But if Whitefield's letters to the peeresses were not always
manly, his *lectures* to the " brilliant circle " at Lady Huntingdon's were evidently as faithful as they were eloquent. The
well-known Countess of Suffolk found them so. Lady Guildford
prevailed on Lady Huntingdon to *admit* this beauty to hear
Whitefield. He, however, knew nothing of her presence. He
drew his bow at a venture : but every arrow seemed aimed at
her. She just managed to sit out the service, in silence ; and
when Whitefield retired, she flew into fury; abused Lady Huntingdon to her face, and denounced the sermon as a deliberate
attack on herself. In vain Lady Betty Jermain tried to appease
the beautiful fury, or to explain her mistake. In vain old
Lady Bertie and the Duchess dowager of Ancaster commanded
her silence. She maintained that she had been insulted. She
was compelled, however, by her relatives who were present, to
apologize to Lady Huntingdon. Having done this with a bad
grace, she left to return no more.

Horace Walpole, unwittingly, has borne testimony to the faithfulness of Whitefield, in the case of Earl Ferrers. " That impertinent fellow," Whitefield, he says, " told his enthusiasts in his sermons, that my Lord's heart was *stone*." So it was, and " harder than the nether millstone." He treated Whitefield courteously; but evinced a reckless contempt for religion. Walpole's own account of Ferrers proves this.

It would hardly be worth while to notice this horrible affair, were it not for the sake of the striking *contrast* between Whitefield and Theophilus Lindsay, when they successively tried to comfort Lady Huntingdon under her calamities. Her son had imbibed the principles of Chesterfield and Bolingbroke ; and her heart brooded in anguish upon his eternal prospects. The Lindsays suggested to her the *possibility* of a temporary hell. Whitefield visited and prayed for her wretched nephew, Ferrers ; but spoke all the truth of his character, and planted no fictions upon his grave.

Horace Walpole, again unwittingly, bears testimony to the uniform consistency of Whitefield's creed and character. When the peace festival was celebrated at Ranelagh, some one asked, in the clique of wits, (most likely himself,) " Has Whitefield *recanted?*" Lady Townshend replied, " O, no ; he has only *canted.*" Walpole thought this a happy hit ; little dreaming it to be a compliment to a man, who might have had preferment at the time, if he would have recanted even his clerical irregularities. This is the original play upon the words, " cant " and " recant ;" which have lately been so happily applied to an ex-patriot, by Lord John Russell.

The following anecdote of Whitefield was communicated by the Countess of Huntingdon to the late Barry, R. A. ; and sent by him to me. I give it in his own words :—" Some ladies called one Saturday morning, to pay a visit to Lady Huntingdon, and during the visit, her Ladyship inquired of them if they had ever heard Mr. Whitefield preach ? Upon being answered in the negative, she said, I wish you would hear him, he is to preach to-morrow evening at such a church or chapel, the name of which the writer forgets (nor is it material) : they promised her Ladyship they would certainly attend. They were as good as their word ; and upon calling on the Monday morning on her Lady-

ship, she anxiously inquired if they had heard Mr. Whitefield on
the previous evening, and how they liked him?—The reply was,
'O my Lady, of all the preachers we ever heard, he is the most
strange and unaccountable. Among other preposterous things,
(would your Ladyship believe it,) he declared that Jesus Christ
was so willing to receive sinners, that he did not object to receive
even the devil's *castaways.*—Now, my Lady, did you ever hear
of such a thing since you was born.' To which her Ladyship
made the following reply: ' There is something, I acknowledge,
a little singular in the invitation, and I do not recollect to have
ever met with it before; but as Mr. Whitefield is below in the
parlour, we'll have him up, and let him answer for himself.'
Upon his coming up into the drawing-room, Lady Huntingdon
said, ' Mr. Whitefield, these ladies have been preferring a very
heavy charge against you, and I thought it best that you should
come up and defend yourself: they say, that in your sermon last
evening, in speaking of the willingness of Jesus Christ to receive
sinners, you expressed yourself in the following terms,—that so
ready was Christ to receive sinners who came to him, that he
was willing to receive even the devil's castaways.'—Mr. Whitefield immediately replied, ' I certainly, my Lady, must plead
guilty to the charge: whether I did what was right or otherwise
your Ladyship shall judge from the following circumstance.—
Did your Ladyship notice, about half an hour ago, a very modest
single rap at the door? It was given by a poor, miserable-look-
ing, aged female, who requested to speak with me.—I desired
her to be shown into the parlour, when she accosted me in the
following manner:—' I believe, Sir, you preached last evening
at such a chapel.'—' Yes, I did.'—' Ah, Sir; I was accidentally
passing the door of that chapel, and hearing the voice of some
one preaching, I did what I have never been in the habit of doing, I went in; and one of the first things I heard you say, was,
that Jesus Christ was so willing to receive sinners, that he did
not object to receiving the devil's castaways. Now, Sir, I have
been on the town for many years, and am so worn out in his service, that I think I may with truth be called one of the devil's
castaways:—do you think, Sir, that Jesus Christ would receive
me?'—Mr. Whitefield assured her there was not a doubt of it,

if she was but willing to go to him.   From the sequel it appeared, that it was the case; and that it ended in the sound conversion of this poor creature; and Lady Huntingdon was assured, from most respectable authority, that the woman left a very charming testimony behind her that, though her sins had been of a crimson hue, the atoning blood of Christ had washed them white as snow."

I shall not soon forget the first use I made of this anecdote. It was handed to me just as I was about to attend the anniversary of the Female Penitentiary.   I told it there, and was pleased, although in nowise surprised, to see tears flowing down the cheeks of the noble chairman, and of honourable women not a few.   I mention this fact, because it is only by such facts, that some minds can be won over to think well of Penitentiaries.   I long questioned their policy.   Even when I became one of the secretaries of the Liverpool Female Penitentiary, I was not sure that I was doing right.   But I soon knew better, when the correspondence of the institution with parents came before me. Indeed, I owe to the *converts* in that house of mercy, and especially to the late Betsy Kenyon, the *relief* of my own mind from the haunting suspicion, that it would be impossible to forget, even in heaven, what certain brands plucked from the burning had been.   I found it impossible, however, to *remember,* even on earth, what that wonderful miracle of grace and martyr of suffering had been, although I knew well her former horrible history.   Then understood I the promise,—"They shall be as though God had not cast them off."   Saints and angels will so resemble each other in the beauty of holiness, that there will be nothing to distinguish them, but the difference of their new song.   I express, I am quite sure, the cherished recollections of many of the greatest and best in the land, in thus recording the *hallowing* influence of Betsy Kenyon's character and spirit.   Her "wings were covered with silver, and her feathers with yellow gold." There ought to be in every large town a female mission, to seek out and bring home the outcasts.

"*A female mission!*"   Yes; the church of Christ flourished most when women "laboured" with Paul "in the gospel," Phil. iv. 3.   He did not, indeed, suffer them to speak *in* the church; but he both employed them to speak *out* of it, and applauded their co-operation in spreading the gospel. He has emblazoned their names, equally with CLEMENT'S, " in the book of life," and in the New Testament. The other apostles also, and all the primitive churches, gratefully accepted and acknowledged female agency. That agency was prolonged in the Western church until the eleventh, and in the Eastern until the end of the twelfth century. The form of prayer used at the ordination of the deaconness is preserved in the " Apostolic Constitutions."

Are we wiser or stronger than the wise and apostolic master-builders of the church, that we can evangelize the world without the co-operation which apostles welcomed, and martyrs honoured, and the fathers immortalized? *(See Clem. Alexand. and Tertullian de Virginn.)* True, ministers and missionaries have freer and fuller access now to all classes, than the apostles and evangelists. Neither the jealousies nor the restraints of the East, exist in the West. What then? Alas, with all our superior facilities, the gospel is not brought home to all classes! There are even hinderances to the spread of it in the metropolis, which no *man* can surmount. Thousands, yea, tens of thousands, of females in London must perish for lack of knowledge, unless the agency of WIDOWS be employed to pluck the brands from the burning! To this extent they have been perishing, and involving, to a still greater extent, the ruin of young men, for ages. No ministry yet has penetrated the haunts of female vice, or the hovels of female ignorance. No *regular* ministry can reach them effectually. Even Whitefield and Wesley could only skirt their borders. Public opinion would not sanction any man to go further at present. It would snatch the *cloak* of character from him, even if he kept his innocence like JOSEPH. His good would be evil spoken of, were he as pure and prudent as an angel. Ministers cannot do nor dare all that their Master did. He could pass, like light, uncontaminated through any medium. He could defy public opinion, or overpower it, by miracles, whenever it was shocked at his condescension to " a woman that was a sinner." No christian man can run such risks with safety. Only christian widows can " follow the Lamb fully in the regeneration of life," in this region of the shadow of death :—and they can follow Him, with equal safety and success. The apostles of the Lamb knew this, and employed them. The apostolic churches knew this, and made deaconesses of many of their *holy widows*. And PRISCILLA too, as well as her husband, was thanked by Paul, in the name of " all the churches of the gentiles," for her services.

This is not the place to reason this question in. I must, however, remind the churches of Britain and America, that they have in the *widowhood* of their fellowship a sisterhood which can be safely and efficiently employed in this work. It would also help many who are " widows indeed," as well as save souls from death.

It will be seen from the anecdote which led to these remarks, that Whitefield was not ashamed nor slow to avow, before any rank, that his commission extended to the chief of sinners. And it is to the credit of Lady Huntingdon and her pious friends, that they were not ashamed of the gospel in this form. They rejoiced in some conversions,—particularly that of Colonel Gumley,—which astonished Doddridge as much as the conversion of Colonel Gardiner. No wonder, therefore, if Horace Walpole wondered, when " Gumley became a methodist." The *wit* was at his " wit's end ;" and could only explain the phenomenon by ascribing to Whitefield the fascinations of Garrick. Even Chesterfield wondered, and offered his chapel at Bretby Hall, in Derbyshire, to such ministers as Lady Huntingdon might introduce to it. She soon introduced Whitefield to Bretby ; and he soon rendered the Hall chapel too small. Bretby park had to accommodate the audience. Whitefield was followed by Romaine, who was not a *field* preacher. The crowd had, therefore, to catch what they could hear in the court of the hall, whilst he spoke only from the pulpit. Both preachers were, however, made very useful on this occasion. Romaine himself says of it, " We had a most refreshing time ; fifteen pulpits open ; showers of grace came down ; sinners in great numbers were awakened, and believers comforted." *Letters.*

These fifteen pulpits were not open to Whitefield. He was too *irregular* for the Derbyshire clergy. He had, however, roused their people so, that it became good policy to admit

Romaine. There was also a better reason. It was a new thing to find Chesterfield patronizing religion ; and therefore wise to make the most of his sanction whilst he was in the humour. Romaine also did well, in continuing regular. But for that, he would have been less useful. It enabled him to introduce the gospel into churches, where there was no leaven in the whole lump. Even in Derby he found his way into " the great church," although " the mayor, and the churchwardens, and the Arian " clergy, opposed him.

Soon after this, Lady Huntingdon summoned Whitefield and Romaine to preach at the opening of her chapel in Bath. Whitefield complied, of course : but Romaine pleaded off. Not, however, from any reluctance to preach with his friend. I say deliberately—his friend. Romaine gloried in the friendship of Whitefield, and cheerfully followed him in the chapels of the Countess. It was the claim of Brighton he pleaded against Bath. " Why should Bath have all, and poor Brighton none? I am at your command to go or stay." The fact is, her Ladyship had invited all her chief clerical friends to the dedication ; and Romaine thought that he might well be excused, especially as he was then labouring with great success at Brighton. The chapel was opened, therefore, by Whitefield, and the rector of Pewsey, the son of the celebrated Alderman Townsend of London. They were soon succeeded by Madan and Romaine.

These services produced a great sensation at Bath. The chapel itself was attractive. Even Horace Walpole said of it, " It is very neat, with *true* gothic windows. I was glad to see that luxury is creeping on them before persecution. They have boys and girls with charming voices, that sing hymns in parts. At the upper end is a broad *hautpas* of four steps, advancing in the middle. At each end of the broadest part are two eagles, with red cushions for the parson and clerk. Behind them rise three more steps, in the midst of which is a third eagle for a pulpit. Scarlet arm-chairs to all three. On either hand a balcony for elect ladies." *Walpole's Letters.*

There was something else which Walpole did not know of ;— a seat for bishops. It was often occupied too ! The witty and eccentric Lady Betty Cobbe, the daughter-in-law of the Archbishop of Dublin, called this curtained seat " The *Nicodemite* corner." She delighted in smuggling in bishops, to see and hear the methodists, unseen. Dr. Barnard, the Bishop of Derry, went thus often. It was he who ordained Maxfield to help Wesley, that that " good man might not work himself to death." Of this chapel Whitefield says, " It is a beautiful original; extremely plain, and equally grand." " Dear Mr. Romaine hath been much owned in" it. In 1766, he and Romaine preached in it alternately, to splendid audiences. Amongst others who heard them with profit, was Lady Glenorchy—the *Selina* of Scotland ; for Lady Huntingdon was her model, although her biographer seems to have forgotten the fact. She derived great spiritual benefit, and caught her inspiration in the cause of God from the example and the chaplains of the countess. It was through her, also, that Lord and Lady Sutherland were introduced into this circle, when they fled from the grave of their eldest daughter, to seek relief in the amusements of Bath. They were led, however, to hear Whitefield, and continued to do so, until their untimely death. They were in the prime of life : and their funeral sermon at the chapel drew out all the nobility, and produced a deep impression. The Duchess dowager of Sutherland, if alive still, knows that Whitefield ministered to her suffering parents, when she was an unconscious infant. A remarkable circumstance aggravated this bereavement to the family. The death of Lady Sutherland had been concealed from her mother, and only that of Lord Sutherland communicated. Lady Alva hastened from the north to Bath, to be with her daughter. She met by the way *two* hearses, and learnt that they were carrying Lord and Lady Sutherland to be interred in the royal chapel at Holyrood. *Evan. Reg.*

Another impressive scene took place at Bath, on the death of the Earl of Buchan. " He died," says Whitefield, " like the patriarch Jacob. He laid his hands on, and blessed, his children; assured them of his personal interest in Jesus; called most gloriously on the Holy Ghost; cried, ' *Happy, happy,*' as long as he could speak." The coffin was removed from Buchan House to the chapel, where it lay a week. Whitefield preached twice a day, and all the family, besides the other

2 L 2

rank in the city, attended. The scene must have been solemn at
the funeral service. In the morning the family attended an
" early sacrament, and seated themselves at the feet of the
corpse," whilst communicating. This was followed by a special
address to them, and closed by the sublime benediction, " The
Lord bless you and keep you ; the Lord lift up the light of his
countenance upon you ; the Lord cause his face to shine upon
you, and give you peace." They then retired to Lady Huntingdon's house, until eleven o'clock, when the public service
began. The chapel was " more than crowded." " Nearly three
hundred tickets, signed by the young earl, were given out to the
nobility and gentry. All was hushed and solemn. Attention
sat on every face, and deep and almost universal impressions
were made," whilst Whitefield preached the funeral sermon.
" The like scene, and, if possible, more solemn, was exhibited
in the evening," and repeated during five days. He says of it,
" A *like* I never expect to see on this side eternity ! Surely the
death of this noble earl, thus improved, will prove the life of
many." It did. Amongst others who publicly avowed themselves, was the young earl. This drew upon him the laugh and
lash of all the wits and witlings of the rooms ; but he " stood
impregnable as a rock."

These were not the first fruits of Whitefield's ministry at
Bath amongst the great. He had often preached to them at
the residence of Lady Gertrude Hotham, the sister of Chesterfield. She was one of his first converts, when he began to preach
at Lady Huntingdon's, in London ; and her own eldest daughter
was amongst the first of them at Bath. Miss Hotham died
early, but happy. There is in the second volume of Whitefield's
Letters a beautiful narrative of his last interview with her.
He wanted her not to sit up in bed, whilst he prayed with her,
because she was very weak. " I can rise to take my physic,"
she said ; " shall I not rise to pray ? " The letter is addressed
to the Countess of Moira, the eldest daughter of Lady Huntingdon ; of whom Horace Walpole says, " The queen of the methodists got her daughter named lady of the bedchamber to the
princesses ; but it is all off again, because she will not let her
play *cards* on Sunday."

The Countess Delitz, one of the daughters of the Duchess of Kendal, and the sister of Lady Chesterfield, was another gem in Whitefield's crown, whom he prized highly. She had much influence upon her nephew, Sir Charles Hotham, when his accomplished wife died suddenly. He had often heard Whitefield at his mother's house in Bath, and had not drunk the poison of his uncle Chesterfield : but he was not a decided character, until he was made a lonely widower. From that time, he defied all the sneers of the court, and dared " to be *singularly* good." He had also some good influence upon the young Earl of Huntingdon, for a time. He was made groom of the bedchamber to George III. ; but he never recovered the shock of his wife's death. He soon relinquished his office, and died. This was a severe blow to his mother, Lady Gertrude ; now old and lonely. It led to her own death, in a painful manner. She had been absorbed whilst reading at night, and the candles set fire to her head-dress. It spread rapidly to her neck and breast. The wounds were so many, that it required an hour and a half every day to dress them. Her composure astonished Adair the surgeon. He used to tell her, " that she *deserved* heaven." This alone discomposed her. She replied, with holy indignation, that there was no merit but in Christ ; and told Adair, that if either of them " escaped eternal death," it must be through the blood and righteousness of the Lamb of God. This account of her death-bed was given by her friend, the late Lady Maxwell of Edinburgh.

Such were Whitefield's trophies in the Chesterfield family. He won souls in it, upon the right hand and the left of the earl ; thus leaving him no excuse for making the exchange of worlds " *a leap in the dark*." His countess made a better choice. Lady Chesterfield was a natural child of George I. For years she was a leading star at court, and in all the spheres of folly. Great, therefore, was their consternation, when they saw her, after hearing Whitefield, lay all her honours and influence at the foot of the cross. Even the king forgot royal decorum so far as to laugh *aloud* in her face, at the simplicity of her dress. There was nothing to laugh at in it, but the chasteness of its beauty. Chesterfield himself had bought it at great expense on the continent; and the earl had certainly quite as much taste as the king.

Pulteney, also, the Earl of Bath, and the well-known political antagonist of Sir Robert Walpole, was deeply impressed under Whitefield's ministry, at the same time as the Countess of Chesterfield. He attended Tottenham Court chapel regularly for some years, and was a munificent benefactor to the orphan-house. Both Lady Huntingdon and Lady Fanny Shirley were his intimate friends. Whatever, therefore, may be thought of his political character, he must have been rather more than *moral*, to have secured their esteem. But amongst the peers, none stood higher in Whitefield's estimation, for piety or prudence, than Lord Dartmouth. George III. confirmed this estimate of Dartmouth's character. Queen Charlotte also thought him " one of the best of men." The king said to Dr. Beattie, the essayist on Truth, " They call his Lordship an *enthusiast;* but surely he says nothing on the subject of religion but what any christian may and *ought* to say." John Newton thought so. Dartmouth was his patron: and to him he addressed the first twenty-six letters of the " *Cardiphonia.*" It was a fit return. Newton had been refused ordination by the Archbishop of York: (not a very *arch* refusal certainly!) and Dartmouth prevailed on Dr. Green, the Bishop of Lincoln, to ordain him; and then gave him the curacy of Olney. How much the church of Christ owes to this act of kindness! Newton's early association with the dissenters, and his methodism, would have shut him out of the church: for it was well known, that Brewer of Stepney recommended him to the dissenters of Warwick, on the removal of Ryland, as a probationer. He preached also in Yorkshire amongst the dissenters. This accounts for the archbishop's refusal. Newton forgot as well as forgave him; but he never forgot nor concealed his connexion with Warwick. Long after his settlement at Olney, he often said, " The very name of Warwick makes my heart leap with joy. There my mouth was first opened. There I met some sweet encouragement on my entrance into the ministry." Thus he loved the people, although he had been an unsuccessful candidate. It is well he was so! He would have been lost amongst the dissenters. I mean, of course, that his *preaching* talents would have given him no distinction amongst them. Even his *pen* they did not want. They welcomed his writings, as they do every thing which is spiritual, in common with all the friends of truth and godliness; but they needed them not for themselves. They read and praised them, that the church might profit by them. This is not the case now. Newton is read by them for their own edification also, and because he was eminently useful in the church. Then, they read him that he might *be* useful, and because there were few Newtons in the church, and still fewer Dartmouths or Thorntons to patronize them.

I have already mentioned Dartmouth's patronage of the college for the American Indians. It is not so generally known, that he was one of the chief patrons of evangelical preaching at the Lock chapel in London. He and Baron Smythe gave the full weight of their rank and influence to that "hill of Zion," on which the dew of heaven has so often and long descended. That influence was not small. Dartmouth stood high at court; and Smythe, besides being the son of Leicester's eldest daughter, was Lord Chief Baron of the Exchequer. Both were the particular friends of Venn also. The latter gave him the living of Yelling, in Huntingdonshire; and Lady Smythe bequeathed to his son the advowson of Bidborough, in Kent.

It was thus Lady Huntingdon and Whitefield, leading each other alternately, and always acting together, drew out and brought into notice the little, but faithful, band of clergymen, who became the *salt* of the church of England. Yes; *they* found out and brought forward these good men, and won for them the patronage which enabled them to do good, as well as created for them the element in which they lived, moved, and had their being. They were, indeed, "independent students of the word of God;" but methodism made them so. This fact is disputed. It cannot, however, be disproved. Why then should it be called in question? It is as impossible to separate the improvement of the church from the direct influence of Whitefield and Wesley, as to separate her corruptions from the name of Laud.

CHAPTER XXX.

WHILST Whitefield was rejoicing over Georgia, applications were pouring in upon him from all quarters, to hasten again to the cities and wildernesses of America. He hardly knew which call was loudest, or " which way to turn" himself. He went, however, first to Philadelphia, after having preached the gospel fully in Savannah. On his arrival he found, he says, "pulpits, hearts, affections as open and enlarged as ever" towards him. Philadelphia could not have given him a more cordial welcome, had she even foreseen that she was to see his face no more: for all the churches as well as the chapels were willingly opened to him, and all ranks vied in flocking to hear him. This free access to the episcopal churches delighted him much, wherever it occurred. He never fails to record both his gratitude and gratification, when he obtains, on any tour, access even to one church. It always did him *good* too. I have often been struck with this, whilst tracing his steps. True; he was at *home* wherever there were souls around him; but he was most at home in a church, except, indeed, when he had a mountain for his pulpit, and the heavens for his sounding-board, and half a county for his congregation. Then, neither St. Paul's nor Westminster had any attractions for him. The fact is, Whitefield both admired and loved the Liturgy. He had the spirit of its compilers and of its best prayers in his own bosom, and therefore it was no *form* to him. It had been the channel upon which the first mighty spring-tides of his devotion flowed, and the chief medium of his communion with heaven, when he was most successful at Tottenham Court and Bath. All his great "days of the Son of Man" there, were associated with the church service. He was, therefore, most in his element *with* it; although he was often equally and more successful *without* it. Accordingly, it would be difficult to say, whether the gospel triumphed most, at this time, in the churches or the chapels of Philadelphia. His prayers for the outpouring of the Holy Spirit went, in an equally "direct line, to heaven," and were equally answered, whether with or without book.

He was now in such good health and spirits, that he preached twice every sabbath, and three or four times a week, although the heat was setting in. During an excursion of a hundred and fifty miles in the province, also, he was able to preach every day, and to "bear up bravely." Indeed, he was so much "better than he had been for many years," that he indulged the hope of returning to Bethesda in the autumn, and of sailing to England again.

In this state of mind and body he arrived at New York, and found not only "congregations larger than ever," but also such a host of invitations from all quarters, that he sent the *bundle* to England as a curiosity. These numerous and loud calls shook his purpose of returning to Georgia in the autumn. "I yet keep to my intended plan," he says, but "perhaps I may not see Georgia until Christmas." A tempting prospect was now held out to him,—of "*fresh work*," at Albany, Great Burrington, Norfolk, Salisbury, Sharon, and New Windsor. This was rendered irresistible by the offer of Kirkland, the Oneida missionary, to accompany him, and to take him to "a great *congress* of the Indians." It does not appear, however, that he went to the Oneida congress. There are, indeed, the names of some Indian towns in his notes of this tour, but no mention is made of Indians.

Whitefield, as might be expected, enjoyed much the scenery of the Hudson, during his sail to Albany; especially in the pass between the Catskill mountains, and not less, when he visited the Cohoes, the falls of the Mohawk, at Schenectady. At both, he could only exclaim, "O thou *wonder-working* God!" (The scenery of America will not long be unknown in Britain. I have seen Bartlett's glorious sketches of it; and some of the en-

gravings are now before me, in the same style as those of Beattie's
Switzerland, Scotland, and Waldenses. The verbal descriptions,
likewise, are equally graphic. The religious public here want
such a work, in order to understand and appreciate Reed and
Cox, and in order to sympathize with Washington Irving, in
their enthusiastic admiration of Transatlantic beauty and sublimity. I need not say that I am not *puffing* the work, even
when I add that it is passing through the press under my own
eye. I have all the reward I wish for, in being the *first* reader
of an illustrative work, worthy of America, and wanted in
Britain. It will enable many, like myself, to trace with the
eyes of the understanding, the steps of Brainerd and Whitefield, of Reed and Cox, and of all tourists who are worth
following.)

I am unable to point out Whitefield's route from Albany back
to New York. It embraced a circuit of more than five hundred miles, and occupied him during the whole of the month of
July. All that he himself records of it—and it is the *last* entry
in his memoranda—is, " Heard afterwards that the word ran
and was glorified. Grace, grace ! " His last letter but *one* to
his friend Keene, is a little more explicit. " All fresh work
where I have been. Congregations have been very large, attentive, and affected. The divine influence hath been as at first.
Oh what a scene of usefulness is opening in various parts of the
new world ! Invitations crowd upon me both from ministers
and people, and from many, many quarters. A very peculiar
providence led me lately to a place where a horse-stealer was
executed. Thousands attended. The poor criminal had sent
me several letters, on hearing I was in the country. The sheriff
allowed him to come and hear a sermon under an adjacent tree.
Solemn, solemn ! After being by himself about an hour—I
walked half a mile with him to the gallows. An *instructive*
walk ! His heart had been softened *before* my first visit.—I
went up with him into the cart. He gave a short exhortation.
I then stood on the coffin ; added, I trust, a word in season,
prayed, and took my leave. Effectual good, I trust, was done.
Grace, grace ! "

From New York he went to Boston, in the middle of Sep-

tember; and again had to say, " Never was the word received
with greater eagerness than now. All opposition seems to
cease for a while. I never was carried through the summer's
heat so well." All this encouraged him to start again upon
another circuit. He therefore went to Newbury; but was
obliged to return suddenly, in consequence of an attack of
cholera in the night. Still, he was not alarmed for his general
health. He soon rallied again, and set off to New Hampshire,
to " begin to begin," as he said, anew !

I have now to transcribe the *last* letter he wrote to England.
It is dated from Portsmouth, *seven* days before he died, and addressed to his friend Keene, one of the managers of the Tabernacle. " My very dear friend, you will see by the many invitations, what a door is opened for preaching the everlasting
gospel. I was so ill on Friday, that I could not preach, although
thousands were waiting to hear. Well; the day of release will
shortly come ;—but it does not seem *yet ;* for, by riding sixty
miles, I am better, and hope to preach here to-morrow. I trust
my blessed Master will accept of these poor efforts to serve him.
Oh for a warm heart ! Oh to stand fast in the faith, to quit ourselves like men, and be strong ! " This prayer was answered,
but his hope " to see all dear friends, about the time proposed,"
was not realized.

At Portsmouth, however, he preached daily, from the 23rd
to the 29th of September, besides once at Kittery and Old York.

On Saturday morning, September 29, he set out for Boston ;
but before he came to Newbury Port, where he had engaged to
preach next morning, he was importuned to preach by the way
at Exeter. At the last he preached in the open air, to accommodate the multitudes that came to hear him, no house
being able to contain them. He continued his discourse near
two hours, by which he was greatly fatigued ; notwithstanding
which, in the afternoon, he set off for Newbury Port, where he
arrived that evening, and soon after retired to rest, being Saturday night, fully intent on preaching the next day. His rest
was much broken, and he awoke many times in the night, and
complained very much of an oppression at his lungs, breathing
with much difficulty. And at length, about six o'clock on

the Lord's day morning, he departed this life, in a fit of the asthma.

Mr. Richard Smith, who attended Mr. Whitefield from England to America the last time, and was his constant companion in all his journeyings while there, till the time of his decease, has given the following particular account of his death and interment :—

" On Saturday, September 29, 1770, Mr. Whitefield rode from Portsmouth to Exeter (fifteen miles) in the morning, and preached there to a very great multitude, in the fields. It is remarkable, that before he went out to preach that day, (which proved to be his last sermon,) Mr. Clarkson, senior, observing him more uneasy than usual, said to him, ' Sir, you are more fit to go to bed than to preach.' To which Mr. Whitefield answered, ' True, Sir ;' but turning aside, he clasped his hands together, and looking up, said—' Lord Jesus, I am weary *in* thy work, but not *of* thy work. If I have not yet finished my course, let me go and speak for thee once more in the fields, seal thy truth, and come home and die.' His last sermon was from 2 Cor. xiii. 5,—' Examine yourselves, whether ye be in the faith ; prove your own selves : know ye not your own selves, how that Jesus Christ is in you, except ye be reprobates ? ' He dined at Captain Gillman's. After dinner, Mr. Whitefield and Mr. Parsons rode to Newbury. I did not get there till two hours after them. I found them at supper. I asked Mr. Whitefield how he felt himself after his journey. He said, ' he was tired, therefore he supped early, and would go to bed.' He ate a very little supper, talked but little, asked Mr. Parsons to discharge the table, and perform family duty ; and then retired upstairs. He said, ' that he would sit and read till I came to him,' which I did as soon as possible ; and found him reading in the Bible, with Dr. Watts's Psalms lying open before him. He asked me for some water gruel, and took about half his usual quantity ; and kneeling down by the bed-side, closed the evening with prayer. After a little conversation, he went to rest, and slept till two in the morning, when he awoke me, and asked for a little cider ; he drank about a wine-glass full. I asked him how he felt, for he seemed to pant for breath. He told me ' his asthma was coming on him again ; he must have two or three days' rest. Two or three days' riding, without preaching, would set him up again.' Soon afterwards, he asked me to put the window up a little higher, (though it was half up all night,) ' for,' said he, ' I cannot breathe ; but I hope I shall be better by and by ; a good pulpit sweat to-day, may give me relief : I shall be better after preaching.' I said to him, I wished he would not preach so often. He replied, ' I had rather *wear* out than *rust* out.' I then told him, I was afraid he took cold in preaching yesterday. He said, ' he believed he had ;' and then sat up in the bed, and prayed that God would be pleased to bless his preaching where he had been, and also bless his preaching that day, that more souls might be brought to Christ ; and prayed for direction, whether he should winter at Boston, or hasten to the southward—prayed for a blessing on his Bethesda college, and his dear family there—for Tabernacle and chapel congregations, and all connexions on the other side of the water ; and then laid himself down to sleep again. This was nigh three o'clock. At a quarter past four he waked, and said, ' My asthma, my asthma is coming on ; I wish I had not given out word to preach at Haverill, on Monday ; I don't think I shall be able ; but I shall see what to-day will bring forth. If I am no better to-morrow, I will take two or three days' ride !' He then desired me to warm him a little gruel ; and, in break- ing the fire-wood, I waked Mr. Parsons, who thinking I knock- ed for him, rose and came in. He went to Mr. Whitefield's bed-side, and asked him how he felt himself. He answered, ' I am almost suffocated. I can scarce breathe, my asthma quite chokes me.' I was then not a little surprised to hear how quick, and with what difficulty, he drew his breath. He got out of bed, and went to the open window for air. This was exactly at five o'clock. I went to him, and for about the space of five minutes saw no danger, only that he had a great difficulty in breathing, as I had often seen before. Soon afterwards he turned himself to me, and said, ' *I am dying.*' I said, ' I hope not, Sir.' He ran to the other window panting for breath, but could get no relief. It was agreed that I should go for Dr. Sawyer ; and on my coming back, I saw death on his face ; and he again said, ' *I am dying.*' His eyes were fixed, his under lip drawing inward every time he drew breath; he went towards the window, and we offered him some warm wine, with lavender drops, which he refused. I persuaded him to sit down in the chair, and have his cloak on ; he consented by a sign, but could not speak. I then offered him the glass of warm wine ; he took half of it, but it seemed as if it would have stopped his breath entirely. In a little time he brought up a considerable quantity of phlegm and wind. I then began to have some small hopes. Mr. Parsons said, he thought Mr. Whitefield breathed more freely than he did, and would recover. I said, ' No Sir, he is certainly dying.' I was continually employed in taking the phlegm out of his mouth with a handkerchief, and bathing his temples with drops, rubbing his wrists, &c. to give him relief, if possible, but all in vain ; his hands and feet were as cold as clay. When the doctor came in, and saw him in the chair leaning upon my breast, he felt his pulse, and said, ' He is a dead man.' Mr. Parsons said, ' I do not believe it ; you must do something, doctor !' He said, ' I cannot ; he is now near his last breath.' And indeed so it was ; for he fetched but one gasp, and stretched out his feet, and breathed no more. This was exactly at six o'clock. We continued rubbing his legs, hands, and feet, with warm cloths, and bathed him with spirits for some time, but all in vain. I then put him into a warm bed, the doctor standing by, and often raised him upright, continued rubbing him and putting spirits to his nose for an hour, till all hopes were gone. The people came in crowds to see him : I begged the doctor to shut the door." *Smith.*

Thus Whitefield died. I need not the apocalyptic voice from heaven in order to " write," nor do you in order to exclaim, " Blessed are the dead who die in the Lord from henceforth : Yea, saith the Spirit, that they may rest from their labours, and their works do follow them :" but the very readiness with which we utter *all* this oracle at his death-bed, should lead us to inquire, why we utter only *part* of it at the death-beds of the righteous in general. I must for my *own* sake, if not for your sake also, meditate on this,

> " In the chamber,
> Where the good man met his fate."

I have not often troubled you with formal reflections in this work. There was no need of them, whilst Whitefield could speak for himself. But he is now dead ; and although "he yet speaketh," his language needs an interpreter, who understands both it and the oracle I have just quoted.

The blessedness of dying in the Lord, is a privilege understood and appreciated by all real christians. Even almost christians see, at a glance, how sweet it must be to sleep in Jesus. Yea, the very BALAAMS of the church, who love gain more than godliness, *feel* what they say, when they exclaim from time to time, " Let me die the death of the righteous, and let my last end be like his." Accordingly, the oracle, " Blessed are the dead which die in the Lord," has passed into a *proverb;* the truth of which no one doubts, and the sweetness of which all acknowledge.

It is a remarkable fact, however, that the last clause of that oracle has not become proverbial, except in its application to very eminent and useful christians. We say of all who die in Jesus, " they rest from their labours :" but of how few we add, with any great emphasis or emotion,—" their *works* do follow them," Rev. xiv. 13. He must have been, if not a *second* Whitefield, at least a very devoted man, of whom we say, with triumph or pleasure, or even without faltering hesitation, " His works do follow him."

It is worthy of special notice, that this hesitation was *foreseen,* and provided against, when the oracle was first given to the church. John says, " I heard a voice from heaven saying unto me, Write, Blessed are the dead which die in the Lord from henceforth." That heavenly voice, however, said no more ; ventured no further. It was the Holy Ghost who added the other parts of the oracle : " Yea, saith the SPIRIT, that they may rest from their labours ; and their works do follow them." Instances of this kind of addition to the amount or the momentum of an oracle, are not uncommon. Hence Paul, when warning the Hebrews by the fate of the church in the wilderness, added to the counsel, " Harden not your hearts," the appeal, " The Holy Ghost saith, To-day if ye will hear his voice," Heb. iii. 7. In like manner the Saviour when expounding the law on the mount, added to his quotations of the law his own injunctions ; prefaced thus,—" But, I say unto you," Matt. v. 20.

Such was the *rule*, in the revelation of some truths. Its *reason* is not, however, so easily explained, in the case of the dead, as in the case of the living. It was a fine measure for giving effect to the tremendous warnings addressed to the Hebrews, to make Paul fall back for a time into the shade, until the Holy Ghost himself said, " I sware in my wrath." After that, the apostle's " Take heed, brethren," and his " Let us fear," could not be wondered at, nor fairly objected to, however solemnly uttered, nor however warmly enforced.

Perhaps this hint will furnish a clue to the reason, why the Holy Spirit took up the subject of future blessedness, where the voice from heaven stopped. He confirmed that voice, so far as it went. " Yea, saith the Spirit," they are blessed who " die in the Lord." Then he added an explanation of that blessedness, which comes better from himself, surely, than it could have come from the lips of either saints or angels in heaven. They, indeed, could have gone a little further than they did, and might have said, (the former from their own experience, and the latter from long observation,) " the dead in Christ *rest* from their labours :"—but it would hardly have *become* saints or angels to complete the explanation of celestial bliss by adding, " their *works* do follow the dead which die in the Lord." Indeed, the more they understood this truth then, the less they would venture to say about it ;—it is so sublime and amazing ! Besides, it was then so *new*, that no one in heaven could well understand it. The fruits and effects of the works of those who had slept in Jesus, were but just beginning to follow them. The *reaction* of their works of faith and labours of love, was only coming into operation on earth ; and thus only " a kind of its first-fruits " had reached heaven ; so that even those who had " turned many unto righteousness," by watching to win souls whilst here, had no idea then of the number of souls they had won by watching. They know better now—and they knew soon after the death of

John, that their labour had not been in vain in the Lord : but when the apocalyptic oracle was first given, they were not *fit* to complete it, either from their own knowledge, or from their own spirit. I mean—they were too much absorbed with a heaven all new to them—with their own personal enjoyment—and especially with the presence of the Lamb slain—to think about their *relative* usefulness on earth. They had *sung* nothing about their works, and thought nothing about them, in heaven, except to blush for their fewness and imperfections ; and, therefore, they *said* nothing about the fruits which followed, when they cried down from their thrones of light and mansions of glory to John, " Write, Blessed are the dead which die in the Lord from henceforth." Here they stopped at once. Then, there was silence in heaven ! But the eternal Spirit did not let the matter rest here. He carried on and completed the revelation of that blessedness. Having " wrought all their works in them ;" having " created them anew in Christ Jesus unto good works ;" and having wrought *by* them in glorifying Christ on earth, the Holy Spirit would not, did not, conceal the sublime fact, that the works of *such* working men do follow them into heaven, in their fruits and effects, as surely as their bodies will follow their souls into heaven.

This is one good reason for the peculiarity of the oracle. It is not, however, the only one worthy of notice. There is in the church on earth, something of the same spirit which kept the church in heaven *silent* on the subject of works. I am aware that we have other reasons for saying nothing about our works, than those had whom John saw. Ours are fewer and feebler than theirs. Some, indeed, do nothing arduous or expensive in the service of God, or for the good of mankind. Many only work enough to prove that they are *unwilling* to work. But such, if they are in the church of Christ, are certainly not of it. On the other hand, however, it is equally true, that in general, the active, the benevolent, and the enterprising, do not allow themselves to take any higher views of their best works, deliberately, than as proofs of faith, love, or sincerity. If their well-doing prove that their faith is unfeigned, they are quite satisfied. Even when they cannot doubt the *usefulness* of their labours of love, nor hide from themselves the fact, that God has honoured their humble efforts to save some, they are only stirred up to watch the more, lest after having preached to others, they themselves should turn out castaways; lest, in keeping the vineyards of others, their own should be neglected. Yes; it is this, more than the dread of legality or of self-complacency, which makes many a faithful servant afraid to call his service, works. He sees clearly in the best of it, so much that is bad in manner and worse in spirit, that he is more ashamed of his good works than Pharisees are of their evil works. " Good " or " faithful servant," is the *last* name of a christian, which he thinks of appropriating to himself. He is even more than content, he is grateful, if he can hope to escape the *branding* name, " wicked and slothful servant." He well understands and approves what one of Whitefield's friends, a devoted minister, said on his death-bed,—" I have been throwing into *one* heap all my bad works and my good works, and carrying both to the foot of the cross."

Thus it is, that the rewardableness of well-doing has hardly any place in the actuating creed of a real christian, whatever theoretic credence he may give to it. He may even be eloquent in speaking of the works of Paul, Luther, Bunyan, Baxter, Whitefield, and Wesley, following them to heaven in forms of good, and as sources of joy,—and yet be more than silent in his own case, although quite sure that his own labour has not been in vain in the Lord.

This is real humility, as well as modesty. Is it, however, as *wise* as it is humble; as scriptural as it is modest? Not if Moses was right in having " respect to the recompence of reward;" not if Daniel was right in saying, that they who turn many to righteousness shall " shine as the stars for ever and ever;" not if Paul was right in anticipating his converts, as his crown and joy in the day of the Lord. It will not weaken the force of this argument to add,—not if Whitefield was right in keeping before himself and his fellow-labourers the prospect of presenting many souls before the throne. He " *hunted* for souls," as well as watched to win souls, because he allowed himself to see—indeed, set himself to study—how the " children "

God gave him as seals to his ministry, would increase his blessedness, when he rested from his labours.   There are many fine specimens of this inspiring hope, in his letters to the Wesleys, the Tennents, and the Welch itinerants.   " I see you with *thousands* around you in glory," is a frequent appeal to them.   And so distinctly and habitually did he realize this scene, that even when writing against Wesley, he closed his remonstrance by saying,—" When I come to judgment, I will thank you before men and angels for what you have, under God, done for my soul."

Even all this, however, does not come up to the full import of " what the Spirit saith unto the churches."   His " Yea, their works do follow them," includes more than the immediate fruits of their labour.   It embraces also all the succession of remote good which their example, labour, and influence might originate and prolong.   And, who can calculate or trace out that? No one understood this *arithmetic* less than Whitefield.   He was all alive to the immediate numbers he could gather into the fold of Christ.   He even revelled in the prospect of meeting them on the right hand of the great white throne, and of spending his eternity with them in heaven; but he did not calculate the consequences of their individual or joint influence upon their contemporaries, or even upon their posterity.   Indeed, the apostles themselves did not allow their eye to run far along the line of their remote influence.   Even they could not " look stedfastly to the END."   We can see the names of " the twelve apostles of the Lamb," on the " twelve foundations " of both the earthly and the heavenly Jerusalem; and can trace Paul planting and Apollos watering yet; and can hear all the dead in Christ, still speaking to the living; and thus can understand how their works are still following them, and will continue to follow them until the end of time, and even how they will be their own reward through eternity: but the workmen could not foresee all this.   It only began to break upon these good and faithful servants, when they entered into the *joy* of their Lord; and then, they were so absorbed with the presence of their Lord himself, that they could not take their eyes off from Him for a moment, to look at any thing beyond the immediate children they had to present before his throne.

2 M 2

It becomes the church, however, now that she has the means of calculating how her well-doing, in the service of God, can multiply and prolong itself from age to age, as well as spread itself over the world,—to search out diligently, what is "the mind of the Spirit," in His "Yea, the works of the dead who die in the Lord do follow them." The workmen "rest from their labour;" but their works are kept up, and carried on, and even carried out, as works which they began: and, therefore, all the dead in Christ are personally interested in all the good now doing in the world, and in all the glory which that good is bringing in to God and the Lamb: for those who rest from their labours enter into the *joy* of their Lord,—which is the many sons He brings to glory.

No one is prepared, or preparing, to enter into the real joy of heaven, who is doing nothing to win souls to Christ on earth. No one can die in the Lord, or enter heaven at all, who has no *works* to follow him there. No wonder! For no christian is so poor, nor so busy, nor so weak, as to be unable to work for God. The weakest and the poorest are able to do work which neither earth nor hell can destroy or stop, and which will be their reward through eternity.

What christian cannot *pray* heartily and habitually for the coming of the kingdom of God? Many of the dead in Christ could do nothing else for his glory. That was *enough*, however, to prepare them to enter into the joy of their Lord; for that connected them with all the grand instrumentality which saves souls. This is too little considered. I am not conscious of being particularly insensible to the natural or the moral *sublime;* but I frankly confess, that I see and feel more sublimity in a *vestry* prayer meeting for the spread of the gospel, than in the most splendid meetings in Exeter Hall. I would rather have been one in the first *nameless* groups, of two or three, who meet together in the name of Christ, to pray in the travail of their souls, that he might "see the travail of His soul and be satisfied," than have been the inventor of the platform. I feel much more sure that prayer meetings will prolong themselves, than that *speech* meetings will keep their place or their power. Prayer " shall be made for Christ continually ;" and those who *began* its concerts in Britain and America, will never be separated from its continuance. Their work has been following them every year since they died, in new and larger meetings for intercession, and in the answers not only to their own prayers, but to all the prayers which their example has thus called forth. They now see the golden censer of the High Priest waving before the throne with a greater weight of prayer, and emitting a larger cloud of incense, than it did when they first entered heaven. They now see the prayers of all saints setting in, like a spring tide, upon all the channels, coasts, and bays of the divine purposes; here, floating the smaller vessels of prophecy over the *bar* of time; and there, beginning to heave afloat the largest and the heaviest of the prophetic *fleet;* and every where rising to the *high-water* mark of "effectual fervent prayer."

Is not this their work *following* them? This prayerfulness in our times was set in motion by their example, just as their prayerfulness was called forth by the example of the first prayer-meetings at Jerusalem. Now, you and I can carry on this good work of intercession and supplication, however little else we can do. We may be both good and faithful servants in this department of labour, and thus be prepared to enter into the joy of our Lord.

It is not splendid works alone, that bring glory to Christ, or that follow christians into heaven in forms of reward. The simple domestic piety of Abraham, Hannah, and Eunice, in training up their children in the nurture and admonition of the Lord, was work which, in its influence, is following them still, and will follow them until the *last* pious family on earth complete "the whole family in heaven." For, what pious father or mother has not been influenced and encouraged by their example and success? Thus the father of the Faithful, and the mothers of Samuel and Timothy, set in motion a system of parental well-doing, which has never stopped entirely since, and which will work on until the end of time, and through eternity be as visible in its effects as the results of the ministry of reconciliation. O parents, what a work, which would follow you like your shadow, you may do for God, by teaching your children to love the Saviour! For who can calculate along the line of posterity, the spreading influence of *one* pious family,

or even of *one* pious child? Only think,—how your own family
may ramify in the next generation, and how it may blend, age
after age, with other families; carrying into them all a sweet
savour of Christ, along with your revered memory, until there
be actually a little *nation* of your descendants, rejoicing in the
God of their fathers? But neglect your son, or leave your
daughter's principles to chance, and you may set in motion a
course of ruin which shall never stop, and be a fountain which
shall originate a stream of evil and woe, that may run, widening
and wasting, through time and eternity!

In those lights, how infinite are the consequences of Sunday
schools! They are now giving a tone and a character to the
rising generation of the poor, which will *tell* for ever upon the
present and future character of the nation, and also upon the
bliss of heaven. That teaching, when well conducted, is a
work, the fruits of which will follow holy teachers, wherever
they follow the Lamb in heaven. It will never stop, until all
shall know the Lord; and even then, that grand consummation
will be in no small measure the fruit of it; and thus the reward
of all who sow, and of all who reap.

In like manner, you may " work a work" for your *neighbourhood*, which shall impress an imperishable character upon its
habits and spirit. You may make and leave it a *nursery* for
holiness, from which you may be regaled every year, until the
end of time, even in Paradise, by *roses* from the wilderness, and
myrtles from the desert. Only sow, plant, and water to the
Spirit, and in due season, and through enduring cycles, you
shall reap, not only life everlasting, but also the *full joy* of that
life, by entering fully into the joy of your Lord.

This is the right improvement of the death of Whitefield. It
would be as easy to write *fine* things upon the subject, as to
read them; but I envy not the taste nor the conscience, that
could be satisfied with *unpractical* truths, at the death-bed of
the most practical man who has appeared since the days of Paul.
I feel that my readers and myself may be Whitefields in *something;* and, therefore, I have written, not for fame, but in order
to be useful. Accordingly, although you *cannot* admire, you
will remember. This is all I want.

CHAPTER XXXI.

RICHARD SMITH'S account of the funeral, like that of the death-bed of Whitefield, needs no commendation; but only some additions.

" The Reverend Mr. Parsons, at whose house my *dear* master died, sent for Captain Fetcomb and Mr. Boadman, and others of his elders and deacons, and they took the whole care of the burial upon themselves, prepared the vault, and sent for the bearers." *Smith.*

Dr. Gillies says, " Early next morning, Mr. Sherburn of Ports-mouth sent Squire Clarkson and Dr. Haven with a message to Mr. Parsons, desiring that Mr. Whitefield's remains might be buried in his own *new* tomb, at his own expense : and in the evening several gentlemen from Boston came to Mr. Parsons, desiring the body might be carried there. But as Mr. White-field had repeatedly desired to be buried before Mr. Parsons' pulpit, if he died at Newbury Port, Mr. Parsons thought him-self obliged to deny both of these requests."

Parsons, in a note to his funeral sermon, says, " At one o'clock all the bells in the town were tolled for half an hour, and all the vessels in the harbour gave their proper signals of mourning. At two o'clock the bells tolled a second time. At three the bells called to attend the funeral. The Reverend Dr. Haven of Portsmouth, and the Reverend Messrs. Rogers of Exeter, Jewet and Chandler of Rowley, Moses Parsons of Newbury, and Bass of Newbury Port, were pall-bearers. Mr. Parsons and his fa-mily, with many other respectable persons, followed the corpse in mourning.

" The procession was only one mile, and then the corpse was carried into the presbyterian church, and placed on the bier in the broad alley; when Mr. Rogers made a very suitable prayer, in the presence of about *six* thousand persons within the walls of the church, while many thousands were on the outside."[*] After singing one of Watts's hymns, " the corpse was put into a new tomb, which the gentlemen of the congregation had had prepared for that purpose; and before it was sealed, Mr. Jewet gave a suitable exhortation." *Parsons.*

" Many ministers of all persuasions came to the house of the Reverend Mr. Parsons, where several of them gave a very particular account of their first awakenings under his ministry, several years ago, and also of many in their congregations, that, to their knowledge, under God, owed their conversion wholly to his coming among them, often repeating the blessed seasons they enjoyed under his preaching: and all said, that this last visit was attended with more power than any other; and that all opposition fell before him. Then one and another of them would pity and pray for his dear Tabernacle and chapel congregations, and it was truly affecting to hear them bemoan America and England's loss. Thus they continued for two hours conversing about his great usefulness, and praying that God would scatter his gifts and drop his mantle among them. When the corpse was placed at the foot of the pulpit, close to the vault, the Rev. Daniel Rogers made a very affecting prayer, and openly confessed, that under God, he owed his conversion to the labours of that dear man of God, whose precious remains now lay before them. Then he cried out, O my father, my father!—then stopped and wept, as though his heart would break, and the people weeping all through the place.—Then he recovered, and finished his prayer, and sat down and wept.—Then one of the deacons gave out that hymn,

'Why do we mourn departed friends?' &c.

some of the people weeping, some singing, and so on alternately.

[*] This church was then (I hope is now) one of the largest in America. *Allen's Dict.*

The Rev. Mr. Jewet preached a funeral discourse, and made an affectionate address to his brethren, to lay to heart the death of that useful man of God; begging that he and they might be upon their watch-tower, and endeavour to follow his blessed example. The corpse was then put into the vault, and all concluded with a short prayer, and dismission of the people, who went weeping through the streets to their respective places of abode." *Smith.*

" The melancholy news of Mr. Whitefield's decease arrived in London, on Monday, November 5, 1770, by the Boston Gazette, and also by several letters from different correspondents at Boston, to his worthy friend, Mr. R. Keene; who received likewise, by the same post, two letters written with his own hand, when in good health, one seven and the other five days before his death. Mr. Keene caused the mournful tidings to be published the same night at the Tabernacle, and the following evening at Tottenham Court chapel. His next step was to consider of a proper person to deliver a funeral discourse, when it occurred to his mind, that he had many times said to Mr. Whitefield, ' If you should die abroad, who shall we get to preach your funeral sermon? Must it be your old friend, the Rev. John Wesley?' And his answer constantly was, ' *He is the man.*' Mr. Keene therefore waited on Mr. Wesley, on the Saturday following, and he promised to preach it on the Lord's day, November 18, which he did, to an extraordinary crowded and mournful auditory; many hundreds being obliged to go away, who could not possibly get within the doors.

" In both the chapel and Tabernacle, the pulpits, &c. were hung with black cloth, and the galleries with fine black baize. Escutcheons were affixed to the fronts of the pulpits; and on each of the adjoining houses, hatchments were put up: the motto on which was—' *Mea vita salus et gloria Christus.*' At the expiration of six months, the mourning in each place of worship, and the escutcheons in the vestries, were taken down. The hatchments remained twelve months, when one was taken down, and placed in the Tabernacle, and the other over a neat marble monument, erected by Mr. Whitefield for his wife, in Tottenham

Court chapel, with a space left for an inscription respecting himself after his decease, as he *wished to be interred in the same vault,* had he died in England. Accordingly the following epitaph was written by the Rev. Titus Knight of Halifax, in Yorkshire."

In Memory of

The Rev. GEORGE WHITEFIELD, A. M.

Chaplain to the Right Honourable the Countess of Huntingdon,

Whose Soul, made meet for Glory,

Was taken to Emmanuel's Bosom,

On the 30th of September, 1770 ;

And who now lies in the silent Grave, at Newbury Port, near Boston,

In NEW ENGLAND ;

There deposited in hope of a joyful Resurrection to Eternal Life and Glory.

He was a Man eminent in Piety,

Of a Humane, Benevolent, and Charitable Disposition.

His Zeal in the Cause of God was singular :

His Labours indefatigable ;

And his Success in preaching the Gospel remarkable and astonishing.

He departed this Life,

In the Fifty-sixth Year of his Age.

————

And, like his Master, was by some despis'd ;
Like Him, by many others lov'd and priz'd :
But theirs shall be the everlasting crown,
Not whom the world, but Jesus Christ will own.

This tribute is as like Knight, as the following epitaph is like Dr. Gibbons.

In Reverendum Virum
GEORGIUM WHITEFIELD,
Laboribus sacris olim abundantem; nunc vero, ut bene speratur
cœlestem et immortalem vitam cum *Christo* agentem,
EPITAPHIM,
(Auctore Thomas Gibbons, S. T. P.)
Electum et divinum vas, Whitefieldi fuisti
Ingenio pollens, divitiisque sacris :
His opibus populo longè latèque tributis,
Tandem perfrueris lætitiâ superum
Inque hanc intrâsti, Domino plaudente ministrum :
Expertum in multis, assiduumque bonum :
Ecce mea portus, et clara palatia cœli
Deliciis plenis omnia aperta tibi.
Dum matutinam Stellam, quam dulce rubentem !
Vivificos roresque ossa sepulta manent.

TRANSLATION.

A vessel chosen and divine, replete
With nature's gifts, and grace's richer stores,
Thou Whitefield wast : these through the world dispens'd,
In long laborious travels, thou at length
Hast reach'd the realms of rest, to which thy Lord
Has welcom'd thee with his immense applause.
All hail, my servant, in thy various trusts
Found vigilant and faithful; see the ports,
See the eternal kingdoms of the skies,
With all their boundless glory, boundless joy,
Open'd for thy reception, and thy bliss !
Mean time, the body in its peaceful cell,
Reposing from its toils, awaits the star,
Whose living lustres lead that promis'd.morn,
Whose vivifying dews thy moulder'd corse
Shall visit, and immortal life inspire.

The following lines are part of a poem on Mr. Whitefield,
written by a *negro servant girl*, seventeen years of age, belonging to Mr. J. Wheatley, of Boston. They are better than *De
Courcy's* Elegy.

" He pray'd that grace in every heart might dwell,
He long'd to see America excel;
He charg'd its youth to let the grace divine
Arise, and in their future actions shine.
He offer'd what he did himself receive,
A greater gift not God himself can give.
He urg'd the need of it to every one;
It was no less than God's co-equal Son!
Take Him, ye wretched, for your only good;
Take Him, ye starving souls, to be your food.
Ye thirsty, come to this life-giving stream;
Ye preachers, take him for your joyful theme.
Take Him, my dear *Americans*, he said,
Be your complaints in his kind bosom laid.
Take Him, ye *Africans*, he longs for you;
IMPARTIAL SAVIOUR, is his title due.
If you will choose to walk in grace's road,
You shall be sons, and kings, and priests to God.
Great *Countess!* we Americans revere
Thy name, and thus condole thy grief sincere.
New England, sure doth feel; the orphan's smart
Reveals the true sensations of his heart.
His lonely Tabernacle sees no more
A Whitefield landing on the British shore.
Then let us view him in yon azure skies,
Let every mind with this lov'd object rise.
Thou, tomb, shalt safe retain thy sacred trust,
Till life divine reanimates his dust."

Cowper's tribute to the memory of Whitefield, although well-known, must not be omitted here.

" LEUCONOMUS (beneath well-sounding Greek
I slur a name, a poet must not speak)
Stood pilloried on infamy's high stage,
And bore the pelting scorn of half an age.
The very butt of slander, and the blot
For every dart that malice ever shot.
The man that mentioned *him*, at once dismiss'd
All mercy from his lips, and sneer'd and hiss'd.
His crimes were such as Sodom never knew,
And perjury stood up to swear all true:
His aim was mischief, and his zeal pretence,
His speech rebellion against common sense:

A knave, when tried on honesty's plain rule,
And when by that of reason, a mere fool.
The world's best comfort was, his doom was pass'd,
Die when he might, he must be damn'd at last.
 Now, truth, perform thine office, waft aside
The curtain drawn by prejudice and pride ;
Reveal (the man is dead) to wond'ring eyes,
This more than monster in his proper guise.
 He lov'd the world that hated him; the tear
That dropp'd upon his Bible was sincere ;
Assail'd by scandal, and the tongue of strife,
His only answer was—a blameless life :
And he that forged, and he that threw, the dart,
Had each a brother's interest in his heart.
Paul's love of Christ, and steadiness unbrib'd,
Were copied close in him, and well transcrib'd.
He followed Paul—his zeal a kindred flame,
His apostolic charity the same:
Like him, cross'd cheerfully tempestuous seas,
Forsaking country, kindred, friends, and ease :
Like him he labour'd, and like him, content
To bear it, suffer'd shame where'er he went.
 Blush calumny ! and write upon his tomb,
If honest eulogy can spare thee room,
Thy deep repentance of thy thousand lies,
Which, aim'd at him, have pierced th' offended skies;
And say, Blot out my sin, confess'd, deplor'd,
Against thine image, in thy saint, O Lord ! "

America did not fail to mark her veneration for Whitefield's memory. It was not alone at Newbury Port that " good men made great lamentation over him." Distant places vied with both Newbury and London, in this tribute of esteem and sorrow. Winter says to Jay, " You have no conception of the effect of Whitefield's death upon the inhabitants of the province of Georgia. All the black cloth in the *stores* was bought up ; the pulpit and desks of the church, the branches, the organ-loft, the pews of the governor and council, were covered with black. The governor and council, in deep mourning, convened at the state-house, and went in procession to church, and were received by the organ playing a funeral dirge. Two funeral sermons were preached by Mr. Ellington and Zubly." *Winter.*

Dr. Gillies has quoted largely from Ellington's sermon. He did not know that it was *composed* by Cornelius Winter. " I was desired to compose" it, says Winter : and he does not add, that he declined the task. I therefore conclude, that he was the real author. Indeed, it is like Winter, and creditable to him, so far as the sentiment and spirit of it go. And it is not less creditable to Ellington, that he *preached* the sermon. Very few clergymen would have consented to utter such truths, at that time. It is not necessary to repeat these truths here. It is enough to say, that they were a transcript of the creed and heart of Cornelius Winter ; and thus they are a *key* to the heart of Ellington. There is, however, one expression in the sermon, which I hesitate to interpret. " It is well known," Ellington says, that Whitefield " had opportunity long since to enjoy *episcopal* emolument." Was it, then, more than a *joke*, when the king suggested to the bench, that they " might *stop* Whitefield's preaching by making a bishop of him ? " A bishopric was, of course, out of the question : but it is quite certain, that he might have had what De Courcy calls " considerable preferment," from the court, as well as from the primate of Ireland.

Dr. Gillies has preserved numerous specimens of the funeral sermons preached on this occasion, in England and America ; and I could add to them. But they are too many to be recorded, and too similar to be distinguished. Their *similarity* is, however, their most instructive and interesting characteristic. It both proves and illustrates the fact, that Whitefield's character and career left the *same* impression upon ministers of different churches, and men of dissimilar talents and temperament. Wesley and Toplady might have written their sermons at the same desk, and compared notes before preaching them. Romaine might have exchanged pulpits with Dr. Pemberton of Boston, and Venn and Newton with Brewer of Stepney, or Dr. Gibbons. They all bear the same testimony, and breathe the same spirit, at the grave of Whitefield.

It was not *Toplady*, but WESLEY, that said of him, " His fundamental point was, Give God all the glory of whatever is good in man : set Christ as high, and man as low as possible, in the business of salvation. All merit is in the blood of Christ, and all power in and from the Spirit of Christ." It was not *Wesley*, but TOPLADY, that said, " He was a true and faithful son of the church of England, and invincibly asserted her doctrines to the last; and that not in a merely *doctrinal* way—though he was a most excellent systematic divine; but with an unction of power from God, unequalled in the present day." It was not a *presbyterian*, but ROMAINE, that said, " Look at the public loss! Oh what has the church suffered in the setting of that bright star, which had shone so gloriously in our hemisphere! We have *none* left to succeed him; none, of his gifts; none any thing *like* him in usefulness." It was not a *methodist*, but VENN, that said, " We are warranted to affirm, that scarce any one of (Christ's) ministers, since the apostles' days, has exceeded, scarce any one has equalled, Whitefield. For such a life, and such a death, though in tears under our loss, we must thank God. We must rejoice—that *millions* heard him so long, so often, and to so much good effect." It was not a *dissenter*, but JOHN NEWTON, that said, " What a change has taken place throughout the land, within little more than thirty years! The doctrines of grace were seldom heard from the pulpit, and the life and power of religion were little known. And how much of this *change* (for the better) has been owing to God's blessing on Whitefield's labours, is well known to many who have lived through this period, and can hardly be denied by those who are *least* willing to allow it." Thus contemporary churchmen thought and wrote of their own accord, when Whitefield died: but since *they* died, his mighty and happy influence upon the church may, it seems, " be controverted!" It *may*: but the evangelical clergy should remember, that they themselves are considered by some of their superiors, as *proofs* of the mighty influence of Whitefield and Wesley upon the church. Venn and Sidney forget, that the anti-evangelical party ascribe to methodism both the rise and progress of evangelical religion in the church. Thus the *blind* see clearly what some of " the children of light" try to conceal.

The following letter, written on the death of Whitefield, suits my limits and design better than formal extracts from the funeral sermons. I do not know who was the author of it; but whoever he was, it will be responded to by all warm hearts.

1771. " A great man is fallen in our Israel—the Rev. Mr. Whitefield is no more! he has left his charge, his flock, and gone to mansions of blessedness.

" I may safely say, a great man, a great christian, a humble follower of the divine Redeemer, and a zealous defender of the doctrines of grace, died, when Whitefield closed his eyes. That voice which was lifted up like a trumpet, and flew around the sacred roof, proclaiming salvation through the dying Jesus, teaching a sinful world the Saviour's name, is now lost in perpetual silence! That man, whose labours in the cause of God have been more abundant, has ceased from his work. That eminent minister of the New Testament, that son of thunder to the careless and secure, that cheering son of consolation to the weary and heavy laden, who has been distinguished as the happy instrument of bringing strayed sheep to the fold of God, is gone to experience the truth of his doctrines; and will one day appear, with all those who have been savingly brought to the knowledge of Jesus by his means, at the right hand of God, to give an account of the ministry he received from him; and in the presence of a surrounding world, say, ' Lord, here am I, and the children thou hast given me.'

" It is an afflictive, awful, and alarming providence to the church of God. A great light extinguished, a bright star set, and a numerous people deprived of their pastor. Who shall supply his place? Who shall, with that pathetic language, strength of argument, and force of persuasion, compel sinners to partake of the gospel feast? Who shall animate our associations, and diffuse a spirit of candour, charity, and moderation, throughout our assemblies? Who shall declare the glories, the riches, the freeness, the fulness of that complete salvation which Messiah finished? Who shall exhort, by precept and example, to that steady, uniform, constant character, which adorns the profession of the gospel? Who shall recommend a life of fellowship and communion with the Father, Son, and Spirit, as the most desirable blessing, and build up the saints in their most holy faith? Who shall?—I am *stopped* by the mouth

of him who says, ' Shall I not do what I will with my own? Is
it not my prerogative to take and leave, as seemeth me good?
I demand the liberty of disposing my servants at my own pleasure. He hath not slept as others do. It is your's to wait and
trust, mine to dispose and govern. On me be the care of ministers and churches—with me is the residue of the Spirit—I set
my labourers to work, and when I please, I take them to the
rest I have appointed for them. My power is not diminished,
my arm not shortened, my love not abated, and my faithfulness
still the same. I know my sheep, and they shall not stray into
forbidden pastures, for want of a shepherd to feed them with
knowledge and understanding.'

" With these thoughts my passions subside, my mind is softened and satisfied. But *now* for the wings of faith and divine
contemplation, to view him among the celestial throng, partaking of the happiness, sharing the joys of yonder blissful
regions—ascribing salvation to Him who loved and washed him
in his blood—having on that perfect robe of immaculate righteousness, wrought out by the dear Redeemer—having on his
head a crown of never-fading glory, and palms of eternal victory in his hands—drinking at the fountain-head of blessedness,
and refreshing himself continually at that river which flows in
sweet murmurs from the right hand of the Majesty on high—
for ever out of the reach of scandal and reproach—where calumny can never penetrate, and the wicked cease from troubling
—where God, even his own God, wipes away all tears from his
eyes—where he will for ever bask in the boundless fruition of
eternal love, continually receiving out of the divine fulness, fresh
supplies of glory for glory, from which on earth he had communication of grace for grace—sees the King in his beauty, rejoices in the beatific vision, follows the Lamb wheresoever he goes
—and with those who are redeemed from among men, rests in
the closest embraces of his Lord.

' And now his voice is lost in death,
Praise will employ his noblest pow'rs,
While life, or thought, or being last,
Or immortality endures!'

" Here we must take our leave of the dear departed saint,
till the happy time takes place, when we shall put off this body,
and enter the confines of unmolested joy.   And oh! in what
elevation of happiness, and refinement of felicity, shall we awake
up in the likeness and express image of that God, who has loved
us, and called us with an holy calling ! Yet let us be persuaded
of this, that when the important period commences, when the
surprising signs, and descending inhabitants of heaven, proclaim
the second coming of our glorious Immanuel—when the heavens
open and disclose his radiant glory, the archangel's trump shall
sound, the Lord himself descend with a shout, and the dead in
Christ arise glorious and immortal—leave corruption, weakness,
and dishonour behind them—we shall with him, and all the
ransomed race, ascend to mansions of glory, bliss, and immortality, and join that universal chorus :—

> ' Say, Live for ever, glorious King !
> Born to redeem, and strong to save :
> Then ask the monster, Where's thy sting ?
> And where's thy victory, boasting grave ? '

" But, my dear Sir, this awful dispensation demands a suitable improvement. The death of ministers, and mankind in
general, are so many mementos ;—' Be ye also ready,' is their
solemn language.   Come then, O my soul, examine with impartiality thy state.   Nothing but an interest in the perfectly
finished, infinitely glorious, and everlastingly sufficient salvation
of Jehovah Jesus, can be of any avail, can be any real ground
of consolation, when the grim tyrant stares thee in the face.
May thy evidence be clear, thy faith strong, and thy hope on
tiptoe ; that when the Bridegroom comes, and summons thy attendance, thou mayst with joy answer, Lord, I come.
" Should not the death of one and another of God's people
give fresh wings to our souls, make life less pleasant, and heaven
more desirable—wean our affections from the beggarly enjoyments of time and sense, and make us long to dwell where
Jesus reveals his beauties, glories, and matchless excellence,
face to face ?   Here on earth we have some faint glimmerings ;
and oh! how ought we to prize them, as they are drops from

the ocean! but the ravishing blaze is reserved for the upper and better world.

" Though our interviews in the church militant are very sweet, yet they are very short. The world's ten thousand baits, the devil's insnaring wiles, but above all, the flesh with its legions of corruptions, enslave the soul, and deaden our relish for divine things. O happy day! O blessed hour! when Christ shall have all his enemies under his feet, and death itself be swallowed up of life—when we shall get within the enclosures of the New Jerusalem, and go out no more for ever!

" If faithful ministers are so soon removed from us, how should we prize them while we have them! Oh let us never give ear to, much less be the means of promoting the malevolent whispers of slander; but esteem them very highly in love for their work's sake! Should it not be our constant care, and studious concern, through divine grace, to improve by every sermon we hear, that the end of all ordinances may be obtained, even an increase in love to Jesus, and fellowship with him? That this desirable end may be answered, let us be earnest and frequent in our address to the throne of grace, for ministers and people, that God may be glorified by bringing home sinners to himself, and in the edification of saints—that each stone in the spiritual fabric may be edified and built up upon the foundation, Christ Jesus, till the top-stone is brought forth with shoutings, Grace, grace, unto it!

" The clock strikes twelve, and tells me to conclude. But how can I do it, without commending you to that God, whose power alone is able to keep you from falling, and at last present you faultless before the presence of his glory with exceeding joy? May he give you continual assurances of his grace, mercy, and love, in his lower courts, thereby making them a heaven upon earth; and cause you at last to join the general assembly and church of the first-born, whose names are written in heaven. This is the hearty, unfeigned, and constant prayer of him, who is, with great esteem and affection,"—

The following eulogium is from the pen of Toplady. " I deem myself happy in having an opportunity of thus publicly avowing the inexpressible esteem in which I held this wonderful man;

and the affectionate veneration which I must ever retain for the memory of one, whose acquaintance and ministry were attended with the most important spiritual benefit to me, and to tens of thousands beside.

" It will not be saying too much, if I term him, THE APOSTLE OF THE ENGLISH EMPIRE ; in point of zeal for God, a long course of indefatigable and incessant labours, unparalleled disinterestedness, and astonishingly extensive usefulness.

" He would never have quitted even the walls of the church, had not either the ignorance, or the malevolence, of some who ought to have known better, compelled him to a seeming separation.

" If the absolute command over the passions of immense auditories, be the mark of a consummate orator, he was the greatest of the age. If the strongest good sense, the most generous expansions of heart, the most artless but captivating affability, the most liberal exemptions from bigotry, the purest and most transpicuous integrity, the brightest cheerfulness, and the promptest wit, enter into the composition of social excellence, he was one of the best companions in the world.

" If to be stedfast, immovable, always abounding in the works of the Lord ; if a union of the most brilliant with the most solid ministerial gifts, ballasted by a deep and humbling experience of grace, and crowned with the most extended success in the conversion of sinners, and edification of saints, be signatures of a commission from heaven, George Whitefield cannot but stand highest on the modern list of christian ministers.

" England has had the honour of producing the greatest men, in almost every walk of useful knowledge. At the head of these are,—Archbishop BRADWARDIN, the prince of divines ; MILTON, the prince of poets ; NEWTON, the prince of philosophers ; WHITEFIELD, the prince of preachers."

Strong as this language is, the sober statements of Cornelius Winter both illustrate and justify it. I therefore shall quote freely from them in the next chapter. In the mean time, I add only his opinion of Toplady's compliment. " Whatever invidious remarks they may make upon his *written* discourses, they cannot invalidate his preaching. Mr. Toplady called him the prince of preachers, and with good reason, for none in our day preached with the like effect." *Jay's Winter.*

Whitefield's successors were very unlike himself, except in piety and sentiment; and yet they nobly sustained the influence of both the Tabernacle and Tottenham Court. This was certainly the more easy, because the stated congregations had never been accustomed to enjoy much of Whitefield's presence: but still, it was an arduous task to succeed him. Mr. Wilks was, however, quite equal to that task. His wisdom *kept* the flock, which Whitefield's eloquence won. He knew the way to the understanding and the conscience, just as well as Whitefield knew the way to the heart. He could dive as far *into* men, as Whitefield could draw them *out* of themselves. If the latter could rouse or melt them, the former could *rivet* them. If Whitefield made them feel, Wilks made them think. Mr. Hyatt had more of Whitefield's tremendous energy. He had, perhaps, *all* his thunder, although but little of his lightning or showers. He was, however, eminently useful in the conversion of sinners. If Wilks *fed* the flock, Hyatt guarded and augmented it. In a word, they were both good shepherds, and each great in his own way.

The body of Whitefield, like that of Moses, although not hid, has been the subject of sharp contention, and has called forth some " railing accusations." In 1790, it was reported in London, that " the body was entire and uncorrupted." In 1801, Mr. Mason of Newbury Port contradicted this, in a letter to the editor of the Gospel Magazine. " We found the flesh," he says, " totally consumed," although " the gown, cassock, and bands, with which he was buried, were almost the same as if just put into the coffin." Until this contradiction appeared, the ignorant welcomed a miracle in the case; the scientific referred it to antiputrescent applications; and the jealous charged the sexton with supplying fresh bodies from time to time.

The facts of the case are these: In 1784, Mr. Brown of Epping Forest visited Newbury Port; and, having heard there that Whitefield's " body was entire," he went, with his wife, to see it. " A lantern and candle being provided, we descended into the tomb. Our guide led me to dear Mr. Whitefield's coffin. He opened the lid down to his breast. I never felt so over a corpse ! His body was perfect. I felt his cheeks and his breast : the skin immediately *rose* after. Even his lips were not consumed, nor his nose. He did not look frightful at all. His skin was considerably discoloured, blackish, through dust and age. His gown was not much impaired, nor his wig.

" I turned to look at Mr. Parsons, who died seven years after him : but there was only a promiscuous show of bones, clean and dry.

" I do but give you the matter of fact. I am well assured the body of Mr. Whitefield was not embalmed. He particularly ordered it should not. The body is open to every visitor." *Brown's Letter.*

This *looks* like truth. Dr. Southey also has quoted from some one, whom he does not name, the following words, " One of the preachers told me the body of Whitefield was not yet putrified : but several other corpses are just in the same state at Newbury Port, owing to the *vast* quantities of *nitre* with which the earth abounds there." This is quoted to prove, that the report does not " seem to have originated in any intention to deceive." Thus there was evidently much truth in it in 1784 ; whereas in 1796, when Mason saw the body, it might be equally true that " the flesh was totally consumed." The skull is, I understand, very perfect still.

It will surprise and grieve not a few on both sides of the At-lantic, when I tell them that the bones of Whitefield are not entire. Part of his *right arm* was sent to this country. I hope it is not here still. If I thought it were not returned, I should feel inclined to tell the American ambassador where to find it, and to urge him to demand it in the name of his country.

About two years ago, a visitor in London invited me to see " a curiosity, sure to *gratify* me." He mistook my taste. I went, and he placed on the table a long narrow box ; defying me to guess its contents. I had no need to guess or hesitate. I said, " It contains the right arm of George Whitefield, and I could *name* both the thief and the receiver. I have known for ten years that it was in your possession : but my organ of *vene-ration* is larger than that of my curiosity ; and, therefore, I never hinted at my knowledge, although I have often visited you on the banks of the Thames, and seen all your other memorials of Whitefield, and reciprocated all your other feelings towards him." I owe it to my friend to add, if the *relic* be still in England, that it could not be in *better* hands than those it was first committed to. Still, I would, if I could, give " *commandment* concerning the bones," as solemnly and authoritatively as dying Joseph. One thing I promise: I will conceal the name of the spoiler, (for I have read his letter,) if the spoil should be returned.

The following inscription was copied by Dr. Reed from the splendid monument erected by Mr. Bartlett, at Newbury Port, to the memory of Whitefield.

THIS CENOTAPH

Is erected, with affectionate Veneration,

To the Memory of

The Rev. GEORGE WHITEFIELD,

Born at Gloucester, England, December 16, 1714,

Educated at Oxford University; ordained 1736.

In a Ministry of Thirty-four Years,

He crossed the Atlantic Thirteen times,

And preached more than Eighteen Thousand Sermons.

As a Soldier of the Cross, humble, devout, ardent,

He put on the whole Armour of God;

Preferring the Honour of Christ to his own Interest, Repose,
Reputation, and Life.

As a Christian Orator, his deep Piety, disinterested Zeal, and vivid
Imagination,

Gave unexampled Energy to his look, utterance, and action.

Bold, fervent, pungent, and popular in his Eloquence,

No other uninspired man ever preached to so large assemblies,

Or enforced the simple Truths of the Gospel, by Motives

So persuasive and awful, and with an Influence so powerful,
On the Hearts of his Hearers.

He died of Asthma, September 30, 1770,

Suddenly exchanging his Life of unparalleled Labours

For his Eternal Rest.

Reed and Matheson's Visit.

CHAPTER XXXII.

I FORESAW, from the commencement of this work, that I was incapable of imbodying the character of Whitefield, at the end, in a form which would satisfy myself. I therefore kept back nothing, for the sake of final *effect;* but allowed him, at every step, to appear all he was at the time and place. His characteristics have thus come out like the stars, now one by one, and anon in constellations, and all "in their season." In this form they have kept alive my own interest in both his Life and Times, whilst writing these pages; and therefore I see no necessity, and feel no inclination, to try my hand at a formal portrait. Whitefield paints *himself* upon every eye that follows him. The only difficulty felt in trying to realize this mighty angel of the everlasting gospel, as he flies in the midst of heaven, arises from the *figure* he presents in almost all the portraits which have accompanied his works hitherto. Indeed, until I saw the full-length engravings of him, from pictures taken when he was in his prime, I found it impossible to associate with his form (except in the case of his uplifted hands and eyes) just ideas of his spirit. This difficulty is now removed, and by no stratagem. The portrait in this volume is a faithful copy (except in length and scenery) of the original engraving, taken from Russell's picture of him, as he appeared in Moorfields in all his glory.

I have another reason for not trying to imbody the whole character of Whitefield: it would present an *inimitable* example; and thus defeat one great purpose I had in writing his life. His image as a whole, is not calculated to multiply itself. Happily this is not the fact, in regard to some features of it.

Some of them, like queen bees, are each capable of producing a whole hive. Indeed, it is impossible that any conscientious minister of the gospel can contemplate Whitefield in this volume, without setting himself to imitate him in something: whereas no one would dream of even trying to imitate him in all things. At least, I never saw the man who could be a *second* Whitefield. Rowland Hill was not that. SPENCER, from all I could learn in Liverpool, during eleven years' occupation of his pulpit, seems to have approached nearest to the pathos and fascination of Whitefield; but he had evidently none of his commanding majesty.

I studied Whitefield until I understood him; and therefore, I have instinctively recognised whatever resembled him, in all the popular preachers of my time. James, of Birmingham, has occasionally reminded me of his alternate bursts of tenderness and terror, in all but their rapidity; Rowland Hill of his *off-hand* strokes of power; and Spring, of New York, his *off-heart* unction, when it fell like dew, copiously and calmly. Baptist Noel also has reminded me of this. Robert Newton has some of Whitefield's oratory, but none of his high passion. Irving had nothing of him but his voice. Cooper, of Dublin, when in his prime, and preaching in the open air, has enabled me to conceive how Whitefield commanded the multitude in Moorfields. I must add,—although I shall not be generally understood,—that Williams of the Wern, and my friend Christmas Evans, of Wales, and Billy Dawson of Yorkshire, have oftener realized Whitefield to me, than any other preachers of my time: and yet these three men do not resemble him, nor each other, in mind or body; but they can *lose* themselves entirely, as he did, in tender and intense love to souls. This is what is wanted; and it will *tell* by any voice or style, and from any eye or stature. Rowland Hill knew and loved one minister in Scotland—the late Cowie of Huntly—for his resemblance to Whitefield. I do not wonder at this. It was Whitefield's likeness to Cowie, that first won my heart. I saw in the busts, and read in the books of George Whitefield, the express image of George Cowie, the pastor of my boyhood. I was not twelve years old when he died: but the majestic music of his voice is yet in my ear, and the angelic benevolence of his countenance yet before my eye. I could weep yet, as I wept when I did not understand him. I wept often then because he was bathed in tears of love. I loved him, because he loved me for my father's sake, when my father died. He then became a father unto me. Whether he *bequeathed* me to Dr. Philip, I do not know: but I can never forget that in his house Dr. Philip adopted me. This he did in the true *spirit* of adoption! I owe every thing, in early life, to this. Even in mature life, I feel the benefit of it every day.

I must not dismiss this reference to Cowie yet. It will help not a few to realize Whitefield. I have often roused the venerable Rowland Hill, in his old age, from absence and depression, when he was not likely to be *himself* in the pulpit, or on the platform, by a timely reference to " our old friend Mr. Cowie." This never failed to quicken him. I was to him so associated with Huntly, that he often called me *Mr. Huntly.* The public are thus indebted to me for not a few of Rowland Hill's last and best eulogiums on Whitefield. He had seen him personified in Cowie, and I kept the image before the good old man, whenever I met him in public or private. The *secret* was this. The chief cause of Mr. Cowie's *excommunication* from the antiburghers, was his cooperation with Mr. Hill, and itinerants of his stamp; and I had been Mr. Cowie's *little* servant on the day he defended himself before the synod. It was a *high* day to me, until I found him condemned. I had carried from his library to the top of his pulpit stairs, the books he intended to quote from; and handed them to him as he required them. It was a long defence; but I felt no weariness, although I did not understand a word of its real merits. There was *Latin* in it—and he had begun to teach *me* Latin; and thus I expected to understand the speech some day. And then it was a perfect stream of eloquence, flowing, now softly as the Boggie, and anon impetuously as the Dovern; the rivers which encircle Huntly. I was sure that nobody could answer him; and so vexed when they tried, that I could have thrown a book at the head of the moderator, and even two or three at some other heads of the synod. True; this was worse than foolish in a boy; but still, it was not more foolish than old men flinging censures at the head of a champion, who was the Whitefield of the north. At this moment, I do not feel that I was the greatest sinner in that assembly.

I thus allow my recollections of Cowie to revel in their own vividness, because they will explain what I have ventured to call my " knowledge of Whitefield." I mean, that I met in the sermons and *vein* of Whitefield, the image of my first friend and pastor ; and Rowland Hill, who knew both parties, attested the likeness. This fact must be my apology for the many instances in this volume, in which I *gossip* about Whitefield, as if I had been brought up at his knee. There is no affectation in this, whatever flippancy it may have betrayed me into. I have been all along at *home*, because in company with Cowie. Besides, only a character which speaks for itself belongs to biography ; and he is no biographer of *it*, who does not speak in its own style.

I have often heard it asked and argued, whether Whitefield would be *popular* now, were he alive ? The late Dr. Ryland used to maintain, that he would be as popular as ever ! The Doctor was right, so far as Whitefield's manner and unction were concerned. Holy *energy* can never be unpopular. Holy *daring* will always wield the multitude. Natural eloquence will find an *echo* for ever in the human heart, however the truth it utters may be evaded or disliked. All ministers who cannot command attention, are *unnatural* in something. Whitefield's sermons, however, would not draw out the same crowd, nor the same classes now, that they did at first. His *doctrine*, as well as his manner, was a novelty then, even in London, to the multitude. They had never heard of regeneration but at the baptismal font ; and *that*, told them of its beginning and completion, in the same breath.

Too little importance, however, has been attached to Whitefield's *manner* of preaching. This is not his fault. He made no secret of his attention to delivery. He commended the study of oratory to the American colleges, and provided for it at Bethesda, and rebuked the neglect of it at Oxford. He was not ashamed to quote *Sheridan's* lectures, in remonstrating with

Durell. "Sorry am I to find so true what a celebrated orator takes the liberty of saying in the University of Oxford, if I mistake not,—'That the state of pulpit elocution in general, in the church of England, is such, that there never was, perhaps, a religious sect on earth, whose hearts were so little engaged in the act of worship, as the members of that church. To be pleased, we must feel; and we are pleased with feeling. The presbyterians are moved; the methodists are moved; they go to their meetings and tabernacles with delight. The very quakers are moved: whilst much the greater part of the members of the church of England are either banished from it through disgust, or reluctantly attend the service as a disagreeable duty.' Thus far Mr. Sheridan."

Whitefield even quotes Betterton the player, and affirms that the stage would soon be deserted if the actors spoke like preachers. "Mr. Betterton's answer to a worthy prelate is worthy of lasting regard. When asked 'how it came to pass that the clergy, who spoke of things *real*, affected the people so little, and the players, who spoke of things barely *imaginary*, affected them so much,' he said, 'My Lord, I can assign but one reason; we players speak of things imaginary as though they were real, and too many of the clergy speak of things real as though they were imaginary.' Thus it was in his, and all know it is too much the case in our time. Hence it is, that even on our most important occasions, the worthy gentlemen concerned in our public churches, generally find themselves more obliged to *musicians* than the preachers; and hence it is, no doubt, that upon our most solemn anniversaries, after long previous notice has been given, and when some even of our lords spiritual do preach, perhaps not two lords *temporal* come to hear them."—*Letter to Durell.*

Whitefield's own maxim was, "to preach as Apelles painted, for ETERNITY." He was first struck with this maxim at the table of Archbishop Boulter in Ireland, where "the great Dr. Delany" said to him, "I wish whenever I go up into a pulpit, to look upon it as the last time I shall ever preach, or the last time the people may hear." He never forgot this. He often said, "Would ministers preach for eternity, they would then act the part of true christian orators, and not only calmly and coolly inform the understanding, but by persuasive, pathetic address, endeavour to move the affections and warm the heart. To act otherwise bespeaks *a sad ignorance of human nature,* and such an inexcusable indolence and indifference in the preacher, as must *constrain* the hearers to suspect, whether they will or not, that the preacher, let him be who he will,—*only deals in the false commerce of unfelt truth.*"

This pointed and perpetual reference to eternity in his preaching, did not divert Whitefield from a due regard to time. He was an ardent admirer, if not imitator, of the character given of one of the German Reformers—*Bucolspherus,* as he calls him. I do not know him, unless Bucholcerus, the young friend of Melancthon, *(Theat. Vir. Erud.)* be referred to; and I doubt whether it could be said of him, " *Vividus vultus, vividi occuli, vividæ manus, denique omnia vivida.*" But whoever he was, Whitefield recognised a living exemplification of him in some of the Romish priests at Lisbon. I must go further, and say, that Whitefield felt it his *duty* to obey the commands given to some of the prophets—to smite with the hand, stamp with the foot, and lift up the voice like a trumpet, as well as to beseech with tears. Winter says of him, " his freedom in the use of his passions often put my pride to the trial. I could hardly bear such unreserved use of tears, and the scope he gave to his feelings; for sometimes he exceedingly wept, stamped loudly and passionately, and was frequently so overcome, that for a few seconds, you would suspect he never could recover; and when he did, nature required some little time to compose herself. I hardly ever knew him go through a sermon without weeping more or less, and I truly believe his were tears of sincerity. His voice was often interrupted by his affections; and I have heard him say in the pulpit,—' You blame me for weeping; but how can I help it, when you will not weep for yourselves, although your immortal souls are on the verge of destruction; and, for aught I know, you are hearing your last sermon, and may never more have an opportunity to have Christ offered to you.'

" I have known him avail himself of the formality of the judge putting on his *black* cap, to pronounce sentence. With his eyes full of tears, and his heart almost too big to admit of speech, he would say, after a momentary pause,—'I am now going to put on my *condemning* cap. Sinner, I MUST do it! I *must* pronounce sentence!' Then, in a strain of tremendous eloquence, he would repeat our Lord's words, 'Depart, ye cursed,' and not without a very powerful description of the nature of that curse. But it was only by hearing him, and by beholding his *attitude and tears*, that a person could well conceive of the effect."

It deserves special notice that Whitefield, whether he stamped or wept, whether he seemed a lion or lamb, was uniformly *solemn*, and allowed nothing to seem at variance with his deep solemnity. "Nothing awkward, nothing careless, appeared about him in the pulpit, nor do I ever recollect his *stumbling* on a word. Whether he frowned or smiled, whether he looked grave or placid, it was *nature* acting in him." *Winter.* This care over his words, tones, and gestures, sustained his own solemnity, and communicated it to others. They neither saw nor heard any thing to weaken the impression. There was no levity in his lively sallies, and no dulness in his reasonings, and no departure from the *spirit* of his mission even when he used "market language." He made all modes of address bear upon *solemn* effect. For *this*—"every accent of his voice spoke to the ear; every feature of his face, every motion of his hands, every gesture, spoke to the eye; so that the most dissipated and thoughtless found their attention involuntarily fixed." *Gillies.* Even when he created a momentary smile, it was to relieve the heart from the tension of an ordinary solemnity, that he might strain it up to an extraordinary pitch.

There was thus much *art* in Whitefield's preaching: I mean, the art of studying to be perfectly *natural* in all things pertaining to real life and godliness. He left nothing to accident that he could regulate by care, in his delivery. Hence practised speakers and shrewd observers could tell at once, whenever he delivered a sermon for the *first* time. Foote and Garrick maintained that his oratory was not at its full height, until he had repeated a discourse forty times. Franklin says, " By hearing him often, I came to distinguish easily between sermons newly composed, and those he had preached often in the course of his travels. His delivery of the latter was so improved by frequent repetition, that every accent, every emphasis, every modulation of voice, was so perfectly tuned and well placed, that, *without* being interested in the subject, (Franklin-like, alas!) one could not help being pleased with the discourse : a pleasure of much the same kind with that received from an excellent piece of music." Dr. Southey shows that he understands *speaking* as well as writing, by his remarks on Whitefield's oratory. —" It was a great advantage, but it was not the only one, nor the greatest, which he derived from repeating his discourses, and reciting instead of reading them. Had they been delivered from a written copy," (only think of Whitefield *reading!)* " one delivery would have been like the last : the paper would have operated as a *spell*, from which he could not depart ;—invention sleeping, while the utterance followed the eye. But when he had nothing before him except the audience whom he was addressing, the judgment and the imagination, as well as the memory, were called forth. Those parts were omitted which had been felt to come feebly from the tongue, and fall heavily on the ear ; and their place was supplied by matter newly *laid in* in the course of his studies, or *fresh* from the feeling of the moment. They who lived with him could trace him, in his sermons, to the book which he had last been reading, or the subject which had recently taken his attention. But the salient points of his oratory were not *prepared* passages—they were bursts of passion, like jets of a GEYSER, when the spring is in full play." *Southey's Wesley.*

David Hume beheld one of these *jets* of the Tabernacle-Geyser, and wondered, despised, and perished! He pronounced Whitefield the most ingenious preacher he ever heard ; and said, it was worth going twenty miles to hear him. " Once, after a solemn pause, he thus addressed his audience :—' The attendant angel is just about to leave the threshold of this sanctuary, and ascend to heaven. And shall he ascend, and not bear with him the news of one sinner, among all this multitude, reclaimed from the error of his ways ?' To give the greater effect to this exclamation, Whitefield stamped with his foot, lifted up his hands and eyes to heaven, and cried aloud, ' Stop, Gabriel, stop, ere you enter the sacred portals, and yet carry with you the news of one sinner converted to God.' " How gladly Gabriel would have carried to the throne the news of Hume's conversion, and told it to his mother in her mansion of glory! But Gabriel did not report Hume's words in heaven, although they were thus complimentary—" This address was accompanied with such animated yet natural action, that it surpassed any thing I ever saw or heard in any other preacher." Dr. Southey says, that this " flight of oratory is not in the *best* taste." Where will he find a better? He himself has quoted worse from Whitefield, without finding fault. But on a question of *taste*, I will not attempt to arbitrate between two historians of acknowledged tact. This flight of oratory will, however, keep itself for ever on all the wings of the wind, even if both judges had found fault with it. It will also be a lasting illustration of the " odd " but not " unapt " expression of the ignorant man, who said " that Whitefield preached like a lion ;" " no unapt notion," says Dr. Southey, " of the force, and vehemence, and passion of that oratory which awed the hearers, and made them tremble like Felix before the apostle."

Such was the *manner* of the preacher, whose spirit has spoken for itself throughout all this volume : and I now ask, was that *spirit* ever trammelled, cooled, or carnalized, by Whitefield's attention to the graces of pulpit eloquence? Did the study of oratory estrange him from his closet, or lessen his dependence on the Holy Spirit, or divert him from living habitually in the light of eternity and the Divine presence? No man ever lived nearer to God, or approached nearer to the perfection of oratory. He was too devotional to be cooled by rules, and too natural to be spoiled by art, and too much in earnest to win souls, to neglect system. He " sought out acceptable " tones, and gestures, and looks, as well as " acceptable words." Was Whitefield right ? Then how many, like myself, are far wrong ! Let the rising ministry take warning ! Awkwardness in the pulpit is a sin—monotony a sin—dulness a sin—and all of them sins against the welfare of immortal souls. These, be it ever remembered, invent too many excuses already for evading the claims of the gospel : do not, therefore, place yourself, STUDENT, among their reasons for rejecting it. It is as easy to be graceful in gesture, and natural in tone, as to be grammatical. You would not dare to violate grammar : dare not to be vulgar or vapid in manner. Your spirituality of mind is too low, and your communion with God too slight, and your love of the truth too cold, if they can be endangered by cultivating an eloquence worthy of the pulpit.

Whitefield's manner fascinated all ranks. I lately visited one of his converts ; now a pilgrim of nearly a century ; and a poor villager, who was never fifty miles from home. I went to see whether old *Father Mead*, of Chinnor, in Oxfordshire, could recognise Whitefield in one of my old prints. To my surprise the veteran himself was not unlike the portrait. Before opening it, therefore, I asked him whether he remembered Whitefield's person? The old man brightened at the question, and said, " Ay, sure : he was a jolly, brave man ; and what a *look* he had when he put out his right hand thus, to rebuke a disturber, as tried to stop him under the pear-tree. The man had been very threatening and noisy : but he could not stand the look. Off he rode, and Whitefield said, There he goes : empty barrels make most din." Father Mead both smiled and wept, as the vision threw him unconsciously into the very attitude and aspect of the preacher. I then asked him, whether he ever saw Whitefield now, in his *dreams*. He paused as if struck by the question. At length he said, " No ; but he was a jolly, brave man, and *sich* a look with him." I then asked if he had ever heard any preacher since, that reminded him of Whitefield? His speaking face sparkled as he looked to his *own* pastor, (who was with me,) and said, " Some reminds me of George." Whitefield seems his perpetual *day-dream ;* for, although almost a pauper, he has not parted with the books which Whitefield wrote or edited. I found him reading one of them, and singing " of mercy and judgment."

This little incident will do more than illustrate the emphatic hints of Cornelius Winter. He characterizes Whitefield's oratory, as we have seen, with great success ; as the following specimens will still further prove.

" As though it were no difficult matter to catch the sound of
the Saviour praying, he would exclaim, ' Hark! hark! do not
you hear him?'—You may suppose that as this occurred frequently, the efficacy of it was destroyed; but, no; though we
often knew what was coming, it was as new to us as though we
had never heard it before.

" That beautiful apostrophe, used by the prophet Jeremiah,
' O earth, earth, earth, hear the words of the Lord,' was very
subservient to him, and never used impertinently.

" He abounded with anecdotes, which, though not always re-
cited verbatim, were very just, as to the matter of them.   One,
for instance, I remember, tending to illustrate the efficacy of
prayer, though I have not been able to meet with it in the
English history—it was the case of the London apprentices
before Henry VIII. pleading his pardon of their insurrection.
The monarch, moved by their sight, and their plea, ' Mercy!
mercy!' cried, ' Take them away, I cannot bear it." The application you may suppose was, that if an earthly monarch of
Henry's description could be so moved, how forcible is the sinner's plea in the ears of Jesus Christ! The case of two Scotchmen, in the convulsion of the state at the time of Charles II.
subserved his design; who, unavoidably obliged to pass some of
the troops, were conceiving of their danger, and meditating what
method was to be adopted, to come off safe : one proposed the
wearing of a scull-cap; the other, supposing that would imply
distrust of the providence of God, was determined to proceed
bare-headed.   The latter, being first laid hold of, and being
interrogated, ' Are you for the covenant?' replied, ' Yes;' and
being further asked, ' What covenant?' answered, ' The covenant of *grace*;' by which reply, eluding further inquiry, he was
let pass : the other, not answering satisfactorily, received a blow
with the sabre, which, penetrating through the cap, struck him
dead.   In the application, Mr. Whitefield, warning against vain
confidence, cried, ' Beware of your scull-caps.' But here likewise the description upon paper, wanting the reality as exemplified by him with voice and motion, conveys but a very faint
idea.   However, it is a disadvantage which must be submitted
to, especially as coming from my pen.

" The difference of the *times* in which Mr. Whitefield made his public appearance, materially determined the matter of his sermons, and, in some measure, the manner of his address. He dealt far more in the explanatory and doctrinal mode of preaching on a sabbath-day morning, than perhaps at any other time; and sometimes made a little, but by no means improper, show of learning. If he had read upon astronomy in the course of the week, you would be sure to discover it. He knew how to convert the centripetal motion of the heavenly bodies to the disposition of the christian toward Christ, and the fatal attraction of the world would be very properly represented by a reference to the centrifugal. Whatever the world might think of him, he had his charms for the learned as well as for the unlearned; and as he held himself to be a debtor both to the wise and to the unwise, each received his due at such times. The peer and the peasant alike went away satisfied.

" As though he heard the voice of God ever sounding in his ears the important admonition, ' Work while it is called to day,' this was his work in London at one period of his life:—After administering the Lord's supper to several hundred communicants, at half an hour after six in the morning; reading the first and second service in the desk, which he did with the greatest propriety, and preaching full an hour, he read prayers and preached in the afternoon, previous to the evening service, at half an hour after five; and afterwards addressed a large society in public. His afternoon sermon used to be more general and exhortatory. In the evening he drew his bow at a venture, vindicated the doctrines of grace, fenced them with articles and homilies, referred to the martyrs' zeal, and exemplified the power of divine grace in their sufferings, by quotations from the venerable Fox. Sinners were then closely plied, numbers of whom from curiosity coming to hear a sentence or two, were often compelled to hear the whole sermon. How many in the judgment day will rise to prove that they heard to the salvation of the soul!

" Perhaps Mr. Whitefield never preached greater sermons than at six in the morning, for at that hour he did preach, winter and summer, on Mondays, Tuesdays, Wednesdays, and

Thursdays. At these times his congregations were of the select description, and young men received admonitions similar with what were given in the society;* and were cautioned, while they neglect the duty required from them under the bond of an indenture, not to anticipate the pleasures and advantages of future life.

" His style was now colloquial, with little use of motion; pertinent expositions, with suitable remarks; and all comprehended within the hour. Christian experience principally made the subject of Monday, Tuesday, Wednesday, and Thursday evening lectures; when, frequently having funeral sermons to preach, the character and experience of the dead helped to elucidate the subject, led to press diligence in the christian course, to reflect upon the blessing of faith on earth, and glory in heaven. Mr. Whitefield adopted the custom of the inhabitants of New England in their best days, of beginning the sabbath at six o'clock on Saturday evenings. The custom could not be observed by many, but it was convenient to a few—a few compared with the multitudes, but abstractedly considered, a large and respectable company. Now ministers of every description found a peculiar pleasure in relaxing their minds from the fatigues of study, and were highly entertained by his peculiarly excellent subjects, which were so suitable to the auditory, that I believe it was seldom disappointed. It was an opportunity peculiarly suited to apprentices and journeymen in some businesses, which allowed of their leaving work sooner than on other days, and availing themselves at least of the sermon; from which I also occasionally obtained many blessings. Had my memory been retentive, and I had studiously treasured up his rich remarks, how much more easily might I have met your wishes, and have answered

* This society, consisting of several hundreds of widows, married people, young men, and spinsters, placed separately in the area of the Tabernacle, used after sermon to receive from Mr. Whitefield, in the colloquial style, various exhortations comprised in short sentences, and suitable to their various stations. The practice of christianity in all its branches, was then usually inculcated, not without some pertinent anecdote of a character worthy to be held up for an example, and in whose conduct the hints recommended were exemplified.

the design of this letter! But though I have lost much of the letter of his sermons, the savour of them yet remains. The peculiar talents he possessed, subservient to great usefulness, can be but faintly guessed from his sermons in print; though, as formerly God has made the reading of them useful, I have no doubt but in future they will have their use. The eighteen taken in short-hand, and faithfully transcribed, by Mr. Gurney, have been supposed to do discredit to his memory, and therefore they were suppressed. But they who have been accustomed to hear him, may collect from them much of his genuine preaching. They were far from being the best specimens that might have been produced. He preached many of them, when, in fact, he was almost *incapable* of preaching at all." *Winter.*

After all, the grand secret of Whitefield's power was, as we have seen and felt, his *devotional* spirit. Had he been less prayerful, he would have been less powerful. He was the prince of preachers *without* the veil, because he was a Jacob " within the veil." His face shone when he came down from the mount, because he had been *long* alone with God upon the mount. It was this won for him the title *seraphic;* not in the scholastic, but in the angelic sense of the term. But he was a *human* seraph; and thus burnt *out* in the blaze of his own fire. What then?—he often ascended in it, as the Angel of the covenant did in the flame of Manoah's sacrifice; and always " did *wondrously*," when he descended. He was so often at the throne, and always so near it, that, like the apocalyptic angel, he came down " clothed with its rainbow."

Whitefield's LETTERS also illustrate both his character and success, as a minister. They are many, and varied, and easy; and must have been very useful. Like the *bulletins* of a general, they were chiefly written on the field of battle; and thus came to his friends associated and enshrined with his victories. No matter, therefore, what they are as epistolary writing; they came from " the conquering hero " of the day, to those who were praying for and expecting him to go on from conquering to conquer. How gratifying, yea, how inspiring, therefore, the briefest and baldest of them must have been, as well as the longest and best, to those who received them! They were all

proofs to them, that he had them in his heart, and that his solicitude and friendship for them followed him like his shadow
wherever he went, and whatever he was doing.　This is the true
light in which to read his letters : and in this light, the wonder
is that they are so many and so good !　The man is to be pitied
who can criticise them ; and so is he who can read them without
being refreshed by them ; for they are only surpassed by Luke's
" Acts of the Apostles."

Whitefield's public character was fully sustained by his private habits.　His vein of humour never betrayed him into
levity, nor his exhaustion into excess, at the social or the domestic table.　He sat down often, of course, to sumptuous
tables, whilst travelling.　Indeed, he could not avoid a succession of such feasts.　Enemies, however, judged of his eating
by the scale of *cooking* in the houses of his hosts.　His corpulency was thus ascribed to " good living."　This needs no refu-
tation, to any one who understands public speaking.　Indulgence
is incompatible with unction, if not with energy also.　Cornelius Winter has thought proper, however, to defend Whitefield ;
and therefore it is my duty to quote the defence :—" He was
unjustly charged with being given to appetite.　His table was
never spread with variety.　A *cow-heel* was his favourite dish ;
and I have known him say cheerfully, ' How surprised would
the world be if they were to peep upon Dr. Squintum, and see
only a cow-heel upon his table ! ' "　He was, however, a *gentleman;* and, therefore, " whether by himself, or having but a
second, his table must be elegantly spread, though it produced
but a loaf and a cheese."　Gillies says, " He was remarkable,
even to a proverb, for moderation in eating and drinking."

This *wise* attention to etiquette he carried into all his habits.
It was a maxim with him, that a minister should be literally
spotless.　" He was neat in the extreme in his person and every
thing about him.　He said, he did not think he could die easy
if he thought his *gloves* were out of their place.　Not a paper
might be out of its place, or put up irregularly.　Each part of
the furniture also must be in its place before we retired to rest.
There was no rest after *four* in the morning, nor sitting up after
ten in the evening.　He was scrupulously exact to break up

parties in time. In the height of a conversation I have heard him say, abruptly, We forget ourselves : come, gentlemen, it is high time for all good folks to be at home." *Jay's Winter.*

Gillies, who knew him in his prime, says, " His person was graceful and well proportioned—his stature above the middle size—his complexion very fair—his countenance manly. His eyes were of a dark blue, and very sprightly. He had a *squint* with one of them. His deportment was decent and easy, without the least stiffness or formality; and his engaging polite manner made his company universally agreeable."

Whitefield's last WILL, also, deserves a place amongst his characteristics. It was brought from America to England by Winter. He felt it to be a *sacred* trust; for during a storm, in which all the sails were blown away, and all the masts bending, and all the dead-lights up, his chief earthly " concern was, that he had Whitefield's will." " I felt sorry," he says, " that by my being lost, his executors would be kept in suspense." Both arrived safe ; but the chief property, Bethesda, was soon destroyed or alienated. It was, I think, Berridge who said, on hearing of the extinction of the orphan-house college, that " God set fire to it, in order to save the founder from becoming the father of a race of unconverted ministers." This is a *just* view of its fate: for, by admitting young men to study for the ministry before their piety or call was ascertained, it was both unfit and unworthy to be a nursery to the church of Christ.

The following are the documents published by the executors. " Mr. Whitefield's executors having received the probate of his will, February 6, 1771, Mr. Keene, who was well acquainted with the whole of his affairs, published it, with the following introduction :

" As we make no doubt the numerous friends of the Rev. Mr. George Whitefield will be glad of an opportunity of seeing a genuine copy of his last will and testament, his executors have favoured us with a copy of the same, transmitted to them from the orphan-house, in Georgia, and which they have proved in the Prerogative Court of Canterbury. And as it was Mr. Whitefield's constant declaration, he never meant to raise either a purse or a party, it is to be remarked, that almost the whole sum he died possessed of, came to him within two or three years of his death, in the following manner, viz: Mrs. Thomson, of Tower Hill, bequeathed him £500 ;—by the death of his wife, (including a bond of £300,) he got £700 ;—Mr. Whitmore bequeathed him £100 ; and Mr. Winder, £100. And it is highly probable, that had he lived to reach Georgia, from his last northern tour, he would have lessened the above sums, by disposing of them in the same noble and disinterested manner, that all the public or private sums he has been intrusted with have been."

" In the name of the Father, Son, and Holy Ghost, three persons, but one God; I, George Whitefield, clerk, at present residing at the orphan-house academy, in the province of Georgia, in North America, being through infinite mercy in more than ordinary bodily health, and a perfectly sound and composed mind, knowing the certainty of death, and yet the uncertainty of the time I shall be called by it to my long-wished-for home, do make this my last will and testament, in manner and form following, viz.

" *Imprimis*—In sure and certain hope of a resurrection to eternal life, through our Lord Jesus Christ, I commit my body to the dust, to be buried in the most plain and decent manner ; and knowing in whom I have believed, being persuaded that he will keep that which I have committed unto him, in the fullest assurance of faith I commend my soul into the hands of the ever loving, altogether lovely, never-failing Jesus, on whose complete and everlasting righteousness I entirely depend for the justification of my person, and acceptance of my poor, worthless, though I trust sincere performances, at that day when he shall come in the glory of his Father, his own glory, and the glory of his holy angels, to judge both the quick and dead. In respect to my American concerns, which I have engaged in simply and solely for his great name's sake, I leave that building, commonly called the orphan-house, at Bethesda, in the province of Georgia, together with all the other buildings lately erected thereon; and likewise all other buildings, lands, negroes, books, furniture, and every other thing whatsoever, which I now stand possessed of in the province of Georgia aforesaid, to that elect lady, that mother in Israel, that mirror of true and undefiled religion, the Right Honourable Selina, Countess dowager of Huntingdon; desiring, that as soon as may be after my decease, the plan of the intended orphan-house, Bethesda college, may be prosecuted, if not practicable, or eligible, to pursue the present plan of the orphan-house academy, on its old foundation and usual channel; but if her Ladyship should be called to enter her glorious rest before my decease—I bequeath all the buildings, lands, negroes, and every thing before mentioned, which I now stand possessed of in the province of Georgia aforesaid, to my dear fellow-traveller and faithful, invariable friend, the Honourable James Habersham, president of his Majesty's Honourable Council : and should he survive her Ladyship, I earnestly recommend him as the most proper person to succeed her Ladyship, or to act for her during her Ladyship's life-time, in the orphan-house academy.—With regard to my outward affairs in England; whereas there is a building, commonly called the Tabernacle, set apart many years ago for divine worship—I give and bequeath the said Tabernacle, with the adjacent house in which I usually reside when in London, with the stable and coach-house in the yard adjoining, together with all books, furniture, and every thing else whatsoever, that shall be found in the house and premises aforesaid; and also the building, commonly called Tottenham Court chapel, together with all the other buildings, houses, stable, coach-house, and every thing else whatsoever, which I stand possessed of in that part of the town, to my worthy, trusty, tried friends, Daniel West, Esq. in Church Street, Spitalfields, and Mr. Robert Keene, woollen draper, in the Minories, or the longer survivor of the two.—As to the monies, which a kind Providence, especially of late, in a most unexpected way, and unthought-of means, hath vouchsafed to intrust me with—I give and bequeath the sum of £100 sterling to the Right Honourable the Countess dowager of Huntingdon aforesaid, humbly beseeching her Ladyship's acceptance of so small a mite, as a pepper-corn acknowledgment, for the undeserved, unsought-for honour her Ladyship conferred upon me, in appointing me, less than the least of all, to be one of her Ladyship's domestic chaplains.

" *Item*—I give and bequeath to my dearly beloved friend, the Honourable James Habersham aforesaid, my late wife's gold watch, and £10 for mourning ;—to my dear old friend, Gabriel Harris, Esq. of the city of Gloucester, who received and boarded me in his house, when I was helpless and destitute, above thirty-five years ago, I give and bequeath the sum of £50 ;—to my humble, faithful servant and friend, Mr. Ambrose Wright, if in my service and employ, either in England or America, or else-where, at the time of my decease, I give and bequeath the sum of £500 ;—to my brother, Mr. Thomas Whitefield, I give and bequeath the sum of £50, to be given him at the discretion of Mr. Robert Keene ;—to my brother-in-law, Mr. James Smith, hosier, in the city of Bristol, I give and bequeath the sum of £50, and £30 also for family mourning ;—to my niece, Mrs. Frances Hartford, of Bath, I give and bequeath the sum of £50, and £20 for family mourning ;—to Mr. J. Crane, now a faithful steward at the orphan-house academy, I give and bequeath the sum of £40 ;—to Mr. Benjamin Stirk, as an acknowledgment of his past services at Bethesda, I give and bequeath the sum of £10, for mourning ;—to Peter Edwards, now at the orphan-house academy, I give and bequeath the sum of £50 ;—to William Trigg, at the same place, I give and bequeath the sum of £50 ; both the sums aforesaid to be laid out, or laid up for them, at the discretion of Mr. Ambrose Wright ;—to Mr. Thomas Adams, of Rodborough, in Gloucestershire, my only surviving first fel-low-labourer, and beloved much in the Lord, I give and bequeath the sum of £50 ;—to the Rev. Mr. Howel Davies, of Pembroke-shire, in South Wales, that good soldier of Jesus Christ ;—to Mr. Torial Joss, Mr. Cornelius Winter, and all my other dearly beloved, present, stated, assistant preachers at Tabernacle and Tottenham Court chapel, I give and bequeath £10 each for mourning ;—to the three brothers of Mr. Ambrose Wright, Ann, the wife of his brother, Mr. Robert Wright, now faithfully and skilfully labouring and serving at the orphan-house academy, I give and bequeath the sum of £10 each for mourning ;—to Mr. Richard Smith, now a diligent attendant on me, I give and be-queath the sum of £50, and all my wearing apparel, which I shall have with me in my journey through America, or on my voyage to England, if it should please an all-wise God to shorten my days in either of those situations.—Finally, I give and bequeath the sum of £100 to be distributed at the discretion of my executors, hereinafter mentioned, for mourning among my old London servants, the poor widows at Tottenham Court chapel, and the Tabernacle poor; especially my old trusty, disinterested friend and servant, Mrs. Elizabeth Wood. All the other residue, if there be any other residues of monies, goods, and chattels, or whatsoever profits may arise from the sale of any books, or any manuscripts that I may leave behind, I give and bequeath to the Right Honourable the Countess dowager of Huntingdon; or in case of her Ladyship being deceased at the time of my departure, to the Honourable James Habersham, Esq. before mentioned, after my funeral expenses and just debts are discharged, towards paying off any arrears that may be due on the account of the orphan-house academy, or for annual prizes as a reward for the best three orations that shall be made in English, on the subjects mentioned in a paper annexed to this my will. And I hereby appoint the Honourable James Habersham, Esq. aforesaid, to be my executor in respect to my affairs in the province of Georgia, and my trusty, tried, dearly beloved friends, Charles Hardy, Esq. Daniel West, Esq. and Mr. Robert Keene, to be executors of this my last will and testament, in respect of my affairs in England, begging each to accept of a mourning ring.

" To all my other christian benefactors, and more intimate acquaintance, I leave my most hearty thanks and blessing, assuring them that I am more and more convinced of the undoubted reality and infinite importance of the grand gospel truths, which I have from time to time delivered; and am so far from repenting my delivering them in an itinerant way, that had I strength equal to my inclination, I would preach them from pole to pole; not only because I have found them to be the power of God to the salvation of my own soul, but because I am as much assured that the great Head of the church hath called me by his word, providence, and Spirit, to act in this way, as that the sun shines at noon-day.—As for my enemies, and misjudging friends, I most freely and heartily forgive them, and can only

add, that the last tremendous day will only discover what I
have been, what I am, and what I shall be, when time itself
shall be no more ; and therefore from my inmost soul, I close all
by crying, *Come, Lord Jesus, come quickly; even so, Lord Jesus.
Amen and Amen !*

GEORGE WHITEFIELD."

" This was written with the testator's own hand, and at his
    desire, and in his presence, sealed, signed, and deliver-
    ed, at the orphan-house academy, in the province of
    Georgia, before us witnesses, Anno Domini, March 22,
    1770.

Signed, { ROBERT BOLTON,
         { THOMAS DIXON,
         { CORNELIUS WINTER."

" N. B. I also leave a mourning ring to my honoured and
dear friends, and disinterested fellow-labourers, the Rev. John
and Charles Wesley, in token of my indissoluble union with
them, in heart and christian affection, notwithstanding our difference in judgment about some particular points of doctrine.
Grace be with all them, of whatever denomination, that love our
Lord Jesus, our common Lord, in sincerity."

" GEORGIA, Secretary's Office.

" A true copy, taken from the original in this office, examined
and certified : and I do further certify, that the same was duly
proved ; and the Hon. James Habersham, one of the executors
therein named, was duly qualified as executor, before his Excellency, James Wright, Esq. governor and ordinary of the said
province, this 10th day of December, 1770.

THOMAS MOODIE, Deputy Secretary."

CHAPTER XXXIII.

THIS volume would be incomplete, for my purpose, without some specimens of Whitefield's preaching. That requires to be *illustrated* as well as analyzed, now that the man, and his message, and his success, are fully before us. It is also necessary to preserve some specimens of his sermons in this record of his life, because his sermons, as such, will hardly perpetuate themselves. His *name* may continue to sell them; but even already they are but seldom read. No minister quotes from them, except when an anecdote of Whitefield brings in some stroke of power or pathos; and no student hears or thinks of them as models. Indeed, they are not models for the *pulpit* but when it stands in the fields; and even there, it must be surrounded by thousands before any man could wield the glittering sword of Whitefield with effect.

Besides; there is not much to be learnt from his sermons now. Their best maxims are but *common-place* to us. They were, however, both new and strange things to the generality of his hearers. He was as much an *original* to them, as Chalmers is to us. And, let it never be forgotten, that Whitefield and Wesley *common-placed*, in the public mind, the great truths of the Reformation, in simple forms and familiar words. If they added nothing to the theology of their country that was either original or valuable, they threw old truths into new proportions and wide circulation. This is forgotten by those who say with a sneer, that there is *nothing* in their sermons. I have often heard this said, by men who never gave *currency* to a single maxim, nor *birth* to a thought worth preserving.

Such critics should be silent.   Their newer modes of thinking and writing will never common-place themselves in the world or the church !

There is one peculiarity about Whitefield's sermons which his critics have not pointed out, and which I should like to commend, if I could do so wisely.   I mean,—his modest *egotism* in preaching.   He is for ever speaking of himself when he touches any experimental point, or grapples with a difficulty. Then he opens his own heart in all its inmost recesses, and details the process by which his own mind was made up; and both without even the appearance of vanity, or of " a voluntary humility."   It is all done with the artless simplicity of child-hood.   He thinks *aloud* about himself, only to enable others to know what to think about their own perplexities, dilemmas, and temptations.   He shows them his own soul, merely to prove that " no strange thing has befallen" their souls.

Nothing is so unlike Whitefield's egotism, however, as the whining confessions of a certain *clique* of preachers, who talk much about the plagues and lusts of their own hearts.   They are theological Rousseaus or Montaignes, foaming out their own shame, if not glorying in it.   Nothing is so disgusting as such obtrusive egotism.   It is, indeed, unblushing effrontery, to *hawk* moral disease thus.   Whitefield spoke of himself in the strong language of the Scriptures; but he did not go into details when applying it to himself, except in the first sketch of his life; and that he carefully pruned in a subsequent edition.

The following passage is a fair specimen of his egotism. " Do not say that I preach despair.   I despair of no one, when I consider how God had mercy on such a wretch as I, who was running in a full career to hell.   I was *hasting* thither; but Jesus Christ passed by and stopped me.   Jesus Christ passed by while I was in my blood, and bid me live.   Thus I am a monument of God's free grace; and, therefore, my brethren, I despair of none of you, when I consider, I say, what a wretch I was.   I am not speaking now out of a false humility, or a pretended sanctity, as the Pharisees call it.   No; the truth in Christ I speak; and therefore, men and devils, do your worst ! I have a gracious Master who will protect me.   It is His work

I am engaged in, and Jesus Christ will carry me above their rage." *Works.*

The following extracts 'will illustrate his vivacity and vehemency, to any one who will consider the scope they afford for the indulgence of both. It must, however, be borne in mind, that his face was a language, and his intonation music, and his action passion. So much was this the case, that GARRICK said of him, he could make men weep or tremble by his varied utterances of the word " Mesopotamia."

PETER ON THE HOLY MOUNT. " ' Peter said unto Jesus, Master, it is good for us to be here : and let us make three tabernacles; one for thee, and one for Moses, and one for Elias: not knowing what he said.' Peter, when he had drank a little of Christ's new wine, speaks like a person intoxicated; he was overpowered with the brightness of the manifestations. ' Let us make three tabernacles ; one for thee, and one for Moses, and one for Elias.' It is well added, ' not knowing what he said.' That he should cry out, ' Master, it is good for us to be here,' in such good company, and in so glorious a condition, is no wonder ; which of us all would not have been apt to do the same ? But to talk of building tabernacles, and one for Christ, and one for Moses, and one for Elias, was saying something for which Peter himself must stand reproved. Surely, Peter, thou wast not quite awake ! Thou talkest like one in a dream. If thy Lord had taken thee at thy word, what a poor tabernacle wouldst thou have had, in comparison of that house not made with hands, eternal in the heavens, in which thou hast long since dwelt, now the earthly house of the tabernacle of thy body is dissolved ! What ! build tabernacles below, and have the crown before thou hast borne the cross ? O Peter, Peter ! ' Master, spare thyself,' sticks too, too closely to thee. And why so selfish, Peter ? Carest thou not for thy fellow-disciples that are below, who came not up with thee to the mount ? carest thou not for the precious souls, that are as sheep having no shepherd, and must perish for ever, unless thy Master descends from the mount to teach, and to die for them ? wouldst thou thus eat thy spiritual morsels alone ? Besides, if thou art for building tabernacles, why must there be three of them, one for

Christ, and one for Moses, and one for Elias? are Christ and
the prophets divided? do they not sweetly harmonize and
agree in one? did they not prophesy concerning the sufferings
of thy Lord, as well as of the glory that should follow? Alas,
how unlike is their conversation to thine! Moses and Elias
came down to talk of suffering, and thou art dreaming of building I know not what tabernacles. Surely, Peter, thou art so
high upon the mount, that thy head runs giddy.

"However, in the midst of these infirmities, there was something that bespoke the honesty and integrity of his heart.
Though he knew not very well what he said, yet he was not so
stupid as his pretended successor at Rome. He does not fall
down and worship these two departed saints, neither do I hear
him say to either, *Ora pro nobis;* he had not so learned Christ;
no, he applies himself directly to the Head, ' he said unto Jesus,
Master, it is good for us to be here.' And though he was for
building, yet he would not build without his Master's leave.
' Master, let us build;' or, as St. Mark words it, ' Wilt thou
that we build three tabernacles, one for thee, and one for Moses,
and one for Elias?' I do not hear him add, and one for
James, and one for John, and one for Peter. No, he would
willingly stay out with them upon the mount, though it was in
the cold and dark night, so that Christ and his heavenly attendants were taken care of. The sweetness of such a heavenly
vision would more than compensate for any bodily suffering
that might be the consequences of their longer abode there.
Nay, further, he does not desire that either Christ, or Moses, or
Elias, should have any trouble in building; neither does he
say, Let my curates, James and John, build, whilst I sit idle and
lord it over my brethren; but he says, ' Let us build;' he will
work as hard, if not harder than either of them, and desire to
be distinguished only by his activity, enduring hardness, and
his zeal to promote the welfare of their common Lord and
Master."

OLD AND INFIRM SAINTS. " Did Moses and Elias appear in
glory? Are there any old saints here? I doubt not but there
are a considerable number. And are any of you afraid of
death? Do any of you carry about with you a body that weighs

down your immortal soul? I am sure a poor creature is preaching to you, that every day drags a crazy load along. But come,
believers, come, ye children of God, come, ye aged, decrepit
saints, come and trample upon that monster death. As thou
goest over yonder church-yard, do as I know an old excellent
christian in Maryland did; go, sit upon the grave, and meditate upon thine own dissolution. Thou mayst, perhaps, have
a natural fear of dying; the body and the soul do not care to
part without a little sympathy and a groan; but O look yonder, look up to heaven, see there thy Jesus, thy Redeemer, and
learn that thy body is to be fashioned hereafter like unto
Christ's most glorious body. That poor body which is now subject to gout and gravel, and that thou canst scarce drag along;
that poor body, which hinders thee so much in the spiritual life,
will ere long hinder thee no more : it shall be put into the
grave; but though it be sown in corruption, it shall be raised
in incorruption; though it be sown in dishonour, it shall be
raised again in glory. This consideration made blessed Paul
to cry out, 'O death, where is thy sting? O grave, where is
thy victory?' Thy soul and body shall be united together
again, and thou shalt be 'for ever with the Lord.' Those
knees of thine, which perhaps are hard by kneeling in prayer;
that tongue of thine, which hath sung hymns to Christ;
those hands of thine, which have wrought for God; those feet
which have ran to Christ's ordinances; shall all, in the twinkling
of an eye, be changed; and thou shalt be able to stand under
an exceeding and an eternal weight of glory. Come then, ye
believers in Christ, look beyond the grave; come, ye dear children of God, and however weak and sickly ye are now, say,
Blessed be God, I shall soon have a body strong, full of vigour
and of glory.

" But as this speaks comfort to saints, it speaks terror to sinners, to all persons that live and die out of Christ. It is the
opinion of Archbishop Usher, that as the bodies of the saints shall
be glorified, so the bodies of the damned shall be deformed.
And if this be true, alas ! what a poor figure will the fine ladies
cut, who die without a Christ ! What a poor figure will the
fine gentleman cut in the morning of the resurrection, that now

2 P

dresses up his body, and at the same time neglects to secure an
interest in Christ and eternal happiness! It is the opinion,
likewise, of Archbishop Usher, that damned souls will lose all
the good tempers they had here; so that though God gave unregenerate people a constitutional meekness, good nature, and
courage, for the benefit of the commonwealth; yet, the use of
these things being over, and they having died without Christ,
and it being impossible there will be an appearance of good in
hell, their good tempers will be for ever lost. If this be so it
is an awful consideration; and I think persons who love their
bodies, should also hence take care to secure the welfare of
their souls."

HEAR CHRIST. "Did the Father say, 'This is my beloved
Son, hear him?' Then let every one of our hearts echo to this
testimony given of Christ, "This is my beloved Saviour.' Did
God so love the world, as to send his only begotten Son, his
well-beloved Son to preach to us? Then, my dear friends, *Hear
Him.* What God said seventeen hundred years ago, immediately by a voice from heaven, concerning his Son upon the
mount, that same thing God says to you immediately by his
word, 'Hear him.' If ye never heard him before, hear him
now. Hear him so as to take him to be your Prophet, Priest,
and your King; hear him, so as to take him to be your God
and your all. Hear him to-day, ye youth, while it is called to-
day; hear him now, lest God should cut you off before you
have another invitation to hear him; hear him while he cries,
'Come unto me;' hear him while he opens his hand and his
heart; hear him while he knocks at the door of your souls, lest
you should hear him saying, 'Depart, depart, ye cursed, into
everlasting fire, prepared for the devil and his angels.' Hear
him, ye old and grey-headed; hear him, ye that have one foot
in the grave; hear him, I say: and if ye are dull of hearing,
beg of God to open the ears of your hearts, and your blind
eyes; beg of God that you may have an enlarged and a believing heart, and that ye may know what the Lord God saith
concerning you. God will resent it, he will avenge himself on
his adversaries, if you do not hear a blessed Saviour. He is
God's Son, he is God's beloved Son; he came upon a great

errand, even to shed his precious blood for sinners ; he came to cleanse you from all sin, and to save you with an everlasting salvation. Ye who have heard him, *hear him again;* still go on, believe in and obey him, and by and by you shall hear him saying, ' Come, ye blessed of my Father, receive the kingdom prepared for you from the foundation of the world.' "

BESEECHING SINNERS. " O my brethren, my heart is enlarged towards you. I trust I feel something of that hidden, but powerful presence of Christ, whilst I am preaching to you. Indeed, it is sweet, it is exceedingly comfortable. All the harm I wish you, who without cause are my enemies, is, that you felt the like. Believe me, though it would be hell to my soul, to return to a natural state again, yet I would willingly change states with you for a little while, that you might know what it is to have Christ dwelling in your hearts by faith. Do not turn your backs ; do not let the devil hurry you away ; be not afraid of convictions ; do not think worse of the doctrine, because preached without the church walls. Our Lord, in the days of his flesh, preached on a mount, in a ship, and a field ; and I am persuaded, many have felt his gracious presence here. Indeed, we speak what we know. Do not reject the kingdom of God against yourselves ; be so wise as to receive our witness. I *cannot,* I *will not* let you go ; stay a *little,* let us reason together. However lightly you may esteem your souls, I know our Lord has set an unspeakable value on them. He thought them worthy of his most precious blood. I beseech you, therefore, O sinners, be ye reconciled to God. I hope you do not fear being accepted in the Beloved. Behold, he calleth you ; behold, he prevents and follows you with his mercy, and hath sent forth his servants into the highways and hedges, to compel you to come in. Remember, then, that at such an hour of such a day, in such a year, in this place, you were all told what you ought to think concerning Jesus Christ. If you now perish, it will not be for lack of knowledge : I am free from the blood of you all. You cannot say I have, like legal preachers, been requiring you to make brick without straw. I have not bidden you to make yourselves saints, and then come to God ; but I have offered you salvation on as cheap terms as you can desire. I have

offered you Christ's whole wisdom, Christ's whole righteousness,
Christ's whole sanctification and eternal redemption, if you will
but believe on him. If you say, you cannot believe, you say
right; for faith, as well as every other blessing, is the gift of
God : but then wait upon God, and who knows but he may have
mercy on thee ? Why do we not entertain more loving thoughts
of Christ ? Or do you think he will have mercy on others, and
not on you? But are you not sinners ? And did not Jesus
Christ come into the world to save sinners ? If you say you are
the chief of sinners, I answer, that will be no hinderance to your
salvation; indeed it will not, if you lay hold on him by faith.
Read the evangelists, and see how kindly he behaved to his disciples who fled from and denied him ; ' Go tell my brethren,'
says he. He did not say, Go tell those traitors ; but, ' Go tell
my brethren, and *Peter ;*' as though he had said, Go tell my
brethren in general, and poor *Peter* in particular, ' that I am
risen :' O comfort his poor drooping heart, tell him I am reconciled to him ; bid him weep no more so bitterly : for though
with oaths and curses he thrice denied me, yet I have died for
his sins, I am risen again for his justification ; I freely forgive
him all. Thus slow to anger, and of great kindness, was our
all-merciful High Priest. And do you think he has changed his
nature, and forgets poor sinners, now he is exalted to the right
hand of God ? No, he is the same yesterday, to-day, and for
ever, and sitteth there only to make intercession for us. Come
then, ye harlots; come, ye publicans ; come, ye most abandoned of sinners, come and believe on Jesus Christ. Though
the whole world despise you and cast you out, yet he will not
disdain to take you up. O amazing, O infinitely condescending
love ! even you he will not be ashamed to call his brethren.
How will you escape, if you neglect such a glorious offer of salvation ? What would the damned spirits, now in the prison of
hell, give, if Christ was so freely offered to their souls ! And
why are not we lifting up our eyes in torments ? Does any one
out of this great multitude dare say, he does not deserve damnation ? If not, why are we left, and others taken away by death?
What is this but an instance of God's free grace, and a sign of
his good will towards us ? Let God's goodness lead us to re-

pentance! O let there be joy in heaven over some of you repenting! Though we are in a *field*, I am persuaded the blessed
angels are hovering now around us, and do long, ' as the hart
panteth after the water-brooks,' to sing an anthem at your conversion. Blessed be God, I hope their joy will be fulfilled.
An *awful silence* appears amongst us. I have good hope that
the words which the Lord has enabled me to speak in your ears
this day, have not altogether fallen to the ground. Your tears
and deep attention, are an evidence that the Lord God is
amongst us of a truth. Come, ye Pharisees, come and see, in
spite of your fanatical rage and fury, the Lord Jesus is getting
himself the victory. And, brethren, I speak the truth in Christ,
I lie not; if one soul of you, by the blessing of God, be brought
to think savingly of Jesus Christ this day, I care not if my
enemies were permitted to carry me to prison, and put my feet
fast in the stocks, as soon as I have delivered this sermon.
Brethren, my heart's desire and prayer to God is, that you may
be saved. For this cause I follow my Master without the camp.
I care not how much of his sacred reproach I bear, so that some
of you be converted from the errors of your ways. I rejoice,
yea, and I will rejoice. Ye men, ye devils, do your *worst :* the
Lord who sent will support me. And when Christ, who is our
life, and whom I have now been preaching, shall appear, I also,
together with his despised little ones, shall appear with him in
glory. And then, what will you think of Christ? I know what
you will think of him. You will think him to be the fairest
among ten thousand : you will then think and feel him to be a
just and sin-avenging Judge. Be ye then persuaded to kiss
him lest he be angry, and so you be banished for ever from the
presence of the Lord. Behold, I come to you as the angel did
to Lot. Flee, flee for your lives; haste, linger no longer in
your spiritual Sodom, for otherwise you will be eternally destroyed. Numbers, no doubt, there are amongst you, that may
regard me no more than Lot's sons-in-law regarded him. I am
persuaded I seem to some of you as one that mocketh : but I
speak the truth in Christ, I lie not ; as sure as fire and brimstone
was rained from the Lord out of heaven, to destroy Sodom and
Gomorrah, so surely, at the great day, shall the vials of God's

wrath be poured on you, if you do not think seriously of, and act agreeably to, the gospel of the Lord's Christ. Behold, I have told you before; and I pray God, all you that forget him may seriously think of what has been said, before he pluck you away, and there be none to deliver you."

CHRISTLESS SINNERS. "My friends, I trust I feel somewhat of a sense of God's distinguishing love upon my heart; therefore I must divert a little from congratulating believers, to invite poor Christless sinners to come to him, and accept of his right-eousness, that they may have life. Alas, my heart almost bleeds! What a multitude of precious souls are now before me! how shortly must all be ushered into eternity! and yet, O cutting thought! was God now to require all your souls, how few, compa-ratively speaking, could really say, The Lord *our* righteousness!

" And think you, *O sinners,* that you will be able to stand in the day of judgment, if Christ be not your righteousness! No; that alone is the wedding garment in which you must appear. O Christless sinners, I am distressed for you! the desires of my soul are enlarged. Oh that this may be an accepted time! that the Lord may be your righteousness! For whither would you flee, if death should find you naked? Indeed there is no hiding yourselves from his presence. The pitiful fig-leaves of your own righteousness will not cover your nakedness, when God shall call you to stand before him. Adam found them ineffectual, and so will you. O think of death! O think of judgment! Yet a little while, and time shall be no more; and then what will become of you, if the Lord be not your righteousness? Think you that Christ will spare you? No, he that formed you will have no mercy on you. If you are not of Christ, if Christ be not your righteousness, Christ himself shall pronounce you damned. And can you bear to think of being damned by Christ? Can you bear to hear the Lord Jesus say to you, ' Depart from me, ye cursed, into everlasting fire, prepared for the devil and his angels?' Can you live, think you, in everlasting burnings? Is your flesh brass, and your bones iron? what if they are? hell-fire, that fire prepared for the devil and his angels, will heat them through and through. And can you bear to depart from Christ? Oh that heart-piercing thought! Ask those holy souls,

who are at any time bewailing an absent God, who walk in darkness, and see no light, though but a few days or hours; ask them
what it is to lose a sight and presence of Christ? See how they
seek him sorrowing, and go mourning after him all the day long!
And if it is so dreadful to lose the sensible presence of Christ
only for a day, what must it be to be banished from him to all
eternity?

" But thus it must be, if Christ be not your righteousness:
for God's justice must be satisfied; and, unless Christ's righteousness is imputed and applied to you here, you must hereafter
be satisfying the divine justice in hell-torments eternally; nay,
Christ himself shall condemn you to that place of torment. And
how cutting is that thought! Methinks I see poor, trembling,
Christless wretches, standing before the bar of God, crying out,
Lord, if we must be damned, let some angel, or some archangel,
pronounce the damnatory sentence: but all in vain. Christ
himself shall pronounce the irrevocable sentence. Knowing,
therefore, the terrors of the Lord, let me persuade you to close
with Christ, and never rest till you can say, ' The Lord our
righteousness.' Who knows but the Lord may have mercy
on, nay, abundantly pardon, you? Beg of God to give you faith;
and, if the Lord give you that, you will by it receive Christ,
with his righteousness, and his all. You need not fear the greatness or number of your sins. For, are you sinners? so am I.
Are you the chief of sinners? so am I. Are you backsliding
sinners? so am I. And yet the Lord, (for ever adored be his
rich, free, and sovereign grace,) the Lord is my righteousness.
Come then, *O young men,* who (as I acted once myself) are playing the prodigal, and wandering away afar off from your heavenly
Father's house, come home, come home, and leave your swine's
trough. Feed no longer on the husks of sensual delights: for
Christ's sake arise, and come home! your heavenly Father now
calls you. See yonder the best robe, even the righteousness of
his dear Son, awaits you. See it, view it again and again. Consider at how dear a rate it was purchased, even by the blood of God.
Consider what great need you have of it. You are lost, undone,
damned for ever, without it. Come then, poor guilty prodigals,
come home: indeed, I will not, like the elder brother in the

gospel, be angry; no, I will rejoice with the angels in heaven. And oh that God would now bow the heavens, and come down! Descend, O Son of God, descend; and as thou hast shown in me such mercy, O let thy blessed Spirit apply thy righteousness to some young prodigals now before thee, and clothe their naked souls with thy best robe!"

PLEADINGS. "My text is introduced in an awful manner, 'Verily I say unto you;' and what Jesus said then, he says now to you, and to me, and to as many as sit under a preached gospel, and to as many as the Lord our God shall call. Let me exhort you to see whether ye are converted; whether such a great and almighty change has passed upon any of your souls. As I told you before, so I tell you again, ye all hope to go to heaven, and I pray God Almighty ye may be all there. When I see such a congregation as this, if my heart is in a proper frame, I feel myself ready to lay down my life, to be instrumental only to save one soul. It makes my heart bleed within me, it makes me sometimes most unwilling to preach, lest that word that I hope will do good, may increase the damnation of any, and perhaps of a great part of the auditory, through their own unbelief. Give me leave to deal faithfully with your souls. I have your dead warrant in my hand: Christ has said it, Jesus will stand to it; it is like the laws of the Medes and Persians, it altereth not. Hark, O man! hark, O woman! he that hath ears to hear what the Lord Jesus Christ says, 'Verily I say unto you, Except ye be converted, and become as little children, ye shall not enter into the kingdom of heaven.' Though this is Saturday night, and ye are now preparing for the sabbath, for what you know, you may yet never live to see the sabbath. You have had awful proofs of this lately; a woman died but yesterday, a man died the day before, another was killed by something that fell from a house, and it may be in twenty-four hours more, many of you may be carried into an unalterable state. Now then, for God's sake, for your own souls' sake, if ye have a mind to dwell with God, and cannot bear the thought of dwelling in everlasting burning, before I go any further, silently put up one prayer, or say *Amen* to the prayer I would put in your mouths; 'Lord, search me and try me; Lord, examine my heart, and let my conscience speak; O let me know whether I am converted or not!' What say ye, my dear hearers? what say ye, my fellow-sinners? what say ye, my guilty brethren? Has God by his blessed Spirit wrought such a change in your hearts? I do not ask you, whether God has made you angels? that I know will never be; I only ask you, whether ye have any well-grounded hope to think that God has made you new creatures in Christ Jesus? so renewed and changed your natures, that you can say, I humbly hope, that as to the habitual temper and tendency of my mind, that my heart is free from wickedness? I have a husband, I have a wife, I have also children, I keep a shop, I mind my business; but I love these creatures for God's sake, and do every thing for Christ: and if God was now to call me away, according to the habitual temper of my mind, I can say, Lord, I am ready; and however I love the creatures, I hope I can say, Whom have I in heaven but thee? whom have I in heaven, O my God and my dear Redeemer, that I desire in comparison of thee? Can you thank God for the creatures, and say at the same time, these are not my Christ? I speak in plain language, *you know my way of preaching:* I do not want to play the orator, I do not want to be counted a scholar; I want to speak so as I may reach poor people's hearts. What say ye, my dear hearers? Are ye sensible of your weakness? Do ye feel that ye are poor, miserable, blind, and naked by nature? Do ye give up your hearts, your affections, your wills, your understanding, to be guided by the Spirit of God, as a little child gives up its hand to be guided by its parent? Are ye little in your own eyes? Do ye think meanly of yourselves? And do you want to learn something new every day? I mention these marks, because I am apt to believe they are more adapted to a great many of your capacities. A great many of you have not that flowing of affection ye sometimes had, therefore ye are for giving up all your evidences, and making way for the devil's coming into your heart. You are not brought up to the mount as ye used to be, therefore ye conclude ye have no grace at all. But if the Lord Jesus Christ has emptied thee, and humbled thee, if he is giving thee to see and know that thou art nothing; though thou art not growing

upward, thou art growing downward; and though thou hast not
so much joy, yet thy heart is emptying to be more abundantly
replenished by and by.

"This may be esteemed as enthusiasm and madness, and as a
design to undermine the established church. No; God is my
judge, I should rejoice to see all the world adhere to her Articles; I should rejoice to see the ministers of the church of
England preach up those very Articles they have subscribed to;
but those ministers who do preach up the Articles are esteemed as madmen, enthusiasts, schismatics, and underminers of the
established church; and though they say these things of me,
blessed be God, they are without foundation. My dear brethren, I am a friend to her Articles, I am a friend to her Homilies, I am a friend to her Liturgy; and, if they did not thrust
me out of their churches, I would read them every day: but I
do not confine the Spirit of God there; for I say it again, I
love all that love the Lord Jesus Christ, and esteem him my
brother, my friend, my spouse; aye, my very soul is knit to
that person. The spirit of persecution will never, indeed it will
never make any to love Jesus Christ. The Pharisees make this
to be madness, so much as to mention persecution in a christian
country; but there is as much the spirit of persecution now in
the world as ever there was: their will is as great, but blessed
be God, they want the power; otherwise, how soon would they
send me to prison, make my feet fast in the stocks, yea, would
think they did God service in killing me, and would rejoice to
take away my life."

MOUNT MORIAH. "'They came to the place of which God
had told Abraham. He built an altar there, and laid the wood
in order, and bound Isaac his son, and laid him on the altar
upon the wood.'

"And here let us pause awhile, and by faith take a view of
the place where the father has laid him. I doubt not but the
blessed angels hovered round the altar, and sang, 'Glory be to
God in the highest,' for giving such faith to man. Come, all
ye tender-hearted parents, who know what it is to look over a
dying child: fancy that you saw the altar erected before you,
and the wood laid in order, and the beloved Isaac bound upon

it : fancy that you saw the aged parent standing by weeping. For, why may we not suppose that Abraham wept, since Jesus himself wept at the grave of Lazarus? Oh what pious, endearing expressions passed now alternately between the father and the son! Josephus records a pathetic speech made by each, whether genuine I know not : but methinks I see the tears trickle down the patriarch Abraham's cheeks ; and out of the abundance of the heart, he cries, ' Adieu, adieu, my son ; the Lord gave thee to me, and the Lord calls thee away; blessed be the name of the Lord : adieu, my Isaac, my only son, whom I love as my own soul ; adieu, adieu.' I see Isaac at the same time meekly resigning himself into his heavenly Father's hands, and praying to the Most High to strengthen his earthly parent to strike the stroke. But why do I attempt to describe what either son or father felt. It is impossible : we may indeed form some faint idea of, but shall never fully comprehend it, till we come and sit down with them in the kingdom of heaven, and hear them tell the pleasing story over again. Hasten, O Lord, that blessed time! O let thy kingdom come ! I see your hearts affected. I see your eyes weep. And, indeed, who can refrain weeping at the relation of such a story? But, behold, I show you a mystery, hid under the sacrifice of Abraham's only son, which, unless your hearts are hardened, must cause you to weep tears of love, and that plentifully too. I would willingly hope you even prevent me here, and are ready to say, ' It is the love of God, in giving Jesus Christ to die for our sins.' "

PETER. " Spiritual sloth, as well as spiritual pride, helped to throw this apostle down. The Sun, that glorious Sun of righteousness, was now about to enter into his last eclipse. Satan, who had left him for a season, or till the season of his passion, is now to be permitted to bruise his heel again. This is his hour, and now the powers of darkness summon and exert their strongest and united efforts. A hymn is a prelude to his dreadful passion. From the communion-table the Saviour retires to the garden. A horrible dread, and inexpressible load of sorrow, begins to overwhelm and weigh down his innocent soul. His body can scarcely sustain it. See how he falters! See how his hands hang down, and his knees wax feeble under the amazing pressure! He is afflicted and oppressed indeed. See, see, O my soul, how he sweats! But what is that which I see? BLOOD—*drops* of blood—*great* drops of blood falling to the ground. Alas, was ever sorrow like unto this sorrow! HARK! what is that I hear? Oh dolorous complaint! ' Father, if it be possible, let this cup pass from me.' HARK! he speaks again. Amazing! the Creator complains to the creature; 'My soul is exceeding sorrowful, even unto death : tarry you here and watch with me.' And now he retires once more. But see how his agony increases—hark! how he prays, and that too yet more earnestly : ' Father, if it be possible, let this cup pass from me.' And will his heavenly Father leave him comfortless? No. An angel (O happy, highly-favoured angel!) is sent from heaven to strengthen him. But where is Peter all this while? We are told that the holy Jesus took him, with James and John, into the garden. Surely he will not leave his Lord in such deep distress! What is he doing? I blush to answer. Alas! he is sleeping : nay, though awakened once by his ago- nizing Lord, with a ' Simon Peter, sleepest thou? what! couldst thou not watch with me one hour?' yet his eyes, not- withstanding his profession of constancy and care, are heavy with sleep. Lord, what is man!" *Works.*

I have now finished my portraiture of Whitefield. It is, I am aware, not fine ; but it is faithful, so far as I know.

THE END.

BUNGAY : PRINTED BY J. R. AND C. CHILDS.